WHO'S WHO IN COUNTRY MUSIC

D0824996

WHO'S WHO IN COUNTRY MUSIC

Hugh Gregory

WEIDENFELD AND NICOLSON
LONDON

First published in Great Britain in 1993 by
Weidenfeld and Nicolson, a division of the Orion Publishing
Group, Orion House, 5 Upper St Martin's Lane, London
WC2H 9EA

Copyright © Hugh Gregory 1993

All rights reserved. No part of this publication may be repro-
duced, stored in a retrieval system, or transmitted in any form
or by any means, electronic, mechanical, photocopying,
recording or otherwise, without the prior permission of the
copyright holder.

A catalogue record for this book is available from the British
Library.

ISBN 0 297 81343 9

Typeset by Selwood Systems, Midsomer Norton
Printed and bound in Great Britain by
Butler & Tanner Ltd, Frome and London

20
-RE
993

INTRODUCTION

Country music has never been so healthy - so we are reliably informed by the media. Certainly in the US, this has been reflected in record sales, with artists like Garth Brooks and Clint Black shifting albums by the truckload. Indeed, record company A&R executives have come up with a new phrase, 'Hat Acts', to describe the plethora of fledgling artists attempting to get record deals. A week seldom passes without the emergence of another Hat Act. While many of these singers pursue the traditional Nashville approach, which can be very staid and veers dangerously close to MOR pop, others take older forms of country music like Western Swing, cajun, bluegrass, Tex-Mex and honky-tonk and adapt them to contemporary requirements. There are many highly individual instrumentalists, such as Peter Rowan, Augie Meyer and J.D. Crowe, who have pursued their careers with a vocational zeal, impervious to the vagaries of fashion.

For UK audiences, country music is still stigmatized by the image of cowboy hats and gaudy costumes, which Hat Acts have done little to dispel. This is a misconception and is responsible for the appalling reputation that country music has in the UK. A recent Country Music Association seminar in London tried to come to terms with how best to redress the imbalance between the US and the UK country markets. Figures were bandied about showing that sales by country artists in the UK were on the increase, but the seminar failed to get to grips with the perceptual problem.

Country music will only expand its market share when record companies push for their US signings to tour the UK, appearing at venues like the London Forum - and when they release the records in the first place. During the early 1970s, the Eagles achieved international celebrity through touring; Ry Cooder packs in audiences whenever he plays; and even the Flying Burrito Brothers were more popular in their halcyon days in Europe than in the US. Though none of these performers reflect Nashville's chosen image of country music, they introduced European audiences to uniquely American styles of music: country rock, Tex-Mex and bluegrass. This generated curiosity, and as a result Commander Cody, Flaco Jimenez and Country Gazette, among others, developed significant European followings.

The time is right now for record companies to apply this modus operandi: the Texas Tornados and the Desert Rose Band, for example, would benefit from promotion in the UK and Europe. Vince Gill played a promotional showcase in London recently performing a handful of his most successful singles and a bluegrass instrumental; the biggest applause of the evening greeted the instrumental. There is a real receptiveness to country music in the UK and Europe, and this book represents an attempt to confound some of these misconceptions by paying equal attention to the writers, producers, session musicians and artists from all genres of country music's long and varied history, as to the new young artists.

The records listed in the discographies are theoretically available in the UK, whether as imports or otherwise, and no distinction has been made as to the format (there are so many different formats now, anyway). In most instances, the discographies are selected, except in the case of specialist US labels, such as Sugar Hill and Rounder, for example, who distribute through specialist record stores in the UK. The absence of any discographical information means there is nothing readily available in the UK, but any specialist shop may have access to US, Japanese or German catalogues, where reissue schedules tend to be more comprehensive. Any corrections or suggestions for the next edition will be gratefully received.

Finally, I have included an index of names who do not have entries of their own. I hope it will prove useful in tracing the connections between country and the wider musical community.

Hugh Gregory
London, May 1993

GLOSSARY

AOR: Album Oriented Radio or Adult Oriented Rock acquired currency in the late 1960s with the emergence of FM radio in the US, whose play-lists were not governed the Top Forty singles charts.

A&R: Artists and Repertoire, the department of the record company that is responsible for signing artists to the label.

Austin: The capital of Texas and the centre of country music in Texas, which has been a magnet for the Outlaw movement, notably **Willie Nelson**, and Tex-Mex artists like **Doug Sahm**. The Armadillo World Headquarters has become one of the best-known bars and dancehalls in the US, because of its appeal to local artists.

Bakersfield: a region in California that, holding out the prospect of work, became the centre for migrating Okies during the 1930s. During the 1960s, it was touted as being a rival to Nashville on account of the pure country styles of **Buck Owens** and **Merle Haggard**.

Bluegrass: a form that had its origins in the Appalachians and featured mainly stringed instruments.

Cajun: Originating in Southern Louisiana, the trademark sound of cajun is the accordion. It combines the traditions of the region's French-speaking population with the rural blues of the black population.

Conjunto music: Derived from *conjunto*, the Spanish for group, this is accordion-led and features *baja sexto* (a sort of twelve-string guitar), bass and drums. The repertoire, comprising polkas and waltzes, is generally sung in Spanish in two-part harmony.

Country boogie: Pianists like **Roy Hall** and **Merrill E. Moore** adopted the boogie-woogie style of Albert Ammons, among others, creating this hybrid, which was a vital step in the evolution of rock 'n' roll.

CMA: The Country Music Association, founded in 1958 to promote the interests of country music within the US and across the world. These aims are achieved through an annual awards ceremony, which is now televised, and record industry seminars and radio shows.

Country Music Foundation: A non-profit-making organization that administers the Country Music Hall of Fame and Museum in Nashville. Among the Foundation's most celebrated achievements is to build up an archive and library of records, tapes, photographs, discs and books dedicated to the study and interpretation of country music's past.

Country Music Hall of Fame: A shrine dedicated to honouring country music's most influential movers. Among those to have been honoured are producers, executives and songwriters, as well as performers.

CMT: Country Music Television, beamed by satellite from Nashville to the UK (since November 1992) and Europe, represents a serious effort to market country music as effectively as in the US.

Countrypolitan: A style that developed through Nashville's desire to become more commercial; producers like **Billy Sherrill** added string arrangements for the benefit of MOR audiences.

Country rock: Groups like the **Eagles** and the **Flying Burrito Brothers** used traditional country styles, such as bluegrass and honky-tonk, but added driving rock-oriented rhythm sections; traditionally, country music rhythm sections are little more than a pulse, pushed back so far in the mix (on records) that they are almost imperceptible.

Country soul: The gospel and R&B influence on secular songs, featuring country arrangements and instrumentation, notably the steel guitar. It should be noted that soul singers like Bobby Womack and Tina Turner have cut country albums.

Grand Ole Opry: Founded by **George D. Hay**, the programme director of Nashville's WSM, in 1925 as an answer to the *National Barn Dance* on WLS, Chicago. At first it was called WSM *Barn Dance*, until on December 10, 1927, it was retitled the *Grand Ole Opry*, starting an unprecedented run that continues to this day. Its first location was in a WSM studio, and up to 1941, this venue was being changed frequently. That year, it made its first broadcast from the Ryman Auditorium, where it remained for over thirty years. Today it is housed in a massive amusement park, fifteen miles from Nashville, called Opryland USA. Over the years, its influence has waned, but it remains the object of desire for most country singers starting out: an appearance in one of their live showcases, or on the show itself, which is now televised, does wonders for an artists career. Although the selection procedure appears conservative and cautious, younger artists like **Vince Gill** and **Garth Brooks** have appeared there in recent years, and their careers have flourished thereafter.

Hat Acts: a record company pejorative loosely applied to the vast number of young artists attempting to get recording contracts. These should not be confused with New Country artists, because Hat Acts depend on their visual appeal on stage or in videos.

Hee Haw: A syndicated TV show that started in 1969 and combined country music with comedy acts. It succeeded it bringing country music to a wider audience and is now broadcast on the Nashville Cable Network, as CBS terminated their license in 1972.

HBO: Home Box Office, a US cable entertainment channel.

Honky-tonk: Derived from the bars of the US southwest, the instrumentation includes steel and electric guitars, and the songs deal with perennial problems like adultery and getting drunk. **Ernest Tubb**, **George Jones** and **Webb Pierce**, among others, were arch-exponents of this genre.

Loew's Theaters: A nationwide chain of theatres and concert halls.

Louisiana Hayride: Following in the tradition of the *Grand Ole Opry* and the *National Barn Dance*, the *Louisiana Hayride* was broadcast from KWKH, Shreveport, on Saturday nights, making its first broadcast on April 3, 1948. One of the reasons for its early popularity was its willingness to break new artists; **Elvis Presley**, **Jim Reeves** and **Hank Williams**, all of whom had been passed over by the *Grand Ole Opry* for one reason or another, first came to attention on the *Hayride*. During the 1960s, it failed to reflect the growing commercialization of country music and was dropped towards the end of the decade.

MOR: Middle Of The Road is the term applied by radio-station programmers and record companies to pop music that caters for an older audience. The main criteria is that it should be easy to listen to.

Nashville: The business centre of country music, in Tennessee. Most of the major record labels have offices in Nashville and focus upon servicing the country music industry. The city also boasts its own satellite television network, TNN, devoted to country music.

Nashville sound: This sound developed in the late 1950s and early 1960s and used lush string arrangements and vocal backing groups. Producers **Chet Atkins** and **Owen Bradley** were its principal proponents.

National Barn Dance: Starting in 1924 in Chicago on WLS, the *National Barn Dance* crystallized the enthusiasm for country music during the 1920s and 1930s. Without the power of the *Barn Dance*, label owners and entrepreneurs like **Ralph Peer** and **Art Satherley** would have had a hard time promoting their records. In 1960, when WLS changed its format and the *Barn Dance* was dropped, the neighbouring WGN picked up the option and ran the show until 1970 when it finally turned up its toes.

New Country: A term applied to the younger artists emerging in the 1980s, who combined the promotional zeal of rock artists with traditional country styles such as Western Swing, honky-tonk and bluegrass.

Old-time(y): The purist form of country music, developed in rural areas. Prime exponents like **Charlie Poole** and **J.E. Mainer** learnt their skills from family and friends. The repertoire comprised traditional regional songs and reflected the concerns of the working man.

Outlaw Movement: Stemming from the album *Wanted: The Outlaws* (1976), the Outlaw Movement revolved around a group of musicians that included **Willie Nelson**, **Waylon Jennings**, **Jessi Colter** and **Tompall Glaser**, who, while stressing the traditional values of country music, collectively rejected the Nashville establishment.

R&B (rhythm & blues): A blanket term covering the black urban music of the 1940s and 1950s, electrically amplified.

Rockabilly: a synthesis of R&B and country that pre-dated rock 'n' roll.

Swamp rock: **Tony Joe White** and **John Fogerty**'s Creedence Clearwater Revival were two notable exponents of this genre, which was guitar-based and fused the rhythmic elements of cajun with rock.

Tex-Mex: A synthesis of R&B, honky-tonk and con-junto, featuring the accordion instead of the steel guitar.

TNN: The Nashville Network is the country music equivalent of MTV. Broadcasting videos and live showcases, round the clock, on cable, it has done more to promote New Country and Hat Acts than anything else. Before its emergence country artists never made promotional videos, now, videos are an integral part of breaking a country artist.

Western Swing: Elements of jazz, blues and country fused together, using fiddles, acoustic guitars and bass.

Zydeco: Indigenous to southwest Louisiana and West Texas, it combines elements of cajun with Caribbean and Creole idioms. The genre's most notable exponents are **Rockin' Dopsie** and **Clifton Chenier**.

ABSHIRE, Nathan

One of the lesser known hybrids of country music is cajun, and one of its most influential movers was accordionist Nathan Abshire.

Abshire was born near Gueydan, Louisiana, on June 27, 1913. His career did not really take off until after the Second World War, despite having recorded as early as 1935 for the Bluebird label. In 1948 he started to appear regularly at the Avalon Club in Basile, Louisiana, and cut 'Pine Grove Blues'; the success of this record did much to augment his own reputation, and also served to elevate the profiles of many fellow accordionists, such as Iry LeJune and Austin Pitre.

The advent of rock 'n' roll in the 1950s militated against the popular acceptance of cajun music, and Abshire had to wait until the 1960s before his reputation rose again with a series of singles for Floyd Soileau's Swallow label and **Jay Miller**'s Kajun.

He performed with most of the celebrated cajun musicians at one time or another, and his records and appearances with the Balfa Brothers (see **Balfa, Dewey**) were pivotal to the renaissance of interest in cajun in the 1970s; this interest was crystallised by a television documentary entitled *The Good Times Are Killing Me*. The title proved prophetic as Abshire died on May 13, 1981.

A CAJUN LEGEND, Swallow (US), 1986
A CAJUN TRADITION, Volumes 1-2, La Louisiane (US), 1987
CAJUNS (with the Balfa Brothers), Sonet, 1973
GOOD TIMES ARE KILLING ME (with the Balfa Brothers), Sonet, 1988
NATHAN ABSHIRE AND OTHER CAJUN GEMS, Arhoolie, 1981
NATHAN ABSHIRE AND THE PINEGROVE BOYS, Flyright, 1986
PINEGROVE BLUES, Ace, 1987

ACUFF, Roy

Roy Acuff has been synonymous with Nashville and country music since the 1940s. While much of his recorded output has been little more than a reaffirmation of the traditional values of republicanism, his contribution to the profile of country music has been of the highest order.

Roy Claxton Acuff was born in Maynardsville, Tennessee, on September 15, 1903. The son of a Baptist minister and one of five children, he learnt to play the harmonica and the jew's harp before turning his attention to baseball. Prevented from playing for the New York Yankees in 1929-30 by severe sunburn, he went to work on the railroad. In 1932 he joined a medicine show, and toured the backwaters of Tennessee and Virginia; and in 1933 he formed the Tennessee Crackerjacks, which included dobroist **Cousin Jody**. He was invited by WROL, the local Knoxville station, to host his own show, before being invited by the rival WNOX to appear regularly on the *Midday Merry-Go-Round*, which was the starting-point for other artists such as **Dottie West** and **Bill Carlisle**. His tenure at WNOX was shortlived, as they turned down his request for a pay rise, and so he returned to WROL, appearing with his band as the Crazy Tennesseans.

After marrying Mildred Douglas in 1936 (she died in 1981), he cut his first sides for the ARC label, which included 'Wabash Cannonball' (featuring vocalist Sam 'Dynamite' Hatcher) and 'The Great Speckled Bird'. In 1938 he made his first appearance on the *Grand Ole Opry*, changing the name of his group - which now included dobroist **Bashful Brother Oswald** and fiddler Howdy Forrester - to the Smokey Mountain Boys. By 1940, Acuff had superseded **Uncle Dave Macon** as the most popular attraction at the *Opry*, and had established significant sponsorship from R.J. Reynolds Tobacco. The war years provided him with a string of hits on the Okeh label, which included 'Wreck On The Highway' and 'Fireball Mail' in 1942, and 'Night Train To Memphis', 'Precious Jewel', 'Pins And Needles' and 'Low And Lonely' in 1943. In some popularity polls he rated higher than Frank Sinatra, and Japanese troops at Okinawa were moved to shout 'To hell with Roosevelt, to hell with Babe Ruth, to hell with Roy Acuff' as they charged the beleaguered US forces.

Acuff's most enduring contribution was the setting up of the music publishers Acuff-Rose, with songwriter **Fred Rose**: it remains to this day the most successful of all Nashville music publishers, and includes the entire catalogues of **Hank Williams** and **Marty Robbins**. This pre-eminence caused him to run for the governorship of Tennessee in 1946 and 1948; an undertaking which, despite its lack of success, succeeded in boosting his reputation.

During the latter half of the 1940s his sales declined drastically and Columbia tried unsuccessfully to persuade him to change his style; Acuff left Columbia, moving first to MGM, and then to Decca and Capitol, but there was little increase of interest. After setting up his own Hickory label with Rose in 1959 he became, in 1962, the first living country musician to be elected to the Country Music Hall Of Fame. In 1965 he was severely injured in a road accident, but was back on the road within months. When the new Opryhouse was opened in 1974, he gave President Nixon an on-stage demonstration of how to play the yo-yo, and continued to perform at the Grand Ole Opry at least twice a week right up to his death on November 23, 1992.

Despite having sold over thirty million records and being dubbed the King of Country Music by its aficionados, Roy Acuff will always be best remembered for his ability to sell Nashville as a place of entertainment as well as a musical centre.

THE ESSENTIAL ROY ACUFF: 1936-49, Sony (France), 1993
FLY, BIRDIE, FLY 1939-41, Rounder, 1988
KING OF COUNTRY MUSIC, Bear Family (Germany), 1993
STEAMBOAT WHISTLE BLUES, Rounder, 1988
TWO DIFFERENT WORLDS, Sundown, 1986

ALABAMA

Alabama was formed in Fort Payne, Alabama, in 1972, and comprised Randy Owen (guitar; born December 13, 1949), Jeff Cook (guitar/fiddle; born August 27, 1949), Ted Gentry (bass; born January 22, 1952) and Rick Scott (drums). After playing in local clubs, including the Bowery in Myrtle Beach, they were signed by the independent MDJ label, and in 1979, just as they were on the point of breaking nationally, Scott was replaced by Mark Herndon (born May 11, 1955).

In 1980 they were signed by RCA where they notched up a string of hits, cut mostly with producers Harold Shedd and Larry McBride, including 'Tennessee River' (C&W#1, 1980), 'Why Lady Why'

(C&W#1, 1980), 'Old Flame' (C&W#1, 1981), 'Feels So Right' (US#20, C&W#1, 1981), 'Love In The First Degree' (US#15, C&W#1, 1981), 'Mountain Music' (C&W#1, 1982), 'Take Me Down' (US#18, C&W#1, 1982), 'Close Enough To Perfect' (C&W#1, 1982), 'Dixieland Delight' (C&W#1, 1983), 'The Closer You Get' (US#38, C&W#1, 1983), 'Lady Down On Love' (C&W#1, 1983), 'Roll On' (C&W#1, 1984), 'When We Make Love' (C&W#1, 1984), 'If You're Gonna Play In Texas (You Gotta Have A Fiddle In The Band)' (C&W#1, 1984), 'A Fire In The Night' (C&W#1, 1985), 'There's No Way' (C&W#1, 1985), 'Forty Hour Week' (C&W#1, 1985), 'Can't Keep A Good Man Down' (C&W#1, 1985), 'She And I' (C&W#1, 1986), 'Touch Me When We're Dancing' (C&W#1, 1986), 'You've Got The Touch' (C&W#1, 1987), 'Face To Face' (C&W#1, 1988) and 'Fallin' Again' (C&W#1, 1988).

In 1989 they parted with their long-standing producer Harold Shedd (he moved over to Polygram); his replacement was the legendary keyboard player from Muscle Shoals Sound Studios, **Barry Beckett**, who continued where Shedd had left off: 'Song Of The South' (C&W#1, 1989), 'If I Had You' (C&W#1, 1989), 'High Cotton' (C&W#1, 1989), 'Pass It On Down' (C&W#3, 1990), 'Jukebox In My Mind' (C&W#1, 1990), 'Forever's As Far As I'll Go' (C&W#1, 1990), 'Down Home' (C&W#1, 1991), 'Born Country' (C&W#2, 1991), 'Take A Little Trip' (C&W#2, 1992) and 'I'm In A Hurry (And I Don't Know Why)' (C&W#1, 1992). Little known outside the US, Alabama have sold well over fifty million records to date.

ALABAMA, RCA, 1984
AMERICAN PRIDE, RCA, 1992
CLOSER YOU GET, RCA, 1985
FEELS SO RIGHT, RCA, 1981
FORTY HOUR WEEK, RCA, 1985
GREATEST HITS, RCA, 1986
JUST US, RCA, 1988
MOUNTAIN MUSIC, RCA, 1984
MY HOME'S IN ALABAMA, RCA, 1980
ROLL ON, RCA, 1984
SOUTHERN STAR, RCA, 1989
THE TOUCH, RCA, 1986

ALLAN, Johnnie

Johnnie Allan enjoyed a brief spell of cult status in the early 1970s with his rip-roaring version of 'Promised Land'. Born John Guillot on March 10, 1938, in Rayne, Louisiana, he made his debut in 1951 as a rhythm guitarist in a local group, but then changed over to steel guitar and joined accordionist Lawrence Walker's band. The band split up in 1957, and Allan became a founder member of the Krazy Kats with **Huey Meaux**'s cousin, fiddler U.J. Meaux. This group had a modest hit with 'Lonely Days, Lonely Nights' (1959) on the local Jin label; the follow-up 'Angel Of Love' (1959) fared less well. Employed as a full-time teacher, Allan quit teaching in 1961 to become a full-time musician; by 1967 he had returned to college, gaining a master's degree, before becoming vice-principal of the Arcadian Elementary School in Lafayette.

In 1974, DJ and author Charlie Gillett picked up Allan's version of Chuck Berry's 'Promised Land' and released it on his Oval label; it turned Allan into a cult hero overnight and made Berry's original version seem sluggish. Re-issued regularly, 'Promised Land' has prompted the re-issue of all the material he recorded for the Jin label. In 1987, he cut *Good Timin' Man* for Flyright.

ANOTHER MAN'S WOMAN, Jin, 1979
DEDICATED TO YOU, Jin, 1979
GOOD TIMIN' MAN, Flyright, 1987
JOHNNIE ALLAN SINGS, Jin, 1979
JOHNNIE ALLAN SINGS CAJUN NOW, Swallow (US), 1987
JOHNNIE ALLAN'S GREATEST HITS, Jin, 1979
LOUISIANA SWAMP FOX, Jin, 1979
PORTRAIT OF JOHNNIE ALLAN, Jin, 1979
PROMISED LAND, Ace, 1992
SOUTH TO LOUISIANA, Ace, 1985
THANKS FOR THE MEMORIES, Jin, 1979

ALLEN, Rex

Rex Allen was born in Willcox, Arizona, on December 31, 1924. Initially a rodeo rider, he learnt to play the guitar and fiddle and, after studying electronics at UCLA, he auditioned successfully for the radio station WTTM in Trenton, New Jersey. By 1951 he had been given his own Hollywood radio show by CBS and appeared in the film *Arizona Cowboy*; he went on to appear in over thirty films between 1950 and 1957, particularly for Disney. His biggest hits were 'Crying In The Chapel' (US#8, 1953) and 'Don't Go Near The Indians' (US#17, 1962).

Although he has long been retired, he still makes appearances at rodeos, and his son Rex Allen Jr (born on August 23, 1947, in Chicago, Illinois) has kept up the family tradition, scoring hits with 'The Great Mail Robbery' and 'Goodbye' (1974) and 'It's Time We Talked Things Over' (1978), and making his first

appearance at the *Grand Ole Opry* in 1980.
BONEY-KNEED, HAIRY-LEGGED COWBOY SONGS, Bear Family, 1984
HAWAIIAN COWBOY, Bear Family, 1986
MISTER COWBOY, Stetson, 1987
UNDER WESTERN SKIES, Stetson, 1985
VOICE OF THE WEST, Bear Family, 1986

ALLEN Jr, Rex See **ALLEN, Rex**

ALLEN, Rosalie

Rosalie Allen was born Julie Marlene Bedra in Old Forge, Pennsylvania, on June 6, 1924, of Polish extraction. After broadcasting on radio during the 1930s, she was signed by RCA, and became known as 'The Prairie Star'; among her biggest hits were 'I Want To Be A Cowboy's Sweetheart' and 'He Taught Me How To Yodel'. These led to an occasional partnership with another distinguished yodeller, **Elton Britt**, which yielded hits like 'Quicksilver', 'Yodel Blues' and 'Beyond The Sunset'. During the 1950s her career slipped into the doldrums after a brief stint as a DJ.

ANDERSON, Bill

While Bill Anderson's public persona embodies the conservative American values that are stereotypically attributed to Nashville and country singers, his contribution to the genre has provided artists such as **Jim Reeves**, **Porter Wagoner**, **Faron Young** and **Hank Locklin** with countless hits. Anderson himself has been a regular visitor to the C&W charts, with a succession of hits - part-spoken and part-sung - that have earned him the moniker Whispering Bill.

He was born on November 1, 1937, in Columbia, South Carolina. Gaining a BA in journalism at the University of Georgia, much of his spare time was spent singing and DJ-ing; after stints with the weekly *DeKalb New Era* and the *Atlanta Journal*, he became a full-time professional singer in 1958 (when **Ray Price** had a million-seller with his composition 'City Lights') and began writing with **Buddy Killen** on songs like 'I May Never Get To Heaven'.

Over the next four years he penned a string of hits for other artists, and in 1962 he broke through on his own account with 'Mama Sang A Song' (C&W#1, 1962). This was followed by 'Still' (US#8, C&W#1, 1963), '8 × 10' (C&W#2, 1963), 'I Get The Fever' (C&W#1, 1966), 'For Loving You' (a duet with **Jan**

Howard; C&W#1, 1967), 'Wild Weekend' (C&W#2, 1968), 'Happy State Of Mind' (C&W#2, 1968), 'My Life' (C&W#1, 1969), 'But You Know I Love You' (C&W#2, 1969), 'The Corner Of My Life' (C&W#2, 1972) and 'World Of Make Believe' (C&W#1, 1974).

During the mid-1960s, he started a parallel career in film and television: he hosted *The Bill Anderson Show* (which was syndicated to 126 cities throughout the US) and presented the television game-show *Fandango*; he appeared in rather undistinguished low-budget films like *Las Vegas Hillbillies* (1966) and *Road To Nashville* (1967); and he established a precedent of sorts when one of his UK concerts was broadcast live to Nashville by satellite. More recently, he has recorded with Mary Lou Turner, scoring with 'Sometimes' (C&W#1, 1976) and 'That's What Made Me Love You' (C&W#3, 1976). In 1989, Longstreet Press published his autobiography *Whispering Bill*.

While others in Nashville have long since eschewed the deep conservatism of the country music establishment, Anderson has continued to espouse its values, his popularity sustained by the silent majority.

BILL ANDERSON STORY, MCA (US), 1986
BRIGHT LIGHTS AND COUNTRY MUSIC, Stetson, 1985
COUNTRY MUSIC HEAVEN, Whispering (US), 1992
LADIES CHOICE, Bulldog, 1982
A PLACE OUT IN THE COUNTRY, Bulldog, 1988

ANDERSON, John

One of the best guitarists and songwriters of the New Country artists, John Anderson was born on December 13, 1954, in Apopka, Florida. In 1972 he moved to Nashville, picking up a string of casual jobs and performing occasionally with his sister Donna, before becoming a member of the group Living End. He obtained his first contract with the small Ace of Hearts label in 1974, before being signed to Warner Bros. in 1977.

Since then he has notched up a string of hits, including 'I'm Just An Old Chunk Of Coal (But I'm Gonna Be A Diamond Someday)' (C&W#4, 1981), 'I Just Came Home To Count The Memories' (1982), 'Wild And Blue' (C&W#1, 1982), 'Swingin'' (C&W#1, 1982), 'Black Sheep' (co-written with film director Robert Altman; C&W#1, 1983) and 'Eyes Of A Hurricane' (1985).

After a fruitless stint with MCA from 1985, he returned with 'Straight Tequila Night' (C&W#1, 1991), 'When It Comes To You' (C&W#3, 1992) and 'Seminole Wind' (C&W#2, 1992) for the BNA label. While many

have compared Anderson to **Lefty Frizzell**, he cites his biggest influences as the **Rolling Stones**, Steppenwolf and Alice Cooper.

GREATEST HITS, Warner Bros., 1986
SEMINOLE WIND, BNA (US), 1992

ANDERSON, Liz

Liz Anderson was born Elizabeth Jane Haaby in Pine Creek, Minnesota on March 13, 1930. On May 26, 1946, she married Casey Anderson and she gave birth to a daughter, **Lynn Anderson**, in 1947. After studying business management and working as a secretary, she secured a contract with RCA as a singer-songwriter. Throughout the latter half of the 1960s she had a succession of hits under her own name with 'Wife Of The Party' (1966), 'The Game Of Triangles' (with **Norma Jean** and **Bobby Bare**; 1966), 'Mama Spank' (1967), 'Tiny Tears' (1967) and 'Husband Hunting' (1970).

As a writer, she provided hits like 'The Fugitive' and '(My Friends Are Gonna Be) Strangers' for **Merle Haggard**. In 1971 she moved to the Epic label, which had previously signed her daughter, before retiring from the music industry in 1976.

ANDERSON, Lynn

Lynn Rene Anderson was born in Grand Forks, North Dakota, on September 26, 1947, the daughter of **Liz Anderson**. She was raised in Sacramento and excelled at horsemanship, winning the California Horse Show Queen title in 1966. Between 1966 and 1968 she sang regularly on Lawrence Welk's weekly television show, which led to a recording contract with the Chart label. Her debut single was a version of one of her mother's compositions, 'Ride, Ride, Ride' (1966); by 1969 she had recorded over a hundred songs for the label, 'That's A No No' being the most succesful.

In 1968 she moved to Nashville and married writer/producer R. Glenn Sutton, who signed her to the Columbia label in 1970. Her first single, 'Stay There 'Til I Get There' (C&W#3, 1970), was written and produced by her husband; the follow-up was the **Joe South** composition 'Rose Garden' (US#3, C&W#1, 1970; UK#3, 1971), a massive hit which won her the CMA Female Singer Of The Year Award. Other hits then followed, including 'You're My Man' (C&W#1, 1971), 'How Can I Unlove You' (C&W#1, 1971), 'Cry' (C&W#3, 1972), 'Listen To A Country Song' (C&W#4,

1972), 'Fool Me' (C&W#4, 1972) 'Keep Me In Mind' (C&W#1, 1973) and 'What A Man My Man Is' (C&W#1, 1974).

In 1977 she divorced Sutton, marrying oilman Harold Stream the following year. She retired from the music industry for a time to look after her children but, after divorcing Stream, she was signed by the independent Permian label, cutting *Back* in 1983. When the label folded, her contract was briefly taken over by MCA, and then Mercury. In 1984 she duetted with **Gary Morris** on 'You're Welcome Tonight', which turned out to be her biggest hit in over a decade. While unable to match the popularity of the early 1970s, she remains a stalwart on the Nashville circuit.

COWBOY'S SWEETHEART, LaserLight (US), 1992
EVEN COWGIRLS GET THE BLUES, CBS, 1981
LYNN ANDERSON, Country Store, 1988
ROSE GARDEN, Mainline, 1990
TWENTY GOLDEN HITS, Spectrum, 1988

ANGLIN, Jack See WRIGHT, Johnny

AREA CODE 615 See MOSS, Wayne

ARNOLD, Eddy

Since his emergence in the mid-1940s, Eddy Arnold has consistently sold records by the truckload; his relaxed style has appealed to successive generations of C&W fans and has made him popular with pop audiences.

He was born Richard Edward Arnold in Henderson, Tennessee, on May 15, 1918; his father, who was a farmer, played the fiddle and taught Arnold how to play the guitar when he was ten. After leaving school to help run the farm, he started performing at local dances; this led to a radio broadcast on Jackson's WTJS in 1936. He made his breakthrough when he joined **Pee Wee King**'s Golden West Cowboys, who regularly appeared on the *Grand Ole Opry*, and he was signed by RCA as a solo artist in 1944. In 1947, his run of hits started with 'What Is Life Without Love' (C&W#1, 1947), which was soon followed by tracks including 'I'll Hold You In My Heart' (US#22, C&W#1, 1947), 'Anytime' (US#17, C&W#1, 1948), 'Bouquet Of Roses' (US#13, C&W#1, 1948), 'Just A Little Lovin' Will Go A Long Way' (US#13, C&W#1, 1948) and 'I Wouldn't Know Where To Begin' (US#22, C&W#1, 1956).

His all-round popularity enabled him to secure guest spots on light entertainment shows hosted by such diverse personalities as Milton Berle, Bob Hope and Dinah Shore. This inevitably led to his own show, *Eddy Arnold Time*, as well as other shows for NBC and ABC. Despite a dip in his record sales (due to the advent of rock 'n' roll), the hits just kept on coming: 'Make The World Go Away' (US#6, C&W#1, 1965; UK#8, 1966), 'I Want To Go With You' (US#36, C&W#1, UK#46, 1966), 'The Last Word In Lonesome Is Me' (US#40, C&W#1, 1966), 'If You Were Mine Mary' (C&W#1, UK#49, 1966), 'Somebody Like Me' (C&W#1, 1967), 'Lonely Again' (C&W#1, 1967), 'Turn The World Around' (C&W#1, 1968) and 'Then You Can Tell Me Goodbye' (C&W#1, 1968).

In the early 1970s he moved to MGM for a brief spell, only to return to RCA in 1976 and continue his run of country hits with 'Let's Get It When The Gettin's Good' and 'That's What I Get For Loving You' in 1980. He was elected into the Country Music Hall Of Fame in 1966.

ANYTIME, Stetson, 1988
CATTLE CALL, Bear Family, 1990
TWENTY OF THE BEST, RCA, 1982

ASHWORTH, Ernie

Ernie Ashworth is one of the legion of country artists whose reputation has been restricted to the cognoscenti. Born in Huntsville, Alabama, on December 15, 1928, he learnt to play the guitar during his adolescence, and started his career by playing in local clubs and doing the odd session for nearby radio stations. In 1955, having moved to Nashville, he broadcasted regularly on WSIX and was signed by MGM, who recorded him under the name of Billy Worth. None of this did much to progress his career, and by 1957 he had returned to Huntsville for a job at the Redstone Arsenal.

In 1960 **Wesley Rose** re-negotiated his contract with Decca, which resulted in a series of hits: 'Each Moment (Spent With You)', 'You Can't Pick A Rose In September' and 'Forever Gone'. His contract with Decca having then expired, Rose signed him to his Hickory label in 1962, and over the next ten years Ashworth was seldom out of the C&W charts: 'Everybody But Me', 'Talk Back Trembling Lips', 'A Week In The Country', 'I Love To Dance With Annie', 'Pushed In A Corner', 'Because I Cared', 'The DJ Cried', 'Sad Face', 'A New Heart' and 'Love, I Finally Found It'.

He won the coveted Most Promising New C&W Artist Award in 1963's *Billboard* poll. His profile today is not as high as it was during the 1960s, but he continues to perform and write material for other artists.

ASLEEP AT THE WHEEL

Asleep At The Wheel have proved to be one of the more durable country-rock outfits, due to their ability to synthesize some of the more diverse elements of country music - such as Western Swing, Tex-Mex and bluegrass - into a readily accessible and identifiable style of their own. While this adaptability has led many of their contemporaries into AOR, Asleep At The Wheel have won admirers among the traditionally-minded country fraternity.

The group was formed by vocalist/guitarist Ray Benson (born March 16, 1951, in Philadelphia) and steel guitarist Lucky Oceans (born Reuben Gosfield on April 22, 1951, in Philadelphia) in California in the late 1960s, and was supplemented by session or local musicians; over the years these have included vocalist/guitarist Leroy Preston, bassist Tony Garnier, fiddler/saxophonist Link Davis, saxophonist Pat 'Taco' Ryan, fiddlers Bill Mabry and **Johnny Gimble** and mandolinist Danny Levin. After moving to a farm in Paw Paw, West Virginia, female vocalist Chris O'Connell (born March 21, 1953, in Williamsport, Maryland) joined the group straight from college as another permanent member.

In 1971 the group moved to San Francisco, where they were joined by pianist Floyd Domino and were signed by United Artists, releasing *Comin' Right At Ya* (1973). The following year they moved to Austin, Texas, and were signed to the Epic label for *Asleep At The Wheel* (1974). After being dropped by Epic, they were signed to Capitol and, building upon their reputation as an enterprising and entertaining live band, cut *Texas Gold*, which included 'The Letter That Johnnie Walker Wrote' (C&W#10, 1975). After recording several more albums for Capitol, they moved to MCA for *Framed* (1986) and then back to Epic for *Ten* (1987).

Despite their lack of commercial success, their albums exhibit an infectious enthusiasm so often lacking in contemporary music, and they have also done much to encourage awareness of **Bob Wills** and the other Western Swing bands of the 1940s.

ASLEEP AT THE WHEEL, MCA (US), 1988
COLLISION COURSE, Capitol, 1978
COMIN' RIGHT AT YA, Edsel, 1986
FRAMED, MCA (US), 1986
JUMPING AT THE WOODSIDE, Edsel, 1986
PASTURE PRIME, Demon, 1985
TEN, Epic, 1987
VERY BEST OF ASLEEP AT THE WHEEL, See For Miles, 1987
WESTERN STANDARD TIME, Epic, 1988
THE WHEEL, Capitol, 1977

ATCHER, Bob

Robert Owen Atcher was born in Hardin County, Kentucky, on May 11, 1914, but moved to North Dakota as a child. His family were all folk singers or fiddlers, twin influences on his own very specific style, which became a fixture on the *National Barn Dance* from 1948 until it finished in 1970. Formerly he had made his debut on Chicago's WJJD and WBBM and, although he recorded for Columbia, Capitol and Kapp, it was through his radio broadcasts that he achieved significant popularity. By the early 1970s, he had stopped performing in favour of a political career that would result in his becoming mayor of Schaumburg, a suburb of Chicago.

ATKINS, Chet

If there is any one individual responsible for the Nashville sound as it is today, that person is Chet Atkins. His finger-picking style - which used three fingers, rather than the thumb and forefinger - has become a benchmark since the late 1950s. However, it is his behind-the-scenes activites that have done so much to shape the Nashville sound.

Chester Burton Atkins was born in Lutrell, Tennessee, on June 20, 1924, and his formative years were heavily influenced by the musicians in his family - his father taught piano and was a voice coach, and his elder half-brother Jimmy was a guitarist in the **Les Paul** Trio. He took up the guitar when he was nine, and by the age of eighteen he had become sufficiently proficient to join WNOX as a fiddler. Over the next five years, he worked at a number of radio stations and studied at music libraries, acquainting himself with different musical styles; this provided him with the raw material for his own highly personal style. After a stint with **Red Foley**, he started to record for RCA in 1947; the relationship would span four decades. Despite his solo sides, he continued working as a sideman with the **Carter Family** and **Homer & Jethro**, among others.

Although his early records for RCA featured vocals,

it was his guitar work on instrumentals like 'Chinatown, My Chinatown', 'Country Gentleman' and 'Downhill Drag' that really caught the imagination. As his role as a session musician increased, he became more influential at RCA, and, in 1955, **Steve Sholes** appointed him manager of RCA's newly opened Nashville Studios. His experience as a session musician enabled him to assemble a stellar line-up of musicians - pianist **Floyd Cramer**, guitarist Hank Garland, bassist **Bob Moore** and drummer Buddy Harman - to back RCA's growing roster of country artists; the formation of a regular studio group giving RCA a headstart over their competitors.

Over the years, Atkins produced or supervised records by the **Everly Brothers**, the **Browns**, **Hank Snow**, **Elvis Presley**, **Bobby Bare**, **Don Gibson**, **Skeeter Davis**, **Jim Reeves**, Al Hirt and Perry Como; and his own hits included 'Poor People In Paris' (1956), 'Boo Boo Stick Beat Beat' (1959), 'One Mint Julep' (1960), 'Teensville' (1960) and 'Yakety Axe' (C&W#4, 1965). While many may contend that much of the output was too poppy - contributing to the perceived view of Nashville as the centre of maudlin kitsch - this view was not shared by audiences, who made country artists pop stars overnight.

As Atkins' creative input was superseded by his administrative duties, the material he recorded became more prosaic. He did nonetheless team up with Ravi Shankar (great idea, shame about the choice of material), **Merle Travis**, **Jerry Reed** and **Doc Watson** for albums of duets, which showed that his abilities as a guitarist were still as acute as ever. In 1981, he left RCA and signed with Columbia; during his long stay with RCA, he had signed **Waylon Jennings**, **Dottie West**, **Connie Smith** and **Charley Pride**, become an Executive Vice-President and been elected to the Country Music Hall Of Fame in 1973. In 1990, he teamed up with Mark Knopfler of Dire Straits for an album that proved to be one of his most successful records in years.

BEST OF CHET ATKINS, RCA International, 1980
CHESTER & LESTER (with Les Paul), RCA, 1977
FAMOUS COUNTRY MUSIC MAKERS, RCA, 1976
IN THREE DIMENSIONS, Stetson, 1988
A MAN AND HIS GUITAR, RCA, 1985
NECK & NECK (with Mark Knopfler), Columbia, 1990
SAILS, Columbia, 1987
STAY TUNED, Columbia, 1985
STREET DREAMS, Columbia, 1986

AUTRY, Gene

Gene Autry, the most popular of all the Singing Cowboys, contributed to many of the most hackneyed stereotypes of country music. However, the country music establishment has never been averse to commercialism, and Autry added lustre to it by aligning himself with Hollywood.

He was born Orvon Gene Autry in Tioga, Texas, on September 29, 1907. Taught to play the guitar by his mother, he joined a medicine show while still at school. After leaving school in 1925, he became a telegrapher for the Frisco Railway Company. In 1929 he went to New York and recorded - often under a pseudonym - for labels like Victor, Okeh and Columbia; at the suggestion of Will Rogers, he landed a job with Tulsa's KVOO as 'Oklahoma's Singing Cowboy'. In 1931 he broadcast regularly on the Sears-sponsored WLS (World's Largest Store) Barn Dance in Chicago. His popularity was increased still further by the release of 'Silver Haired Daddy Of Mine', which went on to sell over five million copies.

His next stop was Hollywood, where he got a role in the Republic B-movie In Old Santa Fe, which led to a starring role in the serial The Phantom Empire. Over the next ten years Autry and his horse, Champion, starred in a string of iffy Westerns, and he notched up a string of hits, most of which were featured over the credits of the films: 'Yellow Rose Of Texas' (1933), 'The Last Roundup' (1934), 'Tumbling Tumbleweeds' (1935), 'Mexicali Rose' (1936), 'Back In The Saddle Again' (1939), 'South Of The Border' (1940), 'You Are My Sunshine' (1941), 'It Makes No Difference Now' (1941), 'Be Honest With Me' (1941) and 'At Mail Call Today' (1945).

With the outbreak of war, Autry enlisted in the US Air Force and became a pilot in Transport Command; at the cessation of hostilities, he returned to Hollywood, where he formed his own film production company, Flying A, and continued making Westerns. While his film career continued apace, his biggest hits of the period were restricted either to seasonal novelty items or children's records: 'Here Comes Santa Claus' (1947), 'Rudolph The Red-Nosed Reindeer' (1948) and 'Peter Cottontail' (1949). His investments included a record company, the California Angels baseball club, a music publishing company, a chain of radio and television stations, as well as interests in oil and property. He was elected to the Country Music Hall Of Fame in 1969.

BACK IN THE SADDLE AGAIN, Platinum, 1989
GENE AUTRY, CBS, 1982

GENE AUTRY 50th ANNIVERSARY, Republic, 1979
LIVE FROM MADISON SQUARE GARDEN, Bulldog, 1982
SINGS SOUTH OF THE BORDER, Bulldog, 1982
TWENTY GOLDEN PIECES, Bulldog, 1982
YELLOW ROSE OF TEXAS, Bear Family, 1986

AXTON, Hoyt

Hoyt Axton is one of a handful of country songwriters who has achieved universal acceptance, through covers of his material by artists as diverse as B.B. King, **Elvis Presley** and Three Dog Night.

He was born on March 25, 1938, in Comanche, Tennessee; his mother was Mae Axton, a songwriter who wrote 'Heartbreak Hotel' for Elvis Presley. Hoyt did a brief stint in the navy before cutting his first record in Nashville, 'Follow The Drinking Gourd'. In 1963 the Kingston Trio had a monster hit with his composition 'Greenback Dollar'. Axton's material consequently became much in demand, and was covered by artists such as **Faron Young**, **Jean Shepard** and **Hank Snow**.

Later he fell foul of the censors, as some of his material - notably 'The Pusher' and 'Snow Blind Friend' (Steppenwolf) - dealt too explicitly with drugs. In spite of this, his reputation spiralled throughout the 1970s, with artists such as Ringo Starr, **Lynn Anderson**, **Tanya Tucker**, **Waylon Jennings**, **Glen Campbell**, **Commander Cody** and Joan Baez covering his songs.

In 1969 he signed with Columbia as a solo artist, cutting *My Griffin Is Gone*, before moving on to Capitol and then A&M. While at A&M, he had minor hits with 'When The Morning Comes' (1974) and 'Flash Of Fire' (1976) and used backing musicians such as **Linda Ronstadt**, **James Burton**, **John Hartford** and guitarist Larry Carlton. After moving to MCA for *Snow Blind Friend* (1977), he scored with 'You're The Hangnail In My Life' and 'Little White Moon' (1977). The following year, he set up the Jeremiah label and charted with 'Della And The Dealer' and 'Rusty Old Halo' (1979). During the 1980s, he launched a parallel film career, appearing in *E.T.* (1983) and *Gremlins* (1984), among others.

AMERICAN ORIGINALS, Capitol (US), 1993
EVERYBODY'S GOIN' ON THE ROAD, Young Blood, 1982
SNOW BLIND FRIEND, MCA (US), 1986
TWENTY GREATEST HITS, Fun (Holland), 1988

BAILES BROTHERS

The Bailes Brothers enjoyed a fleeting spell of celebrity as one of the most popular vocal groups of the 1940s. The group was variously comprised of Kyle, Johnny, Walter and Homer Bailes, but the nucleus consisted of Johnny and Walter. Johnny Bailes was the first member of the family to start performing, when he linked up with **Red Sovine** in 1937; by 1939, Skeets Williamson and his sister, **Molly O'Day**, had joined the group - albeit, briefly. In 1942, the group was auditioned for the *Grand Ole Opry*, which led to a spot on the *Louisiana Hayride*, where they stayed until 1948. While they were appearing at the *Grand Ole Opry*, they recorded for Columbia, contributing songs like 'As Long As I Live', 'I Want To Be Loved' and 'Remember Me'. In 1949 the group disbanded, with each member pursuing separate careers in other professions, although Homer and Kyle made sporadic appearances as gospel singers during the 1950s.

JUST AS THE SUN WENT DOWN, Rounder (US), 1988
TAKE ME BACK TO HAPPY VALLEY, Rounder (US), 1988

BAILEY, DeFord

DeFord Bailey was the first black performer to make regular appearances on the *Grand Ole Opry*. He was born in 1899 in Carthage, Tennessee, and suffered from infantile paralysis when he was three, which stunted his growth. His harmonica version of 'Pan American Blues' was used to open WSM's *Barn Dance*, the billing of which was altered by **George D. Hay** to the *Grand Ole Opry* in 1927. Bailey - known as 'The Harmonica Wizard' - remained an integral part of the *Opry* until 1941, when he was unceremoniously dropped. Although he recorded some sides for Victor from 1927 to 1928, he was always more at home in a live setting and never pursued a recording career. After being dropped from the *Opry*, he ceased to be involved in the music industry and ran a shoeshine stand instead. After years of obscurity, he was tempted out of retirement in 1977 for a series of *Grand Ole Opry* anniversary programmes, before his death in Nashville in 1982.

HARMONICA SHOWCASE (with Bert Bilbro), Matchbox, 1985

BAILEY, Razzy

Erastus Bailey was born on February 14, 1939, near Five Points, Alabama. He made his debut when he was ten for the independent B&K label. By the mid-1960s, he was recording for the Peach label in Atlanta, Georgia, and working the lucrative club circuit of the South. In 1969, **Freddy Weller** produced 'Stolen Moments' for ABC, but it failed to sell and Bailey was left to return to the club circuit playing covers. After two unsuccessful singles for independent labels, and a broken marriage, he cut 'I Hate Hate' for MGM.

His big break came in 1976 when **Dickey Lee** covered Bailey's '9,999,999', which encouraged producer Bob Montgomery to sign Bailey to RCA. With Montgomery at the helm, he chalked up an impressive list of hits: 'What Time Do You Have To Be Back In Heaven' (C&W#9, 1978), 'Loving Up A Storm' (C&W#1, 1980), 'I Keep Coming Back' (C&W#1, 1981), 'Friends' (C&W#1, 1981), 'Midnight Hauler' (C&W#1, 1981), 'She Left Love All Over Me' (C&W#1, 1982), 'Everytime You Cross My Mind' (C&W#10, 1982) and 'Love's Gonna Fall Here Tonight' (C&W#8, 1982).

Unlike many of his compadres, Bailey has retained a strong R&B feel to much of his work - his cover of Wilson Pickett's 'In the Midnight Hour' working surprisingly well. In recent years, the hits have dried up, but his concerts still attract big audiences.

FEELIN' RIGHT, RCA International, 1982
MAKIN' FRIENDS, RCA, 1981
RAZZY BAILEY, RCA, 1981
STILL GOIN' STRONG, Magnum, 1987

BALFA, Dewey

The guiding light behind the traditional cajun band the Balfa Brothers, fiddler Dewey Balfa was born on March 20, 1927, in Mamou, Louisiana, and learnt old songs from his father, who had followed the family tradition by playing the fiddle.

Dewey, with his other brothers, Burkeman, Harry, Rodney and Will, formed the Balfa Brothers band during the late 1930s, collaborating with other prominent Louisiana musicians such as **Nathan Abshire**. Although the group never achieved a solid commercial success, they were sufficiently well-regarded to appear at local functions, and, by the early 1960s, were appearing at folk festivals throughout the US and Europe, and recording for local labels such as Jin and Swallow.

In 1979, the group was decimated by the deaths of Will and Rodney in a car accident, and Dewey was left to continue as a solo artist. While he never made a gainful living from his musical activities, he began to build violins (a natural progression from his regular work as a carpenter) and made albums for Rounder, Sonet and Arhoolie. His importance to cajun music was emphasized in the documentary film *Blues Des Balfas*. Dewey died in 1992.

ARCADIAN MEMORIES (Balfa Brothers), Ace, 1986
CAJUN DAYS (Balfa Brothers), Sonet, 1980
FAIT A LA MAIN, Swallow (US), 1987
LOUISIANA CAJUN MUSIC (Balfa Brothers), Arhoolie, 1981
NEW YORK CONCERTS (Balfa Brothers), Swallow (US), 1987
SOUVENIRS, Swallow (US), 1987
TRADITIONAL CAJUN MUSIC (Balfa Brothers), Ace, 1990

BALLARD, Larry

Larry Ballard's honky-tonk style can be seen as a precursor to New Country, and, while he is much more traditional than, say, **Lyle Lovett**, he is light years away, stylistically, from the old Music City alumni, who have become progressively more pop-orientated.

Larry Ballard was born on November 13, 1946, in Bay City, Michigan. After performing in rock 'n' roll bands during the early 1950s, he switched to country music in 1964. Over the next five years, he toured the Midwest and the West Coast, playing bars and clubs, and by 1973 he had settled in Nashville. After securing a production deal with **Pete Drake**, he landed a contract with the Elektra label, which resulted in the country hit, 'Young Blood And Sweet Country Music' (1974).

BAND, The

Along with **John Fogerty**'s Creedence Clearwater Revival, The Band represented the late 1960s swing towards the appreciation of indigenous American music styles. This had started with the flourishing folk festival circuit of the late 1950s, when traditional styles like cajun, bluegrass and Western Swing began to be seen as significant elements of American cultural history.

Comprising James 'Robbie' Robertson (guitar; born on July 5, 1943, in Toronto, Canada), Garth Hudson (organ; born on August 2, 1937, in London, Canada), Richard Manuel (piano/vocals; born on April 3, 1943, in Stratford, Canada), Rick Danko (bass/vocals; born on December 29, 1942, in Simcoe, Canada) and Levon Helm (drums/vocals; born on May 26, 1943, in Marvell, Arkansas), the group was hired by rockabilly Ronnie Hawkins in 1959 as his backing band, the Hawks. During their time with Hawkins, Robertson demonstrated his flair as a guitarist with his immaculate solo on the group's re-working of Bo Diddley's 'Who Do You Love' (1963).

After finishing with Hawkins in 1963 they took to the open road, playing dancehalls, clubs and bars throughout North America, until they were spotted by John Hammond, the son of the legendary Columbia producer John Hammond. In 1965, they recorded *So Many Roads* with Hammond Jr, before joining **Bob Dylan** for his UK tour. During this tour, music paper headlines screamed 'Bob Dylan Goes Electric!', and Dylan was roundly vilified for moving from pure folk to rock. After the tour, Dylan went to ground in Woodstock in up-state New York with his backing group, now known simply as The Band.

Over the next eighteen months, The Band backed Dylan on a series of tracks that emerged almost immediately on a bootleg album as *The Great White Wonder* (released as *The Basement Tapes* in 1975), while recording their own debut for Capitol. *Music From Big Pink*, was released in August 1968 and generated the type of response generally reserved for long-established artists. It included covers of Dylan songs such as 'I Shall Be Released' and 'This Wheel's On Fire', mixed in with their own compositions like 'The Weight' (UK#21, 1968). The eponymous follow-up in 1969 was a loving representation of a disappearing America: songs like 'The Night They Drove Old Dixie Down' evoked faded photographs in old family albums. Among the other songs were 'Up On Cripple Creek' (US#25, 1969), 'Rag Mama Rag' (UK#16, 1970) and 'King Harvest (Has Surely Come)'. The follow-up *Stagefright* was a slicker affair, but songs like 'The W.S. Walcott Medicine Show', 'Daniel And The Sacred Harp' and 'Stagefright' still retained a patina of rusticity.

Later albums, such as *Cahoots* (1971) and *Northern Lights, Southern Cross* (1975), saw the group's collective edge dissipated by the rigours of life on the road. Their remorseless touring schedule provided the most accurate record of their achievements, and was captured in the live albums *Rock Of Ages* (1972) and *Before The Flood* (with Bob Dylan; 1974). Complete with magnificent horn arrangements by Allen Toussaint, *Rock Of Ages* featured 'Don't Do It' (US#34, 1972) and Chuck Willis's R&B classic 'Hang Up My Rock 'n' Roll Shoes', and anticipated *Moondog Matinée*, which was a collection of R&B standards, including Sam Cooke's 'A Change Is Gonna Come' and Bobby Bland's 'Share Your Love With Me'.

On November 25, 1976, The Band staged their final concert at the Winterland Auditorium in San Francisco; the concert included Van Morrison, Muddy Waters, Eric Clapton, Ronnie Hawkins, Joni Mitchell, **Dr John**, Neil Diamond, Neil Young and Dylan. It was filmed by Martin Scorsese as *The Last Waltz* (1978) and is probably the best film of a live rock concert ever made.

Since The Band's break-up Robbie Robertson has cut a brace of solo albums - *Robbie Robertson* (featuring 'Somewhere Down The Crazy River'; UK#15, 1988) and *Storyville* (1991) - and scored films such as Scorsese's *King Of Comedy* (1983). Levon Helm formed the RCO All Stars, which included Dr John, guitarist Steve Cropper and white bluesman Paul Butterfield, and cut three erratic albums. He also appeared in the biopic of **Loretta Lynn**, *Coal Miner's Daughter* (1980), and in Tom Wolfe's *The Right Stuff* (1983).

Rick Danko cut a fine solo album for Arista in 1978, before joining forces with Levon Helm for a series of reunion gigs (they were later joined by Garth Hudson and Richard Manuel, with Robbie Robertson being replaced by various different session guitarists). After one of these reunion gigs, on March 4, 1986, Richard Manuel hanged himself. While their individual solo projects met with varying degrees of success, nothing matched the imagination and cohesiveness of their work as a unit. A fine group biography by Barney Hoskyns, *Across The Great Divide*, was published in 1992.

THE BAND, Capitol, 1969
BEST OF THE BAND, Capitol, 1987
CAHOOTS, Capitol, 1971
ISLANDS, Capitol, 1977

THE LAST WALTZ, Warner Bros., 1978
MOONDOG MATINEE, Capitol, 1973
MUSIC FROM BIG PINK, Capitol, 1968
NORTHERN LIGHTS, SOUTHERN CROSS, Capitol, 1975
RICK DANKO, Demon, 1978
ROBBIE ROBERTSON, Geffen, 1988
ROCK OF AGES, Capitol, 1972
STAGEFRIGHT, Capitol, 1970
STORYVILLE (Robbie Robertson), Geffen, 1991

BANDY, Moe

Moe Bandy was born in Meridian, Mississippi, on February 12, 1944 into a musical family: his father was a guitarist, his mother a pianist and his grandfather had reputedly been on the railroads with **Jimmie Rodgers**. After the family moved to San Antonio, Texas, he had aspirations to be a rodeo rider, but settled on a musical career when he left school. While working as a metalworker he formed his first group, the Mavericks, and recorded for several local labels.

In 1973 he went solo and recorded 'I Just Started Hatin' Cheatin' Songs Today' (1974) for the GRC label; this was the first of over fifty country hits including 'Honky Tonk Amnesia' (1974), 'It Was Always So Easy To Find An Unhappy Woman' (1975) and 'Bandy The Rodeo Clown' (co-written with **Lefty Frizzell**; 1975). After signing with Columbia in 1975, the hits continued with 'Hank Williams, You Wrote My Life' (C&W#2, 1976), 'I Cheated Me Right Out Of You' (C&W#1, 1979), 'It Took A Lot Of Drinkin' To Get That Woman Over Me' and 'It's A Cheatin' Situation' (C&W#2, 1979). In 1979, he teamed up with **Joe Stampley**; this partnership resulted in a string of hits: 'Just Good Ole Boys' (C&W#1, 1979), 'Hey Joe, Hey Moe' (written by **Boudleaux Bryant**), 'Yesterday Once More' (1980) and 'Where's The Dress' (C&W#2, 1981).

In 1986 he signed with MCA, which rejuvenated his flagging career. Throughout, Bandy has projected the hard-drinkin', womanizing image that has become a cliché within the honky tonk genre, but he does sound as if his tongue is lodged firmly in his cheek.

THE CHAMP, CBS, 1980
FOLLOWING THE FEELING, CBS, 1981
LIVE AT BRANSON, MISSOURI, LaserLight (US), 1992
LIVE FROM BAD BOB'S (with Joe Stampley), CBS, 1985
SHE'S NOT REALLY CHEATIN', CBS, 1982
SONGS OF THE AMERICAN COWBOY, Prism, 1990
YOU HAVEN'T HEARD THE LAST OF ME, MCA, 1987

BANNON, R.C.

Born Daniel Shipley in Dallas, Texas, on May 2, 1945, Bannon sang in the local church choir, played in high-school groups and worked the Texas club circuit, before moving to Seattle. Here he worked as a DJ for a local radio station, adopting the name R.C. Bannon in 1968. After playing support for **Marty Robbins** in 1973, he moved to Nashville in 1976 and became a DJ at Smuggler's Inn, where he met songwriter Harlan Sanders, who secured him a contract with Warner Bros.

Over the next five years, he wrote or co-wrote (usually with John Bettis) 'Only One Love In My Life' (for **Ronnie Milsap**), 'Women Get Lonely' (for **Charly McClain**), and 'Save Me' (1983) and 'Too Hot To Sleep' (1983) (for his wife **Louise Mandrell**). With Louise, he duetted on 'Reunited' (1979) and 'We Love Each Other' (1980), before both switched to RCA. While Louise was far more successful commercially, Bannon chalked up modest solo hits with 'Where There's Smoke There's Fire' (1981) and 'Our Wedding Band' (1982), and worked with his sister-in-law, **Barbara Mandrell**, writing 'One Of A Kind Pair Of Fools' (1983), among others.

BARE, Bobby

Such is the esteem in which Bobby Bare is held by the country music fraternity that when, in 1983, he launched his cable television show *Bobby Bare And Friends* for the Nashville Network, he was able to get all its most successful members to guest. Never one of Nashville's more flamboyant personalities, Bare has been an acute spotter of country trends, picking up writers like **Mickey Newbury**, **Rodney Crowell**, **Guy Clark** and **Shel Silverstein** and performers like **Johnny Rodriguez** early in their careers.

Robert Joseph Bare was born in Ironton, Ohio, on April 7, 1935; his mother died when he was five, and his sister was sent away for adoption. After leaving school at fifteen, he worked first on a farm, and then in a clothing factory; he learnt to play the guitar and eventually joined an amateur country band. In 1958, before being drafted, he recorded the satirical 'The All American Boy' (US#2, 1958), which was credited to a former chum Bill Parsons (Bare benefited little from the song's success, having sold the publishing rights for $50). When he left the army, he was signed by RCA and cut a string of mainly **Chet Atkins**-produced hits, including 'Shame On Me' (US#23, 1962), 'Detroit City' (US#16, 1963), '500 Miles Away From Home' (US#10,

1963), 'Miller's Cave' (US#33, 1964), 'Four Strong Winds' (1964) and **Harlan Howard**'s 'Streets Of Baltimore' (1966).

In 1970 he left RCA for Mercury, and continued to notch up hits such as 'That's How I Got to Memphis' (1970), 'Come Sundown' (1970) and 'Please Don't Tell Me How The Story Ends' (1971). After leaving Mercury, he returned to RCA and recorded *Lullabys, Legends And Lies* and *Singin' In The Kitchen*, both featuring material by Shel Silverstein and including 'Marie Laveau' (C&W#1, 1974) and 'Red-Neck Hippie Romance' (1975). In 1976, he changed labels to Columbia, cutting *As Is* (1981) with Rodney Crowell producing.

In 1976, personal tragedy struck when his fifteen-year-old daughter, Carrie, died from heart failure. While many of his contemporaries have run out of steam, Bare has just kept on going.

AIN'T GOT NOTHING TO LOSE, CBS, 1988
BOBBY BARE, Country Store, 1988
DOWN AND DIRTY, CBS, 1980
ENCORE, CBS, 1984
FAMOUS COUNTRY MUSIC MAKERS, RCA, 1979
MERCURY YEARS: 1970-72, Bear Family (Germany), 1987
MORE TUNES FOR TWO (with Skeeter Davis), RCA International, 1980
TUNES FOR TWO (with Skeeter Davis), RCA, 1975

BAREFOOT JERRY   See **MOSS, Wayne**

BASHFUL BROTHER OSWALD

'Beecher' Pete Kirby, better known as Bashful Brother Oswald, was raised in a family of ten siblings in Sevier County, Tennessee, the son of an accomplished fiddler and guitarist. When Kirby finished school, he worked as a labourer by day, and played guitar in a local club at night. After learning to play the dobro, he moved to Knoxville, Tennessee, and joined **Roy Acuff**'s Crazy Tennesseans.

By 1939, the Crazy Tennesseans had become the Smokey Mountain Boys and were featured on radio station WRL and the *Grand Ole Opry*; as Bashful Brother Oswald, Kirby became one of the star attractions of the performances. In the early 1970s he cut a solo album, produced by **Tut Taylor**, and guested on the influential **Nitty Gritty Dirt Band** album, *Will The Circle Be Unbroken?* Despite failing to achieve international celebrity, his distinctive playing has earned him a legendary status of sorts.

BASHFUL BROTHER OSWALD, Starday (US), 1987
BROTHER OSWALD, Rounder (US), 1988
DON'T SAY ALOHA, Rounder (US), 1988
OZ & CHARLIE (with Charlie Collins), Rounder (US), 1988
THAT'S COUNTRY (with Charlie Collins), Rounder (US), 1988

BATE, Doctor Humphrey, and the Possum Hunters

Doctor Humphrey Bate was born in Summer County, Tennessee, in 1875. Training as a doctor at the Vanderbilt Medical School, he went on to create, with the Possum Hunters, one of the most popular string bands of the 1920s; they appeared first on WSM's *Barn Dance* and then on the *Grand Ole Opry*, and also cut sides for Brunswick. The Possum Hunters variously comprised Bate (harmonica), Oscar Stone (fiddle), Butch Hutcherson (guitar), Walter Leggett (banjo), Staley Walton (guitar), Oscar Albright (bass), Buster Bate (guitar) and Alcyone Beasley, née Bate (vocals and ukelele).

In 1936 Humphrey Bate died, and Stone fronted the group until the reins were taken over by Bate's daughter, Alcyone, and Staley Walton in 1949. The group continued together well into the 1960s, when Alcyone joined the Crook Brothers as pianist.

BECKETT, Barry

Barry Beckett initially achieved celebrity as keyboard player in the house band at **Rick Hall**'s Fame Studios in Muscle Shoals, along with drummer Roger Hawkins, bassist David Hood and guitarist Jimmy Johnson. He has gone on to become one of the more creative country producers in recent years.

He was born in Birmingham, Alabama, in 1944, and moved to Pensacola, Florida, where he played keyboards on sessions with DJ Papa Don Schroeder, who had started to put together his own roster of R&B artists (including Oscar Toney, Mighty Sam and James and Bobby Purify). In 1966, Beckett was invited to fill the keyboard vacancy at Fame. He remained at Fame for two years, leaving to set up the rival Muscle Shoals Sound Studios with Hawkins, Hood and Johnson in 1969; an integral part of the house band, he worked with artists like **Leon Russell**, **Bob Dylan**, **Willie Nelson**, **Tony Joe White**, the Staple Singers and Bobby Womack. After the studios were sold to Malaco in 1985, he concentrated on producing country artists like **Eddy Raven** and **Alabama** and R&B singer Etta James.

BELEW, Carl

Carl Robert Belew was born on April 21, 1931, in Salina, Oklahoma. He came to prominence after securing a spot on the *Louisiana Hayride*, which led to a recording contract with Decca. His first hit was the self-penned 'Am I That Easy To Forget' in 1959. After leaving Decca, he signed with RCA and notched up one hit after another throughout the mid-1960s: 'Hello Out There', 'Crystal Chandelier', 'In The Middle Of A Memory', 'Boston Jail', 'Walking Shadow', 'Talking Memory', 'Girl Crazy', 'Mary's Little Lamb' and 'All I Need is You' (a duet with Betty Jean Robertson). Although the hits have now dried up, he remains a fixture in Nashville.

BELLAMY BROTHERS

The Bellamy Brothers have come to epitomize the soft, close harmonies of much of what is loosely termed 'country-rock'. The brothers - David, born on September 16, 1945, and Howard, born on February 2, 1941, in Derby, Florida - were raised on bluegrass by their musician father. David made his debut in 1964, playing keyboards with the Accidents, a touring band that specialized in backing soul singers like Percy Sledge and Z.Z. Hill. By 1968, he had been joined by his brother Howard in the rock group Jericho; after three years on the road, they turned their attention to composing and writing jingles for commercials, their biggest hit being 'Spiders And Snakes' for Jim Stafford.

In 1975 they secured a contract with Warner Bros., and had a string of hits over the next four years, including 'Nothin' Heavy' (1975), 'Let Your Love Flow' (US#1, UK#7, 1976), 'Satin Sheets' (UK#43, 1976), 'If I Said You Had A Beautiful Body, Would You Hold It Against Me' (US#39, C&W#1, UK#3, 1979), 'Sugar Daddy' (C&W#1, 1980), 'Dancing Cowboys' (C&W#1, 1980) and 'Do You Love As Good As You Look' (C&W#1, 1981). In 1982, they were signed by Elektra - with **Jimmy Bowen** now assisting with the production chores - and the hits kept rolling in: 'For All The Wrong Reasons' (C&W#1, 1982), 'Redneck Girl' (C&W#1, 1982) and 'When I'm Away From You' (C&W#1, 1983).

By 1985 they were being managed by **Mike Curb**, were signed to his MCA-licensed Curb label, and continued to score: 'I Need More Of You' (C&W#1, 1985), 'Old Hippie' (C&W#2, 1985), 'Lie To You For Your Love' (C&W#2, 1985), 'Too Much Is Not Enough' (with the **Forester Sisters**; C&W#1, 1986), 'Kids Of The Baby Boom' (C&W#1, 1987), 'Crazy From The Heart' (C&W#2, 1987) and 'Santa Fe' (1988).

Consistently commercial, the Bellamy Brothers represent the undemanding side of country music; like other 'Top Forty' bands, they have sought instant appeal.

BEAUTIFUL FRIENDS, Warner Bros., 1978
COUNTRY, MCA (US), 1988
CRAZY FROM THE HEART, MCA (US), 1989
GREATEST HITS, MCA, 1987
HOWARD & DAVID, MCA (US), 1986
LET YOUR LOVE FLOW, Warner Bros., 1976
RESTLESS, MCA (US), 1986
SONS OF THE SUN, Warner Bros., 1980

BERLINE, Byron   see COUNTRY GAZETTE

BEVERLY HILLBILLIES   see MANNERS, Zeke

BLACK, Clint

The youngest of four brothers, Clint Black was born in Long Branch, New Jersey, and was raised in Houston, Texas. During his adolescence he played bass in his brother's band, before starting his own outfit in 1987. While working on the club circuit, he met guitarist/fiddler Hayden Nicholas, who had his own home studio. They started working together on material, which resulted in Nicholas auditioning for Z.Z. Top's erstwhile manager, Bill Ham. Ham signed him to a management deal and Black was signed to RCA.

Black's debut, *Killin' Time*, spawned five monsters: 'A Better Man' (C&W#1, 1989), 'Killin' Time' (C&W#1, 1989), 'Nobody's Home' (C&W#1, 1989), 'Walking Away' (C&W#1, 1990) and 'Nothing's News' (C&W#1, 1990). The follow-up, *Put Yourself In My Shoes*, included another wedge of hits: 'Put Yourself In Your Shoes' (C&W#4, 1990), 'Loving Blind' (C&W#1, 1991), 'One More Payment' (C&W#5, 1991) and 'Where Are You Now?' (C&W#1, 1991). *The Hard Way* was released in 1992 with 'We Tell Ourselves' (C&W#1, 1992) following a similar route to its predecessors.

In his short career, Black has become one of the most credible of all the New Country performers, prepared to employ the advances in musical technology without losing sight of diverse inspirations such as **Merle Haggard** and **Jimmy Buffett**.

KILLIN' TIME, RCA, 1989

PUT YOURSELF IN MY SHOES, RCA, 1990
THE HARD WAY, RCA, 1992

BLAKE, Norman

Norman Blake has been justly regarded as one of the most influential session musicians on the circuit, excelling at dobro, mandolin and, most notably, guitar.

He was born in Chattanooga, Tennessee, on March 10, 1938. After leaving high school in Trenton, he joined the Dixieland Drifters, who were regularly featured on local radio in Chattanooga and Knoxville. He recorded an album of duets of Appalachian tunes with banjoist Bob Johnson in 1959, long before interest in traditional music had come into vogue. In 1960 he became a member of **June Carter**'s touring band, and he also duetted with Hylo Brown on West Virginia's WWVA radio station. In 1961, he was drafted into the army for two years, but still managed to find time to cut *Twelve Shades Of Bluegrass*.

On leaving the army, he joined **Johnny Cash**'s backing band, and appeared on his syndicated television series, which began its run in 1969. That year, producer Bob Johnston recruited Blake to appear on the **Bob Dylan** album *Nashville Skyline*. This was followed by more session work, with **Kris Kristofferson**, **Willie Nelson** and Joan Baez. His reputation had now extended beyond the small-print of album covers, and he had the professional clout to form his own groups with other session musicians like **Vassar Clements**, **Tut Taylor** and **John Hartford**; one of the groups was known as the Dobrolic Plectral Society!

In 1977 he was signed to John Fahey's Takoma label, but returned to Rounder in 1980, where he has remained ever since. Touring less and less in recent years, he still works with Johnny Cash, and his exhaustive forays into traditional styles have resulted in a sequence of albums, with Clements, **Tony Rice** and Blake's wife, Nancy, that have done much to foster awareness of the genre.

BLACKBERRY BLOSSOM, Flying Fish, 1979
BLAKE & RICE (with Tony Rice), Rounder (US), 1988
BLIND DOG, Rounder (US), 1988
FIELDS OF NOVEMBER, Flyright, 1989
FULL MOON ON THE FARM, Rounder (US), 1988
HOME IN SULPHUR SPRINGS, Rounder (US), 1987
LIGHTHOUSE ON THE SHORE, Rounder (US), 1985
NASHVILLE BLUES, Rounder (US), 1984
NATASHA'S WALTZ (with Nancy Blake), Rounder (US), 1984
NORMAN BLAKE AND JETHRO BURNS, Flying Fish (US), 1988

NORMAN BLAKE AND TONY RICE, Rounder (US), 1988
NORMAN & NANCY BLAKE, Rounder (US), 1988
OLD AND NEW, Flying Fish (US), 1989
ORIGINAL UNDERGROUND MUSIC FROM THE MYSTE-RIOUS SOUTH, Rounder (US), 1988
RISING FAWN STRING ENSEMBLE, Rounder (US), 1988
SLOW TRAIN THROUGH GEORGIA, Rounder (US), 1988
WHISKEY BEFORE BREAKFAST, Rounder (US), 1988

BLANCHARD, Jack, and Misty Morgan

Jack Blanchard was born on May 8, 1941, and Misty Morgan on May 23, 1945, in Buffalo, New York (coincidentally in the same hospital); both moved to Ohio in their childhood. Blanchard started as a saxophonist in a small instrumental group on the local club circuit, and Morgan played keyboards on the club circuit in Cincinnati.

In the early 1960s, both moved to Florida, where they eventually met and married, and Blanchard began to work on sessions as a pianist and arranger. After five years of conjugal bliss, they started to work together as a duo, attracting the attention of producer Little Richie Johnson, who signed them to the Wayside label. After cutting 'Big Black Bird' in 1969, they finally hit paydirt with the peculiar 'Tennessee Birdwalk' (C&W#1, 1970), which delves into the age-old problem of birdbaths and fowl in underwear! It was followed by another novelty item entitled 'Humphrey The Camel' (C&W#5, 1970), which was their last major hit.

In 1971 they moved to the Mega label, and then to Epic in 1973, but titles like 'You've Got Your Troubles' (1970), 'There Must Be More To Life', 'Somewhere In Virginia In The Rain' and 'I'm High On You' paled into insignificance against the thought-provoking 'Tennessee Birdwalk' and 'Humphrey The Camel'. These two hits have enabled them to get regular television work and keep their engagement diaries full. Jack also worked as a newspaper columnist and drew a comic strip

BLUE GRASS BOYS   see MONROE, Bill

BLUE RIDGE PLAYBOYS   see
TILLMAN, Floyd

BLUE RIDGE RANGERS   see
FOGERTY, John

BLUE SKY BOYS

The Blue Sky Boys are the brothers Bill (born on October 28, 1917) and Earl (born on December 16, 1919), from Hickory, North Carolina. Their father, Garland Bolick, was a tobacco farmer and textile worker. Bill was the first to make his debut in 1935, playing mandolin with the Crazy Hickory Nuts; the same year, the brothers started to perform together on local radio station WWNC in Asheville, North Carolina.

In 1936 they cut their first side for Bluebird, 'The Sunny Side Of Life', written by Bill. Lacking any blues orientation, and wholly influenced by a combination of old-time and religious music, their style differed from that of contemporaries like the **Delmore Brothers** and the **Monroe Brothers**. This made them stalwarts of KWKH's *Louisiana Hayride* for over fifteen years, during which time they had a string of hits: 'Down On The Banks Of The Ohio', 'Story Of The Knoxville Girl', 'Are You From Dixie', 'Turn Your Radio On', 'Short Life Of Trouble' and 'Kentucky'.

Their inflexible conservatism - RCA tried unsuccessfully to persuade them to augment the line-up with an electric guitar - militated against continued popularity, and in 1951 they disbanded. During the mid-1960s, when traditional styles became more appreciated, they teamed up once again to perform at festivals and on the college circuit. The extent of their influence has been clearly reflected in the work of the **Louvin Brothers** and the **Everly Brothers**. Since their rediscovery, the Blue Sky Boys have recorded only occasionally, cutting the odd album for Capitol, Rounder and Starday.

BLUE SKY BOYS, Rounder (US), 1988
IN CONCERT 1964, Rounder (US), 1990
PRESENTING THE BLUE SKY BOYS, Arhoolie (US), 1988
SUNNY SIDE OF LIFE, Rounder (US), 1990

BOGGS, Dock

Moran Lee 'Dock' Boggs was a victim of the period in which he was born - his individual style of banjo-picking would have won him many admirers had he been born twenty years later. Born on February 7, 1898, in Norton, West Virginia, he had to content himself with being a miner for over forty years, as his wife 'held views' on playing the banjo.

In 1927, he caused a certain amount of domestic strife by recording for Brunswick, but it wasn't until his retirement that he came to the attention of Mike Seeger (see **New Lost City Ramblers**), who produced three albums by Boggs for release on the

Folkways label. Unfortunately, it was a case of too little, too late: he died in 1953, and was never able to develop his musical aspirations.

BOGGUSS, Suzy

Since her debut in 1990, Suzy Bogguss has become one of country music's brightest hopes, combining her own material with that of other writers such as **Nanci Griffith** and **John Hiatt**.

A native of Illinois, she graduated from college with a degree in metalwork, and then took to the open road, playing the clubs and bars of the Midwest, building her reputation. In 1990, having been signed by **Jimmy Bowen** to Capitol, she cut *Moment Of Truth*, which was followed by *Somewhere In Between* (1990). While neither made a significant dent in the charts, a relentless touring schedule ensured that her audience kept growing.

The following year, with producer Jimmy Bowen, she cut *Aces* (1991), which failed to provide her with a big hit single but cracked the country Top Ten. It featured a fine version of Nanci Griffith's 'Outbound Plane' and Ian Tyson's (formerly of folk duo Ian & Sylvia) 'Someday Soon', and also featured contributions from **Vince Gill**, fiddler Mark O'Connor and mandolinist Sam Bush (see **New Grass Revival**). In 1992, she cut *Voices In The Wind*, which included covers of two John Hiatt songs, 'Drive South' and 'Lovin' A Hurricane', and a contribution from the **Nitty Gritty Dirt Band**.

ACES, Liberty (US), 1991
MOMENT OF TRUTH, Capitol (US), 1990
SOMEWHERE IN BETWEEN, Capitol (US), 1990
VOICES IN THE WIND, Liberty, 1992

BOND, Johnny

Although Johnny Bond was better known as a Singing Cowboy and an actor, it was his compositional skills that set him apart from his contemporaries. When he ended his career as an entertainer, he started to write - first a biography of **Tex Ritter**, and then his own auto-biography, *Reflections* - both books illustrating an unusual understanding of the evolution of styles in country music.

He was born Cyrus Whitfield Bond on June 1, 1915, in Enville, Oklahoma; during the 1920s, his parents moved to a smallholding in Marietta, Oklahoma. At first he learnt to play the ukelele, before transferring to the guitar, and had mastered them both before leaving high school. In 1934 he made his debut on a radio sta-

tion in Oklahoma City, and three years later he joined **Jimmy Wakely**'s trio, the Bell Boys. In 1940, after travelling to Hollywood, he was signed up to broadcast on **Gene Autry**'s *Melody Ranch*, and remained with the show until 1956. In the meantime, he had signed with Columbia and was rapidly becoming one of the most popular performers in the business, cutting 'Cimarron' (1940), 'I'll Step Aside' (1945), 'Rainbow At Midnight', 'Divorce Me C.O.D', 'Smoke, Smoke, Smoke', 'Tennessee Saturday Night', 'Cherokee Waltz', 'A Petal From A Faded Rose', ''Til The End Of The World', 'Tomorrow Never Comes' and 'I Wonder Where You Are Tonight'.

In 1943, Bond formed the Red River Valley Boys as the backing group for Tex Ritter; this was the beginning of an association that would endure for the rest of their lives, and would result in their forming a music publishing company. In later years, the hits effectively dried up, although 'Hot Rod Lincoln' (US#26, 1960), 'Ten Little Bottles' (C&W#2, 1965) and 'Here Come The Elephants' (1971) were exceptions.

During the 1970s, his career as an author took off and he stopped performing, though he worked on behalf of the Country Music Association. He died on June 12, 1978, in Burbank, California.

BEST OF JOHNNY BOND, Starday (US), 1987
JOHNNY BOND SINGS THE GREAT SONGS OF THAT WILD WICKED BUT WONDERFUL WEST, Official, 1988

BOONE, Debby

Born Deborah Ann Boone on September 22, 1956, in Hackensack, New Jersey, she burst into the charts in 1977 with 'You Light Up My Life' (US#1, C&W#4, UK#48, 1977). This success - combined with her being the daughter of bobby-sox singer Pat Boone and her God-fearing wholesomeness - seemed to indicate that her career in country music would be long and fruitful; but in 1982, after hits like 'My Heart Has A Mind Of Its Own' (1979) and 'Are You On The Road To Lovin' Me Again' (C&W#1, 1980), and after appearing in a revival of the musical *Seven Brides For Seven Brothers*, she went into retirement. Since then she has written her autobiography, *Debby Boone ... So Far*, which is packed with homilies of quite extraordinary banality, and cut religious albums for the Word label.

CHOOSE LIFE, Word, 1985
FRIENDS FOR LIFE, Word, 1989
SURRENDER, Word, 1984

BOWEN, Jimmy

Jimmy Bowen (born on November 30, 1937) has, for over thirty-five years, exerted a considerable influence on the music industry. Having played in a variety of high-school groups, he had his first break by penning 'Party Doll' for rockabilly artist Buddy Knox; this was followed in the same year by 'I'm Stickin' With You' (featuring Bowen on vocals and Knox on guitar; US#14, 1957), which was credited to Jimmy Bowen and his Rhythm Orchids.

By 1963 he had joined Frank Sinatra's Reprise label, where he produced Sinatra, Dean Martin and Keely Smith, among others. When Reprise was absorbed into Warner Bros., Bowen became label head before moving first to Capitol and then, in 1977, to MCA. In 1979, he moved on to Elektra, where he produced **Crystal Gayle** and **Mel Tillis**, among others, before moving to head MCA in Nashville in 1984, where he has produced **George Strait**, the **Bellamy Brothers** and the **Oak Ridge Boys**, and has signed a slew of New Country artists like **Lyle Lovett**, **Steve Earle** and **Reba McEntire**.

In 1989 he set up the Universal label signing artists like **Eddy Raven**, only to dissolve the company a year later, taking all of his signings over to Capitol/Liberty. As head of the label's Nashville operation, he has brought on artists like **Suzy Bogguss** and Billy Dean. Throughout his career as a producer he has notched up about eighty Number Ones in the country charts.

JIMMY BOWEN, Roulette, 1987

BOWMAN, Don

Don Bowman was born on August 27, 1937, in Lubbock, Texas. During his childhood, he sang in church and learnt to play the guitar, and he became a DJ while still at school. After leaving school, he became established as a DJ, working with fellow DJ **Waylon Jennings** and developed a parallel career as a comedian. By 1964, he had come to the attention of **Chet Atkins** who signed him to RCA, resulting in the hit 'Chet Atkins Made Me A Star' (1964), and in 1966 he was nominated Country Comedian of the Year. Despite scoring more hits, with 'For Loving You' (a duet with **Skeeter Davis**; 1968), 'Folsom Prison Blues No. 2' (1968) and 'Old Ugly Gladys Jones' (1969), recent years have seen his career stagnate, although his popularity in the southern states remains as high as ever.

BOXCAR WILLIE

Lecil Travis Martin, better known as Boxcar Willie, was born on September 1, 1931, in Sterrett, Texas. After a successful career in the Air Force, and then as a flight engineer for an airline, he worked as a DJ until starting his own recording career in 1975. By the early 1980s, his part-spoken, part-sung tales of ignominy, marital strife and life on the railroad had become particularly popular in Europe, one of the biggest hits being 'Bad News' (C&W#36, 1982). Despite his late start as a performer, his career has prospered to the extent that he is constantly in demand on television and the club and cabaret circuit, where the trademark overalls, dirty face and floppy hat go down a storm.

BEST LOVED FAVOURITES, Volumes 1-2, RCA, 1988
DADDY WAS A RAILROAD MAN, Big R, 1980
FREIGHT TRAIN BLUES, Colorado, 1985
LIVE AT WEMBLEY, Pickwick,1988
NO MORE TRAINS TO RIDE, Colorado, 1985
SINGS HANK WILLIAMS AND JIMMIE RODGERS, Big R, 1980
TAKE ME HOME, Big R, 1980

BOYD, Bill

Born on a ranch in Fannin County, Texas, on September 29, 1910, Bill Boyd has the dubious distinction of being one of the few performers truly entitled to the label of Singing Cowboy. Forming Alexander's Daybreakers in 1926 with his younger brother Jim, the group had changed their name to the Cowboy Ramblers by 1934, with fiddler Art Davis and banjoist Walter Kirkes making up the line-up. Other later members of the Cowboy Ramblers included guitarist **Charlie Walker** and steel guitarist Lefty Perkins; while his brother Jim played with the **Light Crust Doughboys** from 1938 to 1939.

Having secured a recording contract with the RCA subsidiary Bluebird, they cut cowboy songs or traditional instrumentals: 'Strawberry Roan' (1934), 'Under The Double Eagle' (1935), 'New Spanish Two Step' (1939), 'Spanish Fandango' (1939) and 'Lone Star Rag' (1949). Bill had his own radio show on WRR, Dallas, for many years, and also appeared in several films.

BRADDOCK, Bobby

A fine songwriter, Bobby Braddock was born on August 5, 1940, in Lakeland, Florida, and started his career as a pianist in local groups. In 1964 he moved to Nashville and worked as a session musician, while also honing his songwriting skills. The following year he joined **Marty Robbins**' backing band as pianist and wrote the Robbins hit 'While You're Dancin'' (1965). After leaving Robbins, he became a full-time songwriter and was signed to **Buddy Killen**'s publishing company, Tree.

Over the next few years, with different writing partners such as Sonny Throckmorton and Curly Putman, he co-wrote 'Ruthless' (**Statler Brothers**, 1967), 'D-I-V-O-R-C-E' (**Tammy Wynette**, 1968), 'Did You Ever' (**Charlie Louvin** and **Melba Montgomery**, 1970), 'Golden Ring' (Tammy Wynette and **George Jones**, 1976), 'Thinkin' Of A Rendezvous' (**Johnny Duncan**, 1976), 'He Stopped Loving Her Today' (George Jones, 1980), 'I Feel Like Loving You Again' (**T.G. Sheppard**, 1981) and 'Faking Love' (T.G. Sheppard and **Karen Brooks**, 1983).

During his long career he has picked up several awards from the Country Music Association as well as a Grammy. He also recorded for MGM between 1967 and 1969 (scoring with 'I Know How To Do It' and 'Girls In Country Music'), Elektra from 1979 until 1981, and RCA from 1981 until 1985.

BRADLEY, Harold

The younger brother of producer **Owen Bradley**, guitarist Harold Bradley was born on January 2, 1926, in Nashville, Tennessee. His career started as a guitarist in **Ernest Tubb**'s band in 1943, before working with **Eddy Arnold**, **Pee Wee King** and **Bradley Kincaid** from 1946 until 1948. He then joined the WSM house band and worked on programmes like *Grand Ole Opry* and *Sunday Down South*. From 1950 he was regularly used by his brother Owen as a session guitarist, and during the 1960s recorded a number of bland country-tinged albums of easy-listening music, such as *Bossa Nova Goes Nashville* (1965).

In 1965 he became the musical director of *The **Jimmy Dean** Show* and then formed the Forrest Hills Publishing Company. Throughout the 1970s he continued working on sessions, most notably with **Leon Russell** on *Hank Wilson's Back* (1973). Although he toured with **Slim Whitman** during the mid-1980s, much of his time has been given over to looking after his publishing company.

BRADLEY, Owen

Owen Bradley contributed more to the establishment of Nashville as one of the South's premier recording meccas than, perhaps, anybody else. Bradley's versatility, as an arranger, bandleader, studio owner, record company executive, session musician and producer, was central to the development of the Nashville sound.

He was born on October 21, 1915, in Westmoreland, Tennessee. His career began in the late 1930s as a session pianist and guitarist in Nashville. In 1947 he was signed to the Bullet label, where he remained until moving to Decca in 1949. In his capacity as a recording artist, he cut a string of instrumentals, including 'Blue Eyes Crying In The Rain', 'Blue Danube Waltz' and 'Blues Stay Away From Me'. In 1947 he was appointed leader of radio station WSM's in-house band (which included his brother **Harold Bradley**), as well as being asked by Decca's Paul Cohen to supervise the installation of a recording studio in Nashville. This first studio was completed in 1952, and by 1956 he had built the Quonset Hut (known as Bradley's Barn) on 16th Avenue South (now known as Music Row); Bradley's Barn was acquired by Columbia in 1962, when they established a headquarters in Nashville.

In his capacity as in-house producer for Decca's Nashville set-up, he produced **Ernest Tubb**, **Bill Monroe** and **Kitty Wells**; with these artists, whose individual styles were already fully developed, Bradley proved to be a more-than-sympathetic producer. However, when he was required to produce artists such as **Brenda Lee** and **Patsy Cline**, he tended to use lush orchestral and vocal backing arrangements, which often detracted from their highly personal vocal styles; he also proved distinctly unsuitable when it came to overseeing **Buddy Holly** early in his career, as he was ill-equipped to deal with the rawness of rock 'n' roll.

Despite his pre-eminence at Decca, Bradley was also working independently for Mercury and Dot. This ubiquity, combined with his preference for bland pop arrangements over traditional country fixtures, such as fiddles and steel guitars, gave the Nashville sound a homogeneity and accessibility that did little to enhance the critical reputation of country music. In 1958, he became head of country A&R at Decca, and by 1968 he had become vice-president of their Nashville operation. During the 1960s he stopped recording and concentrated on production, working with **Loretta Lynn**, **Conway Twitty**, **Bill Anderson** and Burl Ives. In 1975 he retired from MCA (Decca became known as MCA in 1974), having been elected to the Country Music Hall Of Fame, but continued to work as an independent producer, on **k.d. lang**'s

Shadowland, among others, and scoring the soundtrack for the Loretta Lynn biopic *Coal Miner's Daughter.*

BIG GUITAR, Charly, 1984

BRIGGS, David
Pianist and guitarist David Briggs was one of the founder members of the soul group the Mark Vs, which gradually metamorphosed into the first house band at the Fame Studios in Muscle Shoals. He was featured on the early hits recorded at Fame by artists like Arthur Alexander, Jimmy Hughes, Tommy Roe and the Tams. While recording at Fame, he toured with the Mark Vs, now renamed Dan Penn and the Pallbearers. In 1964 he left Muscle Shoals for Nashville, where he recorded with **Elvis Presley**, among others, and was a member of the group Area Code 615 (see **Moss**, **Wayne**). By the early 1970s, he had set up the formidably successful Quadrafonic Studios in Nashville with **Jerry Carrigan** and **Norbert Putnam**, backing artists like **Charlie Rich** and **Dobie Gray**.

BRITT, Elton
Despite the multitude of purveyors of western songs and the hosts of yodellers, few have managed to combine those elements as effectively as Britt. He was born James Britt Baker on June 27, 1917, in Marshall, Arkansas. After learning the guitar while at school, he was discovered by talent scouts and given a contract with the Los Angeles radio station, KMPC. On KMPC he broadcast as a solo artist and with the Beverly Hillbillies (See **Manners**, **Zeke**), with whom he cut some sides for Decca and Varsity.

By 1937 he had been signed as a solo artist by RCA; he remained with RCA for twenty-two years, his first hit being 'Chime Bells' (now a yodelling classic), and became the first country artist to win a gold disc in 1942, with his sparkling rendition of 'There's A Star-Spangled Banner Waving Somewhere'. In 1949, having signed with Columbia Pictures the previous year, he appeared in *Laramie*, which was the first of a number of film roles. His pre-eminence as a yodeller ensured that he became a fixture on the *Grand Ole Opry* and WWVA's *Jamboree*. After leaving RCA in 1959, he recorded for ABC, Decca and Ampar. He died on June 23, 1972, having retired to Connellsville, Pennsylvania, some years earlier.

YODEL SONGS, Stetson, 1988

BRODY, Lane
Lane Brody was born in Racine, Wisconsin, and started her career in Chicago singing jingles for McDonalds and Kentucky Fried Chicken. Signed to the GRT label, she was introduced to Steve Wax, who secured her a guest role in the television series *Taxi* and appearances in the television movies *Country Gold* and *Gift Of Life*. Her first hit came in 1983, when 'Over You' was included in Bruce Beresford's movie *Tender Mercies*, starring Robert Duvall; it was nominated for an Academy Award. This provided her with the opportunity to duet with **Johnny Lee** on the theme to NBC's soap, 'The Yellow Rose' (C&W#1, 1984). While her career has failed to pick up momentum since, she is certainly worth earmarking for the future.

BROMBERG, David
Since the late 1960s, David Bromberg's prowess as a session musician has been sought after by artists as diverse as **Bob Dylan**, **Jerry Jeff Walker**, Chubby Checker, Ringo Starr, Gordon Lightfoot and Sha-Na-Na.

He was born on September 19, 1945, in Philadelphia, Pennsylvania, but raised in New York. His earliest influences were folk and blues singers like the Weavers, Big Bill Broonzy and **Doc Watson**. After studying musicology for a year at Columbia, he started to work as a session guitarist, playing with Checker, Walker and Jay & the Americans. Remaining with Walker for two years, he started to record with Bob Dylan in 1970, playing on both *Self Portrait* and *New Morning*. Building up his own following throughout this period - particularly in East Coast clubs like the Bitter End - he secured a contract with Columbia.

He recorded four albums for Columbia: *David Bromberg* (1971), *Demon In Disguise* (1972), *Wanted Dead Or Alive* (1974) and *Midnight On The Water* (1975); they were all considerable critical successes and displayed a keen technical virtuosity. While Bromberg never achieved the same degree of commercial acceptance as **Ry Cooder** and **John Fogerty**, he was one of the first to acknowledge - and pay homage to - his roots, by recording those songs that had initially influenced him. The high esteem in which he was held by his colleagues was illustrated by the featured guest artists on his albums, which variously included Jerry Garcia and Phil Lesh of the Grateful Dead, **Ricky Skaggs**, **Linda Ronstadt**, **Bernie Leadon** and **Dr John**, among others.

ALBUQUERQUE ACADEMY LIBRARY

In 1976, after being dropped by Columbia, he was signed by Fantasy; his first album for them was *How Late'll Ya Play 'Til?*, which was followed by *Hillbilly Jazz*, with **Vassar Clements**, for the independent Flying Fish label. His final album for Fantasy was *You Should See The Rest Of The Band* (1980), after which he went into semi-retirement to build violins.

HILLBILLY JAZZ RIDES AGAIN, Flying Fish, 1987

BROOKS, Garth

Garth Brooks has managed to bust the whole country music market wide open with a trio of albums that have sold over twenty million copies worldwide. Although not a groundbreaker, his unprecedented success has put him firmly in the vanguard of the New Country brigade.

He was born on February 7, 1962, in Oklahoma, and was raised in Yukon. His mother, Colleen Carroll, recorded unsuccessfully for Capitol in the 1950s. Brooks made his debut at a local talent show, which led to a spell with a local group called Nyle. While studying advertising at Oklahoma State University, he played almost nightly at a local pizza parlour. By 1987 he had hooked up with another local group, Santa Fe, and was cutting demos around Nashville. After signing with Capitol, he cut his debut album, *Garth Brooks*, which was produced by **Allen Reynolds**, as were later abums *No Fences* (1990), *Ropin' The Wind* (1991) and *The Chase* (1992).

Brooks has sustained a level of chart consistency matched only by **Ronnie Milsap**, **Randy Travis** and **George Strait**: 'Much Too Young (To Feel This Damn Old)' (C&W#8, 1989), 'If Tomorrow Never Comes' (C&W#1, 1989), 'Not Counting You' (C&W#2, 1990), 'The Dance' (C&W#1, 1990), 'Friends In Low Places' (C&W#1, 1990), 'Unanswered Prayers' (C&W#1, 1990), 'Two Of A Kind, Workin' On A Full House' (C&W#1, 1991), 'The Thunder Rolls' (C&W#1, 1991), 'What's She Doin' Now' (C&W#1, 1991), 'Papa Loved Mama' (C&W#3, 1992), 'The River' (C&W#1, 1992) and 'Somewhere Other Than The Night' (C&W#1, 1992).

While many critics feel that his hi-tech live show is redolent of rock concerts, his songwriting draws from similar traditions to those of country's finest writers, such as **Dallas Frazier**, **Hank Cochran** and **Merle Haggard**.

THE CHASE, Liberty, 1992

GARTH BROOKS, Capitol, 199O
NO FENCES, Capitol, 1990
ROPIN' THE WIND, Capitol, 1991

BROOKS, Karen

Karen Brooks is noted for a purity of voice that is reminiscent of **Emmylou Harris** and **Rosanne Cash**, both of whom have covered her material. Raised in Dallas, Texas, she worked on a ranch in Denton after leaving high school, and then moved to Los Angeles.

Moving again, to Franklin, Tennessee in 1981, she was eventually signed by Warner Bros., where her career started to pick up momentum with modest hits like 'New Way Out' (1982), 'Fakin' Love' (a duet with **T.G. Sheppard**; C&W#1, 1983), 'If That's What You're Thinking' and 'Walk On' (1983), and 'Tonight I'm Here With Someone Else' (1984). In 1985, she cut another duet, this time with **Johnny Cash**, on 'I Will Dance With You', but she hasn't yet managed to consolidate her promise as a performer, despite her songwriting talents.

I WILL DANCE WITH YOU, Warner Bros., 1985

BROWN, Jim Ed

Jim Ed Brown was born on April 1, 1934, in Sparkman, Arkansas, the son of an affluent farmer, and started his career as a member of the sibling group, the **Browns.** In 1965, while still recording with the Browns, he was signed by **Chet Atkins** to RCA as a solo artist, cutting titles like 'I Heard From A Memory Last Night' (1965), 'A Taste Of Heaven' (1966), 'You Can Have Her' (1966) and 'Pop A Top' (C&W#3, 1967). In 1967, when the Browns disbanded, he remodelled his solo career and immediately obtained engagements in Las Vegas. Since then he has managed to notch up a string of hits, including 'Morning' (C&W#4, 1970) and 'Southern Loving' (1973).

In 1976 he teamed up with **Helen Cornelius**, and together they had a number of hits, including 'I Don't Want To Have To Marry You' (C&W#1, 1976), 'Saying Hello, Saying I Love You, Saying Goodbye' (C&W#2, 1977), 'Lying In Love With You' (C&W#2, 1977) and 'Fools' (C&W#3, 1980). His live act, backed by the Gems, combined with his television show, *Nashville On The Road*, has ensured him a constant flow of work, and his popularity seems as great today as it ever was.

BROWN, Milton

Milton Brown was one of the prime movers in the development of Western Swing. Only his death in a car accident stopped him from becoming as well known as **Bob Wills**.

He was born on September 8, 1903, in Stephenville, Texas; in 1918, the family moved to Fort Worth, where Brown went to Arlington Heights High School. In 1925 he joined the police force and then became a salesman. In 1931 he met Bob Wills and joined his group, who performed on local radio under a variety of names, including the Aladdin Laddies and the **Light Crust Doughboys**.

In 1932 Brown left to form his own group, the Musical Brownies, who initially appeared at the Crystal Springs Dance Pavilion, and broadcast on Fort Worth's radio station KTAT. The line-up eventually comprised Brown (vocals), Milton's brother Durwood (vocals and guitar), Cecil Brower (fiddle), Warner Coffman (bass), **Bob Dunn** (steel guitar) and Fred Calhoun (piano); it was this line-up that cut some sides for RCA's Bluebird label. In 1935, the Musical Brownies defined Western Swing with a number of recordings for Decca, blending jazz standards, such as 'St. Louis Blues', 'Hesitation Blues', 'Memphis Blues' and 'Mama Don't Allow', with traditional country items: 'Carry Me Back To The Lone Prairie', 'You're Bound To Look Like A Monkey' and 'Sweet Jennie Lee'. The effect was electrifying, echoing a style that was more in keeping with the Hot Club of France.

In 1936, fiddler **Cliff Bruner** joined the group, but just as their future seemed assured, the tyre of Brown's car burst on the way back from a performance at the Crystal Springs Dance Pavilion, and the car crashed into a telegraph pole, instantaneously killing vocalist Katherine Prehoditch and seriously injuring Brown. He died on April 13, 1936. The group continued for two years after Brown's death, but without his influence their work lacked the potency and immediacy of the earlier records.

DANCE-O-RAMA, Rambler (US), 1981
EASY RIDIN' PAPA, Charly, 1987
TAKING OFF, String, 1981

BROWN, T. Graham

Anthony Graham Brown is one of the new crop of country artists to emerge in the 1980s. Raised on R&B and country, his style echoes the soft country-rock of the **Eagles**.

He was born in Arabi, Georgia, and moved to Nashville in 1982, cutting demos and singing jingles for Disneyland and Budweiser, among others. In 1984 he came to the attention of Capitol, who signed him up, and by 1986 he had teamed up with songwriter **Alex Harvey**, scoring with 'Hell And High Water (C&W#1, 1986), from his debut album *I Tell It Like It Used To Be*. His next single from the album, 'Don't Go To Strangers' (featuring guitarist Brent Rowan; C&W#1, 1987), is notable for its soulful quality, indicating the strong R&B influences of his youth. More hits followed with 'Brilliant Conversationalist', 'She Couldn't Love Me Anymore', 'The Last Resort' and 'Darlene' (C&W#1, 1988).

He has also carved out a niche as a bit-player in movies, such as *Greased Lightning* (with Richard Pryor; 1977), *The Farm* (with **John Schneider**; 1985) and *Heartbreak Hotel* (1988). While his records have tended to be over-produced, his live act has become very popular with the younger audiences who have come to country music via **Garth Brooks**.

BRILLIANT CONVERSATIONALIST, Capitol (US), 1987
BUMPER TO BUMPER, Capitol, 1990
I TELL IT LIKE IT USED TO BE, Capitol (US), 1987

BROWNS

The Browns comprised Ella Maxine Brown (born on April 27, 1932, in Sampti, Louisiana), **Jim Ed Brown** and Bonnie Brown (born on July 31, 1937, in Sparkman, Arkansas). Maxine and Jim Ed started as a duo in 1952, when they won a talent contest on Little Rock's KLRA, which led to a regular spot on *The Barnyard Frolic*. This secured a regular spot on KWKH's *Louisiana Hayride* and a recording contract with Abbot subsidiary, Fabor; their first record was the self-penned 'Looking Back To See' (1954).

In 1954 they became a trio with the addition of younger sister, Bonnie, and headlined at the *Ozark Jubilee* show. In 1956 they were signed to RCA by **Chet Atkins**, on the recommendation of **Jim Reeves**, who had been one of the backing vocalists on the earlier 'Looking Back To See'. While their records with Abbot were very traditional country, their output with RCA was pure pop and more reminiscent of the McGuire Sisters, but they still notched up a number of hits: 'The Three Bells' (US#1, 1959), 'Scarlet Ribbons' (US#13, 1959), 'The Old Lamplighter' (US#5, 1959), 'Send Me The Pillow You Dream On' (1961), 'Ground Hog' (1961), 'I'd Just Be Fool Enough' (1966) and 'Big Daddy' (1967). In 1967, after years of continued popularity, Jim Ed went solo, as both Maxine and Bonnie wanted to devote more time to their families.

LOOKIN' BACK TO SEE, Bear Family (Germany), 1986
ROCKIN' ROLLIN' BROWNS, Bear Family (Germany), 1984

BRUCE, Ed

Edwin Bruce was born in Keiser, Arkansas, on December 29, 1939. He started as a rockabilly singer recording for Sun, while writing for **Jerry Lee Lewis**, **Charlie Rich** and **Johnny Cash**. His own career was greeted with something less than approbation and so he returned to selling used cars on his father's lot. In 1964 he moved to Nashville as a session singer and songwriter, providing 'See The Big Man Cry' for Charlie Louvin (see **Louvin Brothers**) and 'Northeast Arkansas Mississippi County Bootlegger' for **Kenny Price**.

After securing a recording contract with RCA, he cut a number of minor country hits with producer Bob Ferguson: 'Walker's Woods' (1967), 'Last Train To Clarksville' (1967) and 'Painted Girls And Wine' (1968). In 1968 **Fred Foster** of Monument signed him up and he cut *Shades Of Ed Bruce*, which included 'Song For Ginny' and 'Everybody Wants To Go Home' (1969). Moving on once again, this time to United Artists in 1973, he cut 'July You're A Woman' (1973) and 'Mammas Don't Let Your Babies Grow Up To Be Cowboys' (1975). A brief spell at Epic from 1977 was followed by a stint with MCA, where his biggest hits were 'Diane' (1980), 'The Last Cowboy Song' (a duet with **Willie Nelson**; 1981), 'You're The Best Break This Old Heart Ever Had' (C&W#1, 1981), 'My First Taste Of Texas' (1983) and 'After All' (1984). By 1985 he had signed with RCA, cutting *Homecoming*.

Meanwhile his reputation as a writer has flourished, with **Crystal Gayle** covering 'Restless' (1974), **Tanya Tucker** covering 'The Man That Turned My Mama On' and 'Texas (When I Die)' (1975), and **Waylon Jennings** and Willie Nelson covering 'Mammas Don't Let Your Babies Grow Up To Be Cowboys' (1978). He has also joined the Nashville élite, with appearances in *The Chisholms* and in the 1982 *Maverick* series as Tom Guthrie. He has also hosted *American Sports Cavalcade*.

ED BRUCE, MCA (US), 1986
LAST TRAIN TO CLARKSVILLE, RCA International, 1982
NIGHT THINGS, RCA, 1986
ONE TO ONE, MCA (US), 1986
ROCK BOPPIN' BABY, Bear Family (Germany), 1986

TELL'EM I'VE GONE CRAZY, MCA (US), 1986
YOU'RE NOT LEAVING HERE TONIGHT, MCA, 1983

BRUMLEY, Tom

When Tom Brumley joined **Rick Nelson**'s Stone Canyon Band in 1969, he became one of the first country session musicians to embrace the burgeoning hybrid of country-rock that was to become such a lucrative genre in the early 1970s. While groups like **Poco** and the **Eagles** did much to heighten the awareness of country music, it was left to groups like the **Byrds**, **Mike Nesmith**, the **Flying Burrito Brothers** and the Stone Canyon Band to present the less homogenized version of country music.

Brumley was born on December 11, 1935, in Powell, Missouri; his father, Albert, was a composer, and wrote songs like 'Turn Your Radio On' and 'I'll Fly Away'. Brumley quickly assimilated the mores of country music, acquiring his first pedal steel guitar as a teenager, after hearing **Jerry Byrd** and Roy Wiggins. Initially playing the local clubs in Missouri with his four brothers, he was then drafted into the US Army.

After completing his National Service in Germany he headed out west to California, where he met **Buck Owens**; in December 1963 he acquired a full-time position in his group, the Buckaroos, with whom he remained until joining the Stone Canyon Band in 1969. His steel-guitar work helped to characterize the Bakersfield sound, thereby ensuring that California had its own base for country music. Brumley remained with Rick Nelson until the latter's death in 1985, and then concentrated on his steel-guitar manufacturing business, interrupted by the odd bit of session work.

BRUNER, Cliff

Fiddler Cliff Bruner joined the Musical Brownies in 1935, shortly before the death of their founder **Milton Brown**. In the short time the two men worked together they cut over four dozen sides; on these recordings rests the reputation of the Musical Brownies as one of the most innovative of all the Western Swing outfits.

Bruner was born on April 25, 1915, in Houston, Texas, and got his big break when he joined the Brownies. His brief association with the group put him in good stead with their record label, Decca, with whom he was to remain for over ten years. After leaving the Brownies, he formed the Texas Wanderers, also known as Cliff Bruner's Boys, cutting tracks like 'It Makes No Difference Now'. While the line-up of these units varied substantially over the years, the most famous included **Bob Dunn** (steel guitar), **Moon Mullican** (piano), Dickie McBride (guitar), Hezzie Brock (bass) and Will Raley (electric mandolin).

During the 1940s Bruner recorded for the independent Ayo label, but with Western Swing declining in popularity, he gradually stopped performing altogether in the 1950s, becoming an insurance salesman in his hometown, Houston.

BRYANT, Boudleaux and Felice

One of the finest husband-and-wife songwriting teams, Felice and Boudleaux Bryant provided a rich diversity of material for an even wider range of artists. What set them apart was their ability to voice the neuroses of adolescence, backed by strong melodies.

Boudleaux Bryant was born in Shellman, Georgia, on February 13, 1920. After studying the violin and joining the Atlanta Philharmonic Orchestra in 1938, he changed tack and joined a local jazz group; his first excursion into country music came when he joined **Hank Penny**'s group. In 1948 he married Felice Scaduto, who was born in Milwaukee, Wisconsin, on August 7, 1925; they had met when she was an elevator attendant at the Shrader Hotel in Milwaukee. The following year they started to compose together; their first hit was **Little Jimmy Dickens**' version of 'Country Boy'.

With this under their belts, they moved to Nashville, where **Fred Rose** of Acuff-Rose signed them to a publishing deal. Over the next fifteen years or so, they penned one hit after another: 'Bye Bye Love', 'Wake Up Little Susie', 'All I Have To Do Is Dream', 'Bird Dog', 'Problems' and 'Take A Message To Mary' for the **Everly Brothers**; 'Rainin' In My Heart' for **Buddy Holly**; 'I've Been Thinking' and 'The Richest Man' for **Eddy Arnold**; 'Let's Think About Mexico' for **Bob Luman**; 'Baltimore' for **Sonny James**; and 'Come Live With Me' for **Roy Clark**. As an illustration of how effectively their songs have been covered by artists of different musical persuasions, 'Love Hurts' has been recorded by **Roy Orbison**, **Gram Parsons**, the Everly Brothers, Nazareth, Jennifer Warnes, Suzie Quatro, and Jim Capaldi, among others.

In 1979 they departed from the habit of a lifetime by cutting an album of their own compositions, *Surfin' On A New Wave*, for an independent label. Boudleaux died on June 30, 1987.

ALL I HAVE TO DO IS DREAM, DB, 1980

BUCKAROOS   See **OWENS, Buck**

BUFFETT, Jimmy

Jimmy Buffett has always operated on the periphery of the country music industry, as his style owes as much to the singer-songwriter genre of the early 1970s as it does to Nashville. What is intriguing about him is his dilettantism and apparent indifference to the music industry: Buffett spends most of his time kicking around the Florida Keys or the Caribbean on his yacht.

He was born on December 25, 1946, in Mobile, Alabama, and worked for *Billboard* after having graduated in journalism. In 1970 he signed with the Barnaby label, cutting *Down To Earth*. It was a commercial disaster and Barnaby added insult to injury by losing the tapes. He was sufficiently peeved to leave Nashville and head off to Key West. With fresh material, he signed with ABC-Dunhill and recorded *A White Sport Coat And A Pink Crustacean* (1973), which featured guitarist **Steve Goodman** and displayed Buffett's tuneful ear and ironic lyrics. Over the next few years, with the Coral Reefer Band, he cut albums like *Living And Dying In 3/4 Time*, which included 'Come Monday' (US#30, 1974); *Changes In Attitude*, which included 'Margaritaville' (a paean to the joys of inebriation; US#8, 1977), 'Changes In Latitude, Changes In Attitude' (US#37, 1977) and 'Cheeseburger In Paradise' (US#32, 1978); and *Volcano*, which included 'Fins' (US#35, 1979).

By the end of the 1970s, Buffett had cut back his recording activities to concentrate on writing film scripts and novels at his home in Franklin, Tennessee; but he has found the time to cut *Coconut Telegraph* (1980), *Last Mango In Paris* (1985) and *Hot Water* (1988), among others. While many consider him self-indulgent, his levity is a breath of fresh air in an industry noted for its pomposity.

CHANGES IN LATITUDE, CHANGES IN ATTITUDE, MCA (US), 1976
COCONUT TELEGRAPH, MCA (US), 1980
FLORIDAYS, MCA (US), 1987
HAVANA DAYDREAMIN', MCA (US), 1976
LAST MANGO IN PARIS, MCA (US), 1985
LIVING AND DYING IN 3/4 TIME, MCA (US), 1974
OFF TO SEE THE LIZARD, MCA (US), 1989
ONE PARTICULAR HARBOUR, MCA (US), 1982
RIDDLES IN THE SAND, MCA (US), 1984
SOMEWHERE OVER CHINA, MCA (US), 1981
SON OF A SON OF A SAILOR, MCA (US), 1978
VOLCANO, MCA (US), 1979

A WHITE SPORT COAT AND A PINK CRUSTACEAN, MCA (US), 1973

BURGESS, Wilma

Wilma Burgess has never achieved the global celebrity of many of her peers, but has been a consistent hitmaker in the country charts since her debut in 1960.

She was born on June 11, 1939, in Orlando, Florida, and started performing locally while majoring in physical education at Stetson University. Encouraged by her reception, she went to Nashville to cut some demos, which were heard by **Owen Bradley**; and a contract with Decca and an entrée to the lucrative television and club circuit followed. In the mid-1960s, she had a string of minor country hits: 'Baby' (1965), 'Misty Blue' (1966), 'Don't Touch Me' (1966), 'Tear Time' (1967) and 'Lonely For You' (1973). She last recorded between 1977 and 1978 for RCA, but she still appears regularly in and around Nashville.

BURNETTE, Dorsey

As one third of the Rock 'n' Roll Trio, Dorsey Burnette was one of the unsung heroes of rockabilly. It was in his later years, as a songwriter for a number of country artists and as a country singer, that he achieved most success.

He was born on December 28, 1932, in Memphis, Tennessee. In 1956 he formed the Rock 'n' Roll Trio, as a result of the success of another local lad, **Elvis Presley**; the trio comprised his brother, Johnny, and guitarist Paul Burlison. Despite staying together for only a year, they recorded items like the **Delmore Brothers**' 'Blues Stay Away From Me', 'Tear It Up', 'Oh Baby Babe' and 'Train Kept A-Rollin'' for the Coral label, but as they were allegedly too similar to Presley, the trio disbanded. Johnny went on to become a songwriter, and then a teen idol, before dying in 1964 in a boating accident; and Burlison gave up the music business altogether.

Dorsey started to write for other artists, including **Rick Nelson**, as well as recording occasionally with his brother or by himself; as the Burnette Brothers, they cut 'My Honey' for Imperial, and as a solo artist, he had a minor hit with 'Tall Oak Tree' (US#23, 1960) for the Era label. In 1961, he signed to the Dot label, and the country influences became more apparent in his songwriting.

Over the next ten years he recorded for Reprise and Liberty, before signing to Capitol in 1972. Despite

having a number of minor hits in the country charts and cutting the LPs *Here And Now* and *Dorsey Burnette*, it was all a long way from the spirited inventiveness of the Rock 'n' Roll Trio. In 1975 he moved to Motown's Melodyland label, and then to the Calliope label for *Things I Treasure*, as well as writing for **Glen Campbell** and **Jerry Lee Lewis**, among others. He died of a heart attack on August 19, 1979, in Canoga Park, California.

COMPLETE RECORDINGS (Johnny Burnette & the Rock 'n' Roll Trio), Bear Family (Germany), 1988
DORSEY BURNETTE, Volumes 1-2, Hollywood, 1987
THE LEGENDARY JOHNNY BURNETTE ROCK 'N' ROLL TRIO, Charly, 1984
TALL OAK TREE, Era (US), 1987

BURNS, Kenneth 'Jethro'   See **HOMER & JETHRO**

BURTON, James

If it is remotely possible for a session guitarist to become a household name, James Burton is a contender. The list of his past employers includes some of country's most celebrated exponents, whose success is due in part to Burton's distinctive guitar style, a style which has been a significant influence on artists like **John Fogerty** of Creedence Clearwater Revival and Robbie Robertson of **The Band**.

He was born on August 21, 1939, in Shreveport, Louisiana. In 1957 he first made his mark playing sessions with Dale Hawkins, contributing a bluesy staccato solo on 'Suzie Q'; this was followed by a stint with **Bob Luman**, who briefly had aspirations to be a rock 'n' roller. The next year he became a resident member of the studio band, with **Leon Russell** and Delaney Bramlett, on Jack Good's television show, *Shindig*. He then teamed up with bassist James Kirkland to form the nucleus of **Rick Nelson**'s band; it was on records like 'Hello Mary Lou' that Burton developed his highly individual style of playing. In 1964 he left Nelson and started to work with **Buck Owens** and **Merle Haggard**; these collaborations underpinned the Bakersfield sound, which owes as much to rockabilly as to Nashville traditionalism.

In 1969 he formed an alliance with pianist **Glen D. Hardin**, and they were both recruited by **Elvis Presley**, forming the centrepiece of his road and recording unit over the next eight years. In 1972 they both started to record with **Gram Parsons**, being featured on the albums *GP* and *Grievous Angel*. When Parsons died in 1974, and then Presley in 1977, they were enlisted by **Emmylou Harris** to form the Hot Band. In the early 1980s, after several tours and albums with Harris, they both returned to session work.

In 1971 Burton cut the dire *Guitar Sounds Of James Burton*, with a sound reminiscent of muzak, the album proves that a good session man does not necessarily make a good front man.

BUSH, Johnny
Johnny Bush is one of many country artists unknown outside the US. Nominated Most Promising Newcomer in 1968 by *Record World*, he has been one of the many honky-tonk heroes whose melancholic dispositions have found a resonance with the public.

He was born on February 17, 1935, in Houston, Texas; in 1952 he moved to San Antonio, where he got a job at the Texas Star Inn, singing and playing the guitar. By the early 1960s he had become drummer in **Willie Nelson**'s band, which was followed by a spell with **Ray Price**'s Cherokee Cowboys, with whom he stayed for just over three years. At the end of that time, he rejoined Nelson and signed with the independent Stop label as a solo artist, where he had a number of hits: 'You Ought To Hear Me Cry' (1967), 'What A Way To Live' (1967), 'Undo The Right' (1968) and 'You Gave Me A Mountain' (1969).

In 1972, after moving to RCA, he had his biggest hit with 'Whiskey River' (1972). Other lesser hits followed, but by the mid-1970s he had all but given up recording in favour of the lucrative club circuit of Texas and the Deep South.

BUTLER, Carl and Pearl
Carl Robert Butler was born in Knoxville, Tennessee, on June 2, 1927. After starting his career as a songwriter, he obtained a solo contract with Capitol before moving to Columbia in 1960, where he had a number of hits, including 'Honky Tonkitis' (1961) and 'Don't Let Me Cross Over' (C&W#1, 1962). The latter included his wife Pearl Dee (née Jones; born on September 20, 1930, in Nashville, Tennessee) as a backing vocalist, and they decided to form a duo.

With regular appearances at the *Grand Ole Opry* from 1962, they notched up a succession of hits in the late 1960s: 'Loving Arms' (1963), 'Too Late To Try Again' (1964), 'I'm Hangin' Up The Phone' (1964), 'Just Thought I'd Let You Know' (1965), 'Little Pedro' (1966) and 'I Never Got Over You' (1969). Since the

early 1970s, they have curbed their recording activities and concentrated on selected live appearances. Pearl died in March 1988.

BUTTREY, Kenny
Kenny Buttrey has been one of the most visible session drummers in Nashville since the early 1960s, when he joined **Charlie McCoy**'s group, the Escorts, with guitarists Mac Gayden and **Wayne Moss**. He then moved on to the Paramounts, which included soul singer Robert Knight in its line-up. This enabled Buttrey to develop his technique and make contact with producers like **Billy Sherrill**, with whom he would work regularly over the next decade.

During the late 1960s and early 1970s, he was a member of the house band at Monument, and also of Area Code 615 (see **Moss**, **Wayne**) before the group splintered. Buttrey teamed up with **Billy Swan**, forming part of his touring band, and worked on sessions at Nashville principally for Columbia. He remains one of Nashville's most successful drummers.

BYRD, Jerry
When Jerry Byrd decided to quit the music industry and move to Hawaii in the 1950s, country music lost one of its most innovative steel guitarists. He was born on March 9, 1920, in Lima, Peru. He worked as a painter until 1939, when he became a professional musician, after having played with the Pleasant Valley Boys in his free time. After serving in the army, he joined **Ernest Tubb**'s Troubadours for two years, before starting a solo career with the Mercury label in 1949.

Although albums such as *Shores Of Waikiki* (1951) demonstrated a technical prowess and advanced understanding of the Hawaiian guitar, they were difficult to like because the material and arrangements were so crass. Between 1964 and 1968 he was bandleader on television's The **Bobby Lord** Show. He has now retired from the music industry.

BYRDS
Influenced by country music almost from the start, the Byrds' early material belies the notion that the epochal album *Sweetheart Of The Rodeo* was their only real contribution to country music.

The group was formed in the early 1960s as the Beefeaters by Roger McGuinn (born James McGuinn in Chicago, Illinois, on July 13, 1942), David Crosby (born David Van Cortland in Los Angeles, California, on August 14, 1941), **Gene Clark**, **Chris Hillman** and Michael Clarke (born in New York on June 3, 1943). Before its formation, McGuinn had been in the Limeliters and the Chad Mitchell Trio, and Crosby had been a member of Les Baxter's Balladeers. In 1965, the group changed its name to the Byrds.

The first single, a cover of **Bob Dylan**'s 'Mr Tambourine Man' (US#1, UK#1, 1965), featured session musicians like **Leon Russell**, and also featured McGuinn's highly distinctive twelve-string Rickenbacker, whose sonorous jangling was to become the group's trademark in its early years. While covering two more Dylan songs - 'All I Really Want To Do' (US#40, UK#4, 1965) and 'My Back Pages' (US#30, 1967) - the group also started to record their own material, which comprised Gene Clark's plaintive love songs (with strong country overtones), and Crosby's and McGuinn's more folk-orientated material. The Byrds also showed themselves adept at selecting material from disparate sources, and imbuing it with their own distinctive imprimatur: Pete Seeger's 'Turn! Turn! Turn!' (US#1, UK#26, 1965), Jackie DeShannon's 'Don't Doubt Yourself' and Stephen Foster's 'Oh! Susannah'.

In 1966, after the departure of Gene Clark, the group remained a quartet and recorded *Fifth Dimension* and then *Younger Than Yesterday*. These albums were a slight change in direction: McGuinn and Crosby now contributed a larger percentage of the material, with the emergent West Coast sound influencing songs like 'Eight Miles High' (US#14, UK#24, 1966), 'Mr Spaceman' (US#36, 1966) and 'So You Wanna Be A Rock 'n' Roll Star' (US#29, 1967). Hillman also started to develop as a songwriter, his background in bluegrass music ensuring that the rural influence on the group was clearly discernible.

In 1968 Crosby was fired from the group, and they continued as a trio, recording *Notorious Byrd Brothers*, until drummer Michael Clarke left just prior to the album's completion. Superficially a glossy hi-tech album, it showed the group in its best light, maximizing the potential of the recording studio without sacrificing musical integrity; their treatment of Carole King's 'Goin' Back', in particular, transformed a hummable pop song into a nostalgic paean to the lost youth of a generation.

The next line-up included **Gram Parsons**, drummer Kevin Kelley and session musician **Clarence White**; it was substantially this line-up that recorded *Sweetheart Of The Rodeo*, which featured material by the **Louvin Brothers**, **Merle Haggard**, **Woody Guthrie**, soul singer William Bell, Bob Dylan and Gram Parsons. Despite the excellence of this album, and its

subsequent impact on the music industry, it sold poorly at first and was recorded amidst considerable acrimony. After a controversial tour of South Africa, which prompted Parsons' departure, McGuinn found himself the sole survivor, as Hillman had left to join Parsons in the **Flying Burrito Brothers**.

The next line-up, for the album *Dr Byrds And Mr Hyde*, included White, drummer **Gene Parsons** and bassist John York; it was a patchy affair, with McGuinn clearly missing the songwriting input of both Hillman and Parsons. Over the next three years, the line-up stabilized, with Skip Battin replacing York. Although the albums *Ballad Of Easy Rider*, *Untitled*, *Byrdmaniax* and *Further Along* were erratic, there were high points such as 'Ballad Of Easy Rider', 'Chestnut Mare' (US#19, 1971) and 'Just A Season'.

In 1973 McGuinn disbanded the existing line-up, and replaced it with the original line-up for a reunion album, entitled *Byrds*, for the Asylum label: it was a scrappy ill-tempered affair. McGuinn started an erratic solo career, which was interspersed by long silences; he did, nonetheless, record a number of albums, including *Roger McGuinn* (1973), *Cardiff Rose* (1976) and *Thunderbyrd* (1977), and he also joined Bob Dylan's touring caravan, Rolling Thunder Revue.

In 1978, having signed with Capitol, he joined up with Hillman and Gene Clark for *McGuinn, Hillman And Clark* (1979), which included 'Don't You Write Her Off' (US#33, 1979) and *City* (1980), before Clark left to pursue his on-going solo career. McGuinn and Hillman then cut an album of that name, before separating once again. McGuinn toured the club circuit and returned in 1990 with an album for Arista.

BALLAD OF EASY RIDER, Columbia (US), 1970
BYRDS PLAY DYLAN, Columbia (US), 1977
COLLECTION, Castle, 1988
DOCTOR BYRDS AND MR HYDE, Beat Goes On, 1969
FIFTH DIMENSION, Beat Goes On, 1966
GOLDEN HIGHLIGHTS, Columbia (US), 1986
GREATEST HITS, Columbia, 1984
HISTORY OF THE BYRDS, Columbia, 1973
McGUINN, HILLMAN & CLARK, Capitol, 1979
MR TAMBOURINE MAN, Columbia (US), 1965
NOTORIOUS BYRD BROTHERS, Columbia (US), 1968
RETURN FLIGHT (McGuinn, Clark and Hillman), Edsel, 1992
ROGER McGUINN, Edsel, 1973
SWEETHEARTS OF THE RODEO, Columbia (US), 1969
TURN, TURN, TURN, Columbia (US), 1966
ULTIMATE BYRDS, Columbia, 1990
UNTITLED, Columbia, 1970
YOUNGER THAN YESTERDAY, Columbia (US), 1967

CAJUN GIB & GENE see **PARSONS, Gene**

CALE, J.J.
Jean Jacques Cale is one of a small coterie who have evolved such a distinctive guitar style that they transcend genre and have been influenced by the blues, as well as country. He was born on December 5, 1938, in Oklahoma City; after learning the guitar while still at school, he formed the Valentines, which occasionally featured **Leon Russell** and played in and around Tulsa.

By 1959 he had moved to Nashville to build a career as a singer and songwriter, but despite involvement in *Grand Ole Opry* tours, he couldn't penetrate Nashville's close-knit community. In 1964 he went to Los Angeles to seek a publishing deal, and teamed up with Russell and other Oklahomans, Carl Radle and Chuck Blackwell, cutting 'Slow Motion' the following year. For the next four years, he played around Los Angeles, singing in bars and gaining studio experience as a guitarist, arranger and producer, working with Delaney & Bonnie, among others. In 1967 he cut the rock album, *A Trip Down Sunset Strip*, with Russell and producer Snuff Garrett, under the name of the Leathercoated Minds.

In 1968 he returned to Oklahoma, where he built his own studio and started to put together some demos. The demos were passed on to producer Denny Cordell by bassist Carl Radle, and as a result Cordell set up the Shelter label in partnership with Leon Russell. In 1970 Cale had his first hit as a songwriter when Eric Clapton covered 'After Midnight'. In 1972, Cale's debut *Naturally* was issued, produced by Audie Ashworth and featuring **David Briggs**, **Norbert Putnam** and **Jerry Carrigan**, among others. It became a classic and established the standard by which all his later work would be evaluated; it included his only substantial hit 'Crazy Mama' (US#22, 1972). He built a 16-track recording studio in Nashville with some of the proceeds.

The succession of albums he has cut over the years have made absolutely no concession to the demands of commercialism. Both Mark Knopfler and Richard Thompson have acknowledged his influence by appearing on *Eight* (1983); in 1984 he scored the soundtrack to *La Femme De Mon Pote*, starring Isabelle Huppert.

EIGHT, Mercury, 1983
FIVE, Shelter, 1979
GRASSHOPPER, Mercury, 1982
NATURALLY, Shelter, 1972
OKIE, Shelter, 1973
REALLY, Shelter, 1972
SHADES, Mercury, 1981
SPECIAL EDITION, Mercury, 1984
TEN, Silvertone, 1992
TRAVEL LOG, Silvertone, 1989
TROUBADOUR, Mercury, 1976

CALLAHAN BROTHERS
The Callahan Brothers were one of the few vocal/instrumental duos of the 1930s to adapt successfully to the electric country and western fusion of the 1940s.

Bill (guitar and vocals) was born Walter T. Callahan on January 27, 1910, and Joe (guitar, mandolin, bass and vocals) was born Homer C. Callahan on March 27, 1912, in Laurel, North Carolina. Raised on gospel and traditional ballads, they made their debut in 1933 at the Rhododendron Festival at Asheville, North Carolina, where, inspired by the success of **Jimmie Rodgers**, they performed as yodellers. Such was the enthusiasm of the audience that the Callahan Brothers immediately auditioned for radio stations, landing their first engagement at WNOX, Knoxville.

This auspicious start secured them a deal with the ARC label, for whom they recorded fourteen sides. They were featured on radio stations throughout the South and the south-west, settling eventually in Dallas, where they performed daily on KRLD. By the 1940s, they had become one of the more successful Western Swing outfits, enlarging the group - which was known as the Blue Ridge Mountain Folk - and recording regularly for Columbia, as well as ARC. However, they recorded less and less until, by the early 1960s, they had effectively retired. Joe died on September 10, 1971, while Bill continues to work as a photographer and still plays occasionally, providing an invaluable link with the pre-war era.

CAMPBELL, Glen

Glen Travis Campbell, in combining MOR pop with country influences, has succeeded in securing a massive audience. He was born on April 22, 1936, in Delight, Arkansas, and was given his first guitar at the age of four. In 1954 he joined his uncle's group, Uncle Bill's Western Band, and toured New Mexico, before forming his own band, the Western Wranglers.

After marrying Billie Nunley in New Mexico, he moved to Los Angeles in 1958, where he quickly found favour as a session guitarist, and played on the Champs' hit 'Tequila'. From 1960 he sessioned with Frank Sinatra, Jan & Dean, **Rick Nelson**, **Elvis Presley** and the Beach Boys, among others. Capitol signed him as a guitarist, but not before he had had a minor hit with 'Turn Around, Look At Me' for the independent Crest label in 1961.

After more sessions, and a stint in the Beach Boys' touring band (as replacement for Brian Wilson), he had a minor hit with a cover of Donovan's 'Universal Soldier' in 1965. In 1967, he rose to prominence with a cover of **John Hartford**'s 'Gentle On My Mind' (US#39, 1968); he consolidated this success by recording the first of a number of Jim Webb songs, 'By The Time I Get To Phoenix' (US#26, C&W#2, 1967). Over the next dozen years or so, he struck gold time after time: 'I Wanna Live' (US#36, C&W#1, 1968); 'Wichita Lineman' (US#3, C&W#1, 1968; UK#7, 1969) and 'Galveston' (US#4, C&W#1, UK#14, 1969), both composed by Jim Webb; 'Let It Be Me' (US#36, 1969) and 'All I Have To Do Is Dream' (US#27, 1970; UK#3, 1969), with **Bobbie Gentry**; 'Where's The Playground, Susie?' (US#26, 1969); 'True Grit' (US#35, 1969); 'Try A Little Kindness' (US#23, C&W#2, 1969; UK#45, 1970); 'Honey Come Back' (another Webb composition; US#19, C&W#2, UK#4, 1970); 'Oh Happy Day' (US#40, 1970); 'Everything A Man Could Ever Need' (UK#32, 1970); 'It's Only Make Believe' (US#10, UK#4, 1970); 'Dream Baby' (US#31, UK#39, 1971); 'Rhinestone Cowboy' (US#1, C&W#1, UK#4, 1975); 'Country Boy' (US#11, C&W#5, 1975); 'Don't Pull Your Love' (US#27, C&W#5, 1976); 'Southern Nights' (US#1, C&W#1, UK#28, 1977); 'Sunflower' (US#39, C&W#4, 1977) and 'Can You Fool' (US#38, 1978).

In 1969 he started a four-year run of *The Glen Campbell Goodtime Hour* for CBS-TV, as well as co-starring with John Wayne in the film *True Grit*, and starring in the film *Norwood*. In 1981, as the hits decreased, he left Capitol for the Mirage label; in 1983 he moved on to Atlantic's country label, Atlantic America; and in 1987 he signed with MCA, cutting *Still Within The Sound Of My Voice*, which stayed in the country charts for over a year and featured a title track composed by the ubiquitous Webb. Despite the blandness of his work, he has done much to draw the attention of MOR audiences to lesser-known writers.

COMPLETE GLEN CAMPBELL, Stylus, 1989
COUNTRY COLLECTION, Knight, 1990
GLEN CAMPBELL SINGS WITH BOBBIE GENTRY AND ANNE MURRAY, MFP (Holland), 1985
GREATEST HITS, Capitol, 1985
LIVE, RCA, 1981
OLD HOME TOWN, Atlantic, 1984
SOMEBODY LIKE THAT, Liberty, 1992
STILL WITHIN THE SOUND OF MY VOICE, MCA, 1987
WALKIN' IN THE SUN, Capitol, 1990
WICHITA LINEMAN, Connoisseur, 1988

CANNON, Ace

A fine alto saxophonist, Ace Cannon was born on May 5, 1934, and achieved distinction in the late 1950s along with **Boots Randolph** as one of the premier session men. In 1959 he succeeded Martin Willis as the resident saxophonist in Bill Black's Combo, and in 1962 he started a solo career, signing with the Hi label and scoring with 'Tuff' (US#17, 1962) and an instrumental version of the **Delmore Brothers**' 'Blues Stay Away From Me' (US#36, 1963). He continued recording for Hi throughout the 1960s and early 1970s, cutting raunchy instrumental covers of R&B and country classics such as **Charlie Rich**'s 'Behind Closed Doors' and **Tammy Wynette**'s 'Stand By Your Man'. During the late 1970s, he recorded less, but remained active as a session musician and on the club circuit.

CARGILL, Henson

While not quite a one-hit wonder, Henson Cargill's public career was very brief. He was born in Oklahoma on February 5, 1941. His grandfather, who had been Mayor of Oklahoma City, and his father, a leading attorney, were both keen for Henson to follow in the family footsteps. Initially wanting to go into ranching, Cargill settled on a career in the music industry.

After establishing himself on the Las Vegas club circuit in 1966, he went to Nashville and met producer Don Law; their first collaboration was 'Skip A Rope' (US#25, C&W#1, 1968) for Monument. Over the next five years, he scored with 'Row, Row, Row' (1968), 'None Of My Business' (1969) and 'Some Old California Memory' (1973). After spells with different labels, such as Mega (1971), Atlantic (1974) and Elektra (1975), he had another minor hit with 'Silence On The Line' (1979).

CARLISLE, Bill and Cliff

Clifford Raymond Carlisle was a top-notch dobro player, who learnt his craft in vaudeville as a boy. He was born in Taylorsville, Kentucky, on May 6, 1904, and cut his first sides for the Gennett label in 1930, before going on to accompany **Jimmie Rodgers**. While Rodgers was an inspiration for Cliff, Cliff had the purer voice, and his ability to encompass most idioms made him a key influence on later generations of country musicians.

The following year, he formed a duo with his younger brother, William (born in Wakefield, Kentucky, on December 19, 1908), and the pair of them recorded sides for ARC, RCA's Bluebird subsidiary and Decca. They also broadcast regularly on WLAP, Lexington, Kentucky, and WBT, Charlotte, North Carolina. Throughout the 1930s and 1940s, the duo achieved distinction with their train songs (like 'Pan American Man') and 'blue' yodels (both of which had been popularized by Rodgers), as well as with liberal dosings of comedy items (a legacy of Cliff's days in vaudeville). In 1947 Cliff retired and took up residence in Lexington, where he died on April 2, 1983.

Bill formed a new group, the Carlisles, which included various younger members of the family. From 1954 their hits included 'Rainbow At Midnight', 'No Help Wanted' and 'Too Old To Cut The Mustard'; and in that same year they also joined the *Grand Ole Opry*. Bill has become one of the conduits from the traditional hillbilly country of the 1930s to the Nashville of today.

BUSY BODY BOOGIE, Bear Family (Germany), 1985
CLIFF CARLISLE, Volumes 1-2, Old Timey (US), 1988

CARPENTER, Mary-Chapin

Ever since her debut in 1989, Mary-Chapin Carpenter has been justly lionized for the dry perspicacity of her songs. While she has been lumped together with the New Country artists, her songs refuse to lie down in any one particular category. She was born in 1958 in Alexandria, Virginia, and moved to New Jersey. After finishing college, she started a long apprenticeship on the Washington DC folk club circuit where she came to the attention of Columbia's Nashville division.

In 1989, after contributing to **Tony Rice**'s *Native American*, she made her debut with the mature *State Of The Heart*. While it failed to generate hit singles, it sold sufficiently well to get her name around. *Hometown Girl* (1990) and *Shooting Straight In The Dark* (1991) were assured follow-ups, featuring titles such as 'You Win Again' and 'Going Out Tonight', which were neat examinations of the highs and lows in the relationships between men and women.

The follow-up *Come On Come On* in 1992, included singles like 'Passionate Kisses', which in a perfect world would have been a monster hit. However, the success of her singles has become incidental, as her last two albums have gone platinum in the US. She has the potential to rank alongside the very best songwriters of her generation.

COME ON, COME ON, Columbia, 1992
HOMETOWN GIRL, Columbia, 1990
SHOOTING STRAIGHT IN THE DARK, Columbia, 1991
STATE OF THE HEART, Columbia, 1989

CARRIGAN, Jerry

Until his departure with **David Briggs** and **Norbert Putnam** to Nashville in 1964, Jerry Carrigan was the drummer in the Mark Vs, the house band at the Fame Studios in Muscle Shoals. He was featured on that studio's earliest records by artists like Arthur Alexander, Jimmy Hughes, Tommy Roe and the Tams. He became, like other session musicians who customized the great soul records of the early 1960s, one of the stalwarts of the Nashville sound. With Briggs and Putnam, he runs the Quadrafonic Studios, where he has backed artists like **Elvis Presley** and **Charlie Rich**, and worked with producers like **Billy Sherrill** and **Chips Moman**.

CARSON, Fiddlin' John

Fiddlin' John Carson is one of the many mythic characters whose early prowess dragged hillbilly music out of the backwoods, and launched it upon an unsuspecting public. Despite his limited audience, Carson was a model to younger fiddlers and guitarists, leaving a legacy which is still perceptible today.

Carson was born on March 23, 1868, in Fannin County, Georgia. He worked as a jockey, a foreman in a cotton mill, a distiller and a painter, before ending up as a lift attendant. Playing the fiddle in the meantime, he made his radio debut on September 9, 1922. On June 14, 1923, **Ralph Peer** cut Carson's 'The Little Old Log Cabin In The Lane', which is regarded as the first authentic country record. It was put on sale at a fiddlers' convention, sold out within the day, and Carson was signed up by the Okeh label as a result. Between 1923 and 1931 he cut around 150 sides, including 'The Old Hen Cackled And The Rooster's Goin' To Crow', 'You Will Never Miss Your Mother Until She's Gone' and 'Old Dan Tucker'. While most of these sides were solo, he occasionally recorded with the Virginia Reelers, which included his daughter Rosa Lee. From 1931 until 1934 he recorded periodically with RCA. He died on December 11, 1949, in Atlanta.

THE OLD HEN CACKLED AND THE ROOSTER'S GOIN' TO CROW, Rounder (US), 1988

CARSON, Martha

Martha Carson was born Irene Amburgey in Neon, Kentucky, on March 19, 1921. During the 1950s she was one of the most successful vocalists in the US. Her rather anachronistic hybrid of gospel and country appealed to diehard country fanatics, as well the wealthy supper-club circuit, thereby taking the gospel straight to the sinners on their home turf!

Her career started in 1939, when she broadcast on WHIS, Bluefield, West Virginia; shortly afterwards she met and married mandolinist Jack Carson, forming a duo with him and touring the country. Throughout the 1940s they broadcast frequently on WSB's *Barn Dance* in Atlanta, where they were known as the Barn Dance Sweethearts. After divorcing Jack in 1951, Martha turned to gospel and composed around a hundred songs for labels like RCA and Capitol, including 'I'm Gonna Walk And Talk With My Lord', 'I Can't Stand Up Alone', 'Let's Talk About That Old Time Religion' and 'Satisfied'. In recent years, she has gradually slipped into retirement.

EXPLODES, Bear Family (Germany), 1986
SATISFIED, Stetson, 1989

CARTER, Carlene

The daughter of **Carl Smith** and **June Carter**, and the step-daughter of **Johnny Cash**, Carlene Carter at first resisted identification with Nashville, building her career on her own account rather than relying upon her distinguished family connections. Latterly, she has reverted to type, and shows every indication of developing as substantial a career as her half-sister **Rosanne Cash**.

She was born in Nashville, Tennessee, on September 26, 1955, and was taught the guitar by her grandmother, Maybelle Carter (see **Carter Family**). After two unsuccessful marriages and a spell as a model, she moved to London in 1977 and married bassist Nick Lowe, cutting her debut *Carlene Carter* for Warner Bros., with Lowe, guitarist Dave Edmunds and Graham Parker's group, the Rumour. Over the next five years, she was a regular performer on the London club circuit, guesting with her husband's various bands and drawing from a pool of musicians more commonly associated with Squeeze and **Elvis Costello** (she was also briefly signed to the F-Beat label, owned by Elvis's manager Jake Riviera).

Although she had minor hits in the UK - with **Rodney Crowell**'s 'Never Together, But Close Sometimes' (1978), Richard Dobson's 'Baby Ride Easy' (a duet with Dave Edmunds), and Johnny Cash's 'Ring Of Fire' (1980) - she failed to make a big impression. In 1983 she duetted with Robert Ellis Orrall on 'I Couldn't Say No' (US#32, 1983), and the following year she diversified, appearing in the London musical *Pump Boys And Dinettes*, and working on the short film *Too Drunk To Remember* (based on a song of the same name from her 1980 album, *Musical Shapes*).

In 1986 she was due to co-star in another musical, *Angry Housewives*, but left the cast during rehearsals and returned to Nashville. Since her return, she has worked on the club circuit and scored with hits such as 'I Fell In Love' (C&W#3, 1990) and 'Come On Back' (C&W#3, 1990). Her live shows have always been noted for their robust good humour and the ease with which she slips from one style to another.

BLUE NUN, F-Beat, 1981
CARLENE CARTER, Warner Bros., 1978
C'EST SI BON, Epic (US), 1983
MUSICAL SHAPES, F-Beat, 1980

CARTER, June

One of Ezra and Maybelle Carter's (see **Carter Family**) daughters, June Carter was born in Mace

Springs, Virginia, on June 23, 1929, and sang with the Carter Family from 1940 until 1960, when she embarked on a solo career. Her marriage to **Carl Smith** in 1952 resulted in divorce five years later. After starting her solo career, she became an integral part of the **Johnny Cash** roadshow, which resulted in duets with Cash, including 'Jackson' (C&W#2, 1967), 'If I Were A Carpenter' (C&W#2, 1970), 'What Is Truth' (1970) and 'One Piece At A Time' (1976).

In 1968 she married Cash, becaming a regular on his widely syndicated television series, and providing him with the stability to overcome many of the personal problems that had dogged him since childhood. Both **Carlene Carter**, June's daughter from her first marriage, and **Rosanne Cash**, Johnny's daughter from his first marriage, have subsequently become significant additions to the Carter-Cash pantheon.

CARTER, Maybelle   see **CARTER FAMILY**

CARTER, Wilf

Wilf Carter was born in Guysboro, Nova Scotia, on December 18, 1904. After starting out as a rodeo rider, he made his debut on CFCN, Calgary. Here he was principally known for his yodelling, which, although influenced by **Jimmie Rodgers**, possessed a sophistication more attributable to the Swiss. His recording career started with RCA's Bluebird subsidiary, before he moved to New York and landed a regular slot on CBS radio, where he adopted the pseudonym Montana Slim. He composed over five hundred songs, and recorded for Decca and Starday. He retired in 1980.

DYNAMITE TRAIL: The Decca Years, 1954-8, Bear Family (Germany), 1990
MONTANA SLIM, Starday (US), 1987

CARTER FAMILY

The Carter Family, having recorded since 1927, are the first family of country. Their repertoire sets the traditional songs of the South and Old and New World ballads within a populist context.

The original line-up comprised Alvin Pleasant Carter (born on April 15, 1891, at Mace Springs, Virginia), Sara Dougherty Carter (born on July 21, 1898, at Flat Woods, Virginia) and Maybelle Addington Carter (born on May 10, 1909, at Nickelsville, Virginia). One of nine children, A.P. Carter

started his career singing in church alongside his elder sister and two uncles. On June 18, 1915, he married Sara Dougherty, a vocalist who also played the autoharp, guitar and banjo; Maybelle Addington joined the group in 1926 after marrying A.P.'s brother, Ezra.

In 1927, **Ralph Peer** produced their first sides for RCA; this relationship lasted for seven years, during which time they recorded titles like 'Keep On The Sunny Side', 'Bury Me Under The Weeping Willow', 'Wildwood Flower', 'I'm Thinking Tonight Of My Blue Eyes', 'Single Girl' and 'Will The Circle Be Unbroken'. The rise of the Carter Family corresponded with that of fellow RCA recording artist **Jimmie Rodgers**, but while Rodgers' songs espoused the hedonistic doctrine of 'the flesh', the Carter Family remained models of sobriety and advocates of family life (although they did record the occasional risqué number, like 'There'll Be A Hot Time In The Old Town Tonight').

When their contract with RCA expired in 1935, they were signed to ARC, and then to Decca from 1936 to 1938. With Decca, they re-recorded some of their earlier material, but the vitality of their radio broadcasts stimulated constant interest in their work from an increasing audience. The line-up of the group was undergoing regular changes: A.P. Carter had divorced Sara in 1935, while their daughter, Janette (born in Mace Springs in 1923), and Maybelle's daughters, Helen, **June Carter** and Anita (born in Mace Springs on March 31, 1934), more than compensated for the infrequency of A.P.'s appearances. By 1940, after broadcasting regularly on XERF, Del Rio, Texas, they signed with Columbia, cutting 'Wabash Cannonball' and 'Lonesome Valley', among others; this was followed by a two-year stint on WBT, Charlotte, North Carolina.

In 1943, the original line-up disbanded, with Maybelle and her three daughters re-forming as the Carter Sisters & Mother Maybelle. They initially broadcast on WRVA, Richmond, Virginia, where they remained for five years, which galvanized the *Grand Ole Opry* into offering them a regular slot in 1950. In 1952, A.P. Carter and Sara, with their children Janette and Joe, relaunched the Carter Family and recorded for Acme, but they were unable to match Maybelle and her progeny, who were by now regarded as the bona fide Carter Family.

On November 7, 1960, A.P. Carter died; Sara and her children stopped performing, which enabled Maybelle to change the name of her group to the Carter Family, and each member began parallel solo careers. June became the most successful as a result of her marriage to **Johnny Cash** in 1968, which led to regular appearances on his widely syndicated television series; Maybelle and Anita also contributed to this series. In 1967 Sara and Maybelle appeared together at the Newport Folk Festival, and then cut *Historic Reunion* for Columbia. This proved to be Sara's swan song: she died on January 8, 1979, in Lodi, California. Maybelle continued to hold sway as an elder stateswoman of country music, culminating in the election of the Carter Family to the Country Music Hall Of Fame in 1970.

The early recordings by the original group were by now being seen as benchmarks for others to emulate, and artists as diverse as Joan Baez, **Emmylou Harris**, **Flatt & Scruggs** and the **Nitty Gritty Dirt Band** looked to them for material. Maybelle died on October 23, 1978, but the family tradition has been upheld by the rise of **Carlene Carter** (June's daughter by her first marriage to **Carl Smith**) and the durability of the Carter Family Roadshow, which variously includes Helen (with her son, David) and Anita (with her daughter, Lori), as well as other odd nephews and nieces.

CARTER FAMILY ALBUM, Stetson, 1988
CARTER FAMILY ON BORDER RADIO, Arhoolie (US), 1988
COLLECTION OF FAVOURITES, Stetson, 1988
MAYBELLE, ANITA, JUNE & HELEN (Carter Sisters & Mother Maybelle), Bear Family (Germany), 1986
MOTHER MAYBELLE CARTER, EMI, 1973
TWENTY OF THE BEST, RCA (US), 1984
WILDWOOD FLOWER, Mercury, 1989

CARTER SISTERS see CARTER FAMILY

CARVER, Johnny

Johnny Carver was born on November 24, 1940 in Jackson, Mississippi. He sang on a local radio station when he was five as a member of a local gospel group, which included two of his aunts and an uncle, and later graduated to playing one-nighters across the state. By the age of fourteen he had learnt to play the guitar and was fronting his own group. After high school he became a full-time professional musician, touring throughout the South and south-west for the next two years.

In 1961 he moved to Milwaukee and continued to tour, playing the club and bar-room circuit, until he secured a residency at the Palomino Club in Los Angeles in 1965. A recording contract with Imperial

followed and, in 1967, having moved to Nashville, he scored with 'Your Lily-White Hands', which was later followed by 'Hold Me Tight' (1968) and 'Sweet Wine' (1969). In 1973, after a spell with Epic, he was signed to ABC-Dot, where he had hits with covers of ghastly pop songs such as 'Tie A Yellow Ribbon' (1973), 'Afternoon Delight' (1976) and 'Livin' Next Door To Alice' (1977). During the 1980s he has recorded for Equity, Tanglewood and Monument. While never a major-league performer, his relaxed undemanding style is popular on the cabaret circuit.

CASH, Johnny

For many the voice of Johnny Cash is synonymous with country music. Despite a checkered career, which has seen him undergo all sorts of trials and tribulations, his distinctive voice and the enigmatic sobriquet of 'The Man in Black' has given him a mystique that sets him apart from his contemporaries.

He was born in Kingsland, Arkansas, on February 26, 1932. His parents, Ray and Carrie, were impoverished cotton farmers who were resettled on a Government Reserve in Dyess County, Tennessee, in 1935. By 1940 there were seven siblings and the eldest, Roy, had put together a country group, the Delta Rhythm Ramblers, who broadcast on KCLN, Blytheville. In 1950 Cash enlisted in the US Air Force, having previously held down a series of dead-end jobs, such as sweeping floors and working in a car-body plant in Detroit. After his discharge in 1954, he married Vivian Liberto and moved to Memphis, where he became an electrical goods salesman.

There he teamed up with bassist Marshall Grant and guitarist Luther Perkins (both former members of the Delta Rhythm Ramblers), and was signed to **Sam Phillips**' Sun label after broadcasting on KWEM. His work at Sun, often in partnership with producer **Jack Clement**, demonstrated a unique voice, imbued with a sanguine world-weariness that belied his years, and a lyrical facility that owed more to rural blues than to hillbilly: 'Cry, Cry Cry' (1955), 'Folsom Prison Blues' (1956), 'I Walk The Line' (US#17, C&W#1, 1956), 'There You Go' (C&W#1, 1956), 'Ballad Of A Teenage Queen' (US#14, C&W#1, 1958), 'Guess Things Happen That Way' (US#11, C&W#1, 1958) and 'The Ways Of A Woman In Love' (US#24, 1958).

His success was immediate, and a series of nationwide tours and appearances on KWKH's *Louisiana Hayride* followed. After joining the *Grand Ole Opry* in 1957 and appearing in the Hollywood B-movie *Five Minutes To Live*, he was signed to Columbia. The rapidity of his success and the scale of his popularity produced a massive workload: he enlarged his band, adding drummer W.S. Holland, and began consuming vast quantities of amphetamines and alcohol.

In tandem with producer Don Law, and then Bob Johnston, Cash recorded a series of hits for Columbia over the next ten years, including 'All Over Again' (US#38, 1958), 'Don't Take Your Guns To Town' (US#32, C&W#1, 1959), 'I Got Stripes' (1959), 'In The Jailhouse Now' (1962), 'Ring Of Fire' (US#17, C&W#1, 1963), 'Understand Your Man' (US#35, C&W#1, 1964), 'The Ballad Of Ira Hayes' (1964), 'It Ain't Me Babe' (UK#28, 1965), 'Orange Blossom Special' (1965), 'The One On Your Right Is On Your Left' (1966), 'Rosanna's Going Wild' (1967), 'Folsom Prison Blues' (US#32, C&W#1, 1968), 'Daddy Sang Bass' (C&W#1, 1969) and 'A Boy Named Sue' (US#2, C&W#1, UK#4, 1969). More significantly, he cut a number of superb albums during this period - such as *Ride This Train* (1960), *Blood, Sweat And Tears* (1964), *At Folsom Prison* (1968) and *Live At San Quentin* (1970) - which contained an even measure of self-penned material and material derived from traditional country writers and old folk ballads.

Vivian sued him for divorce in 1966. In 1968 he married **June Carter** and cured his amphetamine addiction, and the following year he started his own television show, *The Johnny Cash Show*, elevating his public profile still further by a duet with **Bob Dylan** on his *Nashville Skyline* album, and a string of awards from the CMA. In 1970 he appeared opposite Kirk Douglas in the critically-rated, existential Western *A Gunfight*. Almost as a backlash against his former dissolute lifestyle, he turned increasingly to religion, which tended to distance him from the Outlaw Movement, but continued to rack up hits: 'What Is Truth' (US#19, UK#21, 1970), 'Sunday Morning Coming Down' (C&W#1, 1970), 'Flesh And Blood' (C&W#1, 1971), 'Man In Black' (C&W#3, 1971), 'A Thing Called Love' (C&W#2, UK#4, 1972), 'Kate' (C&W#2, 1972), 'Oney' (C&W#2, 1972), 'Any Old Wind That Blows' (C&W#3, 1973) and 'One Piece At A Time' (US#29, C&W#1, UK#32, 1976).

During the 1980s, Cash participated in a series of projects with colleagues from the Sun years that could have been wallows in nostalgia; but, instead they illustrated his willingness to take creative risks. Firstly, in 1981, he joined **Carl Perkins** and **Jerry Lee Lewis** for *The Survivors*, which was cut in Stuttgart. Then in 1985, under the auspices of producer **Chips Moman**, he teamed up with **Waylon Jennings**, **Kris Kristofferson** and **Willie Nelson** to record *Highwayman*. This proved to be a versatile combination that many had envisaged as being the ultimate country supergroup; the fact that four performers of such stature could work together without treading on one another's toes indicated their mutual admiration. The title track 'Highwayman' (a Jim Webb composition; C&W#1, 1985) became one of the biggest country hits of the 1980s.

In 1986 another reunion album, *The Class Of '55*, featuring Cash, Lewis, Perkins and **Roy Orbison**, was released to rather muted acclaim. The following year, Cash left Columbia for Mercury, and debuted with *Johnny Cash Is Coming To Town*. It was followed in 1988 by *Water From The Wells Of Home*, which included an impressive roster of guest artists, such as Paul McCartney, **Emmylou Harris**, the **Everly Brothers**, Waylon Jennings, his daughter **Rosanne Cash** and her husband **Rodney Crowell**. In 1990 he regrouped with Jennings, Kristofferson and Nelson for another album, *Highwayman 2*, and then toured the world as the Highwaymen, playing Wembley Arena in 1991.

ADVENTURES OF JOHNNY CASH, Columbia (US), 1987

AT FOLSOM PRISON, Columbia, 1968

BEST OF THE SUN YEARS, Music Club, 1992

BIGGEST HITS, Columbia, 1983

BITTER TEARS, Bear Family (Germany), 1990

BOOM CHICKA BOOM, Mercury, 1990

BORN TO LOSE, Instant, 1989

A BOY NAMED SUE, Columbia, 1987

THE CBS YEARS: 1958-86, Columbia, 1987

CLASSIC CASH, Mercury, 1989

COLLECTION, Castle, 1986

COUNTRY BOY, Charly, 1986

FOLSOM PRISON BLUES, Castle, 1968

GREAT SONGS OF JOHNNY CASH, Polydor, 1982

HEROES (with Waylon Jennings), Columbia, 1986

HIGHWAYMAN, (with Waylon Jennings, Kris Kristofferson and Willie Nelson), Columbia, 1985

HIGHWAYMAN 2, (with Waylon Jennings, Kris Kristofferson and Willie Nelson), Columbia, 1990

HOME OF THE BLUES, Charly, 1987

I WALK THE LINE, Charly, 1986

INSIDE A SWEDISH PRISON, Bear Family (Germany), 1982

JOHNNY CASH AT SAN QUENTIN, Columbia (US), 1969

JOHNNY CASH RECORDINGS: 1954-57, Charly, 1988

JOHNNY CASH WITH HIS HOT & BLUE GUITAR, Charly, 1981

JOHNNY CASH'S TOP HITS (with the Tennessee Two), Charly, 1988

JOHNNY & JUNE (with June Carter), Bear Family (Germany), 1984

LAST GUNFIGHTER BALLADS, Columbia, 1977

THE MAN IN BLACK: 1954-58, Bear Family (Germany), 1990

MORE OF OLD GOLDEN THROAT, Bear Family (Germany), 1982

OLD GOLDEN THROAT, Bear Family (Germany), 1982

THE ORIGINAL JOHNNY CASH, Charly, 1986

RIDING THE RAILS, Columbia, 1979

ROCK ISLAND LINE, Sun, 1988

ROCKABILLY BLUES, Columbia, 1980

SILVER, Columbia, 1979

THE SUN YEARS, Sun, 1984

THE SURVIVORS (with Jerry Lee Lewis and Carl Perkins), Columbia, 1982

A THING CALLED LOVE, Columbia, 1972

THE UNISSUED JOHNNY CASH, Bear Family (Germany), 1978

UP THROUGH THE YEARS '57-'58, Bear Family (Germany), 1986

WATER FROM THE WELLS OF HOME, Mercury, 1988

CASH, Rosanne

Rosanne Cash has become one of the most significant of the crop of New Country artists, her songwriting ability, combined with a sense of historical perspective (gained from her father **Johnny Cash**), enabling her to appeal to country and rock fans alike.

She was born on May 24, 1955, in Memphis, Tennessee, and majored in drama at Nashville's Vanderbilt University, before attending Lee Strasberg's Theatre Workshop in California. After being signed by the German Ariola label to record an album (which was never released), she was signed to Columbia. Her first album, *Right Or Wrong*, teamed her with producer **Rodney Crowell**, whom she married on April 7, 1979; this album included her first single, 'No More Memories Hangin' Around' (a duet with **Bobby Bare**).

The title song of the next album, 'Seven Year Ache' (US#22, C&W#1, 1980), established her and her husband in the mainstream of country music, with both of them - individually or together - notching up one hit after another: 'My Baby Thinks He's A Train' (C&W#1, 1981), 'Blue Moon With Heartache' (C&W#1, 1982), 'I Don't Know Why You Don't Want Me' (C&W#1, 1985), 'Never Be You' (C&W#1, 1986), 'The Way We Make A Broken Heart' (C&W#1, 1987), 'Tennessee Flat Top Box' (C&W#1, 1988), 'It's Such A Small World' (a duet with Crowell; C&W#1, 1988) 'If You Change Your Mind' (C&W#1, 1988), 'Runaway Train' (C&W#1, 1988) and

'I Don't Want To Spoil The Party' (C&W#1, 1989).

Through her association with Crowell and father Johnny Cash, Rosanne continues to blend the ethos of traditional country music with that of the new wave of country artists, like **Steve Earle**, **Suzy Bogguss** and **Dwight Yoakam**. Ploughing a furrow between rock and country, she has often recorded songs by artists like **John Hiatt**, Lennon-McCartney and Tom Petty.

INTERIORS, Columbia, 1989

KING'S RECORD SHOP, Columbia (US), 1990

RETROSPECTIVE: 1979-89, Columbia, 1989

RHYTHM AND ROMANCE, Columbia (US), 1986

THE WHEEL, Columbia, 1993

CASH, Tommy

Tommy Cash was born on April 5, 1940, in Mississippi, Arkansas. His elder brother, **Johnny Cash**, was his inspiration, teaching him how to play the guitar. In 1958 he joined the army, and then became a DJ on American Forces Network in Frankfurt. After getting married in Germany and leaving the army, he played the club circuit before signing to the Epic label in 1969, where he had his biggest hits: 'Six White Horses' (1969), 'Rise And Shine' and 'One Song Away' (1970), and 'I Recall A Gypsy Woman' (1973). By 1976 he had moved to Elektra and formed a touring band, the Tomcats. He has recorded a number of modestly successful albums.

CASS COUNTRY BOYS

The Cass Country Boys comprise Fred Martin (accordion and vocals), Jerry Scoggins (guitar and vocals) and Bert Dodson (bass). Although never a major player in the country field, they did appear in an auxiliary capacity in countless **Gene Autry** movies. Recording a number of sides for Decca in the 1930s, which illustrated their impeccable harmonies, they have dated badly and have been unavailable for many years.

CHARLES, Ray

Although known primarily as a soul and jazz singer, Ray Charles's biggest hits were reworkings of country songs, and, as for most residents of the South, country music exerted a fundamental influence of upon his musical development.

He was born Raymond Charles Robinson in Albany, Georgia, on September 23, 1930. When he was seven he contracted glaucoma and went blind. Sent to study piano and clarinet at the Deaf and Blind School in Florida, he was earning his living playing in various bands in and around Florida by the age of sixteen. In 1948 he moved to Seattle, where his next-door neighbour was Quincy Jones, and formed the Maxim Trio with guitarist G. D. McGhee and bassist Milton Gerred. In 1949 they signed with Downbeat Records, who released his first published composition, 'Confession Blues'; he changed his name to Ray Charles that same year, while Downbeat changed their name to Swingtime. From Swingtime he moved to Atlantic, who bought out his contract in 1952.

The emphasis in his repertoire changed from a jazz-tinged flavour to a much harder R&B sound overnight, and throughout the 1950s and early 1960s he enjoyed a reputation (rivalled only by James Brown's) for leading one of the toughest bands in the country. In 1962 he cut *Modern Sounds In Country & Western*, which included two singles, 'I Can't Stop Loving You' (USA#1, UK#1, 1962) and 'You Don't Know Me' (USA#2, UK#9, 1962). The sequel, *Modern Sounds In Country & Western, Volume 2*, spawned a pair of hit singles: 'Your Cheating Heart' (USA#29, UK#13, 1963) and 'Take These Chains From My Heart' (USA#8, UK#5, 1963). These two albums highlighted his strong associations with - and affection for - country music, underlining the symbiotic relationship between soul and country.

In March 1962 he set up his own record label, Tangerine, opening the offices and studios in Los Angeles in March 1963: it was another typical gesture of independence, consolidating his position as a member of the black community who was not going to be subjugated by the predominantly white-owned music business. The release of *Ingredients In A Recipe For Soul* gave him yet another hit single 'Busted' (USA#4, UK#21, 1963), which won a Grammy the following year for Best R&B Record; but his next album, *Sweet And Sour Tears*, produced only a couple of minor hits, lacking the verve and imagination of his earlier records. Although his recent records are often marred by an apparent lack of interest, or by indifferent material, he has occasionally released an album - such as *The Volcanic Action Of My Soul* (1971) - which recaptures some of the visceral energy of the Atlantic material.

In recent years, his better performances have been in supporting roles: a duet with Aretha Franklin at the Fillmore West in 1971; the recording of George Gershwin's *Porgy & Bess* (1976) with Cleo Laine for RCA; his performance in USA For Africa's 'We Are The World' (1985); and his contribution to Quincy Jones's *Back On The Block* (1989). In 1984, the album *Friendship* featured him duetting with a different country artist on each track; among the participants were **Mickey Gilley**, **Willie Nelson** and **Hank Williams, Jr**. Although he will always be most closely associated with R&B, Ray Charles has succeeded - in his idiosyncratic treatment of country songs - in bringing the work of country writers to audiences that would normally never dream of listening to it.

THE COLLECTION, Castle, 1990
FRIENDSHIP, Columbia (US), 1984
FROM THE PAGES OF MY MIND, CBS, 1986
GREATEST COUNTRY & WESTERN HITS, Sequel, 1989
I CAN'T STOP LOVING YOU, Colorado, 1988
JUST BETWEEN US, CBS, 1988
THE RIGHT TIME, Atlantic, 1987
THE SPIRIT OF CHRISTMAS, CBS, 1985

CHENIER, Clifton

Clifton Chenier has long been the most visible and popular of all the zydeco accordionists, providing a starting-point for inheritors of the tradition like **Rockin' Dopsie** and Buckwheat Zydeco.

He was born on June 25, 1925, in Opelousas, Louisiana. In the late 1940s he honed his distinctive style playing the clubs of Port Arthur, Texas, and southern Louisiana. His audience were mostly oil workers or the French-speaking black communities. His sphere of influence expanded as his reputation grew, and he travelled as far afield as California with a band that included pianist Elmore Nixon and Chenier's brother, Cleveland, on rub-board (a ridged metal board played with thimbles on the fingers, rather like a washboard).

By 1955 he was recording for Specialty, on his occasional visits to California, and for the Chess subsidiaries Checker and Argo. From the early 1960s he recorded some definitive albums for the influential Arhoolie label, including *Bon Ton Roulet* (1966) and *Bogalusa Boogie* (1975); these sessions led to a growing popularity on the American and European folk/blues festival circuit. Recording for Arhoolie for over twenty years, he also recorded for Sonet, **Huey P. Meaux**'s Crazy Cajun label, Floyd Soileau's Jin label and, in France, for Freebird and Barclay.

In 1984 his influence was finally acknowledged by the record industry when he won a Grammy for *I'm Here* on Alligator. He continued touring and recording until to

a few weeks before his death on December 12, 1987.
BAYOU SOUL, Maison de Soul, 1979
BLACK SNAKE BLUES, Arhoolie (US), 1981
BOGALUSA BOOGIE, Arhoolie (US), 1987
BON TON ROULET, Arhoolie (US), 1966
BOOGIE 'N' ZYDECO, Sonet, 1980
CAJUN SWAMP, Tomato (US), 1979
CAJUN SWAMP MUSIC LIVE, Tomato (US), 1990
CLASSIC CLIFTON, Arhoolie (US), 1984
CLIFTON CHENIER AND HIS RED HOT LOUISIANA BAND,
Arhoolie (US), 1984
CLIFTON CHENIER AND ROCKIN' DOPSIE, Flyright, 1990
CLIFTON CHENIER IN NEW ORLEANS, GNP (US), 1988
CLIFTON CHENIER SINGS THE BLUES, Arhoolie (US), 1988
COUNTRY BOY NOW, Maison de Soul, 1987
I'M HERE, Sonet, 1982
KING OF THE BAYOUS, Arhoolie, 1981
KING OF ZYDECO, Ace, 1988
LET ME IN YOUR HEART, Arhoolie (US), 1988
LIVE AT A FRENCH DANCE, Arhoolie (US), 1988
LIVE AT MONTREUX, Charly, 1984
LIVE AT THE SAN FRANCISCO BLUES FESTIVAL, Arhoolie
(US), 1985
LOUISIANA BLUES AND ZYDECO, Arhoolie (US), 1981
OUT WEST, Arhoolie (US), 1981
RED HOT LOUISIANA BAND, Arhoolie (US), 1981
SIXTY MINUTES WITH THE KING OF ZYDECO, Arhoolie
(US), 1988
ZYDECO BLUES & BOOGIE, Ace, 1992
ZYDECO LEGEND, Maison de Soul, 1989

CHILDRE, Lew

One of the more endearing characteristics of country
music is the diversity of backgrounds of many of its
exponents. Many performers gained early experience
as comedians and singers in the medicine shows:
Lew Childre was a prime example.

'Doctor Lew' was born in Opp, Alabama, on
November 1, 1901; after establishing himself as a
Hawaiian guitarist and comedian in a medicine show,
he gravitated to the nightclub circuit and a slot on
WWL, New Orleans, with **Curly Fox**. His routine as
Doctor Lew, a purveyor of dubious medical advice,
eventually earned him a slot on the *Grand Ole Opry* in
1945 (working with **Stringbean** until 1948), where he
remained a fixture until his death on December 3,
1961. Although a competent vocalist, he only cut a few
sides for Starday, Gennett and ARC. He was most
effective in his live appearances.

OLD TIME GET TOGETHER, Starday, 1987

CLARK, Gene

One of the highpoints of Gene Clark's career was a
brace of albums he recorded with Doug Dillard (see
the **Dillards**) in the late 1960s, which emphasized the
strong bond between traditional folk music and bluegrass. The partnership, though shortlived, provided -
in adventurousness of style, virtuosity, and quality of
writing - a benchmark for others to follow.

Gene Clark was born in Tipton, Missouri,
on November 17, 1941, and became a member of
the New Christy Minstrels before joining the **Byrds**
in 1964. Clark remained with the Byrds until 1966,
during which time his distinctive vocals and arrangement skills made him a cornerstone of the Byrds'
sound. Leaving the group with the excuse that he
hated touring, he embarked upon an independent
career.

In 1967 he cut *Gene Clark With The Gosdin
Brothers* (see **Gosdin, Vern**), before obtaining a contract with A&M and working with Doug Dillard on *The
Fantastic Expedition Of Dillard & Clark* (1969). The
follow-up was the equally impressive *Through The
Morning, Through The Night* (1969); despite their
excellence, both albums failed to sell and the collaborations ceased.

Clark got his solo career under way with *White Light*
(1971), which was followed by *Roadmaster* (1972);
both outings illustrating the range of his voice and the
perceptiveness of his writing. In 1973 he participated
in the recording of the Byrds' reunion album, *The
Byrds*, after which he resumed his solo career with *No
Other* (1974) - a very bleak offering. Personal problems stopped him from recording, until he teamed up
with Roger McGuinn (see **Byrds**) and **Chris Hillman**
for *McGuinn, Hillman, Clark* (1979) and *City* (1980).
Resuming his solo career, Clark cut *So Rebellious A
Lover* (with Carla Olson; 1987) after years of silence.
He died of a heart attack on May 24, 1991, after years
of erratic health.

GENE CLARK WITH THE GOSDIN BROTHERS, Edsel, 1967
THE FANTASTIC EXPEDITION OF DILLARD & CLARK,
Edsel, 1969
NO OTHER, Edsel, 1974
ROADMASTER, Edsel, 1972
SILHOUETTED IN LIGHT (with Carla Olson), Demon, 1992
SO REBELLIOUS A LOVER (with Carla Olson), Demon, 1987
THROUGH THE MORNING, THROUGH THE NIGHT (Dillard
& Clark), Edsel, 1969
TWO SIDES TO EVERY STORY, Polydor, 1977

CLARK, Guy

Guy Clark has long been regarded as one of the finest of the New Country songwriters. His own records, while excellent, have remained a closely guarded secret.

He was born on November 6, 1941, and raised in Monahans, Texas. His early years were spent at his grandmother's seedy dilapidated hotel - images of this ramshackle joint frequently crop up in his songs - before he moved to Houston in the early 1960s. He secured work as an art director for a Houston-based television station, and met local writers like **Jerry Jeff Walker** and **Townes Van Zandt**. They encouraged him to pursue his writing career and he started to perform on the Texas club circuit in Austin, Dallas and Houston, having formed a group which included **K.T. Oslin**.

After a sojourn in Los Angeles, he moved to Nashville in 1971, and tied up a publishing deal with Sunbury Music: his early songs included 'Desperadoes Waiting For A Train' (covered by **Johnny Cash**, **Kris Kristofferson**, **Waylon Jennings** and **Willie Nelson**), 'L.A. Freeway' and 'The Last Gunfighter Ballad'. After landing a contract with RCA, he recorded his first album; it remains unreleased. In 1975 he issued his ground-breaking debut, *Old No.1*, which established him as one of country's more perceptive writers and performers, the album conveying a spirit of nostalgia and redemption, comparable to films like Howard Hawks' *Red River* and Peter Bogdanovich's *The Last Picture Show*.

The follow-up, *Texas Cookin'*, lacked the impact of its predecessor. Moving to Warner Bros., Clark recorded *Guy Clark* (1978) and *South Coast Of Texas* (1981); despite the dry perceptiveness of the lyrics and the fine laid-back accompaniment, they failed to sell. His most recent album was 1988's solid - but commercially abysmal - *Old Friends*, which included assistance from **Vince Gill**, **Emmylou Harris**, **Rosanne Cash** and **Rodney Crowell**.

His profile as a writer has never been higher, with artists like Vince Gill, Rodney Crowell, **John Conlee** and **Ricky Skaggs** all recording his material. This regard has not yet been translated into album sales, and he remains absurdly underrated.

BEST OF GUY CLARK, RCA International, 1982
BETTER DAYS, Warner Bros., 1983
BOATS TO BUILD, Elektra, 1993
GUY CLARK, Warner Bros., 1978
OLD FRIENDS, Sugar Hill (US), 1988
OLD No. 1, Demon, 1975
SOUTH COAST OF TEXAS, Warner Bros., 1981
TEXAS COOKIN', Demon, 1976

CLARK, Roy

Roy Clark is probably best known as an ambassador for country music. His genial demeanour has made country palatable to a vast number of viewers of the *Hee Haw* television show, which he co-hosted with **Buck Owens**. In 1976 he became the first country artist to visit Russia.

He was born the son of a tobacco farmer, on April 15, 1933, in Meaherrin, Virginia. Moving to Washington, DC, in 1944, he had become a proficient banjo player by the late 1940s, winning the Country Music Banjo Championships in 1949 and 1950. After trials for a baseball team and boxing his way through fifteen bouts, he turned his attention to the entertainment industry.

From 1952, his reputation as an entertainer took hold with a series of performances on the **Jimmy Dean**, **Marvin Rainwater** and **George Hamilton IV** television shows. In 1959 he joined **Wanda Jackson**'s band as arranger and guitarist, which coincided with his own emergence as a solo recording artist. Initially recording for Four Star, followed by Debbie and Coral, he scored his first significant hits for Capitol, with **Bill Anderson**'s 'Tips Of My Fingers' (1963) and 'Through The Eyes Of A Fool' (1964).

Over the next ten years, having moved to Dot, he had a string of hits with titles like 'I Never Picked Cotton' (1970), 'Thank God And Greyhound' (1970), 'A Simple Thing Called Love' (1971), 'Magnificent Sanctuary Band' (1971), 'Yesterday When I Was Young' (US#19, C&W#9, 1973), 'Come Live With Me' (C&W#1, 1973), 'Somewhere Between Love And Tomorrow' (C&W#2, 1974), 'Honeymoon Feeling' (1974) and 'If I Had To Do It All Over Again' (C&W#2, 1976).

In 1972, after only three years, *Hee Haw* was axed, and Clark cut 'The Lawrence Welk Hee-Haw-Counter-Revolution-Polka'. In 1973 he was nominated Entertainer of the Year by the Country Music Association, and during the late 1970s he teamed up with R&B singer Clarence 'Gatemouth' Brown for *Makin' Music*. However, despite his popularity as a musician, he has concentrated on being a 'personality', first and foremost. In 1986 he co-produced and co-starred with **Mel Tillis** in the spoof Western, *Uphill All The Way*, and deputized as host for Johnny Carson on his prestigious *Tonight* show.

BEST OF ROY CLARK, MCA (US), 1987
TWENTY GOLDEN PIECES, Bulldog, 1984

CLARK, 'Yodelling Slim'

'Yodelling Slim' was born Raymond LeRoy Clark on November 12, 1917, in Springfield, Massachusetts. A woodcutter, he made his mark in 1947 by winning the World Yodelling Championship, and was immediately signed up by the Continental label; later records were cut for Remington and Palomino. While not a true original - covering songs by better known yodellers like Montana Slim (see **Carter, Wilf**) and **Jimmie Rodgers** - he continued recording right up to the late 1960s, and his live performances and appearances on the *Grand Ole Opry* were always popular.

CLEMENT, Jack

Producer Jack Clement has made a significant contribution to the growth of country music. Unlike many of his contemporaries, Clement has always been a bit of a maverick, constantly trying out different producion techniques; he has worked with artists as diverse as **Jerry Lee Lewis**, **John Prine**, **Charley Pride**, **Johnny Cash**, **Townes Van Zandt** and Louis Armstrong.

Jack Henderson Clement was born the son of a dentist and a choirmaster on April 5, 1932, in Memphis, Tennessee, and mastered a variety of instruments before joining the Marines. Prior to his discharge he linked up with members of **Ernest Stoneman**'s band, forming a bluegrass outfit who worked first out of Washington, DC, and then Boston. He returned to Memphis in 1954 and formed the Fernwood label with Slim Wallace; their first recording, 'Trouble Bound', by Billy Lee Riley was picked up by **Sam Phillips** at Sun, who signed up Riley and gave Clement a job as a producer and general engineering factotum. During his tenure at Sun, he collaborated not only with Riley but also with Johnny Cash, Jerry Lee Lewis and **Roy Orbison**. While his production credits were impressive, he also wrote songs like 'Ballad Of A Teenage Queen', 'Guess Things Happen That Way' and 'The One On The Right Is On The Left' for Cash. In 1960 he left Sun for RCA, where he produced **Jim Reeves** and **Ed Bruce**.

In 1963 he went to Beaumont, Texas, where he collaborated with Western Swing musicians such as **Moon Mullican** and **Cliff Bruner**, before returning to Nashville and forming Jack Music Publishing. In 1964 he discovered **Charley Pride**, and briefly took over his management; this prompted him to pen '(I Wish I Had) Johnny's Cash And Charley's Pride' some years later. Among the other artists he produced were **Tompall and the Glaser Brothers**, **Doc Watson** and **Mac Wiseman**. In 1970 he built the Jack Clement Studio

and established the JMI record label the following year, with songwriter **Bob McDill**, producer **Allen Reynolds** and **Don Williams**.

After producing the horror film *Dear Dead Delilah*, which lost him most of his money, he closed JMI and formed the Cowboy Ragtime Band. This venture resulted in the peculiar *All I Want To Do In Life* for Elektra in 1978. He has continued producing artists such as Townes Van Zandt, **Waylon Jennings** and Johnny Cash, and since 1980 has also been involved in video distribution.

ALL I WANT TO DO IN LIFE, Elektra (US), 1978

CLEMENTS, Vassar

Vassar 'Superbow' Clements has long been known to readers of record sleeves; in recent years his proficiency on all types of stringed instruments has become known to a wider audience through collaborations with **Norman Blake** and the **Nitty Gritty Dirt Band**.

He was born in April 1928 in Stanard, South Carolina. After learning to play the guitar, he took up the fiddle, which enabled him to join a succession of bluegrass outfits, such as **Bill Monroe**'s Blue Grass Boys, **Jim & Jesse**'s Virginia Boys and the **Earl Scruggs** Revue. As a result of his contribution to the Nitty Gritty Dirt Band's *Will The Circle Be Unbroken?* (which got him known to those outside the inner country circle), he became sought after in his own right during the 1970s, and was signed as a solo artist by Mercury, for whom he cut two over-produced albums: *Vassar Clements* and *Superbow*.

He then formed a band with Norman Blake, **Tut Taylor** and **John Hartford** for a number of impressive albums for the Flying Fish label, including *Hillbilly Jazz* and *Old And New*. After the Mercury contract expired he was signed as a solo artist by Rounder, cutting *Crossing The Catskills*, which was followed by another collaboration with Hartford, and, this time, jazz bassist Dave Holland.

While he continues touring, he has also recorded with Jerry Garcia of the Grateful Dead in the band Old And In The Way. In 1985 he recorded duets with jazz violinist Stéphane Grappelli in Nashville, and his collaborations with other virtuosi musicians from varying backgrounds have ensured that his reputation has continued to grow.

THE BLUEGRASS SESSION, Flying Fish (US), 1989
CLEMENTS, HARTFORD AND HOLLAND, Rounder (US), 1985

CROSSING THE CATSKILLS, Rounder (US), 1987
HILLBILLY JAZZ RIDES AGAIN, Flying Fish (US), 1987
NASHVILLE JAM, Flying Fish (US), 1979
VASSAR, Flying Fish (US), 1988

CLEMENTS, Zeke

A good entertainer and a passable crooner, Zeke Clements (born on September 9, 1911, in Warrior, Alabama) has sustained a long career on the fringes of country music. He made his debut on the *National Barn Dance* in 1928, which was followed by a stint with **Otto Gray**'s Oklahoma Cowboys. By 1933 he had joined the *Grand Ole Opry*, where he dressed as a cowboy (adopting the persona of 'The Alabama Cowboy' in the Bronco Busters), and achieved wider celebrity as the voice of Bashful in Walt Disney's *Snow White And The Seven Dwarfs* (1939).

During the 1940s he made many radio broadcasts and, in 1945, he co-wrote and recorded 'Smoke On The Water', which was the biggest country hit of that year. In later years he appeared on the *Lousiana Hayride*, before moving to Florida in the mid-1960s, where he played banjo in a Dixieland jazz band. He returned to Nashville in 1974.

CLIFTON, Bill

While knowledge of Bill Clifton's output is limited to diehard country fans, his tireless promotion of country music has brought it to audiences in far-flung corners of the world. He was born William Marburg in Riverdale, Maryland, in 1931. During his adolescence he discovered the music of the **Carter Family**, which prompted him to start performing with guitarist Paul Clayton while both were students at the University of Virginia. After graduating he formed his own group, the Dixie Mountain Boys, in 1954. This group established a very strong reputation with bluegrass fans via a number of records for the Starday label, including a collection of Carter Family songs. In 1955 he published a book entitled *150 Old-Time Folk And Gospel Songs*, which has subsequently become a bible for aspiring bluegrass singers.

In 1961 he set up the first one-day festival at Luray, Virginia - folk and country festivals have subsequently flourished from those humble beginnings. In 1963 he moved to the UK, playing the club circuit and touring Europe, and acquainting the uninitiated with the joys of bluegrass. He was given a weekly slot on BBC radio, hosting *Cellar Full Of Folk*. By 1970, having spent three years in the Peace Corps, he had returned to the UK and continued to tour the world, appearing in Japan, the Philippines, the US and Europe, as well as cutting a number of albums for the German label, Bear Family. In 1978, in cahoots with veteran musicians Red Rector and Don Stover, he organised the First Generation band, who toured festivals in the US and Europe. To this day, Clifton pursues his mission with an almost evangelical fervour, his ubiquity seeming to know no bounds.

BEATLE CRAZY, Bear Family (Germany), 1983
BLUE RIDGE MOUNTAIN BLUEGRASS, Westwood, 1982
BLUEGRASS SESSION 1952, Bear Family (German), 1984
MOUNTAIN FOLK SONGS, Starday (US), 1987

CLINE, Patsy

As this book was being compiled in the summer of 1992, the definitive Patsy Cline compilation was loping up the UK album charts; the previous compilation in 1990 also made significant inroads in the charts. This is a remarkable achievement for an artist who died thirty years ago. Possessed of a voice and a vocal 'crying' style that set the tone for her inheritors - from **Tammy Wynette** to **Reba McEntire** - Patsy Cline has become the ad-man's embodiment of country, combining maudlin lyrics with a tragic demise.

She was born Virginia Patterson Hensley in Winchester, Virginia, on September 8, 1932. Displaying considerable precocity, she was an accomplished tap dancer by the age of four and had learnt to play the piano by the age of eight. After singing in local clubs, she auditioned for a trip to Nashville in 1948, where she appeared on the club circuit.

In 1957 she won an *Arthur Godfrey Talent Scouts Show* with her rendition of 'Walking After Midnight', which was then recorded and released by Decca (US#12, 1957). This was the first of a number of hits for that label, including 'I Fall To Pieces' (US#12, C&W#1, 1961), 'Crazy' (US#9, C&W#2, 1961; UK#26, 1990), 'Who Can I Count On' (1962), 'She's Got You' (US#14, C&W#1, UK#43, 1962), 'Heartaches' (UK#43, 1962), 'Strange' (1962) and 'When I Get Thru With You' (1962). This spate of hits guaranteed her a spot at the Grand Ole Opry and established her as the Queen of Country Singers, supplanting **Kitty Wells** - a position that was reinforced by other hits, like 'Imagine That' (1962), 'So Wrong' (1963) and 'Leavin' On Your Mind' (1963).

On March 5, 1963, she was killed in an air crash near Camden, Tennessee, when returning home from a benefit concert in Kansas City; **Hawkshaw Hawkins** and **Cowboy Copas** were also killed in the crash. In subsequent years, her mystique and popularity have grown out of all proportion to that which she enjoyed during her lifetime. Her posthumous hits include 'Sweet Dreams (Of You)', 'Faded Love', 'When You Need A Laugh', 'He Called Me Baby' and 'Anytime'. She was belatedly elected to the Country Music Hall Of Fame in 1973, and in 1981 she was cited in the film *Coal Miner's Daughter* as having been an influence on **Loretta Lynn**. In 1985 Jessica Lange played Cline in *Sweet Dreams*, a film based on her life story.

THE DEFINITIVE, Arc, 1992
LIVE AT THE OPRY, MCA, 1989
NOT FORGOTTEN (with Cowboy Copas and Hawkshaw Hawkins), Starday (US), 1987
THE PATSY CLINE COLLECTION, MCA, 1992
REMEMBERING: PATSY CLINE AND JIM REEVES, MCA (US), 1986

COCHRAN, Hank

Although Hank Cochran recorded regularly for Monument, Liberty and RCA during the 1960s, his principal contribution has been as a songwriter. Born in Isola, Mississippi, on August 2, 1935, he moved to New Mexico during the early 1950s and worked in the oilfields. He then moved to California, where he started to realize some of his aspirations by playing the club circuit. In 1954 he formed a duo with Eddie Cochran (no relation); they remained together for two years.

By 1960 he had met **Harlan Howard** and moved to Nashville, having secured a position as a songwriter with **Ray Price**'s publishing company, Pamper. Over the next few years he provided songs for Price and also wrote 'I Fall To Pieces' (with Howard) and 'She's Got You' for **Patsy Cline**; 'Make The World Go Away' for Price and **Eddy Arnold**; 'I Want To Go With You' for Arnold; 'Willingly' for **Willie Nelson**; 'A Little Bitty Tear' and 'Funny Way Of Laughing' for Burl Ives; and 'Ocean Front Property' and 'The Chair' with Dean Dillon for **George Strait**.

In the early 1960s he managed a few hits on his own account, most notably with 'Sally Was A Good Girl', 'I'd Fight The World' and 'All Of Me Belongs To You', but his heartfelt lyrics have always sounded more poignant coming from the mouths of others.

COE, David Allan

Having spent much of his early life in reform schools, David Allan Coe has better claim than most to the outlaw persona as a means for attracting attention. He was born on September 6, 1939, in Akron, Ohio, and gravitated to Ohio State Penitentiary, where he allegedly killed a fellow prisoner in self-defence and was consigned to Death Row. He was reprieved when the death penalty was abolished in Ohio.

In 1967 he was paroled and was signed to **Shelby Singleton**'s SSS International label on the strength of the songs he had composed while in prison. Two albums resulted: *Penitentiary Blues* and *Requiem For A Harlequin*; starkly arranged, they demonstrated the depth of his allegiance to black music. Thereafter he turned to country, adopting some of the traditional trimmings, such as cowboy outfits, for his performances. He quickly dropped those in favour of the more menacing biker's kit. Possessed of an expressive voice and strong songwriting ability, Coe didn't require these gimmicks, as was demonstrated in songs like 'How High's The Watergate, Martha?' and 'Would You Lay With Me (In A Field Of Stone)' (covered by **Tanya Tucker** in 1975).

Having signed with Columbia in 1974, he released *The Mysterious Rhinestone Cowboy*, which included a cover of **Steve Goodman**'s 'You Never Even Called Me By My Name' (1975). While his albums sold well, the singles did less, but he established himself as a writer, with subject matter veering from worm's-eye views of the underbelly of country music, with 'Willie, Waylon And Me' (1976), 'If That Ain't Country' and 'The Ride' (recounting a meeting with **Hank Williams**' ghost; C&W#2, 1983), to anti-authoritarian tirades, with 'Take This Job And Shove It' (covered by **Johnny Paycheck** in 1977) and 'Need A Little Time Off For Bad Behaviour'.

His songs have always had a strong R&B influence, and the years spent in prison have tagged his work with a greater degree of authenticity than most of his contemporaries. His pre-eminence as a writer has prompted artists such as **Tammy Wynette**, **Johnny Cash**, **George Jones** and **Waylon Jennings** to cover his material, most of which he publishes through his own company. He published his autobiography *Off The Record* in the early 1980s.

FOR THE RECORD, Columbia, 1985
LONGHAIRED REDNECK, Bear Family (Germany), 1993
MYSTERIOUS RHINESTONE COWBOY, Bear Family (Germany), 1993
ONCE UPON A TIME, Bear Family (Germany), 1993

RIDES AGAIN, Bear Family (Germany), 1993
TEXAS MOON, Charly, 1977
UNCHAINED, Columbia, 1986

COHEN, Nudie

Known as Nudie the Tailor, Nudie Cohen was responsible for providing the stars of country music with their magnificent stage costumes. He was born in Brooklyn, New York City, and was briefly a boxer, before turning his attention to the requirements of showgirls. After manufacturing bras and G-strings, he moved to the West Coast just after the First World War, where he made costumes for the Warner Bros. film company.

During the late 1940s, **Tex Williams** approached him to design an outfit for him and his group to wear on stage. For this first assignment, Cohen provided some striking numbers that wowed Williams's admirers, and before long any self-respecting country artist had his own Nudie Suit. As country artists had always favoured western-style outfits, Nudie ran amok with fringes, tassels, sequins and rhinestones. Among his most celebrated designs were the suits worn by the **Flying Burrito Brothers** on the cover of *The Gilded Palaces Of Sin*: each suit was embroidered with the leaves of marijuana plants. He died in Nashville in the late 1980s, but his shop is still in place in Nashville.

COLLINS, Tommy

Tommy Collins was born Leonard Raymond Sipes in Bethany, Oklahoma, on September 28, 1930. Having previously broadcast on Oklahoma City's WKY radio station, he moved to Bakersfield during the 1950s, where he shared an apartment with **Ferlin Husky**, who dubbed him 'Tom Collins'. In Bakersfield, he became a part of the nucleus of musicians who helped to establish it as a haven for the West Coast fraternity. Signed to Capitol, his biggest hits were 'You Better Not Do That' (1954), 'Whatcha Gonna Do Now' (1954), 'You Gotta Have A Licence' (1955) and 'High On A Hilltop' (1955), most of which featured guitarist **Buck Owens**.

His career tailed off for a decade, but he came back in the late 1960s to score a few hits for Columbia: 'If You Can't Bite, Don't Growl' (1966), 'Birmingham' and 'I Made The Prison Band' (1968). Although he seldom works in the US, he still tours Europe, and songs like 'If You Ain't Loving (You Ain't Livin')' have been covered by **George Strait**, among others.

THIS IS TOMMY COLLINS, Stetson, 1988
WORDS AND MUSIC COUNTRY STYLE, Stetson, 1987

COLTER, Jessi

Jessi Colter is the only female artist to be directly associated with the outlaw strand of country music. The calibre of her songwriting and the timbre of her voice has distanced her from mainstream female country singers, placing her in closer proximity to the likes of **Nanci Griffith** and **k.d. lang**, rather than the contemporaneous **Tammy Wynette** and **Dolly Parton**.

She was born Miriam Johnson on May 25, 1947, in Phoenix, Arizona, one of seven children whose father built racing cars. By age of eleven she had mastered the piano sufficiently to play in the local church. In 1963 she married guitarist Duane Eddy, and toured the UK, Europe and South Africa as part of his travelling show. Writing under her married name, Miriam Eddy, her songs were covered by **Don Gibson** and **Dottie West**, until she took the stage name Jessi Colter (her great-great-uncle having been in Jesse James's gang!). She met Eddy's producer, songwriter Lee Hazlewood, and was then signed by the Jamie label, and later by RCA in 1966.

Divorcing Eddy in 1968, she returned to Phoenix and met **Waylon Jennings** (whom she married in 1969); together they cut duets such as 'Suspicious Minds' (1970) and 'Under Your Spell Again' (1971). After signing to Capitol in 1974, she released *I'm Jessi Colter*, which included the self-penned 'I'm Not Lisa' (which won two Grammy awards; US#4, C&W#1, 1975), 'What Happened To Blue Eyes' (1975) and 'You Ain't Never Been Loved (Like I'm Goin' To Love You)' (1976).

In 1976 she contributed to *Wanted: The Outlaws* with Jennings, **Willie Nelson** and Tompall Glaser (see **Tompall and the Glaser Brothers**) and appeared on many of the later tours. In 1982, after touring with Jennings, she cut another album of duets, *Leather & Lace*, but she has recorded less and toured less in recent years, preferring to spend more time with her family. In 1985, she cut a gospel album under her maiden name.

A COUNTRY STAR IS BORN, RCA International, 1982

COMMANDER CODY

Commander Cody and his Lost Planet Airmen were one of the curious amalgams that formed during the mid-1960s, when psychedelia was at its peak. Combining country-rock, R&B and Western Swing, it is often claimed that they were less serious in their vocation than contemporaries such as Dan Hicks and his Hot Licks and **Asleep At The Wheel**.

Commander Cody was born George Frayne in Boise, Idaho, on July 19, 1944. He formed a loose aggregation known as the Lost Planet Airmen while studying art at Michigan University; this line-up eventually coalesced with Cody (keyboards), Bruce Barlow (bass; born on December 3, 1948, in Oxnard, California), Billy C. Farlow (vocals), Bill Kirchen (guitar and vocals; born on June 29, 1948, in Bridgeport, Connecticut), Andy Stein (fiddle and tenor sax; born on August 31, 1948, in New York City), Lance Dickerson (drums; born on October 15, 1948, in Detroit) and John Tichy (guitar). In 1971 Cody took the group out to the West Coast, where he guested on the debut album by the **New Riders of the Purple Sage.**

Having secured a recording contract with Paramount they released *Lost In The Ozone*, which included 'Hot Rod Lincoln' (US#9, 1972); a patchy affair, it nonetheless drew warm praise from critics more accustomed to the bombast of progressive rock. The follow-up, *Hot Licks, Cold Steel And Truckers Favourites*, mixed traditional country-style tunes ('The Kentucky Hills Of Tennessee') with pastiches ('Mama Hated Diesels') and rock 'n' roll ('Rip It Up'). The overall effect was slightly schizoid, yet very effective. In 1974, they moved to Warner Bros., but not before they had issued *Country Casanova*, which included **Merle Travis**'s 'Smoke! Smoke! Smoke! (That Cigarette)', and *Live From Deep In The Heart Of Texas*; which showed them at their wackiest.

The move to Warner Bros. seemed to knock the stuffing out of them, and the only offering of note was the live album, *We've Got A Live One Here*, recorded during their 1976 tour of the UK. The group then disbanded and Cody signed to Arista as a solo artist, cutting *Midnight Man* and *Rock 'n' Roll Again*. In 1980 he cut *Lose It Tonight* with the Moonlighters, which included the minor hit, 'Two Triple Cheese (Side Order Of Fries)'.

The Moonlighters, who included former Airmen Kirchen and Barlow, as well as drummer Tony Johnson and guitarist Austin de Lone, became his official band and together they cut *Let's Rock* (1986) for the independent Special Delivery. This album saw the group returning to their earlier form with such epic tales as 'Truckstop At The End Of The World'. While Cody and the band continue working together as much as possible, they each make their living from lucrative session work and other projects.

CODY RETURNS FROM OUTER SPACE, Demon, 1987
COMMANDER CODY, Warner Bros., 1991
HOT LICKS, COLD STEEL AND TRUCKERS FAVOURITES, MCA (US), 1973
LET'S ROCK, Line (Germany), 1986
LOSE IT TONIGHT, Line, 1980
LOST IN THE OZONE, MCA (US), 1972
VERY BEST OF COMMANDER CODY AND HIS LOST PLANET AIRMEN, See For Miles, 1986
WE'VE GOT A LIVE ONE HERE, Warner Bros., 1976

COMPTON BROTHERS

Harry and Bill Compton are now best known for their ownership of the Weperdol Music Publishers. Raised In St Louis, Missouri, they won a talent contest in 1965 and were signed up by Columbia, and then by Dot. Although they had only had a few minor hits, such as 'Haunted House' (1969) and 'Charlie Brown' (1970), they captured the *Cashbox* Most Promising Vocal Group Award in 1968. While they promised much, obscurity and their publishing interests beckoned and they dutifully complied.

CONLEE, John

A country singer with strong R&B influences, John Conlee has tapped into a growing audience which, raised on rock, is now increasingly turning towards country music. He was born on a tobacco farm in Versailles, Kentucky, on August 11, 1946. After playing in a folk group while at high school, he trained for three years to become a mortician. When he had completed his training, he changed tack and became a DJ at WLAC, Nashville. With the assistance of fellow DJ, Dick Kent, he secured a contract with ABC in 1976, scoring shortly after with the self-penned, honky-tonk-styled 'Rose Coloured Glasses' (C&W#5, 1978).

His later hits were more pop-oriented, reflecting country music's desire to attract younger middle-class audiences: 'Lady Lay Down' (C&W#1, 1979), 'Backside Of Thirty' (C&W#1, 1979), 'Before My Time' (C&W#2, 1980), 'Friday Night Blues' (C&W#2, 1981), 'She Can't Say That Anymore' (C&W#2, 1982), 'Miss Emily's Picture' (C&W#2, 1982), 'Common Man' (C&W#1, 1983), 'I'm Only In It For The Love' (C&W#1, 1983), 'In My Eyes' (C&W#1, 1984), 'As Long As I'm Rocking With You' (C&W#1, 1984), 'Way Back'

(C&W#4, 1985), 'Years After You' (C&W#2, 1985) and 'Old School' (C&W#5, 1986).

At the beginning of 1986 Conlee moved from MCA (ABC had been absorbed into MCA in 1979) and signed with Columbia, retaining the services of his long-time producer Bud Logan. His debut was 'Harmony' (C&W#10, 1986), which was followed by 'Got My Heart Set On You' (co-written by **Dobie Gray**; C&W#1, 1986). After two years with Columbia he changed labels once again, this time signing with Nashville's 16th Avenue label. Although the hits have been less frequent in recent years, he still plays around 120 gigs a year and looks after his 32-acre farm and his parents' 250-acre farm in Kentucky.

GREATEST HITS, Volumes 1-2, MCA (US), 1986
HARMONY, Columbia (US), 1987
ROSE-COLOURED GLASSES, MCA (US), 1979
SONGS FOR THE WORKING MAN, MCA (US), 1986

CONLEY, Earl Thomas

Earl Thomas Conley has become one of country's most prolific hitmakers, with a string of chart-toppers stretching back to the early 1980s. A successful songwriter, Conley is almost unique in his ability to chart consistently with his own material, with the result that he has been able to forge a style that is immediately recognizable and uniquely his own (although the influences of **Merle Haggard** and **George Jones** are clearly discernible).

Born in Portsmouth, Ohio, on October 17, 1941, he didn't take up songwriting until 1968, despite a long-standing interest in music. In 1970 he moved to Huntsville, Alabama, and met a local studio owner, Nelson Larkin. Over the next three years, Conley issued three singles on Larkin's Prize label before moving to the GRT label, where the big break still proved elusive (although **Conway Twitty** covered his composition 'This Time I've Hurt Her More Than She Loves Me'). A brief stint with Warner Bros. and three very minor hits followed.

In 1980 Conley went back to Larkin, who had meanwhile formed the Sunbird label. From the debut album, *Blue Pearl*, two hit singles were issued: 'Silent Treatment' (C&W#7, 1981) and 'Fire And Smoke' (C&W#1, 1981). While retaining the production services of Larkin, RCA bought out his contract with Sunbird and repackaged the debut album. The material on the follow-up, *Somewhere Between Right And Wrong*, was entirely self-penned, with the title track (C&W#1, 1982) and 'I Have Loved You, Girl' (C&W#2,

1983) both becoming substantial hits. The next album, *Don't Make It Easy For Me*, featured five compositions co-written with **Randy Scruggs** and spawned a slew of hits: 'Your Love's On The Line' (C&W#1, 1983), 'Holding Her And Loving You' (voted Song of the Year by the Nashville Songwriters Association for the writers, Walt Aldridge and Tommy Brasfield; C&W#1, 1983), 'Don't Make It Easy For Me' (C&W#1, 1984) and 'Angel In Disguise' (C&W#1, 1984).

The next album, *Treadin' Water*, included 'Chance Of Lovin' You' (C&W#1, 1984), 'Honour Bound' (C&W#1, 1985) and 'Love Don't Care (Whose Heart It Breaks)' (C&W#1, 1985). Just in time for Christmas 1985, RCA issued a *Greatest Hits* album, and to give it a bit more appeal 'Nobody Falls Like A Fool' (C&W#1, 1985) and 'Once In A Blue Moon' (C&W#1, 1986) were recorded specifically for inclusion; it was his first album to top the charts. *Too Many Times* followed the established pattern by providing him with another spate of hits: 'Too Many Times' (a duet with Anita Pointer of the Pointer Sisters; C&W#2, 1986), 'I Can't Win For Losin' You' (C&W#1, 1987), 'That Was A Close One' (C&W#1, 1987) and 'Right From The Start' (which was featured in the Patrick Swayze movie, *Road House*; C&W#1, 1987).

In 1987 Conley parted company with his long-standing producer Nelson Larkin, replacing him with Randy Scruggs and Emory Gordy Jr for *The Heart Of It All*; this change didn't affect his strike rate: 'What She Is (Is A Woman In Love)' (C&W#1, 1988), 'We Believe In Happy Endings' (a duet with **Emmylou Harris**; C&W#1, 1988), 'What I'd Say' (C&W#1, 1989) and 'Love Out Loud' (C&W#1, 1989). Despite his success in the US, he remains largely unknown elsewhere.

GREATEST HITS, RCA, 1989
THE HEART OF IT ALL, RCA (US), 1988

COODER, Ry

A session guitarist whose list of credits reads like a Who's Who, Ry Cooder's versatility seems to know no bounds. At the heart of it lies an all-round knowledge of jazz, country, blues and rock, which has enabled him to record strings of solo albums that have replicated the myriad strands of contemporary US music.

Ryland Peter Cooder was born on March 15, 1947, in Los Angeles. His parents were key members of the Los Angeles folk and blues fraternity, and Cooder was taught for a brief spell by Reverend Gary Davis. Despite the loss of his left eye in an accident, he joined

Jackie DeShannon's backing group as guitarist. He then teamed up with blues guitarist Taj Mahal (another magpie of different styles) to form the Rising Sons; this was followed by a stint with Captain Beefheart's Magic Band, where he showed his adeptness as a slide guitarist. After leaving Beefheart, he started his career as a session musician; this would link him with artists ranging from Randy Newman and Little Feat to the **Rolling Stones** (it was widely suggested that Cooder would become Brian Jones's replacement, and he contributed to the soundtrack of Nicolas Roeg's film *Performance*, starring Mick Jagger).

In 1969, he signed a solo contract with Reprise; his debut *Ry Cooder* featured a mix of blues and hillbilly, livened up by a smattering of obscure R&B songs. If his debut was eclectic, the follow-up *Into The Purple Valley* (1971), which featured a profusion of R&B obscurities and wry social comment, showed a masterful and original hybrid that transcends simple classification. Later albums would tend to examine each strand of this hybrid: *Boomer's Story* (1972) dealt with rural blues; *Chicken Skin Music* (1976) and the live *Showtime* (1977) featured contributions from arch-exponent of Tex-Mex **Flaco Jimenez**, with much of the material being derived from traditional country writers; and *Jazz* (1977) was self-explanatory.

Alongside these specialized offerings he found time to record *Paradise And Lunch* in 1974, which was the logical sequel to *Into The Purple Valley*. In 1979 he issued the lively and accessible *Bop 'Til You Drop*. Since 1980 he has continued issuing solo albums, but has also branched out into film soundtracks: Walter Hill's *The Long Riders* (1980), *Southern Comfort* (1981) and *Crossroads* (1986); Wim Wenders' *Paris, Texas* (1985); and Louis Malle's *Alamo Bay* (1985). In 1991 he formed Little Village with **John Hiatt**, bassist Nick Lowe and drummer Jim Keltner; their debut was issued in 1992.

ALAMO BAY (film soundtrack), London, 1985
BLUE CITY (film soundtrack), Warner Bros., 1986
BOOMER'S STORY, Reprise, 1973
BOP 'TIL YOU DROP, Warner Bros., 1979
BORDERLINE, Warner Bros., 1980
CHICKEN SKIN MUSIC, Reprise, 1976
CROSSROADS (film soundtrack), Warner Bros., 1986
GET RHYTHM, Warner Bros., 1987
INTO THE PURPLE VALLEY, Reprise, 1972
JAZZ, Warner Bros., 1977
LITTLE VILLAGE, Reprise, 1992
PARADISE AND LUNCH, Reprise, 1974

PARIS, TEXAS (film soundtrack), Warner Bros., 1985
RY COODER, Reprise, 1970
SHOWTIME, Warner Bros., 1977
THE SLIDE AREA, Warner Bros., 1982
TRESPASS (film soundtrack), Warner Bros., 1993
WHY DON'T YOU TRY ME TONIGHT, Warner Bros., 1986

COOLEY, Spade

While **Bob Wills** is widely regarded as being the most significant contributor to the evolution of Western Swing, Spade Cooley did much to popularize - and emasculate - the style, by adding lush string arrangements in place of the more feisty horn sections. His band, sometimes containing as many as twenty members, proved to be a useful training ground for young and ambitious musicians, such as steel guitarists Joaquin Murphy and **Speedy West**.

Donnell Clyde Cooley was born on December 17, 1910, at Saddle Creek, Oklahoma, of Scottish-Irish descent, and was dubbed 'Spade' after holding an extraordinary run of spades during a game of poker. Taught to play the fiddle by his father and grandfather, he moved to Southern California in the early 1930s, where he joined **Jimmy Wakely**'s Band. He gravitated to Hollywood where he got work as a film extra, and eventually became **Roy Rogers**' stand-in for a number of films for Republic.

By 1942 he had put together his own orchestra, and was appearing at the regular Western Swing dances at Venice Pier and Redondo Beach. In 1946 he leased the Santa Monica Ballroom on the proceeds of his hit 'Shame On You' (featuring vocalist **Tex Williams**), which had been cut for Columbia the previous year. After Columbia, he moved to RCA Victor, where he remained until 1950, and he then recorded for Decca until 1955. In 1948 he was featured in the KTLA-TV show *The Hoffman Hayride*, and also broadcast widely on radio.

His career slipped into the doldrums in the 1950s, and on April 3, 1961, while doped up and drunk, he murdered his wife, Ella Mae, in front of their daughter, Melody. He was sentenced to life imprisonment on August 25, 1961. His parole was later set for February 2, 1970, but he was allowed to appear at the Alameda County Deputy Sheriffs Association benefit on November 23, 1969. He suffered a fatal heart attack backstage after his performance.

ROMPIN', STOMPIN', SINGIN', SWINGIN' (with Tex Williams), Bear Family (Germany), 1983

COOLIDGE, Rita

Although little has been heard of Rita Coolidge in recent years, she was, during the late 1960s and early 1970s, one of the most sought-after session singers in the US, who bucked the trend by forging her own solo career.

Of part-Cherokee extraction, she was born on May 1, 1944, in Nashville, Tennessee, and made her debut singing radio jingles in Memphis with her sister, Priscilla, before moving to Los Angeles, where she backed Eric Clapton, Boz Scaggs, Stephen Stills and **Leon Russell**. In 1969 Russell recruited her for Joe Cocker's *Mad Dogs And Englishmen* tour, which he was masterminding; this loose agglomeration remained together for almost two years, with Coolidge's version of the Carpenters' 'Superstar' being one of the highlights.

In 1971 she was signed as a solo artist by A&M; she made her debut with *Rita Coolidge* and followed it with an extensive tour. She was backed by the Dixie Flyers, which comprised Jim Dickinson (keyboards), Charlie Freeman (guitar), Mike Utley (keyboards), Tommy McClure (bass) and Sammy Creason (drums). Her early albums, such as *The Lady's Not For Sale*, included compositions by the likes of **Guy Clark**, Eric Kaz and **Kris Kristofferson** (whom she married in 1973).

In 1977 she finally broke through with *Anytime ... Anywhere*, which included Jackie Wilson's 'Higher And Higher' (US#2, UK#48, 1977), Boz Scaggs' 'We're All Alone' (US#7, UK#6, 1977), the Temptations' 'The Way You Do The Things You Do' (US#2O, 1978) and the Bee Gees' 'Words' (UK#25, 1978). In 1980, having divorced Kristofferson, she scored with 'I'd Rather Leave While I'm In Love' (US#38, 1980), which seemed to indicate a move into straight pop, confirmed by 'All Time High' (US#36, UK#75, 1983), the theme for the James Bond film *Octopussy*. She still tours constantly and records when she feels like it.

BREAKAWAY (with Kris Kristofferson), Columbia, 1975
CLASSICS, A&M (US), 1988
INSIDE THE FIRE, A&M, 1989
THE LADY'S NOT FOR SALE, Spot, 1972

COON CREEK GIRLS

The Coon Creek Girls were formed in Kentucky and comprised three sisters, Lily Mae (vocals, banjo and fiddle), Rosie (vocals and guitar) and Susan Ledford (bass), with Daisy Lange (vocals and bass) and Violet Koehler (vocals, mandolin and guitar). They achieved considerable popularity through their broadcasts on **John Lair**'s *Renfro Valley Barn Dance* on WLW, and then WHAS, between 1938 and 1958. Whether this was due to the novelty value of an all-girl band is difficult to say, but the nominal leader, Lily Mae, kept it going right up to her death in 1976, by which time there was nothing remotely novel in the concept.

Although the sides they cut for Vocalion have long since disappeared, they are remembered by some, like **Bill Clifton**, for their timeless theme song 'You're A Flower Blooming There For Me' and the memorable 'How Many Biscuits Can You Eat?'.

COOPER, Stoney, & Wilma Lee

Wilma Lee & Stoney Cooper were one of the *Grand Ole Opry*'s most popular acts right up to Stoney's death in 1977, by which time they had been performing together for almost forty years.

Dale T. 'Stoney' Cooper was born in Harman, West Virginia, on October 16, 1918; his farming family were all proficient musicians. By the early 1930s, Stoney had become an accomplished fiddler and, after leaving school, he joined the gospel vocal group, the Leary Family. Wilma Lee Leary was born in Valley Head, West Virginia, on February 7, 1921; she was a skilful guitarist, pianist, organist and songwriter. Having married in 1939, they remained in the Leary Family until the mid-1940s, when they branched out as a duo.

By 1947 they had joined WWVA's *Wheeling Jamboree* in West Virginia, and after being heard by **Fred Rose** they were signed to Columbia, and then to Rose's Hickory label in 1955. Trained to sing religious songs, Wilma Lee's voice lent a unique soulfulness to old-time traditional material like 'Thirty Pieces Of Silver', 'Tramp On The Street' and 'Legend Of The Dogwood Tree'. After joining the *Grand Ole Opry* in 1957, they recorded a string of hits: 'Come Walk With Me' (1958), 'Big Midnight Special' (1959), 'There's A Big Wheel' (1959), 'Johnny My Love' (1960), 'This Old House' (1960) and 'Wreck On The Highway' (1961).

Despite the paucity of hits after leaving Hickory, Wilma, Stoney and their band, the Clinch Mountain Clan, remained immensely popular at the Opry. On March 22, 1977, Stoney died of a heart attack, but Wilma Lee continued to tour with her daughter, Carol Lee, who was married to **Hank Snow**'s son, Jimmie Rodgers Snow, often performing the old-time songs with which she had grown up.

THE CARTER FAMILY'S GREATEST HITS, Starday (US), 1987
A DAISY A DAY, Rebel, 1975
WHITE ROSE, Rebel, 1975
WILMA LEE COOPER, Rounder (US), 1988
WILMA LEE & STONEY COOPER, Rounder (US), 1988

COPAS, Cowboy

The plane crash that claimed the lives of **Patsy Cline**, **Hawkshaw Hawkins** and Cowboy Copas gave Cline's career an immediate fillip, while both Hawkins and Copas disappeared into obscurity.

Lloyd 'Cowboy' Copas was born on July 15, 1913, in Muskogee, Oklahoma, and was raised on a ranch by his grandfather, who taught him the guitar and a catalogue of songs. By the early 1930s he was traipsing across the country with an Indian fiddler called Natchee, playing clubs, bars and radio stations. In 1940 the duo split up, as Copas had secured a spot on *Boone County Jamboree* on Cincinnati's WLW.

Based in Cincinnati, he commuted regularly to Nashville to buy songs which he duly recorded for **Syd Nathan**'s King label; intriguingly, the writers' credits for these songs were split equally between Copas and Nathan. This proved to be a lucrative arrangement, providing Copas with a number of hits: 'Filipino Baby', 'Tragic Romance', 'Gone And Left Me Blues' and 'Signed, Sealed and Delivered'. In 1946, Copas joined **Pee Wee King**'s Golden West Cowboys as featured vocalist for their performances at the Grand Ole Opry. In 1948 they had a massive hit with 'Tennessee Waltz', before Copas left for a solo career, cutting hits like 'Hangman's Boogie' (1949) and 'Strange Little Girl' (1951).

During the 1950s his career slipped into the doldrums, but was revived by Don Pierce of the Starday label, who encouraged him to return to the *Grand Ole Opry* and start recording again. Among his later hits were 'Alabam' (C&W#1, 1960), 'Flat Top', 'Sunny Tennessee', a re-working of 'Signed, Sealed And Delivered' (1961) and 'Goodbye Kisses' (1963). The plane crash in Camden, Tennessee, on March 5, 1963, swiftly terminated this comeback.

BEST OF COWBOY COPAS, Starday (US), 1980
MISTER COUNTRY MUSIC, Official, 1988
NOT FORGOTTEN (with Patsy Cline and Hawkshaw Hawkins), Starday (US), 1987
OPRY STAR SPOTLIGHT ON COWBOY COPAS, Official, 1988

SIXTEEN GREATEST HITS, Starday (US), 1987

CORNELIUS, Helen

Helen Cornelius was born on December 6, 1950, in Hannibal, Missouri. One of eight siblings, she was raised on a farm and, while still at school, formed a trio with two of her sisters for local engagements. Married at eighteen, she secured work as a secretary and started to cultivate a songwriting career, winning a spot on the talent show *Ted Mack Amateur Hour*.

By 1970, she had signed with Columbia and was developing her career as a performer, but it wasn't until 1975 that, having moved to RCA, she began to attract attention with 'There's Always A Goodbye'. The following year, producer Bob Ferguson suggested that she team up with **Jim Ed Brown** to cut 'I Don't To Have To Marry You' (C&W#1, 1976). This partnership produced other hits, including 'Saying Hello, Saying I Love You, Saying Goodbye' (C&W#2, 1977), 'Lying In Love With You' (C&W#2, 1977), 'Fools' (C&W#3, 1978) and 'You Don't Have To Bring Me Flowers' (1978).

At the end of 1982 the duo went their separate ways, with Cornelius pursuing her songwriting career more assiduously, and partnering Dave Rowland of **Dave & Sugar** in a touring production of *Annie Get Your Gun*. By the end of the 1980s, she had resumed her partnership with Brown.

HELEN CORNELIUS, MCA (US), 1987

COSTELLO, Elvis

Elvis Costello has spent his career vaulting through the spectrum of contemporary music, applying his considerable songwriting abilities to any discipline or genre that catches his imagination. His style is unique, and his sometimes mournful tones are particularly well-suited to country-influenced material.

Born Declan Patrick McManus on August 25, 1955, in Paddington, London, UK, he came to prominence in 1977, when British DJ Charlie Gillett aired some of Costello's demos on his *Honky Tonk* radio show. He was consequently signed to the independent Stiff label by Jake Riviera. Early records like 'Less Than Zero', 'Alison' and 'Watching The Detectives' illustrated his considerable maturity as a songwriter, and his distinctive, slightly hectoring vocals fitted the mood of the era, when high-energy bands like the Clash and the Sex Pistols were eclipsing those staid titans of rock that had come to dominate the British and American music industries.

Over the next four years, Costello recorded one album after another, each as compulsive as its predecessor, until in 1981 he cut *Almost Blue*. On the album cover, a sticky label bore the legend 'This album contains Country & Western music and may produce a radical reaction in narrow-minded people'. It did. It was cut in Nashville with producer **Billy Sherrill**, included covers of compositions by **Hank Williams**, **George Jones**, **Don Gibson** and **Gram Parsons**, and provided Costello with a brace of hits: Jones's 'A Good Year For The Roses' (UK#6, 1981) and **Patsy Cline**'s 'Sweet Dreams' (UK#42, 1981). He had already indicated his interest in country by duetting with Jones on 'Stranger In The House' the previous year, but that didn't prepare audiences for this radical transition.

After the fuss had died down, he reverted to his former rock-oriented stance, but continued appearing with performers like **Delbert McClinton** and **Ricky Skaggs**. In 1985 he joined forces with producer/guitarist T-Bone Burnett, cutting *King Of America*; this, too, marked another change of direction, with Costello embracing different styles like Tex-Mex and cajun, and using musicians such as **James Burton** and drummer Jim Keltner; it featured a classic version of 'Don't Let Me Be Misunderstood' (UK#33, 1986). As if to emphasize his eclecticism, on his most recent work, *The Juliet Letters* (1993), he has partnered classical musicians, the Brodsky Quartet. This, like *Almost Blue*, has elicited howls of rage from the 'rock music press'.

ALMOST BLUE, Demon, 1981
ARMED FORCES, Demon, 1979
BLOOD AND CHOCOLATE, Demon, 1986
GET HAPPY, Demon, 1980
GOODBYE CRUEL WORLD, Demon, 1984
IMPERIAL BEDROOM, Demon, 1982
THE JULIET LETTERS, Warner Bros., 1993
KING OF AMERICA, Demon, 1986
MY AIM IS TRUE, Demon, 1977
OUT OF OUR IDIOT, Demon, 1986
PUNCH THE CLOCK, Demon, 1983
SPIKE, Warner Bros., 1989
TEN BLOODY MARYS, Demon, 1984
THIS YEAR'S MODEL, Demon, 1978
TRUST, Demon, 1981

COTNER, Carl
Carl Cotner's career has been inextricably interwoven with that of **Gene Autry**. Born on April 8, 1916, at Lake Cicot, Indiana, he mastered the fiddle before joining Clayton McMichen's (see **Skillet Lickers**) Georgia Wildcats in 1935. In 1937 he left McMichen to join Gene Autry, and by 1939 he had become musical director of Autry's Melody Ranch band. Apart from his prowess as a fiddler, he took on the chores of arranger and director of many of Autry's television shows, remaining with him when Autry retired to concentrate upon his business interests.

COUNTRY GAZETTE
Country Gazette enjoyed a brief reputation as being one of the more authentic of the bluegrass groups to appear with the rise of interest in country music in the early 1970s. The group comprised Byron Berline (fiddle), Roger Bush (bass), **Herb Pedersen** (banjo and vocals), Kenny Wertz (guitar and vocals) and Roland White (guitar, mandolin and vocals).

Berline, the brains of the outfit, had attended the University of Oklahoma in 1967, and played with **Bill Monroe**, before joining the army. He then became a session musician on the West Coast with Dillard & Clark (see **Clark, Gene**) and the **Flying Burrito Brothers**. After the disintegration of the Flying Burrito Brothers in 1971, he formed Country Gazette with Pederson, Bush (ex-**Clarence White**'s Kentucky Colonels and Flying Burrito Brothers), Wertz (ex-**Country Gentlemen** and Flying Burrito Brothers) and Roland White (see **White**, **Clarence**) .

The group's debut, *Traitor In Our Midst*, for United Artists in 1972, saw them recording traditional bluegrass material, but it failed to cause any waves in the US as their long hair and rock 'n' roll approach had few admirers in bluegrass circles. The tours of the UK and Europe were greeted rapturously on the college and club circuits, where sartorial elegance was not a high priority.

Later albums included *Don't Give Up Your Day Job* and *Sunnyside Of The Mountain*, but their failure to win a significant American following strained the line-up. By 1977 only Alan Munde (who had replaced Pedersen in 1973) and White remained; Berline (who temporarily formed Sundance in 1975) and the others returned to session work on the West Coast. By 1983 all vestiges of the group had finally disappeared.

AMERICAN AND CLEAN, Flying Fish (US), 1989
AMERICA'S BLUEGRASS BAND, Flying Fish (US), 1989
B C H (Byron Berline, Dan Crary and John Hickman), Sugar Hill (US), 1982
BLUEGRASS TONIGHT, Volumes 1-2, Flying Fish (US), 1988
BYRON BERLINE AND L.A. FIDDLE BAND, Sugar Hill (US), 1988

DAD'S FAVOURITES (Byron Berline), Rounder (US), 1987
DOUBLE TROUBLE (Byron Berline and John Hickman), Sugar Hill (US), 1988
FIDDLER'S DREAM (Byron Berline and Sundance), Appaloosa (US), 1985
FROM THE BEGINNING, Liberty, 1978
NIGHT RUN (Byron Berline, Dan Crary and John Hickman), Sugar Hill (US), 1989
NOW THERE ARE FOUR (Byron Berline, Dan Crary and John Hickman), Sugar Hill (US), 1990
OUT TO LUNCH, Flying Fish (US), 1989
OUTRAGEOUS (Byron Berline), Flying Fish (US), 1989
STRICTLY INSTRUMENTAL, Flying Fish (US), 1989
TOGETHER AGAIN - FOR THE FIRST TIME (Sam Bush and Alan Munde), Ridgerunner (US), 1977

COUNTRY GENTLEMEN

The Country Gentlemen were formed in Washington, DC, in 1957, and brought a challenging new direction to bluegrass with their emphasis on instrumental prowess and versatility. Although this tended occasionally to detract from the charm of the more poignant material, their enthusiasm gave bluegrass a much-needed shot in the arm.

The group was formed by Charlie Waller, who was born in Joinerville, Texas, on January 19, 1935, and was raised in Monroe, Louisiana. After touring with Busby's Bayou Boys, he was grounded in Washington, DC, when Busby was injured in a car crash. Waller decided to form the Country Gentlemen and recruited John Duffey (mandolin and vocals; born on March 4, 1934, in Washington, DC), Bill Emerson (banjo) and Jim Cox (string bass and banjo; born on April 3, 1930, in Vansant, Virginia); Eddie Adcock (mandolin; born on June 17, 1938, in Scottsville, Virginia) replaced Bill Emerson in 1959. This line-up remained unchanged until the retirement of Duffey in 1969.

Waller proved his virtuosity on the guitar with scintillating runs executed at a gallop, while Duffey was not averse to employing jazz progressions in his mandolin solos. An entirely acoustic band, their repertoire was drawn from a variety of sources - folk, traditional country, rock and R&B: **Bob Dylan**, **Charlie Poole**, **Molly O'Day**, **Lefty Frizzell**, **Mel Tillis** and Lennon & McCartney were among the writers whose material they covered.

Despite the considerable influence they exerted in the US, they remained completely unknown elsewhere. The group continued recording for Vanguard right into the 1970s; Waller was the only member of the original line-up to remain, while Doyle Lawson (see **Quicksilver**) and **Ricky Skaggs** were notable additions during this period. During the late 1970s they recorded regularly for the Rebel label.

THE AWARD WINNING COUNTRY GENTLEMEN, Rebel, 1975
BLUEGRASS AT CARNEGIE HALL, Gusto (US), 1988
BRINGING MARY HOME, Rebel, 1975
CALLING MY CHILDREN HOME, Rebel, 1975
COUNTRY GENTLEMEN FEATURING RICKY SKAGGS, Vanguard, 1990
COUNTRY SONGS OLD AND NEW, Folkways, 1989
GOOD AS GOLD, Sugar Hill (US), 1989
JOE'S LAST TRAIN, Rebel, 1975
LIVE IN JAPAN, Rebel, 1975
ONE WIDE RIVER, Rebel, 1975
RETURN ENGAGEMENT, Rebel, 1975
RIVER BOTTOM, Sugar Hill (US), 1988
SIT DOWN YOUNG STRANGER, Sugar Hill (US), 1988
SOUND OFF, Rebel, 1975
TWENTY FIVE YEARS, Rebel, 1989
YESTERDAY AND TODAY, Volumes 1-2, Fundamental (US), 1987

COUSIN JODY

Cousin Jody was born James Clell Summey on December 14, 1914, in Sevierville, Tennessee. The early years of his career were passed as dobroist in **Roy Acuff**'s Smoky Mountain Boys, where he was featured on hits like 'Wabash Cannonball' and 'The Great Speckled Bird'. As a result, he became a regular at the *Grand Ole Opry* from 1938 onwards. After leaving Acuff, he joined **Pee Wee King**'s Golden West Cowboys, where he branched out and mastered the electric steel guitar.

His striking craggy features, combined with a propensity for peculiar facial contortions, opened up a fresh career for him as a comedian, initially with Oral Rhodes, and then with **Lonzo & Oscar**. This got him his own spot at the *Opry* for some ten years, before he was stricken with cancer, from which he died in 1976.

COWBOY RAMBLERS   see **BOYD, Bill**

CRADDOCK, Billy 'Crash'

Billy 'Crash' Craddock has become known as Mr Country Rock, due to his penchant for the harder side of country music. He was born in Greensboro, North

Carolina, on June 16, 1939, and was performing with his brothers at local talent shows by the age of ten; this led to him forming the Four Riddles. In the late 1950s he was signed to Columbia, who thought that he had the makings of a pop star; he briefly scored with 'Don't Destroy Me' (1959). Disenchanted with Columbia, he quit the music business and took a series of jobs, including work in a cigarette factory.

In 1970 he was signed to producer Ron Chancey's Cartwheel label; his first single was a re-working of the Dawn song, 'Knock Three Times' (1971). Among his other hits for the label were 'Dream Lover' (1971) and 'I'm Gonna Knock On Your Door'. In 1974 Chancey passed Craddock's contract on to ABC/Dot, and he immediately scored with 'Rub It In' (US#16, C&W#1, 1974), which was followed by 'Ruby Baby' (US#33, C&W#1, 1974), 'Walk Softly', 'You Rubbed It All Wrong' and 'Easy As Pie' (1976), and 'Broken Down In Tiny Pieces' (C&W#1, 1977).

In 1978 he severed his association with Chancey and ABC, teamed up with Dale Morris, and moved to Capitol, where he had hits with 'I Cheated On A Good Woman's Love' (1978), 'My Mama Never Heard Me Sing' (1979), 'I Just Had You On My Mind' and 'Sea Cruise' (1980), and 'Love Busted' (1982). By the end of 1982 he had left Capitol and was recording less and less, preferring to concentrate on touring (particularly in Australia where he has a very substantial following).

BEST OF BILLY 'CRASH' CRADDOCK, MCA (US), 1986
BILLY 'CRASH' CRADDOCK, Capitol, 1978
'CRASH' CRADDOCK, MCA (US), 1986

CRAMER, Floyd

Floyd Cramer's pre-eminence as a session pianist has been based almost exclusively upon his long tenure as one of **Elvis Presley**'s key backing musicians. He was born in Shreveport, Louisiana, on October 27, 1933, but was raised in Hutting, Arkansas. After graduating from high school in 1951, he returned to Shreveport where he obtained work on KWKH'S *Louisiana Hayride*. This led to sessions for the Abbot label, where he was spotted by **Chet Atkins**.

Under the auspices of Atkins, Cramer established himself as one of Nashville's most popular pianists - backing Presley, **Jim Reeves**, **Skeeter Davis** and the **Browns**, among others - and in 1958 he was signed by RCA. His distinctive slipnote style (moving swiftly from one note to the next, enabling him to bend notes a full tone instead of a half tone) was derived from **Don Robertson**. Such was the novelty value of this style

that he notched up a string of hits in his own right: 'Flip, Flop And Bop' (1958), 'Last Date' (US#2, 1960), 'On The Rebound' (US#4, UK#1, 1961), 'San Antonio Rose' (US#8, UK#36, 1961), 'Chattanooga Choo Choo' (US#36, 1962), 'Hot Pepper' (UK#46, 1962) and 'Stood Up'. Despite the absence of hits in recent years, he has continued working with Atkins and still records under his own name.

BEST OF FLOYD CRAMER, RCA International, 1980
DALLAS, RCA International, 1981

CREEDENCE CLEARWATER REVIVAL see FOGERTY, John

CROSS, Hugh

A virtuoso banjo player and guitarist, Hugh Cross started his professional career in 1920, when he joined a medicine show. He was born in 1904 in Tennessee; after his vaudeville career, he joined the Cumberland Ridge Runners (see **Lair**, **John**) in 1930, broadcasting on the *National Barn Dance*. In 1933 he struck out on his own with regular spots on WWVA's *Wheeling Jamboree* and, then, WLW's *Boone County Jamboree*, in partnership with Shug Fisher. By the end of the war, his career was over and he had drifted into obscurity.

CROWE, J.D.

A founder member of **Quicksilver**, banjoist J.D. Crowe has been in the vanguard of the new wave of bluegrass musicians - like Byron Berline (see **Country Gazette**), **Ricky Skaggs** and **Vassar Clements** - who have contributed to the current success of the style. He first came to prominence with **Jimmy Martin**'s Sunny Mountain Boys, and in 1966 he played in a duo with Doyle Lawson (see **Quicksilver**).

In the early 1970s, he formed New South out of the remnants of the Kentucky Mountain Boys. New South drew its membership from a pool of almost interchangeable musicians (such as Skaggs, Lawson and **Tony Rice**) that provided the basis for other bluegrass bands. By 1979 he had again teamed up with Lawson, in Quicksilver.

BLACKJACK, Rebel (US), 1987
BLUEGRASS HOLIDAY, Rebel (US), 1982
J.D. CROWE AND NEW SOUTH, Rounder (US), 1988
LIVE IN JAPAN (with New South), Rounder (US), 1988

★

MODEL CHURCH, Sundown, 1987
MY HOME AIN'T IN THE HALL OF FAME (with New South), Rounder (US), 1988
SOMEWHERE BETWEEN (with New South), Rounder (US), 1988
STRAIGHT AHEAD, Rounder (US), 1987
YOU CAN SHARE (with New South), Rounder (US), 1988

CROWELL, Rodney

Rodney Crowell is one of a group of songwriter-performers who have bridged the gap between rock and country, creating a gutsy hybrid that draws in equal measure from both genres. Born in Houston, Texas, on August 7, 1950, he played in various local Texan bands before moving to Nashville. After washing dishes in a bar for two years, he came to the attention of **Jerry Reed**, and he was recruited for **Emmylou Harris**'s Hot Band in 1975 by producer Brian Ahern. While touring and appearing on her albums, he secured a contract with Warner Bros., and left the Hot Band in 1978 for a solo career. His debut, *Ain't Livin' Long Like This* (1978), featured contributions from **Willie Nelson**, **James Burton** and **Ry Cooder**, but was a commercial flop. The follow-ups, *What Will The Neighbours Think* (1980) and *Rodney Crowell* (1981), although equally impressive, were also commercial failures, and he was dumped by Warner Bros.

His reputation grew during the early 1980s, when his songs were covered by his wife **Rosanne Cash** (they married in 1979), Emmylou Harris, **George Jones**, **Ry Cooder**, Willie Nelson and **Waylon Jennings**, and he concentrated on producing artists like **Albert Lee**, **Guy Clark** and **Bobby Bare**. He also produced *Survivors* (1981), the reunion album featuring **Jerry Lee Lewis**, **Johnny Cash** and **Carl Perkins**.

In 1985 he moved to Columbia and issued *Street Language*: another flop. Forced to re-evaluate his modus operandi, Crowell finally broke through with the follow-up, *Diamonds And Dirt,* which provided him with five hits: 'It's Such A Small World' (a duet with Rosanne Cash; C&W#1, 1988), 'I Couldn't Leave You If I Tried' (C&W#1, 1988), 'She's Crazy For Leaving' (C&W#1, 1989), 'After All This Time' (C&W#1, 1989) and 'Above And Beyond' (C&W#1, 1989). The success of this album has finally placed Crowell among the vanguard of New Country artists.

AIN'T LIVIN' LONG LIKE THIS, Warner Bros., 1978
DIAMONDS AND DIRT, Columbia, 1989
KEYS TO THE HIGHWAYS, Columbia, 1990
LIFE IS MESSY, Columbia, 1992
RODNEY CROWELL, Warner Bros., 1988
THE RODNEY CROWELL COLLECTION, Warner Bros., 1989

CRUM, Simon   see HUSKY, Ferlin

CUMBERLAND RIDGE RANGERS   see LAIR, John

CURB, Mike

Mike Curb became the wunderkind of the US music industry during the 1960s; in the 1990s his prodigious success rate has seen him convert modest-selling artists into household names.

He was born in Savannah, Georgia, on December 24, 1944. In 1964, while still at college, he made his mark by writing the Honda jingle, 'You Meet The Nicest People On A Honda'. Adapting the jingle to 'Little Honda' (later covered by the Beach Boys), the single was put out under the name of the Hondells, who had two more hits with 'My Buddy Seat' and John Sebastian's 'Younger Girl'. In 1966 he formed Sidewalk Productions, which assembled soundtracks for 'youth-exploitation' films like *Wild Angels*, *Riot On Sunset Strip* and *The Trip*; he sold Sidewalk to the Entertainment Company in 1968.

By 1970 he had been appointed president of MGM, ridding the company of its less commercially successful artists, like Frank Zappa and the Velvet Underground, and replacing them with groups like the Osmonds. He also formed the Mike Curb Congregation, a particularly sanitized instrumental and vocal combo that fell somewhere between Ray Coniff and Mitch Miller. After leaving MGM, he set up Curb Productions; among the artists he signed were Shaun Cassidy, **Debby Boone**, the **Bellamy Brothers**, the **Judds**, **Hank Williams, Jr**, and **Sawyer Brown**. In the late 1970s, he was very active on behalf of the Republican Party in California.

CURLESS, Dick

Richard Curless was born in Fort Fairfield, Maine, on March 17, 1932. After leaving school, he joined a local group, the Trail Blazers, and in 1948 he got his own radio show in Massachusetts. In 1951 he was drafted and sent off to Korea, where his experience on radio got him a regular slot on AFN, broadcasting under the pseudonym of the Rice Paddy Ranger. In 1954, he was discharged and returned to playing local clubs. Over the next ten years, his career was erratic, marred by occasional problems with his health.

In 1965 the trucking classic 'A Tombstone Every Mile' landed him a contract with the Capitol subsidiary, Tower, and **Buck Owens** recruited him as a cast member of his *All-American Music Show*. By 1970 he had moved on to the Capitol label, where he had more hits with trucking songs such as 'Big Wheel Cannonball' (1970) and 'Loser's Cocktail' (1971). Curless has recorded less in recent years, but his popularity with truckers remains unchecked and he still tours the north-east.

IT'S JUST A MATTER OF TIME, Stetson, 1990
LONG, LONESOME ROAD, Stetson, 1989
TWENTY GREAT TRUCK HITS, EMI (Sweden), 1983

CURTIS, Sonny

The writer of such classic songs as 'More Than I Can Say', 'I Fought The Law' and 'Walk Right Back', Sonny Curtis was born on May 9, 1937, in Meadow, Texas. He began as a local session musician in Lubbock,

before moving to Nashville to join **Slim Whitman**'s band. In 1959, after **Buddy Holly** moved to New York, leaving the Crickets behind, Sonny Curtis joined Jerry Allison and Joel Mauldin and they continued as a pop group. Curtis's distinctive guitar work was not heard in as sympathetic a light after the group's change of tack, but following the group's break-up in 1965, Curtis's rockabilly inflections graced sessions by **Waylon Jennings**, **Willie Nelson**, **Crystal Gayle**, **Bobby Bare**, **Ricky Skaggs** and Eric Clapton, among others.

In the early 1970s he re-formed the Crickets, in response to the rise of interest in the group and in Texan music; a brace of albums - *Remnants* (1973) and *Long Way From Lubbock* (1974) - were cut for Mercury, and featured guitarist **Albert Lee**. While Lee only remained for these two albums, the group has continued to tour, with Curtis remaining the guiding spirit. At the end of the 1970s he cut two albums for Elektra.

NO STRANGER TO THE RAIN, Ritz, 1990
SPECTRUM, Nightflite, 1987

DAFFAN, Ted

Ted Daffan will always be remembered for contributing a number of songs that have become country standards. These songs have also defined two separate icons in country music: the honky-tonk hero and the trucker.

Theron Eugene Daffan was born in Beauregard, Louisiana, on September 21, 1912, but was raised in Houston, Texas. During his youth he developed a keen interest in steel guitars and electronics; he set up an electronics repair workshop after leaving school, which became a mecca for visiting musicians. **Milton Brown** was one of his earliest clients, and it was through Brown's influence that Daffan joined **Floyd Tillman**'s Blue Ridge Playboys as steel guitarist.

In 1939 he penned the archetypal trucking song, 'Truck Driver's Blues', which was followed by a number of honky-tonk classics, 'Worried Mind' (1940), 'Born To Lose' (1943), 'Headin' Down The Wrong Highway' (1945) and 'I've Got Five Dollars And It's Saturday Night' (1950). From 1944 to 1946 his band held down a residency at the Venice Pier Ballroom, Los Angeles, after which he returned to Houston. During the 1950s, he performed less and less, but compositions such as 'I'm A Fool To Care', 'Blue Steel Blues' and 'A Tangled Mind' were widely covered by **Moon Mullican**, **Cliff Bruner**, **Ernest Tubb** and **Bob Wills**, among others. In 1958 he formed a publishing company with **Hank Snow**, before gradually slipping into retirement.

DALHART, Vernon

Vernon Dalhart was born Marion Try Slaughter, near Jefferson, Texas, on April 6, 1883. During his adolescence he moved to Dallas with his mother and became a piano salesman; other menial jobs followed before he started to attend the Dallas Conservatory of Music. In 1910, having changed his name to Vernon Dalhart (after two small towns in Texas), he moved to New York to study opera, and performed in vaudeville. In 1912 he landed a role in a production of Puccini's

Girls Of The Golden West; and in 1913 he sang in Gilbert & Sullivan's *HMS Pinafore*.

In 1917 he started to record for Thomas Edison. Much of his early output was light operatic pieces and contemporary novelty items, but after scoring with 'The Prisoner's Song' in 1924 he began to delve into the vast archive of hillbilly material. Between 1924 and 1928, he collaborated with **Carson Robison** (who wrote many of his songs), who specialized in setting topical news items to music, such as 'The Death Of Floyd Collins' and 'The John T. Scopes Trial'.

During these years he recorded prolifically for a variety of labels, adopting a multitude of pseudonyms. By the early 1930s he had started to record titles like 'Farm Relief Song' and **Bob Miller**'s '11 Cent Cotton And 40 Cent Meat', both reflecting the depression sweeping the country. In 1939 he cut his final sessions for Bluebird, and by 1942 he was variously employed as a voice coach, a night-watchman in Bridgeport, Connecticut, and a hotel clerk. He died of a heart attack in Bridgeport on September 14, 1948, in total obscurity.

DALTON, Lacy J.

Lacy J. Dalton, in common with Bonnie Raitt, suffers from an age-old problem: nobody knows how best to market her, as her influences draw from folk, blues, country and rock. She was born Jill Byrem on October 13, 1948, in Bloomsbury, Pennsylvania, and started her career as a folk singer, writing protest songs during the mid-1960s. In 1971 she moved to Santa Cruz, California, and, using the name Jill Corston, became the lead singer of the rock band Office. After working on the West Coast, she left Office and cut some demos that eventually came to the attention of **Billy Sherrill**.

In 1979 she was signed to Columbia, scoring with a string of impressive mainly self-penned singles: 'Crazy Blue Eyes' (1979), 'Tennessee Waltz' (1980), 'Hard Times' (1980), 'Takin' It Easy' (1981), '16th Avenue' (1983) and 'Dream Baby' (1983). The bluesy vocals, combined with the dry perceptiveness of the lyrics, were somewhat overwhelmed by Sherrill's production, and a disagreement with Columbia ensued.

The disagreement lasted a year, and when she returned with *Can't Run Away From Your Heart* (1985), some tracks were dropped as they were considered too rock-oriented for a country singer. The follow-up, *Highway Diner* (1986), was reminiscent of John Mellencamp and **Steve Earle**, but it bombed. The following year she cut *Blue-Eyed Blues* (1987), which went some way to re-affirming her status with country audiences. She remains one of the most talented singer-songwriters around, but needs the right producer to fulfil her remarkable potential.

BEST OF LACY J. DALTON, Columbia (US), 1992
BLUE-EYED BLUES, Columbia (US), 1987
CAN'T RUN AWAY FROM YOUR HEART, Columbia, 1985
HARD TIMES, Columbia, 1986
TAKIN' IT EASY, Columbia (US), 1981

DANIELS, Charlie

In the early 1970s, the Deep South was turning out boogie bands faster than Colonel Sanders could turn out fried chicken. While most bands - like the Allman Brothers Band and Lynyrd Skynyrd - were blues-based, the Charlie Daniels Band drew much of their inspiration from bluegrass.

Charlie Daniels was born on October 28, 1937, in Wilmington, North Carolina. In 1959 he joined his first group, the Jaguars, as a fiddler and guitarist; scouted by producer Bob Johnston, the group remained together until 1967, during which time they toured the South, playing every bar and club en route. After the group split up, Daniels settled in Nashville to develop his songwriting career, and obtained regular session work at Columbia, where Johnson was a staff producer; among the artists he backed were Leonard Cohen, **Bob Dylan**, **Flatt & Scruggs**, **Marty Robbins**, **Claude King** and Ringo Starr. In 1969 he moved into production and worked with the Youngbloods, producing four of their albums, including the excellent *Elephant's Memory*.

His reputation had gathered momentum (with artists like **Elvis Presley**, **Tammy Wynette** and **Gary Stewart** recording his material), and he signed with Capitol as a solo artist. His debut, *Charlie Daniels*, led to him forming his own band, which comprised Daniels and Tom Crain (guitars), Joel Di Gregorio (bass), Fred Edwards and Don Murray (drums), and Charlie Hayward (keyboards). In 1971 he signed with the Buddah subsidiary, Kama Sutra, and recorded a

number of albums over the next five years; these included *Fire On The Mountain* (1973), *Way Down Yonder* (1974) and *Nightrider* (1975). With constant touring, they notched up a few hits along the way: 'Uneasy Rider' (US#9, 1973), 'The South's Gonna Do It' (US#29, 1975) and 'Long-Haired Country Boy' (1975).

In 1975, they switched to the Epic label and cut *Saddle Tramp*, *High Lonesome* and *Million Mile Reflections*; the latter included 'The Devil Went Down To Georgia' (US#3, C&W#1, UK#14, 1979), which became their best-selling single and established them with country audiences. Among later notable titles were 'In America' (a reaction to the Iranian hostage crisis; US#11, 1980), 'The Legend Of Woolley Swamp' (US#31, 1980), 'Still In Saigon' (US#22, 1982), 'Drinkin' My Baby Goodbye' (1986) and 'Boogie-Woogie Fiddle Country Blues' (1988).

During the 1980s, the popularity of the group continued with the release of *Powder Keg* (1987) and *Simple Man* (1990), both of which were heavily promoted with punishing touring schedules, a policy which has paid dividends, as the group constantly win awards for their live shows. When not touring, Daniels has played on sessions with the **Oak Ridge Boys, Alabama, George Jones** and **Hank Williams, Jr**.

AMERICA I BELIEVE IN YOU, Liberty (US), 1993
DECADE OF HITS, Epic (US), 1983
ME AND THE BOYS, Epic, 1986
MILLION MILE REFLECTIONS, Epic (US), 1979
NIGHTRIDER, Kama Sutra (US), 1975
POWDER KEG, Epic, 1987
SIMPLE MAN, Epic, 1990
WINDOWS, Epic, 1982

DANKO, Rick   see **BAND, The**

DAVE & SUGAR

Dave & Sugar were formed in the mid-1970s by Dave Rowland, who was born in Anaheim, California, on January 26, 1942. Rowland was a featured vocalist in a local group before he was drafted into the army, where he became a trumpeter with the 75th Army band. He then attended the Stamps School of Music in Texas, which led to membership of the vocal group, the Four Guys. After a tour with **Charley Pride**, he was kicked out of the group because of a variety of personal problems.

In 1975, Dave & Sugar made their debut in

Oklahoma City; Sugar were Vicki Hackman (born in Louisville, Kentucky) and Jackie Franc (born in Sidney, Ohio). Their first single, 'Queen Of The Silver Dollar' (1975), was followed by 'The Door Is Always Open' (C&W#1, 1976). This was the first of a slew of hits that caused some humourists to liken them to Boney M and Abba: 'I'm Gonna Love You' (C&W#3, 1976), 'Don't Throw It All Away' (1976), 'That's The Way Love Should Be' (1977), 'I'm Knee Deep In Loving You' (1977), 'Tear Time' (C&W#1, 1978) and 'Golden Tears' (C&W#1, 1979).

After moving to Elektra in 1981, the hits dried up, with only 'Fool By Your Side' (1981) making any sort of impression. By 1984 Rowland had been dropped by Elektra, after the label amalgamated with Warner Bros., and had joined **Helen Cornelius** in a touring production of *Annie Get Your Gun*. Cutting an album for Dot the following year, they are today a regular feature of the club circuit.

DAVE & SUGAR, MCA (US), 1986
GREATEST HITS, RCA International, 1982

DAVIES, Gail

The first female country singer and songwriter to produce her own records, Gail Davies was born on September 1, 1948, in Broken Bow, Oklahoma. Her father was a studio musician on the *Louisiana Hayride* and her brother was a musician. Davies's songs were first recorded by **Hoyt Axton** and Helen Reddy, which led to a publishing contract with Screen Gems in 1977.

Her marriage broke down and she moved to Los Angeles the following year, where she worked as a session singer, backing Axton, **Linda Ronstadt** and Don Henley (see **Eagles**). She was signed to the Lifesong label, and cut her debut in 1978; it included a number of minor hits: 'Poison Love', 'Someone Is Looking For Someone Like You' and 'No Love Have I' (1978). Lifesong closed down in 1979, and she was signed to Warner Bros., where she scored with the self-produced 'Blue Heartache' (1979), 'I'll Be There' (1980) and 'Singin' The Blues' (1981). After cutting 'Givin' Herself All Away' (1982) she moved to RCA. With *Where Is A Woman To Go?*, which included 'Jagged Edge Of A Broken Heart', 'Break Away' and 'Trouble With Love' (1985), Davies became the first country artist to use promotional videos.

More recently, she has moved to MCA, cutting *Pretty Words* (1989). Despite her lack of international success, Gail Davies has avoided the trap - fallen into by many female country artists - of playing a soft

country-influenced pop: like **Mary-Chapin Carpenter** and **k.d. lang**, she draws from all sources for her inspiration.

THE OTHER SIDE OF LOVE, Capitol (US), 1989
PRETTY WORDS, MCA (US), 1989
WHERE IS A WOMAN TO GO?, RCA, 1985

DAVIS, Betty Jack   see   DAVIS, Skeeter

DAVIS, Danny

A genuine backroom boy, Danny Davis came up with the ruse of adding a brass section to a Nashville rhythm section, and thereby created a country-ish type of muzak. He was born George Nowlam in Randolph, Massachusetts, on April 29, 1925, and started out as a trumpeter in some of the best swing orchestras of the period: Gene Krupa, Bob Crosby and Freddy Martin. By 1958 he had become an arranger and producer for the Joy label, before moving to MGM, where he worked with Connie Francis. He and his brass section, Nashville Brass, were then recruited by **Chet Atkins.** Despite the atrociousness of the resulting records, he cut around a dozen albums and had hit singles with 'Wabash Cannonball' (1969), among others. The best that can be said of his career was that it demonstrated how susceptible the Nashville establishment was to opportunism, and he was duly rewarded with four CMA awards.

DAVIS, Jimmie

The career of James Houston Davis falls into several quite distinct periods: he was first a hillbilly singer-songwriter, then a distinguished gospel singer-songwriter, and finally a politician.

He was born in Quitman, Louisiana, on September 11, 1902, into a sharecropping family. After graduating from Beech Springs Consolidated School, he worked in a sawmill before going to business school in New Orleans. He continued his education by obtaining a BA from Louisiana College in Pineville, and an MA from the Louisiana State University in Baton Rouge. He then taught history and social sciences at Shreveport's Dodd College.

At Louisiana State University he joined a college vocal group, Tiger Four, who performed on campus and in the environs of Baton Rouge. After graduating, he continued to perform, singing on Shreveport's

KWKH. In 1929 he was signed up by an RCA talent scout, and from that time until 1933 he cut sixty-eight sides for the label. Heavily influenced by **Jimmie Rodgers**, Davis's songs dealt with sex in an extremely open and humorous way, employing a language and imagery that was probably well beyond the ambit of his peers. Titles like 'Tom Cat And Pussy Blues', 'Organ Grinder Blues' and 'Sewing Machine Blues' were all quite explicit in their use of sexual imagery.

By the time he started to record for Decca in 1934, much of the lubriciousness had vanished from his songs, and with it, much of the humour, which was replaced by a more commonplace adherence to traditional mores. His style had changed as well, the yodels replaced with a more accessible crooning. At Decca he chalked up a string of hits, with titles like 'Nobody's Darling But Mine' (1935), 'That's Why I'm Nobody's Darling' (1935), 'It Makes No Difference Now' (1938) and 'You Are My Sunshine' (1939). He claimed writer's credit for most of these tracks, but **Floyd Tillman** retrieved co-authorship copyright of 'It Makes No Difference Now' in 1966.

Throughout his career, he had also pursued a role in public life: in 1938 he became Shreveport's Commissioner of Public Safety, and in 1944 he was elected Governor of Louisiana on the Democratic ticket. Apart from an appearance in the film *Louisiana* (1947), he retired from the entertainment industry until the end of his term of office in 1948. Then he turned to gospel and continued to record through the 1950s until, in 1960, he once more successfully ran for State Governor. During this term of office he had a hit with the sacred song, 'Where The Old River Flows'. In 1972, he was elected to the Country Music Hall Of Fame.

BARNYARD STOMP, Bear Family (Germany), 1988
ROCKIN' BLUES, Bear Family (Germany), 1984
YOU ARE MY SUNSHINE, Stetson, 1989

DAVIS, Lynn   see O'Day, Mollie

DAVIS, Mac

In recent years, Mac Davis's career has gone off the boil, due to an unfortunate tendency, common to many country performers, of attempting to become an all-round entertainer. During the mid-1960s and early 1970s, Davis wrote a succession of hit songs that established him as one of the more versatile writers in country music.

He was born on January 21, 1941, in Lubbock, Texas, and much of his adolescence was spent in Atlanta, where he formed an R&B band. In 1961 he joined the Vee Jay label as regional manager, and by 1965 he had moved to Liberty in Hollywood, where he headed the publishing division at Metric Music. Within two years he had caught the writing bug, and was providing material like 'You're Good To Me' for Lou Rawls (1967), 'In The Ghetto' and 'Don't Cry Daddy' for **Elvis Presley**, 'I Believe In Music' for the **Statler Brothers**, and 'Something's Burning' for **Kenny Rogers**.

In 1971 he was signed by Columbia, where he had a number of hits: 'Baby Don't Get Hooked On Me' (US#1, UK#29, 1972), 'One Hell Of A Woman' (US#11, 1974), 'Stop And Smell The Roses' (US#9, 1974), 'Rock 'n' Roll (I Gave You The Best Years Of My Life)' (US#15, 1974) and 'It's Hard To Be Humble' (UK#27, 1980). His success was due to his appeal to both country and pop audiences, and to the marketing knowledge gleaned from his days as a music publisher.

He landed his own television show, which ran from 1974 until 1976; and in 1979 he made his acting debut in *North Dallas Forty*. Although the hits had almost dried up, he was now regularly appearing in cabaret in Las Vegas and on television variety shows. In 1981 he appeared in his second film *Cheaper To Keep Her*. Whether he still composes is a moot point, but then many others have cruised, to far less effect than he, on past glories.

MIDNIGHT CRAZY, Casablanca, 1981
SOFT TALK, Casablanca, 1984
TWENTY GOLDEN SONGS, Astan (US), 1984

DAVIS, Paul

Singer and songwriter Paul Davis was born in Meridian, Mississippi, on April 21, 1948. After learning to play the guitar while at school, he started to play in and around the Deep South. By 1970 he had won his first contract with the Bang label, where he established a reputation as a good all-round writer. In 1974 he had the first of a series of hits, 'Ride 'Em Cowboy' (US#23, 1974), which was followed by 'Superstar' (US#35, 1976), 'I Go Crazy' (US#7, 1977), 'Sweet Life' (US#17, 1978) and 'Do Right' (US#23, 1980).

After leaving Bang in 1980, he signed with the Arista label, and the hits kept on coming: 'Cool Night' (US#11, 1981), '65 Love Affair' (US#6, 1982) and 'Love Or Let Me Be Lonely' (US#40, 1982). After moving to a farm outside Nashville, Davis concentrated on farming and songwriting, providing hits for **Tanya Tucker** and **Dan Seals**, among others, but returned to recording with a brace of collaborations: 'You're Still New To Me' (C&W#1, 1986) with **Marie Osmond**, and 'I Won't Take Less Than Your Love' (C&W#1, 1987) with Tanya Tucker and **Paul Overstreet**. In recent years, the farming has tended to take priority.

COOL NIGHT, Arista, 1982

DAVIS, Skeeter

Skeeter Davis was born Mary Frances Penick on December 20, 1931, in Dry Ridge, Kentucky. The eldest of seven children, she started her career, while still at school, in the Davis Sisters duo with Betty Jack Davis (born in Corbin, Kentucky, on March 3, 1932). After performing throughout Kentucky and southern Ohio, they made occasional broadcasts on the *Kentucky Barn Dance*, which led to a contract with RCA. In 1953, they scored their first hit with 'I Forgot More Than You'll Ever Know' (C&W#1, 1953); their career seemed set, but a car crash en route to Cincinnati, on August 2, 1953, killed Betty Jack outright and critically injured Skeeter.

Traumatized and physically disabled, she didn't return to the music industry until 1958, when she came under the guiding influence of **Chet Atkins**. Despite her lack of experience as a solo artist, Atkins produced a succession of hits, which came close to exemplifying the Nashville sound: '(I Can't Help You) I'm Falling Too' (US#39, 1960), 'My Last Date (With You)' (US#26, 1961), 'The End Of The World' (US#2, UK#18, 1963) and 'I Can't Stay Mad At You' (US#7, 1963). She also recorded duets with a number of other RCA artists like **Porter Wagoner**, **Bobby Bare** and **George Hamilton IV**.

Throughout the latter half of the 1960s she recorded more pop-oriented material, but this ploy didn't really pay the expected dividends, and in the 1970s she returned to traditional country, cutting 'Bus Fare To Kentucky' (1971) and 'I Can't Believe It's All Over' (1973). To this day, she is a devout Christian and owns the Crestmoor Music Publishing Company. Her most recent album, *She Sings, They Play* (1985), featured the eclectic blues band, NRBQ.

BEST OF SKEETER DAVIS, RCA, 1984
HOMEBREAKER, Charly, 1987
SHE SINGS, THEY PLAY (with NRBQ), Rounder (US), 1985
YOU'VE GOT A FRIEND, RCA, 1980

DAVIS SISTERS   see **DAVIS, Skeeter**

DEAN, Eddie

Edward Dean Glossop was born in Posey, Texas, on July 9, 1907. His early career was devoted to gospel, firstly in the James D. Vaughan Quartet and then the V.O. Stamps Quartet. He developed a resonant baritone that enabled him to obtain spots on the *National Barn Dance* in Chicago and on WNAX, Yankton, South Dakota.

In 1937 he moved to Hollywood, where he quickly found work with **Gene Autry** and landed his own series of films for PRC in 1946. Although he had all the credentials to become a massive country star, the right material seemed to elude him and, despite co-writing and cutting titles like 'The Other Has My Heart' and 'I Dreamed Of A Hillbilly Heaven', he never managed to achieve widespread celebrity. Although he continued performing well into his declining years, it was as a guest speaker at film festivals that he found the greatest appreciation of his talents.

DEAN, Jimmy

Jimmy Dean was born Seth Ward on August 10, 1928, on a farm in Plainview, Texas. From a poor family, he formed his first group, the Tennessee Haymakers (which comprised fellow service personnel), in Washington, DC, while in the US Air Force. After his discharge in 1948, he formed the Texas Wildcats, who signed with the Four Star label; they had their biggest hit with 'Bummin' Around' in 1953.

His biggest achievement in the 1950s was his rapid climb up the media ladder, culminating with his nationally syndicated television programme, *The Jimmy Dean Show* (1957). With this massive exposure, he crossed over from country to pop and signed with Columbia, employing a narrative format to most of his hits, which included 'Little Sandy Sleighfoot' (US#32, 1958), 'The Cajun Queen' (US#32, 1958), 'Big Bad John' (US#1, 1961), 'Dear Ivan' (US#24, 1962), 'To A Sleeping Beauty' (US#26, 1962), 'P.T. 109' (US#8, 1962) and 'Little Black Book' (US#29, 1962).

After returning to ABC-TV in the mid-1960s, he moved from Columbia to RCA and released a run of unsuccessful singles: 'Stand Beside Me' (1966), 'A Thing Called Love' (1968) and 'Slowly' (a duet with **Dottie West**; 1971). Another change of label, this time to Casino, brought another hit in the shape of 'I.O.U' (US#35, C&W#1, 1976), which charted again on its re-

release in 1983. During the 1970s, he went into semi-retirement to look after his sausage business.

HIS TOP HITS, Timeless, 1986

DEE, Johnny   see **LOUDERMILK, John D.**

DEE, Tommy   see **LOUDERMILK, John D.**

DELMORE BROTHERS

During the 1930s, record companies seemed to be falling over themselves to sign 'brother acts'; many of these acts were so locked into a specific style that they were incapable of adapting to the changes in fashion and technology. The Delmore Brothers, in their professionalism and their diversity of influences, proved eminently adaptable.

Alton was born on December 25, 1908, and Rabon was born on December 3, 1916, in Elkmont, Alabama. They were brought up on a farm and taught to play the fiddle by their mother, and in 1930 they won a local fiddling contest in Athens. After playing locally, they secured a recording contract with Columbia in 1931. In 1932, they made their first broadcast on WSM's *Grand Ole Opry*, the start of a six-year tenure. Such was their popularity that, from 1932 to 1952 (when Rabon died), they usually held a residency with one radio station or another.

During the late 1930s they recorded for RCA's Bluebird subsidiary, and had a number of hits, including 'Gonna Lay Down My Old Guitar' and 'Brown's Ferry Blues'. (The latter provided the name for a gospel spin-off recording group, Brown Ferry Four, variously featuring the Delmores, **Grandpa Jones**, **Red Foley**, **Cowboy Copas** and **Merle Travis**.) In 1944 the Delmores became, along with Jones and Travis, one of the first signings to **Syd Nathan**'s King label. Their tenure with King saw them moving further away from hillbilly music, in favour of a more blues-oriented style. Among their biggest hits were 'Freight Train Boogie', 'Hillbilly Boogie' and the self-penned 'Blues Stay Away From Me'.

Unfortunately, Rabon had developed lung cancer, from which he eventually died on June 4, 1952. Alton, rather than continuing as a soloist, packed up and moved to Huntsville, Alabama, where he became a travelling salesman. Turning his attention next to writing, he produced short stories for magazines, and then an autobiography, *Truth Is Stranger Than Publicity*. He died of complications arising from a liver disorder on June 9, 1964. The brothers were posthumously elected to the Songwriters' Hall of Fame in 1971.

BEST OF THE DELMORE BROTHERS, Starday (US), 1987
WHEN THEY LET THE HAMMER DOWN, Bear Family (Germany), 1984

DENNY, James

Despite his premature demise, James Denny was a key figure in transforming country music into a multi-million-dollar industry. He was born in Buffalo Valley, Tennessee, on February 28, 1911. After attending school in Nashville, he worked in the post-room at National Life & Accident (the parent company of the local radio station, WSM), when WSM were staging and broadcasting the *Grand Ole Opry*.

By 1951, Denny was talent director of the station, which meant that he effectively decided who would perform on the programme. By 1954, having established Cedarwood music publishing company, he set up the Jim Denny booking agency. By 1961, he was booking country artists worldwide, but on August 27, 1963, he died of a heart attack. His contribution to country was formally acknowledged in 1966, when he was posthumously inducted into the Country Music Hall Of Fame.

DENVER, John

In the early 1970s, John Denver represented the stereotype All-American Boy. In stark contrast to the long-haired, drug-crazed freaks of the east and west coasts, Denver was the clean-living resident of Colorado who exuded health, and his songs dealt with traditonal themes like conservation, falling in love with gingham-clad beauties and nature in all its awe-inspiring grandeur.

He was born Henry John Deutschendorf in Roswell, New Mexico, on December 31, 1943. After studying architecture in Lubbock, Texas, he moved to Los Angeles in 1965, where he got work as a draughtsman. During the evenings, he played the folk clubs and changed his name to Denver (in honour of his favourite city). He auditioned to replace Chad Mitchell in Mitchell's trio, and remained with them until 1968, when he left to embark upon a solo career.

He was signed by RCA the same year and, in 1969, his debut *Rhymes And Reasons* featured 'Leaving On A Jet Plane', which became a massive hit for Peter,

Paul & Mary. While he was now established as a writer, he had to wait until 1971 before he struck gold as a singer with 'Take Me Home Country Roads' (US#2, 1971), which has since become one of those annoyingly infectious songs that is a staple of many repertoires. Other hits followed, including 'Rocky Mountain High' (US#9, 1973), 'Sunshine On My Shoulders' (US#1, 1974), 'Annie's Song' (US#1, UK#1, 1974), 'Back Home Again' (US#5, C&W#1, 1974), 'Sweet Surrender' (US#13, 1975), 'Thank God I'm A Country Boy' (US#1, C&W#1, 1975), 'I'm Sorry' (US#1, C&W#1, 1975), 'Fly Away' (US#13, 1975), 'Looking For Space' (US#29, 1976), 'Like A Sad Song' (US#36, 1976), 'My Sweet Lady' (US#32, 1977), 'Some Days Are Diamonds (Some Days Are Stone)' (US#36, 1981) and 'Shanghai Breezes' (US#31, 1982).

Much of his appeal had initially been to country audiences, but by the end of the 1970s he was firmly ensconced as an MOR entertainer. This new status enabled him to work with artists as diverse as flautist James Galway, the great operatic tenor Placido Domingo, Olivia Newton-John and **Emmylou Harris**, and encouraged ABC-TV to grant him a special, *An Evening With John Denver*, and BBC-TV to give him an entire series. He did not entirely forget his country origins, though, and he was invited to make his debut on the *Grand Ole Opry* in 1976. The same year he formed the Windsong label, which immediately had a monster hit with 'Afternoon Delight' by the Starland Vocal Band. Despite the blandness of much of his work, his sincerity is rather endearing.

BACK HOME AGAIN, RCA, 1974
COLLECTION, Telstar, 1984
FAREWELL ANDROMEDA, RCA, 1984
GREATEST HITS, Volumes 1-3, RCA, 1984
HIGHER GROUND, RCA, 1988
ROCKY MOUNTAIN HIGH, RCA, 1973
WINDSONG, RCA, 1975

DESERT ROSE BAND see HILLMAN, Chris

DEXTER, Al

During the 1940s Al Dexter was an arch-exponent of the Western Swing/honky-tonk sound that proved so popular in California, and his arrangements, which incorporated accordion, steel guitars and brass, had a profound influence on the music of artists such as **Gene Autry**.

He was born Albert Poindexter on May 4, 1902, in Jacksonville, Texas. He initially led the Texas Troopers, with whom he scored his first big hit, 'Honky Tonk Blues' in 1936. In 1942 he hit paydirt with 'Pistol Packin' Mama', which sold millions of copies when it was covered by Bing Crosby, Frank Sinatra and the Andrews Sisters. Recording for a variety of labels, including Columbia, Decca, King and Capitol, he scored hits with 'Too Late To Worry, Too Blue To Cry', 'Rosalita', 'Guitar Polka' and 'So Long Pal'. Throughout the 1950s, he maintained a strong regional following aided by his ownership of the Bridgeport Club in Dallas. He died at Lake Dallas on January 28, 1984.

AL DEXTER SINGS AND PLAYS HIS GREATEST HITS, Stetson, 1989

DIAMOND RIO

One of the few emergent bands to marry the wide-range of country and rock styles successfully, Diamond Rio comprise Marty Roe (vocals and guitar), Jimmy Olander (lead guitar), Gene Johnson (mandolin and vocals), Dan Truman (keyboards), Dana Williams (bass and vocals) and Brian Prout (drums).

Prior to the formation of the band in 1984, each had notable pedigrees as session musicians or with other bands: Roe was in a country band called Windsong while he was studying at Nashville's Lipscomb College; Olander toured and worked on sessions with Duane Eddy, the **Nitty Gritty Dirt Band** and **Rodney Crowell**; Johnson worked with **J.D. Crowe**'s New South and **David Bromberg** and contributes most to Diamond Rio's bluegrass flavour; Dan Truman was a classically-trained pianist from the Brigham Young University, who had toured throughout Europe and the Far-east; Williams, a nephew of the **Osborne Brothers**, worked with **Vassar Clements** and **Jimmy 'C' Newman**, among others; and, native New Yorker Brian Prout was a member of Heartbreak Mountain, which boasted **Shenandoah**'s lead vocalist Marty Raybon in its line-up.

After touring extensively they were finally signed by Arista's Tim DuBois in 1990, and their debut *Diamond Rio* featured hits like 'Meet In The Middle' (C&W#1, 1991), 'Mirror, Mirror' (C&W#4, 1991) and 'Norma Jean Riley' (C&W#2, 1992). The follow-up *Close To The Edge* included 'In A Week Or Two' (C&W#5, 1992), and showed that the group wasn't afraid to bring the rhythm section to the fore (a rarity in country bands), giving them a leaner and harder sound.

CLOSE TO THE EDGE, Arista (US), 1992
DIAMOND RIO, Arista (US), 1991

DICKENS, Little Jimmy

Little Jimmy Dickens pursued a similar avenue to his contemporary **Jimmy Dean**, becoming a versatile entertainer equally at home at the *Grand Ole Opry* as on Johnny Carson's *Tonight* show.

He was born in Bolt, West Virginia, on December 19, 1925, the youngest of thirteen children, and attended the University of West Virginia. In 1942 he secured a spot on a breakfast radio show, where he was required to crow like a rooster; this led to a spot with Johnny Bailes (see **Bailes Brothers**) as Jimmy The Kid, and broadcasts on WIBC Indianapolis, WLW Cincinnati and WKNX Saginaw. A chance meeting with **Roy Acuff** resulted in a guest appearance at the *Grand Ole Opry*, which turned into a residency, and he then secured a contract with Columbia.

Over the next twenty years or so, he strung together a succession of novelty hits like 'Take An Old Cold Tater And Wait' (1949), 'Country Boy' (1949), 'Sleeping At The Foot Of The Bed' (1950), 'Out Behind The Barn' (1952), 'I'm Little But I'm Loud' (1953) and 'May The Bird Of Paradise Fly Up Your Nose' (US#15, C&W#1, 1965). Apart from this propensity for novelty items, he also managed to turn his hand quite effectively to love songs like 'Take Me As I Am' (1951), 'Just When I Needed You' (1953) and 'The Violet And A Rose' (1962).

While none of these were particularly substantial hits, his career as an entertainer enabled him to be a regular guest on *The Jimmy Dean Show*, *Hee Haw* and Johnny Carson's *Tonight* show. He still works the circuit, and appears regularly on television and at the *Grand Ole Opry*.

BEST OF THE BEST OF LITTLE JIMMY DICKENS, Gusto (US), 1988
I GOT A HOLE IN MY POCKET, Revival, 1988
STRAIGHT FROM THE HEART, Rounder (US), 1989

DILLARD & CLARK see CLARK, Gene

DILLARDS

During the mid-1960s the Dillards, by playing the embryonic college circuit, brought bluegrass out of the backwoods and into the open. While they failed to win mass appeal, they (like the **Country Gentlemen**) exerted a considerable influence on musicians such as **Chris Hillman** and **Gram Parsons.**

Rodney Dillard was born on May 18, 1942, and Doug Dillard was born on March 6, 1937, in East St Louis, Illinois. Both grew up in Salem, Missouri, where they played locally, before moving to the West Coast in 1963, where they formed the Dillards with Mitch Jayne and Dean Webb. After signing to the cultish folk label, Elektra, they cut two albums, *Back Porch Bluegrass* (1963) and *Live! Almost!* (1964), and became locked into a rigorous schedule of touring, establishing themselves with rock audiences. Their appearance at the Newport Folk Festival in 1964 worked to their detriment, as it alienated them from the purists, who considered them too rock-oriented.

The release of the excellent *Pickin' And Fiddlin'* (1965), which featured fiddler Byron Berline (see **Country Gazette**), didn't improve their sales record, and Doug left to form Dillard & Clark with **Gene Clark**. Doug's replacement was **Herb Pedersen**, and their next albums, *Wheatstraw Suite* (1968) and *Copperfields* (1970), emphasized their growing allegiance to rock and folk, with covers of material by writers like Tim Hardin, **Bob Dylan**, Lennon & McCartney, **John Prine** and Gordon Lightfoot. While these albums were competent and opened the way for a plethora of country-rock bands, they lacked bite.

As a result, they were dropped by Elektra and signed to United Artists, where their output became even more rock-oriented. After cutting albums such as *Roots And Branches*, they were dropped by United Artists in 1973, and recorded little until 1977. After the shortlived Dillard & Clark disbanded, Doug toured with the **Byrds** and worked on sessions and film soundtracks, like *Bonnie & Clyde* (1967) and *The Vanishing Point* (1971), before organizing the Doug Dillard Band, which cut *Jackrabbit* (1986), among others; Rodney's solo works have been restricted to *Silver Dollar City* (1984).

In 1977 the Dillards re-formed for a number of albums for Flying Fish, including *Decade Waltz*, with Pedersen in 1979; that year, Doug and Rodney joined up with **John Hartford** for *Dillard Hartford Dillard*, and *Homecoming And Family Reunion* was issued, featuring the entire Dillard family. While each maintains his own solo career and plays on sessions, they are at their best when working together on traditional bluegrass material.

COUNTRY TRACKS, Elektra, 1975
DECADE WALTZ, Flying Fish (US), 1979

DILLARD HARTFORD DILLARD, Sonet, 1977
DILLARDS Vs. THE INCREDIBLE L.A. TIME MACHINE, Sonet, 1977
HEARTBREAK HOTEL (Doug Dillard), Flying Fish (US), 1989
HEAVEN (Doug Dillard), Flying Fish (US), 1979
HOMECOMING, Flying Fish (US), 1989
I'LL FLY AWAY, Edsel, 1988
JACKRABBIT (Doug Dillard), Sundown, 1986
MOUNTAIN ROCK, Teldec (Germany), 1988
PERMANENT WAVE (Dillard, Hartford, Dillard), Flying Fish (US), 1989
SILVER DOLLAR CITY (Rodney Dillard), Flying Fish (US), 1986
WHAT'S THAT (Doug Dillard), Flying Fish (US), 1988

DIRT BAND see Nitty Gritty Dirt Band

DOCTOR HOOK

Doctor Hook was initially the mouthpiece for lyricist **Shel Silverstein**, and it was with his material that they showed their true mettle. After the relationship disintegrated, they became just another middle-of-the-road group with strong country leanings, and increased their success rate with a string of anodyne hits.

During the mid-1960s, Ray Sawyer (guitar and vocals; born in Chickasaw, Alabama, on February 1, 1937) formed the Chocolate Papers with Dennis Locorriere (guitar and vocals; born in Union City, New Jersey, on June 13, 1949), who were spotted and signed by Ron Haffkine. In 1969, Sawyer and Locorriere recruited William Francis (keyboards and vocals; born in Mobile, Alabama, on January 16, 1942), George Cummings (steel and lead guitar; born in Meridian, Mississippi, on July 28, 1938), John David (drums; born in Union City on August 8, 1942), Richard Elswit (guitar; born in New York City on July 6, 1945) and Jance Garfat (bass; born in California on March 3, 1944), and the group called itself Doctor Hook and the Medicine Show Band. Haffkine organized a meeting with Silverstein, who was writing the soundtrack for the film *Who Is Harry Kellerman And Why Is He Saying All Those Terrible Things About Me?*, and arranged for the group to appear in the film.

As a result of the film's success, the group were signed by Columbia; their first two albums, *Doctor Hook And The Medicine Show* (1971) and *Sloppy Seconds* (1972), featured Silverstein compositions like 'Sylvia's Mother' (US#5, UK#2, 1972), 'The Cover Of *Rolling Stone*' (US#6, 1973) and 'The Ballad Of

Lucy Jordan'. Their next album, *Belly Up* (1973), featured material which was entirely group-composed and, though attempting to emulate Silverstein's style of writing, lacked any discernible form. It bombed and the group was dropped by Columbia.

In 1975, their name was shortened to Doctor Hook and they were signed by Capitol. Over the next five years, they showed their strong country leanings with a succession of substantial hits: 'Only Sixteen' (US#6, 1976), 'A Little Bit More' (US#11, UK#2, 1976), 'If Not You' (UK#5, 1976), 'More Like The Movies' (UK#14, 1978), 'Sharing The Night Together' (US#6, 1978; UK#43, 1980), 'When You're In Love With A Beautiful Woman' (US#6, UK#1, 1979), 'Better Love Next Time' (US#12, UK#8, 1979), 'Sexy Eyes' (US#5, UK#4, 1980) and 'Years From Now' (UK#47, 1980).

In 1980, a change of label from Capitol to Casablanca resulted in their final hits: 'Girls Can Get It' (US#34, UK#40, 1980) and 'Baby Makes Her Blue Jeans Talk' (US#25, 1982). By 1982 the personnel had undergone a variety of changes, including the departure of Sawyer and Locorriere for solo careers. In 1988 Sawyer re-formed the group, with a completely new line-up, for touring purposes, and they are now firmly entrenched on the concert and cabaret circuit; the hits, however, have remained elusive.

COMPLETELY HOOKED, Capitol, 1992
GREATEST HITS, Capitol, 1987
A LITTLE BIT MORE, Fame, 1975
PLAYERS IN THE DARK, Mercury, 1982
PLEASURE AND PAIN, Capitol, 1979
SYLVIA'S MOTHER, Pickwick, 1989

DOCTOR JOHN

Malcolm John Rebennack was born on November 21, 1941 in New Orleans. By 1957, he had established a reputation for himself as a session pianist, working for labels like Ace, Rex, Ric and Ebb. In 1958, he cut his debut, 'Storm Warning', after co-writing 'Lights Out' for Jerry Byrne (1958). In 1962, he went to Los Angeles and became highly sought after as a session musician by producers like Phil Spector, H. B. Barnum and Harold Battiste, the latter a former acquaintance from New Orleans. Over the next three years, he established a fresh identity as Dr John Creaux, The Night Tripper, fusing the traditional sounds of country and New Orleans R&B with West Coast rock.

In 1968 he released *Gris Gris* for the Atlantic subsidiary, Atco, which, though it failed to sell in large quantities, attracted a substantial following among the cognoscenti. Over the next three years he released three more albums: *Baylon*, *Remedies* and *Dr John, The Night Tripper (The Sun, Moon and Herbs)*, the latter featuring an all-star cast of admirers, including Eric Clapton and Mick Jagger. In 1972 he returned to his roots, with *Gumbo*; it consisted of R&B standards, such as 'Iko Iko', and was produced by Jerry Wexler. The follow-up *In the Right Place* included the singles 'Right Place Wrong Time' (US#9, 1973) and 'Such A Night'; it was followed by *Desitively Bonnaroo* (1974), which was his final offering for Atco. Both albums were produced by Allen Toussaint.

Since 1974, despite being plagued by ill-health, he has continued to record; although the sales of his records have been poor, their eclecticism has guaranteed interest from his long-term admirers. In 1976 he appeared in the Martin Scorsese film of **The Band**'s final concert, *The Last Waltz*, which led to him joining The RCO All Stars, the group formed by The Band's ex-drummer Levon Helm. Throughout his career he has toured constantly, and his extensive knowledge of all styles of music make his live performances a treat to behold. In 1989, he released *In a Sentimental Mood*, which featured a duet with Rickie Lee Jones.

TRIUMVIRATE (with Mike Bloomfield and John Paul Hammond), Edsel, 1971
HOLLYWOOD BE THY NAME, BGO, 1975
DR JOHN PLAYS MAC REBENNACK, Demon, 1981
THE BRIGHTEST SMILE IN TOWN, Demon. 1982
LOSER FOR YOU BABY, Fontana, 1982
I BEEN HOODOOD, Edsel, 1984
SUCH A NIGHT: LIVE IN LONDON, Spindrift, 1984
IN A SENTIMENTAL MOOD, Warner Bros., 1989

DRAKE, Pete

Pete Drake was born on October 8, 1932, in Atlanta, Georgia. He started out as a guitarist, but during the late 1940s changed over to the steel guitar - after hearing **Jerry Byrd** in **Red Foley**'s band - and joined **Ernest Tubb**'s Troubadours. Throughout the 1950s he worked as a session musician in and around his native Atlanta and led his own band, Sons Of The South, until joining **Wilma Lee & Stoney Cooper** in 1958. The following year he moved up to Nashville, where he came to the attention of artists like **Roy Drusky** and **George Hamilton IV**.

In the late 1960s **Bob Dylan** recruited him to work on the albums *John Wesley Harding* (1968) and *Nashville Skyline* (1969); Drake came into his own and

found the approbation of a much wider audience. He went on to produce Ringo Starr's album, *Beaucoups Of Blues* (1970), and then George Harrison enlisted him to play on *All Things Must Pass* (1971). He also worked with artists such as **Leon Russell**, **B.J. Thomas**, **Jim Reeves** and **Ronnie Prophet**, and formed the Stop label in the mid-1970s. He died in Nashville on July 29, 1988.

THE PETE DRAKE SHOW, Stop (US), 1976

DRIFTING COWBOYS

Originally formed by **Hank Williams** as his backing group, the nucleus of the Drifting Cowboys comprised steel guitarist Don Helms (born on February 28, 1927) and guitarist Bob McNett (born on October 16, 1925, in Long Branch, Philadelphia). In 1949 the line-up was supplemented by fiddler Jerry Rivers (born on August 25, 1928, in Miami, Florida) and bassist Hillous Butram (born on April 21, 1928, in Lafayette, Tennessee). This line-up remained with Williams until his death in 1953. After his death, the group joined **Ray Price** and became the core of Price's group, the Cherokee Cowboys.

Individually or collectively, they sessioned for artists such as **Ferlin Husky**, **Carl Smith**, **Marty Robbins** and **Hank Snow**. In 1977 the group started to tour (on the strength of their association with Williams) and also to record, cutting *A Tribute To Hank Williams* (1980), among others. This arrangement continued until 1984, when each moved into retirement. In 1964 Jerry Rivers published a biography of Hank Williams, *From Life To Legend*.

DRIFTWOOD, Jimmie

Jimmie Driftwood, like **Bill Clifton**, has spent most of his working life promoting awareness of traditional country and folk songs, becoming one of country's most significant historians. He was born James Corbett Morris on June 20, 1917, in Mountain View, Arkansas. His childhood and adolescence were spent in the Ozark Mountains, where he learnt to play the guitar, banjo and fiddle, and also began to collect local songs. While still at school, he performed at dances and functions, continuing to do so after he had graduated and qualified as a schoolteacher.

In 1958, having been signed by RCA, he issued the influential *Newly Discovered Early American Folk Songs*. Among the songs included was 'Soldier's Joy' (which provided **Hawkshaw Hawkins** with a country hit in 1959), and a reworking of the fiddle tune 'The Eighth Of January' - better known as 'The Battle Of New Orleans' - which was covered by **Johnny Horton**, **Buck Owens**, the **Nitty Gritty Dirt Band**, Lonnie Donegan and Harper's Bizarre. Driftwood's next album, *The Wilderness Years And Jimmie Driftwood* (1959), was the source of **Eddy Arnold**'s massive hit, 'Tennessee Stud'.

By 1962, after cutting *Songs Of Billy Yank And Johnny Reb* (1961), he had stopped recording to concentrate on administration: he set up the Arkansas Folk Festival and helped to establish the Ozark Folk Center (which has done much to promote understanding of American folk music). He has more recently been involved with the Rackensack Folklore Society, who coordinate the activities of local musicians.

SONGS OF BILLY YANK AND JOHNNY REB, RCA (US), 1961

DRUSKY, Roy

Although Roy Drusky was, during the 1960s, one of country's more consistent hitmakers, his undistinguished style prevented him from achieving wider recognition.

Roy Frank Drusky was born on June 22, 1930, in Atlanta, Georgia. After leaving school he joined the navy and was introduced to country music by fellow shipmates, which encouraged him to learn how to play the guitar. After finishing his tour of duty, he studied veterinary medicine at Emory University until, in 1951, he flunked out of college and formed the Southern Ranch Boys. In 1953 they secured a regular spot on local radio in Decatur and were signed by the Starday label. Although the group were unsuccessful and dropped by Starday, Drusky was given a job by the station as a DJ.

By 1960 he had developed his songwriting skills, penning 'Alone With You' and 'Country Girl' (1959) for **Faron Young**, and also developed his live act with residencies on the club circuit. This resulted in a contract with Decca in Nashville and hits with 'Another' (1960), 'Three Hearts In A Tangle' (1961) and 'Second Hand Rose' (1962). When his contract with Decca lapsed in 1963, he was signed by Mercury, where he continued to notch up hits: 'Peel Me A Nanner' (1963), 'From Now On All My Friends Are Gonna Be Strangers' (1965), 'Yes, Mr Peters' (a duet with Priscilla Mitchell; C&W#1, 1965), 'The World Is Round' (1966), 'If The Whole World Stopped Loving' (1966), 'Where The Blue

And The Lonely Go' (1969), 'Such A Fool' (1969), 'I'll Make Amends' (1970), 'Long, Long Texas Roads' (1970), 'All The Hard Times' (1970) and 'Satisfied Mind' (1973).

In 1970 he appeared in a brace of indifferent movies, *The Golden Guitar* and *Forty Acre Feud*, and after moving from Mercury to Capitol in 1974, his career declined and Capitol dropped him in 1976. Since then he has been signed to a succession of independent labels, including Colorado and Big R. He remains immensely popular in Ireland.

ANYMORE, Stetson, 1987
COUNTRY ROSE, Colorado, 1985
NIGHT FLYING, Big R, 1981
ROY, Big R, 1981

DUDLEY, Dave

Dave Dudley, personifying the swaggering machismo traditionally attributed to the trucker, has been one of the most successful and visible exponents of the trucking song. His version of 'Six Days On The Road' opened up the genre for a whole host of bar-bands and other imitators, which climaxed with the film *Convoy* in 1975.

He was born David Darwin Pudraska on May 3, 1928; initially set to pursue a career as a baseball pitcher, his ambitions were halted by a serious arm injury in 1950. In 1953 he became a full-time professional musician, learning his trade on the club circuit and in bars. On December 3, 1960, he was involved in an almost fatal car accident; his insurance claim paid out $14,000, which he duly invested in starting up his own record label, Golden Wing, and cutting 'Six Days On The Road'.

In 1963 he was enticed to sign with Mercury, for whom he cut a string of hits like 'Last Day In The Mines' (1963), 'Mad' (1964), 'What We're Fighting For' (1965), 'Truck Drivin' Son Of A Gun' (1965), 'Vietnam Blues' (1966), 'There Ain't No Easy Run' (1967), 'George (And The North Woods)' (1969), 'The Pool Shark' (C&W#1, 1970) and 'Me And The Old CB' (1976). After leaving Mercury in 1975, he recorded for labels such as United Artists and Sun, and was given a slot on Nashville's WSM. Although his hits have dwindled in recent years, he holds an annual country festival at his spread in Dudleyville, Wisconsin.

COUNTRY BEST, Bulldog, 1988
ON THE ROAD, IMS, 1981
TRUCK SONGS, Mercury (US), 1984

DUKE OF PADUCAH

The Duke of Paducah has become something of an institution in country circles, having been one of the first comics to bring the homespun values of country music into his routine. Born Benjamin Francis 'Whitey' Ford on May 12, 1901, in De Soto, Missouri, he was raised by his grandmother in Little Rock, Arkansas, and joined the US Navy in 1918. Throughout the 1920s he toured with his own group, playing the banjo, before joining **Otto Gray**'s Oklahoma Cowboys. With this background, he was able to join WLS, Chicago, as an announcer on **Gene Autry**'s radio show, where he was dubbed the Duke of Paducah. His next position was on *Plantation Party* on WLW, Cincinnati; this resulted in a meeting with **John Lair** and **Red Foley**, who were setting up the *Renfro Valley Barn Dance*.

When America entered the war, he toured troop camps; these performances earned him a spot on the *Grand Ole Opry*, where he remained a regular contributor until 1959. Since then he has been a member of the **Hank Williams, Jr**, roadshow and still makes regular appearances on television. In later years he took to the lecture circuit, where his theme was 'You Can Lead a Happy Life!'

DUNCAN, Johnny

A versatile singer-songwriter, Johnny Duncan is one of many artists to have benefited from the influence of producer **Billy Sherrill**. He was born in Dublin, Texas, on October 5, 1938. After leaving school he enrolled at the Texas Christian University, where he met and married his first wife, Betty. In 1959 they moved to Clovis, New Mexico, where he worked with **Norman Petty**. By 1964 the couple had moved once again, this time to Nashville, where Duncan did odd jobs such as bricklaying.

Through some peculiar quirk of fate, he managed to secure an appearance on WSM-TV, Nashville, which was seen by Columbia executive Don Law. In 1967 he had his first minor hit with 'Hard Luck Joe', and worked with **Bobby Goldsboro** and joined the **Charley Pride** roadshow. Despite a number of hits, such as 'There's Something About A Lady' (1971) and 'Sweet Country Woman' (1973), he failed to make the major breakthrough until 1975, when he was teamed with Sherrill and **Janie Fricke**. Discouraged and aggrieved after the break-up of his marriage, his career was apparently washed up, but an introduction to Fricke by **Larry Gatlin** opened fresh vistas. Their first collaboration was 'Jo And The Cowboy', which was followed by a number of hits, including 'Stranger' (C&W#4, 1976),

'Thinkin' Of A Rendezvous' (C&W#1, 1976), 'It Couldn't Have Been Any Better' (C&W#1, 1977), 'A Song In The Night' (1977) and 'Come A Little Bit Closer' (1977).

After his collaborations with Fricke his career began to taper off, with 'She Can Put Her Shoes Under My Bed Anytime' (C&W#1, 1978) being his final significant hit; he was dropped by Columbia in 1982. In 1985, having remarried the previous year, he started to record once again, and although he failed to repeat his former chart success, the popularity of his live act was undiminished by the years of absence.

GREATEST HITS, Columbia (US), 1979
NICE 'N' EASY (with Janie Fricke), Columbia (US), 1981

DUNCAN, Tommy

While many members of **Bob Wills**' Texas Playboys went on to forge highly successful solo careers, it often seemed that the individuals never came close to matching the whole; Tommy Duncan's career bears this out.

Born on January 11, 1911, in Hillsboro, Texas, Duncan was influenced by rural blues and hillbilly. By 1933 he had joined the **Light Crust Doughboys** as the baritone lead vocalist, quitting the Doughboys when Wills left to form the Texas Playboys. Over the next fifteen years or so, Duncan's expressive voice fronted the Playboys on their best known songs, such as 'New San Antonio Rose', 'Blue Yodel No. 1' and 'I Don't Love Nobody', and helped to define the sound of the group in a way that was unmatched by their contemporaries.

By the early 1950s, Duncan had split from the Playboys to front his own group, the Western All Stars, who recorded prolifically for Capitol. Despite the success of these records, they just didn't match up to his efforts with Wills. During the early 1960s, Duncan rejoined the Texas Playboys for a number of albums on the Liberty label. He died of a heart attack on July 25, 1967.

DUNN, Bob

Bob Dunn played both jazz and country during his formative years. He joined **Milton Brown**'s Musical Brownies in 1934, introducing an electrically amplified steel guitar to the line-up - an innovation which proved to be a watershed for country music.

Dunn (born in Braggs, Oklahoma) initially became interested in the Hawaiian guitar through Walter

63

Kolomoku, a native of Hawaii, who instructed him through a series of letters. (Dunn had first seen the instrument in operation in 1917 in Kusa, Oklahoma, when played by a group of Hawaiians.) After playing in vaudeville and in jazz groups he joined the Panhandle Cowboys and Indians in 1927, touring the south-west and broadcasting occasionally on XEPN, Piedras Negras, New Mexico.

In 1934 he joined the Musical Brownies, remaining with them until 1936, when he moved to Houston and formed Dunn's Vagabonds. Although the line-up of the Vagabonds was more or less interchangeable with that of **Cliff Bruner**'s Texas Wanderers, the wailing dissonances of Dunn's guitar set the two groups apart. His other liaisons included a stint with Leon Seph's Blue Ridge Playboys (which also featured notables like Bruner, **Moon Mullican** and **Floyd Tillman**), with whom he cut titles like 'Two More Years'. Dunn had stopped recording by the 1940s; he went on to run a music shop and teach music in Houston until his death in 1970, from cancer.

DUNN, Holly

Holly Dunn was born in San Antonio, Texas; her father was a minister at the Church of Christ, where she frequently sang in the congregation. After winning a number of talent competitions, she joined the Freedom Folk Singers in 1975. While attending Abilene Christian University, she started performing as a solo artist in local venues, as well as appearing with the Hilltop Singers. In 1979, she moved to Nashville and worked for CBS Songs as a staffwriter and receptionist

In 1984 she made her breakthrough by writing 'I'm Not Through Loving You Yet' for **Louise Mandrell**. Her next move was to sign with the MTM label, which finally put her on the map with a number of hits: 'Daddy's Hands' (1986), 'Only When I Love' (1987), '(It's Always Gonna Be) Someday' (1987), 'A Face In The Crowd' (a duet with **Michael Martin Murphey**) and 'Love Someone Like Me' (C&W#2, 1988).

In 1988 the MTM label went to the wall, and Dunn was signed by Warner Bros.; her label debut, *Blue Rose Of Texas*, featured 'Are You Ever Gonna Love Me' (C&W#1, 1989). The following year she scored again with 'You Really Had Me Going' (C&W#1, 1990). This was followed by *Milestones* (1991), a Greatest Hits compilation with a few new tracks added; among them was 'Maybe I Mean Yes', which was withdrawn as she felt that it might reflect adversely on her reputation. While not yet established

beyond the US, she has the potential to be one of country's major stars.

BLUE ROSE OF TEXAS, Warner Bros., 1989
HEART FULL OF LOVE, Warner Bros. (US), 1990
MILESTONES, Warner Bros. (US), 1991
GETTING IT DUNN, Warner Bros. (US), 1992

DYLAN, Bob

Bob Dylan is the critics' favourite whipping-post: while illustrating his iconic status in the popular imagination as an icon, this fails to take into account the enormous influence he exerts on all types of contemporary music.

He was born Robert Allan Zimmerman in the iron-mining town of Hibbing, near Duluth, Minnesota, on May 24, 1941. While at high school, he played with a rock band, the Golden Chords, before joining the Shadows, which was briefly led by Bobby Vee. In 1959 he enrolled at the University of Minnesota and started to play on the emergent college folk-club circuit, changing his name to Bob Dylan (the name derived from the television cowboy character Matt Dillon, while the spelling paid homage to the Welsh poet Dylan Thomas). By 1960 he had dropped out of college and become immersed in the local counter-culture of radical politics and Beat poetry, fuelled by the folk songs of **Woody Guthrie**, the Weavers and Cisco Houston, and the blues of Robert Johnson.

In late 1960 he went to New York to visit Guthrie, and started to play the Greenwich Village club circuit, where he was spotted and signed to the Columbia label by the legendary A&R man John Hammond. His debut, *Bob Dylan* (1961), was a mélange of diverse styles and influences; it displayed his ability as a songwriter with 'Talking New York' (a coolly laconic view of the big city) and 'Song To Woody' (a touching paean to his putative mentor).

The following year, his alignment with the civil rights movement (along with other white middle-class voices like Joan Baez, Phil Ochs, the **New Lost City Ramblers** and Tom Paxton), stimulated the rapid maturing of his songwriting. *The Freewheelin' Bob Dylan* (1963) included the wry 'Blowin' In The Wind' (foreshadowing the mood of pessimism among America's youth), 'A Hard Rain's Gonna Fall' (an unemotional vision of a post-holocaust world) and the fatalistic lovesong, 'Don't Think Twice, It's Alright'. Other albums, such as *The Times They Are A-Changin'* and *Another Side Of Bob Dylan*, backed up by appearances at the Newport Folk Festival, established him as the voice of American youth with his trenchant swipes at the ethics of the establishment; 'The Times They Are A-Changin'' (UK#9, 1965) became a hit when re-released in 1965.

In 1965, he changed from predominantly acoustic instrumentation to electric, cutting *Bringing It All Back Home* (which included 'Subterranean Homesick Blues' (US#39, UK#9, 1965) and 'Maggie's Farm' (UK#22, 1965)), and *Highway 61 Revisited* (which featured session musicians such as organist Al Kooper, harmonica player Paul Butterfield and guitarist Mike Bloomfield). *Highway 61 Revisited* included 'Like A Rolling Stone' (US#2, UK#4, 1965), which marked the coming of age of rock 'n' roll, with its length (over six minutes) and bittersweet lyrics (formerly they would have been published in a volume of poetry). While these albums were lambasted by folk purists, they marked the development of folk-rock, which, as the decade progressed, would become the most populist of all styles. At the end of 1965 he released 'Positively 4th Street' (US#7, UK#8, 1965), which was followed by 'Can You Please Crawl Out Your Window' (UK#17, 1965).

After teaming with the Hawks (later **The Band**) for a UK tour, he cut the double album *Blonde On Blonde*, which was recorded in Nashville and New York; this included 'Desolation Row', 'One Of Us Must Know (Sooner Or Later)' (US#7, UK#33, 1966), 'Rainy Day Nos.12 & 35' (US#2, UK#7, 1966), 'I Want You' (US#20, UK#16, 1966) and 'Just Like A Woman' (US#33, 1966). A serious motorbike accident put him out of action, and he retired to Woodstock to work with The Band on the *Basement Tapes* (these formed the basis of the first internationally successful bootleg album, *The Great White Wonder*, and were not officially issued until 1975).

In 1967 he went to Nashville to cut the country-tinged *John Wesley Harding* with session men such as **Charlie McCoy**, **Kenny Buttrey** and **Pete Drake**. It represented a return to the stark simplicity of *Freewheelin'*: the gentle, compassionate 'I Pity The Poor Immigrant', the touching 'I'll Be Your Baby Tonight' and the allegorical 'All Along the Watchtower' emphasized this change. In 1969, the transitional move to country was completed with *Nashville Skyline*; using the same body of session musicians as its predecessor, it included a great duet with **Johnny Cash** on 'Girl From The North Country' (later covered by the British folk singer Roy Harper), 'I Threw It All Away' (UK#30, 1969) and the mellow 'Lay Lady Lay' (US#7, UK#5, 1969).

His output thereafter varied wildly: *Self Portrait* (1970) was a scrapbook of bits and pieces (including covers of other people's songs and reworkings of his own compositions), while *New Morning* (1970) retained the gentle country feel of *Nashville Skyline*. In 1971 he joined George Harrison and Eric Clapton at the first charity rock concert, in aid of Bangladesh, and followed his appearance with two singles: 'Watching The River Flow' (featuring **Leon Russell**; UK#24, 1971) and 'George Jackson' (dedicated to the black activist who was shot in a jailbreak attempt; US#33, 1971). In 1973, his erratic film career kicked off with a supporting role in Sam Peckinpah's *Pat Garrett And Billy The Kid* (starring **Kris Kristofferson**; 1973); the soundtrack featured Dylan's elegiac 'Knockin' On Heaven's Door' (US#12, UK#14, 1973), which was later replicated, with greater commercial success, by Eric Clapton.

At the end of his contract with Columbia, he moved temporarily to the Asylum label for *Planet Waves* (1973), on which he was backed by The Band; this prefaced a lengthy tour with The Band, the highlights of which were captured on *Before The Flood* (1974). As with the earlier *Basement Tapes*, The Band imbued Dylan's work with a mystical, rural feel of a disappearing America. This evocative spirit was present on *Blood On The Tracks* (1974), most notably on the western fable 'Lily Rosemary And The Jack Of Hearts' and the love song 'Tangled Up In Blue' (US#31, 1975).

He then participated in a tour, named the Rolling Thunder Revue, with Joni Mitchell, Joan Baez, **Roger McGuinn**, Mick Ronson (formerly of Mott The Hoople and David Bowie's band) and poet Allen Ginsberg. *Desire* (1976) violinist Scarlet Rivera and **Emmylou Harris**, and marked his return to the political protest arena with 'Hurricane' (based on the wrongful conviction of boxing champion Hurricane Carter; US#33, UK#43, 1976). *Street Legal* (1978) included 'Baby Stop Crying' (UK#13, 1978) and 'Is Your Love In Vain' (a passing nod to bluesman Robert Johnson; UK#56, 1978).

After *Bob Dylan At Budokan* (1979), which documented his 1978 world tour, he cut *Slow Train Coming*, with producers Jerry Wexler and **Barry Beckett**; it included 'Gotta Serve Somebody' (US#24, 1979). This marked a new stage in his career as he claimed to have converted to Christianity; critics wailed in horror at the prospect of a Dylan full of evangelical fervour, not realizing that it was just another one of his phases. *Saved* (1980) and *Shot Of Love* (1981) unconvincingly continued the religious theme, before Dylan turned to consorting with rock musicians such as Mark Knopfler of Dire Straits, Dave Stewart of the Eurythmics, the

Grateful Dead, Tom Petty and guitarist Carlos Santana.

The records from this period demonstrate Dylan's apparent preoccupation with a role as elder statesman of rock, and his appearances at star-studded 'fests' like Live Aid and Farm Aid seemed to vindicate this view. In 1988 he teamed up with George Harrison, Jeff Lynne of the Electric Light Orchestra, Tom Petty and **Roy Orbison** for *The Travelling Wilburys, Volume 1*. This was followed by *Oh Mercy* (1989), produced by Daniel Lanois, who had previously worked with Robbie Robertson (see **The Band**), and a tour with the Grateful Dead.

Such is Dylan's iconoclasm that it is as impossible to write him off as a spent force (he regularly stages comebacks), as it is to subject him to simple musical classification. The all-purpose chameleon, his songs have been covered by everyone, from Johnny Mathis and John Lennon to **Willie Nelson** and **Rodney Crowell**.

ANOTHER SIDE OF BOB DYLAN, Columbia, 1964
BASEMENT TAPES, Columbia, 1975
BEFORE THE FLOOD, Columbia, 1974
BIOGRAPH, Columbia, 1985
BLONDE ON BLONDE, Columbia, 1966
BLOOD ON THE TRACKS, Columbia, 1974
BOB DYLAN, Columbia, 1961
BOB DYLAN AT BUDOKAN, Columbia, 1979
BRINGING IT ALL BACK HOME, Columbia, 1965
DESIRE, Columbia, 1975
DOWN IN THE GROOVE, Columbia, 1988
EMPIRE BURLESQUE, Columbia, 1985
THE FREEWHEELIN' BOB DYLAN, Columbia, 1963
GOOD AS I BEEN TO YOU, Columbia, 1992
GREATEST HITS, Columbia, 1967
HARD RAIN, Columbia, 1976
HIGHWAY 61 REVISITED, Columbia, 1965
INFIDELS, Columbia, 1983
JOHN WESLEY HARDING, Columbia, 1968
KNOCKED OUT LOADED, Columbia, 1986
MORE GREATEST HITS, Columbia, 1971
NASHVILLE SKYLINE, Columbia, 1969
NEW MORNING, Columbia, 1970
OH MERCY, Columbia, 1989
PAT GARRETT AND BILLY THE KID, Columbia, 1973
PLANET WAVES, Columbia, 1973
REAL LIVE, Columbia, 1984
SAVED, Columbia, 1980
SELF PORTRAIT, Columbia, 1970
SHOT OF LOVE, Columbia, 1981
SLOW TRAIN COMING, Columbia, 1979
STREET LEGAL, Columbia, 1978
THE TIMES THEY ARE A-CHANGIN', Columbia, 1963

EAGLES

When the Eagles formed in 1971 as **Linda Ronstadt**'s backing band, they constituted a distillation of the many disparate influences implicit in West Coast rock. This synthesis was critical in establishing them as the most successful of the multitude of country-rock bands that emerged in the early 1970s.

In August 1971 the band was persuaded by David Geffen (the head honcho of the Asylum label) to go to Aspen, Colorado, and play a round of club dates to tighten up their live act. The band called themselves the Eagles and comprised **Bernie Leadon** (guitar and vocals), Glenn Frey (guitar and vocals; born on November 6, 1948, in Detroit), **Randy Meisner** (bass and vocals) and Don Henley (drums and vocals; born on July 22, 1947, in Gilmer, Texas).

In April 1972 they cut their first album, *The Eagles*, in the UK with producer Glyn Johns. This album included the Jackson Browne song 'Take It Easy' (US#12, 1972), which was emblematic of the California lifestyle, and was a harbinger of the group's musical direction in later years. Other singles from the album were 'Witchy Woman' (US#9, 1972) and 'Peaceful Easy Feeling' (US#22, 1973), both of which helped to establish the group on the international festival circuit.

The follow-up *Desperado* was probably the most country-influenced of all their albums, attempting to evoke the passing of an era and the demise of the Old West, in much the same way as John Wayne films like *The Searchers* and *Red River* had done. While the album was modestly successful, the singles 'Tequila Sunrise' and 'Outlaw Man' (1973) only scratched around in the lower reaches of the charts. The next album, *On The Border*, saw a change of producer, with Glyn Johns being replaced by Bill Szymczyk, and the line-up being augmented by the inclusion of Don Felder (slide guitar; born on September 21, 1947, in Topanga Canyon, Los Angeles). These changes emphasized the gradual hardening of the group's sound, and also pushed the band further into the mainstream with a number of singles including 'Already Gone' (US#32, 1974) and 'Best Of My Love' (US#1, 1974).

In 1975 *One Of These Nights* emerged, hot on the heels of a performance, supporting Elton John, in front of 100,000 people at Wembley Stadium in London. Although this album - which featured the singles 'One Of These Nights' (US#1, UK#23, 1975), 'Lyin' Eyes' (US#2, UK#23, 1975) and 'Take It To The Limit' (US#4, UK#12, 1976) - was to be the group's UK breakthrough, there was growing dissent within the band over their musical direction. This culminated in Leadon's departure at the end of the year; his replacement was Joe Walsh.

From that point onwards, the Eagles were just another close-harmony rock band and, although songs like 'New Kid In Town' (US#1, 1976; UK#2O, 1977), 'Hotel California' (US#1, UK#8, 1977), 'Heartache Tonight' (US#1, UK#40, 1979), 'The Long Run' (US#8, UK#66, 1979) and 'I Can't Tell You Why' (US#8, 1979) proved that they were undoubtedly the market leaders of that particular genre, it had always been Leadon's country-influenced guitar work that set them apart. Both Don Henley and Glen Frey went on to have very successful solo careers.

BEST OF THE EAGLES, Asylum, 1985
DESPERADO, Asylum, 1973
THE EAGLES, Asylum, 1972
EAGLES LIVE, Asylum, 1980
HOTEL CALIFORNIA, Asylum, 1977
LONG RUN, Asylum, 1979
ON THE BORDER, Asylum, 1974
ONE OF THESE NIGHTS, Asylum, 1975

EARLE, Steve

In the vanguard of the New Country artists, Steve Earle's blend of rock 'n' roll and country forms the ideal backdrop for his tales of drifters and brawlers and bikers and no-hopers. While some see similarities to Bruce Springsteen, Earle's characters are not seen through the shimmering haze of a wet windshield, but in eyeball-to-eyeball confrontation.

He was born in Fort Monroe, Virginia, on January 17, 1955, and grew up in San Antonio, Texas. After leaving San Antonio in 1971 he moved to Nashville, in the glory days of the outlaw movement, and became influenced by writers such as **Kris Kristofferson**, **Guy Clark** and **Townes Van Zandt**. He spent the next fifteen years writing songs, covered by artists such as **Carl Perkins**, **Waylon Jennings** and **Connie Smith**, and playing the club circuit. In 1986 his persistence paid off with a contract with MCA. His debut, *Guitar Town,* combined the instrumental muscle of rock 'n' roll with acute lyrical sensitivity.

After forming the Dukes in 1987, which includes Zip Gibson (guitar), Kelly Looney (bass), Ken Moore (keyboards), Craig Wright (drums) and Bucky Baxter (steel guitar), Earle embarked upon a remorseless coast-to-coast touring schedule that still continues today; in summer 1989 he toured with **Bob Dylan**, and cut the live *Copperhead Road*. With an aversion to rigid formulaic music, Earle's writing and playing is consistently improving, as his most recent album, *Shut Up And Die Like An Aviator*, testifies (1992).

BBC RADIO 1 LIVE IN CONCERT, Windsong, 1992
COPPERHEAD ROAD, MCA, 1989
ESSENTIAL, MCA, 1993
EXIT 0, MCA, 1987
GUITAR TOWN, MCA, 1986
THE HARD WAY, MCA, 1990
SHUT UP AND DIE LIKE AN AVIATOR, MCA, 1992
WE AIN'T NEVER SATISFIED, MCA, 1991

EATON, Bob see EATON, Connie

EATON, Connie

Connie Eaton was born on March 1, 1950, in Nashville; her father, Bob Eaton, celebrated her birth with his biggest hit 'Second Hand Heart'. In 1968, after studying drama, Connie met her future husband, Cliff Williamson (who was A&R director of the Chart label), who introduced her to the world of television.

After winning various talent shows she started to appear regularly on *The Lawrence Welk Show*, *Hee Haw* and the *Arthur Godfrey Talent Scout Show*. By 1970 she had been nominated for awards by Cashbox, and had had a modest hit with 'Angel Of The Morning'. After spells with labels like Stax, ABC and GRC her career slipped into the doldrums. Partial resuscitation occurred with the hit 'Lonely Men, Lonely Women' (1975), but she retired from the music industry to spend time with her family.

EDWARDS, Stoney

Criminally underrated, Stoney Edwards - like **O.B. McClinton** - is one of the finest exponents of 'country-soul'. He was born on December 24, 1937, in Oklahoma, and worked as a farm labourer, truck driver and concierge, before moving to Oakland, California, where he sang in clubs. He signed with Capitol in 1970, adopting the honky-tonk sound of Bakersfield and **Buck Owens**, and scored with 'Poor Folks Stick Together' (1971), 'She's My Rock' (1972), 'Hank And Lefty Raised My Country Soul' (1973), 'Mississippi You're On My Mind' (1975), 'If I Had To Do It All Over Again' (1978) and 'No Way To Drown A Memory' (1980). His career went into decline during the 1980s, and he has since sunk into obscurity.

ELLIOTT, Ramblin' Jack

In developing a hybrid style that owes as much to folk as it does to country, the iconoclastic performer Ramblin' Jack Elliott provided a model for many younger artists, such as **Bob Dylan**, John Sebastian, Jesse Colin Young and **Ry Cooder**, who emerged in the 1960s.

Elliot Charles Adnopoz was born into a Jewish family in Brooklyn, New York, on August 1, 1931, the son of a doctor. His first real influence was cowboy music, and in 1947 he changed his name to Buck Elliott and ran away to join Colonel Jim Eskew's rodeo. In 1951 he met **Woody Guthrie** in Greenwich Village, the start of a friendship that would last until Guthrie's death in 1967; it was with Elliott that Guthrie made his final recordings in 1955 for Moe Asch's Folkways label.

By 1955, Buck Elliott had become Ramblin' Jack Elliott and was a fixture on the burgeoning New York folk circuit; while he included many songs by Guthrie in his repertoire, he also sang songs by **Hank Williams**, **Jimmie Rodgers** and the **Carter Family**. After travelling to Europe, he met some of the leading lights of the nascent English folk scene, including Ewan MacColl and Peggy Seeger, and recorded for the UK label, Topic. Throughout the 1960s, he was a fixture at most of the US folk festivals and recorded extensively for labels like Fantasy, Vanguard, Folkways, Delmark and Prestige.

In 1968 he was signed by Reprise and cut a brace of rather unsatisfactory albums, including *Young Brigham*. Dylan recruited him to appear in the Rolling Thunder Revue (1976), an account of which later appeared as the film *Renaldo And Clara*. Many of his contemporaries and influences have long since died, but Elliott is still regarded as one of the few genuine interpreters of traditional American music.

HARD TRAVELLIN' SONGS BY WOODY GUTHRIE, Big Beat, 1990
KEROUAC'S LAST DREAM, Folk Freak, 1988
MULESKINNER, Topic, 1981
ROLL ON BUDDY, Topic, 1981
TALKING WOODY GUTHRIE, Topic, 1981

ELY, JOE

Joe Ely established his reputation as one of the front-runners in the New Country movement of the late 1970s, with an imaginative hybrid of Tex-Mex, honky-tonk, R&B and 'garage-rock'. He was born on February 9, 1947, in Amarillo, Texas, and moved to Lubbock in 1958. After leaving school, he played in local bars and toured Europe with a theatre group, before returning to Texas to form an acoustic country group, the Flatlanders, with **Butch Hancock** and **Jimmie Dale Gilmore**. Working throughout the south-west, they cut *One More Road* (1971) before splitting up.

Ely formed his own band and built a reputation in the clubs and bars of the south-west, until being signed by MCA in 1975. His debut, *Joe Ely* (1977), failed to sell in quantity as the driving rhythm section was deemed too rock-oriented, but the minor hit 'All My Love' and the three Butch Hancock compositions, 'Suckin' A Big Bottle Of Gin', 'She Never Spoke Spanish To Me' and 'Tennessee's Not The State I'm In', demonstrated his natural affinity with country. The follow-up, *Honky Tonk Masquerade* (which included the Gilmore-penned title song; 1978), established Ely with European audiences, but success remained elusive in the US.

In 1979, in an attempt to achieve a wider audience, **Bob Dylan**'s former producer Bob Johnston was brought in for *Down On The Drag*. This did little to raise his profile in the US, but he was venerated by many in Europe, including the Clash, with whom he toured and recorded the energetic *Live Shots* (1981). Taking a sabbatical from touring, and concentrating on writing, he produced little over the next three years. When he re-emerged with *High Res* (1984), its sophisticated studio technology alienated many of his longest-standing supporters, who felt that he was selling out.

After cutting *Lord Of The Highway* (1987), he decided to leave MCA and release the album on the independent Hightone label. While it was his best album to date (demonstrating his growth as a writer and his mastery of studio technique), Hightone were ill-equipped to market it to the full; the follow-up, *Dig All Night*, emerged in 1988. In 1990, he appeared at the **Roy Orbison** Tribute Concert and at Farm Aid, before re-signing with MCA for *Live At Liberty Lunch* (1990) and *Love And Danger* (1992). Although his European reputation is assured (particularly in Ireland), he remains very underrated.

DIG ALL NIGHT, Demon, 1988
DOWN ON THE DRAG, MCA (US), 1979
HI-RES, MCA, 1984
JOE ELY, MCA, 1981
LIVE AT LIBERTY LUNCH, MCA, 1990
LIVE SHOTS, MCA (US), 1981
LORD OF THE HIGHWAY, Hightone (US), 1987
LOVE AND DANGER, MCA, 1992
MILKSHAKES AND MALTS, Sunstorm, 1988
MUSTA NOTTA GOTTA LOTTA, MCA (US), 1981
ONE MORE ROAD (Flatlanders), Charly, 1989
WHATEVER HAPPENED TO MARIA, Sunstorm, 1989

EMMONS, Buddy

One of the doyens of the studio session, Buddy Emmons has played with everyone from Henry Mancini through to **Ray Charles**, gaining lengthy sojourns with **Ernest Tubb** and **Ray Price** en route. While his reputation is based upon his prowess on the steel guitar, he is an extremely versatile musician, capable of playing almost any instrument.

He was born on January 27, 1937, in Mishawaka, Indiana. After learning to play a rather primitive version of the Hawaiian guitar when he was eleven, he studied at the Hawaiian Conservatory of Music in South Bend, Indiana, from the age of sixteen. He began to gig in clubs in Calumet City, Illinois, during the week, travelling up to Chicago at the weekends to jam. Within a couple of years he had relocated to Detroit, where he secured a permanent position with **Little Jimmy Dickens**' band, resulting in a number of appearances at the Grand Ole Opry.

Based in Nashville, he joined Ernest Tubb before moving on to Ray Price's Cherokee Cowboys. After setting up a company to market pedal steel guitars, he became bassist in **Roger Miller**'s band in 1969, which involved moving out to Los Angeles. Here he became one of the most sought-after session musicians on the West Coast, working with Judy Collins, **Linda Ronstadt** and **Merle Haggard**.

After leaving Miller in 1973, he returned to playing in the Nashville session circuits, and promoted understanding of the steel guitar, with his business partner Shot Jackson, through the Sho-Bud Guitar Company, issuing several instruction albums on his own Emmons label. He also recorded several solo albums for the specialist Flying Fish label, notably *Buddy Emmons Sings Bob Wills* (1973), *Steel Guitar* (1975) and *Minors Aloud* (1979).

BUDDY EMMONS SINGS BOB WILLS, Sonet, 1976
MINORS ALOUD, Flying Fish (US), 1979
STEEL GUITAR, Sonet, 1976

ENGLAND DAN see SEALS, Dan

EVANS, Dale see ROGERS, Roy

EVERLY BROTHERS

During the 1970s, it was rumoured that the Everly Brothers were, due to fraternal animosity, no more. This was a greater disaster than a plague of locusts, because the Everly Brothers, like the late **Elvis Presley** and the late **Buddy Holly**, had been there during the 1950s, providing the soundtrack to countless childhoods. And when, in 1983, the Everlys started playing together again, it was as if they had never been away. Not because they started churning out hits all over again, but because their seamless harmonies and impeccable choice of material echoed a bygone era, and to hear them was to feel the years fall away.

Don was born on February 1, 1937, and Phil Everly was born on January 19, 1939, in Brownie, Kentucky. Their parents, Margaret and Ike, were country artists and had their own radio show on KMA, Shenandoah, Iowa; this imbued both with a sense of showmanship, and enabled Don to secure his own radio programme, *The Little Donnie Show*. After Phil's graduation from high school in 1954, the family moved to Knoxville and the brothers went to Nashville in search of a recording deal.

After a round of rejections, Don sold his composition 'Thou Shalt Not Steal', which became a hit for **Kitty Wells**: they were offered a contract by Columbia as a result. One single, 'Keep On Loving Me' (produced by **Chet Atkins**), materialized before they were dropped. Atkins introduced them to **Wesley Rose**, who became their manager and signed them to his publishing company, Acuff-Rose. Rose went on to introduce them to the songwriting team of **Felice and Boudleaux Bryant** and the label boss of Cadence, Archie Bleyer. Most of their hits for Cadence were written by the Bryants, and produced by Chet Atkins, who combined the maudlin teenage angst of the lyrics and the brothers' plaintive, whining harmonies with a rock 'n' roll backbeat, thereby creating an intoxicating confection that was to influence the Beatles, Paul Simon and Crosby, Stills and Nash.

Between 1957 and 1960 they notched up ten hits for Cadence: 'Bye Bye Love' (US#2, UK#6, 1957), 'Wake Up Little Susie' (US#1, UK#2, 1957), 'All I Have To Do Is Dream' (US#1, UK#1, 1958), 'Bird Dog' (US#1, UK#2, 1958), 'Problems' (US#2, UK#6, 1958), 'Take A Message To Mary' (US#16, UK#20, 1959), '('Til) I Kissed You' (US#4, UK#2, 1959), 'Like Strangers' (US#22, UK#11, 1959), 'Let It Be Me' (US#7, UK#13, 1960) and 'When Will I Be Loved' (US#8, UK#4, 1960). In addition to the singles, they cut the magnificent *Songs Our Daddy Taught Us* (1958), a collection of traditional country songs.

In 1960 they left Cadence and signed with the Warner Bros. label. The following year a dispute over royalties broke out between them and their manager Wesley Rose, as they had written '('Til) I Kissed You' and 'When Will I Be Loved' and had not been fully reimbursed for their efforts. This rift meant that they were denied access to the Bryants' songs and the Nashville session men but, despite these changes, the hits kept rolling: 'Cathy's Clown' (US#1, UK#1, 1960), 'Lucille' (US#21, UK#4, 1960), 'Walk Right Back' (US#7, UK#1, 1961), 'Temptation' (US#27, UK#1, 1961), 'Don't Blame Me' (US#20, UK#20, 1961), 'Crying In The Rain' (US#6, UK#6, 1962), 'How Can I Meet Her' (UK#12, 1962), 'That's Old Fashioned (That's The Way Love Should Be)' (US#9, 1962) and 'No One Can Make My Sunshine Smile' (UK#11, 1962).

In 1963 the US music industry was turned on its head by the invasion of British bands like the Beatles and the Hollies. Despite the fact that many of these bands had been decisively influenced by the Everlys, the Everlys now seemed out of step with the times, and the hits became commensurately smaller and less regular: 'So It Always Will Be' (UK#23, 1963), 'It's Been Nice' (UK#26, 1963), 'The Girl Sang The Blues' (UK#25, 1963), 'Ferris Wheel' (UK#22, 1964), 'Gone Gone Gone' (US#31, UK#36, 1964), 'That'll Be The Day' (UK#30, 1965), 'The Price Of Love' (UK#2, 1965), 'I'll Never Get Over You' (UK#35, 1965), 'Love Is Strange' (UK#11, 1965), 'Bowling Green' (US#40, 1967) and 'It's My Time' (UK#39, 1968).

Though their personal relationship deteriorated, the

brothers maintained a steady flow of concert appearances, particularly in the UK and Europe. In 1971 Don started a solo career, cutting *Don Everly* for Lou Adler's Ode label; the following year they signed a new recording contract with RCA, debuting with *Stories We Could Tell*; featuring a star-studded cast of contributors, like **Ry Cooder**, John Sebastian, David Crosby (see **Byrds**) and Graham Nash, it included material from a whole host of contemporary writers, such as Sebastian and Jesse Winchester. It failed to sell, as did the excellent follow-up, *Pass The Chicken And Listen* (1973), which marked their return to Nashville and to producer Chet Atkins. *Pass The Chicken* proved to be their last album for ten years, as in the middle of a concert appearance in Hollywood, Phil smashed up his guitar and stormed off the stage, leaving Don to complete the final set alone.

Towards the end of 1973, Phil made his solo debut with *Star-Spangled Springer*, featuring contributions from **James Burton**, among others. Over the next ten years both brothers recorded solo albums for a variety of different labels, but neither achieved much success. In 1982 Phil Everly had a solo hit with 'Louise' (UK#47, 1982), which was followed by a duet with Cliff Richard, 'She Means Nothing To Me' (featuring guitarist Mark Knopfler; UK#9, 1983). The reunion concert in London in 1983 proved to be an emotional occasion for all concerned, and the subsequent live album, *Reunion*, hit the UK album charts.

The success of the reunion prompted them to sign with Mercury, and guitarist Dave Edmunds was installed as producer for the ensuing *Everly Brothers* (1983) and *Born Yesterday* (1986). Despite a combination of old and new material, the only song to catch the public imagination was written for them by Paul McCartney, 'On The Wings Of A Nightingale' (UK#41, 1984). After being inducted into the Rock 'n' Roll Hall Of Fame, they released *Some Hearts* (1988).

BOTH SIDES OF AN EVENING, Rollercoaster, 1985
BROTHER JUKEBOX (Don Everly), Sundown, 1988
CADENCE CLASSICS, Rhino (US), 1986
A DATE WITH THE EVERLY BROTHERS, Rollercoaster, 1985
THE EVERLY BROTHERS, Bear Family (Germany), 1981
THE EVERLY BROTHERS, Warner Bros., 1988
THE EVERLY BROTHERS SING GREAT COUNTRY HITS, Rollercoaster, 1985
THE FABULOUS STYLE OF THE EVERLY BROTHERS, Ace, 1960
GOLDEN HITS, Warner Bros., 1987
GREATEST RECORDINGS, Ace, 1986
INSTANT PARTY, Rollercoaster, 1962

IT'S EVERLY TIME, Rollercoaster, 1960
LOUISE (Phil Everly), Magnum Force, 1988
MERCURY YEARS: 1984-86, Mercury, 1992
NEW ALBUM, Warner Bros., 1977
PASS THE CHICKEN AND LISTEN, Edsel, 1992
PERFECT HARMONY, Knight, 1990
PHIL EVERLY, Capitol, 1983
REUNION CONCERT, Mercury, 1986
ROCKIN' IN HARMONY, Crown, 1986
SOME HEARTS, Mercury, 1989
SONGS OUR DADDY TAUGHT US, Ace, 1958
SUZIE Q, Magnum, 1988
WALK RIGHT BACK, Warner Bros., 1975
THE WARNER BROTHERS YEARS, Volumes 1- 2, Ace, 1989

EXILE

Exile became a household name in the late 1970s, when their monster hit, 'Kiss You All Over' (US#1, UK#6, 1978), sold over four million copies worldwide. A six-piece outfit from Lexington, Kentucky, Exile had been formed in 1963 (as the Exiles) by guitarist and writer J.P. Pennington, whose mother, Lily Mae Ledford, had been a member of the **Coon Creek Girls**. By 1978, Pennington was the sole survivor of the original line-up. The remainder of the group comprised Sonny Lemaire (bass), Les Taylor (guitar), Steve Goetzman (drums), Marlon Hargis (keyboards) and Jimmy Stokely (vocals). Unable to sustain the momentum of 'Kiss You All Over', they scored modestly with their later records: 'You Thrill Me' (US#40, 1979), 'How Could This Go Wrong' (UK#67, 1979) and 'Heart And Soul' (covered by Huey Lewis & the News; UK#54, 1985).

By 1981 Jimmy Stokely had left the group, and the remainder had returned to Lexington to play in local clubs. Their manager, Jim Morey, introduced them to veteran producer **Buddy Killen**, who secured a deal for them with Epic. Their first single, 'The High Cost Of Leaving', was followed by a string of hits, which included 'Woke Up In Love' (C&W#1, 1984), 'I Don't Have To Be A Memory' (C&W#1, 1984), 'Give Me One More Chance' (C&W#1, 1984), 'Crazy For Your Love' (C&W#1, 1984), 'She's A Miracle' (C&W#1, 1985), 'Hang On To Your Heart' (C&W#1, 1985), 'I Could Get Used To You' (C&W#1, 1986), 'It'll Be Me' (C&W#1, 1986), 'She's Too Good To Be True' (C&W#1, 1987), 'I Can't Get Close Enough' (C&W#1, 1987) and 'Just One Kiss' (C&W#9, 1988).

In 1987, Hargis was replaced by Lee Carroll; and the following year, Taylor left to pursue a solo career, being replaced by Paul Martin. After ending their association with Buddy Killen, they took up with Elliot Scheiner and, in 1990, they signed with Arista for *Still Standing*, which included 'Nobody's Talking' (C&W#2, 1990). Apart from their work with the group, Pennington and Lemaire have also written hits for **Alabama**, among others.

EXILE, Epic, 1984
EXILE, Arista, 1991
SUPER HITS, Epic (US), 1992

FAIRCHILD, Barbara

Barbara Fairchild was born on November 12, 1950, in Knoble, Arkansas. While attending high school in St. Louis, Missouri, she broadcast on a local radio station and appeared on local television. After her graduation she moved to Nashville, where she was signed as a writer by MCA's Jerry Crutchfield (her songs have been covered by artists including **Loretta Lynn** and **Conway Twitty**). This won her a recording contract with Kapp, but she spent most of her time cutting demos until, in 1968, she was spotted by **Billy Sherrill**, who signed her to Columbia.

Over the next few years she notched up a series of minor hits, including 'Love Is A Gentle Thing' (1969), 'A Girl Who'll Satisfy Her Man' (1970), '(Loving You Is) Sunshine' (1971), 'Love's Old Song' (1971) and 'Thanks For The Memories' (1972). She finally hit pay-dirt with 'The Teddy Bear Song' (US#32, C&W#1, 1972), which labelled her a writer of children's songs - evidenced by her next two hits, 'Kid Stuff' (C&W#2, 1973) and 'Baby Doll' (C&W#6, 1974). Other lesser hits followed, such as 'You've Lost That Lovin' Feeling' (1975), 'Cheatin' Is' (1976) and 'Let Me Love You Once Before You Go' (1977). Her career declined after she moved to Texas and, apart from duets with **Billy Walker** on *The Answer Game* (1982), little has been heard from her since.

MISSISSIPPI, Columbia (US), 1977

FAITHFULL, Marianne

One of the most versatile female vocalists of her generation, Marianne Faithfull has worked as an actress in films and theatre in addition to her career as a singer. She was born in Hampstead, London, UK, on December 29, 1946, the daughter of a British university lecturer and an Austrian baroness.

She started her career as a protégée of the **Rolling Stones**' manager Andrew Loog Oldham, whom she met at a London party. Signed to the Decca label by Oldham in 1964, she scored with a string of gentle, folkish ballads, such as the Mick Jagger and Keith Richards' composition 'As Tears Go By' (UK#9, 1964); **Bob Dylan**'s 'Blowin' In The Wind'; 'Come And Stay With Me' (UK#4, 1965); **John D. Loudermilk**'s 'This Little Bird' (UK#6, 1965) and 'Summer Nights' (UK#10, 1964); 'Yesterday' (UK#36, 1965) and 'Is This What I Get For Loving You' (UK#43, 1967).

By the end of 1968, after appearing in the cult film *Girl On A Motorcycle* (directed by Alain Delon), her relationship with Mick Jagger, which had started in 1966, became the object of considerable speculation by the tabloid press. Her recording career suffered as a consequence, with 'Something Better' (1970) being her final single for Decca. Taking a break from recording, she appeared at London's Royal Court Theatre in Chekhov's play, *Three Sisters* (1969), and at London's Roundhouse in Shakespeare's *Hamlet* (1970) as Ophelia.

Over the next five years, little was heard from her as she tried to avoid the intense scrutiny of the media. In 1975 she resumed recording with a tasteful cover of **Allen Reynolds**' 'Dreaming My Dreams', which failed to chart but encouraged her to cut *Faithless* (1978). Her occasionally fragile-sounding voice gave an added dimension to country songs like **Jessi Colter**'s 'I'm Not Lisa' and 'Honky Tonk Angels'. Given a hammering by the critics at the time of its release, the sparse country arrangements foreshadowed the rise of interest in country music that was to occur three years later.

In 1979, after signing to the Island label, she cut *Broken English*, which featured a great version of **Shel Silverstein**'s 'Ballad Of Lucy Jordan' (UK#48, 1979) and an intense, vitriolic version of John Lennon's 'Working Class Hero'. Later albums included *Dangerous Acquaintances* (1981) and *Strange Weather* (1987). She remains a true original, who has kept going despite the prurient interest of the press in her private life.

AS TEARS GO BY, Decca, 1981
BROKEN ENGLISH, Island, 1979
A CHILD'S ADVENTURE, Island, 1983
DANGEROUS ACQUAINTANCES, Island, 1981

DREAMIN' MY DREAMS, Nems, 1977
STRANGE WEATHER, Island, 1987

FARGO, Donna

Donna Fargo, like **Lynn Anderson**, **Crystal Gayle**, **Billy Jo Spears** and **Dottie West**, has built her career on middle-of-the-road material with country-styled arrangements.

Yvonne Vaughn was born in Mount Airey, North Carolina, on November 10, 1949, where her father farmed tobacco. She was educated at High Point, North Carolina, before attending a teachers' training college; she went on to study at the University of Southern California, singing in bars during the evenings; she then became a teacher and continued to sing. In 1969, having met her future husband, producer Stan Silver, she moved to Phoenix, Arizona, cutting a few unsuccessful sides for the Ramco label. She then cut some more unsuccessful sides for Challenge, which prompted ABC-Dot to sign her.

Their faith was amply rewarded, as she charted regularly from 1972 with a string of predominantly self-penned hits: 'Happiest Girl In The Whole USA' (US#11, C&W#1, 1972), 'Funnyface' (US#5, C&W#1, 1972), 'Super Man' (C&W#1, 1973), 'You Were Always There' (C&W#1, 1973), 'Little Girl Gone' (C&W#2, 1973), 'I'll Try A Little Bit Harder' (C&W#6, 1974), 'You Can't Be A Beacon' (C&W#1, 1974) and 'Don't Be Angry' (C&W#3, 1976).

In 1976 she moved from Dot to Warner Bros., and maintained a reasonably impressive strike rate: 'Mockingbird Hill' (C&W#9, 1977), 'That Was Yesterday' (C&W#1, 1977), 'Somebody Special' (1979), 'Walk On By' (1980) and 'Lonestar Cowboy' (1981). In June 1978 she was diagnosed as having multiple sclerosis; she fought the disease and scored with 'It's Hard To Be The Dreamer' (1982) for RCA and 'The Sign Of The Times' (1983) for the Cleveland International label. She has become less active of late.

SHAME ON ME, Warner Bros., 1978

FEATHERS, Charlie

While **Sam Phillips** proved to be immensely successful with most of the artists he signed to his Sun label (most notably **Johnny Cash**, **Elvis Presley** and **Jerry Lee Lewis**), there were some, like **Warren Smith** and Charlie Feathers, who just never managed to make the grade. Feathers was nonetheless one of the greatest exponents of rockabilly, drawing heavily from blues and country boogie.

He was born on June 12, 1932, in Myrtle, Mississippi. After learning the guitar from black sharecropper Junior Kimball, he went to work as a session musician in Memphis. In 1954 he was signed to Sun by Phillips and cut songs such as 'I Forgot To Remember To Forget', 'Send Me The Pillow That You Dream On' and 'Gone Gone Gone'. While these records found favour with a few discerning fans, Feathers lacked the gimmicks that helped launch other Sun artists into the big time. After being dropped by Sun he was signed by a succession of independent labels, such as Meteor (for whom he recorded the classic 'Tongue-Tied Jill'; 1956), King, Kay, Rollin' Rock and Holiday Inn, and took to the club circuit.

In 1991 *Charlie Feathers* was released by Elektra, featuring contributions from former Sun musicians such as Stan Kesler. Still based in Memphis, he continues to tour the UK and Europe - playing with his son, Bubba, and daughter, Wanda - but his activities have been proscribed by diabetic neuropathy, which has caused a partial loss of the use of his legs.

ALL TORE UP, ZuZazz, 1988
CHARLIE FEATHERS, Elektra, 1991
GOOD ROCKIN' TONIGHT, Edsel, 1992
HONKY-TONK MAN, New Rose, 1988
JUNGLE FEVER, Kay, 1987
ROCKABILLY'S MAIN MAN, Charly, 1985

FELTS, Narvel

Narvel Felts, like **Razzy Bailey**, **Billy 'Crash' Craddock** and **Earl Thomas Conley**, is one of country's more rock-influenced singers. Born in Missouri on January 11, 1938, the schoolboy Felts won a talent contest in 1956 with his rendition of 'Blue Suede Shoes'. This led to a position as bassist in Jerry Mercer's Band, which was followed by assignments with **Conway Twitty** and **Charlie Rich**. His first solo contract was with Mercury, which was followed by a contract with the Pink label and a minor hit with 'Honey Love' (1959).

Having moved to Nashville and spent years in semi-obscurity, he formed his own label, Cinnamon, with DJ John Morris in 1972; this set-up brought him a number of moderate hits: 'Drift Away' (1973), 'All In The Name Of Love' (1973) and 'When Your Good Love Was Mine' (1974). In 1975 Cinnamon went out of business and he joined the Dot label, where he scored with 'Reconsider Baby' (C&W#2, 1975), **Willie Nelson**'s 'Funny How Time Slips Away' (1975), 'Somebody Hold Me' (1975),

Lonely Teardrops' (1976), 'The Feeling's Right' (1977) and 'Everlasting Love' (1979).

Dropped by Dot (when it was assimilated into MCA), he has since recorded for independent labels, such as Compleat and Evergreen. Still touring with his backing group, the Rockets, his lack of strong self-penned material has militated against international recognition.

MEMPHIS DAYS, Bear Family (Germany), 1990
A TEEN'S WAY, Bear Family (Germany), 1987

FENDER, Freddy

Since the early 1970s, the number of Tex-Mex artists has proliferated and its popularity has boomed accordingly, with **Flaco Jimenez**, **Doug Sahm** and Freddy Fender being some of the most notable. While other Chicanos, such as **Johnny Rodriguez**, tended to eradicate most of the Mexican influences from Tex-Mex, Fender has remained authentic, specializing in a variant of the polka and the waltz known as *conjunto*.

He was born Baldemar G. Huerta on June 4, 1936, in San Benito, South Texas, to a family of migrant workers, who encouraged him to play the guitar. After dropping out of school at sixteen, he joined the Marines for three years. On his return he started to play the bars and dances of San Benito, before turning professional and adopting the name Freddy Fender in 1957. Initially recording in Spanish for the Falcon label, he went on to sign to the Duncan label (distributed by Imperial), cutting the original version of 'Wasted Days And Wasted Nights' (1960).

His career was interrupted in 1960, when he was jailed for five years for possession of marijuana. In 1963 he was paroled from Angola State Penitentiary, Louisiana, by State Governor **Jimmie Davis**, on the understanding that he quit the music business. After working as a mechanic and attending college he returned to playing the bars of San Benito. In 1974 he was introduced to producer **Huey P. Meaux**, who was quick to spot the potential in Fender's voice and signed him to ABC - Fender went on to have a string of hits throughout the late 1970s: 'Before The Next Teardrop Falls' (US#1, C&W#1, 1975), 'Wasted Days And Wasted Nights' (US#8, C&W#1, 1975), 'Secret Love' (US#20, C&W#1, 1975), 'You'll Lose A Good Thing' (US#32, C&W#1, 1976), 'Vaya Con Dios' (C&W#7, 1976), 'Living It Down' (C&W#2, 1976), 'The Rains Came' (C&W#4, 1977) and 'Walkin' Piece Of Heaven'.

After a spell with Meaux's Starflite label from 1979,

he moved on to Warner Bros. in 1982. In 1987 he appeared in the Robert Redford film, *The Milagro Beanfield War* and, in 1990, he formed a band called the Texas Tornados, which included Sahm, Jimenez and **Augie Meyer** in its line-up. While this group has had little commercial success (it is mainly a performance outfit), their individual and collective contributions have done much to increase the awareness of Tex-Mex.

BEFORE THE NEXT TEARDROP FALLS, Charly, 1987
BEST OF FREDDY FENDER, MCA (US), 1984
CRAZY BABY, Starburst, 1987
EARLY YEARS: 1959-63, Krazy Kat, 1986
FREDDY FENDER, Country Store, 1989

FIREFALL see ROBERTS, Rick

FLATLANDERS see ELY, Joe

FLATT & SCRUGGS

As the first of **Bill Monroe**'s many sidemen to leave and start up their own group, Flatt & Scruggs have become synonymous with bluegrass. Writing or rearranging many of the standards of the genre, much of what is now referred to as bluegrass was pioneered by the duo.

Lester Raymond Flatt was born on June 19, 1914, in Overton County, Tennessee, and Earl Eugene Scruggs was born on January 6, 1924, in Cleveland County, North Carolina. Both came from musical families: Flatt's parents played the banjo, and encouraged him to play both banjo and guitar and to sing in the church choir; while Scruggs, raised in the Appalachians, was accustomed to the 'three-finger banjo' technique indigenous to the region.

After a spell as a textile worker, Flatt formed a hill-billy group and in 1939 turned professional. Over the next few years he played on WDBJ, Roanoke, before being hired by **Charlie Monroe** as a member of the Kentucky Pardners in 1943; he was hired by Bill Monroe the following year. Meanwhile, Scruggs - who had been performing since he was six with his brothers - had played with the **Morris Brothers** on WSPA, Spartanburg, South Carolina, before going into the textile industry during the war years. After a spell with 'Lost' John Miller, broadcasting on WSM, Nashville, Scruggs was enlisted by Monroe.

With Monroe, each was able to develop his own

technique within the context of a larger group, with Flatt taking over principal vocal duties. While they remained with Monroe for only four years, the media coverage, derived from regular radio broadcasts and records for Columbia, made them stars: Flatt's guitar runs, combined with his emotive vocals, and Scruggs' pioneering banjo style made the Blue Grass Boys one of the best bluegrass outfits in the business.

In 1948, Flatt and Scruggs left Monroe within a few months of each other, and formed the Foggy Mountain Boys. The early line-up of this group included **Mac Wiseman** and Curly Seckler (mandolin), and former Monroe sidemen Jim Shumate (fiddle) and Cedric Rainwater (bass). Over the next five years, despite switching from Mercury to Columbia to Decca, they cut a number of definitive sides: 'Foggy Mountain Breakdown' (1949); 'Roll In My Sweet Baby's Arms' and 'Old Salty Dog Blues' (1950); and 'Earl's Breakdown' and 'Flint Hill Special' (1952). Not content to be mere virtuosi, the duo were constantly expanding the parameters of their instruments, and in 1951 Scruggs developed the 'Scruggs Peg', in order to facilitate swift retuning of the banjo's B and G strings ('Earl's Breakdown' is the earliest example of its use).

In 1953 they started to appear with **Ernest Tubb** and **Lefty Frizzell**, before joining Nashville's WSM to broadcast on *Martha White Biscuit Time*. In 1955 they joined the *Grand Ole Opry* and landed a syndicated television show, which gave them a wider audience. Over the next few years they fuelled the revival of interest in traditional music with appearances at New York's Carnegie Hall. The line-up of the group changed, with fiddler Paul Warren joining in 1954. Scruggs was now regarded as the arch-exponent of the banjo, having recorded a number of tutorial albums, and in 1962, they cut 'The Ballad Of Jed Clampett' (C&W#1, 1962) as the theme to the TV series *The Beverly Hillbillies*.

By 1969 they had tired of one another. Flatt formed Nashville Grass with Curly Seckler and then cut an album of duets with Mac Wiseman, while Scruggs formed the Earl Scruggs Revue, which would become the training-ground for his sons, Gary, Steve and **Randy Scruggs**. The break brought a divergence: Flatt wanted to continue with the traditional acoustic sound of bluegrass, while Scruggs wanted to experiment, and became the catalyst for the **Nitty Gritty Dirt Band**'s seminal *Will The Circle Be Unbroken?* by providing introductions to many of the older artists.

In 1975 the Earl Scruggs Revue issued a brace of albums to commemorate his twenty-five years with Columbia; they featured a whole host of guest contributors, like **Johnny Cash**, **Bob Dylan**, **Buffy Sainte-Marie**, Billy Joel and Leonard Cohen. Flatt died on May 11, 1979, but Nashville Grass continued under the guiding hand of Seckler throughout the 1980s. Scruggs has worked less and less with his revue in recent years, preferring to concentrate on tuition manuals. With an influence that extends throughout all of country music, it is difficult to over-emphasize their impact.

DON'T GET ABOVE YOUR RAISIN', Rounder (US), 1988
FANTASTIC PICKIN' (Lester Flatt and Nashville Grass), CMH, 1976
FLATT & SCRUGGS, Columbia (US), 1982
GOLDEN ERA, Rounder (US), 1988
GOLDEN HITS, Gusto (US), 1988
LESTER & MAC (Lester Flatt and Mac Wiseman), Stetson, 1988
LESTER FLATT'S BLUEGRASS FESTIVAL (Lester Flatt and Nashville Grass), CMH, 1977
LESTER RAYMOND FLATT, Flying Fish (US), 1989
LIVE AT THE BLUEGRASS FESTIVAL, RCA (US), 1986
LIVE BROADCAST, Sandy Hook (US), 1986
MERCURY SESSIONS, Volumes 1-2, Rounder (US), 1987
TOP OF THE WORLD (Earl Scruggs), Columbia, 1983
YOU CAN FEEL IT IN YOUR SOUL, Rounder (US), 1988

FLYING BURRITO BROTHERS

The Flying Burrito Brothers were formed in 1968 by **Gram Parsons** and **Chris Hillman** in the wake of their departure from the **Byrds**. While it was their first two albums that made waves, influencing a generation of young rock musicians, they continued as a constantly changing aggregation until the mid-1980s. The line-up initially comprised Parsons (guitar and vocals), Hillman (guitar, mandolin and vocals), Chris Ethridge (bass), Sneaky Pete Kleinow (pedal steel guitar) and Jon Corneal (drums).

After being signed by A&M, their debut *The Gilded Palaces Of Sin* (1969) illustrated Parsons' ability to wrest every last drop of emotion from a song in much the same way as the more intuitive country singers like **George Jones** and **Hank Williams** had done before him. His compositional talents were highlighted by titles like 'Sin City', which conveyed twentieth-century images in the traditional vernacular of country music. While the album was being recorded, Jon Corneal jumped plane and joined Dillard & Clark (see **Clark, Gene**); his replacement was Michael Clarke (see **Byrds**).

Just before the start of the sessions for the next album, Ethridge left and Hillman took over as bassist, while **Bernie Leadon** joined from Dillard & Clark. The follow-up, *Burritos Deluxe* (1970), was recorded in a spirit of considerable acrimony, mainly because Parsons was consuming vast quantities of pharmaceuticals and was becoming increasingly paranoid. At the end of the sessions, Parsons left and was replaced by **Rick Roberts**. The next album, *Flying Burrito Brothers* (1971), was notable only for the absence of the cutting edge that Parsons' vocals and songwriting had provided.

Both Leadon and Kleinow left the group in the summer of 1971; the former joined the **Eagles** and the latter returned to session work. They were replaced by Al Perkins (steel guitar), Byron Berline (fiddle), Roger Bush (bass) and Kenny Wertz (guitar) for the live *Last Of The Red Hot Burritos* (1971). The album was recorded in October, and the group fell apart soon after, with Perkins and Hillman joining Stephen Stills' Manassas and Clarke moving to Hawaii. Rick Roberts took over the reins, recruiting Don Beck (pedal steel guitar), Alan Munde (banjo) and Erik Dalton (drums) for a tour of Europe that resulted in *Live In Amsterdam*. On their return the group fell apart once again: Roberts started Firefall, while Berline, Bush and Wertz formed **Country Gazette** with **Herb Pedersen**.

Founder members Chris Ethridge and Sneaky Pete Kleinow revived the name in 1975, and were signed to Columbia for *Flying Again*; the line-up was completed by Gib Guilbeau (fiddle; see **Parsons, Gene**), Joel Scott-Hill (bass) and **Gene Parsons** (drums). In 1976 another album, *Airborne*, emerged, but Ethridge had disappeared again, and had been replaced by Skip Battin from **New Riders of the Purple Sage.**

Over the next couple of years they toured the US and Japan; the line-up was still in a state of flux, and by 1981 they were known simply as the Burrito Brothers. In 1985, the group - which now comprised Kleinow, Battin, Greg Harris (guitar) and Jim Goodall (drums) - disintegrated once and for all. The group's *joie de vivre* had effectively vanished by the end of 1971, and their later records were pretty lacklustre affairs.

BURRITOS DELUXE, Edsel, 1970
DIM LIGHTS, THICK SMOKE AND LOUD MUSIC, Edsel, 1987
GILDED PALACES OF SIN, Edsel, 1969
HOLLYWOOD NIGHTS: 1979-81, Sundown, 1990
LAST OF THE RED HOT BURRITOS, A&M, 1971
LIVE FROM TOKYO, Sundown, 1986

SLEEPLESS NIGHTS, A&M (US), 1976
SOUTHERN TRACKS, Dixie Frog (US), 1990

FOGERTY, John

Inspired by the rockabilly singers of the 1950s, Creedence Clearwater Revival's guitar-based, riff-laden songs made them the most popular singles band in the US in the late 1960s. The man behind the band was John Fogerty.

He was born John Cameron Fogerty on May 28, 1945, in Berkeley, California, and formed his first group, the Blue Velvets, while at El Cerrito high school in 1959. The Blue Velvets comprised Fogerty (guitar), his elder brother Tom (vocals and guitar; born on November 9, 1941, in Berkeley), Stu Cook (bass; born on April 25, 1945, in Oakland, California) and Doug Clifford (drums; born on April 24, 1945, in Palo Alto, California). In 1961 they recorded some sessions with the San Francisco Orchestra, while continuing to play high-school dances.

In 1964, they changed their name to the Golliwogs and were signed to the Fantasy label. While they cut several singles, including a cover of Van Morrison's 'Brown-Eyed Girl' (1966), the growth of psychedelia on the West Coast made the 'beat-group sound' outdated. The owner of Fantasy, Saul Zaentz, suggested they adopt a more traditional approach, based on country and rock 'n' roll. With the same line-up, they changed their name to Creedence Clearwater Revival in 1967, and John became the main writer and lead vocalist, taking over the latter role from his brother Tom. Their eponymous debut in 1968 included covers of Dale Hawkins' 'Suzie Q' (US#11, 1968) and Screamin' Jay Hawkins' 'I Put A Spell On You'.

The follow-up, *Bayou Country*, illustrated John's growth as a writer - with songs such as 'Proud Mary' (US#2, UK#8, 1969) and 'Keep On Chooglin'' - and the group's development as arch-exponents of 'swamp rock', along with **Tony Joe White**. Over the next three years, the band cut some of the finest sides of the era: 'Bad Moon Rising' (US#2, UK#1, 1969), 'Green River' (US#2, UK#19, 1969), 'Down On The Corner' (US#3, UK#31, 1969), 'Travellin' Band' (US#2, UK#8, 1970), 'Up Around The Bend' (US#4, UK#3, 1970), 'Lookin' Out My Back Door' (US#2, 1970), 'Long As I Can See The Light' (UK#20, 1970), 'Have You Ever Seen The Rain' (US#8, UK#36, 1971), 'Sweet Hitch-Hiker' (US#6, UK#36, 1971) and 'Someday Never Comes' (US#25, 1972).

While the singles were successful, the albums,

such as *Willie And The Poor Boys* (1969) and *Cosmo's Factory* (1970), were impeccable, and included ambitious reworkings of seemingly unimprovable classics, such as Marvin Gaye's 'I Heard It Through The Grapevine' and **Elvis Presley**'s 'My Baby Left Me'.

In 1971, Tom Fogerty left the group for a solo career. It proved to be an error of judgement as his solo albums, including *Excalibur* (1973), *Rock And Roll Madness* (1978) and *Deal It Out* (1981), were unexceptional. He died of a heart attack on September 6, 1990. After Tom's departure, John relinquished sole control of the group, with Clifford and Cook contributing to the songwriting chores. *Pendulum* (1971) and *Mardi Gras* (1972) lacked the cohesiveness of earlier efforts, and the group disbanded in 1972. Clifford and Cook went to work with **Doug Sahm** on *Groover's Paradise* (1974), and then the Don Harrison Band, before moving into session work and production.

Fogerty returned to his roots with *Blue Ridge Rangers* (1973), a collection of lovingly re-created traditional country songs, such as **Hank Williams**'s 'Jambalaya', **Dickey Lee**'s 'She Still Thinks I Care' and **Merle Haggard**'s 'Today I Started Loving You Again'. Fogerty played every single note on the album, but, attempting to maintain the illusion that Creedence actually existed, did not credit himself anywhere on the album sleeve.

After two years of silence, Fogerty returned with his debut for Asylum, *John Fogerty*. It included 'Rockin' All Over The World' (covered by Status Quo in 1977 and Dave Edmunds in 1981; US#27, 1975) and reworkings of Frankie Ford's 'Sea Cruise' and Jackie Wilson's 'Lonely Teardrops'. The follow-up *Hoodoo* was never released (although bootlegs have been circulating for some time) and Fogerty disappeared into retirement.

In 1985 he broke his silence with the immaculate *Centrefield* for Warner Bros., which included 'The Old Man Down The Road' (US#10, 1985) and 'Rock And Roll Girls' (US#20, 1985). As if to indicate the extent to which Fogerty had dominated the sound of Creedence, Fantasy tried to sue him for infringing their exclusive copyright of the Creedence material (this was mainly due to the fact that Fogerty had included the libellous 'Zaentz Can't Dance', but the title was changed to 'Vance Can't Dance'). The follow-up, *Eye Of The Zombie* (1986), was a sombre affair, with Fogerty's writing showing a marked disaffection with the music industry and Reagan's US. Nothing has been heard from him since.

BAYOU COUNTRY (Creedence Clearwater Revival), Fantasy, 1969
BLUE RIDGE RANGERS, Fantasy, 1973
CENTREFIELD, Warner Bros., 1985
CHOOGLIN' (Creedence Clearwater Revival), Fantasy, 1992
CHRONICLE, Volumes 1-2 (Creedence Clearwater Revival), Fantasy, 1987
THE CONCERT (Creedence Clearwater Revival), Fantasy, 1981
COSMO'S FACTORY (Creedence Clearwater Revival), Fantasy, 1970
CREEDENCE CLEARWATER REVIVAL, Fantasy, 1968
CREEDENCE CLEARWATER REVIVAL HITS ALBUM, Fantasy, 1982
CREEDENCE COUNTRY (Creedence Clearwater Revival), Fantasy, 1992
EYE OF THE ZOMBIE, Warner Bros., 1986
GREEN RIVER (Creedence Clearwater Revival), Fantasy, 1969
JOHN FOGERTY, Fantasy, 1975
LIVE IN EUROPE (Creedence Clearwater Revival), Fantasy, 1990
MARDI GRAS (Creedence Clearwater Revival), Fantasy, 1972
PENDULUM (Creedence Clearwater Revival), Fantasy, 1971
WILLY AND THE POOR BOYS (Creedence Clearwater Revival), Fantasy, 1970

FOGGY MOUNTAIN BOYS see FLATT & SCRUGGS

FOLEY, Red

The records that Red Foley cut during the 1930s and 1940s were geared to the requirements of national radio audiences, and were consequently a touch bland. He broke loose and showed his real colours during the 1950s, cutting material that was more influenced by R&B and boogie-woogie.

He was born Clyde Julian Foley on June 17, 1910, in Blue Lick, Kentucky. He had all the makings of a supreme athlete, but these inclinations quickly gave way when he won a talent contest. In 1930 he moved to Chicago and joined **John Lair**'s Cumberland Ridge Runners, who were regular contributors to the *National Barn Dance* on WLS. The association with Lair was to continue in later years when they both began the *Renfro Valley Barn Dance*, before joining the *Grand Ole Opry* in 1947, which led to the television series, *Ozark Jubilee*, from Springfield, Missouri.

In 1941 he signed with Decca, and strung together

a succession of hits over the next fifteen years: 'Old Shep' (1941); 'Foggy River' (1947); 'Tennessee Saturday Night' (1948); 'Candy Kisses', 'Tennessee Polka' and 'Sunday Down In Tennessee' (1949); 'Chattanooga Shoeshine Boy', 'Steal Away', 'Just A Closer Walk With Thee', 'Birmingham Bounce', 'Mississippi' and 'Sugarfoot Rag', featuring guitarist Hank Garland (1950); 'Peace In The Valley', 'Hot Rod Dance' and 'Alabama Jubilee' (1951); 'Midnight' (1952); 'Don't Let The Stars Get In Your Eyes' and 'Hot Toddy' (1953); and 'One By One' (a duet with **Kitty Wells**; 1954).

After cutting R&B and rockabilly titles like 'Shake A Hand' (1953), 'Jilted' (1954), 'Hearts Of Stone' (1954) and 'Crazy Little Guitar Man' (1958), he worked as an actor for a spell, appearing in the ABC-TV series *Mr Smith Goes To Washington* from 1961 to 1962. In 1967 he was elected to the Country Music Hall Of Fame, and continued to make personal appearances right up to his death on September 19, 1968, in Fort Wayne, Indiana.

COMPANY'S COMING, Stetson, 1989
RED & ERNIE (with Ernest Tubb), Stetson, 1985
THE RED FOLEY SHOW, Stetson, 1986
THE RED FOLEY STORY, MCA (US), 1986
TENNESSEE SATURDAY NIGHT, Charly, 1984

FORD, Mary see PAUL, Les

FORD, Tennessee Ernie

In the mid-1950s, *basso profundo* Tennessee Ernie Ford dominated the airwaves with a distinctive combination of religious and country songs. While his country material tended to reflect his personal pride in the US, with songs chronicling the Civil War, the War of Independence and tales of everyday strife in urban communities, his religious songs were a mixture of hymns and spirituals.

Ernie Jennings Ford was born on February 13, 1919, in Bristol, Tennessee. While at school he played trombone and sang in the choir, but also spent a lot of time hanging out at the local radio station, WOAL. By 1937 he had worked his way up the station hierarchy to become an announcer; this was followed by a stint at the Cincinnati Conservatory of Music. In 1941 he joined the US Air Force, as a bombardier and then as an instructor.

After his discharge he moved to southern California, where **Cliffie Stone** introduced him to the Capitol label. From 1948, he started a run of hits that would continue until the end of the 1950s: 'Mule Train', 'Smokey Mountain Boogie' and 'Anticipation Blues' (1949); 'I'll Never Be Free' (with Kay Starr), 'The Cry Of The Wild Goose' and 'Shotgun Boogie' (1950); 'Give Me Your Word' (UK#1, 1955); 'Ballad Of Davy Crockett' (US#5, 1955; UK#3, 1956); **Merle Travis**'s 'Sixteen Tons' (US#1, 1955; UK#1, 1956); 'That's All' (US#17, 1956); and 'In The Middle Of An Island' (US#23, 1957).

In 1955, having had his own syndicated radio shows with both the CBS and ABC networks, he was given his own television show by NBC. During the 1960s his personal appearances decreased, while his commitment to 'affairs of the spirit' increased. Curiously, it is the non-secular records that have endured, with many remaining in the catalogue long after the others have been deleted. He died on October 17, 1991.

COUNTRY COLLECTION, Knight, 1990
FARMYARD BOOGIE, See For Miles, 1989
FORD FAVOURITES, Stetson, 1987
OL' ROCKIN' ERN, Stetson, 1987
SIXTEEN TONS, Bear Family (Germany), 1990

FORESTER SISTERS

During the 1980s, the Forester Sisters became one of the first all-girl country groups. Kathy, June and Kim Forester were raised in Lookout Mountain, Georgia, and, after singing in church and completing college, they began to work as backing vocalists with local groups. By 1982 they had inducted another sister, Christy, into the fold, and had launched themselves as a group in their own right, touring with **Alabama**, **Ronnie Milsap**, **George Jones** and **John Anderson**. In 1984, having cut a demo at the Muscle Shoals Sound Studios, they secured a recording contract with Warner Bros.

Their first single, '(That's What You Do) When You're In Love', was followed by 'I Fell In Love Again Last Night' (C&W#1, 1985), 'Just In Case' (C&W#1, 1985), 'Mama's Never Seen Those Eyes' (C&W#1, 1986), 'Lonely Alone' (C&W#2, 1986), 'Too Much Is Not Enough' (with the **Bellamy Brothers**; C&W#1, 1986), 'Too Many Rivers' (C&W#5, 1987), 'You Again' (C&W#1, 1987), 'Lyin' In His Arms Again' (1987), 'Letter Home' (1988), 'Sincerely' (1988), and 'Love Will' and 'Don't You' (1989).

Their touring schedule is intense, and their ability to project themselves well on television, combined with the strength of their material (from writers like **Paul Overstreet**), has added to their popularity.

ALL I NEED, Warner Bros., 1989
PERFUME, RIBBONS AND PEARLS, Warner Bros., 1987
SINCERELY, Warner Bros., 1988
YOU AGAIN, Warner Bros., 1987

FOSTER, Fred

Fred Foster was born in Rutherford, North Carolina. In 1954 he joined Mercury to work in field promotion, and in 1956 he joined ABC-Paramount, where he signed R&B artist Lloyd Price. In 1958 he set up the Monument label in Nashville and struck gold immediately with **Billy Grammar**'s 'Gotta Travel On', followed later by **Pee Wee King**'s 'Bonaparte's Retreat'. This success was consolidated when he signed **Roy Orbison** in 1960.

In 1963 he established the subsidiary label, Sound Stage Seven (which was devoted to soul and R&B), and enlisted the services of DJ John Richbourg to oversee the development of the artist roster. In 1967 he signed **Dolly Parton**, who scored immediately with 'Dumb Blonde'.

In 1970 Monument signed a distribution deal with CBS/Columbia, and also set up its own house band, which comprised bassist Tim Drummond, guitarists **Troy Seals**, **Wayne Moss** and Mac Gayden, pianist Bob Wilson, drummer **Kenny Buttrey** and **Charlie McCoy** on harmonica. While the Sound Stage Seven label failed to survive the Columbia distribution deal, Foster was quick to give his session men their heads, and artists like McCoy and Moss (with Barefoot Jerry) were signed to the label to pursue their own projects. Among the other artists signed to the label were **Tony Joe White**, **Billy Swan**, **Grandpa Jones** and, of course, Roy Orbison. Although the label has been less active in recent years, Foster's extensive publishing interests ensure that he doesn't starve.

FOWLER, Wally

Wally Fowler (born in 1917 in Bartown County, Georgia) deserves some sort of accolade for being one of country's more enterprising opportunists. At the time when the US dropped the bomb on Hiroshima, on August 6, 1945, Wally Fowler was a member of the gospel group, the Georgia Clodhoppers, who were based in the town of Oak Ridge, where the bomb had been developed as part of the Manhattan Project. Fowler, seeing little potential in the name the Georgia Clodhoppers, renamed the group the Oak Ridge

Quartet; during the 1960s the group changed their name to the **Oak Ridge Boys**. Fowler recorded for Decca and King, penned titles like 'I'm Sending You Red Roses' and 'That's How Much I Love You, Baby', and caught the public imagination with his evangelical zeal, specializing in religious promotional gimmicks such as all-night singing.

FOX, Curly, and Texas Ruby

Curly Fox and Texas Ruby were one of the best-loved husband-and-wife teams to play the *Grand Ole Opry* during the late 1930s and 1940s. Ruby's sultry tones, offset by Fox's fiddling, gave their hillbilly songs a resonance lacking in most hillbilly material.

Curly Fox was born Arnim LeRoy Fox on November 9, 1910, in Graysville, Tennessee. In 1923 he joined a medicine show as a fiddler, and by 1929 he had joined the Roane County Ramblers. Within three years, he had formed his own group, the Tennessee Firecrackers, securing a regular slot on WSB, Atlanta, as well as playing on other stations like WWL, New Orleans, with **Lew Childre**.

Texas Ruby was born Ruby Owens, the sister of **Tex Owens**, in Wise County, Texas, on June 4, 1910. In 1934, as a member of **Zeke Clements**' group, the Bronco Busters, she broadcasted on the *Iowa Barn Dance Frolic* on WHO, Des Moines, before moving to Nashville to perform at the *Grand Ole Opry*. After meeting Fox in 1937, they started to work together, and by 1939 they had married.

Throughout the 1940s they played the *Opry*, where Fox's showmanship (learnt from his years with the medicine show) was spectacular on titles like 'Orange Blossom Special' and 'Listen To The Mockingbird'. By 1945 they had started to record for Columbia, and in 1947 they changed to the King label. In 1948 they moved to New York, before travelling down to Houston, where they were featured on KPRC-TV, becoming one of the first country acts to hold down their own television show.

After seven years, they returned to Nashville and the *Grand Ole Opry*. Now contracted to Starday, they cut a brace of albums before Ruby was killed in a domestic fire in March, 1963. Fox went into retirement and lived the life of a hermit for many years, until re-emerging in the 1970s to appear at local festivals.

FRAZIER, Dallas

Dallas Frazier has, since the late 1950s, been one of the most adaptable and skillful writers working in the

US. He was born on October 27, 1939, in Spiro, Oklahoma, and his family moved to Bakersfield (the mecca of Californian country music) during the 1940s. After winning a talent contest sponsored by **Ferlin Husky**, he landed a guest spot on Husky's syndicated television show, which resulted in a recording contract with Capitol. His next stop was Nashville to promote himself as a songwriter, where he became a regular radio and television contributor.

It was as a songwriter that he achieved most distinction, penning titles like the novelty song 'Alley Oop' for the Hollywood Argyles; 'There Goes My Everything' for Englebert Humperdinck and **Elvis Presley**; 'Elvira' for the **Oak Ridge Boys**; 'Son Of Hickory Holler's Tramp' for O.C. Smith; 'Timber, I'm Falling' for Ferlin Husky; 'California Cottonfields' for **Merle Haggard**; 'Then Who Am I' for **Charley Pride**; 'Mohair Sam' for **Charlie Rich**; and 'Beneath Still Waters' for **Emmylou Harris**.

While titles like 'Alley Oop' indicated a strong streak of opportunism, his ability to deal incisively with social issues made his songs appealing to performers with social consciences. He had a modest hit in his own right with his version of 'Elvira' in 1966.

FRICKE, Janie

Janie Fricke's nomination for the CMA Female Artist of the Year in 1983 was quite an achievement for someone who seven years earlier had been scratching a living as a Nashville session singer. The catalyst for her solo career was, typically, producer **Billy Sherrill**, who had partnered her with **Johnny Duncan** and signed her to Columbia in 1978.

She was born in South Whitley, Indiana, on December 19, 1947. After studying at the University of Indiana, she began to work on a teaching diploma in Memphis and took up singing lessons. Upon graduation she moved west to Los Angeles, back to Memphis and then on to Nashville, all the while singing in clubs, on commercials and as a session singer. After joining the Lea Jane Singers, she started to tour, backing artists such as **Johnny Rodriguez**, which drew her to the attention of Sherrill.

Her first credited hit was a duet with **Charlie Rich**, 'On My Knees' (C&W#1, 1978). By 1980 she had been teamed with producer Jim Ed Norman, but the only substantial hit to emerge from this liaison was 'Don't Worry 'Bout Me Baby' (C&W#1, 1982). In 1982 she changed producer and was teamed with Bob Montgomery. *It Ain't Easy* spawned four hits: 'It Ain't Easy Being Easy' (C&W#1, 1982), 'You Don't Know

Love' (C&W#4, 1983) 'He's A Heartache (Waitin' For A Place To Happen)' (C&W#1, 1983) and 'Tell Me A Lie' (C&W#1, 1983).

Since then, she has notched up hits such as 'Let's Stop Talkin' About It' (C&W#1, 1984), 'If The Fall Don't Get You' (C&W#8, 1984), 'Your Heart's Not In It' (C&W#1, 1984), 'A Place To Fall Apart' (with **Merle Haggard**; C&W#1, 1984) and 'Always Have, Always Will' (C&W#1, 1986). Although her success rate is undeniably impressive, like many others she seems to have settled for the bland 'countrypolitan' sound.

BLACK AND WHITE, Columbia, 1986
FIRST WORD IN MEMORY, Columbia, 1985
LABOUR OF LOVE, Columbia, 1989
LOVE NOTES, Columbia, 1979
VERY BEST OF JANIE FRICKE, Columbia, 1986

FRIEDMAN, Kinky

One of country music's few eccentrics, Kinky Friedman has long relished his chosen vocation as gadfly to the Nashville establishment. His commercial acceptance may be minimal, but he has won admirers in the rock fraternity, and brought country music to those otherwise put off by its conservatism.

He was born Richard Friedman in Rio Duckworth, Texas, on October 31, 1944; his father was a professor at the University of Texas in Austin. While at university he formed his first band, King Arthur and the Carrots. He then joined the Peace Corps and worked in Borneo on agricultural projects, where he introduced the natives to the Frisbee.

On his return, he assembled the Texas Jewboys (which included **Billy Swan** in its line-up) and started to play club gigs on the West Coast, making his debut for Vanguard with *Sold American* (1973). While his pithy wit found many admirers, there were some who considered his stance anti-Semitic and un-American. The album failed to sell and he was dropped from the label. The follow-up, for ABC, contained another selection of acerbic songs; it also flopped and he was dropped again.

In 1976, having this time signed to Epic, he cut *Lasso From El Paso*, which featured contributions from Eric Clapton, **Bob Dylan**, **Doug Sahm** and **John Fogerty**. This was another flop, and Friedman stopped recording, concentrating instead upon touring and writing detective novels.

OLD TESTAMENTS & NEW REVELATIONS, Fruit Of The Tune 777 (US), 1993

FRITTS, Donnie

Donnie Fritts was born and raised in Florence, Alabama, where he met local songwriter Tom Stafford. In 1959 Stafford set up the publishing outlet Spardus, and in 1960 he invited Fritts and **David Briggs** to become partners. After **Rick Hall** set up Fame, Fritts became one of Dan Penn's songwriting partners, as well as playing drums in a local R&B group, Hollis Dixon. By the mid-1960s Fritts had joined the growing body of writers and musicians migrating to Nashville.

In 1974 he recorded *Prone To Lean* for Atlantic, recorded at Muscle Shoals Sound Studios and produced by Jerry Wexler and **Kris Kristofferson**. Since then he has continued to play sessions with Kristofferson and **Billy Swan**, among others, and write songs.

FRIZZELL, David

While David Frizzell never achieved the status of his elder brother, **Lefty Frizzell**, he came into his own during the 1980s with a number of duets with **Shelly West**. He was born on September 26, 1941, in Texas, and made his debut performances in his brother's travelling roadshow. By the age of thirteen, he had performed a selection of **Elvis Presley** songs at the Rainbow Gardens in Bakersfield. He signed with Columbia in 1958, and cut a series of unsuccessful songs. After spending four years in the US Air Force, he resumed his career, but still failed to make a significant impression on his own account.

In 1980 he teamed up with Shelly West and producer Tommy 'Snuff' Garrett, striking gold with 'You're The Reason God Made Oklahoma' (which was featured in the Clint Eastwood film *Any Which Way You Can*; C&W#1, 1981), followed by three more hits: 'A Texas State Of Mind' (1981), 'Another Honky-Tonk Night On Broadway' (1982) and 'I Just Came Here To Dance' (1982). After this joint success, both started solo careers, Frizzell scoring first with the touching 'I'm Gonna Hire A Wino To Decorate Our Home' (C&W#1, 1982), which was followed by 'Lost My Baby Blues' (1982) and 'Where Are You Spending Your Nights These Days' (1983). Unable to sustain a pattern of recording success, he returned to the comparative security of regular touring.

FRIZZELL, Lefty

Lefty Frizzell is one of the great undervalued stylists of country music. Despite his impact, his influence on **Merle Haggard** and **John Anderson** has never been

properly acknowledged. His influence is still felt in the work of **George Strait**, **Randy Travis** and **Clint Black.**

William Orville Frizzell was born on March 31, 1928, in Corsicana, Texas, the son of an itinerant oil worker. Initially influenced by **Jimmie Rodgers**, he was playing the bars of Dallas at the age of seventeen, evolving the honky-tonk style that would become a *leitmotiv* for the duration of his career. However, an abortive stab at the Golden Gloves Boxing Championship intervened, and he was dubbed Lefty after knocking out several opponents with his left hand.

By 1950 he had come to the attention of Columbia A&R man Don Law, who put him under contract and set him to work in Jim Beck's Dallas studio. Over the next fifteen years or so, he notched up a number of hits: 'I Love You A Thousand Ways' (1950), 'If You've Got The Money, Honey, I've Got The Time' (C&W#2, 1950), 'I Want To Be With You Always' (C&W#1, 1951), 'Mom And Dad's Waltz' (1951), 'Always Late' (C&W#1, 1951), 'Travellin' Blues' (1951), 'Give Me More, More, More' (1951), 'Don't Stay Away' (1952), 'Forever' (1952) and 'I'm An Old, Old, Old Man' (1952).

In 1952 he joined the *Grand Ole Opry*, before moving to the West Coast and joining *Town Hall Party* in Compton, Los Angeles. Although the hits decreased in number, he scored with 'I Love You Mostly' (1955), 'Cigarettes And Coffee Blues' (1958) and 'Long Black Veil' (1959), and cut a tribute to Rodgers with *Lefty Frizzell Sings The Songs Of Jimmie Rodgers*. In 1962 he moved back to Nashville and scored with 'Saginaw, Michigan' (C&W#1, 1964) and 'She's Gone, Gone, Gone' (1965).

During the 1960s his health gradually declined, brought on by a combination of drinking and arduous touring. After being signed by ABC in 1973, he had a few minor hits with 'The Way Love Goes' (1973), 'I Never Go Around Mirrors' (1974) and 'Watermelon Time In Georgia' (1974), until on July 19, 1975, he died of a heart attack. *The Legendary Last Sessions* was issued posthumously in 1986.

HIS LIFE HIS MUSIC, Bear Family (Germany), 1984
HONKY TONKIN', Flyright, 1986
LEFTY FRIZZELL, Columbia (US), 1982
LEFTY FRIZZELL GOES TO NASHVILLE, Rounder (US), 1988
THE LEGENDARY LAST SESSIONS, MCA (US), 1986
TREASURES UNTOLD, Rounder (US), 1988
TWENTY GOLDEN HITS, Gusto (US), 1988

FROMHOLZ, Steve

Steve Fromholz, like **Kinky Friedman**, is a Texan with a distinctly offbeat view of humanity. While success has constantly eluded him, he has found a niche within Austin's floating musical community.

He was born on June 8, 1945 in Temple, Texas. In 1963, while studying at North Texas State University, he met up with **Michael Martin Murphey** and they formed a duo, which quickly became part of the Denton and Dallas club circuit. They then joined the Dallas County Jug Band, which was cut short by Fromholz being drafted into the Navy. After leaving the Navy, he formed Frummox with Dan McCrimmon, cutting *From Here To There* (1969) for the ABC subsidiary Probe. In 1971 he briefly joined Stephen Stills' band, and then made his debut for **Mike Nesmith**'s Countryside label, cutting the unreleased *How Long Is The Road To Kentucky*.

In 1974 he moved to Austin, where he fell in with **Willie Nelson** (who covered 'I'd Have To Be Crazy') and started to appear at dancehalls such as the Armadillo World Headquarters. His appearance in Austin coincided with a growth of interest in Texan music, which resulted in him securing a deal with Capitol. In 1976 his debut solo album emerged, *A Rumour In My Own Time* featuring Nelson, Doug Dillard (see **Dillards**) and John Sebastian. The following year, after cutting a sequel, *Frolicking In The Myth*, he was dropped by Capitol, and was signed to Nelson's Lone Star. His first outing, *Just Playing Along* (1979), failed to generate much interest, despite its high quality. He still plays on the Texas club circuit.

FURAY, Richie see POCO

GATLIN, Larry

Larry Gatlin represents the new wave of country performers who have accrued considerable wealth through writing their own material and performing on the cabaret circuit for the well-heeled, God-fearing Middle American. With this wealth he has established his own merchandising operation and invested astutely in property, making him one of Nashville's richest.

Larry Gatlin was born on May 2, 1948, in Odessa, Texas, one of six siblings whose father was an oil driller. Larry made his debut in the local church as a robust five-year-old, adapting contemporary pop songs by substituting religious lyrics. He and his brothers, Steve (born on April 4, 1951) and Rudy (born on August 20, 1952), performed regularly as the Gatlin Brothers on an Abilene television show hosted by Slim Willett, which resulted in a gospel album for the Sword and Shield label. With this under his belt, Larry attended the University of Houston, studying English, but this came to a close when he joined a gospel group called the Imperials.

Dottie West heard him performing with the group on *The **Jimmy Dean** Show* in Las Vegas and paid for him to go to Nashville, where she signed him to her publishing company, First Generation, and recorded two of his compositions. Meanwhile, Steve, Rudy and their sister, LaDonna, had joined **Tammy Wynette**'s backing band. In 1973 he was signed to Monument by **Fred Foster** at the suggestion of **Kris Kristofferson**.

Between 1974 and 1977 he charted with 'The Bigger They Are, The Harder They Fall' (1974); 'Delta Dirt' (1975); 'Broken Lady' and 'Statues Without Hearts' (1976); 'I Don't Wanna Cry' and 'Love Is Just A Game' (1977); and 'I Just Wish You Were Someone I Love' (C&W#1, 1977). In 1976, Steve, Rudy and LaDonna had become part of Larry's roadshow, which was billed as Larry Gatlin with Brothers and Friends; this was later to become Larry Gatlin and the Gatlin Brothers Band.

By 1979, with hits like 'Night Time Magic' (C&W#2, 1978) and 'I've Done Enough Dyin' Today' (1978), Gatlin, having had his contract taken over by

Columbia, was moving rapidly towards the top flight of country entertainers. He charted with 'All The Gold In California' (C&W#1, 1979); 'Take Me To Your Lovin' Place' (1980); 'It Don't Get No Better Than This' and 'What Are We Doin' Lonesome' (1981); 'Sure Feels Like Love' (1982); 'Houston (Means I'm One Day Closer To You)' (C&W#1, 1983); 'Denver' (1984); and 'She Used To Be Somebody's Baby' and 'Talkin' To The Moon' (1985).

While the Gatlins have numbered such distinguished followers as Ronald Reagan and George Bush among their fans, Larry was hospitalized and put on the 'programme' to overcome drug abuse in 1984. In 1988 he signed with Universal, cutting *Pure 'n' Simple* (with Bee Gee Barry Gibb and **Roy Orbison**; 1988) and *Larry Gatlin And The Gatlin Brothers* (1989). By 1992 he had moved on yet again, signing with Liberty; his first release was *Adios*, which was prefaced by a year-long tour, and produced by **Jimmy Bowen**. He has become a fixture on the booming cabaret circuit, his popularity remaining as high as ever despite a marked decrease in hits.

ADIOS, Liberty (US), 1992
GREATEST HITS, Columbia (US), 1979
GREATEST HITS ENCORE, Liberty (US), 1992
HELP YOURSELF, Columbia, 1981
LARRY GATLIN AND THE GATLIN BROTHERS, MCA (US), 1989
PURE 'N' SIMPLE, MCA (US), 1989
STRAIGHT AHEAD, Columbia, 1980

GAYLE, Crystal

The purity of her voice has done much to make Crystal Gayle one of the most commercially successful country artists. She has developed a type of supper-club country music, which has been described as 'countrypolitan'.

She was born Brenda Gail Webb in Paintsville, Kentucky, on January 9, 1951, the younger sister of **Loretta Lynn**. Raised in Wabash, Indiana, she joined her sister's roadshow in 1967 (along with another sister, Peggy Sue) as the Loretta Lynn Sisters. Her own debut came three years later with 'I Cried The Blue Right Out Of My Eyes' for Decca, which failed to score, but featured the achingly tremulous voice which became her trademark. In 1972 she was signed by United Artists, who teamed her with producer **Allen Reynolds**; he set about arranging her songs to create a more pop-oriented style.

The fruits of this liaison paid dividends: 'Wrong Road Again' (C&W#6, 1974), 'Somebody Loves You' (C&W#8, 1975), 'I'll Never Get Over You' (C&W#1, 1976), 'You Never Missed A Real Good Thing ('Til He Says Goodbye)' (C&W#1, 1976), 'I'll Do It All Over Again' (C&W#2, 1977), 'Don't It Make My Brown Eyes Blue' (US#2, C&W#1, UK#5, 1977), 'Ready For The Times To Get Better' (C&W#1, 1978), 'Talking In Your Sleep' (US#18, C&W#1, UK#11, 1978) and 'Why Have You Left The One You Left Me For' (C&W#1, 1978). During this period, a succession of albums established her as one of the most successful female artists: *We Must Believe In Magic* sold over a million copies.

In 1979 she moved from United Artists to Columbia. The hits continued with 'Half The Way' (US#15, C&W#2, 1979), 'It's Like We Never Said Goodbye' (C&W#1, 1980), 'If You Ever Change Your Mind' (C&W#1, 1980) and 'Too Many Lovers' (C&W#1, 1981), but her music had become increasingly formulaic.

In 1982 she moved to Elektra, and was teamed with **Eddie Rabbit** for a duet on 'You & I' (C&W#1, 1982), and with Tom Waits on the soundtrack of the Francis Ford Coppola film *One From The Heart*; these recordings, like later releases, showed her embracing a more traditional feel. However Reynolds, who had contributed so much to her success, was unhappy with her new label, and the first album, *True Love*, included three tracks produced by label boss **Jimmy Bowen**, who would assume greater control over her career in later months. None of this affected her commercial viability, and the hits continued to roll: ''Til I Gain Control Again' (C&W#1, 1983), 'Our Love Is On The Faultline' (C&W#1, 1983), 'Baby What About You' (C&W#1, 1983), 'The Sound Of Goodbye' (C&W#1, 1983), 'I Don't Want To Lose Your Love' (C&W#2, 1984), 'Turning Away' (C&W#1, 1984) and 'Me Against The Night' (C&W#4, 1984).

In 1985 she changed producer and started to work with Jim Ed Norman, who teamed her with **Gary Morris** for the duet 'Makin' Up For Lost Time' (C&W#1, 1986), which was followed by 'Cry' (C&W#1, 1986) and 'Straight To The Heart' (C&W#1, 1986). In 1987 she teamed up with Morris for an album of duets, and

toured with her sister Loretta Lynn in 1988, after co-headlining shows at Lake Tahoe. In 1989, she resumed her working relationship with Allen Reynolds and was signed to Capitol.

AIN'T GONNA WORRY, Capitol, 1990
BEST OF CRYSTAL GAYLE, Warner Bros. (US), 1987
COLLECTION, Columbia, 1982
COLLECTION, Knight, 1990
CRYSTAL GAYLE, Capitol, 1988
FAVOURITES, EMI America, 1988
NOBODY'S ANGEL, Warner Bros., 1988
SINGLES ALBUM, Liberty, 1980
STRAIGHT TO THE HEART, Warner Bros., 1986
TALKING IN YOUR SLEEP, EMI, 1988
TRUE LOVE, Elektra, 1982

GENTRY, Bobbie

In the summer of 1967 'Ode To Billy Joe' told the enigmatic tale of a suicide in a distant corner of the Deep South. It became a massive international hit, the character of Billy Joe generating such interest that a film was constructed around the character.

Bobbie Gentry, the author of this mini-soap opera, was born Roberta Streeter in Chickasaw County, Mississippi, on July 27, 1944. In 1957 she moved to California, where she studied music, before starting to work the club circuit. By 1967 she had secured a contract with Capitol, making her debut with 'Ode To Billy Joe' (US#1, UK#13, 1967); it was followed by 'Okohona River Bottom Band' (1967), 'Fancy' (US#31, 1967), 'Chickasaw County Child' (1968), 'I'll Never Fall In Love Again' (UK#1, 1969), 'Raindrops Keep Falling On My Head' (UK#13, 1970) and two duets with **Glen Campbell**, 'Let It Be Me' (US#36, 1969) and 'All I Have To Do Is Dream' (US#27, UK#3, 1969), both covers of **Everly Brothers**' songs.

By the early 1970s her career had undergone a sea-change and she was working in Las Vegas. Although her career was rekindled by the emergence of the film *Ode To Billy Joe* in 1976, she married songwriter Jim Stafford in 1978 and promptly disappeared into obscurity.

BEST OF BOBBIE GENTRY, EMI (Germany), 1983

GIBBS, Terri

Terri Gibbs was born on June 15, 1954, in Augusta, Georgia. Blind from birth, she was raised on gospel and learnt to play the piano, forming her own group in

1974 called Sound Dimension. Between 1975 and 1980, she worked in an Augusta Steak House. After being signed by MCA in 1980, she scored a hit with 'Somebody's Knockin'' (US#13, 1981). While hardly setting the world on fire, she has established herself as one of the more gospel-oriented country singers. After leaving MCA in 1983, she signed with Warner Bros.

GIBSON, Don

During the 1950s, Don Gibson composed some of country music's most celebrated songs, covered by artists like **Ray Charles**, **Willie Nelson**, **Ronnie Milsap** and **Patsy Cline**. Although he is known as 'Mr Country Soul', slick productions by **Chet Atkins** have neutralized much of the latent emotion.

Gibson was born on April 3, 1928, in Shelby, North Carolina; by his teens he had already become a proficient guitarist and was playing clubs and honky-tonks in the surrounding district. In 1946 he moved to Knoxville, broadcast on WNOX's *Tennessee Barn Dance* and started to record for local independent labels. In 1954 he was signed by music publishers **Acuff-Rose**, and by 1957 Chet Atkins had signed him to RCA. His first success as a writer came when **Faron Young** recorded 'Sweet Dreams'; this was later to be recorded by Patsy Cline and was the title of the 1985 film starring Jessica Lange.

The following year when **Kitty Wells** covered 'I Can't Stop Loving You', Gibson cut his own version, coupled with 'Oh Lonesome Me' (US#7, C&W#1, 1958), which became his first hit. Later successes included 'Blue Blue Day' (US#20, C&W#1, 1958), 'Give Myself A Party' (1958), 'Don't Tell Me Your Troubles' (1959), 'Just One Time' (US#29, C&W#2, 1960), 'Sweet Dreams' (1960), 'Sea Of Heartbreak' (US#21, C&W#2, UK#14, 1961), 'Lonesome Number One' (C&W#2, UK#47, 1962), 'Country Green' (C&W#5, 1971) and 'Woman (Sensuous Woman)' (C&W#1, 1972). In 1970 he was signed to the Hickory label, and cut some duets with **Sue Thompson**. After re-joining the *Grand Ole Opry*, he recorded again for Warner Bros., ABC and RCA.

COLLECTION, Castle, 1987
DON GIBSON AND LOS INDIOS TABAJARAS, Bear Family (Germany), 1986
EARLY DAYS, Bear Family (Germany), 1986
A LEGEND IN MY TIME, Bear Family (Germany), 1987
ROCKIN' ROLLIN' GIBSON, Volumes 1-2, Bear Family (Germany), 1984

GILL, Vince

One of country's better and brighter newcomers, Vince Gill's career has been overshadowed by **Garth Brooks** and **Clint Black**. His music reveals an understanding of the roots of country that far exceeds some of the more flamboyantly successful artists, and he wields his Telecaster with such conviction that Mark Knopfler offered him a job in Dire Straits in 1990.

Born in Norman, Oklahoma, on April 4, 1957, Gill played the guitar and banjo well enough to join a bluegrass outfit, Mountain Smoke, while still at high school. Among their achievements was opening a concert for the **Pure Prairie League**, who were later to have a substantial bearing on his career. After leaving school and considering a career as a professional golfer, he was invited to join the Bluegrass Alliance, who, like the **Dillards** and the **Country Gentlemen** before them, had a progressive approach to bluegrass. He remained with them until 1978, when he moved out to Los Angeles and joined Byron Berline (see **Country Gazette**) in Sundance. He remained with Sundance until 1979, when he auditioned for the Pure Prairie League, and landed the job.

Over the next three years Gill's vocals contributed to the renaissance of the Pure Prairie League, putting them back into the charts. However, during his days as a member of Sundance, he had met **Rodney Crowell**, who had invited him to join his band, the Cherry Bombs. He initially declined, but took him up on his offer after cutting another album with Pure Prairie League. Through this association he met Tony Brown, the former pianist in **Emmylou Harris**'s Hot Band.

When Brown moved to A&R at RCA in 1984, Gill was one of his first signings, but before they could cut any records together, Brown had moved on to MCA. At RCA, Gill was teamed with Emmylou's former bassist, Emory Gordy, and over the next five years Gill strung together a number of medium-sized hits, including 'If It Weren't For Him' (a duet with **Rosanne Cash**), 'Oklahoma Borderline', 'Cinderella' and 'Everybody's Sweetheart' (1985).

In 1989 Gill moved to MCA with Tony Brown, who gave him his head to draw from a wide range of styles - bluegrass, Western Swing and contemporary pop music. The first album, *When I Call Your Name*, featured four hits: 'Never Alone', 'Oklahoma Swing' (a duet with **Reba McEntire**), 'When I Call Your Name' (featuring **Patti Loveless**; C&W#2, 1990) and 'Never Knew Lonely' (C&W#3, 1990). The follow-up in 1991, *Pocket Full Of Gold*, spawned other hits, including 'Liza Jane' and 'Take Your Memory With You' (C&W#2,

1992). In 1992 *I Still Believe In You* proved to be the most well-rounded album of the lot, including hits like 'I Still Believe In You' (C&W#1, 1992) and 'Don't Let Our Love Start Slippin' Away' (C&W#1, 1992).

I STILL BELIEVE IN YOU, MCA, 1992
POCKET FULL OF GOLD, MCA, 1991
VINCE GILL, RCA (US), 1985
WHEN I CALL YOUR NAME, MCA (US), 1989

GILLEY, Mickey

Mickey Gilley initially got into the record business because he was the first cousin of **Jerry Lee Lewis**, and imitated his style. He soon developed his own style, which owed more to traditional country than to the rambunctious rock 'n' roll of Lewis.

Gilley was born in Natchez, Louisiana, on March 9, 1936; after moving to Houston in 1956, he started recording for the Minor label and playing in local clubs. Over the next ten years he recorded for a succession of different labels, including Dot, Rex, Paula, 20th Century and his own Astro label, which he formed in 1964. While his hits - 'Is It Wrong' (1960), 'Lonely Wine' (1964) and 'Now I Can Live Again' (1966) - were few and modest, he had overcome the histrionic flamboyance that characterized many of his Lewis impressions.

Having signed with Hugh Hefner's Playboy label in 1974, he hit paydirt with 'Room Full Of Roses' (C&W#1, 1974), which was followed by 'I Overlooked An Orchid' (C&W#1, 1974), 'City Lights' (C&W#1, 1974), 'Window Up Above' (C&W#1, 1975), 'Overnight Sensation' (C&W#7, 1975), 'Don't The Girls All Get Prettier At Closing Time' (C&W#1, 1976), 'Bring It On Home To Me' (C&W#1, 1976) and 'She's Pulling Me Back Again' (C&W#1, 1977).

In 1970 he bought a down-at-heel dive in Houston called Shelley's, which he refurbished and transformed into a salubrious 1,500-seater nightspot called Gilley's, where he often provided the entertainment himself. In 1980 the club was used as a location for the film *Urban Cowboy*, starring John Travolta; the soundtrack of this movie became one of the year's great success stories, with Gilley hitting the charts with 'Stand By Me' (US#22, C&W#1, 1980). By 1987, the club had run into legal problems that resulted in Gilley terminating his partnership with the manager, Sherwood Cryer, and winning $17 million in lieu of unpaid royalties for T-shirt sales; the club closed in 1989.

During the 1980s, after moving to Epic in 1978, he continued to hit the charts: 'Here Comes The Hurt Again' (C&W#9, 1978), 'True Love Ways' (C&W#1, 1980), 'That's All That Matters' (C&W#1, 1980), 'A Heartache Tomorrow (Or A Heartache Tonight)' (C&W#1, 1981), 'You Don't Know Me' (C&W#1, 1981), 'Lonely Nights' (C&W#1, 1981), 'Tears Of The Lonely' (C&W#3, 1982), 'Put Your Dreams Away' (C&W#1, 1982), 'Talk To Me' (C&W#1, 1982), 'Fool For Your Love' (C&W#1, 1983), 'You've Really Got A Hold On Me' (C&W#3, 1983) and 'Paradise Tonight' (a duet with **Charly McClain**).

In 1985 he duetted with **Ray Charles** on 'It Ain't Gonna Worry My Mind'; this was included on Charles's *Friendship* album, which featured contributions from a variety of other country artists. While Gilley has in recent years been overshadowed by young turks such as **Clint Black** and **Dwight Yoakam**, he remains one of the most respected entertainers on the circuit.

DOWN THE LINE, Charly, 1981
FROM PASADENA WITH LOVE, Sundown, 1985
THAT'S ALL THAT MATTERS TO ME, Columbia, 1980
TWENTY GOLDEN SONGS, Astan (US), 1984

GILLILAND, Henry See ROBERTSON, Eck

GILMORE, Jimmie Dale

During the 1970s, the Flatlanders (see **Ely, Joe**) emerged as one of the more influential Texan bands; its alumni, including **Joe Ely**, **Butch Hancock** and Gilmore, have since gone on to front their own bands.

Gilmore was raised in Lubbock, Texas, and quickly broke into the flourishing club circuit, where performers like **Guy Clark**, **Lyle Lovett** and Joe Ely were all starting to make an impression. With Ely, Gilmore has composed such titles as 'Treat Me Like A Saturday Night' and 'Dallas', and as a member of the Flatlanders he cut *One More Road* (1971) for the independent Hightone label, before the group split. Gilmore went on to cut a brace of albums, *Jimmie Dale Gilmore* and *Fair And Square*, that sold reasonably well locally.

In 1990, Gilmore and Hancock toured Australia; one of the gigs was recorded, resulting in *Two Roads*, which was released by Virgin later the same year. In 1991 he was signed to Elektra, cutting *After Awhile*, which included a splendid contribution from Hancock on 'My Mind's Got A Mind Of Its Own'. While his songwriting skills are becoming more widely acknowledged, his own recordings appear undervalued.

AFTER AWHILE, Elektra, 1991
FAIR AND SQUARE, Demon, 1987
JIMMIE DALE GILMORE, Demon, 1989
TWO ROADS (with Butch Hancock), Virgin, 1990

GIMBLE, Johnny

Johnny Gimble has, since his comeback in 1968, been one of the most sought-after fiddlers on the circuit, recording and touring with performers as varied as **Asleep At The Wheel**, **Merle Haggard**, **Johnny Rodriguez**, **George Strait** and **Loretta Lynn**.

He was born in 1926 in Tyler, Texas, where he was raised on a farm. By the late 1930s he was in a group with his brothers (Gene, Jerry, Jack and Bill) called the Rose City Hipsters, who played dances, clubs and broadcast on KGKB, Tyler. In 1943 he joined the **Shelton Brothers** and broadcast on KWKH, Shreveport, before being enlisted by **Jimmie Davis**. After two separate spells with **Bob Wills**' Texas Playboys, he retired from the music business in the early 1950s, when Western Swing had gone out of fashion.

For the next ten years or so, he worked as a barber and in a hospital until 1968, when he was encouraged to take up the fiddle once again. He has cut a number of solo albums, including *Fiddlin' Around* and *Texas Dance Party*, and is a sought-after session musician. Groups like **Commander Cody** and the **Nitty Gritty Dirt Band** have adopted many of his stylistic traits.

STILL SWINGIN', CMH (US), 1976
TEXAS FIDDLE COLLECTION, CMH (US), 1976
TEXAS HONKY TONK HITS, CMH (US), 1976

GIRLS OF THE GOLDEN WEST

Dolly and Millie Good struck an early blow for female emancipation when they became one of the first female groups to break out on their own account. Adopting many of the traditional appurtenances of the cowboy image, they became one of the first duos to bring yodelling out of the backwoods.

Dorothy Laverne (Dolly) was born on December 11, 1915, and Mildred Fern (Millie) was born on April 11, 1913, in Illinois (although their agent put it about that they hailed from Muleshoe, Texas). They started their career on WIL and KMOX, St Louis, and then XER in New Mexico, before moving to WLS, Chicago, and broadcasting regularly on the *National Barn Dance* between 1933 and 1937. After relocating to Cincinnati,

they built up an even larger following on the *Boone County Jamboree* and the *Mid-Western Jamboree* on the local WLW station, and recorded for RCA, Columbia, Conqueror and FJC.

By the 1950s they had become anachronisms and, by the early 1960s, they had ceased to perform altogether. The independent Bluebonnet label put together a ' comprehensive retrospective of their career in the early 1960s, but Dolly's death, on November 12, 1967, put paid to any thoughts of a reunion. Millie still lives in the environs of Cincinnati.

GLASER, Jim

As a member of the Glaser Brothers, Jim (born on December 16, 1937, in Spalding, Nebraska) was overshadowed by the family firm of **Tompall and the Glaser Brothers** spearheaded by the eldest brother, Tompall.

The group began as session musicians for artists like **Marty Robbins** and **Johnny Cash**. By 1971, the Glaser Brothers were trying to break away from being known as Tompall's backing group. Jim broke away from the group and secured his first solo contract with the Monument label, but, unable to establish himself as a solo artist, he returned to the fold.

In 1982, Don Tolle, a former promotion man with A&M, decided to sign Glaser to his new independent label, Noble Vision. The debut *Man In The Mirror* included 'When You're Not A Lady' and 'You're Gettin' To Me Again' (C&W#1, 1984), but the label folded due to financial problems. Glaser returned to session work as a guitarist and vocalist, working with Tompall, as well as with others like **Ronnie McDowell**.

JIM GLASER, Country Store, 1988
MAN IN THE MIRROR, Range (US), 1984

GLASER, Tompall   See **TOMPALL & The Glaser Brothers**

GOLDEN WEST COWBOYS   See **KING, Pee Wee**

GOLDSBORO, Bobby

Bobby Goldsboro is one of those MOR balladeers who has strayed into country more by accident than by design. Although, in recent years, he has signally failed to come to the attention of anyone other than the 'chicken-in-the-basket' audiences, his one massive hit, 'Honey', has ensured that they will keep on flocking to see him perform.

He was born on January 18, 1941, in Marianna, Florida, and got his first taste of the high life as guitarist in **Roy Orbison**'s touring band, the Candy Men, in 1960. By 1962, he had had his first hit with 'Molly' for the Laurie label. The following year he was signed to the United Artists label, and started a succession of pop hits that continued until the early 1970s: 'See The Funny Little Clown' (US#9, 1964), 'Whenever He Sees You' (US#39, 1964), 'Little Things' (US#13, 1965), 'Voodoo Woman' (US#27, 1965), 'It's Too Late' (US#23, 1966), 'Blue Autumn' (US#35, 1967), 'Honey' (C&W#1, UK#2, 1968), 'Autumn Of My Life' (US#19, 1968), 'The Straight Life' (US#36, 1968), 'Watching Scotty Grow' (US#11, 1971), 'Summer (The First Time)' (US#21, UK#9, 1973) and 'Hello Summertime' (UK#14, 1974).

During the 1970s, as he turned increasingly to country music, cutting titles like 'I Believe The South Is Gonna Rise Again', and changing labels regularly, he couldn't arrest his inexorable decline into the supper-club circuit.

GOODMAN, Steve

With his dry perceptive wit, Steve Goodman promised to become one of the more acute documentarists of American life until his demise at thirty-six from leukaemia. He was born on July 25, 1948, in Chicago, Illinois, and studied political theory at the University of Illinois, where he assimilated many of the stylistic patterns of American folk songs. He started to play on the thriving club circuit (where he met songwriter **John Prine**) and began writing jingles.

In 1971 he was signed to Buddah and cut *Steve Goodman* in Nashville, with **Kris Kristofferson** and **Norbert Putnam** producing; it included 'City Of New Orleans' which later became a hit for **Arlo Guthrie** and **Willie Nelson**. In 1973, the follow-up, *Somebody Else's Troubles*, included contributions from **Bob Dylan** (under the pseudonym of Robert Milkwood Thomas) and showed a healthy wit, taking potshots at a variety of targets, including the continued involvement of the US in Vietnam in 'The Ballad Of Penny Evans'.

After signing to Asylum he cut *Jessie's Jigs And Other Favourites* (1975), *Words We Can Dance To* (1976), *Say It In Private* (1978) and *Hot Spot* (1980). He became a regular visitor to festivals in the UK and Europe, where his effortless ability to move from one style to another often stole shows from other more celebrated participants.

In 1983, having tired of the major labels, he set up his own Red Pajamas label and issued *Artistic Hair* (1983) and *Santa Ana Winds* (1984). He died on September 20, 1984, in Seattle, shortly after the release of the latter. On November 3, 1984, a tribute concert was staged at the Pacific Amphitheatre in Costa Mesa, California; among those who appeared were Willie Nelson, **Emmylou Harris**, Jackson Browne, **Jimmy Buffett**, **Rosanne Cash** and **Rodney Crowell**. Another benefit was staged the following year in Chicago with the **Nitty Gritty Dirt Band**, **John Hartford**, Richie Havens, Bonnie Raitt, **David Bromberg**, John Prine and Bonnie Koloc; it was released as *A Tribute To Steve Goodman* (1985).

SAY IT IN PRIVATE, Asylum, 1978
WORDS WE CAN DANCE TO, Asylum, 1976

GOSDIN, Vern

Vern Gosdin was born on August 5, 1934, in Woodland, Alabama, the sixth of nine children. During his teens, Gosdin and two of his brothers broadcast as a gospel vocal group on WVOK, Birmingham. By 1960 he had attempted, unsuccessfully, to launch a career in country music, and had moved to Chicago where he ran a club called the D&G Tap. That year he formed the bluegrass group the Golden State Boys, with his brother, Rex; this would later evolve into the Hillmen, with **Chris Hillman**. When Hillman left to join the Beefeaters (see **Byrds**) in 1963, Gosdin moved to Georgia and set up a glass company, resuming his career briefly in 1967 to record *Gene Clark With The Gosdin Brothers* for Columbia.

Music beckoned again in 1976, and he cut demos of 'Hangin' On' (1976) and 'Yesterday's Gone' (featuring **Emmylou Harris**; 1977); both were issued by Elektra and became modest hits. Over the next few years he cut a number of songs for a variety of labels, including 'Till The End', 'Dream Of Me', 'If You're Gonna Do Me Wrong (Do Me Right)' and 'Way Down Deep', and went on to cut 'I Can Tell By The Way You Dance (You're Gonna Love Tonight)' (C&W#1, 1984), 'What Would Your Memories Do' (C&W#10, 1984) and 'Slow Burning Memory' (C&W#10, 1985) for Compleat.

In 1986 Compleat went out of business, and Gosdin was left without a recording contract. In 1988, with the assistance of **Hank Cochran**, he secured an offer from Columbia, and his debut, *Chiselled In Stone*, included 'Do You Believe Me Now' (C&W#4, 1988),

'Set 'Em Up Joe' (C&W#1, 1988) and 'Chiselled In Stone' (C&W#6, 1988). The follow-up, *Alone*, included 'I'm Still Crazy' (C&W#1, 1989). While Gosdin, who was dubbed 'The Voice', has had an erratic career, he remains one of the few to stay true to his roots: the influences of bluegrass and of more traditional artists like **Ernest Tubb** are just as conspicuous now as they were twenty years ago.

CHISELLED IN STONE, Columbia (US), 1988
NICKELS & DIMES, Columbia (US), 1991

GRAMMER, Billy

Billy Grammer is one of the few guitarists to have his name immortalized in a type of guitar: the Grammer guitar, a flat-top instrument, was installed in the Country Music Hall Of Fame in 1969.

He was born on August 28, 1925, in Benton, Illinois, one of thirteen siblings whose father was a coal miner. Grammer first caught the ear in 1947, broadcasting over WRAL, Arlington, and by 1955 he had become a regular on The ***Jimmy Dean*** Show. After being signed by **Fred Foster** to Monument in 1958, he notched up a few hits inspired by traditional country: the Weavers' 'Gotta Travel On' (US#4, 1958) and 'Bonaparte's Retreat', and 'The Kissing Tree' (1959).

After joining the *Grand Ole Opry* in 1959, he continued notching up hits for a succession of different labels: 'I Wanna Go Home' (1963), 'The Real Thing' (1966), 'Mabel' (1967), 'Ballad Of John Dillinger' (1968) and 'Jesus Is A Soul Man' (1969). By the end of the 1960s, he was concentrating on the development of technical improvements to his guitar.

GRAY, Claude

Claude Gray was born on January 26, 1932, in Henderson, Texas. He scored his first hit in 1960 with a cover of the **Willie Nelson** composition 'Family Bible', which encouraged Mercury to sign him. He struck immediately with 'I'll Just Have Another Cup Of Coffee' (C&W#5, 1961) and 'My Ears Should Burn' (C&W#4, 1961). He remained with Mercury until 1965, when he was signed by Columbia; the following year he had a modest hit with 'Mean Old Woman'. Dropped by Columbia that same year, he was signed to Decca, where he scored with 'I Never Had The One I Wanted' (1966), 'How Fast Them Trucks Can Go' (1967) and 'Woman Ease My Mind' (1973). Although not a household name, Gray has managed to find an audience with those who like their music to espouse the gentle down-home doctrines of Middle America.

GRAY, Dobie

Although Dobie Gray's claim to fame was 'Drift Away' (US#5, 1973), he initially came to prominence as early as 1965 with the dance-floor classic 'The In Crowd' (which was something of a deviation from his country-soul *métier*; US#13, 1965).

He was born Leonard Victor Ainsworth on July 26, 1942, in Brookshire, Texas, the son of a sharecropper. In 1963 he cut 'Look At Me', which was the first of a number of dance-floor hits. After this brief spell of celebrity, his career slipped into the doldrums and he turned to acting, appearing with Rip Torn in productions of *The Beard* and *The Balcony*, and then in *Hair*. In 1969 he returned to the music industry, joining an iffy progressive rock band called Pollution, with whom he cut a mediocre album.

In 1971 he met songwriter Mentor Williams (the brother of the songwriter Paul Williams), and over the next three years he recorded *Drift Away* and *Loving Arms* (1973), and *Hey Dixie* (1974) for MCA. The fact that they were recorded in Nashville with **David Briggs**, Reggie Young, **Charlie McCoy** and **Troy Seals** only emphasized the strong bond between soul and country. Both *Loving Arms* and *Hey Dixie* suffered from poor promotion and confusion about 'country-soul', which resulted in Gray being dropped by MCA.

He was signed by Capricorn for *New Ray Of Sunshine* (produced by Seals; 1975), but it, too, sank without trace. After a few years of obscurity, he returned with the disco-oriented single 'You Can Do It' (produced by **Rick Hall**). More years of obscurity followed, during which he cut the odd single for independent labels, like Inferno, until in 1986, with Seals collaborating, he had a minor hit with 'The Dark Side Of Town' for Capitol. Since then he has continued to play around the South.

GRAY, Otto

Otto Gray was one of the first performers to incorporate the spirit of vaudeville within a western setting. He established a strong following, with very commercialized music, through his tours of the RKO stations in the north.

Gray was born in Stillwater, Oklahoma, the son of a well-to-do rancher. By 1923, he had assumed leadership of a string band called Bill McGinty's Cowboys, and changed the name of the group to the Oklahoma

Cowboys. Over the next few years, the slick sounds of the Cowboys were a regular feature of stations like WLS and WHN, New York, and, despite many sides recorded for labels like Okeh and Vocalion, they were mainly known for the radio work. The act, revolving around Otto's wife 'Mommie' Gray (a performer of old western songs), was somewhat anachronistic, but an effective money-spinner.

Gray also encouraged other entertainers, like the **Duke Of Paducah** and **Zeke Clements**, to branch out and evoke the imagery of the Old West in their performances. Gray ran his band well into the 1940s, by which time they had become even more anachronistic.

GREEN, Lloyd

One of the finest steel guitarists in Nashville, Lloyd Green has for over thirty years been one of the busiest session men on the circuit. He was born in Mobile, Alabama, on October 4, 1937, and started to learn the steel guitar when he was seven, mastering it sufficiently to play professionally by the age of ten. While at high school he played bars and dances, drawing his repertoire from the popular songs of the day. After studying psychology at the University of South Mississippi, he moved to Nashville and obtained work with **Hawkshaw Hawkins** and **Jean Shepard**.

In 1957 he broke into the highly competitive world of session playing, and has, over the years, worked with artists such as **Johnny Gimble**, **George Jones**, **Faron Young**, **Lynn Anderson**, **Billy 'Crash' Craddock**, **Crystal Gayle**, **Don Williams** and **Tammy Wynette**. He has also found the time to record a number of distinguished solo albums, such as *Stainless Steel* (1978).

GREEN VELVET, President, 1982
STEEL RIDES, Monument, 1976
SWEET CHEEKS, President, 1988
TEN SHADES OF GREEN, President, 1977

GREENBRIAR BOYS

The Greenbriar Boys made their reputation through the emergence of the folk and country festivals in the late 1950s and early 1960s, which provided the setting for some of the best bluegrass music. While the Greenbriar Boys, like the **Dillards** and the **Country Gentlemen**, achieved a modicum of celebrity with their progressive style, their recorded output lacked continuity due to rapid turnover within the band.

The group was formed in 1958 in New York by Eric Weissberg, John Herald, Ralph Rinzler and Bob Yellin; Rinzler, the former manager of **Bill Monroe**, provided much of the drive. In 1962 they recorded *Greenbriar Boys* for Elektra, but they changed labels to Sam Charters' Vanguard (which had, under the auspices of Rinzler, recently signed **Doc Watson**). There they cut albums like *Ragged But Right* (1964) and *Better Late Than Never* (1967), and appeared with, or on the same bill as, Watson.

Weissberg, Yellin and Herald had all left the group at various stages, and Weissberg was the only one to make a significant comeback, via session work and playing the celebrated banjo part on 'Duelling Banjos' (US#2, UK#17, 1973) featured in the film *Deliverance*; with Steve Mandel on guitar, the track was based on 'Feuding Banjos', originally performed by **Don Reno** and **Arthur 'Guitar Boogie' Smith**. Among the other musicians to pass through the ranks were mandolinist Frank Wakefield and fiddler Buddy Spicher, both of whom would later have successful careers as session men. By the end of the 1960s the group had disbanded, although Rinzler continued to champion the cause of old-time traditional music with occasional impromptu sessions.

BEST OF THE GREENBRIAR BOYS, Vanguard, 1972
DELIVERANCE (Original Soundtrack; Eric Weissberg & Steve Mandel), Warner Bros., 1972

GREENE, Jack

Jack Henry Greene was born on January 7, 1930, in Maryville, Tennessee, and, in common with many other performers could play the guitar almost before he could walk. In 1944 he made his debut on WGAP, Tennessee, becoming a full-time musician with the Atlanta-based Cherokee Trio. In 1950 he became a member of the Rhythm Ranch Boys, before joining the army. Two years later, after his discharge, he joined the Peachtree Cowboys, who also came from Atlanta.

His big break came in 1962, when he was recruited by **Ernest Tubb** to be a member of his band, the Texas Troubadours. In 1965, with the long production experience of **Owen Bradley** behind him, he started a solo career that provided him with hits such as **Dallas Frazier**'s 'There Goes My Everything' (C&W#1, 1966), 'All The Time' (C&W#1, 1967), 'What Locks The Door' (C&W#2, 1967), 'You Are My Treasure' (C&W#1, 1968), Frazier's 'Until My Dreams Come True' (C&W#1, 1969), 'Statue Of A Fool' (C&W#1, 1969) and 'Back In The Arms Of Love' (C&W#4, 1969).

★

In 1969 he joined forces with **Jeannie Seely** on Ernest Tubb's *Midnight Jamboree*, and assembled a roadshow featuring his backing band the Jolly Giants (in honour of his nickname). Their first duet, 'Wish I Didn't Have To Miss You' (C&W#2, 1969), consolidated the partnership. While the hits may have dried up, the roadshow continues to attract large audiences, and he still records for Frontline and CMH.

GREATEST HITS, Starday (US), 1988
GREATEST HITS (with Jeannie Seely), Starday (US), 1988

GREENE, Richard see ROWAN, Peter

GREENWOOD, Lee

The gruff, smoky timbre of Lee Greenwood's voice has caused many to compare him with **Kenny Rogers**. As he picks up one Country Music Association award after another, it would seem that the future of country music lies with those with a pop sensibility.

Greenwood was born on October 27, 1942, in Los Angeles; his parents divorced in 1943 and he moved to Sacramento to live with his grandparents. By 1956 he had learnt to play the saxophone, and over the next seven years or so he played in a variety of groups, including **Del Reeves**' band. In 1963, having moved to Las Vegas with his group the Apollos (who promptly split up), he worked there as a bandleader, arranger and vocalist.

After stints with a variety of bands (at one point he had the opportunity of joining the Rascals), he was signed by the Paramount label in 1971. He returned to Los Angeles, but for the next five years Paramount steadfastly refused to let him out of his contract while refusing to release any of his records. With his career grounded he did a variety of menial tasks, including frying chicken in a fast-food joint, before moving back to Las Vegas to work the casinos and clubs as a dealer and a singer.

In 1980 he moved to Nashville, and was signed by producer Jerry Crutchfield to MCA. His 1981 debut, 'It Turns Me Inside Out', set in motion a succession of hits: 'Ring On Her Finger, Time On Her Hands' (C&W#5, 1982), 'She's Lying' (C&W#7, 1982), 'Ain't No Trick (It Takes Magic)' (C&W#7, 1982), 'Somebody's Gonna Love You' (C&W#1, 1983), 'Going, Going, Gone' (C&W#1, 1984), 'Dixie Road' (C&W#1, 1985), 'I Don't Mind The Thorns (If You're The Rose)' (C&W#1, 1985), 'Don't Underestimate My Love For You' (C&W#1, 1985), 'Hearts Aren't Made To

Break (They're Made To Love)' (C&W#1, 1986) and 'Mornin' Ride' (C&W#1, 1987).

In 1987 **Jimmy Bowen** took over the production chores, maintaining Greenwood's impressive strike rate with 'Someone', 'If There's Any Justice' and 'Touch And Go Crazy' (1987). After Bowen's departure for Capitol, Jerry Crutchfield took over as producer and Greenwood partnered **Barbara Mandrell** on an album of duets. While the size and regularity of the hits decreased, he scored with 'Holdin' A Good Hand' (C&W#2, 1990) and managed to maintain a foothold with his roadshow. Apart from his recording career, he has also worked on commercials for McDonalds and Coors.

GREATEST HITS, Volumes 1-2, MCA (US), 1989
GREENWOOD & MANDRELL (with Barbara Mandrell), MCA (US), 1988
HOLDIN' A GOOD HAND, MCA (US), 1990
IF ONLY FOR ONE NIGHT, MCA (US), 1989
INSIDE OUT, MCA (US), 1983
LOVE WILL FIND ITS WAY TO YOU, MCA (US), 1987
SOMEBODY'S GONNA LOVE YOU, MCA (US), 1984
STREAMLINE, MCA (US), 1986
WIND BENEATH MY WINGS, MCA (US), 1984
YOU'VE GOT A GOOD LOVE COMIN', MCA (US), 1988

GRIFF, Ray

Despite prodigious musical abilities (he was a drummer in a band at the age of eight, proficient on the piano and the guitar, and a bandleader by the time he was eighteen), Ray Griff has never managed to make the big time as a performer, but has established himself through songwriting.

He was born on April 22, 1940, in Vancouver, British Columbia, but moved on to Calgary, Alberta, in the early 1950s. He started to write in the late 1950s, coming to prominence when **Johnny Horton** recorded his composition 'Mr Moonlight'; this was consolidated when **Jim Reeves** cut a Griff song, 'Where Do I Go', in 1962. As the years passed, other performers, such as **Porter Wagoner**, **George Hamilton IV**, **Dolly Parton**, **Wilma Burgess**, **Faron Young** and **Jerry Lee Lewis**, all dipped into the Griff songbook.

He moved to Nashville in 1964 at the suggestion of Jim Reeves, and quickly became involved as a singer, recording for the RCA subsidiary Groove. He recorded 'Your Lily White Hands' (1967) for MGM, 'Sugar From My Candy' (1968) for Dot, and a cover of Norman 'General' Johnson's 'Patches' (1970) and

'The Morning After Baby Let Me Down' (1971) for Royal American. These modest hits encouraged Capitol to sign him, and he scored with 'You Ring My Bell' (1975) and 'Let Her Come In' (1976), among others. Since the late 1970s, most of his energies have been directed towards running his own music publishing company, Blue Echo.

GRIFFIN, Rex
Rex Griffin (born on August 22, 1912, in Gadsden, Alabama) was one of the few genuine itinerant songsters, and he chose to tour the radio stations of the South (including WSB, Atlanta), rather than perform at hoe-downs and bars. Though best known for his tear-stained composition, 'The Last Letter', his reworkings of **Jimmie Rodgers**' songs, and his version of the Emmett Miller yodelling classic, 'Lovesick Blues', have added to his reputation.

By the 1940s he was presenter of *Texas Round-Up* on KRLD, Dallas. However, his restless spirit left him with a serious drinking problem, which eventually killed him on October 11, 1959. In a sense, he was one of the first - and last - twentieth-century troubadours.

GRIFFITH, Nanci
In the late 1970s the UK was gripped by punk; there was a similar revolution taking place in the US. While not as radical as its English counterpart, the US revolution was to have far-reaching effects on country music, with songwriters such as **Butch Hancock**, **Jimmie Dale Gilmore** and Griffith utilizing the traditional imagery of country music in their lyrics, but drawing their arrangements from a variety of different styles, such as rockabilly, folk, Western Swing and Tex-Mex.

Born on July 6, 1953, in Austin, Texas, Griffith began singing in local honky-tonks when she was fourteen. Although she trained as a teacher, she continued to write and perform her songs until, in 1978, she secured a contract with the local independent Philo label, issuing *There's A Light Beyond These Woods* (1978). This debut, the blueprint of what she would later describe as 'folkabilly', displayed finely wrought vignettes, which chronicled life without rose-tinted glasses. The release of this album secured Griffith a host of admirers, particularly in Ireland.

The follow-up, *Once In A Very Blue Moon* (1984), emerged six years later, and in the interim she had toured on the flourishing club and folk festival circuits and had continued to teach. *The Last Of The True*

Believers (1985) won her a Grammy for Best Folk Album; it was followed by *Poet In My Window* (1986). Both contained some material by other writers, such as Pat Alger and Fred Koller, which tended to complement her own songs.

In 1987 she made her breakthrough by signing to MCA and cutting *Lone Star State Of Mind* (1987), which included 'From A Distance', a Number One hit in Ireland. The move to MCA gave her albums a slightly harder edge, and brought her more into contact with the mainstream. *Little Love Affairs* (1987), *One Fair Summer Evening* (1988), *Storms* (1989), *Late Night Grande Hotel* (1991) and *Other Voices, Other Rooms* (1993) all managed to broaden her appeal. The focus of her music had by now expanded, drawing in reference points beyond the confined and somewhat parochial atmosphere of Nashville, including influences from Irish writers and performers like Mary Black and Maura O'Connell. Her songs have been covered by **Suzy Bogguss**, **Kathy Mattea** and **Lynn Anderson**, among others.

THE LAST OF THE TRUE BELIEVERS, Demon, 1985
LATE NIGHT GRANDE HOTEL, MCA, 1991
LITTLE LOVE AFFAIRS, MCA, 1987
LONE STAR STATE OF MIND, MCA, 1987
ONCE IN A VERY BLUE MOON, MCA, 1984
ONE FAIR SUMMER EVENING, MCA, 1988
OTHER VOICES, OTHER ROOMS, MCA, 1993
POET IN MY WINDOW, MCA, 1986
STORMS, MCA, 1989
THERE'S A LIGHT BEYOND THESE WOODS, MCA, 1978

GRISMAN, David
A true all-round musician, David Grisman was born in Hackensack, New Jersey, in 1945, and became a proficient mandolinist, guitarist and saxophonist. After joining folk group the Even Dozen Jug Band, which included John Sebastian (later a founder member of the Lovin' Spoonful) and vocalist Maria Muldaur, he met Jerry Garcia (later a founder member of the Grateful Dead) and then **Peter Rowan**. In 1967 he formed Earth Opera with Rowan, but the group split up in 1969, having cut *Earth Opera* and *The Great American Eagle Tragedy* for Elektra.

Working as session musicians, Grisman and Rowan formed Muleskinner with Richard Greene in 1972. The following year, Grisman and Rowan joined Jerry Garcia's occasional band, Old And In The Way, with fiddler **Vassar Clements**. Over the next three years Grisman formed a number of different outfits, including the Great American Music Band with Greene, and worked as a session musician on film soundtracks, before forming the David Grisman Quintet in 1977. Over the next four years Grisman cut *Hot Dawg* (1979) and *Mondo Mando* (1981), among others.

While the repertoire of the group was drawn from the old-time traditional hillbilly music of the 1920s and 1930s, the arrangements were jazz-influenced. In 1981 Grisman and Stéphane Grappelli played a number of concerts - the highlights appearing in *Live* - and then teamed up with legendary Danish violinist Svend Asmussen for *Swingin' With Svend* (1986). He is the publisher of *Mandolin World News*.

ACOUSTIC CHRISTMAS, Rounder (US), 1988
DAVID GRISMAN QUINTET, Kaleidoscope (US), 1979
DAVID GRISMAN ROUNDER ALBUM, Rounder (US), 1988
EARLY DAWG, Sugar Hill (US), 1988
HERE TODAY, Rounder (US), 1988
HOME IS WHERE THE HEART IS, Rounder (US), 1988
HOT DAWG, Mobile Fidelity Sound Lab (US), 1989
MANDOLIN ABSTRACTIONS, Rounder (US), 1988

GUILBEAU, Gib see PARSONS, Gene

GUITAR, Bonnie

Bonnie Guitar was born Bonnie Buckingham on March 25, 1934, in Auburn, Washington. From a musical household, she started playing the clarinet before moving to the guitar. While at school, she played in various groups, and after leaving school she worked the clubs, playing in pop, C&W and R&B bands.

In 1955 she cut a demo, which found its way to producer Fabor Robison; at Fabor's Studios, she learnt every aspect of recording, from sound mixing to playing on sessions. Among the artists she worked with were **Dorsey Burnette** and Ned Miller. In 1957 Miller wrote the big hit 'Dark Moon' (US#6, 1957) for her (although Gale Storm's cover fared better). Failing to chart again, she formed her own label, Dolton, which released a succession of hits for the Fleetwoods.

In the early 1960s, she worked for the Dot label as head of A&R of the country department. After leaving Dot she returned to performing and recording, cutting 'I'm Living In Two Worlds' (1966), 'A Woman In Love' (1967), 'I Believe In Love' (1968), 'Happy Everything' (1972) and 'Honey On The Moon' (1980).

DARK MOON, MCA (US), 1992

GULLY JUMPERS

Comprising Paul Warmack (mandolin and guitar), Charlie Arrington (fiddle), Roy Hardison (banjo) and Burt Hutcherson (guitar), the Gully Jumpers were, along with **Doctor Humphrey Bate and his Possum Hunters** and the Crook Brothers, one of the more innovative string bands. Formed by car mechanic Warmack in 1923, as an occasional diversion, by 1928 they had established themselves as one of the most popular bands at the *Grand Ole Opry*, and had recorded a bunch of sides for RCA. The line-up remained unchanged for over twenty years, but by the early 1960s, Burt Hutcherson was the only remaining member of the original group.

GUNTER, Arthur 'Hardrock'

Sidney Louie Gunter was born on September 18, 1918, in Birmingham, Alabama. He began in the music business as a DJ in 1939, and by the late 1940s his recording career had got under way. While his success rate was hardly extraordinary, his 'Birmingham Bounce' was covered with spectacular results by **Red Foley**, who took it to the top of the charts; the R&B singer Amos Milburn contributed his own version a couple of years later. What was significant about Gunter was that his brand of rockabilly predated the 'official' emergence of rock 'n' roll by some years. He recorded for a variety of different labels, such as Bama, Bullet and Decca; for the latter, he cut a libidinous version of 'Sixty Minute Man' with Roberta Lee and the self-penned 'Baby Let's Play House'.

In 1951 he was conscripted; he became a First Lieutenant and was stationed at Fort Jackson in South Carolina. After being demobbed in 1953, he cut a brace of sides for MGM. The following year he recorded for Sun, and broadcast on WWVA's *Wheeling Jamboree*. Unable to sustain his career (despite cutting a number of sides for labels like King and Emperor), he had disappeared into obscurity by the early 1960s, emerging only to cut the atrocious 'Hillbilly Twist', and then again, in 1972, to cut an album of **Hank Williams** songs.

BLACK & BLUES, Excello (US), 1979
BOOGIE WOOGIE ON A SATURDAY NIGHT, Charly, 1984

GUTHRIE, Arlo

Arlo Guthrie has done much to keep alive the spirit and memory of his father, **Woody Guthrie**, through his highly individual, unfailingly evocative reworkings of his father's songs. He has also established himself as a witty writer and performer in his own right.

Arlo was born on July 10, 1947, in New York, and launched his career in 1967 with 'Alice's Restaurant', a nineteen-minute talking blues which formed the basis for the film of the same name two years later. While it failed to hit, it picked up a lot of airplay on the rock-oriented FM radio stations, establishing Arlo as a performer at festivals and on the club circuit. Over the years, albums like *Hobo's Lullaby* (1973) and *Last Of The Brooklyn Cowboys* (1977) showed him getting to grips with material from diverse sources. His only hit was the **Steve Goodman** composition, 'City Of New Orleans' (US#18, 1973).

During the 1970s Arlo collaborated with one of his father's best friends, Pete Seeger, and together they cut the live album *In Concert* (1974), and *Precious Friend* (1981). In 1987 Arlo contributed to the excellent television programme, *A Vision Shared*, which was a Library of Congress film celebrating the lives of both Woody Guthrie and Leadbelly; other contributors included Seeger, Robbie Robertson (see **The Band**), **Emmylou Harris**, John Mellencamp, Bono of U2 and Bruce Springsteen.

GUTHRIE, Jack

The cousin of **Woody Guthrie**, Leon 'Jack' Guthrie was born in 1915 in Olive, Oklahoma. In 1932 he moved to California to get into the music business. While his style was modelled on **Jimmie Rodgers**, he approached the business of making music with the seriousness of a documentarist. Once in Los Angeles, he teamed up with Woody, broadcasting on KFVD, and together they wrote titles like 'Oklahoma Hills' and 'Reno Blues'; the former became one of the biggest hits of 1945.

After joining the Capitol label, he was drafted into the army and stationed on the South Pacific island of Le Shima. Here he was critically wounded and contracted a wasting disease from which he never fully recovered. After being demobbed, he recommenced his recording career, which proved short-lived as he was hospitalized in a Veteran's hospital in 1947, and died on January 15, 1948. To this day, Jack Guthrie remains grievously underrated, and his records are hard to find.

HIS GREATEST SONGS, Stetson, 1989

GUTHRIE, Woody

The music of Woody Guthrie occupies a very special place in the history of the US. He became the voice of the people in the Depression of the 1930s, when his songs spoke graphically of the plight of the many migrant workers, and provided them with a message of hope.

He was born Woodrow Wilson Guthrie on July 14, 1912, in Okemah, Oklahoma; after his mother's death from Huntington's Chorea (a chronic nerve disorder), and his father's financial problems, he moved to Pampa, Texas to live with an uncle. This uncle, a keen fiddler, taught him how to play the guitar and introduced him to the old traditional tunes, which Woody adapted with his own lyrics. His first composition, 'Dusty Old Dust' (1935) was written to the tune of **Carson Robison**'s 'The Ballad Of Billy The Kid'. For the next two years, he travelled the country drawing inspiration from hymns, ballads, the blues and dance tunes.

In 1937, having based himself in Los Angeles, he started to work with his cousin, **Jack Guthrie**, and broadcast over KFVD. Much of his material was drawn from his developing repertoire of 'dust bowl ballads' and traditional songs, including titles like 'Pretty Boy Floyd', 'Dust Bowl Refugees', 'I Ain't Got No Home', 'Gypsy Davy', 'Oklahoma Hills', 'This Land Is Your Land' and 'John Henry'.

As his profile grew, so did his commitment to political reform and socialist principles. The significance of his work was quickly grasped by official bodies like the Library of Congress, for whom he recorded many hours of material under the guidance of Alan Lomax in 1940. The following year, he was commissioned to write a song cycle celebrating the building of hydro-electric dams in the Pacific North-West, which included 'Grand Coulee Dam' and 'Pastures Of Plenty'.

By 1943, his overt Communist sympathies had started to land him in serious trouble with the authorities, and toleration of his outspokenness had given way to outright hostility, culminating in a ban from all the US radio networks. This had little real effect on him, because his autobiography, *Bound For Glory*, was published to considerable acclaim. The following year, he was signed up by Moe Asch to cut a number of albums for Folkways, albums which included songs such as 'Plane Wreck At Los Gatos (Deportees)' and 'Going To The Zoo'. The former was based around a newspaper article about an aeroplane full of migrant workers that crashed with no survivors; this song, like many others in Woody's repertoire, showed his

★

compassion for, and anger at, the suffering of others. Subsequent versions by the **Byrds**, **Dolly Parton** and **Emmylou Harris** retain that sense of indignation and outrage.

By 1950, he had started his long fight against the Huntington's Chorea that was to claim his life seventeen years later. While he physically declined, his reputation increased, with his songs being covered by **Ramblin' Jack Elliott**, the **Carter Family**, the Weavers, Pete Seeger, Ewan MacColl, **Bob Dylan** and many others. On October 3, 1967, Guthrie died; in the wake of his death his songs have continued to be covered by artists too numerous to mention, and the sphere of his influence shows no sign of letting up. His song 'This Land Is Your Land', in particular, has become a more potent US national anthem than 'The Star-Spangled Banner' will ever be. In 1976, his autobiography was turned into a movie starring David Carradine; and in 1980 Joe Klein wrote a biography, *Woody Guthrie: A Life*.

COLUMBIA RIVER COLLECTION, Topic, 1988
DUST BOWL BALLADS, Rounder (US), 1988
LIBRARY OF CONGRESS RECORDINGS, Volumes 1-3, Rounder (US), 1988
SONGS FROM BOUND FOR GLORY, Warner Bros., 1977
STRUGGLE, Special Delivery, 1990
THIS LAND IS YOUR LAND, Folkways (US), 1988
A TRIBUTE TO WOODY GUTHRIE (Various Artists), Columbia, 1988
THE VERY BEST OF WOODY GUTHRIE, Music Club, 1992
WOODY GUTHRIE SINGS FOLK SONGS (with Sonny Terry and Cisco Houston), Folkways (US), 1988
WOODY GUTHRIE SINGS FOLK SONGS OF LEADBELLY, Folkways (US), 1988

HACKBERRY RAMBLERS

During the 1930s, the pathbreaking Hackberry Ramblers established themselves as one of the premier cajun bands. Comprising Luderin Darbonne (fiddle), Lennis Sonnier (guitar and vocals), Edwin Duhon (mandolin), Joe Werner (guitar), Lonnie Rainwater (guitar) and Floyd Rainwater (bass), they initially recorded for the RCA subsidiary, Bluebird, singing in both English and French. The band broke up in 1939, only to be re-formed by Darbonne in the early 1960s to cut *The Hackberry Ramblers* for Arhoolie and to tour the festival circuit.

FIRST RECORDINGS: 1935-48, Folklyric (US), 1988
LOUISIANA CAJUN MUSIC, Arhoolie (US), 1988

HAGGARD, Merle

Merle Haggard remains one of the most impressive country singers and songwriters of all time. Having never repressed or hidden the poverty of his early life, Haggard has drawn liberally from those experiences to compose songs that evoke human frailty.

He was born on April 6, 1937, in Bakersfield, California, in a converted boxcar, where his parents had been forced to take up residence after being driven from their farm in East Oklahoma. His father was an adequate fiddler, but never managed to play professionally as a result of his wife's devout Christianity - professional musicians being sinners! After his father's death in 1946, Merle took to petty crime, and his mother had him committed to a juvenile detention centre. He spent the 1950s in and out of jail, but by 1960, after meeting **Johnny Cash** (who came to perform at San Quentin while Haggard was serving a stretch for attempted burglary), he determined to clean up his act and attempt to make a living as a performer.

Based in the fast-growing music community of Bakersfield, he befriended **Buck Owens** and **Bonnie Owens** (Buck's ex-wife, whom Haggard would later marry) and also met his future manager, a local musician called Fuzzy Owen. In 1962, after joining a band

and playing in Las Vegas, Haggard recorded some sides for the Tally label, which Fuzzy Owen had acquired from his cousin. Over the next two or three years, he cut titles such as 'Sing A Bad Song', 'Sam Hill', 'All My Friends Are Gonna Be Strangers' and 'I'm A Lonesome Fugitive' (C&W#1, 1967), the last two written by Casey and **Liz Anderson**. Haggard was now signed to Capitol by producer Ken Nelson, as the Tally label had been taken over. His backing group (which included **Johnny Gimble**) was called The Strangers in honour of his first major hit, 'All My Friends Are Gonna Be Strangers'.

Over the next ten years, he put out a string of blues-influenced hit records that eschewed the traditional optimism of country music: 'Branded Man' (C&W#1, 1967), 'Sing Me Back Home' (C&W#1, 1967), 'The Legend Of Bonnie And Clyde' (C&W#1, 1968), 'Mama Tried' (C&W#1, 1968), 'I Take A Lot Of Pride In What I Am' (C&W#3, 1968), 'Hungry Eyes' (C&W#1, 1969), 'Workin' Man Blues' (C&W#1, 1969), 'Okie From Muskogee' (C&W#1, 1969), 'The Fighting Side Of Me' (C&W#1, 1970), 'Jesus Take A Hold' (C&W#3, 1970), 'I Can't Be Myself' (C&W#3, 1970), 'Soldier's Last Letter' (C&W#3, 1971), 'Someday We'll Look Back' (C&W#2, 1971), 'Daddy Frank (The Guitar Man)' (C&W#1, 1971), 'Carolyn' (C&W#1, 1971), 'Grandma Harp' (C&W#1, 1972), 'It's Not Love (But It's Not Bad)' (C&W#1, 1972), 'I Wonder If They Ever Think Of Me' (C&W#1, 1973), 'The Emptiest Arms In The World' (C&W#3, 1973), 'Everybody's Had The Blues' (C&W#1, 1973), 'If We Make It Through December' (US#28, C&W#1, 1973), 'Things Aren't Funny Anymore' (C&W#1, 1974), 'Old Man From The Mountain' (C&W#1, 1974), 'Kentucky Gambler' (C&W#1, 1974), 'Always Wanting You' (C&W#1, 1975), 'Movin' On' (C&W#1, 1975), 'It's All In The Movies' (C&W#1, 1975), 'The Roots Of My Raising' (C&W#1, 1976) and 'Cherokee Maiden' (C&W#1, 1976).

In 1977 he left Capitol and signed with MCA. The 1970s had also seen Haggard pursuing other objectives like cutting *A Tribute To The Best Damn Fiddle Player In The World (My Salute To **Bob Wills**)* (1970), and in 1980 he duetted with Clint Eastwood on 'Bar

Room Buddies' (C&W#1, 1980), which was featured in the movie *Every Which Way But Loose*. While his time with MCA was not unproductive, his only significant hit was 'I Think I'll Just Stay Here And Drink' (C&W#1, 1980).

In 1981 he published his autobiography, *Sing Me Back Home*, and was signed by Epic; these twin events revived interest in his career and the hits started to flow again: 'My Favourite Memory' (C&W#1, 1981), 'Big City' (C&W#1, 1982), 'Are The Good Times Really Over (I Wish A Buck Was Still Silver)' (C&W#2, 1982), 'Going Where The Lonely Go' (C&W#1, 1982), 'You Take Me For Granted' (C&W#1, 1983), 'That's The Way Love Goes' (C&W#1, 1984), 'Someday When Things Are Good' (C&W#1, 1984), 'Let's Chase Each Other Around The Room' (C&W#1, 1984), 'Natural High' (C&W#1, 1985) and 'Twinkle Twinkle Lucky Star' (C&W#1, 1988). He released an album of duets with **George Jones**, which included 'Yesterday's Wine' (C&W#1, 1982); and then, the first of two albums of duets with **Willie Nelson** (featuring musicians like **Grady Martin** and **Chips Moman**), which included 'Pancho & Lefty (C&W#1, 1983). Another collaboration followed, this time with **Janie Fricke** on 'A Good Place To Fall Apart' (C&W#1, 1984).

One of the striking features of Haggard's career is that he has remained creative and never become complacent and coasted on past triumphs, despite having been showered with every possible accolade the Country Music Association could bestow upon him.

BRANDED MAN, Capitol, 1985
CAPITOL COUNTRY CLASSICS, Capitol, 1980
EPIC COLLECTION, Epic (US), 1984
5.01 BLUES, Epic, 1989
A FRIEND OF CALIFORNIA, Epic,1986
GOIN' WHERE THE LONELY GO, Epic, 1982
GREATEST HITS AND BEST OF MERLE HAGGARD, MCA (US), 1988
HEART TO HEART (with Leona Williams), Mercury, 1983
I'M A LONESOME FUGITIVE, See For Miles, 1966
MERLE HAGGARD, Epic (US), 1986
MERLE HAGGARD, Capitol, 1990
MERLE HAGGARD SINGS COUNTRY FAVOURITES, EMI, 1987
STRANGERS, Stetson, 1990
SWINGING DOOR, See For Miles, 1986
25th ANNIVERSARY ALBUM, EMI, 1989
THE VERY BEST OF MERLE HAGGARD, EMI, 1988
WALKING THE LINE (with George Jones and Willie Nelson), Epic (US), 1987
THE WAY I AM, MCA (US), 1988

HALE, Monte see WILLING, Foy

HALE, Theron

Fiddler Theron Hale (born in 1883, in Pikeville, Tennessee) and his daughters, Elizabeth (fiddle) and Mamie Ruth (piano), were one of the early Grand Ole Opry bands, who flourished in the late 1920s and early 1930s. While little remains of their recorded output for RCA Victor, they are noted for a genteel musical style almost unique in that period, and became best known for their version of 'Listen To The Mockingbird'. By the end of the 1930s, they had ceased performing altogether. Theron is thought to have died in 1954, while Elizabeth and Mamie Ruth vanished into obscurity.

HALEY, Bill

Along with **Elvis Presley**, Bill Haley and the Comets became synonymous with the emergent rock 'n' roll of the mid-1950s. An unlikely focal point of teenage rebellion, the rather portly Haley rose to prominence as a result of the adroitness of the film industry, which was quick to seize upon 'Rock Around The Clock' and include it in a number of films, such as *The Blackboard Jungle*, and even to base an entire film (aptly entitled *Rock Around The Clock*!) around it.

William John Clifton Haley was born on July 6, 1925, in Highland Park, Michigan and grew up in Chester, Pennsylvania. He joined Shorty Cook's Downhomers in 1944 (replacing the ace yodeller **Kenny Roberts**), with whom he toured the north and Midwest. In 1946 he joined WPWA, Chester, as musical director, before forming his own group, Bill Haley and the Four Aces of Swing. Although cutting material by great artists such as **Hank Williams** and **Red Foley**, the Four Aces failed to establish a clear identity and were gradually superseded by the Saddlemen. At this point Haley began to infuse his music with a much harder R&B sound, and by 1951, with a cover of Jackie Brenston's 'Rocket 88' (arguably the first ever rock 'n' roll record), the country element had all but evaporated from Haley's style.

In 1953 Haley changed the name of the group to the Comets and cut 'Crazy Man Crazy'. Haley now abandoned the image of a country band and adopted the vernacular of the street, which, combined with the slap bass of Al Rex, embodied the emergent hybrid of rock 'n' roll. In spite of their inventiveness, the Comets were not immune to lapses of taste, cutting rubbish like 'Pat-a-Cake'.

Haley joined Decca in 1954 (having been previously signed to a variety of independent labels), and cut 'Dim, Dim The Lights (I Want Some Atmosphere)' (US#11, 1954), 'Shake Rattle And Roll' (UK#4, 1955), 'Mambo Rock' (US#17, UK#14, 1955), 'Birth Of The Boogie' (US#26, 1955) and the epoch-making 'Rock Around The Clock' (US#1, UK#1, 1955).

'Rock Around The Clock' has, over the years, become a classic, mainly because it has sold over 25 million copies. The rimshot drumming of Billy Guesack and the liquid guitar work of Danny Cedrone became synonymous in the public imagination with the new phenonenon of rock 'n' roll. Though at first it failed to make an impact, its inclusion in *The Blackboard Jungle* guaranteed 'Rock Around The Clock' almost unprecedented exposure. Haley responded quickly by recruiting new sidemen for the Comets - only Rex remained after a round of financial finagling - who were not only better musicians, but also better showmen.

While unable to match the charisma of Presley or the lyricism of Chuck Berry, Bill Haley and the Comets developed a stage act that fulfilled the high-octane requirements of rock 'n' roll: Rex would spin his bass and new sax player Rudy Pompilli would lie on his back, while everyone else would cavort around. Other hits followed with a monotonous regularity; some plumbed the depths of crassness while others were just about passable: 'Rock A-Beatin' Boogie' (UK#4, 1955), 'Razzle Dazzle' (US#15, 1955; UK#13, 1956), 'Burn That Candle' (US#9, 1955), 'See You Later Alligator' (US#11, UK#7, 1956), 'The Saints Rock 'n' Roll' (UK#5, 1956), 'Rockin' Through The Rye' (UK#3, 1956), 'R-O-C-K' (US#16, 1956), 'Rip It Up' (US#25, UK#4, 1956), 'Rudy's Rock' (US#34, UK#26, 1956), 'Rock The Joint' (UK#20, 1957), 'Don't Knock The Rock' (UK#7, 1957) and 'Skinny Minnie' (US#22, 1958).

Haley's success was almost wholly derived from his being in the right place at the right time. The fact that he was an indifferent country singer with no compositional ability was highlighted in later years, when 'Rock Around The Clock' was reissued for the umpteenth time to coincide with yet another world tour. From the early 1960s, Haley's star was in the descendant, and despite the periodic reissues and the endless revival tours, his health started to decline. He died of heart failure brought on by excessive drinking on February 9, 1981.

DECCA YEARS AND MORE, Bear Family (Germany), 1990
GREATEST HITS, MCA, 1985
ROCKIN' ROLLIN' BILL HALEY, Bear Family (Germany), 1984

HALL, Rick

Rick Hall was born in Franklin County, Alabama on January 31, 1932. In 1957 he joined the country group Carmol Taylor and the Country Pals, where he met **Billy Sherrill**. By 1958 he and Sherrill had formed the Fairlanes, which featured vocalist Dan Penn. In 1959, Fame (Florence Alabama Music Enterprises) was launched. At first it was situated above a drugstore belonging to the father of a local songwriter, Tom Stafford. Word got around, and a group of aspiring local musicians (including **David Briggs**, **Norbert Putnam**, **Jerry Carrigan**, **Donnie Fritts**, Spooner Oldham, Roger Hawkins, David Hood, Jimmy Johnson and Penn) gravitated quickly to the studios.

In 1961, Hall had his first hit with 'You Better Move On' by soul singer Arthur Alexander. He set up the Fame studios in new premises in neighbouring Muscle Shoals with the accompanying royalties, and he assembled the first of several versions of the house band from his assortment of inexperienced musicians. He was also the catalyst for the songwriting partnerships Penn formed with Fritts and Oldham.

In 1964, following the departure of the nucleus of the first house band - Briggs, Carrigan and Putnam - for Nashville, Hall put in place Mark 2; it consisted of Roger Hawkins (drums), Jimmy Johnson (guitar), Junior Lowe (bass) and Spooner Oldham (keyboards). Lowe was replaced by bassist Tommy Cogbill in 1967 and then by David Hood, but it was the early combination that put Muscle Shoals on the international map. Over the next four years a steady stream of artists and producers came to Hall's front door: Aretha Franklin and Wilson Pickett with Jerry Wexler and Tom Dowd; Joe Tex with **Buddy Killen**, among others; as well as artists that Hall was producing himself, such as Clarence Carter and Etta James.

In 1969, Johnson, Hood, Hawkins and **Barry Beckett** left Fame to set up their own operation, Muscle Shoals Sound Studios in Sheffield (Beckett had been Spooner Oldham's replacement when he joined Dan Penn at **Chips Moman**'s American studios). After their departure, Junior Lowe moved back into the frontline, supplemented by Travis Wammack (guitar), Freeman Brown (drums), Jesse Boyce (bass) and Clayton Ivey (keyboards). Hall, however, had begun to devote more and more of his energy to recording pop and country music by artists like **Mac Davis**, **Tom Jones**, **Bobbie Gentry**, the Osmonds and Paul Anka. In 1974 he closed the Fame label for good, and by the end of the 1970s, Hall had reverted to production and was concentrating upon his publishing interests. Among those to benefit from his experience were **Dobie Gray**, **T.G. Sheppard** and **Shenandoah**.

HALL, Roy

Alcohol consumption has always been a source of inspiration to country artists. For some performers it has become an integral part of their modus operandi: Roy Hall is one.

He was born James Faye 'Roy' Hall on May 7, 1922, in Big Stone Gap, Virginia, in the foothills of the Appalachians. By the age of twenty he had mastered the piano, and was an accomplished player of a hybrid of hillbilly and boogie-woogie. After leaving home in 1949, he put together his own band, the Cohutta Mountain Boys. Touring the South and the Midwest, they cut their first sides for the Fortune label. While songs like 'Never Marry A Tennessee Girl' were pretty standard hillbilly fare, other titles (such as 'Dirty Boogie') were crude rockers, which gave full vent to Hall's barroom piano technique.

The following year he headed for Nashville and cut a couple of records for the Bullet label; more significantly, though, he opened his own bar and gambling den, which were to become the sanctuary for many of Nashville's finest artists. One such artist was **Webb Pierce**, who hired Hall to be his pianist and managed to get him signed to Decca in 1955. Showing that he was a rock 'n' roller at heart, Hall cut 'Whole Lotta Shakin' Goin' On' (written under the pseudonym of Sunny David) which became a big hit only later when recorded by **Jerry Lee Lewis**. Hall remained with Pierce for over six years, and then went on to play the Nashville club circuit, until his death on March 2, 1984.

BOOGIE ROCKABILLY, Rock & Country, 1988
DIGGIN' THE BOOGIE, Charly, 1984
HANK 'N' THE HOUND, Rock & Country, 1988

HALL, Tom T.

Tom T. Hall's two superlative albums, *In Search Of A Song* (1971) and *The Storyteller* (1973), contain some of the best examples of narrative songs. His songs reflect the day-to-day trials and tribulations of life in small close-knit communities, where the tiniest occurrence assumes disproportionate significance. No other writer is as perceptive in his analysis of the 'small-town mentality'.

Born in Olive Hill, Kentucky, on May 25, 1936, he began his career first as a bluegrass musician and

then as a DJ; he started writing songs during his conscription in the 1950s. He began civilian life writing advertising copy, before moving on to Nashville, where **Jimmy 'C' Newman** turned his song 'DJ For A Day' into a hit. Over the next four years, he wrote songs for **George Jones**, **Bobby Bare** and **Dave Dudley**, and wrote a massive hit, 'Harper Valley P.T.A.', for **Jeannie C. Riley.**

With Riley's hit behind him, he was signed by producer **Jerry Kennedy** to Mercury, and scored his own first hit with 'Ballad Of Forty Dollars'; this was followed by 'A Week In A Country Jail' (C&W#1, 1970), 'Shoeshine Man' (C&W#8, 1970), 'Salute To A Switchblade' (C&W#8, 1971), 'The Year That Clayton Delaney Died' (C&W#1, 1971), '(Old Dogs, Children And) Watermelon Wine' (C&W#1, 1972), 'I Love' (C&W#1, 1972), 'That Song Is Driving Me Crazy' (C&W#2, 1974), 'Country Is' (C&W#1, 1974), 'Sneaky Snake' (C&W#1, 1975), 'Faster Horses (The Cowboy And The Poet)' (C&W#1, 1976), 'Fox On The Run' and 'Your Man Loves You, Honey'.

Hall moved to RCA in 1977, but only managed a couple of hits with 'What Have You Got To Lose' and 'The Old Side Of Town'. In 1984 he returned to Mercury and scored with 'P.S. I Love You' (C&W#8, 1984). With the passage of time, his recording and touring commitments have given way to other interests: he has written books (*How I Write The Songs*, *The Storyteller's Nashville*, *The Laughing Man Of Woodmont Cove* and *Christmas In The Old House*) and presented the television show *Pop Goes Country*.

GREATEST HITS, Volumes 1-3, Mercury (US), 1983
IN CONCERT, RCA (US), 1986
NATURAL DREAMS, Mercury (US), 1984
NEW TRAIN, SAME RIDER, RCA (US), 1979
PLACES I'VE DONE TIME, RCA (US), 1979
SOLDIER OF FORTUNE, RCA (US), 1980
STORYTELLER AND THE BANJO MAN (with Earl Scruggs), Columbia, 1982
WORLD CLASS COUNTRY, Range, 1985

HALL, Wendell

Wendell Hall was born in St George, Kansas, on August 23, 1896. After attending the University of Chicago, he was conscripted for military service during the First World War. At the end of hostilities, he took to the vaudeville circuit playing the ukelele, and scored a massive hit with 'It Ain't Gonna Rain No Mo''. This encouraged labels like Edison, Gennett and Victor - and later, WLS, Chicago - to record some of his songs. He then went on to cut some duets with **Carson Robison**, including 'Whistling The Blues Away' and 'I'm Telling The Birds, I'm Telling The Bees (How I Love You)'. During the 1930s, he directed a number of radio shows (including *Gillette's Community Sing*, with comedian Milton Berle), before retiring from the music business to take up a position with an advertising agency. He died on April 2, 1969.

HAMBLEN, Stuart

Stuart Hamblen was born in Kellyville, Texas, on October 20, 1908. After graduating from the McMurray Teachers' College in Abilene in the 1920s, he moved to Hollywood (where he started to get bit-parts in Westerns) and built a radio career singing (and writing) cowboy songs, including 'My Mary', 'My Brown-Eyed Texas Rose', 'But I'll Go Chasin' Women' and '(Remember Me) I'm The One Who Loves You'. A man with an almost unbridled capacity for self-promotion, Hamblen was also instrumental in launching the careers of other artists, including **Patsy Montana**.

In 1952 he ran for the Presidency on a prohibition ticket - an attempt which failed, as had his earlier candidacy for Congress. In 1954 he penned 'This Ole House' (US#26, C&W#2, 1954), which later became a monster hit for Rosemary Clooney. With the passage of time he turned increasingly to God, composing a multitude of non-secular items that sold by the truck-load. He died on March 8, 1989, of a brain tumour.

HAMILTON IV, George

While George Hamilton IV has for many years been accorded a limited celebrity status in the US, he has achieved greater stardom overseas, through a relentless touring schedule that has even included Russia. He was born on July 19, 1937, in Matthews, North Carolina, and raised in Winston Salem, North Carolina. He was inspired by the movies of **Tex Ritter**, **Roy Rogers** and **Gene Autry** to take up the guitar, buying his first one at the age of twelve. An avid follower of the *Grand Ole Opry*, he formed a group at school in Winston, and cut a demo of the **Little Jimmy Dickens** song 'Out Behind The Barn', which enabled him to win a slot on *Arthur Godfrey's Talent Scouts*.

Over the next few years he scored a number of hits for ABC-Paramount, starting with 'A Rose And A Babe Ruth' (US#6, 1956), which initially tagged him with the label of 'teen idol' and consigned him to a series of package tours with **Buddy Holly**, the **Everly Brothers**, Gene Vincent and Bobby Vee. He was quick to rectify the situation by cutting titles like 'Why Don't They Understand' (US#10, 1957; UK#22, 1958), 'Only One Love' (US#33, 1957), 'Now And For Always' (US#25, 1958) and 'I Know Where I'm Going' (US#23, 1958).

After signing to RCA, the hits continued with 'Abilene' (US#15, C&W#1, 1963), 'Steel Rail Blues' and 'Early Morning Rain'. While his style had become more folk-oriented, he still played the country circuit and appeared on television and radio throughout the world. Such was his success that he secured a regular television series with the BBC and has become a regular visitor to the Country Music Festival in London.

In recent years he has embraced Christianity and cut albums of religious material. He returned to the secular with *American Country Gothic* (1989), which was produced by **Chet Atkins** and included a brace of songs written by **John D. Loudermilk**.

AMERICAN COUNTRY GOTHIC, Conifer, 1989
BEST OF GEORGE HAMILTON IV, RCA, 1974
BLUEGRASS GOSPEL, Word, 1982
CUTTING ACROSS THE COUNTRY, RCA, 1981
FAMOUS COUNTRY MUSIC MAKERS, RCA, 1979
HYMNS COUNTRY STYLE, Word, 1985
MUSIC MAN'S DREAMS, Range, 1984

HANCOCK, Butch

Butch Hancock was one of the key members of the Texas New Country artists, emerging in the early 1970s as a member of **Joe Ely**'s influential band, the Flatlanders. Born George Hancock on July 12, 1945, in Lubbock, Texas, he dropped out of architectural studies to work on his father's farm. By 1970 he had started to write songs (inspired by **Bob Dylan** and Peter, Paul & Mary), and joined the Flatlanders. The group was signed to **Shelby Singleton**'s Plantation label and cut *One More Road*. In 1973 - Ely having left the band for a solo career - Hancock moved to Clarendon, Texas, and took to writing songs in an old jailhouse.

He moved to Austin in 1975, formed his own label, Rainlight, and started to issue albums on a regular basis; these included *West Texas Waltzes And Dust-Blown Tractor Tunes* (1978), *The Wind's Dominion* (1979) and *Diamond Hill* (1980). Although he never had a regular band, he drew from a pool of Austin musicians, such as Ely and **Jimmie Dale Gilmore**. Between 1981 and 1985 he took a sabbatical from music and concentrated on painting.

In 1986 he returned to the music industry and

toured London with Wes McGhee. In 1990 he teamed up with Gilmore, cutting *Two Roads* for the Virgin label, which was recorded live while the two were touring Australia. Although he has never achieved much commercial success, his songs have been covered by McGhee, Ely, Gilmore, **Jerry Jeff Walker** and **Doug Sahm**, among others, and his unpretentious concerts are always excellent.

DIAMOND HILL, Rainlight (US), 1980
OWN & OWN, Demon, 1989
TWO ROADS (with Jimmie Dale Gilmore), Virgin, 1990
WEST TEXAS WALTZES AND DUST-BLOWN TRACTOR TUNES, Rainlight (US), 1978
THE WIND'S DOMINION, Rainlight (US), 1979
YELLOW ROSE, Rainlight (US), 1985

HARDEN, Arlene

During 1966, the Harden Trio - comprising Arlene (born on March 11, 1945) and brother Bobby and sister Robbie, from England, Arkansas - notched up a substantial hit with 'Tippy Toeing' (C&W#3, 1966), which stayed in the charts for almost six months. This proved to be their most significant contribution to country music, and secured them a membership of the *Grand Ole Opry* which lasted until 1968.

After a number of other inconsequential hits, including 'Seven Days Of Crying', 'Sneakin' Across The Border' and 'Everyone Wants To Be Someone Else', the trio split up and Arlene pursued a solo career with United Artists, having modest hits with 'He's A Good Ole Boy' (1968), 'Lovin' Man' (1970) and 'Married To A Memory' (1971). After moving to Capitol she cut *I Could Almost Say Goodbye* (1975), and gradually disappeared into the void of the Nashville circuit. Bobby Harden recorded for Columbia and United Artists.

HARDEN, Bobby   see HARDEN, Arlene

HARDEN TRIO   see HARDEN, Arlene

HARDIN, Glen D.

Glen D. Hardin (born on March 18, 1939) is a superior session pianist with impeccable credentials: the list of artists to benefit from his sterling work have included the Crickets (during the early 1960s) and **Elvis Presley** (from 1969 until his death in 1977), with whom Hardin both toured and recorded. From 1969 he struck up a partnership with guitarist **James Burton**, and the two of them formed the nucleus of **Gram Parsons**' band; after Parsons' death, they formed the nucleus of **Emmylou Harris**'s Hot Band. After leaving the Hot Band, Hardin returned, in the 1980s, to the less gruelling routine of session work.

HARGROVE, Linda

Little known beyond Nashville, Linda Hargrove, who was born - and raised - in Tallahassee, Florida in 1951, is one of country music's unrevealed talents. After learning the piano and the French horn she moved to Nashville in 1970, having subsequently taken up the guitar. While providing material for the **Sandy Posey** comeback album, she befriended **Pete Drake**, who offered her use of his studio in return for bits of general dogsbodying and session work.

Her first solo project was an album for **Mike Nesmith**'s Countryside label, but the label went bust before the album could be released. With her songs now being picked up by a multitude of artists (including **Leon Russell**, **Jan Howard**, **Melba Montgomery** and **Billie Jo Spears**), she secured a fresh deal with Elektra, cutting the striking *Music Is Your Mistress* (1972), before moving on to Capitol where she cut a number of albums, including *Just Like You* (1976).

A somewhat idiosyncratic female country performer, Hargrove has had to satisfy herself with ploughing a furrow somewhere between the country and folk audiences, where she has at least been able to confirm her excellence as a guitarist.

HARRELL, Kelly

One of **Ralph Peer**'s protégés, vocalist Kelly Harrell was born Crockett Kelly Harrell in Drapers Valley, Virginia, on September 13, 1899. Having learnt a vast number of traditional songs during his formative years, he travelled around Virginia singing at hoedowns and bars, accompanied by whoever happened to be around at the time. In 1927 he settled in Fieldale, Virginia, where he worked on the looms at the Fieldcrest Mill.

After meeting Peer in 1925, he started cutting sides for Victor, and by 1927, with a group comprising Posey Rorer (fiddle; see **Poole, Charlie**), R.D. Huntley (banjo) and Alfred Steagall (guitar), he recorded some of the finest ever examples of Virginian country music (an area in which the **Carter Family** excelled). Among the songs he recorded were 'I Wish I Was Single Again', 'The Butcher Boy', 'Nobody's Darlin' But Mine' and 'Chateau Giteau'. Before the Depression in 1929, he recorded some sides with **Henry Whitter** for the Okeh label and penned the **Jimmie Rodgers** classic 'Away Out On The Mountain' and **Ernest Stoneman**'s 'The Story Of The Mighty Mississippi'. As the Depression took hold he stopped performing professionally and continued working at the mill until his death from asthma on July 9, 1942.

HARRIS, Emmylou

Emmylou Harris has bridged the gap between rock and country without suffering too much from those purists on either side who accuse her of having 'sold out'. The purity of her soprano voice wins over even the staunchest critic.

She was born on April 2, 1947, in Birmingham, Alabama, and spent an erratic childhood moving from place to place with her father's army postings. After attending the University of North Carolina, she went to Washington, D.C., where she played in folk clubs, before moving to New York and hitting the folk-club circuit of Greenwich Village. Here she played with musicians such as **Jerry Jeff Walker** and cut her first album, *Gliding Bird* (1969), for the Jubilee label. The label closed down and she continued playing the club circuit, where she was rediscovered by **Gram Parsons**.

She featured prominently on Parsons' first two solo albums, *GP* and *Grievous Angel*, and became a member of his backing group, the Fallen Angel Band. When Parsons died in 1973, she took over the Fallen Angel Band and toured extensively, drawing her repertoire from country and pop writers, ancient and modern. In 1975 she cut her first album for Reprise, *Pieces Of The Sky*, which included the self-penned 'From Boulder To Birmingham' and the **Louvin Brothers**' 'If I Could Only Win Your Love' (C&W#4, 1975). It was followed by *Elite Hotel*, which included three Parsons compositions ('Sin City', 'Oooh Las Vegas' and 'Wheels') and **Buck Owens**' 'Together Again' (C&W#1, 1976) and 'Sweet Dreams' (C&W#1, 1976). She married her producer, Brian Ahern, the following year and remained with him until 1983.

Her group, now known as the Hot Band, comprised Byron Berline (fiddle; see **Country Gazette**), **James Burton** (guitar), **Glen D. Hardin** (piano), Hank DeVito (steel guitar), John Ware (drums) and Emory Gordy (bass). For Harris's next album, *Luxury Liner* (1977) - which included '(You Never Can Tell) C'est La Vie' and

'Making Believe' - Burton and **Bernie Leadon** were replaced by **Albert Lee** and **Rodney Crowell**, respectively. In 1978 Harris released *Quarter Moon In A Ten Cent Town*, which included **Delbert McClinton**'s 'Two More Bottles Of Wine' (C&W#1, 1978); and in 1979 *Blue Kentucky Girl* spawned a trio of hits: 'Save The Last Dance For Me' (C&W#4, 1979), 'Blue Kentucky Girl' (C&W#6, 1979) and 'Beneath Still Waters' (C&W#1, 1980).

In 1980 she released her most traditional album to date, *Roses In The Snow* (which featured **Ricky Skaggs**, **Tony Rice** and **Herb Pedersen** on songs like 'Wayfaring Stranger' and 'Miss The Mississippi And You'), and she duetted with **Roy Orbison** on 'That Lovin' You Again Feeling'. After *Cimarron* (1982), she cut the live *Last Date* album, which included '(Lost His Love) On Our Last Date' (C&W#1, 1982); this was followed by *White Shoes* (1983), featuring 'In My Dreams' and 'Pledging My Love'.

After cutting a concept album *The Ballad Of Sally Rose* (1985) with her new husband **Paul Kennerly**, she collaborated with **Dolly Parton** and **Linda Ronstadt** on *Trio* (1987), which featured revivals of 'To Know Him Is To Love Him' (C&W#1, 1987), 'Telling Me Lies', 'Those Memories Of You' and 'Wildflowers'. Another duet followed, this time with **Earl Thomas Conley**: 'We Believe In Happy Endings' (co-produced by **Randy Scruggs**; C&W#1, 1988).

While the hits have decreased in recent years, she regularly appears as a guest artist on other people's records and maintains her own rigorous recording and touring schedule.

THE BALLAD OF SALLY ROSE, Warner Bros., 1985
BLUE KENTUCKY GIRL, Warner Bros., 1979
BLUEBIRD, Reprise, 1989
BRAND NEW DANCE, Reprise, 1990
THE CHRISTMAS ALBUM, Warner Bros., 1979
CIMARRON, Warner Bros., 1982
DUETS, Warner Bros., 1990
ELITE HOTEL, Reprise, 1976
EMMYLOU HARRIS AND THE NASH RAMBLERS, Reprise, 1992
EVANGELINE, Warner Bros. (US), 1981
LAST DATE, Warner Bros., 1984
LUXURY LINER, Warner Bros., 1977
PIECES OF THE SKY, Reprise, 1975
PROFILE, Warner Bros., 1983
QUARTER MOON IN A TEN CENT TOWN, Warner Bros., 1978
ROSES IN THE SNOW, Warner Bros. (US), 1980
THIRTEEN, Warner Bros., 1987

TRIO (with Linda Ronstadt and Dolly Parton), Warner Bros., 1987

WHITE SHOES, Warner Bros., 1983

HART, Freddie

Born Freddie Segrest in Lochapka, Alabama, on December 21, 1928, he ran away from home and became a cotton picker, a sawmill worker, a pipeline layer and a dishwasher, before joining the Marines. He moved to Los Angeles in 1951, where he taught karate at the Police Academy.

In 1953 he met **Lefty Frizzell**, who appeared regularly on *Town Hall Party* on KFI, Compton. Frizzell sponsored Hart's (as he had now become) first broadcast. A contract with Capitol followed shortly after. Over the next ten years Hart recorded for a variety of labels, and had a few minor hits in 1959 with 'The Wall', 'Chain Gang' and 'The Key's In The Mailbox'.

After being re-signed by Capitol in 1969, he struck gold with 'Easy Loving' (US#17, C&W#1, 1971), which was the first of a series of hits in the early 1970s: 'My Hang-Up Is You' (C&W#1, 1972), 'Bless Your Heart' (C&W#1, 1972), 'Got The All Overs For You' (C&W#1, 1972), 'Super Kind Of Woman' (C&W#1, 1973), 'Trip To Heaven' (C&W#1, 1973), 'If You Can't Feel It (It Ain't There)', 'The Want To's', 'My Woman's Man', 'Hang In There Girl' (C&W#2, 1974), 'The First Time' (C&W#1, 1975) and 'When Lovers Turn To Strangers'.

At the end of 1979 he moved from Capitol to the independent Sunbird label, and had a minor hit with 'Sure Thing'. Recent investments (in a trucking company, bull breeding and acres of plum trees!) have meant that Freddie Hart has reduced his recording commitments. His touring schedule (backed by his group, the Heartbeats) is still intensive, and he regularly appears at the *Grand Ole Opry*.

MY LADY, Capitol (US), 1979

HARTFORD, John

A songwriter, fiddler, banjoist and guitarist, John Hartford defies categorization. He was born John Harford on December 30, 1937, in New York, but was raised in St Louis, where he became besotted with bluegrass and steamboats. He had mastered the banjo and the fiddle by the time he was thirteen, and performed regularly at square dances; he developed his talents by learning dobro and guitar. After leaving school he worked as a commercial artist, a deckhand on a Mississippi riverboat and a DJ. In 1965 he

married and moved to Nashville, where he became a session musician and was signed to RCA (who added the 't' to his name).

His first recordings for RCA included 'Gentle On My Mind', which was turned into a multi-million seller by **Glen Campbell** and then Dean Martin. This success guaranteed him a certain amount of autonomy, and his work became more eccentric (although he now appeared frequently on *The Glen Campbell Goodtime Hour*). He left RCA for Warner Bros. in 1970, and cut *Aero-Plain*, which had strong bluegrass influences and included 'They're Gonna Tear Down The Grand Ole Opry'. In 1972, disenchanted by the commercial process, he retired to his boat to paint.

After four years in retirement, he signed with the independent Flying Fish label and recorded with **Tut Taylor**, **Vassar Clements** and **Norman Blake**; other collaborations included a stint with the **Dillards**, which emphasized his commitment to traditional music. His live performances harked back to his youth by including square dances. After years of playing the folk circuits, he returned to the mainstream by signing with a major label, MCA, and cutting the album *Annual Waltz* with his own string-band backing group. He appears at bluegrass festivals to this day.

ALL IN THE NAME OF LOVE, Flying Fish (US), 1989
ANNUAL WALTZ, MCA (US), 1987
DOWN ON THE RIVER, Flying Fish (US), 1988
GUM TREE CANOE, Sundown, 1987
JOHN HARTFORD, MCA (US), 1988
MARK TWANG, Flying Fish (US), 1989
ME OH MY, HOW TIME DOES FLY, Flying Fish (US), 1989
MYSTERY BELOW, Flying Fish (US), 1989
NOBODY KNOWS WHAT YOU DO, Flying Fish (US), 1989
SLEEPIN' ON THE CUMBERLAND, Flying Fish (US), 1979
YOU AND ME AT HOME, Flying Fish (US), 1989

HARVEY, Alex

Alex Harvey was born in Brownsville, Tennessee, in 1945. He obtained a degree in music from Murray State University in Kentucky, and became conductor of the university's symphony orchestra. During the mid-1960s he moved to Nashville, where he established himself as a songwriter - penning titles like 'Molly' for **Jim Glaser** and 'Reuben James' for **Kenny Rogers** - and landed the television series *Fun Farm*.

He moved to Hollywood in 1970, where he wrote 'Delta Dawn' for Helen Reddy and 'Rings' for **Tompall and the Glaser Brothers**. In 1972 Kenny Rogers cut *Ballad Of Calico*, which was devoted to compositions by Harvey. Although he has recorded under his own name for Capitol and Kama Sutra, among others, his compositions have been more successful when covered by other artists, such as **David Houston** and **Tanya Tucker**. In recent years he has written with **T. Graham Brown**, one of their most successful joint ventures being 'Hell And High Water' in 1986.

HARVEY, Roy see POOLE, Charlie

HAWKINS, Hawkshaw

Prior to his untimely death in 1963, it looked as if Hawkshaw Hawkins was going to become one of the few honky-tonk singers able to move from the esoteric backwaters of hillbilly music to the mainstream. He was born Harold Franklin Hawkins on December 22, 1921, in Huntington, West Virginia. During his adolescence, he broadcast on WSAZ, Huntington, as a result of winning a talent contest. After the bombing of Pearl Harbor in 1942, he enlisted and was sent to the South Pacific. In 1946 he resumed his career, broadcasting on WWVA's *Wheeling Jamboree* and recording for the King label. After a number of hits, with 'Sunny Side Of The Mountain', 'I Wasted A Nickel' and 'Slow Poke', he was signed by RCA. In 1954, his matinee-idol good looks won him a slot on the ABC-TV *Ozark Jubilee*, which was followed by recruitment to the *Grand Ole Opry* in 1956. Over the next six years he enjoyed little success, apart from a minor hit with 'Soldier's Joy' for Columbia.

In 1962, following his marriage to **Jean Shepard**, he cut the **Justin Tubb** composition 'Lonesome 7-7203' (C&W#1, 1963). On March 5, 1963, Hawkins died in the same aeroplane crash that claimed the lives of **Patsy Cline** and **Cowboy Copas.**

HAWKSHAW HAWKINS, Sing, 1988
HAWKSHAW HAWKINS SINGS, Stetson, 1989
NOT FORGOTTEN (with Cowboy Copas and Patsy Cline), Starday (US), 1987
SIXTEEN GREATEST HITS, Starday (US), 1987

HAY, George D.

'The Solemn Old Judge' (as he came to be known) was the single most influential factor in the establishment of the *Grand Ole Opry*. These broadcasts, over Nashville's WSM, were of such significance that a venue called the Grand Ole Opry was established; it was this venue which gave country music its popular focus.

George Dewey Hay was born in Attica, Indiana, on November 9, 1895. After the end of the First World War, he became a reporter on the *Memphis Commercial Appeal* and started going to the occasional hoedown. In 1924 the newspaper diversified into radio, setting up WMC, for whom Hay became a radio editor. He then moved on to WLS, Chicago, as an announcer; here he pioneered the *National Barn Dance* in 1925, which led to his appointment as programme director for WSM in Nashville.

Inevitably, he set up the *WSM Barn Dance* which, on December 10, 1927, was renamed the *Grand Ole Opry*: the *Opry* has since become the longest-running show in broadcasting history. He remained with WSM until his retirement in 1951, during which time he diversified the programme's itinerary to include regular live events. On his retirement he went to live with his daughter at Virginia Beach, Virginia, where he died on May 9, 1968. He was elected to the Country Music Hall Of Fame in 1966.

HAYNES, Henry see HOMER & JETHRO

HEAD, Roy

Roy Head's flirtation with stardom lasted for approximately six months in 1965, when he was widely touted as being the definitive 'blue-eyed soul boy'. Born in Texas on January 9, 1943, he started his career as a vocalist in the Traits, who were discovered by **Huey Meaux**. At Meaux's instigation, Head left the Traits and embarked upon a solo career, recording the singles 'Treat Her Right' (USA#2, UK#30, 1965) and 'Apple Of My Eye' (USA#32, 1965) for Don Robey's Back Beat label; both were produced by Meaux. After recording briefly for Scepter, cutting 'Just A Little Bit' (USA#39, 1965), he returned to playing the club circuit to fans of his energetic live act.

By the end of the decade - and after a brief spell with Steve Cropper's (formerly of Booker T and the MGs) production company, TMI - he stopped singing soul and began singing country. Based once again in Texas, he joined forces with Meaux and recorded for Dot and Elektra; his biggest country hit to date has been 'Come To Me' (1977).

ROY HEAD AND THE TRAITS, TNT, 1987

HEBB, Bobby

Bobby Hebb was born in Nashville on July 26, 1941. His career started in 1953, when he was recruited by **Chet Atkins** to play the spoons for **Roy Acuff**'s Smoky Mountain Boys, thereby becoming one of the first black artists to appear on the *Grand Ole Opry*. In 1955, DJ John Richbourg signed him to his Rich label and he cut 'Night Train To Memphis'. He continued to play in and around Nashville until 1961, when he teamed up with Sylvia Shemwell and recorded as Bobby & Sylvia until 1963.

In 1966, after signing with Philips, he had a massive hit with 'Sunny' (US#2, UK#12, 1966); it wasn't a particularly distinguished song, but has become a standard of sorts, being a particular favourite of cabaret artists. It was followed by his version of the **Porter Wagoner** composition 'A Satisfied Mind' (US#39, 1966), which, though it failed to match the success of its predecessor, showed quite clearly that Hebb's real métier was country.

In the early 1970s, having concentrated upon country-ish material, he scored again with 'Love Love Love' (UK#32, 1972). Recent years have seen him coursing towards middle of the road, where he has attained a soulfulness comparable to that of **Charley Pride**.

HELM, Levon see BAND, The

HELMS, Bobby

Bobby Helms was born on August 15, 1935, in Bloomington, Indiana; he made his radio debut when he was thirteen, and made his first broadcast on the *Grand Ole Opry* four years later. In 1957, having been signed to Decca and to the music publishers **Acuff-Rose**, he scored with 'Fraulein' (US#36, C&W#1, 1957); it was followed by a cover of the **Johnny Duncan** composition 'My Special Angel' (US#7, UK#22, 1957), the appalling 'Jingle Bell Rock' (US#6, 1957), 'No Other Baby' (UK#30, 1958), 'Jacqueline' (UK#20, 1958) and 'Just A Little Lonesome'.

The hits had stopped rolling in by the end of the 1950s (apart from the seasonal disinterment of 'Jingle Bell Rock'), and Helms slipped into obscurity, re-emerging periodically to record for independent labels, such as Little Darlin' and Certron.

MY SPECIAL ANGEL, President, 1988

HIATT, John

Ever since his emergence in the early 1970s, John Hiatt has been one of a handful of writers who can turn their hands effectively to any style of music. The result is an authentic hybrid, and not a pastiche. Born in 1952 in Indianapolis, Indiana, he moved to Nashville at the end of the 1960s to work for a music publishing company as a staff writer. One of his first successful songs was 'Heavy Tears', which was covered by **Conway Twitty**. This gave him the impetus to cut two albums, *Hangin' Around The Observatory* (1974) and *Overcoats* (1975), with producer **Norbert Putnam**. Although neither fared well commercially, they established him as an artist of great promise.

After touring with his own band, he signed to MCA in 1978 and cut the critically acclaimed *Slug Line* (1979) and *Two Bit Monsters* (1980). Both generated sufficient interest for other artists, such as Dave Edmunds, Nick Lowe, **Ry Cooder** and **Rick Nelson**, to start covering his songs. Furthermore, he was enlisted to contribute to the soundtracks of the movies *American Gigolo* (1980) and *Cruising* (1980). In 1980 he joined Ry Cooder's band, with whom he co-wrote the score to the movie *The Border*. His next album, *All Of A Sudden* (produced by Tony Visconti and featuring contributions from David Bowie; 1982), was cut in London for the Geffen label.

Throughout the 1980s he cut albums at regular intervals, interspersed by stints touring as sideman with artists such as **Buffy Sainte-Marie** and T-Bone Burnett. In 1987, guitarist Cooder, bassist Lowe and drummer Jim Keltner played on his *Bring The Family* album, and the seeds were sown for the four of them to work together on a more regular basis. In 1991 this came to fruition with the formation of Little Village whose debut album emerged the following year to be followed by a tour of Europe and the US.

BRING THE FAMILY, Demon, 1987
LITTLE VILLAGE, Reprise, 1991
SLUG LINE, MCA, 1979
TWO BIT MONSTERS, MCA, 1980

HIGHWAY 101

Highway 101 was the brainchild of the **Nitty Gritty Dirt Band**'s manager, Chuck Morris, who decided that a country band fronted by a woman would be commercially successful. The woman in question was Paulette Carlson from Minnesota, who, in conjunction with Jack Daniels (guitar), Curtis Stone (bass) and Cactus Moser (drums), formed the group in 1986.

Carlson's career had started in 1983 with a contract with RCA, but her producer Paul Worley introduced her to Morris, who set the wheels in motion for the group.

With Worley producing and songwriters like John Scott Sherrill, **Rodney Crowell** and **Harlan Howard** composing the songs, the group started off with a string of hits that included 'The Bed You Made For Me' (C&W#4, 1987), 'Whisky, If You Were A Woman' (C&W#2, 1987), 'Somewhere Tonight' (C&W#1, 1987), 'Cry Cry Cry' (C&W#1, 1988) and '(Do You Love Me) Just Say Yes' (C&W#1, 1988). In common with so many country outfits, Highway 101 have not managed to break out beyond the US.

HIGHWAYMEN see CASH, Johnny

HILL, Goldie

Goldie Hill was born on January 11, 1933, in Karnes County, Texas, and began her recording career with Decca. Assisted by broadcasts on the *Louisiana Hayride*, she joined the *Grand Ole Opry* in 1953, after having a hit with 'Don't Let The Stars Get In Your Eyes'. After taking to the club circuit, she toured extensively with **Carl Smith**, whom she married in 1957. Although thought by many to be a serious contender for **Kitty Wells**' title of Queen of Country, Hill moved into semi-retirement after her marriage, and has only had occasional hits since, including 'Yankee Go Home' (1959) and 'Loveable Fool' (1968).

HILLMAN, Chris

Chris Hillman (born on December 4, 1942, in Los Angeles) has for over twenty-five years been one of the most significant contributors to the country-rock movement. In the early 1960s, having mastered the guitar, mandolin and bass, he formed his first group, the Scottsville Squirrel Barkers, and then a bluegrass outfit called the Hillmen with Don Parmley and Rex and **Vern Gosdin**. In 1964 he joined the Beefeaters, who were later to become the **Byrds**. By 1969, having helped to forge the development of country-rock, he left the Byrds, along with **Gram Parsons**, to form the influential **Flying Burrito Brothers**, with whom he remained until 1973.

His next stop was Stephen Stills' Manassas, with whom he stayed until 1974, when he formed the Souther, Hillman, Furay Band. This band, comprising Hillman, songwriter J.D. Souther and former **Poco** gui-

tarist Richie Furay, were a pale imitation of the **Eagles**, with whom they shared a label, Asylum, and a manager, Irving Azoff. After two albums, *The Souther, Hillman, Furay Band* (1974) and *Trouble In Paradise* (1975), and one modest hit ('Fallin' In Love'; UK#27, 1974), the group disbanded.

Hillman then launched a solo career, cutting a brace of competent solo albums, *Slippin' Away* (1976) and *Clear Sailing* (1977). In 1978 he got back together with Roger McGuinn (see **Byrds**) and **Gene Clark**, recording *McGuinn, Hillman And Clark* (1979) and *City* (1980) for the Capitol label. Clark then left to resume his solo career, leaving McGuinn and Hillman to record another album at the end of 1980. Over the next few years he linked up with Rex and Vern Gosdin again for a traditional bluegrass album, *The Hillmen*, for the Sugar Hill label, before cutting two more solo albums, *Morning Sky* (1982) and *Desert Rose* (1984).

Hillman's next venture came about when working as a session musician for Dan Fogelberg. It was 1985, and Fogelberg was about to tour; Hillman was asked to put together an acoustic band to open the performances - this band was to form the nucleus of the Desert Rose Band. Initially comprising Hillman (guitar, mandolin and vocals), **Herb Pedersen** (guitar), John Jorgenson (guitar) and Bill Bryson (bass), the group was augmented by Jay Dee Maness (steel guitar) and Steve Duncan (drums) after the tour. They began to play club dates in and around Los Angeles and were signed to the Curb label, cutting *Desert Rose Band* (1988).

Hillman was to enjoy more commercial success with this group than he had had since the early days of the Byrds - a string of hit singles soon followed: 'Love Reunited' (C&W#6, 1987), 'One Step Forward' (C&W#2, 1987), 'He's Black And I'm Blue' (C&W#1, 1988), 'Summer Wind' (C&W#2, 1988), 'I Still Believe In You' (C&W#1, 1989) and 'She Don't Love Nobody' (C&W#3, 1989). The group have become one of the most entertaining and authentic of all the West Coast country outfits, and it is gratifying to see that Hillman's patience has at last been rewarded with a measure of commercial acceptance.

CLEAR SAILING, Asylum, 1977
DESERT ROSE, Sundown, 1984
DESERT ROSE BAND, MCA (US), 1988
MORNING SKY, Sundown, 1982
MORNING STAR, Sugar Hill (US), 1981

HOLLY, Buddy

Buddy Holly died over thirty years ago: he has become a role model for more groups than one could possibly mention. Buddy Holly and the Crickets were the first truly self-contained group: they wrote, they played all the instruments on their records and they performed live. Holly's compositional powers were intuitive, the trademark hiccups were spontaneous, and the instrumental prowess of the Crickets came from years of assimilating country music - an assimilation which was combined with a somewhat notional interpretation of rock 'n' roll.

Charles Hardin Holley (the 'e' was dropped when he signed his first recording contract) was born in Lubbock, Texas, on September 7, 1936. During his childhood he mastered the piano and the guitar, and listened to the blues, Country & Western and R&B; he later teamed up with a fellow schoolboy, Bob Montgomery, and broadcast over KDAV as Buddy & Bob, with **Sonny Curtis** in the line-up. In 1955 they got their first break by opening for **Elvis Presley** and **Ferlin Husky**, among others, and Holly was signed to Decca as a result.

In 1956 Holly travelled to Nashville and cut some sides with producer **Owen Bradley**; while these sides included an early version of 'That'll Be The Day', Bradley's slick approach did little for Holly, and he was dropped by Decca. After this setback, Holly formed a new band with Jerry Allison (drums), Niki Sullivan (guitar) and Joe Mauldin (bass), and went to Clovis, New Mexico, to cut some sides with producer **Norman Petty**, who had recently made his mark with 'Party Doll' for Buddy Knox.

Petty negotiated two separate deals: one for the Crickets (the name the group had settled upon during a recording session) with Brunswick, and another one for Holly with Coral. The sides Holly cut as a member of the Crickets included 'That'll Be The Day' (US#1, 1957), 'Oh, Boy!' (US#10, 1957), 'Maybe Baby' (US#17, 1958) and 'Think It Over' (US#27, 1958). His solo sides included 'Peggy Sue' (US#3, UK#6, 1957), 'Listen To Me' (UK#16, 1958), 'Rave On' (US#37, UK#5, 1958), 'Early In The Morning' (US#32, UK#17, 1958) and 'Heartbeat' (UK#30, 1959). Buddy Holly and the Crickets became regular members of the rock 'n' roll package tours that played throughout the US and the UK.

By October 1958, Holly and the Crickets had separated, with Holly (who had moved to New York) pursuing a solo career with a new group that included **Waylon Jennings** (bass), Carl Bunch (drums) and Tommy Allsup (guitar). In January 1959 they started a nationwide package tour, but midway through the tour, on February 2, after playing at the Surf Ballroom in Clear Lake, Iowa, the light aeroplane in which they were travelling crashed just minutes after take-off, killing Holly, the Big Bopper, Richie Valens and all the other passengers. Being the first internationally known rock 'n' roll star to be cut off in his prime, Holly's death caused a *frisson* of panic in the entertainment world, comparable to that of James Dean. In the wake of his death, tribute records started to emerge, culminating in Don McLean's 'American Pie' (1972).

Over the next five years, material culled from Holly's final recording sessions in New York, and unreleased material from the Petty sessions, gradually began to see the light of day. A string of posthumous hits followed, including: 'It Doesn't Matter Anymore' (US#13, UK#1, 1959), 'Midnight Shift' (UK#26, 1959), 'Peggy Sue Got Married' (UK#13, 1959), 'True Love Ways' (UK#25, 1960), 'Learnin' The Game' (UK#36, 1960), 'What To Do' (UK#34, 1961), 'Baby I Don't Care' (UK#12, 1961), 'Reminiscing' (UK#36, 1962), 'Brown-Eyed Handsome Man' (UK#3, 1963), 'Bo Diddley' (UK#4, 1963), 'Wishing' (UK#10, 1963), 'You've Got Love' (UK#40, 1964) and 'Love's Made A Fool Of You' (UK#39, 1964).

Buddy Holly continues to be big business: Paul McCartney has acquired the rights to his publishing catalogue; and the Crickets, having been a going concern ever since they separated from Holly back in 1958, are regularly featured on the international 'oldies' circuit. After the film biography, *The Buddy Holly Story* (1978), starring Gary Busey, the musical *Buddy* came to London's West End and is running to this day.

BUDDY HOLLY, MCA, 1986
BUDDY HOLLY AND THE CHIRPIN' CRICKETS, MCA, 1986
THE COMPLETE BUDDY HOLLY SET, MCA, 1989
FOR THE FIRST TIME ANYWHERE, MCA, 1983
FROM THE ORIGINAL MASTER TAPES, MCA, 1985
REMINISCING, Castle, 1963
WORDS OF LOVE, MCA, 1993

HOLLY, Doyle

Doyle Holly was born in Perkins, Oklahoma, on June 30, 1936. Having learnt to play the bass guitar, he formed a group with his brothers and started to play at rodeos and dances. By the age of thirteen he was working in the Kansas oilfields prior to joining the army in 1953. After being discharged in 1957 he returned to the oilfields, this time in Bakersfield, where he became an occasional member of Johnny Burnette's (see **Burnette, Dorsey**) group. This led to him joining **Buck Owens**' group, the Buckaroos, with whom he remained from 1963 until 1970, when he left to form the Vanishing Breed. During the early 1970s they had a couple of modest hits with 'Lila' and 'Queen Of The Silver Dollar', before returning to the comparative safety of the Bakersfield club circuit.

HOMER & JETHRO

Raised in Knoxville, Tennessee, Homer was born Henry D. Haynes on July 29, 1917, and Jethro was born Kenneth C. Burns on March 10, 1923. They made their debut on WNOX, Knoxville, and soon won a regular slot with their parodies on the *Renfro Valley Barn Dance*. They began as an instrumental duo, with Homer on guitar and Jethro on mandolin, but such was the biting wit of their comedy routines that their music took second place.

Both were conscripted when war broke out, but resumed their partnership in 1945 as regular members of the *National Barn Dance* on WLS. This led to a recording contract with RCA, where they had a number of hits over the next fifteen years: 'Baby It's Cold Outside' (with **June Carter**), 'That Hound Dog In The Window', 'Hernando's Hideaway', 'The Battle Of Kookamonga' (US#14, 1959) and 'I Want To Hold Your Hand'. While these hits were overt novelty items, they went on to demonstrate their instrumental ability as members of an occasional recording group known as the Nashville String Band, which teamed them with **Chet Atkins**. These recordings showed the complementary virtuosity of each performer, and displayed Jethro's exemplary jazz-influenced mandolin work. After Homer's death on August 7, 1971, Jethro continued to play right up to his own death from cancer on March 4, 1989.

ASSAULT THE ROCK 'N' ROLL ERA, Bear Family (Germany), 1989
BACK TO BACK (Jethro Burns and Tiny Moore), Kaleidoscope (US), 1979
BAREFOOT BALLADS, Stetson, 1988
JETHRO BURNS, Flying Fish (US), 1989
JETHRO LIVE, Flying Fish (US), 1989
NORMAN BLAKE AND JETHRO BURNS, Flying Fish (US), 1988
TEA FOR ONE (Jethro Burns), Kaleidoscope (US), 1988

HOOSIER HOT SHOTS

The Hoosier Hot Shots were a group of vaudevillians who used their hillbilly backgrounds to develop a combination of music and comedy. Comprising Gabe Ward (clarinet), Hezzie Triesch (whistle, drums and washboard), Kenny Triesch (banjo, tenor guitar and horn) and Frank Kettering (banjo, guitar, flute, bass and piano), they started as an instrumental combo, until their propensity for jollying along their act with zany humour became increasingly prominent. After joining the cast of the *National Barn Dance* in 1935 their popularity boomed and they took to the road as regular members of the *Barn Dance* roadshows. In spite of making recordings for Vocalion, it was the knockabout routines in their stage act that made them memorable. After the war, they all moved to the West Coast and made occasional film appearances.

HOPKINS, Doc

Doctor Howard Hopkins was born on January 26, 1899, in Harlan County, Kentucky. His guitar and mandolin work was to be inspirational for younger musicians, particularly **Karl & Harty**, who played with him in the Cumberland Ridge Runners (see **Lair, John**) from 1930 to 1936. After the Ridge Runners split up, Hopkins continued to perform on the *National Barn Dance* until 1949, singing traditional mountain ballads which would otherwise have been forgotten. Despite recording for ARC, Paramount and Decca, Hopkins remains little known, and much of his contribution to the preservation of traditional American music has been overshadowed by the commercial zeal of others, like Lair.

HORTON, Johnny

While Johnny Horton was best known for singing the theme songs to a number of movies (including *Sink The Bismarck* and *North To Alaska*) and 'historical saga songs', he was primarily a honky-tonk singer. Born on April 30, 1927, in Tyler, Texas, he attended college in Jacksonville and Kilgore, Texas, and then enrolled at the University of Seattle, prior to joining the fishing industry. Changing jobs, he started to perform as 'The Singing Fisherman', broadcasting regularly on KXLA, Pasadena's *Hometown Jamboree* and the *Louisiana Hayride*.

After recording for a number of labels, such as Dot, Mercury and Abbott, he was signed by Columbia and had a succession of hits that included 'Honky Tonk Man' (C&W#1, 1956), 'When It's Springtime In Alaska'

(C&W#1, 1959), 'Battle Of New Orleans' (a **Jimmie Driftwood** composition, also covered by Lonnie Donegan; US#1, UK#16, 1959), 'Johnny Reb', 'Sink The Bismarck' (US#3, 1960), 'North To Alaska' (US#4, 1960; UK#23, 1961), 'Sleepy Eyed John' and 'All Grown Up'. On November 5, 1960, he was killed in a car crash just outside Milano, Texas, en route to Nashville. His widow, Billie Jean, had previously been widowed by **Hank Williams**.

MORE SPECIALS, Stetson, 1987
ROCKIN' ROLLIN', Volumes 1-2, Bear Family (Germany), 1988

HOUSTON, David

Singer David Houston (a descendant of Robert E. Lee) was born in Shreveport, Louisiana, on December 9, 1938, and raised by his aunt in Bossier City. In 1950 he secured a guest spot on the *Louisiana Hayride*, which led to his permanent membership of the cast. After finishing his education at Centenary College in Shreveport, he consolidated his musical reputation through an uninterrupted touring schedule, whilst also starting work as an insurance underwriter.

After a short spell with Sun in 1957, he was signed by **Billy Sherrill** to Epic in 1963, a move which was to kick-start Sherrill's career as a writer and producer and provide Epic with its first major successes. The debut single, 'Mountain Of Love' (C&W#2, 1963), signalled the beginning of a string of successful releases: 'Livin' In A House Full Of Love' (C&W#3, 1967), 'Almost Persuaded' (US#24, C&W#1, 1966), 'With One Exception' (C&W#1, 1965), 'You Mean The World To Me' (C&W#1, 1967), 'My Elusive Dreams' (with **Tammy Wynette**; C&W#1, 1967), 'Have A Little Faith' (C&W#1, 1968), 'Already It's Heaven' (C&W#1, 1968), 'Baby, Baby (I Know You're A Lady)' (C&W#1, 1969), 'I Do My Singing At Home', 'After Closing Time' (with **Barbara Mandrell**; C&W#6, 1970), 'Wonders Of The Wine', 'A Woman Always Knows' (C&W#2, 1971), 'Nashville', 'Home Sweet Home', 'Soft Sweet And Warm', 'Good Things' (C&W#2, 1973), 'She's All Woman' and 'The Woman On My Mind'.

Towards the end of the 1970s, incapacitated by hearing difficulties and by cartilage problems in his knees and an elbow, Houston drastically curtailed his workload; he did, however, continue to make periodic appearances at the *Grand Ole Opry*, of which he had been a member since 1971, and had one minor hit, 'So Many Ways' (1977), for Starday.

BEST OF DAVID HOUSTON, First Base, 1985

HOWARD, Harlan

Harlan Howard is one of a fistful of songwriters who, while regarded principally as country writers, have also been successful in other genres. He was born in Lexington, Kentucky, on September 8, 1929, and was raised in Detroit, where he began writing songs at the age of twelve. After graduating from high school, he spent four years as a paratrooper, based at Fort Benning, Georgia. Upon leaving the army Howard moved to California, working as a bookbinder, until meeting **Johnny Bond**, who published and recorded his songs. His songs were consequently picked up by **Wynn Stewart**, **Kitty Wells**, **Guy Mitchell** and **Buck Owens**, with Owens cutting 'Above And Beyond', 'Excuse Me, I Think I've Got A Headache' (1960) and 'Foolin' Around' (1961).

Howard's first big hit, 'Pick Me Up On Your Way Down', was written for **Ray Price** but passed on to Price's protégé, **Charlie Walker** (Price himself recorded 'Heartaches By The Number' at a later date). After moving to Nashville in 1960, Howard started to churn out hits in quick succession, which included 'Three Steps To A Phone' for **George Hamilton IV** (1961), 'I Fall To Pieces' (co-written with **Hank Cochran**) for **Patsy Cline** (1961), 'Busted' for **Johnny Cash** and **Ray Charles** (1963) and 'Streets Of Baltimore' (co-written with Tompall Glaser; see **Tompall and the Glaser Brothers**) for **Bobby Bare** (1966).

Although his efforts today are centred on managing his extensive song copyrights, he still finds time to write, teaming up most recently with **Rodney Crowell** on 'Somewhere Tonight' for **Highway 101** (1987). He has also occasionally recorded his own songs, his most notable effort being *Down To Earth* (1968).

SINGS HARLAN HOWARD, Stetson, 1987

HOWARD, Jan

Despite being married to **Harlan Howard** (one of Nashville's most prolific songwriters) during the 1960s, Jan Howard's biggest successes were her duets with **Bill Anderson**, in which her easy vocal style was perfectly complemented by his warm baritone.

She was born on March 13, 1932, in West Plains, Missouri, to a Cherokee mother and an Irish father. After meeting **Johnny Cash** and **June Carter** in the late 1950s, she started a tour with **Johnny Horton**. In 1960 she cut 'Yankee Go Home' (with **Wynn Stewart**) for the Challenge label, later followed by 'The One You Slip Around With'.

By the mid-1960s she had moved to Nashville and teamed up with Anderson, becoming a regular member of his roadshow and television series; among the duets they recorded together were 'I Know You're Married' (1966), 'For Loving You' (C&W#1, 1967), 'If It's All The Same To You' (1969), 'Someday We'll Be Together' (1970) and 'Dissatisfied' (1971). She also issued a number of solo singles, including 'Evil On Your Mind' (C&W#5, 1966), 'Bad Seeds' (1966), 'Count Your Blessings, Woman' and 'My Son' (dedicated to her second son who died in the Vietnam War; 1968). In the early 1970s she retired from recording, and only performed as a member of the **Carter Family** entourage in their roadshow.

THE DOT SERIES, MCA, 1987

HOWARD, Paul

While **Spade Cooley** and **Bob Wills** represented the popular side of Western Swing, Paul Howard and his Arkansas Cotton Pickers were just as proficient, but never managed to achieve the same level of popularity.

Howard was born in Midland, Arkansas, on July 10, 1908. Having caught the Western Swing bug in the 1930s he joined the *Grand Ole Opry* as a vocalist, and there began to assemble his own backing band, the Arkansas Cotton Pickers, which had up to a dozen members. After recording for Columbia and King, he moved away from Nashville and the *Grand Ole Opry* (as Western Swing wasn't really appreciated in the southeast), and settled in Shreveport in 1949. From Shreveport, he travelled throughout the southwest with his band, playing radio stations and dancehalls. His records have been unavailable for some years

HUNTER, Ivory Joe

A fine R&B singer, Ivory Joe Hunter was one of the first black artists to acknowledge the strong influence of country music in his songs. He was born on October 10, 1914, and brought up in Kirbyville, Texas. During the 1930s he performed gospel in and around Texas, but by the 1940s had gravitated to the West Coast, where he put out records on his own Ivory label. In 1947 he signed to the King label (recording songs which included 'Jealous Heart'), but switched labels again in 1949, this time to MGM (the home of **Hank Williams**), where he stayed for the next five years, recording his own compositions such as 'I Almost Lost My Mind' and 'I Need You So'.

In 1954 Hunter signed with Atlantic, for whom he continued to write and record his own compositions, and scored with 'Since I Met You Baby' (USA#12, 1956), 'Empty Arms' and **Bill Anderson**'s 'City Lights'. Throughout the 1960s he continued to record for a series of labels: Capitol, Veejay, Stax, Goldwax, Sound Stage Seven and Epic. In 1970 he appeared with the Johnny Otis Show in Monterey (the concert was later issued as a double album), and in 1973 he released his final album, aptly entitled *I've Always Been Country*, which featured guitarists Reggie Young and Tommy Cogbill.

On November 8, 1974, he died of cancer, aged sixty. Held in high esteem by the country music establishment, a benefit concert (which featured **George Jones**, **Tammy Wynette** and Isaac Hayes) was held in his name at the *Grand Ole Opry* shortly before his death.

THE ARTISTRY OF IVORY JOE HUNTER, Bulldog, 1982
THE HITS, Official, 1988
77th STREET BOOGIE, Route 66, 1980
SIXTEEN ALL-TIME HITS, King, 1989
THIS IS IVORY JOE, Ace, 1984

HUSKY, Ferlin

Ferlin Husky was one of country's more curious performers, moving between his rustic, vaguely humourous alter-ego 'Simon Crum' and the lugubrious country-pop of 'Gone'.

He was born in Flat River, Missouri, on December 3, 1927. After a spell in the merchant navy he became a DJ in St Louis, before moving to Bakersfield, where he was discovered by **Tennessee Ernie Ford**'s manager, **Cliffie Stone**, who signed him to the Capitol label. Adopting the pseudonym of Terry Preston (which he later dropped), and creating his comic character, Simon Crum, he started to play throughout California, appearing on the *Hometown Jamboree* in Los Angeles.

In 1953 he was teamed with **Jean Shepard** for two duets inspired by the war effort in Southeast Asia: 'Dear John Letter' (US#4, 1953) and 'Forgive Me John'. Other hits followed with 'I Feel Better All Over', 'Gone' (US#4, 1957) and, as Simon Crum, 'Country Music Is Here To Stay' (C&W#2, 1958). In 1958 he appeared in the movie *Country Music Holiday* with **Faron Young** and Zsa Zsa Gabor, as well as being a regular guest on television series like *Kraft TV Theatre*, *The Steve Allen Show* and *The Ed Sullivan Show*. In 1960 he cut a strange version of the gospel standard

'On The Wings Of A Dove' (US#12, 1960), and had other hits with 'A Fallen Star', 'The Waltz You Saved For Me', 'Once' and 'Just For You'.

After leaving Capitol in 1973, he moved to ABC (latterly MCA) and toured frequently with his backing band, the Hush Puppies. From 1977, after suffering a stroke, he cut back his performances.

DOT SERIES, MCA, 1987

FAVORITES OF FERLIN HUSKY, Starday (US), 1987

FERLIN HUSKY, Capitol, 1989

JACKSON, Alan

Although **Garth Brooks** and **Clint Black** have managed to attract a large international audience, Alan Jackson has been one of their closest rivals in the US. He was born in Newman, Atlanta, in 1960, where his father was a mechanic. By the time he was twelve he had got his first job and had married by the age of twenty. Over the next few years he did a variety of jobs, until finally deciding to make the move to Nashville to try to break into the music business. His big break came when his wife, Denise, who was working as an airline stewardess, met **Glen Campbell** and told him of her husband's plans to move to Nashville. Campbell gave her his business card and told her to get in touch.

Through this contact with Campbell, Jackson eventually got a publishing contract and a recording deal with Arista. His debut, *Here In The Real World*, was released in 1990 and was an immediate success, yielding hits like 'Here In The Real World' (C&W#3, 1990), 'Wanted' (C&W#3, 1990), 'Chasin' That Neon Rainbow' (C&W#2, 1990) and 'I'd Love You All Over Again' (C&W#1, 1990). The follow-up, *Don't Rock The Jukebox* (1991), was equally successful and included hits such as 'Don't Rock The Jukebox' (C&W#2, 1991), 'Dallas' (C&W#1, 1992) and 'Midnight In Montgomery' (C&W#3, 1992).This was followed by *A Lot About Livin'*, which included 'Love's Got A Hold On You' (C&W#1, 1992) and 'She's Got The Rhythm' (C&W#1, 1992).

His songs, while paying lip-service to traditional country styles such as honky-tonk, avoid the cloying sentimentality evident in so much of country music, and it can only be a matter of time before he achieves international recognition.

A LOT ABOUT LIVIN', Arista (US), 1992
DON'T ROCK THE JUKEBOX, Arista, 1991
HERE IN THE REAL WORLD, Arista, 1990

JACKSON, Aunt Molly

Born Mary Magdalene Garland in 1880 in Clay County, Kentucky, Aunt Molly Jackson's life was beset by abject poverty and tragedy: her mother died of starvation, her brother, husband and son all died in mining accidents, while her father and another brother were both blinded in further colliery incidents. It comes as no surprise, then, that throughout most of her working life she put everything she had into fighting the venal system that permitted such horrors. She was jailed regularly, eventually culminating in her being barred from all the collieries in Kentucky.

In 1936 she moved to New York and organized union activities, singing on picket lines and at demonstrations. To this day little recorded material remains, apart from 'Kentucky Miner's Wife' on Columbia and material cut for the Library of Congress, both of which illustrate the hardships of rural life: they are protest songs far removed from the glamour of Nashville. She died on September 1, 1960.

JACKSON, Carl

One of the most impressive of the new generation of bluegrass musicians, Carl Jackson's banjo-pickin' has made him a highly sought-after session musician, and a regular member of the **Glen Campbell** roadshow.

Born in 1953, in Louisville, Mississippi, he was taught to play the banjo when he was five and joined a bluegrass band that included his uncle and father. While at school he was recruited by **Jim & Jesse** as a member of their touring band and, having left school, cut his first solo album, *Bluegrass Festival* (1970), for the independent Prize label.

In 1972 he met Larry McNeely, Campbell's banjo player, who was on the verge of leaving the group, and was immediately recruited as his replacement. The following year he was signed by Capitol and cut his debut, *Banjo Player* (1973). Since that time he has continued to do session work (for artists including **Merle Haggard** and **Buck Owens**) and work for Campbell, whilst also pursuing a solo career and releasing *Banjo Man: A Tribute To Earl Scruggs* (see **Flatt & Scruggs**) and *Song Of The South*, which included contributions from **Emmylou Harris** and Jesse McReynolds (see **Jim & Jesse**).

BANJO HITS, Sugar Hill (US), 1989
BANJO MAN: A Tribute To Earl Scruggs, Sugar Hill (US), 1980
SONG OF THE SOUTH, Sugar Hill (US), 1981

JACKSON, Stonewall

Named after the Confederate general, Stonewall Jackson has lived up to his namesake by espousing an extremely virulent republicanism. He was born in Tabor City, North Carolina, on November 6, 1932, and had learnt to play the guitar by the age of ten. After finishing his schooling he joined the navy, serving in submarines.

In 1956 he went to Nashville, and **Wesley Rose** (of Acuff-Rose) signed him to a publishing contract, which enabled him to secure a recording contract with Columbia. His first country hit, 'Life To Go' (1958), was followed by the international pop hit 'Waterloo' (nothing to do with the Abba song; US#4, C&W#1, UK#24, 1959); this opened the door to membership of the *Grand Ole Opry* and appearances on Dick Clark's *American Bandstand*. Among his other hits were 'Why I'm Walkin' (1960), 'A Wound Time Can't Erase' (1962), 'B.J. The D.J.' (1963), 'Don't Be Angry' (1964), 'Mary Don't You Weep' (1965), 'I Washed My Hands In Muddy Waters', 'Help Stamp Out Loneliness' (1967) and 'Me And You And A Dog Named Boo' (1971). Despite a pronounced lack of chart activity since the early 1970s, he still plays the club and cabaret circuit.

MY FAVOURITE SIN, President, 1988
UP AGAINST THE WALL, Allegiance, 1984

JACKSON, Wanda

Wanda Jackson cut a number of classic tracks that came as close to embodying the essence of rockabilly as anything to emerge from the Sun Studios in Memphis. She was born Wanda Lavonne Jackson on October 20, 1937, in Maud, Oklahoma. She made her debut in 1951 singing on Oklahoma's KPLR, which led to a tour with **Hank Thompson**'s band, the Brazos Valley Boys. Billy Gray, the leader of Thompson's band, recommended her to Decca and she cut a number of tearjerking ballads, including 'The Right To Love' and 'You Can't Have My Love' (C&W#8, 1954).

A tour with **Elvis Presley** encouraged her to change tack and embrace rockabilly; producer Ken

Nelson, having signed her to Capitol, provided her with backing musicians, which included pianist **Merrill Moore** and guitarists **Buck Owens**, **Joe Maphis** and **Merle Travis**. Rousing titles like 'Honey Bop', 'Fujiyama Mama', 'Whole Lotta Shakin' Goin' On', 'Mean, Mean Man' (UK#40, 1961) and 'Let's Have A Party' (US#37, UK#32, 1960) were some of the best ever rock 'n' roll records - her voice having the strength and range of a gospel singer.

By 1962 she had changed direction: assisted by **Roy Clark**, on titles such as 'Right Or Wrong' (US#29, 1961) and 'In The Middle Of A Heartache' (US#27, 1961), she recorded songs that were more reminiscent of the material she had sung in the early stages of her career. In 1973, having become a born-again Christian, she signed with the gospel label Word and cut several albums. Still regularly touring the country circuit, she makes it a condition of appearance that she be allowed to preach.

COUNTRY GOSPEL, Word, 1982
EARLY WANDA JACKSON, Bear Family (Germany), 1984
LET'S HAVE A PARTY, Charly, 1987
RIGHT OR WRONG, Bear Family (Germany), 1992
WANDA JACKSON, Capitol, 1993

JAMES, Sonny

Nicknamed 'The Southern Gentleman', Sonny James (born in Hackleburg, Alabama, on May 1, 1929) has, since he first appeared with 'For Rent' in the 1950s, been a model of consistency. Born Jimmy Loden, into a showbusiness family, he started his career aged four. By the age of seven, he had learnt to play the violin and was broadcasting on regional radio stations. After being conscripted in 1953, he spent fifteen months in Korea, and was signed by Capitol on his return from service in 1955.

His first hit, 'For Rent' (1956), started a pattern that would continue, almost uninterrupted, well into the 1970s. Most of his biggest hits were pop hits for other artists that James merely re-arranged for the country market: 'The Cat Came Back' (UK#30, 1956), 'Young Love' (previously a hit for Tab Hunter; US#1, UK#37, 1957), 'First Date, First Kiss, First Love' (US#25, 1957), 'The Minute You're Gone' (a hit for Cliff Richard), 'You're The Only World That I Know' (C&W#1, 1964), 'Behind The Tear' (C&W#1, 1965), 'I'll Keep Holding On' (C&W#2, 1965), 'True Love's A Blessing' (C&W#3, 1966), 'Take Good Care Of Her' (C&W#1, 1966), 'Need You' (C&W#1, 1967), 'I'll Never Find Another You' (a hit for the Seekers; C&W#1, 1967), 'It's The

Little Things' (C&W#1, 1967), 'A World Of Our Own' (also a Seekers hit; C&W#1, 1968), 'Heaven Says Hello' (C&W#1, 1968), 'Born To Be With You' (a hit for the Chordettes; C&W#1, 1968), 'Only The Lonely' (a hit for **Roy Orbison**; C&W#1, 1969), 'Running Bear' (a hit for Johnny Preston; C&W#1, 1969), 'Since I Met You Baby' (a hit for **Ivory Joe Hunter**; C&W#1, 1969), 'It's Just A Matter Of Time' (a hit for Brook Benton; C&W#1, 1970), 'My Love' (a hit for Petula Clark; C&W#1, 1970), 'Don't Keep Me Hanging On' (C&W#1, 1970), 'Endlessly' (another Brook Benton hit; C&W#1, 1970), 'Empty Arms' (another Ivory Joe Hunter hit; C&W#1, 1971), 'Bright Lights, Big City' (a hit for Jimmy Ree; C&W#1, 1971), 'Here Comes Honey Again' (C&W#1, 1971) and 'That's Why I Love You Like I Do' (C&W#1, 1972).

In 1972 he signed with Columbia (after the retirement of his mentor at Capitol, Ken Nelson) and the hits continued to flow: 'When The Snow Is On The Roses' (C&W#1, 1972), 'White Silver Sands' (C&W#5, 1972), 'I Love You More And More Everyday' (C&W#4, 1973), 'Is It Wrong (For Loving You)' (C&W#1, 1974), 'When Something's Wrong With My Baby', 'The Prisoner's Song' and 'Come On In'. In 1973 he also took up the role of producer, producing **Marie Osmond**'s debut hit 'Paper Roses'.

Despite moving from Columbia to Dimension, and then to Monument in the early 1980s, James's hits began to dry up. He began to conduct so-called 'Christian' crusades against homosexual rights and abortion, giving him the reputation for being a bit of a reactionary. While not the most original of performers, it is surprising that he has never won an award from the Country Music Association, despite his sixteen Number Ones.

SONNY, Stetson, 1988
SONNY JAMES, Capitol, 1990

JASON

Guitarist Jason Ringenberg was born on November 22, 1959, in Illinois, very close to the Rock Island Line. During his teens he played with a variety of local country and bluegrass bands, until forming Jason and the Scorchers in 1981 with guitarist Warner Hodges (born in Tennessee on June 4, 1959) and drummer Perry Baggs (born in Illinois on March 22, 1962). A guitar-based country-rock group, they specialized in thunderous riffs that showed a debt to the garage and punk bands of the late 1970s, such as the Clash.

They were signed by EMI America in 1982, making their debut with the EP *Reckless Country Soul*; this was followed by the mini-album, *Fervor* (1983), which included a storming cover of **Bob Dylan**'s 'Absolutely Sweet Marie' and Jason's self-penned 'Pray For Me Mama (I'm A Gypsy Now)'. In 1985 they released *Lost And Found*, which included a rip-roaring cover of **Hank Williams**' 'Lost Highway', as well as original songs such as 'Shop It Around'. *Still Standing* followed in 1986, but while the band had a hard core of fans, they couldn't make the vital breakthrough and they went their separate ways in 1988.

After a long absence, and still with EMI, Jason returned as a solo artist in 1992 with *One Foot In The Honky Tonk*, which showed him in fine fettle, particularly on the rousing 'Hard Luck Boy' and the honky-tonk styled 'Wild About Me'. Like **Steve Earle**, he has a range of styles at his disposal, but Jason seems to be a guitar-slinging rock 'n' roller at heart, which may work against him with the staunchly conservative country audiences.

ONE FOOT IN THE HONKY TONK, Liberty, 1992

JENNINGS, Waylon

In recent years there has been much press interest in what has come to be known as New Country. Waylon Jennings was among the first - along with **Willie Nelson** and **Tompall Glaser** - to challenge the authority of the country music establishment. In the early 1970s, Jennings began to eschew the traditional motifs of country by embracing contemporary topics and using lesser-known writers, such as **Billy Joe Shaver** and **Rodney Crowell**. Though the establishment came to regard him as treasonous, his attitude encouraged many artists (including **Steve Earle**, **Lyle Lovett** and **Guy Clark**) to adopt a fresher approach to country music.

Born into a musical family on June 15, 1937, in Littlefield, Texas, Jennings had, by the age of only twelve, a sufficient mastery of the guitar to win a spot on the local radio station, KDOV. In 1955 he moved to Lubbock and became a DJ; his first single on the Brunswick label, 'Jolé Blon', emerged three years later, and was produced by **Buddy Holly** and featured saxophonist King Curtis. When Holly left the Crickets later that year, Jennings was recruited as bassist and narrowly avoided being killed in the crash that claimed Holly's life, having given his seat on the aeroplane to the Big Bopper.

Traumatized by the crash, Jennings returned to Lubbock to continue his career as a DJ and vocalist, cutting some sides for the Trend label. After a brief spell with A&M, where Herb Alpert tried to turn him into a pop singer, he was signed to RCA by **Chet Atkins** in 1965, where he remained for twenty years. A number of albums, with producers such as **Chips Moman** and Richie Allbright (the drummer from his backing group, the Waylors), developed his reputation as one of Nashville's more intrepid sons: *Waylon Jennings Sings Ol' Harlan* (covering songs by **Harlan Howard**; 1966), *Ladies Love Outlaws* (1971), *Honky Tonk Heroes* (1973), *Outlaws* (with **Jessi Colter**, Willie Nelson and Tompall Glaser; 1976), *Ol' Waylon* (1977) and *Waylon & Willie* (an album of duets with Nelson; 1978).

Over the years an impressive sequence of hits established him as one of country's most consistent hitmakers, these included: 'Only Daddy That'll Walk The Line' (C&W#2, 1968), 'This Time' (C&W#1, 1974), 'I'm A Ramblin' Man' (C&W#1, 1974), 'Rainy Day Woman' (C&W#2, 1975), 'Are You Sure Hank Done It This Way' (C&W#1, 1975), 'Good Hearted Woman' (with Willie Nelson; US#25, C&W#1, 1976), Chips Moman and **Buddy Emmons**'s 'Luckenbach, Texas (Back To The Basics Of Love)' (US#25, C&W#1, 1977) and 'The Wurlitzer Prize (I Don't Want To Get Over You)' (C&W#1, 1977), **Ed Bruce**'s 'Mammas, Don't Let Your Babies Grow Up To Be Cowboys' (also with Willie Nelson; C&W#1, 1978), 'There Ain't No Good Chain Gang' (with **Johnny Cash**; C&W#2, 1978), 'I've Always Been Crazy' (C&W#1, 1978), **Bob McDill**'s 'Amanda' (C&W#1, 1979), 'Come With Me' (C&W#1, 1979), **Rodney Crowell**'s 'I Ain't Living Long Like This' (C&W#1, 1980), 'Theme From The Dukes Of Hazzard (Good Ol' Boys)' (US#21, C&W#1, 1980), 'Just To Satisfy You' (with Willie Nelson; C&W#1, 1982), 'Lucille (You Won't Do Your Daddy's Will)' (C&W#1, 1983), 'Highwayman' (with Willie Nelson, Johnny Cash and **Kris Kristofferson**; C&W#1, 1985) and 'Rose In Paradise' (C&W#1, 1987).

After recording two more albums of duets with Willie Nelson, *Waylon & Willie II* (1982) and *Take It To The Limit* (1983), he recorded *Waylon & Company*, a series of duets with different artists, such as **Emmylou Harris**, **Hank Williams Jr.**, **Ernest Tubb**, **Jerry Reed**, **Jessi Colter** and **Tony Joe White**. In 1985 Jennings moved to MCA, and although there were indications that he was slowing down (having undergone heart surgery and overcome a serious cocaine problem), he has started diversifying into other areas, such as marketing his own brand of barbecue sauce. His later albums, such as *Hangin' Tough* (1987), still adhere to the tried and tested formulas that have proved so successful throughout his career, and his continuing eagerness to use the material of up-and-coming writers makes him one of country's more forward-looking performers.

BURNING MEMORIES, Castle, 1986
DIAMOND SERIES, RCA, 1988
THE EAGLE, Epic, 1990
FILES: Volumes 1-15, Bear Family (Germany), 1985
GREATEST HITS, RCA, 1990
HANGIN' TOUGH, MCA, 1987
HONKY TONK HEROES, RCA (US), 1973
LADIES LOVE OUTLAWS, RCA (US), 1971
MOST WANTED NASHVILLE REBEL, RCA (US), 1984
NEW CLASSIC WAYLON, MCA, 1989
OL' WAYLON, RCA, 1977
RAVE ON, Bear Family (Germany), 1985
SINGER OF SAD SONGS, RCA International, 1980
THIS TIME, RCA, 1984
WANTED: THE OUTLAWS (with Willie Nelson), RCA, 1976
WAYLON, RCA, 1983
WAYLON & COMPANY, RCA, 1983
WAYLON & WILLIE (with Willie Nelson), RCA, 1979
WAYLON JENNINGS, MCA (US), 1988
WAYLON MUSIC, RCA, 1980
WILL THE WOLF SURVIVE, MCA, 1986

JETHRO   See HOMER AND JETHRO

JIM & JESSE

The brothers Jim (guitar; born on February 13, 1927) and Jesse McReynolds (mandolin and fiddle; born on July 9, 1929) were raised in Coeburn, Virginia, and were encouraged by their grandfather, who had been an old-time fiddler, to take up music professionally. Inspired by the work of the **Blue Sky Boys**, the **Delmore Brothers** and the **Louvin Brothers**, they made their radio debut on WNVA, Norton, Virginia, in 1947.

At first their repertoire, as the Virginia Trio (with Larry Roll), was gospel-oriented and featured songs like 'God Put A Rainbow In The Clouds'. However, the influence of **Earl Scruggs**' syncopated banjo style encouraged Jesse to adopt a similar approach on the mandolin. After cutting sides for the Kentucky label, they moved to Capitol and cut bluegrass titles like the Louvins' 'Are You Missing Me' and 'My Little Honeysuckle Rose', but their progress was halted when Jesse was conscripted and sent to Korea.

On his return in 1954 the duo resumed their work

with a regular spot on WNOX's *Barn Dance*. By the early 1960s they had formed the Virginia Boys, which included **Vassar Clements**, and had signed to Epic, cutting 'Cotton Mill Man' (1964), 'Diesel On My Trail' (1967), 'Ballad Of Thunder Road' (1967) and 'Golden Rocket' (1968), among others. In 1971, they returned to Capitol and had an instant success with 'Freight Train'. Despite having been members of the *Grand Ole Opry* since the early 1960s, they have managed to keep their feet in both the country and the folk camps, with appearances at the Newport Folk Festival.

EPIC BLUEGRASS HITS, Rounder (US), 1985
A HANDFUL OF GOOD SEEDS, Canaan, 1982
IN THE TRADITION, Rounder (US), 1988
JIM & JESSE STORY, CMH (US), 1988
JIM & JESSE TODAY, CMH (US), 1988

JIMENEZ, Flaco

In recent years Flaco Jimenez has become one of the most celebrated exponents of Tex-Mex. While many contend that the original purity of 'conjunto' has been - through the influence of **Ry Cooder** and other non-Hispanic practitioners - sacrificed for popularity, were it not for these influences Flaco Jimenez would probably be an obscurity still playing in bars down Mexico way.

He was born on March 11, 1939, in San Antonio, Texas, where his father Santiago was a prominent local accordionist. With this distinguished pedigree, Flaco (meaning 'the skinny one') learnt to play the accordion and was soon developing his skills throughout the border bars. In the 1960s he came to the attention of **Doug Sahm**, and also of Chris Strachwitz, owner of the roots label Arhoolie, for whom he recorded a number of albums. In 1976 he was recruited by Cooder for the *Chicken Skin Revue*, where he brought the repertoire of Tex-Mex - polkas, waltzes, mazurkas and 'canciones' (songs in two-part harmony) - to a larger audience.

As a result of this wave of interest in Tex-Mex music, a documentary was made (called *Chulas Fronteras*) which galvanized international enthusiasm and enabled him to tour Europe on a regular basis, while European-based independent labels (such as Waterfront and Sonet) showed a much greater interest than their US counterparts in issuing his records. In 1990 he formed an occasional group with **Freddy Fender**, **Augie Meyer** and Doug Sahm called the Texas Tornadoes, and, in 1992, he made his debut *Partners* for a major label, Reprise.

ACCORDION STRIKES BACK, Waterfront, 1987
ARIBA EL NORTE, Zensor (Germany), 1990
AY TE DEJO EN SAN ANTONIO, Arhoolie, 1986
EL SONIDO DE SAN ANTONIO, Arhoolie, 1981
ENTRE HUMO Y BOTELLAS, Rounder (US), 1989
FLACO JIMENEZ AND HIS CONJUNTO, Arhoolie (US), 1981
FLACO'S AMIGOS, Cooking Vinyl, 1988
PARTNERS, Reprise, 1992
SAN ANTONIO SATURDAY NIGHT, Sonet, 1986
THE SAN ANTONIO SOUND, Waterfront, 1985
TEX-MEX BREAKDOWN, Sonet, 1987
VIVA SEGUIN, Rogue, 1986

JIMMY & JOHNNY see MATHIS, Country Johnny

JOHNNY & JACK see WRIGHT, Johnny

JOHNSON, Michael

Michael Johnson was born on August 8, 1944, in Denver, Colorado, and learnt to play the guitar from his brother Paul when he was thirteen. In 1965 he went to Barcelona to study classical guitar under the tutelage of Graciano Tarrago. When he returned to the US, he joined the Chad Mitchell Trio, which included **John Denver** in its line-up.

In 1971 he started his solo career under the auspices of producer Phil Ramone; in 1978, having signed with EMI America, he scored three hits: 'Bluer Than Blue' (US#12, 1978), 'Almost Like Being In Love' (US#32, 1978) and 'This Night Won't Last Forever' (US#19, 1979). After being dropped by the label, he made a conscious decision to change tack and become a country artist.

In 1985 he was signed by RCA producer Brent Maher, his debut being a duet with **Sylvia**, 'I Love You By Heart'. It was followed by a number of other hits, including 'Give Me Wings' (C&W#1, 1986), 'The Moon Is Still Over Her Shoulder' (C&W#1, 1987), 'Crying Shame' (1987), 'I Will Whisper Your Name' (1988) and 'That's That' (1988). The most distinctive feature of Johnson's work to date has been the Spanish influences in his guitar work.

LIFE'S A BITCH, RCA, 1990
MICHAEL JOHNSON, RCA (US), 1993

JONES, George

George 'Thumper' Jones (so named after his switch from country to rockabilly) remains one of the most emotive and evocative performers in contemporary music. His lyrical intensity reflects many personal vicissitudes, but he has always managed to transcend the mawkish sentimentality that so often bedevils country music.

He was born in Saratoga, Texas, on September 12, 1931, and was raised, by musical parents, on a heady diet of both religious and secular music. After learning the guitar at the age of nine, he performed in his local church until joining the Marines and being dispatched to Korea. By 1954 he had left the Marines and was performing in local bars, subsidizing himself by house-painting. He was signed by 'Pappy' Daily at Starday, where he cut 'Why Baby Why' before assuming the alias of Thumper Jones and cutting 'Rock It' and 'Heartbreak Hotel'.

In 1958 he moved to the Mercury label, where he cut classic honky-tonk titles like 'Treasure Of Love' and 'White Lightning' (C&W#1, 1959), and moved on to the United Artists label in 1961. Despite being primarily a country singer, his church-singing background enabled him to draw from gospel music, giving his work an emotional intensity lacking in many of his contemporaries. With United Artists he cut some of his best songs, including 'Tender Years' (C&W#1, 1961), 'Window Up Above', 'She Still Thinks I Care' (C&W#1, 1962), 'We Must Have Been Out Of Our Minds' (1963) and 'The Race Is On' (1964).

In 1965 he moved to the Musicor label, founded by Pappy Daily. Although this should have been a prolific period for Jones, Daily was a clueless producer, and Jones's output was consequently patchy, with songs like 'Walk Through This World With Me' (C&W#1, 1966) and 'When The Green Grass Grows Over Me' (1968) being the cream of the crop.

In 1969 he married **Tammy Wynette**, and started a production relationship with **Billy Sherrill** that would outlive his marriage. With Sherrill, the turbulence of Jones's marriage was immortalized in song, often in duets with Tammy, where the mutual recrimination frequently lurked just beneath the surface.

Throughout this period he enjoyed a greater level of chart consistency than ever before: 'A Good Year For The Roses' (1970), 'We're Gonna Hold On' (with Tammy Wynette; C&W#1, 1973), 'The Grand Tour' (C&W#1, 1974), 'The Door' (C&W#1, 1974), 'These Days (I Barely Get By)', 'Her Name Is ... ' (C&W#3, 1976), 'Golden Ring' (with Tammy Wynette; C&W#1, 1976), 'Near You' (with Tammy Wynette; C&W#1, 1976), 'Southern California' (C&W#5, 1977), 'Two Story House' (with Tammy Wynette; C&W#2, 1980), 'He Stopped Loving Her Today' (C&W#1, 1980), 'I'm Not Ready Yet' (C&W#2, 1981), 'Still Doin' Time' (C&W#1, 1981), 'Same Ole Me' (C&W#5, 1982), 'Shine On' (C&W#3, 1983), 'I Always Get Lucky With You' (C&W#1, 1983), 'Tennessee Whisky' (C&W#2, 1983), 'She's My Rock' (C&W#2, 1984), 'You've Still Got A Place In My Heart' (C&W#3, 1984), 'Who's Gonna Fill Their Shoes' (C&W#3, 1985) and 'The One I Loved Back Then (The Corvette Song)' (C&W#3, 1986).

After being divorced by Tammy Wynette in 1975, he embarked upon a course of alcohol and drug abuse of such severity that it almost finished his career. In 1979 he went into a rehabilitation centre. Meanwhile he had still, amazingly, found time to collaborate with singers such as **Willie Nelson**, **Emmylou Harris**, **Linda Ronstadt** (on *My Very Special Guests*; 1979) and **Elvis Costello**. In recent years he has recorded less (cutting *Too Wild Too Long* in 1988), and has been spending more time with his wife, Nancy Sepulveda, whom he married in 1983. He still plays the cabaret circuit, where his reputation has - despite his tumultous former marriage - remained untarnished.

BEST OF SACRED MUSIC, Gusto (US), 1988
BURN THE HONKY TONK DOWN, Rounder (US), 1988
COLLECTION, Knight, 1990
DON'T STOP THE MUSIC, Ace, 1987
GOLDEN HITS, Gusto (US), 1988
A GOOD YEAR FOR THE ROSES, Castle, 1986
GREAT SONGS OF LEON PAYNE, Gusto (US), 1988
GREATEST HITS (with Tammy Wynette), Epic, 1977
HEARTACHES & HANGOVERS, Rounder (US), 1988
I AM WHAT I AM, Epic, 1981
JONES COUNTRY, Epic, 1983
LADIES CHOICE, Epic, 1985
LONE STAR LEGEND, Ace, 1985
MY FAVOURITES OF HANK WILLIAMS, Stetson, 1990
MY VERY SPECIAL GUESTS, Epic, 1979
THE RACE IS ON, Capitol, 1988
SIXTEEN GREATEST HITS, Starday (US), 1987
STILL THE SAME OLE ME, Epic, 1982
TEXAS TORNADO, Ace, 1986
TOGETHER AGAIN (with Tammy Wynette), Epic, 1981
TOO WILD TOO LONG, Epic, 1988
WALLS CAN FALL, MCA (US), 1992
WINE COLOURED ROSES, Epic, 1986
YOU OUGHT TO BE HERE WITH ME, Epic, 1990
YOU'VE STILL GOT A PLACE IN MY HEART, Epic, 1984

JONES, Grandpa

Grandpa Jones has, since his emergence in the late 1920s, been one of the most versatile entertainers in country music, being both witty raconteur and thoroughly proficient musician. He was born Louis Marshal Jones on October 20, 1913, in Henderson County, Kentucky. By the age of sixteen he won a talent contest, sponsored by **Wendell Hall**, for his guitar work. While working with **Bradley Kincaid** in 1935, he started to adopt the persona of Grandpa Jones and changed from guitar to banjo, emulating the flamboyant style of **Uncle Dave Macon**. After leaving Kincaid he formed his own outfit, known as Grandpa Jones and his Grandchildren, which became regulars first on WWVA's *Wheeling Jamboree*, and then on WLW's *Barn Dance* (where he met and married the fiddler Ramona Riggins).

When the King label was formed in 1944, Jones was one of the first to be signed, cutting sides with **Merle Travis**, the **Delmore Brothers** (known then as the gospel group, the Brown's Ferry Four) and as a solo performer. That same year he was conscripted and posted to Germany until 1946. He joined the *Grand Ole Opry* upon his return, and during this tenure he recorded a string of songs including 'Mountain Dew', 'Tragic Romance', 'Eight More Miles To Louisville' and 'Old Rattler' for Decca during the 1950s. After moving to Monument he cut 'All American Boy' (1959) and the **Jimmie Rodgers** classic 'T For Texas' (1962) and then became a regular member of the cast of *Hee Haw*, following its establishment in 1969.

In the 1970s, Jones became one of the more vocal critics of the increasing liberalism within the country music fraternity (songs about sex were a prime target). In 1983 he appeared at the CMA's twenty-fifth anniversary concert in Washington, with Ronald and Nancy Reagan in attendance. While increasingly reducing his musical workload, he still finds time to appear at the *Opry*.

FAMILY ALBUM, CMH (US), 1976
THE MAN FROM KENTUCKY, Bulldog, 1982
THE OTHER SIDE OF GRANDPA JONES, King (US), 1982
SIXTEEN GREATEST HITS, Starday (US), 1987
TWENTY OF THE BEST, RCA International, 1984

JONES, Tom

Tom Jones has always been sensationalized for his big balladeering style that has women ripping their kit off; it is seldom observed that most of his successful material has actually been derived from country writers and that his background in a Welsh mining community has parallels with that of **Loretta Lynn**.

He was born Thomas Jones Woodward on June 7, 1940, in Treforest, Pontypridd, Wales. He formed his first group, Tommy Scott and the Senators, in 1963; they recorded some sides for EMI, with Joe Meek producing. In 1964 he was spotted by Gordon Mills, was renamed Tom Jones (echoing the successful Tony Richardson film of the same name) and signed to Decca. His first hit 'It's Not Unusual' (US#10, UK#1, 1965) was written by Mills and Les Reed, and became his theme song, providing him with ample scope for cavorting around the stage.

After recording the film title songs 'What's New Pussycat' (US#3, UK#11, 1965) and 'Thunderball' (US#25, UK#35, 1966), he maintained a steady stream of hits, which included **Porter Wagoner**'s 'Green Green Grass Of Home' (US#11, 1967; UK#1, 1966), **Mel Tillis**'s 'Detroit City' (US#27, UK#8, 1967), **Mickey Newbury**'s 'Funny Familiar Forgotten Feelings' (UK#7, 1967), 'I'll Never Fall In Love Again' (US#10, 1969; UK#2, 1967), 'I'm Coming Home' (UK#2, 1967), 'Delilah' (US#15, UK#2, 1968), 'Help Yourself' (US#35, UK#5, 1968), 'Love Me Tonight' (US#13, UK#9, 1969), 'Without Love' (US#5, UK#10, 1969), 'Daughter Of Darkness' (US#13, UK#5, 1970), 'I (Who Have Nothing)' (US#14, UK#16, 1970), 'She's A Lady' (US#2, UK#13, 1971), 'Till' (UK#2, 1971) and 'The Young New Mexican Puppeteer' (UK#6, 1972).

He began to tour the US immediately after making his mark in the UK, and his stage show went down a storm on the American supper-club cabaret circuit. By 1969 he had his own television show, *This Is Tom Jones*, and was well on the way to becoming one of the highest-paid performers in Las Vegas. Throughout the mid-1970s he spent most of his time in the US, and in 1977 he was signed by Epic, scoring with 'Say You'll Stay Until Tomorrow' (US#15, C&W#1, UK#40, 1977). Veering increasingly towards country music, he recorded several albums for Mercury including *Darlin'*, from which 'Touch Me (I'll Be Your Fool Once More)' (1981) was extracted. Dissatisfied with this move to country music, as it had effectively typecast him and was proving too restricting, he went into retirement.

In 1987 he returned to participate in a project based on the life of the bullfighter El Cordobes, which had been written and developed by Edward Seago and Mike Leander, and featured 'A Boy From Nowhere' (UK#2, 1987). This was followed by a collaboration with the English band, The Art Of Noise, on a cover of a Prince composition, 'Kiss' (UK#5, 1988); his most recent album, *Carrying A Torch* (1991), featured contributions from Van Morrison.

CARRYING A TORCH, Dover, 1991
THE COMPLETE TOM JONES, London, 1992
DARLIN', Mercury (US), 1987

JORDANAIRES

Lead tenor Gordon Stoker formed the Jordanaires in 1948; the line-up changed regularly over the years with Stoker the common denominator. They began as a barbershop quartet in 1948, in Springfield, Missouri, singing gospel. The following year they secured their first date at the *Grand Ole Opry* and then were featured on the **Red Foley** version of 'Just A Closer Walk With Thee' (1950).

Due to their involvement with **Elvis Presley** they have, over the years, become the most popular and influential of all session vocalists, accompanying nearly every major artist in Nashville. They have also lent their voices to innumerable film soundtracks.

JORDANAIRES SING ELVIS'S GOSPEL FAVOURITES, Magnum Force, 1986

JUDDS, The

The Judds have, since their emergence in 1983, become one of the most successful groups in the US, through a combination of sound judgement on the part of their long-time producer, Brent Maher, and through their carefully selected choice of material, which appeals to MOR audiences as well as country aficionados.

Born - and raised - in Ashland, Kentucky, in 1948, Naomi Judd moved to the West Coast with her husband and two-year-old daughter Wynonna in 1968. After her marriage broke down she returned to Ashland with Wynonna and Ashley (born in Los Angeles, California, in 1970) and worked as a nurse. In 1979 she moved to Nashville, where she worked as a nurse at the Williamson County Hospital. In 1983 she met Diana Maher, wife of the RCA producer Brent Maher, who had been involved in a car crash; she gave her a tape of herself and Wynonna singing.

In 1983 the Judds were signed to the RCA label, scoring their first hit with 'Had A Dream'; it was followed by a string of other hits, including 'Mama He's Crazy' (C&W#1, 1984), 'Why Not Me' (C&W#1, 1984), 'Girls' Night Out' (C&W#1, 1985), 'Love Is Alive' (C&W#1, 1985), 'Have Mercy' (C&W#1, 1985),

'Rockin' With The Rhythm Of The Rain' (C&W#1, 1986), 'Grandpa (Tell Me About The Good Old Days)' (C&W#1, 1986), 'Cry Myself To Sleep' (C&W#1, 1986), 'I Know Where I'm Going' (C&W#1, 1987), 'Maybe Your Baby's Got The Blues' (C&W#1, 1987), 'Turn It Loose' (C&W#1, 1988), 'Change Of Heart' (C&W#1, 1988), 'Young Love' (C&W#1, 1989) and 'Let Me Tell You About Love' (C&W#1, 1989).

In 1991 they undertook their final concert tour (Naomi's health had suffered as a consequence of constant touring) and Wynonna started a solo career. The following year she made her solo debut with *Wynonna* (1992), which included the following hits: 'She Is His Only Need' (C&W#1, 1992), 'I Saw The Light' (C&W#1, 1992) and 'No One Else On Earth' (C&W#1, 1992).

GIVE A LITTLE LOVE, RCA, 1987
GREATEST HITS, RCA, 1988
LOVE CAN BUILD A BRIDGE, RCA, 1990
RIVER OF TIME, RCA, 1989
ROCKIN' WITH THE RHYTHM, RCA, 1986
WHY NOT ME, RCA, 1985
WYNONNA, Curb, 1992

JUSTIS, Bill

Bill Justis, along with **Scotty Moore** and Bill Black, was one of the key movers behind the success of **Sam Phillips**' Sun label, particularly through their discovery of **Charlie Rich**.

He was born on October 14, 1927, in Birmingham, Alabama, and grew up in Memphis, where he learnt about music from his mother who was a concert pianist. In 1942, having taken up the saxophone, he formed a jazz band and then went on to study music at college.

In 1957 he joined the Sun label as an A&R man and an arranger; one of his first projects was to cut the instrumental track 'Raunchy' with Sun session musicians. Although later records by Justis, such as 'College Man' and 'Flea Circus', proved to be unsuccessful, Justis showed his mettle by discovering Charlie Rich, who was at that time singing jazz. With Rich, Justis produced 'Whirlwind' and 'Lonely Weekends', before being fired by Phillips for 'insubordination' in 1961.

He was immediately employed by RCA, and was followed there by Rich, who cut a version of the Jimmy Reed song 'Big Boss Man'. His next move was to **Fred Foster**'s Monument and Sound Stage Seven labels. His career lost its momentum during his later years, and he died on July 15, 1982.

KANE, Kieran see O'KANES

KAPP, Jack
Jack Kapp was one of the early record company moguls who, through his policy of scouting for talent by making regular trips into rural areas, managed to build up an unmatched roster of black and country artists at Decca. He was born on June 15, 1901, in Chicago, Illinois. At the age of seventeen he joined Columbia as a salesman, and remained with them for seven years. In 1925 he joined the Brunswick label as A&R director and made successful pioneering trips down to the South, procuring artists such as Louis Armstrong and **Buell Kazee**.

In 1933 he resigned from Brunswick and set up the American Decca label, with financial backing from Edward Lewis, the managing director of its English counterpart. Over the next fifteen years he signed artists such as **Jimmie Davis**, **Ernest Tubb**, **Roy Acuff** and **Milton Brown**, as well as non-country artists such as Bing Crosby, Guy Lombardo, the Ink Spots and Armstrong. He was also the first record company executive to realize the potential of the film soundtrack album: *The Wizard Of Oz* (1939) being the first example. He died on March 25, 1949, in New York City, of a heart attack.

KARL & HARTY
Karl Victor Davis (born on December 17, 1905) and Hartford Connecticut Taylor (born on April 11, 1905) were brought up in Mount Vernon, Kentucky. They became known through their membership of **John Lair**'s Cumberland Ridge Runners, who were one of the better known outfits on WLS's *National Barn Dance*. After the group disintegrated, this t wosome remained on the show for a further fifteen years and recorded extensively for ARC and then Capitol.

Their close harmonies, combined with mandolin and guitar instrumentation, were to be an influence on other duos (including the **Blue Sky Boys**). Apart from his expertise as a mandolinist, Karl penned titles which included 'I'm Just Here To Get My Baby Out Of Jail' (1934), 'The Prisoner's Dream' and 'They're All Going Home But One' (1936), and 'Kentucky' (1938); many of his songs have cropped up in the repertoires of artists such as the Blue Sky Boys, **J.E. Mainer**, the **Everly Brothers**, **Hank Locklin**, **Emmylou Harris** and **Linda Ronstadt**. Both retired from the music business in the 1950s.

KAZEE, Buell
Buell Kazee was born on August 29, 1900, in Magoffin County, Kentucky. Displaying an erudition that was well beyond most hillbillies, he became a Missionary Baptist minister when he was seventeen, before enrolling at Georgetown College to study music and voice. While majoring in English at Georgetown, he studied Elizabethan literature and discovered that many of the folk songs and ballads he had grown up with originated in that period. Between 1927 and 1929 he recorded some of these songs for Brunswick, including 'The Butcher's Boy', 'The Lady Gay' and 'Faded Coat Of Blue'.

While his religious convictions prohibited him from enjoying the commercial benefits of his records, his concerts were entertaining for the casual listener, as well as informative for students of the genre. Although little remains of his original work, later recordings during the 1960s for the Library of Congress show that his voice had remained unaffected by the passing of the years. He died on August 31, 1976.

KEEN, Robert Earl
One of the new wave of singer-songwriters who have emerged in the last ten years, Robert Earl Keen's songs draw from all aspects of traditional American music. He was born in Houston, Texas, on January 11, 1956, and started performing and writing songs while at the University of Houston. After leaving university he played throughout Texas, until meeting **Lyle Lovett** in 1986 and co-writing 'This Old Porch', which appeared

on Lovett's debut album. This encouraged the Philo label to sign him as a solo artist.

His debut, *No Kinda Dancer*, emerged in 1988 and was swifly followed by *The Live Album*. Although Keen has failed to secure major hits in his own right, his reputation as a writer has flourished, with artists such as **Reba McEntire** and **Nanci Griffith** recordings his songs.

BIGGER PIECE OF SKY, Sugar Hill (US), 1993
LIVE ALBUM, Sugar Hill (US), 1988
NO KINDA DANCER, Rounder (US), 1988
WEST TEXAS, Special Delivery, 1990

KEMP, Wayne

Best known for his compositional skills, Wayne Kemp was born in Muldrow, Oklahoma, in 1941. Although he had shown an adolescent fondness for motor racing (his father was a mechanic), he formed a band during the late 1950s which toured throughout the southwest and came to the attention of **Buddy Killen**, who signed him to a publishing and recording contract with Dial.

While his own records generated little response, he had more success as a writer, scoring a hit in 1965 with 'Love Bug' for **George Jones**. After leaving Dial he joined the Jab label, cutting 'The Image Of Me' (1966); **Conway Twitty** heard it and cut his own version, which further established Kemp's credentials as a writer. Twitty went on to cut other Kemp songs, such as 'Next In Line', 'Darling You Know I Wouldn't Lie' and 'That's When She Started To Stop Loving You'. Through his association with Twitty, Kemp was signed by Decca and notched up a number of modest hits for the label, including 'Bar Room Habits' (1969), 'Who'll Turn Out The Lights' and 'Did We Have To Come This Far' (1971). After being dropped by Decca he was signed by Dot, but still failed to generate significant interest in his own recorded output.

KENDALLS

A native of St Louis, Royce Kendall (born on September 25, 1934) began his professional career on the West Coast during the late 1950s, performing as half of a duo with his brother Floyce. After returning to St Louis, Royce worked as a barber and his wife Melba as a beautician, until in 1969, following a long tradition of family duos in country music, he started to sing with his daughter Jeannie (born on November 13, 1954). The family moved to Nashville, where father

and daughter (now known as the Kendalls) were signed by **Pete Drake** to his Stop label.

After several other changes of label, including spells with Dot and United Artists, the Kendalls signed to Ovation, where they achieved their breakthrough with the first of a number of cheating songs (about adultery), 'Heaven's Just A Sin Away' (C&W#1, 1977), which was followed by other hits, including 'It Don't Feel Like Sinnin' To Me' (1977), 'Pittsburgh Stealers' (1978), 'Sweet Desire' (C&W#1, 1978), 'I'm Already Blue' and 'Put It Off Until Tomorrow' (1980).

In 1981 they signed with Mercury, cutting 'Teach Me To Cheat' and 'If You're Waiting On Me (You're Backing Up)'. In 1983 they cut *Movin' Train*, using three separate producers: Brian Ahern at Magnolia Sound, Hollywood, with harmony vocals from **Emmylou Harris**; Jerry Gillespie at Muscle Shoals, Alabama; and Blake Mevis at Music City Hall, Nashville. This album yielded three hits: 'Thank God For The Radio' (C&W#1, 1984), 'Movin' Train' (1984) and 'Precious Love' (1985). In 1986 they changed labels once again, signing with MCA and cutting *Fire At First Sight*. While they have been less active of late, they still tour and have become regulars on the *Grand Ole Opry*.

BEST COUNTRY DUO 1978, Gusto (US), 1979
FIRE AT FIRST SIGHT, MCA, 1987
MOVIN' TRAIN, Mercury, 1983
SIXTEEN GREATEST HITS, Gusto (US), 1988

KENNEDY, Jerry

One of the most successful Nashville producers, Jerry Kennedy was instrumental, during the latter half of the 1960s, in establishing and consolidating the role of Mercury as one of America's most consistent labels.

He was born in Shreveport, Louisiana, and won a **Bob Wills** talent contest when he was ten, before finding work as a guitarist on the *Louisiana Hayride* during the mid-1950s. After touring with **Johnny Horton**, he moved to Nashville where he became a session musician. He then gravitated to production in 1963, and worked with artists including **Tom T. Hall**, **Faron Young**, **Roger Miller**, **Charlie Rich**, **Johnny Rodriguez** and the **Statler Brothers**. While head of Mercury's Nashville Division, he still retained a creative producer/artist role that was comparatively rare for a label boss.

KENNERLEY, Paul

Paul Kennerley was raised in the UK and worked for many years in advertising, until the arrival of punk in 1976. Although his preferences were for groups like the Clash, the Sex Pistols and the Stranglers, he started to develop an interest in country music. Two concept albums, *White Mansions* (1978) and *The Legend Of Jesse James* (1980), materialized, featuring artists like **Emmylou Harris** and **Waylon Jennings**.

In 1983 he made a permanent move to Nashville, married Emmylou Harris and started writing hits for artists like the **Judds** ('Have Mercy', 'Cry Myself To Sleep' and 'Young Love'), Sweethearts of the Rodeo ('Chains Of Gold'), Emmylou Harris ('In My Dreams'), **Nanci Griffith** ('Let It Shine On Me') and **Patti Loveless** ('Blue Side Of Town').

KENTUCKY COLONELS see WHITE, Clarence

KENTUCKY RAMBLERS see PRAIRIE RAMBLERS

KERR, Anita

Doyennes of back-up vocalists, the Anita Kerr Singers established themselves during the 1950s in pretty much the same way as the **Jordanaires**. Anita Kerr was born on October 13, 1927, in Memphis, Tennessee. Her first vocal group, the Grilli Sisters, was assembled before she started high school. In 1941 she joined the staff of the Memphis station WMPS as an arranger. By 1949 she had moved to Nashville and had quickly established one of the best vocal back-up groups in the business.

Over the years she has worked with almost every major country artist, including **Ray Price**, **Jim Reeves**, **Chet Atkins** and **Eddy Arnold**. She has also cut a number of mediocre albums under her own name - dreary middle-of-the-road material, ideally suited to shopping malls. Her smooth vocal arrangements, however, became a trademark of the Nashville sound.

KERSHAW, Doug

Cajun fiddler Doug Kershaw was born on January 24, 1936, at Teil Ridge, Louisiana, and grew up on an island in the Gulf of Mexico. He made his debut at the Bucket of Blood, Lake Arthur, accompanying his mother who was a guitarist and fiddler. In 1948 he

formed the Continental Cowboys, with his brothers Pee Wee and Rusty (born on February 2, 1938, at Teil Ridge, Louisiana), winning a spot on KPLC-TV, Lake Charles, and then going on to broadcast regularly on the *Louisiana Hayride*.

In 1953, as the duo Rusty & Doug, they recorded in Nashville for the Hickory label, accompanied by **Floyd Cramer** and **Pete Drake**, among others. In 1958 they scored their first hit with **Boudleaux Bryant**'s 'Hey Sheriff', which was followed by 1961's 'Louisiana Man' (a self-penned track which secured Doug's reputation) and 'Diggy Liggy Lo' (1961). In 1964 the duo separated and Doug unleashed his ferocious style upon the session circuit, recording with **John Stewart**, Longbranch Pennywhistle and Grand Funk Railroad. He came to the attention of rock audiences towards the end of the 1960s through his session work for artists such as **Bob Dylan**, **Johnny Cash** and Earl Scruggs (see **Flatt & Scruggs**).

His solo career started first with Mercury and then MGM, before **Buddy Killen** landed him a contract with Warner Bros. in 1969. Most of his albums for Warner Bros. (including *Spanish Moss* and *Mama Kershaw's Boy*) displayed an uncomfortable eclecticism that failed to show the virtuosity of his fiddling, and it was only when he really let rip on *The Ragin' Cajun* that his prowess was allowed to shine. As for his brother, Rusty, he battled vigorously against alcoholism until 1970, when apparently cured, he cut *Cajun In The Blues Country* for the Atlantic subsidiary, Cotillion. Having been dropped some years back by Warner Bros., Doug continues to play sessions and appear at festivals.

CAJUN COUNTRY ROCKERS (Rusty & Doug), Bear Family (Germany), 1984
HOT DIGGITY DOUG, Sundown, 1989
LOUISIANA MAN (Rusty & Doug), Sundown, 1985
MORE CAJUN COUNTRY ROCK (Rusty & Doug), Bear Family (Germany), 1984
RUSTY, DOUG, WILEY & FRIENDS (with Wiley Barkdull), Flyright, 1989

KERSHAW, Sammy

Although Sammy Kershaw has only hit the high spots in recently, he has been performing since he was twelve, and as a result he has a flair for making concert audiences eat out of the palm of his hand.

He was born in 1958 in Kaplan, South Louisiana, the nephew of Rusty and **Doug Kershaw**. His father died of lung cancer in 1969 and his mother worked as a waitress to make ends meet, and the following year she arranged for him to work with a local musician, J.B. Perry, as a roadie. He remained with Perry for the next eight years and was often allowed to do a turn on stage, solo or with Perry, when they opened for Nashville's finest, including **George Jones**, **Ray Charles** and **Charlie Rich**. During the late 1970s and early 1980s, he played the local club circuit and worked as a carpenter and welder, among other things. His club act proved so popular that he joined a local band, Blackwater, and toured throughout the southwest, until packing up the music industry to work for the Wal-Mart Corporation redesigning their shops. While working on a shop in Texas, he was approached by a Nashville entrepreneur, Barry Jackson, which resulted in an audition for Harold Shedd of Mercury.

He was signed to the label in 1990, making his debut with *Don't Go Near The Water*, which included 'Cadillac Style' (C&W#3, 1991). This was followed by *Haunted Heart* in 1992, which included 'She Don't Know She's Beautiful'. The quality of his live act and the strong cajun influence set him apart from the majority of the New Country artists, but greater selectivity in his material would improve his reputation.

DON'T GO NEAR THE WATER, Mercury (US), 1991
HAUNTED HEART, Mercury (US), 1992

KETCHUM, Hal

Born in New York in 1953, Hal Ketchum was raised on a diet of Duke Ellington and trumpeter Dizzy Gillespie. Throughout his adolescence he was drummer in an R&B outfit. After finishing high school he worked as a carpenter until moving to Texas in the late 1980s. The change in musical atmosphere encouraged Ketchum to write songs in the evenings.

Although his early influence was jazz, his songs were reminiscent of **George Jones**, and he was signed to the independent Sawdust label, making his debut with *Threadbare Alibis* in 1990. After meeting Terrell Tye (whom he later married), the president of Forerunner Music, he was signed by **Mike Curb** to the Curb label. He immediately established himself as one of the best up-and-coming singer-songwriters with titles like 'Small Town Saturday Night' (1991), 'Past The Point Of Rescue' (C&W#2, 1992), 'I Know Where Love Lives' (1992) and 'Sure Love' (1993).

PAST THE POINT OF RESCUE, Curb (US), 1991
SURE LOVE, Curb (US), 1992
THREADBARE ALIBIS, Sawdust, 1990

KILGORE, Merle

Merle Kilgore achieved some distinction as a solo performer with a few hits in the 1950s, but it was as a writer that he became best known, co-writing 'Ring Of Fire' with **June Carter** for **Johnny Cash**. He was born Wyatt Merle Kilgore on September 8, 1934, in Chickasha, Oklahoma, and moved to Shreveport, Louisiana, during his childhood. After learning to play the guitar, he joined Shreveport's KENT as a DJ in 1950, and scored a hit with his composition 'More, More, More' in 1952. He was subsequently invited to join the resident band on the *Louisiana Hayride*, where he remained for the duration of the 1950s.

Although he was now working for the American Optical Company, he continued to pursue his musical career with Starday, charting with 'Dear Mama' (1959) and 'Love Has Made You Beautiful' and 'Gettin' Old Before My Time' (1960); in addition, **Johnny Horton** covered 'Johnny Reb', turning it into a huge hit. In 1962 he collaborated with Carter on 'Ring Of Fire' and **Claude King** on 'Wolverton Mountain'.

As his career in the music industry was on the decline, he began to appear in films for director Henry Hathaway, such as *Nevada Smith* (starring Steve McQueen; 1966) and *Five Card Stud* (starring Dean Martin and Robert Mitchum; 1968). He has since apparently vanished into obscurity.

KILLEN, Buddy

Buddy Killen was born in Florence, Alabama, and secured session work as a bassist at the *Grand Ole Opry*, until joining **Hank Williams**' **Drifting Cowboys**. After Williams' death in 1953, he toured with **Ray Price** and **Jim Reeves**, before joining Jack Stapp, who had recently founded the publishing company Tree; they became partners in 1957.

After discovering soul singer Joe Tex, Killen decided to oversee his career and produce him for his own Dial label; at **Rick Hall**'s Fame studios in Muscle Shoals, Tex cut his first hit, 'Hold What You Got'. Tex's success prompted Killen to expand his roster of R&B artists to include the veteran Clarence 'Frogman' Henry, Paul Kelly and Bobby Marchan and to add cajun fiddler **Doug Kershaw**.

Tex died in 1982, and Killen then reverted to managing his own substantial publishing interests (which exceeded those of **Acuff**-**Rose**) and working in Nashville as a producer. Among the artists he has worked with are **Exile** and **T.G. Sheppard**.

KINCAID, Bradley

Bradley Kincaid made a major contribution to the popularization of traditional American folk songs - for the rather banal reason that he possessed a clear singing voice (untinged by an impenetrable 'hillbilly drawl') which meant that everyone understood what he was singing! He was a staunch upholder of traditional values and detested being associated with hillbillies, whom he considered 'ill-educated bums'.

He was born in Garrard County, Kentucky, on July 13, 1895, and was educated at Berea College. After moving to Chicago to further his studies, he auditioned for WLS and was given the opportunity to sing folk songs to his own guitar accompaniment on the *National Barn Dance*. Achieving instant popularity, he secured a deal with Gennett in 1928, cutting sides like 'Barbara Allen', 'Fatal Derby Day', 'Sweet Kitty Wells' and 'I'll Be All Smiles Tonight'.

In 1930 he moved from WLS to WLW, Cincinnati, before joining forces with **Grandpa Jones** in 1935. Throughout the late 1930s he travelled extensively, sometimes with Jones, sometimes alone, broadcasting at one radio station after another. In 1942 he returned to WLW and became a regular on the *Boone County Jamboree*. While he continued to record for a succession of different labels, his radio broadcasts emphasized the timelessness of folk songs. By 1944 he had joined Nashville's WSM and broadcast on the *Grand Ole Opry*. Although his style was overshadowed by the flamboyance of other artists, his method of collecting songs from rural backwaters - and updating and reworking them with contemporary arrangements (often with the help of prospective performers) - proved to be a highly profitable exercise.

In the course of his career he published over three hundred songs in a dozen individual songbooks. By the early 1960s he had retired to Springfield, Ohio, to run a record shop. In 1963 he came out of retirement to record in Fort Worth for the Bluebonnet label; and in 1973 he recorded for the McMonigle label. His influence is still felt today in the work of artists such as the **Carter Family**.

KING, Claude

Claude King was born on February 5, 1933, in Shreveport, Louisiana. After attending the University of Idaho, he returned to Shreveport to attend business school. Having learnt the guitar while at school, he now started to play local clubs and appear on radio and television, before being signed to Columbia in 1961.

Over the next decade he notched up a series of hits with saga songs that celebrated the ruggedness of America: 'Big River Big Man' and 'The Comancheros' (1961); 'Wolverton Mountain' (co-written with **Merle Kilgore**; US#6, 1962); 'Burning Of Atlanta' and 'I've Got The World By The Tail' (1962); 'Sheepskin Valley', 'Building A Bridge', 'Hey Lucille' and 'Sam Hill' (1963); 'Tiger Woman' (1965); 'All For The Love Of A Girl' and 'Friend, Lover, Woman, Wife' (1969); and 'Mary's Vineyard' (1970). During the 1970s his career slipped into decline and, despite an attempt to revitalize it with a 'greatest hits' compilation in 1980, he died in obscurity in 1983.

BEST, Gusto (US), 1980

KING, Pee Wee

While Pee Wee King was the first Western Swing bandleader to feature an electric guitarist and drummer in his line-up on the *Grand Ole Opry*, he was first and foremost a showman, who was prepared to use gimmicks - like electric guitars and drums and cowboy outfits - and was able to employ a succession of highly-talented musicians.

He was born Frank Arthur Kuczynski, on February 18, 1914, in Abrams, Wisconsin, of Polish extraction. After training as a draughtsman and learning to play the fiddle, harmonica and accordion, he led his first band in 1933 with regular spots on WIS, Milwaukee, before moving, in 1934, to WHAS, Louisville, where he dubbed his band the Golden West Cowboys. This was followed by a sojourn with WLS, Chicago, on the *National Barn Dance*, before moving to WSM and the *Grand Ole Opry* in 1937.

By this time his band had acquired considerable prestige, and was being viewed as a training ground for aspiring artists: **Eddy Arnold**, **Redd Stewart**, **Cowboy Copas**, **Ernest Tubb** and **Cousin Jody** all passed through the ranks. During this period he recorded for a string of labels, including Bullet, King and RCA Victor, and had hits with 'Bonaparte's Retreat' (1948), 'Tennessee Waltz' (US#30, 1948), 'Slow Poke' (US#1, 1951), 'Silver And Gold' (1952) and 'Bimbo' (1954), all co-written with Redd Stewart.

During the 1950s, the rise of rock 'n' roll made King and his band seem old-fashioned, and his popularity suffered accordingly. After enduring various financial problems, he disbanded the Golden West Cowboys and replaced them with a touring unit for the express purpose of accompanying **Minnie Pearl**. In 1965, 'Tennessee Waltz' was nominated the official anthem of the State of Tennessee, and he retired from performing in 1969. He was elected to the Country Music Hall Of Fame in 1974, and has since become a director of the Country Music Foundation.

Despite his tremendous influence in Nashville, his music lacked the originality of **Bob Wills**'s band or the **Skillet Lickers**, but this deficiency was compensated for by his showmanship, which at the peak of his career was given much exposure on syndicated television shows.

BALLROOM KING, Detour, 1980
BEST OF PEE WEE KING, Starday (US), 1987
HOG WILD TOO, Zu Zazz, 1990
ROMPIN', STOMPIN', SINGIN', SWINGIN', Bear Family (Germany), 1984

KIRBY, Beecher Pete see BASHFUL BROTHER OSWALD

KIRK, Eddie

Eddie Kirk was born in Greeley, Colorado, on March 21, 1919. He first made his mark as an amateur flyweight boxer, before winning him the National Yodelling Championships in 1935 and 1936. Thereafter he became a singer and guitarist with the Beverly Hillbillies (see **Manners, Zeke**). His melodic crooning drew him to the attention of **Gene Autry**, who gave him a regular spot on his radio show, and Kirk subsequently went on to appear on KFI, Compton's *Town Hall Party*.

In 1947 he was signed by Capitol and cut a version of 'Blues Stay Away From Me' with **Tennessee Ernie Ford** and **Merle Travis**. Other solo hits followed, including 'Candy Kisses' and 'The Gods Were Angry With Me'. During the 1950s he moved away from the music industry, and took up a lucrative line in film bit-parts.

KNOBLOCH, Fred see OVERSTREET, Paul

KRISTOFFERSON, Kris

Kris Kristofferson was born on June 22, 1936, in Brownsville, Texas, the son of an Air Force major-general, and grew up in various military camps. While living in San Mateo, he attended Pomona College and participated in the Golden Gloves boxing championship. In 1958 he won a Rhodes Scholarship to Oxford University, but became sidetracked by his attempts at writing novels; all his efforts were rejected by publishers and he dropped out of university and tried his luck as a songwriter under the auspices of UK impresario, Larry Parnes. This, too, proved abortive and he returned to the US, joining the army in 1960.

He was discharged in 1965 and spent the next four years living on the edge in Nashville, trying to build a career as a songwriter. One of the new wave of country writers, he (along with **Mickey Newbury**, **Rodney Crowell**, **Shel Silverstein** and **John Hartford**) came to prominence with compositions that drew their inspiration from life and literature. In 1969 **Roger Miller** picked up 'Me And Bobby McGee' and turned it into a hit, which prompted Janis Joplin and **Jerry Lee Lewis** to do their versions. Janis Joplin's version was so successful that Kristofferson became the songwriter of the moment and his other songs were widely covered: 'Sunday Morning Coming Down' (**Johnny Cash** and Hank Ballard), 'For The Good Times' (**Ray Price**, **Stoney Edwards** and Perry Como) and 'Help Me Make It Through The Night' (Gladys Knight and the Pips, Lou Rawls and **Sammi Smith**).

After being signed by **Fred Foster** to the Monument label, he cut some albums, including *Me And Bobby McGee* (1970) and *The Silver Tongued Devil And I* (1971), which established his credentials as a performer and provided the hit 'Loving Her Was Easier (Than Anything I'll Ever Do Again)' (US#26, 1971). Later albums, such as *Jesus Was A Capricorn* and *Easter Island*, were patchy, but the former yielded the hit 'Why Me?' (US#16, C&W#1, 1973); other collaborations with his wife, **Rita Coolidge**, such as *Full Moon* and *Breakaway*, were equally patchy.

Kristofferson's highly successful acting career got off the ground in 1971 with the soundtrack for Dennis Hopper's *The Last Movie*. His next film was the superb *Cisco Pike* (co-starring Gene Hackman); other films included Sam Peckinpah's *Pat Garrett And Billy The Kid* (co-starring **Bob Dylan**; 1973), *Alice Doesn't Live Here Anymore* (co-starring Ellen Burstyn; 1974), *A Star Is Born* (co-starring Barbra Streisand; 1976), Sam Peckinpah's *Convoy* (co-starring Ali MacGraw and based on the **C.W. McCall** song of the same name; 1978) and Michael Cimino's *Heaven's Gate* (1980).

After some years in the recording wilderness, he joined forces with **Willie Nelson**, **Waylon Jennings** and Johnny Cash for *Highwayman*, the title track of which became a substantial hit. His solo career was revitalized by signing to Mercury and teaming with **Billy Swan**, cutting *Repossessed* (1987) and *Third World Warrior* (1990).

HELP ME MAKE IT THROUGH THE NIGHT, Columbia, 1984
REPOSSESSED, Mercury (US), 1987
SONGS OF KRISTOFFERSON, Monument (US), 1982
THIRD WORLD WARRIOR, Mercury, 1990
TO THE BONE, Monument, 1981

LA COSTA

La Costa Tucker was born on December 12, 1949, in Snyder, Texas, the elder sister of **Tanya Tucker**. Her childhood was nomadic as her father, Beau, was a building contractor and was always on the move. She won her first talent contest when she was four, and during her teens she and Tanya worked with the band Country Westerners between 1968 and 1970. After marrying Daryl Sorenson she moved to Toltrec, Arizona, and became a medical records clerk at the local hospital.

In 1972 her sister's career began to blossom and La Costa decided to take another stab at the music industry. She was immediately signed by Capitol and her first record, 'I Wanna Get To You' (1973), was a modest hit; other hits included 'Get On My Love Train' (C&W#3, 1974) and 'Western Man' (1974). During the late 1970s her career faded, but she returned with 'Love Take It Easy On Me' (1982) for Elektra.

While La Costa has never achieved the super-stardom attained by her sister, she, with the Stone Bridge Band, has carved a niche on the cabaret and television circuit that has included appearances on *The Bob Hope Show* and with **Hoyt Axton**.

LAIR, John

John Lair has managed to do for country music what Allen Lomax did for the blues: he brought many old songs out of the back porch and into the homes of thousands of radio listeners. Born on July 1, 1894, in Livingston, Kentucky, his career got into swing in 1927 when he joined WLS, Chicago, as a radio producer. In this capacity he organized friends and acquaintances into a loose aggregation known as the Cumberland Ridge Runners, which comprised **Doc Hopkins** (guitar and vocals), Linda Parker (guitar, banjo, dulcimer and vocals), **Hugh Cross** (banjo), Slim Miller (fiddle), Karl Davis (mandolin; see **Karl & Harty**), Harty Taylor (guitar; see **Karl & Harty**) and **Red Foley** (bass).

Their regular broadcasts on the *National Barn Dance* contributed to the enormous popularity of barn dances in the 1930s, and, although by 1936 the Cumberland Ridge Runners had become dated, Lair was able to establish the *Renfro Valley Barn Dance* from WLW in Cincinnati, and then from WHAS in Louisiana, with the help of Red Foley and the **Duke Of Paducah**. He retained his interests in the show until selling them in 1968.

LANE, Christy

Christy Lane was born Eleanor Johnston on January 8, 1940. Her career started in 1972 when her husband, Lee Stoller, concluded that she had potential as a singer. They moved from Peoria to Nashville (where Stoller set up his own record label, LS), and Eleanor Stoller became Christy Lane.

Her career initially took second place to raising her family, but as the children grew older, she concentrated more on recording. Her first hits were 'Tryin' To Forget About You' and 'Let Me Down Easy' (1977). In 1979 United Artists bought out her contract, and she had a string of hits with 'Simple Little Words' (1979), 'One Day At A Time' (C&W#1, 1980), 'Ask Me To Dance' (1980) and 'Slippin' Up, Slippin' Round' (1980). 'One Day At A Time' has subsequently become a gospel standard, featured on innumerable compilation albums. While Christy Lane has never managed to match that early triumph, she has become a popular member of the *Grand Ole Opry*.

ASK ME TO DANCE, Liberty (US), 1980

LANE, Red

A songwriter of some distinction, Red Lane has collaborated with other major writers such as **Hank Cochran** and Curly Putnam. He was born in Bogaloosa, Louisiana, before moving up to Michigan, where he got his first break as a guitarist. In the early 1960s he moved to Nashville and secured work as a session guitarist; his next move was to join **Justin Tubb**'s backing band and, in 1967, he became a member of **Dottie West**'s outfit, the Heartaches.

The following year he collaborated with West, co-writing 'Country Girl'; this gave him the incentive to focus upon a solo career, and he was signed by RCA. Among his hits were 'The World Needs A Melody' and 'Set The World On Fire' (1971); his other songs have included 'Mississippi Women', 'One Row At A Time', 'All The Way In Or All The Way Out' and 'Charleston Cotton Mill'. In recent years, despite being without a recording contract, he still continues to contribute songs to artists of high calibre, such as **Waylon Jennings**.

LANG, K.D.

Kathy Dawn Lang has, through her refusal to be tied to a specific genre, become one of the most celebrated icons in the music industry of the last few years. While some of her material can loosely be termed country, she is first and foremost a highly individual stylist.

She was born in 1961 in Consort, Alberta, Canada, and studied classical music for three years. In 1970 she wrote 'Hoping All My Dreams Come True', which she sent to **Anne Murray**, and the following year changed tack, playing the guitar instead of the piano. After studying music at Red Deer College, Alberta, she appeared in the stage show *Country Chorale*, which led to her joining a country outfit called Dance Party, based in Edmonton.

The group's first album, *A Truly Western Experience*, was produced by Lang and appeared on the independent Vancouver-based label Bumstead; it combined many of her most disparate influences - from Yoko Ono to **Patsy Cline** - and encouraged Sire to sign her. Her debut, *Angel With A Lariat*, was a critical success but signally failed to ignite the charts; this would prove to be a recurrent problem.

The next album, *Shadowland*, did much to foster the general perception of her as a country singer: recorded in Nashville, with **Owen Bradley** producing, it featured vocal assistance from **Loretta Lynn**, **Brenda Lee** and **Kitty Wells** on 'The Honky Tonk Angels Medley'. Other notable collaborations followed, including a duet with **Roy Orbison** on 'Crying' (UK#7, 1992); and in 1992 a duet with Jane Siberry on 'Calling All Angels' was included on the soundtrack of the Wim Wenders film, *Until The End Of The World*.

In 1989 she released *Absolute Torch And Twang*; featuring her long-standing backing group, the Reclines, it illustrated the extent to which she had matured into an all-round performer, able to encompass many styles. This was emphasized still further by 1992's *Ingénue* - a collection of ballads and torch songs - which distanced her from her early type-casting as 'just another country singer'.

Alongside her blossoming musical career, Lang has won many followers in the feminist camp by her avowed sexual ambivalence, which has contributed to her iconic status. An appearance in Percy Adlon's *Salmonberries* in 1991 fuelled speculation that she might be one of the few contemporary musicians able to make a successful transition from vinyl to celluloid.

ABSOLUTE TORCH AND TWANG, Sire, 1989
ANGEL WITH A LARIAT, Sire, 1987
INGENUE, Sire, 1992
SHADOWLAND, Sire, 1988

LAWSON, Doyle See QUICKSILVER

LEADON, Bernie

Bernie Leadon was born on July 19, 1947, in Minneapolis, Minnesota. After moving to the West Coast in 1964 he joined **Chris Hillman**, first in the Scottsville Squirrel Barkers and then in the Hillmen. When Hillman joined the Beefeaters, Leadon moved on to Hearts and Flowers, remaining with them until May 1968, when he joined Dillard & Clark (see **Clark, Gene**). When Dillard & Clark separated after two albums, Leadon joined **Linda Ronstadt**'s backing group, the Corvettes. He lasted five months before going on to replace Chris Ethridge in the **Flying Burrito Brothers** in September 1969.

His tenure with the Burritos was marred by personality clashes with other members of the group, which caused him to leave in April 1971, and return to the harmonious atmosphere of Ronstadt's band. Shortly after his return the band became the **Eagles**, and Leadon led them through their most successful years until his departure in 1976. Since then he has worked principally as a session guitarist (with artists including **David Bromberg**, **Rita Coolidge**, Chris Hillman, Helen Reddy, Stephen Stills and Andy Fairweather-Low), apart from a brief stint in 1977, when he fronted his own group with Michael Georgiades.

LEE, Albert

Albert Lee has, since the early 1970s, been widely regarded as the English equivalent to US session guitarists like **James Burton**. Where Lee has triumphed over his US counterparts, however, has been in his ability to make excellent solo albums.

He was born in Leominster, Herefordshire, UK, on December 21, 1943. In 1959 he joined the UK R&B band Chris Farlowe and the Thunderbirds, remaining with them until 1967; among his most significant contributions was a particularly rousing solo on 'Stormy Monday Blues', the T-Bone Walker song. After leaving the group he played sessions for Joe Cocker among others, before taking to the club circuit with Country Fever and recording with Black Claw. While the group never made any recordings, they were part of a growing body of English bands (like Brinsley Schwartz) who were influenced as much by country as by R&B.

His next venture was to team up with songwriter Tony Colton and Chas Hodges (more recently in Chas & Dave), forming Poet and the One Man Band, who cut one album for Verve before changing their name to Head, Hands & Feet. Considerably more successful in the US, the group disbanded after cutting three albums (*Head, Hands & Feet*, 1971; *Tracks*, 1972; and *Old Soldiers Never Die*, 1973) which did much to raise Lee's US profile.

Settling in the US, he joined **Sonny Curtis**'s Crickets, who had managed to revive their career with the growing popularity of 'all things Texan'. In 1976 he started a liaison with **Emmylou Harris** (in the Hot Band) that resulted in Lee cutting his first solo album, *Hiding* (1979), produced by Emmylou's husband, Brian Ahern.

Such was the impact of his presence on the Hot Band that Lee became sought after on sessions in Nashville, as well as Los Angeles and the UK, contributing to albums by artists such as the **Everly Brothers**, **Juice Newton**, **Jerry Lee Lewis**, Eric Clapton, Jackson Browne and Dave Edmunds. Other solo albums followed, including *Albert Lee* (1982) for Polydor, *Country Guitar Man* (1986) for Sundown, and *Speechless* (1987) for MCA.

BLACK CLAW AND COUNTRY FEVER, Line (Germany), 1991
COUNTRY GUITAR MAN, Sundown, 1986
GAGGED BUT NOT BOUND, MCA (US), 1988
HIDING, A&M, 1979
SPEECHLESS, MCA, 1987

LEE, Brenda

'Little Miss Dynamite' exploded onto the scene in 1949, at the age of five. She has since maintained a presence as a country-ish rock 'n' roll singer, and then as a middle-of-the-road country singer. Closely involved with the country music establishment, she became a director of the Country Music Association in the 1980s.

Born Brenda Mae Tarpley on December 11, 1944, in Lithonia, Georgia, she won a talent contest when she was five. Six years later she won another talent contest which was heard by **Red Foley**, who invited her to appear on the *Ozark Jubilee Show*. This impressed Dub Albritton (Foley's manager), and he signed her to Decca.

Lee's first record, the **Hank Williams** composition 'Jambalaya', was followed by a number of rambunctious titles - including 'Let's Jump The Broomstick' (UK#12, 1961) - which opened the floodgates for a string of **Owen Bradley**-produced hits that stretched through the early 1960s: 'Sweet Nothin's' (US#4, UK#4, 1960), 'I'm Sorry' (US#1, UK#12, 1960), 'I Want To Be Wanted' (US#1, UK#31, 1960), 'Rockin' Around The Christmas Tree' (US#14, 1960; UK#6, 1962), 'Emotions' (US#7, UK#45, 1961), 'You Can Depend On Me' (US#6, 1961), 'Dum Dum' (US#4, UK#22, 1961), 'Fool No.1' (US#3, UK#38, 1961), 'Break It To Me Gently' (US#4, UK#46, 1962), 'Speak To Me Pretty' (UK#3, 1962), 'Here Comes That Feeling' (UK#5, 1962), 'Everybody Loves Me But You' (US#6, 1962), 'Heart In Hand' (US#15, 1962), 'All Alone Am I' (US#3, 1962; UK#4, 1963), 'Your Used To Be' (US#32, 1963), 'Losing You' (US#6, UK#10, 1963), 'I Wonder' (US#24, UK#14, 1963), 'The Grass Is Greener' (US#17, 1963), 'Sweet Impossible You' (UK#4, 1963), 'As Usual' (US#12, 1963; UK#5, 1964), 'Think' (US#25, UK#26, 1964), 'Is It True' (US#17, UK#17, 1964), 'Christmas Will Be Just Another Lonely Day' (UK#29, 1964), 'Thanks A Lot' (UK#41, 1965), 'Too Many Rivers' (US#13, UK#22, 1965), 'Rusty Bells' (US#33, 1965), 'Coming On Strong' (US#11, 1966) and 'Ride, Ride, Ride' (US#37, 1967).

While many of the earlier hits adopted the 'crying style' that **Patsy Cline** had popularized, she became progressively outmoded as groups such as the Beatles began to emerge. By the end of the 1960s she was no longer a force in the pop charts, but made inroads into the country charts with titles like 'If This Is Our Last Time' (1971), 'Nobody Wins' (C&W#5, 1973), 'Big Four Poster Bed' (1974) and 'He's My Rock' (1975), and also recorded a duet with **George Jones**, singing the **Ray Charles** classic 'Hallelujah I Love Her So' (1984). By the end of the 1980s she had become a fixture on the cabaret circuit, and was appearing regularly in Las Vegas.

BEST OF BRENDA LEE, MCA, 1986

LOVE SONGS, MCA, 1986
VERY BEST OF BRENDA LEE, Volumes 1-2, MCA, 1990

LEE, Dickey
Under his original name of Dickey Lipscomb, Lee has achieved immortality through the composition of the **George Jones** hit 'She Still Thinks I Care' (1962) - one of the most frequently recorded songs in the country canon. Born in Memphis on September 21, 1941, his career started while still at school when his group won a talent contest, the prize being a fifteen-minute slot on a radio station in Santa Barbara, California. In 1957 he joined the Sun label, cutting 'Good Lovin'', and then won a boxing scholarship to Memphis State University, becoming its welterweight champion. Moving on to the Philips subsidiary Smash, he had hits with 'Patches' (US#6, 1962), 'I Saw Linda Yesterday' (US#14, 1962) and 'Laurie (Strange Things Happen)' (US#14, 1965).

In 1970, having meanwhile pursued a career as a songwriter, he was signed by **Chet Atkins** to RCA and cut titles such as 'The Mahogany Pulpit' (1971), 'Never Ending Song Of Love' (C&W#8, 1971), 'Rocky' (C&W#1, 1975), 'Angels, Roses And Rain' and '9,999,999 Tears' (1976) with producer **Allen Reynolds**. His career took a nosedive after signing to Mercury, and he reverted to songwriting, penning titles such as 'You're The First Time I've Thought About Leaving' (**Reba McEntire**), 'Let's Fall To Pieces Together' (**George Strait**) and 'I've Been Around Enough To Know' (**John Schneider**).

LEE, Ernie
Radio and television presenter *par excellence*, Ernest Eli Cornelison was born near Berea, Kentucky, and made his debut on the *Renfro Valley Barn Dance* in 1940, taking over as host on **Red Foley**'s departure. His next step was to become host of the *Midwestern Hayride* on WLW, Cincinnati, and in 1947, when the programme transferred from radio to television, he continued to host it until 1953.

After leaving WLW he spent a year in Dayton, Ohio, before retiring to Florida to fish. The strain of fishing proved too much and he quickly established himself on WSUN, St Petersburg, where he remained until 1958. After moving to WTVT, Tampa, he hosted a breakfast show until the early 1980s. While he cut the odd record, such as 'Hominy Grits' (1947) for RCA, it is his charm as a presenter that has earned him respect.

LEE, Jimmy   see **MATHIS, Country Johnny**

LEE, Johnny
Born John Lee Hamm on July 3, 1946, in Alta Loma, Texas, he formed Johnny Lee and the Road Runners while at school in Santa Fe. In 1970 he met **Mickey Gilley**, who recruited him as a trumpeter/vocalist in his touring band; this led to a residency at Gilley's club in Pasadena, Texas. From 1975 he recorded with local labels, cutting 'Sometimes' (1975) and 'This Time' (1978), among others. His career leapfrogged when 'Lookin' For Love' (US#5, C&W#1, 1980) was featured in the film *Urban Cowboy* (1980); most of the film's action was based around Gilley's club.

After the success of 'Lookin' For Love' Lee was signed to Asylum and notched up other hits, such as 'One In A Million' (C&W#1, 1980), 'Pickin' Up Strangers' (C&W#3, 1981), 'Prisoner Of Hope' (C&W#3, 1981), 'Bet Your Heart On Me' (C&W#1, 1981), 'The Yellow Rose' (with **Lane Brody**; C&W#1, 1984), 'You Could've Heard A Heart Break' (C&W#1, 1984), and 'Rollin' Lonely' and 'Save The Last Chance' (1985).

After being dropped by the label in 1986, he spent some months in litigation with his former manager Sherwood Cryer, until being signed in 1989 by **Mike Curb** to the Curb label and releasing *New Directions*.

JOHNNY LEE, Audio Fidelity (US), 1984

LEWIS, Bobby
No relation to the Bobby Lewis who scored a monster hit in the early 1960s with 'Tossin' & Turnin'', Bobby Lewis was born in Hodgensville, Kentucky, on May 9, 1946, and made his debut at the age of eleven on Lexington's *Kentucky Barn Dance*, where he remained until 1959. In 1958 he appeared on CBS's *Saturday Night Country Style*, and by 1964 he was appearing on the television programme *Hi-Varieties Show*.

During the mid-1960s he was signed to United Artists, scoring hits with 'How Long Has It Been' (1964), 'Love Me And Make It Better' (1967), 'From Heaven To Heartache' (1968), 'Hello Mary Lou' (1970) and 'She's Been Keeping Me Up Nights' (1979). Although 'From Heaven To Heartache' secured him a Grammy nomination for Best Male Performer of 1969, he has remained a little-known figure, noted for playing a lute with guitar strings.

LEWIS, Jerry Lee

So much has been written about Jerry Lee Lewis that mythology has come to obscure his prodigious abilities as a musician. Although accused of moral misdemeanors, Lewis's position as one of the most innovative country-based performers of all time is beyond question. His passion and fervour has transformed many a maudlin song into a manic tour de force.

He was born in Ferriday, Louisiana, on September 29, 1935, a cousin of **Mickey Gilley** and the evangelist Jimmy Lee Swaggart. Inspired by pianists **Moon Mullican** and **Del Wood**, Lewis had mastered the piano by the age of nine. Other early influences included the showmanship of Al Jolson, an influence which proved vital in enabling him to win one of Ted Mack's talent shows, which in turn granted him a slot on WNAT, Natchez, that lasted until 1951. He then took up a diploma in theology in Texas, with a view to becoming a preacher. In 1952 he married Jane Mitcham (the first of six wives) and their son, Jerry Lee, Jr, was born on November 2, 1953.

After auditioning for **Slim Whitman** on the *Louisiana Hayride* (Whitman organized one of the *Louisiana Hayride* roadshows), he was signed in 1956 by **Sam Phillips** as a putative replacement for **Elvis Presley**. Although not a prolific writer, he demonstrated an idiosyncratic style even on his first record, 'Crazy Arms' (a hit for **Ray Price**), which carried the trademarks that were to figure throughout his career. A tour with **Johnny Cash** and **Carl Perkins** was crucial in breaking him, and a succession of hits followed: 'Whole Lotta Shakin' Goin' On' (US#3, C&W#1, UK#8, 1957), 'Great Balls Of Fire' (US#2, C&W#1, UK#1, 1957), 'Breathless' (US#7, UK#8, 1958), 'High School Confidential' (US#21, 1958; UK#12, 1959), 'Lovin' Up A Storm' (UK#28, 1961), 'Baby Baby Bye Bye' (UK#47, 1961), 'What'd I Say' (US#30, UK#10, 1961), 'Sweet Little Sixteen' (UK#38, 1962) and 'Good Golly Miss Molly' (UK#31, 1963).

The modest chart success of these songs was not commensurate with his standing as a live performer. This was due to hostility from radio stations over the alleged obscenity of some of his lyrics, and was exacerbated still further by his marriage to Myra Gail, his thirteen-year-old cousin, which caused a tour of the UK to be cancelled at the last minute. In 1963 Lewis moved to the Mercury subsidiary, Smash, run by **Jerry Kennedy**. He was here encouraged to embrace a more traditional type of country music, moving away from the raucous rock 'n' roll that had made him famous; two of his best albums were cut during these

years: *The Greatest Live Show On Earth* (1965) and *More Of The Greatest Live Show On Earth* (1966).

Although beset by many personal problems (some self-inflicted), he continued, from the 1960s onwards, to establish himself as a country singer with a string of hits: 'Another Time, Another Place' (C&W#4, 1968), 'What's Made Milwaukee Famous (Has Made A Loser Out Of Me)' (C&W#2, 1968), 'She Still Comes Around' (C&W#2, 1968), 'To Make Love Sweeter For You' (C&W#1, 1969), 'One Has My Name (The Other Has My Heart)' (C&W#3, 1969), 'She Even Woke Me Up To Say Goodbye' (C&W#2, 1970), 'Once More With Feeling' (C&W#2, 1970), 'There Must Be More To Love Than This' (C&W#1, 1970), 'Touching Home' (C&W#3, 1971), 'Me And Bobby McGee' (US#40, C&W#1, 1972), 'Chantilly Lace' (C&W#1, UK#33, 1972), 'Let's Put It Back Together Again' (1976), 'Middle Age Crazy' (C&W#4, 1977) and 'I'll Find It Where I Can' (1978).

During the 1970s and 1980s, his status as a legend was confirmed when a bunch of younger rock musicians (including **Albert Lee**, Rory Gallagher, Peter Frampton and Alvin Lee) collaborated with him on *The Session* (1973), and when German television staged a concert with Lewis, Carl Perkins and Johny Cash, which was released as *The Survivors* on Columbia in 1982.

In 1979 he moved to Elektra, and scored with 'Over The Rainbow' and 'Thirty Nine And Holding' (C&W#4, 1981); and in 1981 he moved on again (this time to MCA) and cut *My Fingers Do The Talking* (1983) and *I Am What I Am* (1985). In 1989 Dennis Quaid played him in the biopic, *Great Balls Of Fire*, and Nick Tosches wrote his biography, *Hellfire*. While his health has caused concern over the years, his touring schedule has changed little, with appearances in Las Vegas and Europe displaying a charisma rivalled only by artists like James Brown and Little Richard.

CLASSIC JERRY LEE LEWIS, Bear Family (Germany), 1989
COMPLETE LONDON SESSIONS, Volumes 1-2, Bear Family (Germany), 1986
THE ESSENTIAL JERRY LEE LEWIS, Charly, 1986
FERRIDAY FIREBALL, Charly, 1986
GREAT BALLS OF FIRE, Charly, 1989
KILLER: 1963-77, Volumes 1-3, Mercury/Bear Family (Germany), 1989
KILLER COUNTRY, Edsel, 1981
LIVE AT THE VAPORS CLUB, Ace, 1991
NUGGETS, Volumes 1-2, Charly, 1977
ORIGINAL JERRY LEE LEWIS, Charly, 1976
RARE & ROCKIN', Charly, 1987

ROCKET, Instant, 1990
ROCKIN' MY LIFE AWAY, Tomato (US), 1990
THE SUN YEARS, Sun, 1989
SURVIVORS (with Johnny Cash and Carl Perkins), Columbia, 1982
UP THROUGH THE YEARS: 1955-63, Bear Family (Germany), 1986
WHEN TWO WORLDS COLLIDE, Elektra, 1980

LIGHT CRUST DOUGHBOYS

Exponents of Western Swing, the Light Crust Doughboys proved the value of sponsorship in the early days of radio as they were formed - by Wilbert Lee O'Daniel (born on March 11, 1890, in Malta, Ohio), the rising star of the Burrus Mill Flour Company - to promote 'Light Crust Flour' on KFJZ, Fort Worth. This support ensured that, with regular radio broadcasts, Western Swing began to reach a much larger audience, laying the foundation for struggling musicians (such as **Bob Wills**, **Johnnie Lee Wills**, **Milton Brown**, **Leon McAuliffe** and Herman Arnspiger) to find wider popularity and greater distinction in later years. Bob Wills, Brown and Arnspiger were all themselves employees of Burrus Mill, and their group, the Aladdin Laddies, formed the nucleus of the Doughboys.

Once the popularity of the group took hold, O'Daniel became MC and wrote songs such as 'Beautiful Texas' and 'Put Me In Your Pocket'. After leaving the company in 1935, he set up the Hillbilly Flour Company and organized W. Lee O'Daniel and the Hillbilly Boys. His political ambitions, however, were of more importance to him, and he eventually went on to became Governor of Texas. One of the most skilful manipulators of music, he used his position with the group as a propaganda platform to vilify his opponents. The Light Crust Doughboys, with an ever-changing line-up, have continued on an on-off basis ever since.

LIVE: 1936, Jambalaya, 1990

LINDE, Dennis

While having little success in his own right, Dennis Linde (born on March 18, 1943) is one of many writers to flourish in Nashville. During the mid-1960s he came to prominence with a band called the Starlighters before moving to Nashville and cutting *Linde Manor* (1968) for the Intrepid label. After meeting up with **Kris Kristofferson**, he joined his backing band, which also included **Billy Swan** and a former member of the Lovin' Spoonful, Zally Yanofsky.

After recording a one-off album, *Jubal*, for Elektra, he went on to cut *Dennis Linde* (1973) and *Trapped In The Suburbs* (1974). While neither were commercial successes, he was signed by **Fred Foster** to Monument as a solo artist, cutting *Surface Noise* (1976). As a writer, he came into his own when **Elvis Presley** recorded 'Burning Love' (1972), which encouraged artists such as **Roy Orbison** and the **Everly Brothers** to start recording his songs. He rejoined Kristofferson's touring band as a session guitarist (along with Billy Swan) in 1986.

LITTLE VILLAGE see HIATT, John

LLOYD, Jimmie see LOGSDON, Jimmie

LOCKLIN, Hank

One of many performers to have made an impact upon the Irish community in both the US and Eire, Hank Locklin has a laid-back vocal style that was echoed to great success by **Don Williams**. Born Lawrence Hankins Locklin on February 15, 1918, in McLellan, Florida, he won an amateur talent contest in 1928, but when the Depression struck in the early 1930s, he struggled to survive, working at a variety of jobs including labouring and sharecropping. After the Second World War he joined the *Louisiana Hayride* and recorded for Decca and Four Star, where he cut 'The Same Sweet Girl' (1949) and 'Let Me Be The One' (1953).

'Let Me Be The One' caught the ear of **Chet Atkins**, who signed him to RCA; in later years he would record with the session combo Nashville Brass (see **Davis, Danny**). Among the hits that followed were 'Geisha Girl' (1957), 'Send Me The Pillow You Dream On' (C&W#5, 1958), 'It's A Little More Like Heaven' (1958), 'Please Help Me I'm Falling' (US#8, C&W#1, UK#9, 1960), 'Happy Birthday To Me' (1961), 'From Here To There To You' (UK#44, 1962), 'We're Gonna Go Fishing' (UK#18, 1962), 'Happy Journey', 'I Feel A Cry Coming On' (UK#28, 1962) and 'Country Hall Of Fame' (1967).

While his touring schedule has remained as intensive as ever, the chart action was over by the end of the 1960s and, having moved to Houston, Texas, he concentrated on television work, appearing on KTR-TV and KRID's *Big D Jamboree*. In 1975 he changed labels and signed with MGM, since when he has recorded little. Many compilations of his material are still available.

FAMOUS COUNTRY MUSIC MAKERS, RCA, 1975
FOREIGN LOVE, Stetson, 1989
FROM HERE TO THERE TO YOU, Bulldog, 1985
IRISH SONGS, COUNTRY STYLE, RCA, 1984

LOCORRIERE, Dennis see DOCTOR HOOK

LOGSDON, Jimmy

Jimmie Logsdon (born on April 1, 1922, in Panther, Kentucky) is one of many hillbilly singers to have spent most of their careers in obscurity. His father was a church minister constantly on the move, but the family finally settled in Ludlow, near Cincinnati. In 1944 Logsdon was drafted into the airforce and learnt about electronics; after the war he opened a radio repair shop in Louisville, which also did a line in records. Logsdon began to play guitar after hearing **Hank Williams**; by 1948 he was sufficiently good to land a slot on WLOU, Louisville.

In 1952 he left WLOU to become an announcer on the neighbouring WKYW, and was booked to open for Hank Williams; Williams was so impressed by Logsdon that he introduced him to Paul Cohen, the head of Decca in Nashville. Over the next three years he cut a number of singles for the label, including 'As Long As We're Together', 'Where The Old River Flows' and 'The Death Of Hank Williams', backed by Williams' group, the Drifting Cowboys. After failing to get a hit, he was dropped by Decca, and signed to Dot, cutting 'Midnight Blues'; this, too, failed.

With his career heading nowhere fast, he checked into a hospital to overcome pill and alcohol habits. In 1957 he cut 'I've Got A Rocket In My Pocket' as Jimmie Lloyd (presumably to avoid the wrath of his God-fearing parents) for Roulette. This stab at immortality may have been pretty impressive, but the punters were content to let it pass them by. Returning to Louisville as a DJ he recorded a few sides for King in 1964, before hanging up his guitar for good in 1972 and getting work in Kentucky for the state authorities.

LONDIN, Larrie

One of the best ever session drummers, Larrie Londin was born Ralph Gallant, near Detroit, in 1944. He started to play the drums when he was fifteen, but his first professional engagement was as a vocalist with the Headliners, a white band who were signed to Motown. While the Headliners failed to make any waves, he started to play sessions for Motown artists such as the Temptations, Junior Walker, Marvin Gaye and the Supremes. Londin struck up a friendship with **Chet Atkins** and **Jerry Reed** during this period, who encouraged him to move to Nashville to work on sessions.

The drumming techniques that Londin demonstrated in Nashville - he was one of the first to use electronic drums - encouraged other RCA artists, such as **Waylon Jennings**, **Elvis Presley** and **Dolly Parton**, to enlist his services. His years at Motown had endowed him with an ability to adapt to virtually any style, and he played sessions for artists as varied as **Emmylou Harris**, **Linda Ronstadt**, **Randy Travis**, **Albert Lee**, **Neil Young**, **Reba McEntire**, Joe Cocker, B.B. King, Johnny Mathis, Adrian Belew and Journey. He began recording with the **Everly Brothers** when they regrouped, and became a part of their roadshow. On August 31, 1992, he died of cancer.

LONZO & OSCAR

As Lonzo & Oscar, the Sullivan brothers occupied a place in the hearts of many for their comedy act at the *Grand Ole Opry*. While their brand of humour would now leave most cold, they reigned supreme for over twenty years.

Hailing from Edmonton, Kentucky, John (Lonzo) was born on July 7, 1917, and Rollin (Oscar) was born on January 19, 1919. Before the war, Rollin was partnered by Ken Marvin (whose real name was Lloyd George) as Lonzo, and together they had a hit with 'I'm My Own Grandpa' (1940) and broadcast on WTJS, Jackson, until the outbreak of hostilities in 1942.

After the war, Ken Marvin retired and Rollin's brother, John Sullivan, took over the Lonzo role, which he held until his death in 1967. Touring at first with **Eddy Arnold**, they secured a regular spot on the *Grand Ole Opry*, becoming firm favourites and recording for RCA, Columbia and Starday, among others. When John died, Rollin put the act in mothballs until he recruited Dave Hooten in 1968. Although they continue to work, their humour is now somewhat dated.

LORD, Bobby

Bobby Lord was born on January 6, 1934, in Sandford, Florida. After graduating from the University of Tampa, he joined **Red Foley**'s outfit on the *Ozark Jubilee*, which enabled him to secure a contract with the Hickory label and become a cast member of the *Grand Ole Opry*. In the 1960s he had a number of modest hits, including 'Hawkeye', 'Life Can Have Meaning' (1964) and 'You And Me Against The World' (1970), and his own TV show, but by the turn of the 1970s he had disappeared into obscurity.

LOUDERMILK, John D.

The distinguished songwriter John D. Loudermilk was born on March 31, 1934, in Durham, North Carolina, the son of a carpenter. During his childhood he played drums in the Salvation Army Band, before making his first radio broadcast when he was ten; in 1946 he made his first television appearance on a talent show hosted by **Tex Ritter**.

After attending the University of North Carolina, he joined Durham's WTVD as a musician, and was occasionally allowed to perform his own songs. **George Hamilton IV** heard and recorded Loudermilk's composition 'A Rose And Baby Ruth' (1956) and turned it into a massive hit. Over the next fifteen years Loudermilk went on to have hits with songs like 'Sittin' In The Balcony' (Eddie Cochran), 'Waterloo' (**Stonewall Jackson**), 'Ebony Eyes' (**Everly Brothers**), 'Sad Movies (Make Me Cry)' and 'Norman' (**Sue Thompson**), 'Abilene' (George Hamilton IV), 'Tobacco Road' (Nashville Teens) and 'Indian Reservation' (Paul Revere & the Raiders and Don Fardon).

During the late 1950s and early 1960s he made his mark as a performer, cutting 'Sittin' In The Balcony' (US#38, 1957) as Johnny Dee, and 'Three Stars' (a tribute to **Buddy Holly**, the Big Bopper and Ritchie Valens; US#11, 1959) as Tommy Dee. Under his own name, 'Language Of Love' (US#32, UK#13, 1961), 'Thou Shall Not Steal' (1962), 'Road Hog' (1962) and 'Blue Train' (1963) all became hits and he would have, in all probability, had many more had he not been so reluctant to tour. By the end of the 1960s his ample royalties enabled him to concentrate on fishing and studying ethnomusicology, although he has appeared on several occasions at London's Country Music Festival in Wembley; his folk songs, performed to his own guitar accompaniment, have an enduring appeal which transcends the quirks of fashion.

BLUE TRAIN: 1961-2, Bear Family (Germany), 1989
IT'S MY TIME, Bear Family (Germany), 1989
TWELVE SIDES OF LOUDERMILK, RCA (US), 1987

LOUVIN BROTHERS

The vitality of the Louvin Brothers' records has made them one of the most influential of duos; their influence has been wide-ranging - the **Everly Brothers**, the **Byrds** and **Emmylou Harris** have all fallen under their spell.

Raised in Henagar, North Alabama, Ira (born on April 21, 1924, in Rainesville, Alabama) and Charlie Loudermilk (born on July 7, 1927, in Jefferson City, Missouri) grew up listening to the **Blue Sky Boys** and the **Delmore Brothers**. Ira learnt to play the mandolin, while Charlie learnt the guitar; in 1943 they won a talent contest in Chattanooga, Tennessee, their prize being a slot on a breakfast radio show, broadcasting as the Foggy Mountain Boys.

In 1946, after military service, they changed their name to Louvin and hit the road with a vengeance, touring radio stations, which culminated with a residency on *Midday Merry-Go-Round* on WNOX, Knoxville. After signing to MGM they cut a string of gospel songs between 1949 and 1951, including 'The Family Who Prays', 'Preach The Gospel' and 'Satan Lied To Me'. They moved to Capitol in 1951 and cut sides, such as 'Are You Missing Me?' and 'Childish Love' (1952), that - despite the brothers' resistance to any form of labelling - were pure bluegrass. Among their later hits for Capitol were 'When I Stop Dreaming' (1955), 'You're Running Wild' (1956), 'I Don't Believe You've Met My Baby' (C&W#1, 1956) and 'My Baby's Gone' (1959).

In 1956 they cut *Tragic Songs Of Life* (a collection of old-time ballads and folk songs), which included the classic 'Knoxville Girl'. Over the next six years, having joined the cast of the *Grand Ole Opry*, their sound became less individual as **Chet Atkins** was drafted in to streamline their sound. In 1963 the partnership, which had always been volatile, split up, with each brother pursuing a solo career. Charlie had hits with 'I Don't Love You Anymore' (C&W#4, 1964), 'See The Big Man Cry' and 'Less And Less' (1964).

On June 20, 1965, Ira and his wife Florence were killed in a head-on collision, his long-deleted debut solo album was released posthumously. Charlie continued working as a solo artist, although he duetted with **Melba Montgomery** and, some years later, Emmylou Harris. He also appeared in films such as *Music City USA* and *Golden Guitar*.

BEST OF THE EARLY LOUVIN BROTHERS, Rebel, 1985
CHARLIE LOUVIN, President, 1986
I FORGOT TO CRY (Charlie Louvin), Stetson, 1990
IRA & CHARLIE, Stetson, 1988

LIVE AT THE NEW RANCH RIVER, Copper Creek (US), 1989
LOUVIN BROTHERS, Capitol, 1992
MY BABY'S GONE, Stetson, 1986
SING THEIR HEARTS OUT, See For Miles, 1989
SONGS THAT TELL A STORY, Sundown, 1988
TRAGIC SONGS OF LIFE, Stetson, 1987

LOVELESS, Patty

Patty Loveless is one of the new breed of country singer, combining the rock inflections of **Linda Ronstadt** with the robust traditionalism of Loveless's relation, **Loretta Lynn**. She was born Patty Ramey in Pikeville, Kentucky, in 1957. A teenage member of the **Wilburn Brothers'** roadshow, she did not impress Teddy Wilburn, and so, after marrying the Wilburns' drummer, Terry Lovelace, she moved to North Carolina in 1974, altering the spelling of her married name to Loveless to avoid confusion with actress Linda Lovelace. For the next decade she played the club circuit, until returning to Nashville in 1985 and being signed by producer Tony Brown to MCA.

In 1988 she broke through with 'If My Heart Had Windows'; this was followed by 'A Little Bit In Love' and 'Blue Side Of Town' (1988), 'Don't Toss Us Away' (1989), 'Timber I'm Falling In Love' (C&W#1, 1989), 'The Lonely Side Of Love' (1989) and 'On Down The Line' (1991). At present she is one of country's brightest stars; she trumpets the cause of lesser-known writers, such as Kostas and **Paul Kennerley**, by covering their songs.

HONKY TONK ANGEL, MCA, 1989
IF MY HEART HAD WINDOWS, MCA, 1988
ON DOWN THE LINE, MCA, 1990
PATTI LOVELESS, MCA, 1987

LOVETT, Lyle

Lyle Lovett has become one of the more iconoclastic members of the New Country movement, with a lyrical style that places many of the old values of country music within a contemporary setting. Unlike many of his counterparts he has managed to forge an album-based career; this has made him much more attractive to rock audiences than to the traditional singles-oriented country market.

He was born on November 1, 1957. After leaving school he studied German before moving into journalism and starting to write songs. In 1979 he made his perfroming debut, but was not signed until 1986, when MCA promoted him and his band as a Western Swing outfit. *Cowboy Man* emerged that year and included 'Cowboy Man' (C&W#10, 1986), 'Closing Time' and **Robert Earl Keen**'s 'This Old Porch' (1986).

The follow-up, *Pontiac* (1987), established him with contemporaries such as Randy Newman, **Guy Clark** and **Emmylou Harris**, who all employed him as an opening act on their respective tours. 1989's *Lyle Lovett & His Large Band* included a cover of **Tammy Wynette**'s 'Stand By Your Man' (1989), which reputedly is a gay classic. As a writer, his songs have been covered by Harris, **Lacy J. Dalton** and **Nanci Griffith**. His 1991 appearance in Robert Altman's movie *The Player* affirmed the public perception of him as an enigmatic figure; while 1992's *Joshua Judges Ruth* showed that as a songwriter and performer he was going from strength to strength.

COWBOY MAN, MCA, 1987
JOSHUA JUDGES RUTH, MCA, 1992
LYLE LOVETT AND HIS LARGE BAND, MCA, 1989
PONTIAC, MCA, 1988

LUKE THE DRIFTER see WILLIAMS, Hank

LULU BELLE & SCOTTY

Lulu Belle & Scotty were one of many husband-and-wife duos that flourished in the 1930s and 1940s. Though their output was bland, they commanded substantial fees wherever they played.

Lulu Belle was born Myrtle Eleanor Cooper on December 24, 1913, in Boone County, North Carolina. In 1932, having learnt the guitar while at school, she auditioned successfully for the *National Barn Dance* and, subsequently, partnered a number of artists, including **Red Foley**. The following year Scott Wiseman joined the cast.

Wiseman was born on November 8, 1909, in Spruce Pine, North Carolina; before joining the *National Barn Dance* he broadcast on WRVA, Richmond, and WMMN, Fairmont. On joining the *Barn Dance*, Wiseman started to perform with Lulu Belle as a duo; they married in 1934. In 1936 Lulu Belle won an award for being the most popular female entertainer in the US, and over the next twenty years they were regularly featured on the *Barn Dance*, popularizing songs such as 'Remember Me (When The Candle Lights Are Gleaming)' (1935), 'Brown Mountain Light' (1935) and 'Have I Told You Lately That I Love You' (1936). They broadcast on the *Boone County Jamboree* from WLW, Cincinnati, between 1938 and 1941, had their own television programme on WNBQ from 1949 until 1957, and recorded for many labels, including Vocalion, Starday, Okeh, Mercury and London.

They retired from public performances in 1958; Scotty became a full-time teacher and Lulu Belle joined the North Carolina legislature. Scotty died on February 1, 1981, in Gainesville, Florida.

SWEETHEARTS, Starday, 1987
SWEETHEARTS OF COUNTRY MUSIC, Starday, 1987

LUMAN, Bob

Bob Luman was uncertain whether to pursue a career in music or in baseball; the prevailing mood of the time, with **Elvis Presley**'s success as a rockabilly singer, ensured that music won.

He was born Robert Glyn Luman on April 15, 1938, in Nacogdoches, Texas; his father was a fine fiddler and all-round musician and encouraged him to play the guitar. Though his energies were diverted by the offer of a trial with the Pittsburgh Pirates, he began to make records for an independent label, which resulted in a spot on KWKH's *Louisiana Hayride* as a replacement for **Johnny Cash**. In 1960, after spells with Imperial and Capitol and an appearance in the film *Carnival* (1957), he broke through with **Boudleaux Bryant**'s 'Let's Think About Living' (US#7, UK#6, 1960) on Warner Bros.; this was followed by 'Why Why Bye Bye' (UK#46, 1960) and 'The Great Snowman' (UK#49, 1961).

The momentum was broken when he was called up for military service. Luman found, after discharge, that rockabilly had become obsolete with the rise of the **Rolling Stones**, and he turned to country, signing with Hickory in 1964 and scoring a minor hit with 'The File' (1964). Two years later he moved to Epic and notched up hits that included 'Ain't Got Time To Be Unhappy' (1968), 'When You Say Love', 'Lonely Women Make Good Lovers' (1972), 'Neither One Of Us' (1973) and 'Still Loving You' (1974). In 1977 he signed with Polydor, scoring with 'The Pay Phone' and cutting *Alive And Well*, which was produced by Johnny Cash. His career was cut short when he died tragically of pneumonia on December 27, 1978.

CARNIVAL ROCK, Bear Family (Germany), 1988
LET'S THINK ABOUT LIVING, Sundown, 1961
LORETTA, Sundown, 1989
MORE ROCKABILLY ROCK, Bear Family (Germany), 1987
STILL ROCKIN', Bear Family (Germany), 1984
WILD-EYED WOMAN, Bear Family (Germany), 1988

LUNN, Robert

Lunn was born in Franklin, Tennessee, on November 28, 1912. He joined the *Grand Ole Opry* in 1938, after having performed vaudeville, remaining there (except for a break during the war) until 1958. As his voice was mediocre he adopted the 'talking blues', which enabled him to improvise lengthy recitations. In later years **Woody Guthrie** and **Bob Dylan** would adopt the 'talking blues', but with a greater degree of trenchancy than Lunn.

In common with many other former vaudevillians, he seldom recorded - being more at ease in live performance. He retired in 1958 and died of a heart attack on March 8, 1966.

LUTHER, Frank

Frank Luther (like **Vernon Dalhart** and his erstwhile colleague, **Carson Robison**) was a writer with eyes fixed on both the past and present; he adapted a number of folk songs, making them suitable as either novelty items or children's songs: 'Barnacle Bill The Sailor', 'Home On The Range' and 'What Good Will It Do'.

He was born Francis Luther Crow on August 5, 1905, in Larkin, Kansas, and was raised in Bakersfield. He studied music while at college, before joining the church as a minister. In 1926 he joined the DeReszke Singers as the lead tenor and piano accompanist and, the following year, joined another vocal group, the Revellers, who had a following on the local radio networks.

He moved to New York in 1928 and started to record extensively for a variety of major labels, including Victor and Decca; some of these recordings were duets with Carson Robison, under the name of Bud & Joe Billings. They also broadcasted with Ethel Park Richardson, who did much to get city dwellers interested in pastoral pleasures with her series of programmes on NBC and WOR.

During the 1930s he recorded with his trio, which included Leonard Stokes and his wife, Zora Layman, with **Ray Whitley** as a later addition. In the latter half of the 1930s he recorded children's songs based on *Snow White And The Seven Dwarves*, *Mother Goose's Rhymes* and *Babar The Elephant*. He retired from performing after the Second World War, became director of children's programmes for a New York radio station and wrote a book on the history of American folk music, *Americans And Their Songs*.

LYNN, Judy

An all-round entertainer, little known beyond Las Vegas, Judy Lynn was born the daughter of band-leader Joe Voiten in Boise, Idaho, on April 12, 1936. During her teens she was a rodeo rider, 'Queen of the Snake Valley Jamboree' in 1952, and a beauty queen, representing Idaho in the Miss America finals of 1955. The following year she was pulled in as a replacement for **Jean Shepard** (who had been taken ill) at the Grand Ole Opry roadshow. This led to a recording contract with Dot, and was followed by her nomination as co-host (with **Ernest Tubb**) of the first national transmission of the *Grand Ole Opry*. While her live appearances and television performances were plentiful and successful, she has had very few hits: 'Footsteps Of A Fool' (1961), 'My Secret', 'My Father's Voice' (1963) and 'Married To A Memory' (1971).

LYNN, Loretta

The story of Loretta Lynn's travails prior to super-stardom was brought into focus in 1980, with the hugely successful film adaptation of her autobiography: *Coal Miner's Daughter* won Sissy Spacek an Oscar for her performance as Lynn. This was a story without rose-tinted spectacles, and it demonstrated just how little her success has affected her music.

She was born Loretta Webb on April 14, 1935, in Butcher's Hollow, Kentucky, one of eight siblings (including **Crystal Gayle**), whose father, Melvin Webb, was a miner. She married Oliver 'Moonshine' Lynn at the age of thirteen, and during the 1950s she moved with him to Custer, Washington, and started a family - her husband supporting them by garage work. Encouraged to sing at family gatherings during her childhood, Loretta now began to write songs and play with a band. She cut her first record, 'I'm A Honky Tonk Girl', in 1960 for the Zero label, which impressed the **Wilburn Brothers** enough to invite the band to Nashville.

In 1961 **Owen Bradley** signed her to the Decca label; her first hit prophetically titled 'Success' (1962), showed her ability as a songwriter and illustrated the extent of the influence of **Kitty Wells** and **Patsy Cline** on her vocal style. She cut a string of hits throughout the 1960s, which included 'Don't Come Home A-Drinkin' (With Lovin' On Your Mind)' (C&W#1, 1966), 'Fist City' (C&W#1, 1968), 'You Ain't Woman Enough' (C&W#2, 1968), 'You've Just Stepped In (From Steppin' Out On Me)' (C&W#2, 1968), 'Your Squaw Is On The Warpath' (C&W#3, 1969), 'Woman Of The World' (C&W#1, 1969), 'Coal Miner's Daughter' (C&W#1, 1970), 'I Wanna Be Free' (C&W#3, 1971), 'You're Lookin' At Country' (C&W#5, 1971), 'One's On The Way' (C&W#1, 1971), 'Rated X' (C&W#1, 1973), 'Love Is The Foundation' (C&W#1, 1973), 'Hey Loretta' (C&W#3, 1973), 'They Don't Treat 'Em Like My Daddy' (C&W#4, 1974), 'Trouble In Paradise' (C&W#1, 1974), 'The Pill' (C&W#5, 1975), 'Somebody Somewhere (Don't Know What He's Missin' Tonight)' (C&W#1, 1976), 'She's Got You' (C&W#1, 1977) and 'Out Of My Head And Back In My Bed' (C&W#1, 1977).

Almost as impressive were her duets with **Conway Twitty**: 'After The Fire Is Gone' (C&W#1, 1971), 'Lead Me On' (C&W#1, 1971), 'Louisiana Woman, Mississippi Man' (C&W#1, 1973), 'As Soon As I Hang Up The Phone' (C&W#1, 1974), 'Feelins' (C&W#1, 1975), 'The Letter' (C&W#3, 1976), 'I Can't Love You Enough' (C&W#2, 1976), 'It's True Love' (C&W#5, 1979) and 'I Still Believe In Waltzes' (C&W#2, 1981). Although the success of her records has been restricted to the country charts, the book and the film *Coal Miner's Daughter* did much to regenerate interest in country music when its popularity was on the wane. The book was at the top of the *New York Times* best-seller list for nine weeks.

Her business interests reflect the extent of her success, with ownership of the town of Hurricane Mills, Tennessee (where she lives) and holdings in a rodeo production company and the now defunct United Talent agency (which she co-owned with Conway Twitty). Over the years she has won more Country Music Association awards than any other female performer, and in 1978 was given a 'star' on the Hollywood Walk of Fame. Although her records today are not guaranteed the success of former years, her roadshow is still a *tour de force* and her music remains unadorned by the trappings of stardom.

COAL MINER'S DAUGHTER, MCA (US), 1986
GOLDEN GREATS, MCA, 1986
LORETTA LYNN, MCA (US), 1988
TWENTY GREATEST HITS, MCA (US), 1989
THE VERY BEST OF CONWAY & LORETTA, MCA (US), 1986
WE'VE COME A LONG WAY BABY, MCA (US), 1979

MAC & BOB

Arguably the first exponents of guitar and mandolin duets, Mac (Lester McFarland; born on February 2, 1902, in Gray, Kentucky) and Bob (Robert Alexander Gardner; born on March 16, 1897, in Oliver Springs, Tennessee) met at the Kentucky School for the Blind in 1915, where both were studying. After playing at hoedowns and acquiring a considerable reputation for their duets, they started to record for Brunswick in 1926; this was followed by contracts with other labels (including Conqueror, ARC and Columbia), where they recorded songs such as 'When The Roses Bloom Again', ''Tis Sweet To Be Remembered', 'Twenty-One Years', 'That Little Boy Of Mine', 'I'm Forever Blowing Bubbles' and 'Eastbound Train'.

Although their records didn't fare well, they had a number of lengthy sinecures with radio stations (including WNOX, Knoxville) and on the *National Barn Dance* for WLS, Chicago; the latter lasted until 1951, when both musicians retired. During their careers they exercised considerable influence on the **Monroe Brothers**, the **Blue Sky Boys** and the **Delmore Brothers**, who managed to take their style and popularize it. Both are reputed to be alive and well today.

McAULIFFE, Leon

Few performers have exerted as much influence on Western Swing as Leon McAuliffe. During his membership of the Texas Playboys, **Bob Wills**'s admonition, 'Take It Away, Leon!', was a hallmark of the group's performances of the 1930s.

Leon McAuliffe was born on January 3, 1917, in Houston, Texas, and joined the **Light Crust Doughboys** in 1933, at the age of sixteen. Two years later he joined the Texas Playboys, and (along with **Bob Dunn**) laid down the parameters for future steel guitarists, figuring prominently on titles such as 'Steel Guitar Rag', 'Panhandle Rag' and 'Bluebonnet Rag'. In 1942 he joined the war effort; he remained in the army until 1946, when he set up his own band, the Cimarron Boys.

Over the next ten or so years he recorded for Dot, Starday, ABC and Stoneway, cutting titles such as 'Blacksmith Blues'. As interest in Western Swing declined he started to involve himself in other projects, including the running of two radio stations in Arkansas. In the late 1960s, the emergence of groups like **Asleep At The Wheel** revived interest in Western Swing, which encouraged Bob Wills and McAuliffe to re-form the Texas Playboys in a line-up which included many of the original members. McAuliffe led the group after Wills' death in 1975, and continued playing dates and recording until his death in 1988.

COZY INN, ABC, 1987
EVERYBODY DANCE, EVERYBODY SWING, Stetson, 1989

McCALL, C.W.

For a few short months in 1975 the airwaves were full of jargon about CB radios; this was prompted by the success of a song called 'Convoy'. Its author was one C.W. McCall, who was born William Fries on November 15, 1929, in Audobon, Iowa. McCall was brought up in a musical environment (his parents were accompanists for silent movies in cinemas) and studied music at the University of Iowa; he dropped out and became a journalist before joining the advertising agency, Bozell & Jacobs, where he developed the characters of 'C.W. McCall' and the waitress 'Mavis' for an advertising campaign.

His first hit, 'Old Home Filler-Up An' Keep On-A-Truckin' Café' (1974), was based on commercials he scripted for the Old Home bread company. It was followed by other hits with 'Wolf Creek Pass' (US#40, 1975) and 'Classified', before he cut 'Convoy' (US#1, C&W#1, UK#2, 1975). At the last count 'Convoy' had sold over seven million copies and was adapted as a film by Sam Peckinpah in 1978, starring **Kris Kristofferson** and Ali McGraw. With this success behind him he became Mayor of Olathe, Colorado.

McCLAIN, Charly

A country-pop singer, Charlotte Denise McClain was born in Jackson, Tennessee, on March 25, 1956, and made her debut as bassist with her brother's band before appearing on *Mid-South Jamboree*, where she became a frequent contributor. She then joined the local band, Shylo, where she met producer Larry Rogers.

In 1976 she was signed by Epic, making her chart debut with 'That's What You Do To Me' in 1978; this was followed by 'I Hate The Way I Love It' (a duet with **Johnny Rodriguez**; 1979), 'Surround Me With Love' (C&W#2, 1980), 'Men' (C&W#2, 1980), 'Who's Cheating Who' (C&W#1, 1981), 'Sleepin' With The Radio On' (1981), 'Dancing Your Memory Away' (1982), 'Paradise Tonight' (a duet with **Mickey Gilley**; C&W#1, 1983), 'Candy Man' (another duet with Gilley) and 'Radio Heart' (C&W#1, 1985).

In 1984 she married Wayne Massey, and together they cut a number of duets, including 'With Just One Look In Your Eyes' (1984) and 'You Are My Music, You Are My Song' (1985). She changed record labels in 1988 and signed with Mercury, while Massey took over the production chores.

I LOVE COUNTRY, Columbia, 1987
WOMEN GET LONELY, Epic (US), 1982

McCLINTON, Delbert

Singer and guitarist Delbert McClinton was born on November 4, 1940, in Lubbock, Texas, and was a key figure on the Texas club circuit throughout the early 1960s, achieving a reputation as a harmonica player with his solo on Bruce Chanel's monster hit, 'Hey Baby'. In 1964 he joined the Ron-Dels, recording 'If You Really Want Me To, I'll Go', which became a local hit. After moving to the West Coast in 1970 he teamed up with Glen Clark to form the duo, Delbert & Glen. In the mid-1970s he returned to Texas and recorded two solo albums for ABC, *Victims Of Life's Circumstances* (1975) and *Love Rustler* (1977), before moving to Capricorn for *Second Wind* (1978) and *Keeper Of The Flame* (1979).

In 1980, having signed with Capitol, he hit the big time with 'Giving It Up For Your Love' (US#8, 1980), which was extracted from the **Barry Beckett**-produced album *The Jealous Kind*. During the 1980s he returned to the club circuit, cutting *Live From Austin* (1989) for the Alligator label. This was followed by *I'm With You* (another Beckett production; 1991). His compositions have been regularly covered by other artists, including **Emmylou Harris** in 1978 with 'Two More Bottles Of Wine'. As a performer, however, McClinton has always kept his solo career low-key, preferring the comparative intimacy of the Texas club circuit to constant international touring.

FEELIN' ALRIGHT, Astan (US), 1984
I'M WITH YOU, Curb, 1991
THE JEALOUS KIND, Capitol (US), 1981
LIVE FROM AUSTIN, Alligator, 1989

McCLINTON, O.B.

Known mainly as a songwriter, O.B. McClinton is one of the few black performers to cross over into country music and achieve a reasonable level of acceptance. He was born Obie Burnett McClinton on April 25, 1942 in Senatobia, Mississippi, one of seven children. His father was a minister and owned a seven-hundred-acre farm. In 1962 O.B. began attending Rust College in Holly Springs in Mississippi, on a choral scholarship. When he graduated four years later he joined WDIA, Memphis, before joining the US Air Force in 1966. While in the Air Force he appeared on various talent shows and was discovered by Quinton Claunch, the owner of the Memphis soul label Goldwax.

During this period he started to build a reputation as a songwriter, penning titles like 'Keep Your Arms Around Me' (Otis Redding), 'You Can't Miss What You Can't Measure' (Clarence Carter), 'Back Road Into Town' (Willie Hightower), 'She's Better Than You', 'You Got My Mind Messed Up' and 'A Man Needs A Woman' (James Carr). This success as a writer led to a contract with the famous soul label, Stax, in 1971, where he cut albums including *Country* (1971) and *Obie From Senatobia* (1973); the latter included a version of **Merle Haggard**'s 'Okie From Muskogee'.

When Stax went out of business in 1975, he signed first with Mercury, and then Dot and Epic. At Epic he was produced by **Buddy Killen**, and cut titles like 'Hello, This Is Anna' and 'Natural Love'. He then moved to the Sunbird label, cutting *Chocolate Cowboy* (1981). By the mid-1980s he had become seriously ill with cancer, which killed him on September 23, 1987, in Nashville.

McCOY, Charlie

Charlie McCoy has long had the reputation for being the best harmonica player in Nashville. He was born on March 28, 1941, in Oak Hill, West Virginia. After forming his own group, the Escorts, which included

Wayne Moss, **Kenny Buttrey** and Mac Gayden, he joined **Stonewall Jackson**'s touring band for a brief period. He then rejoined his former colleagues from the Escorts on the Nashville session circuit. As a member of the house band at Monument, he secured a solo contract with the label in 1969, and then joined the group of session men known as Area Code 615 (see **Moss, Wayne**). His harmonica work on Area Code 615's 'Stone Fox Chase' became famous through its use as the signature tune to the BBC's *Old Grey Whistle Test*.

In recent years he has established himself in the more general field of popular music, working with artists such as **Bob Dylan**, **Waylon Jennings**, **Ivory Joe Hunter**, **Dobie Gray**, **B.J. Thomas** and Quincy Jones.

APPALACHIAN FEVER, Monument (US), 1979
BOOGIE WOOGIE HIT MAN, Monument, 1988
GREATEST HITS, Monument, 1990
NASHVILLE SOUND, Monument, 1988

McDANIEL, Mel

Mel McDaniel has, over the years, developed a reputation as a solid all-round live performer. He first performed as long ago as 1958 in Okmulgee, Oklahoma, after which he moved first to Nashville and then to Anchorage, Alaska, where he held down a residency at King X's Lounge. In 1975 he returned to Nashville, working as a songwriter at Combine Music and singing demos.

This led to a contract with Capitol in 1976. After early difficulties, it took the services of songwriter **Bob McDill** and producer **Jerry Kennedy** to establish his career. Among his earlier hits were 'Louisiana Saturday Night', 'Right In The Palm Of Love', 'I Call It Love' and 'Baby's Got Her Blue Jeans On' (C&W#1, 1984). He made his debut on the *Grand Ole Opry* in 1986. In recent years he has slipped into obscurity.

GREATEST HITS, Capitol (US), 1988

McDILL, Bob

One of Nashville's most successful songwriters, Bob McDill's songs reflect a lyrical maturity very much at odds with the machismo of much country music. He was born on April 4, 1944, in Beaumont, Texas, and attended Lamar University prior to spending a couple of years in the army. After his discharge he went to Memphis and wrote songs for Sam the Sham & the

Pharaohs, among others, before moving to Nashville in 1969, at the suggestion of **Allen Reynolds**, and signing to **Jack Clement**'s publishing company JMI; in 1972, with Clement and Reynolds, he formed the JMI record label.

At JMI he forged a relationship with **Don Williams**, providing him with hits such as '(Turn Out The Light) Love Me Tonight', 'Say It Again', 'Rake And Ramblin' Man' and 'Good Ole Boys Like Me', which resulted in Williams being lionized by rock musicians such as Pete Townshend and Eric Clapton. Among the songs he has written or co-written for other artists are 'Catfish John' and 'Red Necks, White Socks and Blue Ribbon Beer' (Johnny Russell); 'Song Of The South' (**Alabama** and **Tom T. Hall**); 'Don't Close Your Eyes' (**Keith Whitley**); 'Amanda' (**Waylon Jennings**); 'Just Like Real People' (**Kendalls**); 'Nobody Likes Sad Songs' with Wayland Holyfield (**Ronnie Milsap**), and 'Louisiana Saturday Night', 'Right In The Palm Of Love', 'I Call It Love' and 'Baby's Got Her Blue Jeans On' (**Mel McDaniel**). In 1986 he was elected to the Songwriters' Hall of Fame.

McDONALD, Skeets

Skeets McDonald was born Enos William McDonald on October 1, 1915, on a farm near Greenaway, Arkansas. In 1932, having finished school, he left Arkansas, travelling north to Michigan, where he formed a hillbilly boogie outfit, the Lonesome Cowboys. By 1937 the group had secured regular work on Royal Oak's WXEL; this was followed by a stint on Flint's WFDF, and then Pontiac's WCAR. In 1943 the group disbanded to join the war effort and McDonald headed off to the Pacific, where he remained until 1946. On his return he immediately re-formed the Lonesome Cowboys.

By 1950 McDonald had cut the dirge-like 'Please Daddy Don't Go To War' for the London label, but recovered his former *joie de vivre* when he teamed up with Johnny White and his Rhythm Riders as lead vocalist, cutting 'Mean And Evil Blues' and 'The Tattooed Lady' in Detroit for the Fortune label. Both songs were, as music writer Nick Tosches would have it, 'expressions of his devotion to the flesh of the lesser sex'. Unwilling to let the grass grow beneath his feet, McDonald moved to Los Angeles and was promptly signed to Capitol, who proved to be completely unaware of how best to market him. He had to wait until 1952 before having a hit with the self-penned 'Don't Let The Stars Get In Your Eyes' (C&W#2, 1952).

Over the next four years he continued recording,

but further success proved elusive, and although Capitol issued a series of rockabilly records (such as 'You Ought To See Grandma Rock' and 'You Gotta Be My Baby' - some of the most visceral songs of the era), the record-buying public remained unimpressed. After his stint with Capitol he went to Nashville and was signed to Columbia, where he remained until 1967. His output there (which included minor hits with 'Call Me Mr Brown' and 'You Took Her Off My Hands') can best be described as pedestrian. On March 31, 1968, McDonald suffered a heart attack from which he failed to recover.

DON'T LET THE STARS GET IN YOUR EYES, Bear Family (Germany), 1986
GOING STEADY WITH THE BLUES, Stetson, 1990
ROCKIN' ROLLIN', Bear Family (German), 1986

McDOWELL, Ronnie

Ronnie McDowell was born on March 26, 1950, in Portland, Tennessee, and gained a spurious reputation as an **Elvis Presley** imitator after recording 'The King Is Dead' (US#13, 1977). Although it was his only national hit, it was a launch pad for his career as a country singer.

Buddy Killen took him to the Epic label in 1979, where he notched up a number of hits, including 'Wandering Eyes' (C&W#2, 1981) and 'Older Women' (C&W#1, 1981), both of which were written by Jamie O'Hara of the **O'Kanes**; 'Watchin' Girls Go By' (C&W#4, 1982); 'You're Gonna Ruin My Bad Reputation' (C&W#1, 1983); 'You Made A Wanted Man Of Me' (C&W#3, 1983); 'In A New York Minute' (1984); 'Love Talks'; and 'All Tied Up' (1986).

In 1987 he changed labels, moving to Curb, and scored with an incongruous remake of the **Conway Twitty** song 'It's Only Make Believe'. His recording career has been less active of late, but his live shows, particularly when he reprises 'The King Is Dead', are reputedly very entertaining!

ALL TIED UP IN LOVE, MCA (US), 1987

McENERY, 'Red River' Dave

One of country music's more eccentric personalities, 'Red River' Dave McEnery managed to cash in on a trend for cowboy and saga songs in the late 1930s, and was cutting these dire heart-rending tales well into the 1970s.

He was born on December 15, 1914, in San Antonio, Texas, and started his career in 1935, broadcasting on a variety of radio stations across the US. He ended up at WHN, New York, in 1938, and developed a considerable reputation with titles such as 'Amelia Earhart's Last Flight'. In 1941 he returned to San Antonio, playing the bars and radio stations in the border country. He also recorded for labels like Decca, MGM, Continental and Savoy, among others, where titles like 'The Blind Boy's Dog' elicited mirth rather than pathos.

As westerns were still popular, he was able to pick up bit parts in films such as *Swing In The Saddle* (1948) and *Hidden Valley* (1949). Despite a lull in his career during the 1950s and 1960s, he returned with titles like 'The Ballad Of Francis Gary Powers', 'The Flight Of Apollo Eleven', 'The Ballad Of Emmett Till' and 'The Ballad Of Patty Hearst'.

McENTIRE, Reba

Reba McEntire has been nominally associated with New Country, which is something of a fallacy given that her music is saturated with references to country's most enduring legends. She was born on March 28, 1954, in McAlester, Oklahoma, and made her first record in the early 1970s with the family group, the Singing McEntires. She was 'discovered' in 1974 by vocalist **Red Steagall** at the National Rodeo Finals in Oklahoma City, while she was still attending South-Eastern State University in Durant, Oklahoma. Steagall encouraged her to get studio time and cut some demos, which eventually found their way to Mercury boss, **Jerry Kennedy**.

Her debut, 'I Don't Want To Be A One Night Stand', appeared during her graduation from South-Eastern State University, and was followed by **Don Gibson**'s 'Sweet Dreams' (1979), '(You Lift Me) Up To Heaven' (1980), 'Today All Over Again', 'I'm Not That Lonely Yet' (1982), 'Can't Even Get The Blues' (C&W#1, 1982), 'You're The First Time I've Thought About Leaving' (C&W#1, 1983) and 'Why Do We Want (What We Know We Can't Have)'.

She left Mercury in 1984, was signed by MCA and was initially teamed with producer Harold Shedd, cutting songs like 'How Blue' (C&W#1, 1984) and **Harlan Howard**'s 'Somebody Should Leave' (C&W#1, 1985). For the next round of recording McEntire took over the production chores, with **Jimmy Bowen** assisting. This new combination not only produced a number of highly successful records, but also gave her the confidence and freedom to experiment with her own material and that of lesser-known writers, as well as doing creditable covers of classics such as 'Cathy's Clown'. A string of hits followed: 'Whoever's In New England' (C&W#1, 1986), 'Little Rock' (C&W#1, 1986), 'What Am I Gonna Do About You' (C&W#1, 1986), 'Let The Music Lift You Up' (C&W#4, 1987), 'One Promise Too Late' (C&W#1, 1987), 'The Last One To Know' (C&W#1, 1987), 'Love Will Find Its Way To You' (C&W#1, 1988), 'I Know How He Feels' (C&W#1, 1988), 'New Fool At An Old Game' (C&W#1, 1989) and the **Everly Brothers**' 'Cathy's Clown' (C&W#1, 1989).

In 1989 Tony Brown took over as her co-producer, collaborating on *Rumour Has It* (1990), *For My Broken Heart* (1991) and *It's Your Call* (1992), which collectively spawned hits such as 'Walk On' (C&W#2, 1990), 'You Lie' (C&W#1, 1990), 'Rumour Has It' (C&W#3, 1990), 'Is There Life Out There?' (C&W#1, 1991) and 'The Greatest Man I Ever Knew' (C&W#3, 1992). *It's Your Call* featured a duet with **Vince Gill** on 'The Heart Won't Lie'. She has also embarked on an acting career, appearing first in the sci-fi/horror film *Tremors*; and then co-starring in the NBC-TV mini-series *The Gambler IV* with **Kenny Rogers**.

On March 16, 1991, band members Kirk Capello (keyboards), Tony Saputo (drummer), Larry Cigainero (guitar), Terry Jackson (bass), Michael Thomas (guitar), Paula Kay Evans (vocals) and Chris Austin (fiddle, guitar and vocals) and road manager, Jim Hammon, were killed when the Piper aircraft in which they were travelling crashed on Otay Mountain near San Diego, California. There were no survivors.

BEHIND THE SCENES, Mercury (US), 1983
FOR MY BROKEN HEART, MCA, 1991
GREATEST HITS, MCA (US), 1987
HAVE I GOT A DEAL FOR YOU, MCA (US), 1985
IT'S YOUR CALL, MCA, 1992
JUST A LITTLE LOVE, MCA (US), 1984
LAST ONE TO KNOW, MCA (US), 1987
MY KIND OF COUNTRY, MCA (US), 1984
REBA, MCA (US), 1989
REBA NELL McENTIRE, Mercury (US), 1986
RUMOUR HAS IT, MCA (US), 1990
UNLIMITED, Mercury (US), 1983
WHAT AM I GONNA DO ABOUT YOU?, MCA (US), 1986
WHOEVER'S IN NEW ENGLAND, MCA, 1987

McGEE, Sam & Kirk

In the early years, when country music first began to acheive popular acclaim, **Uncle Dave Macon** exerted a prodigious influence on the generation of young up-and-coming artists. Two performers that fell under his spell were the brothers Sam (guitar and banjo; born on May 1, 1894) and Kirk McGee (guitar and fiddle; born on November 4, 1899), from Franklin, Tennessee.

Sam and Kirk were initially encouraged into music by their fiddle-playing father and the local rural blues. In 1924 they struck up a friendship with Macon and joined his group, the Fruit Jar Drinkers; they remained with him until 1930 and appeared with him on the *Grand Ole Opry* broadcasts. In 1930 they formed the Dixieliners with **Fiddlin' Arthur Smith**, cutting sides like 'Railroad Blues' and 'Buck Dancer's Choice' for Bluebird and appearing on WSM's *Barn Dance*, where Sam was one of the first to use an electric guitar. After the war they slipped gradually into obscurity, with both opting to pursue separate careers.

Their careers were revived in the 1960s, and they started to record for labels such as Arhoolie and Starday; this renewed interest prompted them to start playing many of the folk and country festivals, where McGee's finger-picking style was imitated by many young guitarists.

COUNTRY GUITAR (Sam McGee), Arhoolie (US), 1981

McGUINN, Roger see BYRDS

MACK, Warner

A prolific songwriter, Warner Mack has never quite managed to reach the top as a performer, but has nevertheless had a creditable number of hits. He was born Warner McPherson on April 2, 1938, in Nashville, and was brought up in Vicksburg, Mississippi. He played the guitar at a number of local dances during his school years and hit the club circuit on graduation, enabling him to secure regular slots on the *Louisiana Hayride* and the *Ozark Jamboree*.

In 1957 he had his first hit with 'Is It Wrong'; he was credited on the label with the name 'Warner Mack', a name which he has used ever since. In 1964, having signed to Decca, he had a string of hits including 'Surely' (1964), 'The Bridge Washed Out' (1965), 'Talkin' To The Wall' (1966) and 'How Long Will It Take' (1967). He has, since the early 1970s, recorded less and less, but is still reputedly performing on the club circuit.

PRINCE OF COUNTRY BLUES, Sundown, 1988

McMICHEN, Clayton see SKILLET LICKERS

★

MACON, Uncle Dave

One of the biggest and brightest stars of the *Grand Ole Opry*, Uncle Dave Macon straddled the thin line between vaudeville and hillbilly, where his larger-than-life personality caused him to be given nicknames such as 'The Dixie Dewdrop', 'The King of the Hillbillies' and 'The King of the Banjo Players'.

He was born David Harrison Macon in Smart Station on October 7, 1870; his parents managed the Broadway Hotel in Nashville, which was frequented by musicians and entertainers. After his marriage to Mathilda Richardson in 1889 he moved to Readyville, Tennessee, and set up a transportation company. Raised in a musical environment, he was a gifted banjo player, but remained an amateur until the early 1920s, when he met the fiddler Sid Harkreader; together they toured the South on the vaudeville circuit, appearing at the Loew's theatres.

The tour led to a series of Vocalion recording sessions in New York, accompanied by **Sam McGee**, where Macon recorded a number of titles, including 'Keep My Skillet Good And Greasy'. Among the other labels he recorded for were Brunswick, Okeh, Gennett and Folkways. While noted for his jocularity, he also addressed contemporary issues in songs such as 'Farm Relief' and 'Tennessee Gravy Train'.

In 1926 he made his debut on the *Grand Ole Opry*, accompanied by his son, Dorris. His performances were a skilful blend of vaudevillian light entertainment and traditional folk songs. After forming the Fruit Jar Drinkers, which also featured **Sam & Kirk McGee** and the old-time fiddler Mazy Todd, he continued to broadcast on the *Grand Ole Opry*. During the 1930s he performed regularly with the McGees and the **Delmore Brothers**, appearing on the *Opry* road-shows.

In 1940 the movie *Grand Ole Opry* was released, with Macon stealing the thunder of other more widely known artists such as **Roy Acuff**. He continued to perform and tour right up to the time of his death on March 22, 1952. He was elected to the Country Music Hall Of Fame in 1966.

AT HOME IN 1950, Bear Family (Germany), 1987
LAUGH YOUR BLUES AWAY, Rounder (US), 1988
OVER THE MOUNTAIN: 1935-38, Old Homestead (US), 1987
WAIT TILL THE CLOUDS, Historical (US), 1990

MADDOX, Rose

Rose Maddox and her brothers Henry (mandolin and guitar), Calvin (guitar and harmonica), Fred (bass) and Don (fiddle), became one of the most popular vocal and instrumental groups in the 1940s and early 1950s. Based in the Los Angeles area, Rose became one of the first successful female country stars.

She was born Rosea Arbana Brogdon on August 15, 1925, in Boaz, Alabama; in 1933 the family joined the trail of Okies heading west to the orange groves of California, and settled in Modesto. In 1937 Rose and her brothers won sponsorship to broadcast on the local radio station, KTRB, which led to a syndicated show on KFBK, Sacramento. When war broke out, the brothers were enlisted for military service and, on their return in 1946, they re-grouped with Rose, becoming one of the most popular acts up and down the western seaboard, popularizing songs like 'Milk Cow Blues', 'Philadelphia Lawyer' and 'Blue Eyes Crying In The Rain'. Parading in loud and gaudy costumes, they found an immediate and enthusiastic audience in the military personnel and factory workers, with Rose the undisputed star of the show. They started to broadcast on the *Louisiana Hayride* and the *Grand Ole Opry*, before disbanding in 1956.

Rose launched a solo career in 1958, signing with Capitol and, over the years, had hits with 'Gambler's Love' (1959), 'Kissing My Pillow' (1961), 'Sing A Little Song Of Heartache' (1962), 'Lonely Teardrops', 'Somebody Told Somebody' (1963), 'Bluebird' and 'Loose Talk' (a duet with **Buck Owens**; 1964). In 1963 she cut *Rose Maddox Sings Bluegrass*, with accompaniment from banjoist **Don Reno** and **Bill Monroe**.

She went into temporary semi-retirement during the mid-1960s, before returning to the club circuit and cutting *Reckless Love And Bold Adventure* (1972) for John Fahey's Takoma label, while the Arhoolie label reissued much of the material she had cut in the 1940s with her brothers for the Four Star label.

FAMILY FOLKS, Bear Family (Germany), 1984
MADDOX BROTHERS AND ROSE: 1946-51, Volumes 1-2, Arhoolie (US), 1988
MADDOX BROTHERS AND ROSE ON THE AIR, Volumes 1-2, Arhoolie (US), 1986
ROCKIN' ROLLIN', Bear Family (Germany), 1984

MAINER, J.E.

J.E. Mainer's Mountaineers were among the first string bands to have their music recorded, translating many of the rural styles - breakdowns, reels and ballads - into what became generically known as bluegrass.

Joseph Emmett Mainer was born in Weaversville, North Carolina, on July 20, 1898. He worked in a cotton mill until he formed his first group with his brother **Wade Mainer**, which featured Zeke Morris (see **Morris Brothers**) and Papa John Love. In 1934 they started to broadcast on WBT, Charlotte, North Carolina, as the Crazy Mountaineers (in deference to their sponsor, the Crazy Water Crystals Company), and began a long recording relationship with RCA, cutting tracks such as 'Maple On The Hill', 'John Henry' and 'Light In The Valley'.

Throughout the 1940s - his brother having left to assemble his own group - he recorded with labels including King, and broadcast on WPTF, Raleigh, North Carolina. Despite a slump in his popularity during the 1950s, he recorded occasionally until the 1960s, and then retired to repair fiddles. During the 1960s he came out of retirement to re-record most of his old material for the Rural Rhythm label, until his death on June 2, 1971.

J.E. MAINER AND HIS MOUNTAINEERS, Arhoolie (US), 1981
J.E. MAINER'S MOUNTAINEERS, Volumes 1-2, Old Timey (US), 1988

MAINER, Wade

Banjoist Wade Mainer was born in Weaversville, North Carolina, on April 21, 1907. Following in the footsteps of **J.E. Mainer**'s Mountaineers (of which he was a founder member), he formed the Sons of Mountaineers, which variously comprised **Clyde Moody** and Wiley and Zeke Morris (see **Morris Brothers**). Despite the group's impeccable credentials, they failed to capitalize on the success of the Mountaineers, scoring only with 'Sparkling Blue Eyes'. In the post-war years Mainer recorded for King, before moving into retirement in North Carolina, and then working for Chevrolet in Flint, Michigan. During the 1970s, he cut a number of albums for the Old Homestead label that reprised his best-known material of the 1930s and 1940s.

MANDRELL, Barbara

Barbara Mandrell's early career was founded on her interpretation of soul and R&B material. She has latterly moved more towards the mainstream of country, and has become one of the most successful white exponents of country-soul.

Born into a musical family on December 25, 1948, in Houston, Texas, she was brought up in Los Angeles. By 1959 she had become a capable steel guitarist and was performing on the nightclub circuit in Las Vegas, which she continued to do throughout her years at school. This led to a regular spot on the television programme, the *Town Hall Party Show* (on the suggestion of **Joe Maphis**), and then to a tour with **Johnny Cash** as part of the Mandrells, which also featured her parents, Mary and Irby.

After recording for the Mosrite label, the family moved to Tennessee and, in 1969, she signed with Columbia. Her first hits were covers of soul classics, such as Otis Redding's 'I've Been Loving You Too Long' (1969), Dan Penn and **Chips Moman**'s 'Do Right Woman - Do Right Man' (1971), Shirley Brown's 'Woman To Woman' (1972), Denise LaSalle's 'Married, But Not To Each Other' (1972) and Joe Tex's 'Show Me' (1972); she was also teamed with **David Houston** for the duet 'After Closing Time' (1970).

In 1975 she joined the Dot label and embarked upon the most successful phase of her career, notching up a number of major hits including 'Standing Room Only' (C&W#5, 1975), 'Sleeping Single In A Double Bed' (C&W#1, 1978), '(If Loving You Is Wrong) I Don't Want To Be Right' (C&W#1, 1979), 'Years' (C&W#1, 1979), 'I Was Country When Country Wasn't Cool' (with **George Jones**; C&W#1, 1981), 'Wish You Were' (C&W#2, 1981) ,'Til You're Gone' (C&W#1, 1982), **R.C. Bannon**'s 'One Of A Kind Pair Of Fools' (C&W#1, 1983), 'Happy Birthday Dear Heartache', 'Only A Lonely Heart Knows', 'Fast Lanes And Country Roads' and 'I Wish That I Could Fall In Love Today'.

In 1980 she was given a show by the NBC-TV network, *Barbara Mandrell And The Mandrell Sisters* (Irlene and **Louise Mandrell**), which ran for two years. Barbara followed this with a special, *The Lady Is A Champ*, for the HBO cable channel in 1983. Despite being concussed in a car accident in 1984, Barbara was back on the road within nine months, maintaining her hefty touring schedule. Although the hits have not been as plentiful in recent times - Mandrell having been partially eclipsed by younger artists such as **Reba McEntire** and **Lorrie Morgan** - she remains highly successful on the cabaret circuit.

CLEAN CUT, MCA, 1984
GET TO THE HEART, MCA (US), 1986
GREATEST HITS, MCA (US), 1986
LIVE, MCA (US), 1981
LOOKING BACK, Columbia, 1982
NO NONSENSE, EMI America (US), 1990
SURE FEELS GOOD, EMI America (US), 1987

MANDRELL, Louise

One of **Barbara Mandrell**'s sisters, Louise was born on July 13, 1955, in Corpus Christi, Texas, and learnt to play the guitar, banjo and fiddle during her childhood, becoming a bassist in Barbara's band in 1971. After a brief spell as a featured vocalist on Stu Phillips's television show between 1973 and 1974, she joined the **Merle Haggard** roadshow as a backing vocalist. After leaving Haggard in 1977, she signed to Epic and scored with 'Put It On Me' (1978), 'Everlasting Love' (1979) and 'Reunited' (a duet with husband **R.C. Bannon**; 1979).

After switching to RCA in 1981, she continued notching up hits with 'You Sure Know Your Way Around My Heart' (1981), 'Some Of My Best Friends Are Old Songs' (1982), 'Runaway Heart' (1982), Bannon's 'Save Me' (1983), Bannon's 'Too Hot To Sleep' (1983) and **Holly Dunn**'s 'I'm Not Through Loving You Yet' (1984). Between 1980 and 1982 she appeared on the NBC-TV network show *Barbara Mandrell And The Mandrell Sisters*.

LOUISE MANDRELL, Epic, 1982

MANNERS, Zeke

Accordionist Zeke Manners was born Leo Mannes in California and became the guiding star for the old-time string band, the Beverly Hillbillies, when assembled by Glen Rice for radio station KEJK (later KMPC) in 1928. Although the group initially comprised Zeke and Tom Manners, Hank Skillet and Ezra Paulette, it was a line-up that was constantly changing, and through its ranks passed some of the most influential figures in western music. These guys were not just singing cowboys, but experienced musicians with keen ears for the hybridization of western and hillbilly music. Among those who first found fame with group were **Elton Britt**, **Stuart Hamblen** and Wesley Tuttle.

When Britt joined the group in 1932, it signalled the beginning of a partnership with Manners that would take both of them to New York to join a flourishing community of writers and singers - including **Carson Robison**, **Frank Luther**, **Tex Ritter** and **Ray Whitley** - who were all attempting to keep traditional music alive. Manners also recorded obscure solo sides for RCA, Bluebird and Variety.

MAPHIS, Joe

Joe Maphis was one of the most influential figures in the development of the Bakersfield sound, and also one of the first to incorporate the finger-picking technique on rock 'n' roll records, playing on sides by artists such as **Rick Nelson** and **Wanda Jackson**.

He was born Otis W. Maphis in Suffolk, Virginia, on May 12, 1921, and was raised in Cumberland, Maryland. In 1932 he joined his father's group, the Railsplitters, and in 1938 he became a full-time professional musician, joining Sunshine Sue Workman's group; this was followed by stints on the *National Barn Dance* and WRVA, Virginia's *Old Dominion Barn Dance*. On the latter he met Rose Lee, in 1947; they married a year later and moved to Los Angeles to appear on Compton's *Town Hall Party* and **Cliffie Stone**'s *Hometown Jamboree*.

These appearances made him a highly sought-after session musician, working with Rick Nelson, Wanda Jackson and on soundtracks for films and television. His own work included *Joe & Rose Lee Maphis* for Starday and the classic honky-tonk composition, 'Dim Lights, Thick Smoke (And Loud, Loud Music)'. He also recorded a number of gospel albums, and was instrumental in helping to promote the career of his niece, **Barbara Mandrell**. In 1971 they briefly moved to Nashville to continue session work, but returned to Los Angeles, where Joe died on June 27, 1986.

JOE MAPHIS AND ROSE LEE WITH THE BLUE RIDGE MOUNTAIN BOYS, Stetson, 1987

MARTELL, Linda

Linda Martell made a fleeting impression at the end of the 1960s by becoming the first black woman to appear at the *Grand Ole Opry*. Born in South Carolina, she was a soul singer, playing the Charleston Air Force base, until **Shelby Singleton** realized her potential as a country artist and signed her to his Plantation label. A number of modest hits followed, including 'Colour Him Father' (1969) and 'A Bad Case Of The Blues' (1970), but obscurity beckoned and she disappeared from sight.

MARTIN, Grady

One of Nashville's premier guitar-pickers, Grady Martin has been one of the top session musicians for over forty years. He was born on January 17, 1929, near Chappel Hill, Tennessee. In 1944 he moved into Nashville and, two years later, made his debut as a fiddler on the *Grand Ole Opry*. After cutting 'Chattanooga Shoeshine Boy' he went on to record with **Hank Williams**, **Marty Robbins**, **Merle Haggard**,

Floyd Cramer and Bing Crosby. He also established himself at RCA as one of the studio's principal guitarists (along with **Chet Atkins** and Hank Garland), and in 1979 he became a regular member of **Willie Nelson**'s band.

While he has avoided cutting solo records, he has occasionally turned his hand to writing, his most successful composition being 'Snap Your Fingers', which has been covered by **Dick Curless**, **Don Gibson**, **Ronnie Milsap**, Dean Martin and Barbara Lewis.

GUITAR GENIUS (with Les Paul and Hank Garland), Charly, 1985

MARTIN, Jimmy

One of the nattiest dressers to emerge from Nashville, Jimmy Martin was also one of the best bluegrass singers in the business, but a difficult man to work with. His group, the Sunny Mountain Boys, never achieved the level of recognition that lay within their grasp. Martin, through steadfastly clinging to the 'old ways', has been an invaluable influence on the younger generation.

He was born James Henry Martin in Sneedville, Tennessee, on August 10, 1927. His first break came in 1949 when he was hired as an occasional vocalist on the local radio station in Morristown, Tennessee. He was consequently hired by **Bill Monroe** to replace **Mac Wiseman** in the Blue Grass Boys for two spells between 1949 and 1954, broken only by a stint with the **Osborne Brothers**. During these years he acquired a reputation for the strength and authenticity of his voice, singing lead on such Monroe classics as 'The Little Girl And The Dreadful Snake', 'On The Old Kentucky Shore' and 'Voice From On High'. With the Osborne Brothers he cut titles like 'Blue-Eyed Darlin'' and 'You'll Never Be The Same'.

After leaving Monroe in 1954 he teamed up with the Osborne Brothers, forming the Sunny Mountain Boys. They remained together until 1955 - working on the radio station WJR and cutting titles like '20/20 Vision' - when the Osbornes moved away from Detroit. After their departure he managed to recruit a string of highly talented musicians, including the mandolinists Earl Taylor, Doyle Lawson (see **Quicksilver**) and Paul Williams, and banjoists Sam Hutchins, **J.D. Crowe**, Alan Munde (see **Country Gazette**) and Bill Emerson (see **Country Gentlemen**).

After signing to Decca in 1956 he cut a number of sides, including the hits 'Widow Maker' (1964), 'Sunny Side Of The Mountain' (1965) and 'Freeborn Man'

(1968), and from 1956 broadcast regularly on the *Louisiana Hayride* and the *Grand Ole Opry*. Dropped by MCA (formerly Decca) in 1976, he went on to record for Starday. In recent years he has been a frequent guest on the international festival circuit.

GREATEST BLUEGRASS HITS, Gusto (US), 1988
SING, Stetson, 1988
WILL THE CIRCLE BE UNBROKEN, Gusto (US), 1980
YOU DON'T KNOW MY MIND, Rounder (US), 1990

MARVIN, Frankie

Frankie Marvin was born in 1905 in Butler, Oklahoma, and started his career in New York with his elder brother, **Johnny Marvin**, as a steel guitarist and comedian. This was followed by a spell with the **Duke Of Paducah** and then **Gene Autry**, whom he had got to know while working in New York in 1929. In the mid-1930s he moved to Hollywood with Autry, and became an integral part of his roadshow for over twenty years, playing the steel guitar for Autry's ensemble. He left the show and retired in 1955.

MARVIN, Johnny

Johnny Marvin was born in 1898 in Butler, Oklahoma, and ran away from home at the age of twelve. Having worked his way to New York, he began his career on the vaudeville circuit, ending up on Broadway as an all-round entertainer, singing and playing the guitar. This led to a contract with Victor, where he cut titles like 'Just Another Wasted Day' and 'Wait For Me At The Close Of A Long, Long Day'. With his brother, steel guitarist **Frankie Marvin**, he worked with **Gene Autry** and became the producer of his Melody Ranch radio programme. During the war he entertained the troops in the South Seas, where he contracted the disease from which he eventually died in 1945.

MASSEY, Louise, and the Westerners

Louise Massey was one of the first performers to capitalize upon the exploitative potential of country music by adopting a gaudy style of garb that was loosely based on traditional costumes. The celebrated rhinestone Nudie Suits (see **Cohen, Nudie**), indissolubly linked to the traditional image of C&W, came to prominence as a result of the showmanship of these early performers.

The first group formed by vocalist Louise Massey was the Musical Massey Family, who then became the nucleus of the Westerners; the group included her brothers (Curt and Allen Massey), her father, husband (Milt Mabie) and Larry Wellington. In 1928 they became one of the first regular acts on the *National Barn Dance* (from WLS, Chicago). They recorded for a variety of different labels, such as ARC, Okeh and Vocalion, scoring with 'The Honey Song' and 'My Adobe Hacienda', but are best remembered for their live shows. Louise continued to work on the cabaret circuit until the late 1950s, while her brother, Curt, went on to become an influential composer of television themes like *The Beverly Hillbillies*.

MATHIS, Country Johnny

At the peak of his popularity during the 1950s and 1960s, Country Johnny Mathis (not to be confused with the MOR singer) wrote material for **George Jones**, **Webb Pierce** and **Johnny Paycheck**; as his popularity has declined, so too has the demand for his songs. He was born on September 28, 1933, in Maud, Texas, and made his debut on Dallas's *Big D Jamboree* in 1952, where he stayed until 1954. His residency on the *Big D Jamboree* won him a recording contract with the Chess label, where he was teamed with another country singer, Jimmy Lee, for a series of duets as Jimmy & Johnny. The duo had only one significant hit, 'If You Don't Somebody Else Will' (1954), before separating.

Jimmy Lee vanished into obscurity, and Mathis started to record for Decca in 1957 and remained with the label until the early 1960s, when he was signed by United Artists. He scored just one hit for United Artists, 'Please Talk To My Heart' (1963), before being dropped by the label in 1966. In 1967 he started to record religious material for different labels such as Little Darlin' and Hilltop. He still tours periodically, where his laid-back style, similar to that of **Bill Anderson**, has its admirers.

COUNTRY HEARTFELT, President, 1980

MATTEA, Kathy

A highly successful country-pop singer, Kathy Mattea was born in Cross Lanes, West Virginia, on June 21, 1959, and played the guitar with a bluegrass group called Pensboro while at the state university. After leaving university she went to Nashville where she got a job as a guide at the Country Music Hall Of Fame and Museum. She then worked as a waitress at a fast-food joint, while also singing sessions, recording

demos and providing back-up vocals for **Bobby Goldsboro**.

In 1983 she was signed to Mercury and teamed with producer **Allen Reynolds**; her first two albums bombed, but the third, in 1986, included four hits with 'Love At The Five And Dime' (C&W#1, 1986), the title track 'Walk The Way The Wind Blows', 'You're The Power' and 'Train Of Memories'. The follow-up, *Untasted Honey*, yielded hits including 'Goin' Gone' (C&W#1, 1988) and 'Eighteen Wheels And A Dozen Roses' (C&W#1, 1988), and she went on to score with tracks such as 'Untold Stories' (C&W#4, 1988), 'Life As We Knew It' (C&W#4, 1989), 'Come From The Heart' (C&W#1, 1989), 'Burnin' Old Heart' (C&W#1, 1989) and 'She Came From Fort Worth' (C&W#2, 1990).

Having won the CMA Female Vocalist of the Year award in 1989, she represents the new breed of artist - preferring to play gigs to her fans and avoiding the lucrative nightclub circuit in Las Vegas. She has hitherto played safe by sticking to the middle of the road, but has the potential to be as influential as **Nanci Griffith** or **Emmylou Harris**.

LONESOME STANDARD TIME, Mercury, 1992
UNTASTED HONEY, Mercury, 1988
WALK THE WAY THE WIND BLOWS, Mercury (US), 1987
WILLOW IN THE WIND, Mercury (US), 1989

MEAUX, Huey P.

Huey P. Meaux was born on March 10, 1929, in Kaplan, Louisiana; his father, an occasional accordionist, raised him on a diet of Tex-Mex and cajun music. After doing his national service, Meaux opened a barber's shop in Winnie, Texas, but soon turned the shop into a makeshift studio, where he recorded some demos. These came to the attention of Floyd Soileau of Jin Records, who leased 'Breaking Up Is Hard To Do' by Jivin' Gene (a Louisiana-based pop singer) for distribution to Chess's subsidiary, Argo. After this moderate success Meaux sold the barber's shop to concentrate on talent scouting and production, discovering Joe Barry, who recorded 'I'm A Fool To Care' (US#24, 1961); it was leased by Soileau to Smash.

With the proceeds Meaux set up his own network of labels in Houston, which included Crazy Cajun, Tribe, Teardrop and Jetstream. Among the artists he produced were **Roy Head**, **Doug Sahm**, Barbara Lynn, T-Bone Walker and Johnny Copeland. In the late 1960s he was jailed for fourteen months for conspiring to contravene the Mann Act: a girl he had taken to a DJ's convention started to work as a prostitute and then told the police about her activities.

In 1974 he was introduced to **Freddy Fender**, whom he signed to ABC, and produced a string of hits for him throughout the late 1970s: 'Before The Next Teardrop Falls', 'Wasted Days And Wasted Nights', 'Secret Love', 'You'll Lose A Good Thing', 'Vaya Con Dios', 'Living It Down', 'The Rains Came' and 'I'm Leaving It All Up To You'. During the 1980s he has continued to work with other local Texans, like Sahm and **Kinky Friedman**, and in 1986 he appeared as a DJ in the David Byrne film *True Stories* (Byrne is the guiding spirit of Talking Heads).

MEISNER, Randy

Bassist Randy Meisner (born on March 8, 1946, in Scottsbluff, Nebraska) has been one of the mainstays of the Los Angeles session fraternity. From 1964 he was a member of the band Poor, before co-founding **Poco** in August, 1968. He remained with Poco until April, 1969, leaving to join **Rick Nelson**'s Stone Canyon Band, and then moved quickly on to join **Linda Ronstadt**'s backing band, who later achieved success in their own right as the **Eagles**. He remained with the Eagles until September 1977, when, fed up with living out of a suitcase, he left to launch a solo career and work as a session musician.

Having signed a solo deal with the Asylum label, *Randy Meisner* emerged in 1978, which replicated the sound of the Eagles. After signing to Epic he cut *One More Song* in 1980, which included 'Deep Inside My Heart' (US#22, 1980) and 'Hearts On Fire' (US#19, 1981). Another untitled album came out in 1982, which included 'Never Been In Love' (US#28, 1982). In 1984 the original Poco line-up re-formed to record *Inamorata* and play a few gigs in the US; it was a short-lived exercise and Meisner returned to session work.

MENDOZA, Lydia

Known as 'the Lark of the Border' (la Alondra de la Frontera), Lydia Mendoza (born on May 31, 1916, in Houston, Texas) has been the most influential exponent of Tex-Mex since the 1930s. She began performing with her family during the 1920s in clubs and bars, building up a repertoire of ballads and *corridos* (song stories). By 1934 she had branched out to become a solo performer, accompanying herself on the twelve-string guitar and scoring a substantial local hit with 'Mal Hombre'.

Her reputation gradually increased over the next thirty years, and she recorded for international labels like Columbia and Victor and local labels such as Azteca; she remained, however, a secret to all but the most diligent followers of Tex-Mex. By the 1970s her reputation had extended beyond Spanish-speaking audiences and she was being internationally acclaimed, with **Doug Sahm** and **Flaco Jimenez** acknowledging her influence. In 1976 the documentary film *Chulas Fronteras* appeared and the Arhoolie label issued *La Gloria De Texas*. Sadly, she remains little-known.

MEYER, Augie

Augie Meyer, in conjunction with **Doug Sahm**, has done much - from the early days with the Sir Douglas Quintet (see **Sahm, Doug**) and producer **Huey Meaux**, to the present day with the Texas Tornados (see **Sahm, Doug**) - to popularize Tex-Mex.

He was born August Meyer on May 31, 1940, in San Antonio, Texas, and teamed up with Doug Sahm to form the Sir Douglas Quintet in the early 1960s. The group split up after having a number of hits (including 'She's About A Mover'), but Sahm and Meyer remained together, with Meyer's keyboard work being the trademark of Sahm's later records. Still based in San Antonio, they recorded with many of the leading lights of the border musical communities, including **Flaco Jimenez**, **Jimmie Dale Gilmore** and **Joe Ely**.

While Sahm's albums always reflected his keen interest in R&B and country, Meyer's solo albums reflected his enthusiasm for the waltzes and polkas of Tex-Mex in its purest form. In 1983 he moved to New York (where he popularized Tex-Mex), and recorded *August In New York* with other Texans such as **Asleep at the Wheel** and **Jerry Jeff Walker**. After returning to Texas and the club circuit, he cut *San Antonio Saturday Night* (1985), among others. In 1990 he founded the Texas Tornados, with Sahm, Jimenez and **Freddy Fender**.

AUGIE'S BACK, Sonet, 1986
AUGUST IN NEW YORK, Sonet, 1984
FINALLY IN LIGHTS (with Doug Sahm), Sonet, 1986
STILL GROWING, Sonet, 1982

MILLER, Bob

Bob Miller, one of the great songsmiths of the 1920s and 1930s, was noted for a hillbilly musical style and topical lyrical content. Born in Memphis, Tennessee on September 20, 1895, during his adolescence he became a pianist on the riverboat line that ran up and down the Mississippi. His next position was to lead the Idlewild orchestra and also to publish jazz and blues material. He moved to New York in 1928 to work for Irving Berlin's publishing company, before establishing the Bob Miller publishing company in the Brill Building on Broadway - New York's 'Tin Pan Alley'.

In 1928 he cut his first record, 'Eleven Cent Cotton, Forty Cent Meat', as a critique on the poor standards that farmers were expected to endure; later songs included 'There's A New Star Up In Heaven (Baby Lindy Is Up There)', inspired by the Lindbergh kidnapping case. Among the topics he targeted were prohibition, banking, politics and crime; other songs, such as 'Little Sweetheart Of The Prairie', 'Sipping Cider' and 'Rockin' Alone (In An Old Rockin' Chair)', were more typical hillbilly fare.

In 1931 he joined ARC as recording manager, working for **Art Satherley**. His songs were covered during the 1930s with most success by **Carson Robison**, the **Carlisles** and **Vernon Dalhart**; and during the Second World War he published **Elton Britt**'s 'There's A Star Spangled Banner Waving Somewhere', the biggest hit of the war years.

After the war, as Nashville became the epicentre of country music, the country sound became more streamlined and hillbilly music slipped out of fashion. He died on August 26, 1955, having lived off old royalties in his later years.

MILLER, Jay

During the 1950s Jay Miller became one of the most successful producers in southern Louisiana, mainly because of his willingness to cut any kind of music that came his way.

He was born on May 5, 1922, in El Campo, Texas, and started to sing cowboy songs on KPLC, Lake Charles in the 1930s. In 1937 he moved to Crowley, Louisiana and realized - having seen artists such as the **Hackberry Ramblers** and Happy Fats and the Rayne-Bo Ramblers - the vast under-exploited potential of rural music. After the war he set up the Fais Do Do label, releasing records by Happy Fats and fiddler Doc Guidry; this expanded to incorporate the Feature label, which issued titles by **Jimmy 'C' Newman** and **Doug Kershaw**. He also wrote songs, including 'It Wasn't God Who Made Honky Tonk Angels', which became a huge hit for **Kitty Wells**.

In 1954 he diversified still further by developing a roster of blues artists, including Slim Harpo, and establishing different labels for the cajun releases

(Cajun Classics and Kajun) and the R&B releases (Rocko and Zynn). His studios, which had the reputation of being the best in southern Louisiana, were widely used by other producers like Floyd Soileau and George Khoury.

Throughout the 1960s he cut a number of oddball comedy records that were issued on his Rebel label, but by 1970 he had stopped producing and was concentrating on managing his diverse investments. His vast back catalogue has been re-issued by the UK-based roots label, Flyright.

JAY MILLER STUDIO BAND: 1961-63, Flyright, 1985

MILLER, Jody

Jody Miller has always been an enigma: no record company has ever known whether to market her as a country, folk or pop singer. Born into a musical family (her father was a fiddler) on November 29, 1941, in Phoenix, Arizona, she moved with them to Oklahoma in the 1950s. She sang in the Melodies with some friends during her school years, and after graduating launched her own solo career. This career was already taking shape when she broke her neck in a car accident; on her recovery she got a spot on a local television show with folk singer and songwriter Tom Paxton.

In 1963 she was signed by Capitol to record folk songs, including 'He Walks Like A Man', 'Queen Of The House' (her 'answer record' to **Roger Miller**'s 'King Of The Road'; US#12, 1965) and 'Home Of The Brave' (US#25, UK#49, 1965). After retiring to raise her daughter Robin, she returned to recording in 1970, having been signed to Epic by **Billy Sherrill**. She notched up a string of hits with country versions of pop classics, including the Chiffons' 'He's So Fine' (1971), Barbara Lewis's 'Baby I'm Yours' (1971), the Ronettes' 'Be My Baby' and the Shirelles' 'Will You Love Me Tomorrow' (1976). Since the early 1980s she has retired to breed horses in Blanchard, Oklahoma.

MILLER, Ned

A distinguished songwriter, Henry Ned Miller was born on April 12, 1925, in Raines, Utah. He worked as a pipefitter, and wrote songs with his wife Sue in his spare time. In 1956 he signed with the music publishers and record label, Fabor, and his songs started to be picked up and covered by artists such as **Bonnie Guitar**, **Jim Reeves** and **Sonny James**. In 1962 he scored in his own right with 'From A Jack To A King'

(US#6, C&W#2, 1962; UK#2, 1963); in the course of the next few years he had other hits, such as 'Invisible Tears' and 'Do What You Do Do Well' (UK#48, 1965). After stints with Capitol in 1965 and **Gene Autry**'s Republic label in 1970, he moved to Prescott, Arizona.

MILLER, Roger

Roger Miller came to represent the sound of Nashville in 1960s' Britain through his success with a number of country novelty items. Although Miller's musical style (which can be charitably described as country-pop) was light years away from Nashville traditions, his witty country-influenced lyrics created an interest in country music beyond the US, an interest that had previously been hindered by its image as all cowboys and maudlin reminiscences.

He was born on January 2, 1936, in Fort Worth, Texas, and brought up in Erick, Oklahoma. Influenced by **Hank Williams**, he learnt the guitar and worked in a variety of jobs before being dispatched to Korea with the US Army. On his return he went to Nashville and started to write songs which were picked up by a number of artists, including **Ray Price** (Miller's first beneficiary, with 'Invitation To The Blues'), **Ernest Tubb**, **Jim Reeves** and **George Jones**.

In 1958 he was signed to Starday, but moved on to RCA in 1960, scoring with 'You Don't Want My Love' (1960) and 'When Two Worlds Collide' (co-written with **Bill Anderson**; C&W#6, 1961). This was followed by a spell with **Faron Young**'s band as a drummer, during which time he penned 'Swiss Maid' for Del Shannon. In 1964 he was signed by **Jerry Kennedy** to the Smash label, and he immediately struck gold with a succession of hits, including 'Dang Me' (US#7, C&W#1, 1964), 'Chug-A-Lug' (US#9, 1964), 'Do Wacka Do' (US#31, 1965), 'King Of The Road' (US#4, UK#1, C&W#1, 1965), 'Engine, Engine No.9' (US#7, UK#33, 1965), 'One A-Dyin' And A-Buryin'' (US#34, 1965), 'Kansas City Star' (US#31, UK#48, 1965), 'England Swings' (US#8, UK#13, 1965), 'Husbands And Wives' (US#26, 1966), 'You Can't Roller Skate In A Buffalo Herd' (US#40, 1966), 'Walkin' In The Sunshine' (US#37, 1967) and 'Little Green Apples' (US#39, UK#19, 1968).

In 1966, his appearances on *The Johnny Carson Show* and *The Andy Williams Show* showed his versatility as an all-round entertainer, and he was rewarded with *The Roger Miller Show* on NBC. At the beginning of the 1970s he started to diversify, establishing a chain of motels called King of the Road, and providing music for Disney Movies (including *Robin Hood*; 1973) and for the Broadway musical *Big River* (1985), based on *The Adventures Of Huckleberry Finn* by Mark Twain.

Although his career as a performer had long since evaporated (not even a collaboration with **Willie Nelson** on *Old Friends* (1982) could revive it), his lucrative royalties and the success of his hotel chain ensured that he was financially secure. He died in Los Angeles on October 25, 1992, of cancer.

THE BIG INDUSTRY, Fundamental, 1988
KING OF THE ROAD, Bear Family (Germany), 1990
MOTIVE SERIES, Mercury, 1981
OLD FRIENDS (with Willie Nelson), Columbia, 1982
ROGER MILLER, MCA (US), 1987
ROGER MILLER'S GREATEST HITS, RCA, 1985
WHAM ON EXPRESS, SST (US), 1990

MILSAP, Ronnie

Ronnie Milsap (born blind in Robbinsville, North Carolina, on January 16, 1944) is one of those country artists whose adaptability has enabled him to play any type of music. A capable musician on the piano, guitar and violin by the age of twelve, he attended the Morehead School for the Blind in Raleigh and developed an interest in classical music, but formed a rock band, the Apparitions, on graduating from high school. He stopped studying - having won a scholarship to read law at Emory University - to play with **J.J. Cale**.

In 1965 he formed an R&B band and was signed by Scepter, cutting 'Never Had It So Good', which led to tours with bluesman Bobby Bland, Little Anthony & the Imperials and the Miracles. By 1969 he had moved to Memphis, securing a residency at TJ's club; this resulted in a contract with the Chips label, where he cut 'Loving You Is A Natural Thing'. After signing with Warner Bros. he cut *Ronnie Milsap* (with songwriter Dan Penn producing); it included compositions by **Kris Kristofferson**, **Roy Orbison**, Chuck Berry and Dan Penn & Spooner Oldham.

Poor sales prompted him to move to Nashville in 1972, where he played piano at **Roger Miller**'s King of the Road motel. There he was spotted by **Charley Pride**'s manager, Jack D. Johnson, who secured him a contract with RCA and persuaded him to put his rock 'n' roll years behind him and turn to country. Unfortunately, while his voice was well suited to honky-tonk, many of his best records were cluttered with superfluous arrangements.

This did not stop him from becoming one of

the most successful country artists of the next two decades, with a long list of hits: Dan Penn's 'I Hate You' (1973), **Eddie Rabbitt**'s 'Pure Love' (C&W#1, 1974), Kristofferson's 'Please Don't Tell Me How The Story Ends' (C&W#1, 1974), **Don Gibson**'s '(I'd Be) A Legend In My Own Time' (C&W#1, 1974), 'Daydreams About Night Things' (C&W#1, 1975), 'Just In Case' (C&W#6, 1975), 'What Goes On When The Sun Goes Down' (C&W#1, 1976), '(I'm A) Stand By Your Woman Man' (C&W#1, 1976), 'Let My Love Be Your Pillow' (C&W#1, 1976), 'It Was Almost Like A Song' (US#16, C&W#1, 1977), 'What A Difference You've Made In My Life' (C&W#1, 1977), 'Only One Love In My Life' (C&W#1, 1978), 'Let's Take The Long Way Around The World' (C&W#1, 1978), 'Back On My Mind Again' (C&W#2, 1978), **Bob McDill** and Wayland Holyfield's 'Nobody Likes Sad Songs' (C&W#1, 1979), 'Get It Up' (C&W#6, 1979), Bob McDill's 'Why Don't You Spend The Night' (C&W#1, 1980), 'My Heart' (C&W#1, 1980), 'Cowboys And Clowns' (C&W#1, 1980), 'Smoky Mountain Rain' (US#24, C&W#1, 1981), 'Am I Losing You' (C&W#1, 1981), '(There's) No Gettin' Over Me' (US#5, C&W#1, 1981), 'I Wouldn't Have Missed It For The World' (US#20, C&W#1, 1981), 'Any Day Now' (US#14, C&W#1, 1982), 'He Got You' (C&W#1, 1982), 'Inside' (C&W#1, 1982), 'Stranger In My House' (US#23, C&W#5, 1983), 'Don't You Know How Much I Love You' (C&W#1, 1983), 'Show Her' (C&W#1, 1984), 'Still Losing You' (C&W#1, 1984), 'Prisoner Of The Highway' (C&W#5, 1984), 'She Still Keeps The Home Fires Burning' (C&W#1, 1985), 'Lost In The Fifties Tonight (In The Still Of The Night)' (partly based on the 1950s hit 'In The Still Of The Night' by the Five Satins; C&W#1, 1985), 'Happy Happy Birthday Baby' (C&W#1, 1986), 'In Love' (C&W#1, 1986), 'How Do I Turn You On' (C&W#1, 1986), 'Snap Your Fingers' (C&W#1, 1987), 'Make No Mistake, She's Mine' (a duet with **Kenny Rogers**; C&W#1, 1987), 'Where Do The Nights Go' (C&W#1, 1987), 'Old Folks' (a duet with writer Mike Reid; C&W#2, 1988), **Hank Cochran**'s 'Don't You Ever Get Tired (Of Hurting Me)' (C&W#1, 1989), 'Houston Solution' (C&W#4, 1989), 'A Woman In Love' (C&W#1, 1989), 'Stranger Things Have Happened' (C&W#2, 1990) and 'Are You Lovin' Me Like I'm Lovin' You' (C&W#3, 1991).

He is one of the few artists to remain both popular and commercially successful alongside the young turks of New Country, who have successfully eclipsed the chart careers of many other performers. His consistency is due to a relentless touring schedule, which ensures promotion for every record he releases.

GREATEST HITS, Volumes 1-2, RCA (US), 1986
IMAGES, RCA (US), 1979
INSIDE, RCA (US), 1982
IT WAS ALMOST LIKE A SONG, RCA (US), 1977
KEYED UP, RCA, 1983
A LEGEND IN MY TIME, RCA, 1979
LIVE, RCA (US), 1979
LOST IN THE '50's TONIGHT, RCA, 1986
ONE MORE TRY FOR LOVE, RCA, 1984
ONLY ONE LOVE IN MY LIFE, RCA (US), 1978
SPINNING WHEEL, Sundown, 1987
20-20 VISION, RCA (US), 1976

MOMAN, Chips

A producer of impeccable credentials, Moman has worked with **Elvis Presley**, **Waylon Jennings**, **Willie Nelson**, Aretha Franklin and Bobby Womack, among others. Although his principal impact has been as a producer, his guitar work for Gene Vincent and producer Jerry Wexler, with soul singers Franklin and Wilson Pickett, has left few doubting his capability.

He was born in LaGrange, Georgia, in 1936, and started to work as a musician after leaving school. By 1957, after working his way to Los Angeles as a member of **Dorsey Burnette**'s road group, he worked as a session guitarist at the Gold Star Studios. In 1959 he became a member of Gene Vincent's group, the Bluecaps, only to leave when they reached Memphis. In Memphis he met up with the owner of the Satellite label, Jim Stewart, and encouraged him to concentrate upon signing R&B acts, rather than country.

During the formative years of Stax (a threatened injunction caused them to change the name from Satellite), Moman's influence coursed through the veins of the operation, as he produced and played on early hits like Carla Thomas's 'Gee Whiz', the Mar-Keys 'Last Night' and William Bell's 'You Don't Miss Your Water'. In late 1962 Moman left Stax to set up his own studio, American, at 827 Thomas Street, Memphis. It opened in 1964.

Between 1964 and 1971, Moman's American Studios turned out a succession of hits for artists like Merilee Rush ('Angel Of The Morning'), **Sandy Posey**, Elvis Presley, James Carr, the Box Tops, Bobby Womack, Joe Tex and Joe Simon. The house band consisted of Reggie Young (guitar), Bobby Emmons and Bobby Wood (keyboards), Tommy Cogbill and Mike Leech (bass) and Gene Chrisman (drums); songwriters Dan Penn and Spooner Oldham left **Rick Hall**'s Fame Studios to work for Moman. This nucleus of musicians and writers from disparate musical backgrounds helped him transcend musical barriers: Elvis Presley's 'Suspicious Minds' is a hybrid of pop, soul and country.

In 1972, in a fit of pique, Moman shut down the studio in Memphis and reopened it in Atlanta; his wrath was caused by a reluctance on the part of the musical establishment to give him any credit for his achievements. It turned out to be a false move. In 1975 he moved to Nashville and set up studios on Music Row, where he produced **Ronnie Milsap**, **B.J. Thomas**, **Jessi Colter**, Waylon Jennings and Willie Nelson.

His collaborations with Jennings and Nelson on their albums of duets - *Waylon & Willie* (1977), *WWII* (1982) and *Take It To The Limit* (1983) - contributed to the gradual acceptance of country music in the mainstream. In 1985 he was recruited to produce 'Highwayman', which evolved into an album of the same name featuring the combined talents of **Johnny Cash**, **Kris Kristofferson**, Jennings and Nelson, the follow-up, *Highwayman II*, emerged in 1987. His restless enthusiasm has recently driven him to forsake Nashville and return to Memphis.

MONROE, Bill

Bill Monroe contributed more to establishing the parameters of bluegrass than any other single individual: while **Flatt & Scruggs** helped to popularize it, it was Bill who developed the hybrid from the string bands and close harmony singing of the southeastern states, providing the inspiration for countless younger musicians.

He was born the youngest of eight children, on September 13, 1911, in Rosine, Kentucky, and raised on a farm. Coming from a large family and suffering from poor eyesight, he became very shy and developed an interest in music. While the whole family was musical (with brothers Birch and **Charlie Monroe** playing the fiddle and guitar, respectively), Bill was the most academic in his approach, being influenced by church hymns as well as blues and string bands like the North Carolina Ramblers (see **Poole, Charlie**).

In 1929 he left home to join his brothers, Birch and Charlie, who had moved to Indiana in search of work. They did a variety of manual jobs during the day, and played at dances during the evening. Given the opportunity to join WLS, Chicago on the *National Barn Dance* as square dancers, in 1934 they were employed by the station as musicians, but Birch decided to quit music and return home.

Inspired by the success of other duos, such as **Mac & Bob** and **Karl & Harty**, the Monroe Brothers came into being, with Bill playing mandolin, and Charlie, guitar. Touring the Midwest, they ended up in North Carolina in 1935 and were sponsored by the Crazy Water Crystal Company to broadcast on WBT, Charlotte, alongside **J.E. Mainer**'s Mountaineers. In 1936 they cut their first sides for the RCA subsidiary, Bluebird; these included titles like 'On The Banks Of The Ohio' and 'What Would You Give (In Exchange For Your Soul)'.

In 1938 the brothers parted company, and Bill moved on to radio station KARK, Little Rock, and formed the Kentuckians, who evolved into the first line-up of the Blue Grass Boys when starting to broadcast on WSB, Atlanta's *Crossroads Follies*. The group made its debut on the *Grand Ole Opry* the following year, and Bill started to compose, contributing titles like 'Muleskinner Blues'. While he had not yet fully evolved his distinctive style, recordings from this period show the process was well on its way. In 1945 the accordion was dispensed with, and banjoist Earl Scruggs joined the group, bringing with him a fast, driving syncopated style that characterized the group's sound. The same year, having signed to Columbia, Bill cut titles like 'Blue Moon Of Kentucky', 'I Hear A Sweet Voice Calling' and 'Mother's Only Sleeping'.

In 1946, with a line-up that comprised Bill (mandolin and vocals), Scruggs (banjo), Lester Flatt (guitar), Chubby Wise (fiddle) and Howard Watts (bass), the archetypal bluegrass band came into existence. While this line-up only remained together until 1948 (when Flatt and Scruggs left), the Columbia sides have an inventive, rough-and-ready freshness that make his later records sound overly slick. After a disagreement with Columbia, he joined Decca and recorded titles including 'Uncle Pen', 'Roanoke', 'Scotland', 'My Little Georgia Rose' and 'New Mule Skinner Blues'.

Over the years, the Blue Grass Boys has been the university for a vast number of musicians, including **Jimmy Martin**, **Vassar Clements**, **Don Reno**, **Mac Wiseman**, **Clyde Moody**, Sonny Osborne (see **Osborne Brothers**), **Peter Rowan** and Buddy Spicher. Bill continued to tour and record throughout the 1950s, cutting albums like *Knee Deep In The Bluegrass*. His manager, Ralph Rinzler (formerly of the **Greenbriar Boys**), helped him break established patterns by introducing him into the flourishing folk circuit; this was consolidated in 1963 by his appearance at the University of Chicago Folk Festival.

His appeal to younger folk-oriented audiences encouraged the spread of interest in bluegrass, which, ultimately, was responsible for the formation of later groups such as the **Dillards**, **Country Gazette**, **Country Gentlemen**, **Quicksilver** and New Country (see **Crowe, J.D.**). While still under contract to Decca, he continued issuing albums, which, although recorded in Nashville with producer **Owen Bradley**, illustrated his continuing allegiance to traditional bluegrass. In 1970 he was elected to the Country Music Hall Of Fame, and he went on to cut excellent albums in the following years, including *Bill Monroe's Uncle Pen* (1972) and *Master Of Bluegrass* (1981). In 1986 he cut *Bill Monroe And The Stars Of The Bluegrass Hall Of Fame* for MCA, which featured **Jim & Jesse**, Mac Wiseman and Ralph Stanley (see **Stanley Brothers**). While he has toured less and less in recent years, he still makes the occasional appearance at the *Grand Ole Opry*.

BEST OF BILL MONROE, MCA, 1986
BLUEGRASS: 1950-58, Bear Family (Germany), 1989
CLASSIC BLUEGRASS INSTRUMENTALS, Rebel, 1990
CLASSIC BLUEGRASS RECORDINGS, Volumes 1-2, County (US), 1981
COUNTRY MUSIC HALL OF FAME, MCA (US), 1986
EIGHTY SEVEN, MCA (US), 1988
FATHER OF BLUEGRASS MUSIC, RCA, 1987
IN THE PINES, Rebel, 1990
KNEE DEEP IN THE BLUEGRASS, Stetson, 1985

MONROE, Charlie

While not exerting as great an influence on the development of bluegrass as his younger brother **Bill Monroe**, Charlie Monroe and his group, the Kentucky Pardners, were a capable and entertaining hillbilly outfit.

He was born on July 4, 1903, in Rosine, Kentucky, and learnt the guitar by the age of eleven. After moving to Indiana, with his brothers Birch and Bill, he joined the *National Barn Dance* on WLS, Chicago. When Birch returned to Kentucky, Bill and Charlie continued as the Monroe Brothers until 1938, when Bill went off to form the Kentuckians, and Charlie formed the Kentucky Pardners.

While this group was much more extrovert in its performances than Bill's counterparts, Charlie was constantly trying to find a mandolinist of his brother's calibre, and there were a string of players - including Curly Seckler, Ira Louvin (see **Louvin Brothers**), Lester Flatt (see **Flatt & Scruggs**) and Red Rector - passed through the ranks. The group remained essentially a hillbilly outfit, their best-known songs being 'Rose Conley' and 'Bringing In The Georgia Mail'.

Charlie retired in the mid-1950s, re-emerging briefly to appear on the bluegrass circuit, before dying from cancer of the lymph on September 27, 1975 in Reidsville, North Carolina.

MONTANA, Patsy

A star of the silent screen, Patsy Montana was born Rubye Blevins on October 30, 1914, in Hot Springs, Arkansas. Her singing career started with **Jimmie Davis** in 1932 before she joined the **Prairie Ramblers**, a four-piece string band, who had established themselves at the same time as the **Girls of the Golden West** on the *National Barn Dance*. In 1935 they accompanied her on 'I Wanna Be A Cowboy's Sweetheart' for the ARC label, which became the first million-seller by a female vocalist. She continued her partnership with the group for over fifteen years, yodelling her way through countless cowboy scenarios.

In 1952 she parted company with the group and moved out to the West Coast, where she retired from the music industry in order to devote more time to raising her daughters, Judy and Beverly. During the 1970s she occasionally came out of retirement to perform and to record for Starday.

MONTANA, Slim see CARTER, Wilf

MONTGOMERY, Melba

Melba Montgomery was born in Iron City, Tennessee, on October 14, 1938, and raised in Florence, Alabama. She started to sing during childhood at the local church, where her father gave singing lessons. Throughout the 1950s she entered a number of talent contests and eventually, in 1958, won a contest at the WSM Studios in Nashville, which was seen by **Roy Acuff**. She was recruited to Acuff's camp, the start of a four-year association.

In 1962 she went solo, and cut a number of singles, including 'Just Another Fool Along The Way', and was then teamed with **George Jones** for duets such as 'We Must Have Been Out Of Our Minds' (C&W#3, 1963) and 'Let's Invite Them Over' (1964). Her solo career continued with other hits, such as 'Hall Of Shame' (1963) and 'The Greatest One Of All' (1963). After finishing her collaborations with Jones she was signed to Capitol, where she was teamed with Charlie Louvin (see **Louvin Brothers**) and producer/steel guitarist **Pete Drake**, scoring with 'Something To Brag About' (1970).

In 1973 she changed labels once more, this time signing to Elektra, who had just opened a country division; among her hits were 'Wrap Your Love Around Me' (1974), 'He'll Come Home' (1975) and 'No Charge' (written by **Harlan Howard**; C&W#1, 1976). In 1977 she changed labels once more, signing with United Artists, where she had a modest hit with a reworking of 'Angel Of The Morning' (1977). While her voice has remarkable purity and range, she has never managed to project a strong enough image to compete with **Tammy Wynette**, **Dolly Parton** or **Barbara Mandrell**.

DO YOU KNOW WHERE YOUR MAN IS?, Playback (US), 1993

MOODY, Clyde

During the 1930s Clyde Moody was one of the many musicians to pass through **Bill Monroe**'s Blue Grass Boys and go on to achieve considerable distinction under his own name. Born in 1915 in Cherokee, North Carolina, he was recruited to **Wade Mainer**'s Sons Of Mountaineers in 1936. After leaving Mainer he formed the Happy-Go-Lucky Boys with Jay Hugh Hall, and then moved on to join Monroe. He stayed with him for some years, contributing 'Six White Horses' to the Monroe canon, until joining **Roy Acuff**'s Crazy Tennesseeans.

After the formation of the King label by **Syd Nathan** in 1944, Moody was one of the first to be signed, with a succession of solo hits, including 'Shenandoah Waltz', 'Carolina Waltz', 'Next Sunday Darling Is My Birthday' and 'I Know What It Means To Be Lonesome' (1944). In the late 1940s he moved to Washington, DC, to work in television, but relocated to his native North Carolina when he was given his own long-running television series. He has, more recently, returned to the music business in Nashville and started to play on the prosperous festival circuit.

MOORE, Bob

A founder member of the band that played sessions at RCA and jammed with **Chet Atkins** at Nashville's Carousel Club, bassist Bob Moore (born on November 30, 1932) was the lynchpin of the group. The band was made up of **Floyd Cramer** (piano), Buddy Harman (drums) and **Boots Randolph** (saxophone). Among the artists Moore has backed are **Jim & Jesse**, **Roy Orbison**, **Red Foley**, **Jim Reeves**, **Skeeter Davis**, **Porter Wagoner**, **Brenda Lee**, **Elvis Presley** and Connie Francis. His solitary hit, 'Mexico'

(US#7, 1961), was credited to Bob Moore and his Orchestra, which comprised session musicians. He has now retired.

MOORE, Merrill E.

Merrill Moore took the pumping, boogie-woogie piano style of jazzman Albert Ammons and adapted it to rockabilly in the early 1950s. His ferocious style predated that of Jerry Lee Lewis by some years, and although he was signed by different record companies, his records were never marketed properly.

He was born on September 23, 1923, in Algona, Iowa, and started to play the piano while still at school, during which time he came across records by artists such as Ammons, Jelly Roll Morton and Pete Johnson. During the war he served in the Navy and married at the end of hostilities, before moving to Tucson in late 1945. In Tucson, he played in hotel bars until moving to San Diego in 1948, where he continued to do more of the same until 1950, when he formed his first band, the Saddle Rock and Rhythm Boys.

In 1952 they were signed by Capitol, cutting titles such as **Bob Wills**'s 'She's Gone', **Hank Thompson**'s 'Doggie House Boogie', 'House Of Blue Lights' and 'Down The Road A-Piece'. After being dropped by Capitol in 1958, Moore slipped back into the old routine of playing the bars in the environs of San Diego. A couple of anthologies of his work were issued in 1969.

BOOGIE MY BLUES AWAY, Bear Family (Germany), 1990
TWENTY GOLDEN PIECES, Bulldog, 1982

MOORE, Scotty

When **Sam Phillips** teamed **Elvis Presley** with Bill Black and Scotty Moore, he must have had little conception of the impact upon popular music that would occur as a result of this apparently innocuous decision. Quite apart from the effect that Presley had on youth culture, Moore's guitar work influenced successive generations of rock 'n' roll guitarists.

Winfield 'Scotty' Moore was born on December 27, 1931, in Gadsden, Tennessee. Initially a member of Doug Poindexter's Starlite Wranglers with Bill Black, he was lured to the Sun label by Phillips in 1954. After working on the first Elvis Presley sessions, Moore became Presley's first manager, and organized all of the club bookings until Memphis DJ Bob Neal took over in early 1955. The same year, drummer D.J. Fontana was brought in to the group and, with Moore and Black (who both stopped touring with Presley in

1957 because of the atrocious wages), backed Presley on his records until 1958. Some of the best rock 'n' roll records of all time were cut during those years.

After Presley was drafted into the army in 1958, Moore worked on sessions in Nashville. In 1960, when Presley came out of the army, Moore returned to working on Presley's sessions, doing so, off and on, until 1968. In the late 1960s he opened his own studios, Music City Recorders, Nashville, where he worked as producer and engineer with artists such as **Tracy Nelson** (1970) and **Carl Perkins** (1975).

THE GUITAR THAT CHANGED THE WORLD, Epic (US), 1983

MORGAN, George

A smooth crooner, George Morgan - widely touted as the man most likely to represent a serious threat to the popularity of **Eddy Arnold** during the late 1940s - was born in Waverly, Tennessee, on June 28, 1925, and raised in Barberton, Ohio. When he finished his schooling, he undertook a series of part-time jobs while performing at local venues during the evening. His big break came when he secured a regular spot on WWVA's *Wheeling Jamboree*, which led to a contract with Columbia and his first big hit, 'Candy Kisses' (C&W#1, 1949). Joining the *Grand Ole Opry* that year, he scored with other hits, such as 'Rainbow In My Heart' (1949), 'Room Full Of Roses' (C&W#4, 1949), 'Cry Baby Heart' (1949), 'Almost' (1952), 'I'm In Love Again' (1959) and 'You're The Only Good Thing' (1960). From 1966 he recorded for Starday (having previously left Columbia), Pete Drake's Stop label and Decca; other minor hits followed, but his career had lost its momentum. He died of a heart attack on July 7, 1975, in Madison, Tennessee.

BEST OF GEORGE MORGAN, Starday (US), 1987

MORGAN, Lorrie

The daughter of **George Morgan**, Loretta Lynn Morgan was born on June 27, 1960, in Nashville, Tennessee, making her debut on the *Grand Ole Opry* in 1973. In 1979 she launched her recording career with 'Two People I Love' for the Hickory label, which failed to make an impact, and she moved on to record for MCA and Four Star. In 1986 she married **Keith Whitley**, and together they cut the duet "Til A Tear Becomes A Rose', which was nominated by the CMA

as the best duo performance of the year. By 1988 she had signed with RCA, cutting *Leave The Light On*, which included 'Trainwreck Of Emotion' (C&W#4, 1988) and 'Five Minutes' (C&W#1, 1990). Later hits included 'We Both Walk' (C&W#3, 1991), 'Watch Me' (C&W#2, 1992) and 'What Part Of No' (C&W#1, 1992).

Despite the death of her husband in 1989, her traditional Nashville background and Whitley's influence have provided her with the pedigree to become one of the most significant vocalists of her generation.

LEAVE THE LIGHT ON, RCA, 1989
SOMETHING IN RED, RCA, 1991
WATCH ME, BNA (US), 1992

MORGAN, Misty   See **BLANCHARD, Jack**

MORRIS, Gary

Gary Morris was born on December 7, 1948, in Fort Worth, Texas. During his childhood he excelled at sports, particularly athletics, and participated in the Little League World Series at the age of eleven. After leaving high school, he played throughout Texas in clubs and bars, honing his songwriting skills. His big break into the music industry came in 1976, when he performed at Democrat conventions during Jimmy Carter's presidential campaign. When Carter was elected, he threw a special 'thank you' party for the Country Music Association, with Morris performing. At this party he was spotted by Norro Wilson, head of A&R for Warner Bros.

Two years later Morris began looking for a recording contract, and was immediately signed up by Wilson. He established himself with his third single, 'Headed For A Heartache' (C&W#8, 1981), and continued with a string of hits, including 'Velvet Chains' (1982), 'The Love She Found In Me' (1982), 'The Wind Beneath My Wings' (1983), 'You're Welcome Tonight' (a duet with **Lynn Anderson**, 1984), 'Baby Bye Bye' (C&W#1, 1985), 'I'll Never Stop Loving You' (C&W#1, 1985), 'Makin' Up For Lost Time' (a duet with **Crystal Gayle**; C&W#1, 1985), '100% Chance Of Rain' (C&W#1, 1986) and 'Leave Me Lonely' (C&W#1, 1987).

Apart from his success as a country artist, he also appeared alongside **Linda Ronstadt** in an off-Broadway production of *La Bohème*; in 1986 he appeared in the ABC-TV soap, *Dynasty II: The Colbys*; and in 1987 he appeared in the Broadway production of *Les Miserables*. That same year he cut an album of duets with Crystal Gayle entitled *What If We Fall In Love*. Morris has consistently managed to maintain a high profile, with regular appearances at the *Grand Ole Opry* and a rigorous touring schedule.

SECOND HAND HEART, Warner Bros. (US), 1986

MORRIS BROTHERS

Wiley and Claud 'Zeke' Morris were one of several influential duos to emerge from North Carolina during the 1930s. Initially playing with **J.E. Mainer**, **Wade Mainer** and **Charlie Monroe**, they later came together to form the Morris Brothers. Although they cut songs such as 'Salty Dog Blues', 'Tragic Romance' and 'You Give Me Your Love And I'll Give You Mine', they were at their peak on their radio broadcasts from stations like WSPA, Spartanburg, South Carolina, in 1939. The line-up of the Morris Brothers was often supplemented by musicians like Earl Scruggs (see **Flatt & Scruggs**) and **Don Reno**, both of whom would go onto bigger things.

The brothers retired from the music industry after the 1940s, but in later years they re-emerged to participate in television specials and to appear on the festival circuit, most notably at the Newport Folk Festival in 1959.

MOSS, Wayne

Wayne Moss was born in Charleston, West Virginia, and had learnt the guitar by the age of twelve. After joining a variety of R&B groups, he spent two years playing in **Brenda Lee**'s backing group. He then joined the Escorts, which included **Charlie McCoy** and **Kenny Buttrey**. When the group disbanded he became one of Nashville's top session men and joined the house band at Monument, which came to be known as the Music City Five; it included Buttrey, McCoy, Tim Drummond and **Troy Seals**.

In 1969 he co-founded Area Code 615 (the Nashville telephone code), with McCoy (harmonica) and Buttrey (drums). This group comprised other session musicians, such as Mac Gayden (guitar), Bobby Thompson (banjo), Weldon Myrick (steel guitar), **Norbert Putnam** (bass), Ken Lauber (keyboards) and Buddy Spicher (fiddle). The group's debut featured a fine selection of country instrumentals, all executed with consummate skill. The follow-up, *Trip In The Country* (which featured 'Stone Fox Chase', the theme from BBC TV's *Old Grey Whistle Test*), included the same line-up, although **David Briggs** replaced Lauber on keyboards. The group broke up in 1971, with Moss forming Barefoot Jerry.

This group comprised Jim Colvard (guitar), Warren Hartman (keyboards), Russ Hicks (steel guitar), Terry Dearmore (bass and vocals) and Si Edwards (drums). Throughout the 1970s the group recorded for Monument, Capitol and Warner Bros. with little commercial success. Moss remains one of Nashville's top session guitarists and runs his own studios, Cinderella, which he acquired in the early 1960s.

WATCHIN' TV (Barefoot Jerry), Houdini, 1980

MOTHER EARTH see NELSON, Tracy

MOTHER MAYBELLE see CARTER FAMILY

MULESKINNER see ROWAN, Peter

MULLICAN, Moon

One of the finest ever boogie-woogie pianists, Aubrey 'Moon' Mullican (born on March 27, 1909, near Corrigan, Polk County, Texas) exerted a decisive influence upon **Jerry Lee Lewis**. He initially played the old pump organ that his father had acquired for his daughters to play religious music, but Moon had other ideas about its uses. In 1930 he travelled to Houston, where he acquired the moniker 'Moon' from his habit of sleeping during the day and playing the piano in bars and brothels by night.

In 1937 he joined **Cliff Bruner** and his Texas Cowboys, and developed the 'three-finger style' that characterized his later solo recordings and exerted such a huge influence upon the youthful Jerry Lee. His next move was to join Leon Seph's Blue Ridge Playboys in 1940. This was followed by a flourishing solo career with the King label, during which time he had a string of hits, which included 'New Jole Blon' (an adaptation of the old cajun classic; 1947), 'I'll Sail My Ship Alone' (1950), 'Mona Lisa' (1950) and 'Cherokee Boogie' (1951). These hits predated the emergence of rock 'n' roll by several years and were dubbed 'hillbilly boogie'.

He toured the South with **Red Foley** and **Tennessee Ernie Ford** during the latter half of the 1950s, before joining Governor **Jimmie Davis**'s band and staff in 1960. In 1961 he had one final hit with

'Ragged But Right' for Starday, but the following year suffered from a heart attack caused by obesity (he weighed 275 pounds); on New Year's Eve, 1966, he succumbed to a fatal attack and died on January 1, 1967, in Beaumont, Texas.

GREATEST HITS, Starday (US), 1987
HIS ALL-TIME GREATEST HITS, Sing, 1988
THE OLD-TIME TEXAN, King (US), 1990
SEVEN NIGHTS TO ROCK, Western (US), 1989
SWEET ROCKIN' MUSIC, Charly, 1984

MURPHEY, Michael Martin

One of the Austin musical community, country-rock singer-songwriter Michael Martin Murphey was born in Oak Cliff, Texas. He moved out to the West Coast to study English at UCLA in 1970, and started to perform locally at Ledbetter's in Westwood. Moving to Austin in 1971, where he remained for the next three years, he was signed by A&M, had a hit with 'Geronimo's Cadillac' (US#37, 1972) and rubbed shoulders with groups like the Flatlanders (see **Ely, Joe**). In 1974 he moved to Colorado, where, having signed to Epic, he notched up a number of hits including 'Wildfire' (US#3, 1975), 'Carolina In The Pines' (US#21, 1975) and 'Renegade' (US#39, 1976).

By 1982, having moved to New Mexico, he cut the minor country hit 'The Two-Step Is Easy' (1982); this was followed by 'What's Forever For' (US#19, C&W#1, 1982), 'Still Taking Chances' (1982), 'Will It Be Love By Morning' (1983), 'I'm Gonna Miss You, Girl' (1983), 'From The Word Go' (1984) and 'A Long Line Of Love' (C&W#1, 1987). Charting erratically, he seems to have joined a long list of artists that have turned to country more out of desperation than commitment.

MICHAEL MARTIN MURPHEY, Liberty (US), 1983
WIDE OPEN COUNTRY, Warner Bros. (US), 1992

MURRAY, Anne

A very successful country-pop singer of the 1970s, Anne Murray was born in Spring Hill, Nova Scotia, Canada, on June 20, 1946. After obtaining a degree from the University of New Brunswick, she began training as a physical education teacher, until making her debut on Canadian television's *Let's Go*, alongside the rock band Guess Who. She became a regular on the Halifax TV programme *Singing Jamboree*, which led to a contract with the ARC label, with Brian Ahern (who later produced and married **Emmylou Harris**) producing. In 1970 she moved to the Capitol label, and started an impressive sequence of hits that included 'Snowbird' (US#8, 1970), Kenny Loggins' 'Danny's Song' (US#7, 1973), 'Love Song' (US#12, 1974), **Dickey Lee**'s 'He Still Thinks I Care' (the personal pronoun was altered from 'She' to 'He' by Murray; C&W#1, 1974) and Lennon - McCartney's 'You Won't See Me' (US#8, 1974).

In 1974 she retired from the music business for four years to raise a family. On her return she was teamed with producer Jim Ed Norman, and the hits resumed: the **Everly Brothers**' 'Walk Right Back' (C&W#4, 1978), 'You Needed Me' (US#1, 1978), 'I Just Fall In Love Again' (US#12, C&W#1, 1979), 'Shadows In The Moonlight' (US#25, C&W#1, 1979), 'Broken Hearted Me' (US#12, C&W#1, 1979), **John Stewart**'s 'Daydream Believer' (US#12, 1980), 'Could I Have This Dance' (from the soundtrack of the movie *Urban Cowboy*; US#33, C&W#1, 1980), 'Blessed Are The Believers' (US#34, C&W#1, 1981), 'A Little Good News' (C&W#1, 1983), 'Just Another Woman In Love' (C&W#1, 1984), 'Nobody Loves Me Like You Do' (a duet with Dave Loggins; C&W#1, 1984), 'Time Don't Run Out On Me' (C&W#2, 1985) and 'Now And Forever (You And Me)' (C&W#1, 1986).

Her relationship with producer Jim Ed Norman terminated in 1985, when he became head of the Warner Bros. Nashville Division. From that point on she worked with a variety of producers who directed her towards pop - rather than country - audiences, as was borne out by *Something To Talk About* (1986) and *Harmony* (1987); this policy was neither a critical nor a commercial success. More recently she has established herself on the lucrative Las Vegas cabaret circuit.

BOTH SIDES NOW, Castle, 1986
SPECIAL COLLECTION, Capitol, 1990

MUSICAL BROWNIES see BROWN, Milton

NATHAN, Syd

Syd Nathan became one of the principal conduits between R&B and country music by establishing one of the first genuine independent record labels; his roster of R&B artists drew liberally from the repertoires of his country artists, and vice versa.

He was born on April 27, 1904, in Cincinnati, Ohio. Initially a furniture salesman, he opened a record shop in 1938. In 1944 he founded the King label, which began to record Country & Western; among his early signings were **Merle Travis**, **Grandpa Jones**, the **Carlisle Brothers**, the **Delmore Brothers**, **Cowboy Copas** and **Hank Penny**. He quickly diversified when he saw the potential in the gospel and R&B markets. In 1947 he appointed Henry Glover musical director for the label, with Ralph Bass in place as the head of A&R and of the subsidiary, Federal. During the 1950s his roster of R&B artists flourished, with signings like Billy Ward and the Dominoes, Little Willie John, Hank Ballard and the Midnighters, the Five Royales and James Brown; the hillbilly and country roster also prospered, with signings such as **Moon Mullican**, **Hawkshaw Hawkins** and the **Stanley Brothers**.

Nathan died in 1968, and King was sold to Nashville's Starday label shortly after his death. The entire Starday-King catalogue was then sold to songwriters Leiber & Stoller, who themselves sold it on - to yet another Nashville-based record company, Gusto, in 1975.

NAYLOR, Jerry

Jerry Naylor was one of the polymorphous Crickets' first frontmen, following **Buddy Holly**'s defection for greater things. He was born on March 6, 1939, in Stephenville, Texas, and in 1953 formed his first group, who were good enough to warrant a slot on the *Louisiana Hayride*. While at high school he became a DJ on a local radio station in San Angelo, and, on graduation, studied electronics, prior to joining the army as an engineer on the American Forces Network in Germany. After sustaining an injury to his spine, he was discharged from the army and returned to the US.

He cut some sides for the independent Skyla label on his return, and met **Glen Campbell**. In 1961 they moved to Los Angeles and Naylor joined the radio station KRLA, and then KDAY. Later that year he was recruited to replace Joe Mauldin in the Crickets; the line-up of the group at this juncture was Naylor, Jerry Allison, **Sonny Curtis** and **Glen D. Hardin**. Plagued by ill health he left the group in 1964, having suffered a heart attack, and started a career in television. In the early 1970s he began a solo career as a country artist, recording for Columbia, Tower and Melodyland. Success was elusive, with only one modest hit materializing: 'Is That All There Is To Honky Tonk'.

NELSON, Rick

Ricky Nelson came to prominence in the early 1950s in the syndicated television series *The Adventures Of Ozzie And Harriet*, which starred his parents Ozzie and Harriet Nelson. This provided the springboard for a career as one of the first immaculately groomed teen idols, out of a similar mould to Pat Boone. Where Nelson differed from Boone, though, lay in the quality of his material and productions, which featured some of Los Angeles' finest session musicians, most notably guitarists **James Burton** and **Joe Maphis**.

He was born Eric Hilliard Nelson on May 8, 1940, in Teaneck, New Jersey. In 1949 he joined the cast of his parents' television show (along with his brother David), and became the first soap-opera teen idol. In 1957 he was signed to the Verve label and scored with the double A-side, 'I'm Walkin''/'A Teenager's Prayer' (US#2, 1957), which featured jazz guitarist Barney Kessel; this was followed by 'You're My One And Only' (US#14, 1957).

He was then signed to the Imperial label, and notched up a string of hits that included 'Be Bop Baby' (US#3, 1957), 'Stood Up' (US#2, 1957; UK#27, 1958), 'Believe What You Say' (US#4, 1958), 'Poor Little Fool' (US#1, UK#4, 1958), 'Lonesome Town' (US#7, 1958), 'Never Be Anyone Else But You' (US#6, UK#14, 1959), 'It's Late' (US#9, UK#3, 1959), 'Just A Little Too Much' (US#9, UK#11, 1959), 'I Wanna

Be Loved' (US#20, 1959; UK#30, 1960), 'Young Emotions' (US#12, UK#48, 1960), 'I'm Not Afraid' (US#27, 1960), 'You Are The Only One' (US#25, 1961), 'Travellin' Man' (US#1, 1961), 'Hello Mary Lou' (US#9, UK#2, 1961), 'A Wonder Like You' (US#11, 1961), 'Young World' (US#5, UK#27, 1962), 'Teenage Idol' (US#5, UK#39, 1962) and 'It's Up To You' (US#6, 1962; UK#27, 1963).

In 1962 he moved to Decca, changing his name to Rick Nelson, and had a few more hits, including 'String Along' (US#25, 1963), 'Fools Rush In' (US#12, UK#12, 1963), 'For You' (US#6, UK#14, 1964) and 'The Very Thought Of You' (US#26, 1964), until the emergence of the Beatles and the **Rolling Stones** rendered Nelson and others of his ilk obsolete overnight. Despite James Burton's membership of the band, his move from rockabilly to out-and-out country failed to make an impression, in spite of the excellence of *Bright Lights And Country Music* (1966) and *Country Fever* (1967). Other albums featured material by contemporary songwriters such as **Bob Dylan**, Tim Hardin, Tom Paxton and Randy Newman.

By the late 1960s he had formed the Stone Canyon Band with sidemen like **Tom Brumley** and **Randy Meisner**, and cut albums such as *Rick Sings Nelson* and *Rudy The Fifth*. From this period he cut two final hits, a memorable version of Dylan's 'She Belongs To Me' (US#33, 1970) and 'Garden Party' (US#6, UK#41, 1972) - the latter directed at those who felt that he should just sing his old hits. Throughout the remainder of the 1970s and early 1980s his recording career went into a decline: he was dropped by MCA after the release of *Windfall*, then by Epic after cutting *Intakes* (1977), and finally by Capitol after releasing *Playing To Win* (1981).

These albums were victims of fashion: the emergence of trends like disco tended to overshadow the work of stalwarts like Nelson. Touring regularly throughout the US and Europe, he died in an aeroplane crash on December 31, 1985, on his way to a concert in De Kalb, Texas.

BEST OF RICKY NELSON, Liberty, 1985
COMES OF AGE, See For Miles, 1987
COUNTRY FEVER, BRIGHT LIGHTS AND COUNTRY MUSIC, See For Miles, 1987
GARDEN PARTY, Beat Goes On, 1972
GOLDEN GREATS, MCA, 1987
INTAKES, Epic, 1977
JUST FOR YOU, CRC (US), 1989
LEGENDARY MASTERS, EMI America, 1990
ROCKIN' ROCK, MCA (US), 1979

SINGS SONGS FOR YOU, MCA, 1990
STRING ALONG WITH RICK, Charly, 1984

NELSON, Tracy

Tracy Nelson emerged during the mid-1960s as a folk singer, before getting involved with the psychedelic explosion on the West Coast in 1967, as lead singer of the band Mother Earth. This band failed to make any significant commercial inroads, but they did have, in Tracy Nelson, arguably one of the most pliant and expressive voices of that period - she never gained anything like the credit that was her due.

Born in Madison, Wisconsin, on December 27, 1944, she started with the group Fabulous Imitations, before moving on to the R&B band White Trash. In early 1967 she headed for the coast and joined Mother Earth, who performed mainly original material drawing heavily from traditional folk, country and blues repertories. During the early 1970s the band split up, and she cut a number of distinguished albums for various labels, including *Tracy Nelson* for Atlantic. She then hit the lucrative session circuit, where her talents were rewarded by the likes of **Waylon Jennings**, **Linda Ronstadt** and Allen Toussaint.

COME AND SEE ABOUT ME, Flying Fish (US), 1989
DOIN' IT MY WAY, Adelphi, 1981
HOMEMADE SONGS, Flying Fish (US), 1989

NELSON, Willie

One of the leading figures of the Outlaw Movement, Willie Nelson has, as both writer and performer, drawn from traditional country styles, as well as the blues, to create a unique hybrid which has influenced the development of contemporary country music.

He was born in Abbott, Texas, on April 30, 1933; after his parents divorced, he was raised by his grandparents, who taught him the rudiments of the guitar. In 1950 he joined the Air Force, remaining there until discharged in 1952. After a series of dead-end jobs, he became a disc-jockey and started to compose songs. In 1959 he moved to Nashville, and was signed to **Ray Price**'s publishing company, Pamper, joining his band as bassist.

Signed to RCA, he recorded a string of self-composed songs that were often covered by others: 'Crazy' (**Patsy Cline** and **Linda Ronstadt**), 'Hello Walls' (**Faron Young**), 'Night Life' (Ray Price), 'Pretty Paper' (**Roy Orbison**) and 'Funny How Time Slips Away' (Dorothy Moore). He also scored a number of hits in his own right during his years at RCA, including 'Touch Me', 'The Party's Over' and 'Willingly'. His sparse, bluesy style was very much at odds with the tendency at RCA to swamp the productions with lush string arrangements - while this complemented the music of some artists, it detracted from the emotional impact of Nelson's songs.

In 1971 he left RCA and moved to Austin, Texas, signing with the newly formed country division of Atlantic, and cutting two albums, *Shotgun Willie* and *Phases & Stages*, that were produced by Jerry Wexler and Arif Mardin, respectively. Both these albums - by using producers who were better known for their work with black R&B artists - showed Nelson in an entirely different light: the stark uncluttered arrangements underlined Nelson's lyrical debt to the blues, and emphasized his disenchantment with the whole attitude towards recording in Nashville. These albums were commercial disasters, and in 1974 he was signed by Columbia after Atlantic shut down their Nashville operation.

Over the next decade or so he cut albums such as *Red Headed Stranger* and *Sound In Your Mind*, which established him as one of the most creative forces in country music. Collaborations with **Waylon Jennings**, **Jessi Colter** and Tompall Glaser (see **Tompall and the Glaser Brothers**) established this breakaway movement of musicians known as the 'Outlaws' (stemming from the album of the same name). The commercial success of *Wanted: The Outlaws* enabled them all to have carte blanche over their recording careers.

Nelson himself struck a vein of hit singles, as a soloist and with other artists, that stretched into the mid-1980s: 'Blue Eyes Crying In The Rain' (US#21, C&W#1, 1975), 'Good Hearted Woman' (with Waylon Jennings; US#25, C&W#1, 1976), 'If You've Got The Money, I've Got The Time' (C&W#1, 1976), **Ed Bruce**'s 'Mammas Don't Let Your Babies Grow Up To Be Cowboys' (with Waylon Jennings; C&W#1, 1978), 'Georgia On My Mind' (C&W#1, 1978), 'Blue Skies' (C&W#1, 1978), 'Help Me Make It Through The Night' (C&W#3, 1979), 'Heartbreak Hotel' (with **Leon Russell**; C&W#1, 1979), 'My Heroes Have Always Been Cowboys' (C&W#1, 1980), 'Midnight Rider' (C&W#6, 1980), 'On The Road Again' (US#20, C&W#1, 1980), 'Angel Flying Too Close To The Ground' (C&W#1, 1981), 'Always On My Mind' (US#5, C&W#1, 1982), 'Let It Be Me' (US#40, 1982), 'Just To Satisfy You' (with Waylon Jennings; C&W#1, 1982), 'Pancho & Lefty' (with **Merle Haggard**; C&W#1, 1983), 'To All The Girls I've Loved Before' (with Julio Iglesias;

US#5, C&W#1, 1984), 'City Of New Orleans' (C&W#1, 1984), 'Seven Spanish Angels' (with **Ray Charles**; C&W#1, 1985), 'Forgiving You Was Easy' (C&W#1, 1985), 'Highwayman' (with Waylon Jennings, **Johnny Cash** and **Kris Kristofferson**; C&W#1, 1985), 'Living In The Promised Land' (C&W#1, 1986) and 'Nothing I Can Do About It Now' (C&W#1, 1989).

While some of the collaborations - particularly with Julio Iglesias - could be considered slightly off the wall, Nelson tackled any new venture with spirited enthusiasm. This enthusiasm was applied to other ventures, such as his annual Independence Day picnics (which were essentially outdoor festivals), and a parallel film career, in which he appeared in Sidney Pollack's *The Electric Horseman* (1979) with Jane Fonda and Robert Redford, Jerry Schatzberg's *Honeysuckle Rose* (1980), Fred Schepsi's *Barbarosa* (1981), Michael Mann's *Thief* (1981) and Alan Rudolph's *Songwriter* (1984).

As a result of the 'Live Aid' event of 1985, Willie Nelson instigated 'Farm Aid' to benefit impoverished American rural communities: the first show featured appearances by artists including Nelson, Merle Haggard, **John Conlee**, **Tanya Tucker**, John Mellencamp and Foreigner. By the end of the 1980s, despite having been declared bankrupt (with exorbitant debts to the Internal Revenue Service), he remained as popular and influential as ever. In 1993, he cut *Across The Borderline*, which marked a return to the peak of his powers.

ACROSS THE BORDERLINE, Columbia, 1993
ALWAYS ON MY MIND, Columbia, 1982
BLUE SKIES, Columbia, 1981
COLLECTION, Columbia, 1988
DIAMOND SERIES, RCA, 1988
FAMILY BIBLE, MCA, 1986
GREATEST HITS (AND SOME THAT WILL BE), Columbia, 1992
HALF NELSON, Columbia, 1985
HELP ME MAKE IT THROUGH THE NIGHT, RCA, 1984
HORSE CALLED MUSIC, Columbia, 1989
I LOVE COUNTRY, Columbia, 1987
ISLAND IN THE SEA, Columbia, 1987
LONGHORN JAMBOREE, Charly, 1977
LOVE SONGS, Columbia, 1990
ONE FOR THE ROAD (with Leon Russell), Columbia (US), 1979
OUTLAWS (with David Allan Coe), Charly, 1986
PROMISED LAND (with David Allan Coe), Columbia, 1986
RED HEADED STRANGER, Pickwick, 1989
SOUND IN YOUR MIND, Columbia, 1983

TAKE IT TO THE LIMIT (with Waylon Jennings), Columbia, 1983
WHAT A WONDERFUL WORLD, Columbia, 1988
WITHOUT A SONG, Columbia, 1985
YESTERDAY'S WINE, RCA, 1980

NESMITH, Mike

A founder member of the Monkees, Mike Nesmith left the group in 1969 to pursue his first love, country music. Although much maligned, due to the fact that their huge commercial success was contrived by television producers, the Monkees notched up a string of tuneful hits. It later became clear - through Nesmith's solo career - that the success of the band had not been entirely attributable to their zany television antics.

Nesmith was born on December 30, 1942, in Houston, Texas. He was conscripted into the Air Force at eighteen, and started to play the guitar and write songs after his discharge in 1962. After joining the Monkees in 1966, Nesmith's interest in country music became evident in the choice of some of the group's material, particularly with their massive hit of **John Stewart**'s 'Daydream Believer' in 1967. By the time he left the group in 1969 he had composed songs like 'Different Drum', which was recorded by **Linda Ronstadt**, and cut an album of instrumentals, *Wichita Train Whistle Sings*.

On his departure he formed the First National Band, which included steel guitarist **Red Rhodes** in its line-up. The group's debut for RCA, *Magnetic South* (1970), featured 'Joanne' (later covered by Andy Williams; US#21, 1970); two other albums followed: *Loose Salute* (1971) and *Nevada Fighter* (1972), the latter featuring contributions from **James Burton** and **Glen D. Hardin**. Although the First National Band had split, with Rhodes and Nesmith remaining, other albums, such as *Tantamount To Treason* (1972), *And The Hits Just Keep On Coming* (1972) and *Pretty Much Your Standard Ranch Stash* (1973), ensured that Nesmith remained in the vanguard of country-rock artists.

Nesmith left RCA in 1973 to found the Countryside label, issuing albums by Rhodes and Ian Matthews. It was a shortlived venture as Elektra, which had backed Countryside, underwent major personnel changes (with David Geffen replacing Jac Holzman as the head honcho), and backing was withdrawn. In 1975 he established Pacific Arts Corporation, a film and multi-media company, and scored a hit with 'Rio' (UK#28, 1977). *Infinite Rider Of The Big Dogma*, released in 1979, was followed by a quieter recording period as Nesmith became more involved with his film company, which co-produced Alex Cox's *Repo Man* (1984).

While never coming close to achieving the Monkees' success, he has written some fine songs over the years, including 'Silver Moon' and 'Some Of Shelley's Blues'.

AND THE HITS JUST KEEP ON COMIN', Awareness, 1972
FROM A RADIO ENGINE TO A PHOTON WING, Awareness, 1976
INFINITE RIDER OF THE BIG DOGMA, Awareness, 1979
THE NEWER STUFF, Awareness, 1990
THE OLDER STUFF (BEST OF THE EARLY YEARS), Awareness, 1992
PRETTY MUCH YOUR STANDARD RANCH STASH, Awareness, 1973
THE PRISON, Awareness, 1990
TANTAMOUNT TO TREASON, Awareness, 1973

NEW COUNTRY see Crowe, J.D.

NEW GRASS REVIVAL

This group, like **J.D. Crowe**'s New Country, **Country Gazette** and **Quicksilver**, has based its reputation on an ability to draw extensively and authentically from the traditional bluegrass repertoire. They have also succeeded in maintaining interest from younger audiences by constantly experimenting with other musical forms.

New Grass Revival was formed in 1972 by fiddler and mandolinist Sam Bush, one of the younger generation of bluegrass musicians. The group evolved out of the remnants of another outfit, Bluegrass Alliance, which featured Curtis Burch (guitar and vocals), Dan Crary (guitar), Lonnie Peerce (fiddle) and Bush. Bush and Courtney Johnson (banjo) had joined the Alliance in 1970 from another group, Poor Richard's Almanac. In forming New Grass Revival, with Burch and Ebo Walker (bass), they became one of the most respected bluegrass bands on the circuit.

Although the line-up has changed over the years, Bush has remained centre stage, cutting albums for Starday and Flying Fish like *Fly Through The Country* (1974) and *The Storm Is Over* (1979), and teaming up with **Leon Russell** for *The Live Album* on Warner Bros. in 1981. In 1987 they cut their major label debut for EMI America, which was modestly successful. Since that time they have continued to work the clubs and the festival circuit, while Bush has become highly sought-after as a session musician, working most recently with **Suzy Bogguss** on *Aces* (1991).

BARREN COUNTRY, Flying Fish (US), 1979
COMMONWEALTH, Flying Fish (US), 1989
FLY THROUGH THE COUNTRY, Flying Fish (US), 1979
FRIDAY NIGHT IN AMERICA, Capitol (US), 1989
HOLD ON TO A DREAM, Capitol (US), 1988
LATE AS USUAL (Sam Bush), Rounder (US), 1988
NEW GRASS REVIVAL, EMI America (US), 1987
ON THE BOULEVARD, Sugar Hill (US), 1985
THE STORM IS OVER, Flyright, 1979
TOGETHER AGAIN - FOR THE FIRST TIME (Sam Bush and Alan Munde), Ridgerunner (US), 1977
TOO LATE TO TURN BACK, Sonet, 1978

NEW LOST CITY RAMBLERS

The New Lost City Ramblers emerged in the late 1950s on the back of the explosion of interest in traditional American music. The group was founded by folk singer Pete Seeger's half-brother, Mike Seeger (born in New York in 1933), John Cohen (born in New York in 1932) and Tom Paley (born in New York on March 19, 1928). Seeger's father, Charles, was a keen devotee of hillbilly music and passed this interest on through the family, with Mike becoming an accomplished string instrumentalist and himself encouraging veteran musicians, like **Dock Boggs** and **Eck Robertson**, to record in their later years.

Cohen, a graduate of Yale, developed his interest in folk music through his dalliances on the New York club circuit while working as a photographer. Paley had been brought up on a steady diet of classical music by his mother, a piano teacher. While studying mathematics, he started to learn the banjo and guitar, acquiring such proficiency that he later taught **Ry Cooder**.

The group was formed in 1958, cutting a number of albums for the Folkways label; these albums featured old songs that had been popularized by artists such as **Charlie Poole**, Gid Tanner (see **Skillet Lickers**), **Uncle Dave Macon** and **Fiddlin' John Carson**. In 1959 the group appeared at the Newport Folk Festival, and became regular features on the East Coast club circuit. In 1962 Tracey Schwarz (born in New York in 1938) replaced Paley, bringing a more flexible approach to the group. Other albums followed, including *American Moonshine And Prohibition Songs* (1963), and in 1964 Cohen and Seeger compiled

some of the better known songs in their repertoire as *The New Lost City Ramblers Songbook*.

By the end of the 1960s the group had drifted apart, with each member continuing to further knowledge of traditional music in varying capacities elsewhere: Seeger continued collecting songs and organized a festival of old-time music at Rockbridge, Virginia; Cohen played with a number of different groups, including the Putnam County String Band, and became a documentary film-maker; Schwarz joined up with the Balfa Brothers (see **Balfa**, **Dewey**) on odd occasions for festival appearances, as well playing regularly with members of his family; and Paley, having moved to the UK, worked the club and festival circuit in Europe and the US. In 1988, the group reformed for a reunion concert.

20th ANNIVERSARY CONCERT, Flying Fish (US), 1987
TWENTY YEARS, Flying Fish (US), 1979

NEW RIDERS OF THE PURPLE SAGE

The New Riders of the Purple Sage were initially a loose aggregation of musicians revolving around Grateful Dead guitarist Jerry Garcia. By the early 1970s, with the spiralling interest in country-rock nearing its zenith, the band became a full-time operation and Garcia effectively ceased to be involved with the running of the group. The New Riders, however, did remain a satellite of the Grateful Dead, with current and former members of the latter moving in and out of their line-up: drummer Mickey Hart, bassist Phil Lesh, keyboardist Keith Godchaux and his vocalist wife, Donna, all put in spells with the group. Other distinguished members included former Jefferson Airplane drummer Spencer Dryden and **Byrds** bassist Skip Battin. The group's main contributors were guitarist Dave Torbert and steel guitarist Buddy Cage, who, after Garcia's departure, became the lynchpin of the band.

Signed by Columbia in 1971, their most successful albums were *Powerglide* (1972) and *Gypsy Cowboy* (1972), with the former offering the most consistent indication of the group's abilities. By 1976 they had signed with MCA and become established as a live outfit, often supporting the Grateful Dead; their albums now sounded increasingly strained, and the band stopped recording by the end of 1970s.

ADVENTURES OF PANAMA RED, Beat Goes On, 1973
MARIN COUNTY LINE, MCA, 1978
NEW RIDERS OF THE PURPLE SAGE, Edsel, 1970

NEWBURY, Mickey

The writer of 'An American Trilogy', memorably recorded by **Elvis Presley**, Mickey Newbury has acquired a reputation within country circles for composing songs more literate than is usual among country writers - **Johnny Cash** has referred to him as a poet.

Milton Newbury was born in Houston, Texas, on May 19, 1940. After leaving school he played in bars and fished in the Gulf of Mexico, before joining the Air Force in 1960. Discharged after four years, he moved to Nashville and devoted all his time to songwriting. His first hit was 'Funny Familiar Forgotten Feeling', which was covered by **Don Gibson** and **Tom Jones**. Among the other songs he composed were 'Just Dropped In (To See What Condition My Condition Was In)' for **Kenny Rogers**, 'She Even Woke Me Up To Say Goodbye' for **Jerry Lee Lewis**, 'Frisco Mabel Joy' for Joan Baez, 'Sweet Memories' for Andy Williams, 'You've Always Got The Blues' for Bobby Bland and 'Time Is A Thief' for Solomon Burke.

His own records (which he cut for RCA, Elektra, Mercury and ABC) were less successful, but included a version of 'The American Trilogy' (US#26, 1971) - his biggest hit to date.

AFTER ALL THESE YEARS, Mercury (US), 1981

NEWMAN, Jimmy 'C'

Born of French extraction in Big Mamou, Louisiana, on August 27, 1927, Jimmy 'Cajun' Newman was brought up on the sounds of cajun music. He started his career in 1946, working the clubs and bars of Lake Charles. By 1954 he had crossed over from the relative purity of cajun into a more general country-pop, backed up by regular appearances on the *Louisiana Hayride*, and, by 1956, at the *Grand Ole Opry*.

Signed by Dot, he strung together a number of hits, including 'Cry Cry Darling' and 'A Fallen Star' (US#23, 1957). In 1958, he was signed to MGM and cut a string of hits which included 'You're Making A Fool Out Of Me' (1958) and 'Grin And Bear It' (1960). Newman changed labels again in 1960, this time to Decca, and continued to have hits throughout the 1960s, which included 'Bayou Talk' (1962), 'Artificial Rose' (1965), 'Back Pocket Money' (1966) and 'Born To Love You' (1968).

Although acquitting himself well on most types of country music, he is really in his element when reverting to cajun, a 1962 album, *Folk Songs Of The Bayou*, being particularly impressive.

ALLIGATOR MAN, Charly, 1984
BOP A HULA, Bear Family (Germany), 1990
CAJUN COUNTRY CLASSICS, Charly, 1986
FOLK SONGS OF THE BAYOU, Stetson, 1962
JIMMY 'C' NEWMAN AND CAJUN COUNTRY, MCA (US), 1986
LOUISIANA SATURDAY NIGHT, Charly, 1987

NEWTON, Juice

Representing the swing towards pop prevalent in country music during the late 1970s and early 1980s, Juice Newton, with roots in country-rock, became one of the more successful of the new breed of country artist. She was born Judy Kay Newton on February 18, 1952, in Lakehurst, New Jersey, and raised in Virginia Beach, Virginia. In 1974, she moved to California and teamed up with Otha Young and Tom Keely to form the group Silver Spur. They cut their first album for RCA the following year, and after two further albums she launched a solo career as Juice Newton.

In early 1981, having signed with Capitol, she scored her first major hit with a remake of the Merilee Rush title, 'Angel Of The Morning' (US#4, 1981); it was followed by a slew of hits over the next five years: 'Queen Of Hearts' (US#2, 1981), 'The Sweetest Thing (I've Ever Known)' (US#7, C&W#1, 1981), 'Love's Been A Little Hard On Me' (US#7, 1982), 'Break It To Me Gently' (US#11, C&W#2, 1982), 'Heart Of The Night' (US#25, 1982) and 'Tell Her No' (US#27, 1983).

After leaving Capitol she joined RCA and scored with 'You Make Me Want To Make You Mine' (C&W#1, 1985), 'Hurt' (C&W#1, 1986), 'Old Flame', 'Both To Each Other (Friends And Lovers)' (a duet with **Eddie Rabbitt**; C&W#1, 1986), 'Cheap Love' and 'What Can I Do With My Heart' - all of which were taken from the *Old Flame* album. 'Tell Me True' in 1987 proved to be her final hit to date and she took to the cabaret circuit.

CAN'T WAIT ALL NIGHT, RCA, 1984
COUNTRY CLASSICS, RCA (US), 1992

NITTY GRITTY DIRT BAND

The Nitty Gritty Dirt Band were, along with the **Byrds**, one of the first country-rock bands. There was a fundamental difference between the two: while the Byrds had their roots in contemporary American folk music, the Nitty Gritty Dirt Band had their origins in traditional American folk music. They proved their credentials with their triple album *Will The Circle Be Unbroken?* (1972).

The group was formed as the Illegitimate Jug Band in 1966 by Bruce Kunkel (born in 1948, in Long Beach, California) and Jeff Hanna (born on August 11, 1947, in Detroit, Michigan) in Long Beach and became a floating aggregation of performers of differing musical persuasions. The group initially comprised musicians such as Jimmy Fadden (born on March 9, 1948, in Long Beach, California), John McEuen (born on December 19, 1945, in Long Beach, California) and Chris Darrow, with John McEuen's brother, Bill, becoming the group's manager.

After signing to Liberty, the band's early recordings combined a hybrid of blues, bluegrass and old-time, with songs by writers like Jackson Browne - an erstwhile member - and Kenny Loggins. In 1968, they appeared in the movie *Paint Your Wagon* with Lee Marvin and Clint Eastwood; and in the following year they had their first hit with the **Mike Nesmith** composition, 'Some Of Shelley's Blues'. In 1971 *Uncle Charlie And His Dog Teddy* emerged: this album featured a reworking of the **Jerry Jeff Walker** song 'Mr Bojangles' (US#9, 1971), but also showed the group's versatility.

The following year *Will The Circle Be Unbroken?* was released: whereas earlier country-rock records - by the Byrds, for instance - had been treated with suspicion or complacency by the traditionalists in Nashville, this album featured bastions of the country music fraternity, such as **Merle Travis**, **Roy Acuff**, Maybelle Carter (see **Carter Family**) and **Doc Watson**, and was impossible to ignore. It vindicated attempts by many less tradition-bound performers, like **Commander Cody** and **Country Gazette**, to work - and build up a following - within the established country music network. This ultimately assisted the endeavours of artists like **Willie Nelson** and **Waylon Jennings**, both of whom were keen to break the monopoly of Nashville. Furthermore, John McEuen galvanized the group's record label, Liberty/United Artists, into repackaging **Bob Wills**'s records, which had been deleted from catalogues for a number of years.

The group's reputation expanded through the latter half of the 1970s, with a tour of Russia in 1977, and a collaboration (under the name of the Toot Uncommons) with comedian Steve Martin on 'King Tut' (US#17, 1978). After shortening their name to the Dirt Band, they cut *Make A Little Magic*, and scored with the **Rodney Crowell** composition 'An American Dream' (featuring **Linda Ronstadt**; US#13, 1980), and 'Make A Little Magic' (US#25, 1980).

In 1983 the group reverted to their former full name,

and started to put together a number of country hits: 'Shot Full Of Love', 'Dance Little Jean', 'Long Hard Road (The Sharecropper's Dream)' (C&W#1, 1984), 'I Love Only You', 'High Horse', 'Modern Day Romance' (C&W#1, 1985), 'Home Again In My Heart', 'Partners, Brothers And Friends', 'Stand A Little Rain', 'Baby's Got A Hold On Me' (C&W#2, 1987) and 'Fishin' In The Dark' (C&W#1, 1987). In 1989 they cut *Will The Circle Be Unbroken? Volume 2*; this album, while not as influential as the previous volume, included contributions from Roger McGuinn (see **Byrds**), **Chris Hillman**, **Johnny Cash**, **Ricky Skaggs**, **John Prine**, **Emmylou Harris** and **John Denver**. Despite the departure of founder member John McEuen, the group has managed to consolidate itself as the world's premier country-rock band.

ALL THE GOOD TIMES, Beat Goes On, 1972
AMERICAN DREAM (Dirt Band), Liberty (US), 1979
BEST OF THE NITTY GRITTY DIRT BAND, EMI, 1988
DIRT, SILVER AND GOLD, United Artists, 1976
EARLY DIRT: 1967-70, Charly, 1986
JEALOUSY (Dirt Band), Liberty, 1982
MAKE A LITTLE MAGIC (Dirt Band), Liberty, 1981
REST OF THE DREAM, MCA, 1990
STARS & STRIPES FOREVER, Beat Goes On, 1974
TWENTY YEARS OF DIRT, Warner Bros., 1987
UNCLE CHARLIE AND HIS DOG TEDDY, Beat Goes On, 1971
WILL THE CIRCLE BE UNBROKEN?, Volume 2, MCA, 1989
WORKIN' BAND, Warner Bros., 1988

NOACK, Eddie

A minor performer, but an influential songwriter, Eddie Noack was born Armond A. Noack on April 29, 1930, in Houston, Texas. After graduating in journalism and English from the University of Houston, he decided to launch a career as a vocalist. In 1947 he won a talent contest at Houston's Texas Theater, which led to his first radio broadcast in Bayton, Texas.

In 1949 he signed his first record deal with Gold Star, cutting 'Gentlemen Prefer Blondes'; he recorded for other minor labels (such as Four Star and TNT) over a two-year period, before landing up at Starday. At Starday he met **Hank Snow**, when both were appearing with **Hank Williams**. Snow was impressed by Noack's songwriting and cut a version of Noack's 'These Hands'. This encouraged other artists to pick up his songs, including **George Jones**, **Hawkshaw Hawkins**, **Ray Price**, **Ernest Tubb** and **Lefty Frizzell.** Although he remained with Starday until 1958, he started to record under the pseudonym of Tommy Wood for Pappy Dailey's D label, scoring a minor hit with 'Have Blues Will Travel'. When the label was sold to Mercury, Noack moved away from performance to concentrate on writing, striking up a particularly strong bond with George Jones, who scored with titles like 'For Better Or For Worse' and 'Barbara Jay'. In recent years he has returned to recording, cutting a number of sides for a variety of minor labels, culminating with a compilation of his better-known sides, entitled *Gentlemen Prefer Blondes*, for the independent Del Rio label in 1985.

NORMA JEAN

During the 1960s, Norma Jean acquired quite a reputation through her long-term association with the **Porter Wagoner** television show. She was born Norma Jean Beasler on January 30, 1938, in Wellstown, Oklahoma, and was brought up in Oklahoma City, where she learnt to play the guitar. In 1958, having played at local dances, she joined **Red Foley**'s *Ozark Jubilee* television show, which led to her selection by Wagoner as a member of the cast.

Between 1964 and 1967 she notched up a string of hits with 'Let's Go All The Way', 'Go Cat Go' (1964), 'I Wouldn't Buy A Used Car From Him' (1965) and 'Heaven Help The Poor Working Girl'. In 1967 **Dolly Parton** replaced Norma Jean on Wagoner's television show and she gradually slipped out of the picture, retiring to Oklahoma to look after her family.

NORTH CAROLINA RAMBLERS see POOLE, Charlie

NUDIE THE TAILOR see COHEN, Nudie

OAK RIDGE BOYS

In 1945, **Wally Fowler**, a member of the Georgia Clodhoppers, renamed the group the Oak Ridge Quartet. Over the years, as a gospel group, the line-up underwent myriad changes, until in 1957 Smitty Gatlin upgraded the old model from a part-time group to a full-blown professional outfit. This outfit had, by 1971, recorded for labels like Starday, Warner Bros., Checker, Cadence and Columbia.

Towards the end of the 1960s the group had become the Oak Ridge Boys, and the personnel were now sporting long hair and various other rock 'n' roll accoutrements. Staunch gospel adherents criticized them for their apparent lack of God-fearing respect, and by 1973 the group, while retaining a high percentage of gospel in their live act, had crossed over to country.

Comprising lead vocalists Duane Allen (born in Taylortown, Texas, on April 29, 1943) and Bill Golden (born in Brewton, Alabama, on January 12, 1939), tenor vocalist Joe Bonsall (born in Philadelphia on May 18, 1948) and bass vocalist Richard Sterban (born in Camden, New Jersey, on April 24, 1943), the group maintained a level of consistency matched only by **Alabama**. The succession of hits started in 1977, when they signed to ABC/Dot with producer Ron Chancey at the tiller: 'Y'all Come Back Saloon' (C&W#3, 1977), 'You're The One' (C&W#2, 1978), 'I'll Be True to You' (C&W#1, 1978), 'Sail Away' (C&W#2, 1979), 'Leaving Louisiana In The Broad Daylight' (C&W#1, 1979), 'Trying To Love Two Women' (C&W#1, 1980), 'Heart Of Mine' (C&W#3, 1980), 'Beautiful You' (C&W#3, 1980) 'Elvira' (US#5, C&W#1, 1981), 'Fancy Free' (C&W#1, 1981), 'Bobbie Sue' (US#12, C&W#1, 1982), 'I Wish You Could Have Turned My Head (And Left My Heart Alone)' (C&W#2, 1982), 'Thank God For Kids' (C&W#3, 1982), 'American Made' (C&W#1, 1983), 'Love Song' (C&W#1, 1983), 'Ozark Mountain Jubilee' (C&W#5, 1983), 'I Guess It Never Hurts To Hurt Sometime' (C&W#1, 1984), 'Everyday' (C&W#1, 1984), 'Make My Life With You' (C&W#1, 1984), 'Little Things' (C&W#1, 1985), 'Touch A Hand, Make A Friend' (C&W#1, 1985), 'It Takes A Little Rain (To Make Love Grow)' (C&W#1, 1987), 'This Crazy Love' (C&W#1, 1987) and 'Gonna Take A Lot Of River' (C&W#1, 1988).

In 1987, Bill Golden (who joined the group in 1965, and was its longest-standing member) was asked to leave, his replacement being Steve Sanders, a guitarist in the group's backing band; Golden eventually filed a $40 million suit against the other members of the band for wrongful dismissal (they settled out of court). The other major change had been the replacement of their producer, Ron Chancey, by MCA vice-president **Jimmy Bowen**. Still immensely successful, they represent the undemanding, easy-listening side of country music, with trite lyrics and pleasant innocuous harmonies.

AMERICAN DREAMS, MCA, 1989
BOBBIE SUE, MCA (US), 1982
DELIVER, MCA (US), 1984
FANCY FREE, MCA, 1981
GREATEST HITS, MCA (US), 1986
HEARTBEAT, MCA (US), 1989
THE OAK RIDGE BOYS HAVE ARRIVED, MCA (US), 1988
ROOM SERVICE, MCA (US), 1988
SEASONS, MCA (US), 1986
SENSATIONAL, Starday (US), 1987
STEP ON OUT, MCA (US), 1985
TOGETHER, MCA (US), 1980
WHERE THE FAST LANE ENDS, MCA, 1987
Y'ALL COME BACK SALOON, MCA (US), 1978

O'DANIEL, W. Lee see LIGHT CRUST DOUGHBOYS

O'DAY, Molly

Despite her comparatively brief career, Molly O'Day carved a reputation, which still lingers with some old-timers, as the best country singer of all time. Her métier was religious songs and romantic ballads, having little time for the rowdy wit of contemporaries like **Rose Maddox**.

She was born LaVerne Lois Williamson on July 9, 1923, in McVeigh, Pike County, Kentucky. In 1939 she started her career as a professional vocalist, under the pseudonym of Mountain Fern, with her brother, Cecil (Skeets), and Johnny Bailes (see **Bailes Brothers**) on WCHS, Charleston. On April 5, 1941, she married another member of her backing group, Lynn Davis (born Leonard Davis on December 15, 1914, in Paintsville, Kentucky) and together they formed their own outfit, known as the Cumberland Mountain Folks, which later included **Mac Wiseman**.

After the marriage, the couple toured radio stations, broadcasting on the *Early Morning Frolic* on WHAS, Louisville, the *Renfro Valley Barn Dance* on WLW, Cincinnati, and *Midday Merry-Go-Round* on WNOX, Knoxville. This exposure brought them into contact with **Fred Rose** in 1946, who signed them to Columbia, where they cut titles like 'The Tramp On The Street', 'Six More Miles', 'Black Sheep Returned To The Fold' and 'Drunken Driver'. Between 1947 and 1951, she scored a number of minor hits with songs like 'I'll Never See Sunshine Again', 'At The First Fall Of Snow', 'Poor Ellen Smith', 'Matthew Twenty-Four' and 'I Heard My Mother Weeping'.

In 1952 O'Day contracted tuberculosis and, with her husband, quit the music business: they both become ministers in the Church of God. By 1974 they had established a Christian station, WEMM-FM in Huntingdon, West Virginia, where they made their home. She died on December 5, 1987.

THE SOUL OF MOLLY O'DAY, Volumes 1-2, Old Homestead (US), 1987

O'DONNELL, Daniel

One of the best-selling Irish country singers of all time, Daniel O'Donnell has begun to make waves in the US as well as in Ireland and the UK. He was born in Kincasslagh, Co. Donegal, Ireland, on December 12, 1961. His solo career started in 1983 after several years working in his sister Margo's band. He initially failed to make any impact, and was on the verge of emigrating to Canada, when he was signed by the Ritz label in 1985, who began to promote him.

Over the next six years, songs such as 'A Veil Of White Lace' (1985), 'Take Good Care Of Her', 'Don't Forget To Remember' and 'I Need You' (1987), 'Far Far From Home' (1988), 'My Shoes Keep Walking Back To You' (1989) and 'Last Waltz Of The Evening' (1990) established him as Ireland's most popular singer. In the UK, most of his album catalogue is in the country Top Twenty at any given time, and his videos are formidably successful.

While he has yet to break in a big way in the US, 1990's *The Last Waltz* was recorded in Nashville with producer **Allen Reynolds**, which was followed by appearances on the *Grand Ole Opry* and a short concert tour. His most recent album, *Follow Your Dream*, stayed at the top of the UK and Irish country charts for what seemed an eternity.

THE BOY FROM DONEGAL, IMH, 1987
DON'T FORGET TO REMEMBER, Ritz, 1987
FAVOURITES, Ritz, 1990
FOLLOW YOUR DREAM, Ritz, 1992
FROM THE HEART, Telstar, 1988
I NEED YOU, Ritz, 1987
THE LAST WALTZ, Ritz, 1990
THOUGHTS OF HOME, Telstar, 1989
TWO SIDES OF DANIEL O'DONNELL, Ritz, 1985

O'HARA, Jamie   See **O'KANES**

O'KANES

Kieran Kane was born in Queens, New York, and started his career playing bluegrass with his brother Richard before moving to Boston. From Boston he moved to Los Angeles in the early 1970s, where he toured with groups like the Steve Miller Band. During the late 1970s he moved to Nashville in an attempt to make the grade as a songwriter, and was signed by **Buddy Killen**'s publishing company, Tree, as a writer and performer. After a spell with Elektra in 1980, followed by a stint with Warner Bros. in 1983, he started to write with fellow Tree writer, Jamie O'Hara.

O'Hara was born in Toledo, Ohio, where he had been a footballer, before moving to Nashville and starting to work the club circuit. After signing to Tree he wrote 'Wandering Eyes' and 'Older Women' (1981) for **Ronnie McDowell**, and 'Grandpa (Tell Me About The Good Old Days)' (1986) for the **Judds**. In 1986 he started to work with Kane, calling themselves the O'Kanes. At the suggestion of Killen they cut a number of demos, and secured a contract with Columbia.

Their debut, 'Oh Darlin'' (1987), cracked the Top Ten, and the follow-up, 'Can't Stop My Heart From Loving You' (C&W#1, 1987) established them. Other hits, such as 'Daddies Need To Grow Up Too' and 'Just Lovin' You' (1987), and 'One True Love' and 'Blue Love' (1988), followed, but their pared-down sound failed to win a regular audience with the traditionalists and the New Country aficionados and they separated in 1990.

IMAGINE THAT, Columbia, 1990
O'KANES, Columbia, 1987
TIRED OF RUNNING, Columbia (US), 1988

ORBISON, Roy

Many contemporary rock musicians have cited Roy Orbison as a major influence, but few would have imagined that his career would have revived so spectacularly in the years before his death.

He was born Roy Kelton Orbison, the son of an oilman, on April 23, 1936, in Vernon, Texas. In 1949 he formed his first group, the Wink Westerners, and while at high school he played with a rockabilly outfit, the Teen Kings, who made their recording debut with the Orbison-penned 'Ooby Dooby' at **Norman Petty**'s studio for the Jewel label in 1955. In 1956 Orbison moved to the Sun label, re-recording tracks such as 'Ooby Dooby'. By 1958, following the **Everly Brothers** rendition of 'Claudette', he stopped performing to concentrate on songwriting.

After a brief spell with RCA, he was signed by **Fred Foster** to the fledgling Monument label in 1960. Over the next five years he cut a string of highly effective, emotionally charged sides such as 'Only The Lonely' (US#2, UK#1, 1960), 'Blue Angel' (US#9, UK#11, 1960), 'I'm Hurtin'' (US#27, 1960), 'Running Scared' (US#1, UK#9, 1961), 'Crying' (US#2, UK#25, 1961), 'Dream Baby' (US#4, UK#2, 1962), 'The Crowd' (US#26, UK#1, 1962), 'Leah' (US#25, 1962), 'In Dreams' (US#7, UK#6, 1963), 'Falling' (US#22, UK#9, 1963), the double A-side 'Mean Woman Blues'/'Blue Bayou' (US#5, UK#3, 1963), 'Pretty Paper' (US#15, 1963; UK#6, 1964), 'Borne On The Wind' (UK#15, 1964), 'It's Over' (US#9, UK#1, 1964), 'Oh, Pretty Woman' (US#1, UK#1, 1964), 'Goodnight' (US#21, UK#14, 1965), '(Say) You're My Girl' (US#39, UK#23, 1965).

After leaving Monument in 1965 his career slipped into the doldrums, hastened by a series of personal tragedies: his wife Claudette was killed in a motorcycle accident in 1965, and two of his children died in a fire at his house in 1968. He was signed by MGM, but contractual problems and unsympathetic producers rendered most of his work from this period inferior by comparison with the high standards of his years at Monument. The hits from this period include 'Ride Away' (US#25, UK#34, 1965), 'Crawlin' Back' (UK#19, 1965), 'Breakin' Up Is Breakin' My Heart' (US#31, UK#22, 1966), 'Twinkle Toes' (US#39, UK#29, 1966), 'Lana' (UK#15, 1966), 'Too Soon To Know' (UK#3, 1966), 'There Won't Be Many Coming Home' (UK#19, 1966), 'So Good' (UK#32, 1967), 'Walk On' (UK#39, 1968), 'Heartache' (UK#44, 1968), 'My Friend' (UK#35, 1969) and 'Penny Arcade' (UK#27, 1969).

Throughout the late 1970s, he maintained his popularity in Europe by touring regularly, cutting *I'm Still In Love With You* for Mercury (1976) and returning to Monument for *Regeneration* (1977). In 1979 he moved to Elektra for *Laminar Flow*, which was followed by a duet with **Emmylou Harris** on 'That Lovin' You Again Feeling', featured in the film *Roadie*. This duet marked the beginning of a major revival of interest in his work, spurred by the inclusion of 'In Dreams' on the soundtrack of David Lynch's movie *Blue Velvet* (1986).

The following year T-Bone Burnett produced *In Dreams*, with Orbison reworking his best-known songs. The same year, Orbison, **Bob Dylan**, George Harrison (of the Beatles), Jeff Lynne (of the Electric Light Orchestra) and Tom Petty formed the Travelling Wilburys, and the debut featured 'Handle With Care' (UK#21, 1988) and 'End Of The Line' (UK#52, 1989). In the months before his fatal heart attack (on December 6, 1988, in Hendersonville, Tennessee), he recorded *Mystery Girl* (1989) and *King Of Tears* (1992); both were issued posthumously, with the former including 'You Got It' (UK#3, 1989) and 'She's A Mystery To Me' (UK#27, 1989). The latter included a duet with **k.d. lang** on his old composition 'Crying' (UK#7, 1992).

The success he found in later years with rock musicians was hardly surprising, considering the fact that he - and he alone - had managed to withstand the British beat-group invasion of the US in the early 1960s, maintaining a level of popularity and credibility that outstripped his contemporaries.

ALL TIME GREATEST HITS, Monument, 1973
THE BIG O, Charly, 1985
BLACK & WHITE NIGHT, Virgin, 1989
THE CLASSIC ROY ORBISON, Ocean, 1989
GO GO GO, Charly, 1986
GOLDEN DECADE BOXED SET, Knight, 1990
I'M STILL IN LOVE WITH YOU, Mercury, 1989
IN DREAMS, Virgin, 1987
KING OF TEARS, Virgin, 1992
MYSTERY GIRL, Virgin, 1989
RCA SESSIONS (with Sonny James), Bear Family (Germany), 1987

ROY ORBISON, Charly, 1990
ROY ORBISON AT ROCK HOUSE, Charly, 1981
THE SUN YEARS, Charly, 1984
TRAVELLING WILBURYS, Volume 1, Warner Bros., 1988

OSBORNE BROTHERS

Following in the footsteps of **Bill Monroe**, the Osborne Brothers blazed a trail for progressive bluegrass bands like the **Country Gentlemen** and **Quicksilver** to follow. Hailing from Hyden, Kentucky, Bobbie was born on December 7, 1931, and Sonny was born on October 29, 1937. Bobbie started his career in 1949 as a member of the Lonesome Pine Fiddlers, while Sonny began his career with Monroe in 1952. The following year they pooled their resources and made their first radio broadcast on WROL, Knoxville. In 1954 they moved to Detroit and recorded briefly with **Jimmy Martin**, before establishing themselves on WJR and then joining WWVA's *Wheeling Jamboree*.

In 1956 they signed to MGM, cutting tracks including 'Ruby' and 'Once More', before transforming themselves three years later into a trio, with the addition of lead vocalist Benny Birchfield. From 1959 they became fixtures at the folk festivals and on the college circuits. Evolving into an electric bluegrass band (having added steel guitar, drums and keyboards to the line-up - anathema to most purists), they began to secure dates on the nightclub circuit. In 1963 they were signed by Decca (later MCA), and cut records such as 'The King Of Woman I Got', 'Rocky Top', 'Tennessee Hound Dog' and 'Georgia Pinewoods', all of which became modest hits. They remain the only contemporary bluegrass band to be nominated for CMA awards.

BLUEGRASS COLLECTION, CMH (US), 1978
BLUEGRASS CONCERTO, CMH (US), 1979
BOBBY AND HIS MANDOLIN, CMH (US), 1980
ESSENTIAL BLUEGRASS, CMH (US), 1978
FROM ROCKY TOP TO MUDDY BOTTOM, CMH (US), 1977
I CAN HEAR KENTUCKY CALLING ME, CMH (US), 1980
MODERN SOUNDS OF BLUEGRASS MUSIC, Stetson, 1988
ONCE MORE, Volumes 1-2, Sugar Hill (US), 1989
OSBORNE BROTHERS, Rounder (US), 1988
OSBORNE BROTHERS AND RED ALLEN, Stetson, 1988
SINGING, SHOUTING PRAISES, Sugar Hill (US), 1989
SOME THINGS I WANT TO SING ABOUT, Sugar Hill (US), 1985
VOICES IN BLUEGRASS Stetson, 1985

OSLIN, K.T.

Kay Toinette Oslin emerged in the mid-1980s as a country singer, having spent many years in the heart of the entertainment business. She was born in 1942 in Crossit, Arkansas, and raised in Houston, Texas. After graduating from Milby High School she studied drama at Lon Morros College, before joining a folk group with **Guy Clark**. In 1966 she joined the chorus of a touring production of *Hello, Dolly!*, and then moved to New York, securing parts in *West Side Story* and *Promises, Promises*.

Over the next fifteen years or so, she parlayed her talents singing advertising jingles into work as a sessions backing vocalist. She also developed a career as a songwriter - her songs have been covered by artists including Judy Rodman, the **Judds** and **Dottie West**. After a brief stint with Elektra, where she cut the self-penned 'Clean Your Own Tables', she resumed session work until 1985, when she moved to Nashville and was spotted by producer Harold Shedd. They cut some demos together which eventually landed her a contract with RCA, where she scored with titles like '80's Ladies' (C&W#7, 1987), 'Do Ya' (C&W#1, 1987), 'I'll Always Come Back' (C&W#1, 1988), 'Money', 'Hold Me' (C&W#1, 1988), 'Hey Bobby' (C&W#2, 1989), 'This Woman' (C&W#5, 1989) and 'Come Next Monday' (C&W#1, 1990).

In her short career, her songwriting abilities and her wealth of theatrical experience have established her as one of Nashville's most convincing performers.

EIGHTIES LADIES, RCA, 1988
LOVE IN A SMALL TOWN, RCA, 1990
THIS WOMAN, RCA, 1988

OSMOND, Marie

Marie Osmond was overshadowed in her early career by the flatulent bombast of her brothers' pop group, the Osmonds. Although the Osmonds have, in recent years, turned increasingly to country music, Marie, having started her career in a country vein, never had to make such compromises with pop.

She was born a Mormon on October 13, 1959, in Ogden, Utah. With the staggering success of the Osmonds in the background, MGM label boss **Mike Curb** persuaded **Sonny James** to produce her debut, 'Paper Roses' (US#5, C&W#1, UK#2, 1973); with this success behind her she was teamed with brother Donny for a series of duets and their own television show, which ran from 1976 until 1978. The duets - all revivals - included 'I'm Leaving It (All) Up To You'

(Dale & Grace; US#4, UK#2, 1974), 'Morning Side Of The Mountain' (Tommy Edwards; US#8, UK#5, 1974), 'Make The World Go Away' (**Eddy Arnold**; UK#18, 1975), 'Deep Purple' (Nino Tempo & April Stevens: US#14, 1975; UK#25, 1976), 'Ain't Nothing Like The Real Thing' (Marvin Gaye & Tammi Terrell; US#21, 1976) and '(You're My) Soul And Inspiration' (Righteous Brothers; US#38, 1978).

While these hits did much to focus attention on her abilities as an entertainer, they did little to establish her credentials with country audiences. She eventually achieved this support by endless rounds of touring on the cabaret circuit. By 1985, having signed with Capitol, a duet with **Dan Seals** on **Paul Davis**'s 'Meet Me In Montana' (C&W#1, 1985) won her the approbation she had been seeking. Other hits then followed, including 'There's No Stopping Your Heart' (C&W#1, 1986), 'You're Still New To Me' (a duet with Paul Davis; C&W#1, 1986), 'Everybody's Crazy About My Baby' (1987), 'Cry Just A Little' (1987) and 'All In Love' (1988).

I ONLY WANTED YOU, Capitol (US), 1986
THERE'S NO STOPPING YOUR HEART, Capitol (US), 1986

OVERSTREET, Paul

Paul Overstreet came to prominence in the mid-1980s as a songwriter, contributing titles like 'On The Other Hand' for **Randy Travis** and 'You're Still New To Me' for **Marie Osmond** and **Paul Davis**. In 1986, in conjunction with two other writers, Thom Schuyler and Fred Knobloch, he formed S.K.O. Although each had previously performed as solo artists, only Knobloch had achieved any measurable success, with hits including 'Why Not Me' (US#18, 1980), 'Memphis' and 'Killin' Time' (a duet with actress Susan Anton; US#28, 1980). Signed to Mary Tyler Moore's label, MTM, they scored immediately with 'You Can't Stop Love' (C&W#9, 1987) and 'Baby's Got A New Baby' (C&W#1, 1987). In late 1987 Overstreet left the group for a solo career, and the group recruited Craig Bickhardt for one final single, 'Givers And Takers', before disbanding.

Before his solo career got under way, he teamed up with **Tanya Tucker** and Paul Davis for 'I Won't Take Less Than Your Love' (C&W#1, 1988). This was followed by solo hits such as 'Seein' My Father In Me' (C&W#2, 1990), 'Richest Man On Earth' (C&W#3, 1990) and 'Daddy's Come Around' (C&W#1, 1990). Since then he has sought, in his solo work, to transmit his religious convictions rather than achieve substantial commercial success.

LOVE IS STRONG, RCA (US), 1992
SOWIN' LOVE, RCA (US), 1989

OVERSTREET, Tommy

Little known beyond the US, Tommy Overstreet is one of many performers able to ply his trade on the strength of television appearances (on *Hee Haw* and *Midnight Special*, among others) and a thorough touring schedule (with his band Nashville Express).

He was born on September 10, 1937, in Oklahoma. After moving to Houston, Texas, he obtained work as Tommy Dean on the local television station, before going to the University of Texas in 1956 to study radio and television production. On graduation he joined the army and, on completion of his service in 1961, toured with his cousin, vocalist Gene Austin, until 1962. In early 1963 he started to work the Texas club circuit, until moving to Nashville in 1967, where he was employed by the Dot label to run their local office.

By 1969 he had been signed to Dot and began notching up a series of modest hits: 'Rocking A Melody' (1969), 'If You're Looking For A Fool' (1970), 'Heaven Is My Woman's Love' (1972), 'Send Me No Roses' (1973), 'If I Miss You Again' (1974), 'Here Comes That Girl Again' (1976), and 'If Love Was A Bottle Of Wine' and 'Don't Go City Girl On Me' (1977). In recent years he has recorded less, but he still retains a substantial following on the club circuit.

SOLID GOLD HITS, Bulldog, 1982

OWENS, Bonnie

It is unfortunate that Bonnie Owens has only had the reputation for being the best back-up vocalist in the business: successively married to two of country's biggest stars - **Buck Owens** and then **Merle Haggard** - she has been overshadowed by them.

She was born Bonnie Campbell on October 1, 1932, in Blanchard, Oklahoma. During the early 1950s she sang in clubs, before meeting and marrying Buck Owens; they performed together over KTYL, Mesa, Arizona, on the *Buck & Britt Show*. They moved to Bakersfield, California, in 1951 and Bonnie concentrated on raising their family. After divorcing Owens in 1955 she recorded for local labels like Marvel and Tally, cutting 'Daddy Don't Live Here Anymore' (1964) and 'Don't Take Advantage Of Me' (1965).

In 1965 she married Haggard, with whom she cut a collection of duets, *Just Between The Two Of Us*; this was followed by 'Number One Heel' and 'Lead Me

On'. In 1975 she retired from performing to look after Haggard's business affairs. She divorced him in 1976, but continues to look after his business affairs.

JUST BETWEEN THE TWO OF US (with Merle Haggard), Stetson, 1966

OWENS, Buck

In the hype surrounding the arrival of New Country, many have overlooked its natural antecedents. Buck Owens and his band, the Buckaroos, combined rockabilly and honky-tonk and thus paved the way for New Country artists like **Dwight Yoakam** and **Randy Travis**.

He was born Alvis Edgar Owens, the son of a sharecropper, on August 12, 1929, in Sherman, Texas, but was raised in Mesa, Arizona. Despite leaving school prematurely to work as a labourer with his parents, he became a proficient guitarist and mandolinist. He initially performed with his wife **Bonnie Owens** on the *Buck & Britt Show* on KTYL, Mesa; after their divorce, Owens moved on to Bakersfield, joining Bill Woods' band as a guitarist.

Based in Bakersfield, he started to develop a reputation as an outstanding session musician, backing artists like **Wanda Jackson**, **Sonny James**, **Tommy Collins**, **Tennessee Ernie Ford** and **Faron Young** and appearing as a sideman on KTTV's *Town Hall Party* from Compton. In 1956 he recorded briefly for the local Pep label, and in 1957 was signed by Capitol.

Over the next twenty or so years, he notched up a string of hits that, combined with the success of **Merle Haggard**, established Bakersfield as the hottest centre on the map for genuine hard-edged country music (Nashville, throughout these years, had been larding its sound with lush string arrangements and ethereal choirs). The Buckaroos, featuring steel guitarists like Ralph Mooney and **Tom Brumley**, bassist **Doyle Holly** and fiddler and guitarist **Don Rich**, provided accompaniment for the best of his work during these years, evident on hits like 'Second Fiddle', 'Under Your Spell Again', 'Above And Beyond', 'Excuse Me, I Think I've Got A Heartache', 'Fooling Around', 'Under The Influence Of Love', 'Act Naturally' (C&W#1, 1963), 'My Heart Skips A Beat' (C&W#1, 1964), 'Love's Gonna Live Here' (C&W#1, 1964), 'I've Got A Tiger By The Tail' (C&W#1, 1965), 'Buckaroo' (C&W#1, 1965), 'Waitin' In The Welfare Line' (C&W#1, 1966), 'Sam's Place' (C&W#1, 1967), 'How Long Will My Baby Be Gone' (C&W#1, 1968), 'Who's Gonna

Mow Your Grass' (C&W#1, 1969), 'Johnny B. Goode' (C&W#1, 1969), 'Tall Dark Stranger' (C&W#1, 1969) and 'Made In Japan' (C&W#1, 1972).

His career during the 1960s was fuelled by appearances at such prestigious venues as the White House, the Houston Astrodome, Carnegie Hall, Madison Square Garden and London's Royal Albert Hall, and by his own television show, *Buck Owens' Ranch*. In 1969 he began co-hosting *Hee Haw* with **Roy Clark**, a position he held until until 1986. The 1970s saw him establishing his commercial interests in management and publishing, while maintaining his studio complex in Bakersfield. By 1980, following a duet with **Emmylou Harris** on 'Play "Together Again" Again' and an uninspired sojourn with Warner Bros. (whom he joined in 1976), he retired from recording and performing.

In 1988 he emerged from retirement to duet with Dwight Yoakam at the Country Music Association's awards presentation: the result was a tingling version of a song he had recorded over fifteen years previously, 'Streets Of Bakersfield' (C&W#1, 1988); this encouraged him to go back into the studio, and, having re-signed with Capitol, he started recording again.

ACT NATURALLY, Capitol, 1990
BLUE LOVE, Sundown, 1987
BUCK OWENS, Audio Fidelity (US), 1984
HOT DOG, Capitol, 1989

OWENS, Ruby   See **FOX, Curly, and Texas Ruby**

OWENS, Tex

Tex Owens was born in 1892 in Wise County, Texas and enjoyed a brief spell of popularity as a Singing Cowboy with his 1935 Decca recording of 'Cattle Call' (later covered by **Eddy Arnold**). His principal success came through his radio broadcasts on KMBC's *Brush Creek Follies* and WLW's *Boone County Jamboree*. After the war he disappeared into obscurity, but the family tradition was sustained by his sister Ruby (see **Fox, Curly, and Texas Ruby**), and his daughter, Laura Lee (who sang with **Bob Wills**). Tex died in Baden, Texas, in 1962.

OXFORD, Vernon

Vernon Oxford has proved to be an unusual country artist: he has built up a considerable following in the

UK and the rest of Europe, but failed to make any waves in the US. Born on June 8, 1941, in Benton County, Arkansas, he was one of seven siblings whose father was a fiddler. After several years on the move his family finally settled in Wichita, Kansas, where Vernon joined the local church choir and started to play the fiddle. He toured the Midwest throughout the 1960s, but having been rejected by record labels for being too purist, he started to tour Europe. Finally securing a contract with RCA in 1965, he was dropped after only a few singles. In 1974, he was re-signed by RCA and scored minor hits with 'Redneck' and 'Shadows Of My Mind' (1976).

Now more popular than ever in Ireland and Europe, he makes regular appearances at the annual Country Festival at Wembley, London. He left RCA in 1978 and recorded for Rounder, cutting *If I Had My Wife To Love Over* (1978) and *Keepin' It Country* (1985), the latter featuring stellar session musicians such as **Charlie McCoy**, **Pete Drake**, **Kenny Buttrey** and **Lloyd Green**.

A BETTER WAY OF LIFE, Sundown, 1987
HIS & HERS, Rounder (US), 1988
I LOVE TO SING, Bear Family (Germany), 1986
IF I HAD MY WIFE TO LOVE OVER, Rounder (US), 1978
KEEPIN' IT COUNTRY, Sundown, 1985
POWER IN THE BLOOD, BBC, 1989

PARKER, Andy, and the Plainsmen

Andy Parker was one of the few Singing Cowboys to make the transition from purveying glamourized views of the Old West to leading a creditable old-time and Western Swing group, the Plainsmen. He was born near Mangum, Oklahoma, on March 17, 1913, and started his broadcasting career in 1929 on KGMP, Elk City, Oklahoma. In the mid-1930s he moved to San Francisco and became the Singing Cowboy on NBC's *Death Valley Days* in 1937 - a role he maintained until 1941, when he went to work in a Los Angeles munitions factory.

In 1944 he formed the Plainsmen, which included such luminaries as Joaquin Murphy (steel guitar), George Bamby (accordion and arrangements; formerly of **Spade Cooley**'s outfit), Charlie Morgan (lead guitar) and Clem Smith (bass). Based in Hollywood and broadcasting on KNX, they appeared with **Eddie Dean** in a number of films and secured a recording contract with Capitol in 1947. Unfortunately the few sides they cut for Capitol made little impact and the group disbanded. A grave heart condition curtailed Parker's activities and he moved into a premature retirement in the mid-1950s.

PARSONS, Bill see BARE, Bobby

PARSONS, Gene

One of the many peripatetics to have spent most of their careers working with other former members of the **Byrds**, guitarist and drummer Gene Parsons was born on April 9, 1944. In 1963 he started his career with the Castaways, remaining with them until 1966, when he teamed up with cajun fiddler Floyd 'Gib' Guilbeau and formed the duo Cajun Gib & Gene. His association with Guilbeau brought him into contact with **Clarence White**, and, in 1968, the three of them formed Nashville West, bringing in bassist Wayne Moore. While this band was shortlived, it stimulated interest in traditional country music among college students.

In September 1968 the group disbanded when White joined the Byrds, followed two months later by Parsons, who replaced drummer Kevin Kelley. Parsons remained with the Byrds until 1972, when he embarked on a solo career, cutting *Kindling* for Warner Bros., before teaming up with Guilbeau again and touring as a duo. In 1974, Parsons and Guilbeau joined the new line-up of the **Flying Burrito Brothers** and cut *Flying Again*. In 1976 Parsons left the group and took another stab at a solo career with an eponymous solo album, before joining Warner Bros. as an A&R man. Guilbeau remained with the Flying Burrito Brothers until 1982, when he reverted to playing traditional cajun music on the club circuit and on sessions.

GENE PARSONS, Sierra, 1979
TOE TAPPIN' MUSIC (Gib Guilbeau), Shiloh, 1979

PARSONS, Gram

The lachrymose passion of country music and the immediacy of rock were first fused into country-rock in the music of Gram Parsons, who became a role model for countless imitators. Despite his lack of commercial acceptance during his short life, his influence is perceptible in the work of **Emmylou Harris**, **Elvis Costello** and **Marianne Faithfull**.

He was born Cecil Connor on November 5, 1946, in Winterhaven, Florida, the son of country singer and composer 'Coon Dog' Connor; his early years were spent in Georgia where he learnt to play the guitar. His father committed suicide in 1959, and Parsons adopted the name of his mother's second husband. Throughout his adolescence, he was constantly running away from home and often forming bands, including the Shilos (which featured Jim Stafford and Kent LaVoie, a.k.a. Lobo). In 1965 he briefly attended Harvard as a theology major, before dropping out to form the International Submarine Band, who recorded arguably the first country-rock album, *Safe At Home* (1967), for Lee Hazelwood's LHI label.

In 1968 he joined the **Byrds**, with whom he cut the

majestic *Sweetheart Of The Rodeo*: His influence permeates the record and makes plain the link between soul and country in readings of songs like William Bell's 'You Don't Miss Your Water'; his own compositional talents hint at future success in songs like 'Hickory Wind'.

After leaving the Byrds he formed the **Flying Burrito Brothers**; their debut, *The Gilded Palaces Of Sin*, follows on from where *Sweetheart Of The Rodeo* left off. Among the songs included is a version of Dan Penn's classic, 'Dark End Of The Street', which evokes a sense of brooding foreboding, and the self-composed 'Sin City', which crystallizes the impossibility of redemption. The follow-up, *Burritos Deluxe*, was a much more rock 'n' roll affair, and Parsons, in his personal life, now began to adopt the accoutrements of the lifestyle by knocking around with Keith Richards and Mick Jagger of the **Rolling Stones**.

In 1972 he was signed by Reprise and cut his first solo album, *GP*. This was a logical development from *The Gilded Palaces Of Sin*, and included a band which comprised **James Burton** and **Glen D. Hardin**, and introduced Emmylou Harris to the world stage. In 1974 *Grievous Angel* appeared, featuring substantially the same band and containing versions of songs including **Felice and Boudleaux Bryant**'s 'Love Hurts' (a magnificently aching duet with Harris), and self-penned items like '$1000 Wedding' and 'In My Hour Of Darkness'.

Parsons was dead by the time it was released: he suffered a fatal heart attack on September 19, 1973, precipitated by a combination of drug and alcohol abuse. Curiously, a post mortem was never carried out, as his manager and close friend Phil Kaufman kidnapped the corpse and took it to Joshua Tree in the California desert and cremated it. It is foolish to speculate on just how significant his contribution would have been had he lived, but Emmylou Harris has kept his legacy alive.

THE EARLY YEARS, Magnum, 1984
GP, Reprise, 1973
GRAM PARSONS, Warner Bros., 1982
GRIEVOUS ANGEL, Reprise, 1974
LIVE (with Emmylou Harris), Sundown, 1989
MELODIES, Sundown, 1984
SAFE AT HOME (International Submarine Band), Sundown, 1991
WARM EVENINGS, PALE MORNINGS, BOTTLED BLUES, 1963-73, Raven, 1992

PARTON, Dolly

Elevated to iconic status, Dolly Parton has managed to make her presence felt throughout every facet of the international entertainment business. She was born Dolly Rebecca Parton, the fourth of twelve children, on January 19, 1946, in Locust Ridge, Tennessee. In 1956 she made her radio debut on WNOX, and by 1959 she had made her first appearance at the *Grand Ole Opry*. In 1964 she graduated from Sevier County High School and moved to Nashville, where she worked as a songwriter. Within three years she had been signed to the Monument label by **Fred Foster**, and scored her first hits with 'Dumb Blonde' and 'Something Fishy' (1967).

In 1967 she replaced **Norma Jean** as the featured singer on television's ***Porter Wagoner*** *Show* and was signed by RCA, where she had an immediate hit duetting with Wagoner on Tom Paxton's 'Last Thing On My Mind' (C&W#7, 1967). Over the years they cut a number of duets, including 'We'll Get Ahead Someday', 'If Teardrops Were Pennies', 'Please Don't Stop Loving Me' (C&W#1, 1974) and 'Making Plans' (C&W#2, 1980). She remained with Wagoner until 1974.

Her solo career had picked up steam with self-penned songs such as 'Just Because I'm A Woman', 'In The Good Old Days', 'My Blue Ridge Mountain Home', 'Joshua' (C&W#1, 1970), 'Coat Of Many Colours' (C&W#4, 1971), 'Jolene' (C&W#1, 1974; UK#7, 1976), 'I Will Always Love You' (which was covered by Whitney Houston in 1992, and featured on the soundtrack of *The Bodyguard*; C&W#1, 1974), 'Love Is Like A Butterfly' (C&W#1, 1974) and 'The Bargain Store' (C&W#1, 1975). In 1977 she started to record in Los Angeles, broadening her horizons with songs like 'Here You Come Again' (US#3, C&W#1, 1977; UK#75, 1984), 'It's All Wrong, But It's All Right' (C&W#1, 1978), 'Two Doors Down' (US#19, 1978), 'Heartbreaker' (US#37, C&W#1, 1978), 'Baby I'm Burning' (US#25, C&W#1, 1978), 'You're The Only One' (C&W#1, 1979), 'Starting Over Again' (written by soul singer Donna Summer; US#36, C&W#1, 1980) and 'Old Flames Can't Hold A Candle To You' (C&W#1, 1980).

She took on her first movie role in 1980, co-starring with Jane Fonda and Lily Tomlin in *9 To 5*; her performance established her beyond any doubt as a national institution, and the movie became the basis for a television series in 1982. The theme song, '9 To 5' (US#1, C&W#1, 1980; UK#47, 1981) became her biggest national hit, launching her onto the lucrative Las Vegas cabaret circuit. Her country hits meanwhile continued with 'But You Know I Love You' (C&W#1, 1981).

In 1982 she starred with Burt Reynolds in the movie *The Best Little Whorehouse In Texas*, featuring 'I Will Always Love You' (C&W#1, 1982), which became one of only a few records in the history of country music to top the charts on two separate occasions. The following year she was teamed with **Kenny Rogers** on the Bee Gees' composition 'Islands In The Stream' (US#1, C&W#1, UK#7, 1983). In 1984 she appeared with Sylvester Stallone in the mediocre movie *Rhinestone*, based on the **Glen Campbell** song 'Rhinestone Cowboy'; among the songs featured on the soundtrack was 'Tennessee Homesick Blues' (C&W#1, 1984).

After the success of the duet with Kenny Rogers, she toured with him in 1985, recording another duet 'Real Love' (C&W#1, 1985), which was featured on the HBO special *Kenny Rogers And Dolly Parton Together* and was the title track of the album that also included 'Think About Love' (C&W#1, 1986). In 1986, the much-vaunted collaboration with **Emmylou Harris** and **Linda Ronstadt** finally took place with *Trio* (1987), which featured revivals of 'To Know Him Is To Love Him' (C&W#1, 1987), 'Telling Me Lies', 'Those Memories Of You' and 'Wildflowers'.

After the project with Harris and Ronstadt, she was signed by the ABC-TV network to star in a variety series *Dolly*, earning her $44 million. In late 1987 she changed record labels and signed with Columbia. Her debut for the label was *Rainbow*, which was followed by *White Limozeen*: produced by **Ricky Skaggs** it included 'Why'd You Come In Here Looking Like That' (C&W#1, 1989) and 'Yellow Roses' (C&W#1, 1989). Towards the end of 1989 her fourth film, *Steel Magnolias*, was released, featuring stars such as Sally Field, Shirley MacLaine, Julia Roberts and Darryl Hannah. In 1991 she teamed up with **Ricky Van Shelton** for the duet 'Rockin' Years' (C&W#1, 1991), and followed it up with *Slow Dancing At the Moon* (1993).

COLLECTION, Castle, 1992
THE DOLLY PARTON STORY, Columbia, 1977
GREATEST HITS, RCA, 1992
THE LOVE ALBUM, RCA, 1989
RAINBOW, Columbia,1988
SLOW DANCING AT THE MOON, Columbia,1993
TRIO, (with Linda Ronstadt & Emmylou Harris), Warner Bros., 1987
WHITE LIMOZEEN, Columbia,1989
WINNING HAND, (with Willie Nelson, Kris Kristofferson & Brenda Lee), Monument, 1983
YOU ARE, RCA, 1980

PAUL, Les, and Mary Ford

One of the most innovative guitarists of his day, Les Paul left a legacy in the solid-body guitar he designed for the Gibson company, in the overdubbing techniques that his knowledge of electronics enabled him to develop, and with the hits he had with his wife Mary Ford in the early 1950s.

He was born Lester William Polfus on June 9, 1916, in Waukesha, Wisconsin. A proficient guitarist by the age of twelve, he started his career in 1929, playing guitar and harmonica in the duo Sunny Joe & Rhubarb Red with Joe Wolverton. In 1933 he toured with Rube Tronson and his Texas Playboys, before being bitten by the jazz bug and starting to play in orchestras. By 1935 his versatility had secured him a slot on WJJD, Chicago, as Rhubarb Red, playing country, and on WIND, as Les Paul, playing jazz. While his jazz work was strongly influenced by Django Reinhardt and Eddie Lang, the fluid style of his country work was light years away from the traditional country pickers.

In 1936 he formed the Les Paul Trio with bassist Ernie Newton and Jim Atkins (the older half-brother of **Chet Atkins**). After moving to Los Angeles in 1941 he played in Ben Bernie's Orchestra, started doing sessions for artists like Nat 'King' Cole and Bing Crosby and also recorded under his own name, scoring hits with 'It's Been A Long Long Time' (US#1, 1945), 'Lover' (US#1, 1948) and 'Nola' (US#1, 1950).

In 1947 he teamed up with Mary Ford (born Colleen Summers on July 7, 1924, in Pasadena, California), who was also an expert guitarist, having played with **Gene Autry** and **Jimmy Wakely**. The couple married in 1949 and began recording together the following year. The combination of Ford's vocals and Paul's lyrical guitar-work provided him with a perfect opportunity to demonstrate the wide applications and potential of overdubbing; their biggest hits, however, were surprisingly bland: 'Tennessee Waltz', 'Just One More Chance', 'Mockingbird Hill' (US#2, 1951), 'How High The Moon' (US#1, 1951), 'The World Is Waiting For Sunrise' (US#2, 1951), 'Vaya Con Dios' (US#1, UK#7, 1953) and 'I'm A Fool To Care'.

With the emergence of rock 'n' roll in the mid-1950s, the duo's style became hideously dated, and while his solid-body guitar was an essential item for every professional guitarist, his recordings were increasingly safe: 'Hummingbird' (US#7, 1955), 'Amukiriki' (US#38, 1955), 'Cinco Robles' (US#35, 1957), 'Put A Ring On My Finger' (US#32, 1958) and 'I Swear I Love You' (US#37, 1961). In 1963 the couple divorced, and Paul, who was suffering from hearing difficulties, retired to his electronics workshop. Ford gave up performing and died on September 30, 1977. Paul made a limited comeback in 1974, recording *Chester & Lester* (1976) and *Guitar Monsters* (1978) with Chet Atkins for RCA; both albums show two tireless technicians at their best.

CHESTER & LESTER (with Chet Atkins), RCA, 1977
GUITAR GENIUS (with Grady Martin and Hank Garland), Charly, 1985
THE LEGEND AND THE LEGACY (Les Paul), Capitol, 1991

PAYCHECK, Johnny

Johnny Paycheck was born Donald Eugene Lytle on May 31, 1941, in Greenfield, Ohio. He started his career as bassist in **Porter Wagoner**'s Wagonmasters, then joined **Faron Young**'s Deputies, and followed with stints with **Ray Price** and **George Jones**. His own recording career started in 1959 as a rockabilly artist with Decca, under the pseudonym of Donny Young, where he cut titles which included 'Shaking The Blues'. After another spell with George Jones, he signed to Mercury as Johnny Paycheck (after a small-time heavyweight boxer who was knocked out by Joe Louis in 1940) scoring modest hits with 'A-11' (1965) and 'Heartbreak, Tennessee' (1966).

In 1966 he co-founded the Little Darlin' label, and scored his biggest hit to date with 'The Lovin' Machine' (1966); he also started to achieve recognition as a writer, penning titles like 'Apartment No. 9' for **Tammy Wynette** and 'Touch My Heart' for Ray Price. After a few years in obscurity, he was signed by **Billy Sherrill** to the Epic label, where he scored a string of hits which included 'She's All I Got' (C&W#2, 1971), 'Someone To Give My Love To', 'Mr Lovemaker', 'Song And Dance Man', 'For A Minute There', 'Take This Job And Shove It' (C&W#1, 1978) and 'Maybellene' (a duet with George Jones; 1978). In 1981 he cut a fine live album, *New York Town*, and *Mr Hag Told My Story*, a tribute to **Merle Haggard.**

His aggressiveness has landed him in trouble with the police on several occasions, and he has often been on the brink of bankruptcy. On December 19, 1985, a shooting in a bar in Hillsboro, Ohio, resulted in him being sent to prison for nine-and-a-half years. He was released on appeal in early 1987, and was signed to Mercury, where he cut *Modern Times*, which included 'Old Violin' (1987).

APARTMENT No. 9, President, 1986
BIGGEST HITS, Epic, 1983

GOLDEN CLASSICS, Gusto (US), 1988
HONKY TONK & SLOW MUSIC, Sundown, 1988
I DON'T NEED TO KNOW THAT RIGHT NOW, Allegiance, 1984
SIXTEEN GREATEST HITS, Gusto (US), 1988
SURVIVOR, Dixie Frog, 1990

PAYNE, Leon

Leon Payne's smooth tenor voice characterized a style of crooning popular with fans of artists like **Eddy Arnold**, **George Morgan** and **Hank Locklin**. Though he never achieved their success, he did establish a successful songwriting career.

Born blind on June 15, 1917, in Alba, Texas, Payne attended the Texas School for the Blind from 1924 until graduation in 1935, and learnt to play a variety of instruments, including the keyboards, guitar, drums and trombone. On graduation he became a professional musician, appearing with a variety of local bands including **Bob Wills**'s Texas Playboys. After stints with Jack Rhodes' band he formed his own group, the Lonesome Buddies, and broadcast on the *Grand Ole Opry*.

His reputation as a writer increased simultaneously, with **Hank Williams** covering 'Lost Highway' and 'They'll Never Take Her Love From Me'. Among his other compositions were 'I Love You Because', 'Blue Side Of Lonesome' and 'You'll Still Have A Place In My Heart'; the former, which was dedicated to his wife, provided him with his only hit and has been covered by artists including **Jim Reeves**, **Elvis Presley** and **Ernest Tubb**.

He recorded with labels such as MGM, Starday, Decca and Capitol until, after a heart attack in 1965, he retired from performing. He died of another heart attack on September 11, 1969.

PEARL, Minnie

The character 'Minnie Pearl' was created by Sarah Ophelia Colley in 1936, and helped to make the *Grand Ole Opry* broadcasts accessible to the masses. Colley was born in Centreville, Tennessee, on October 25, 1912, and studied drama at the prestigious Ward-Belmont College in Nashville during the 1920s. In 1934 she joined an Atlanta-based production company as a drama coach, and in 1936, after spending the night with an impoverished family in the backwoods of Alabama, she came up with the character 'Minnie Pearl'.

In the late 1930s she toured the South in this role,

until, in 1940, she made her debut on the *Grand Ole Opry*. While her jokes, and indeed the whole routine - with Colley wearing a straw hat covered in flowers and an old summer dress - were as corny as it gets, she nonetheless became one of the first highly visible stars of the developing country music culture. Although she recorded for a number of labels, it was her stage act that made her memorable. She was elected to the Country Music Hall Of Fame in 1975.

PEDERSEN, Herb

Stalwart of the country music session circuit, banjoist/guitarist Herb Pedersen was born on April 27, 1944, in Berkeley, California, and made his debut in 1968 as a member of the **Dillards**, before leaving to form **Country Gazette** in 1971. He remained with them until 1973, when he left to join the session circuit, playing with artists including Dan Fogelberg, **Emmylou Harris**, **Linda Ronstadt** and **John Denver**.

In 1982 he teamed up with **Chris Hillman** for some of Hillman's solo projects, and ended up forming the Desert Rose Band (see **Hillman, Chris**), which, as the 1980s gave way to the 1990s, remained the one of the few country-rock band prepared to draw effectively from country music's rich heritage.

LONESOME FEELING, Sugar Hill (US), 1984

PEER, Ralph

Ralph Sylvester Peer was one of the first talent scouts to recognize the immense potential value of acquiring copyrights of hillbilly songs and jazz compositions. To this day, the Peer-Southern Organization ranks as one of the largest holders of international copyrights in the music publishing industry.

He was born on May 22, 1892, in Kansas City, Missouri, the son of a phonograph dealer. After joining Columbia's Kansas office in 1911 he moved on to the Okeh label, and in 1920 made one of the first pioneering field trips, recording the blues singer Mamie Smith. In 1923 he recorded **Fiddling John Carson**, cutting the first ever genuine country sides. Throughout the 1920s, he made regular field trips and signed artists like the **Carter Family** and **Jimmie Rodgers** to Victor.

In 1928 he formed Southern Music, having concluded a deal with Victor that would secure him the publishing rights of their entire jazz and country catalogues. In 1932 he gained full control of Southern Music from Victor, and started to publish popular music by writers like Hoagy Carmichael. During the 1940s he obtained the copyright to all the incidental music used in Walt Disney movies, and in the 1950s he had publishing interests in the catalogues of artists such as **Buddy Holly**, **Mel Tillis** and Little Richard. His later years were spent pursuing his interest in horticulture. He died on January 19, 1960, in Hollywood, California. His son Ralph Peer II now controls his multi-million-dollar company.

PENNY, Hank

In recent years Hank Penny has worked as a comedian on the West Coast, but his career stretches back to the 1930s, when he led the Radio Cowboys, who were an amalgam of influences drawn from the big bands of the era and Western Swing outfits like **Milton Brown**'s Musical Brownies and **Bob Wills**' Texas Playboys.

He was born Herbert Clayton Penny on September 17, 1918, in Birmingham, Alabama. He made his debut as a banjoist for Hal Burns in 1933 on WAPI, Birmingham, before moving to WWL, New Orleans, as a vocalist and guitarist. After hearing the Musical Brownies he formed the Radio Cowboys, which included Noel Boggs, trombonist Eddie Duncan and **Boudleaux Bryant**. They were signed by **Art Satherley** to Vocalion in 1938, and commenced a tour of the radio stations of Tennessee and Alabama. The following year they joined the cast of *Crossroads Follies* on WSB, Atlanta, and cut some sides for Vocalion, including 'Hesitation Blues' and 'Hot Time Mama'.

In 1942 the Radio Cowboys disbanded and Penny moved to WLW, Cincinnati, to broadcast on *Midwest Hayride* and *Boone County Jamboree*, and to start recording for the local King label with session musicians such as **Merle Travis** and **Speedy West**. He stayed with King until 1950, cutting sides like 'Hillybilly Bebop', 'Open The Door Richard', 'Jersey Bounce', 'Tuxedo Junction' and 'Bloodshot Eyes'. In 1945 he moved to Los Angeles, where he formed another Western Swing outfit and worked as a comedian on the ABC radio show *Roundup Time*.

After fulfilling his commitments to King, he started to record for RCA in 1950, before moving on to Decca in 1952. Throughout the 1950s, his band included steel guitarist Herb Remington and vocalist **Sue Thompson**. By the late 1950s he had joined the migration to the Las Vegas cabaret circuit, where he employed Thompson and **Roy Clark**, among others. He moved back to the coast in 1975 and has appeared in a number of films including Mel Brooks' *Silent Movie*.

ROMPIN', STOMPIN', SINGIN', SWINGIN', Bear Family (Germany), 1984
TOBACCO STATE SWING, Rambler (US), 1981

PERKINS, Carl

A formative figure in the early days of rock 'n' roll, Carl Perkins' career was put on the skids by a serious car crash, ending his contention for the crown that for so long rested uneasily on **Elvis Presley**'s head. He has, nonetheless, succeeded in influencing a plethora of other artists, such as the Beatles, Dave Edmunds, **Ry Cooder** and **John Fogerty.**

Born into an extremely poor farming family on April 9, 1932, in Tiptonville, Tennessee, Carl Perkins was raised with the blues and country music. He was taught the guitar by a black sharecropper, and he, in turn, taught his brothers Jay and Clayton. They made their debut playing the local bars and radio stations as the Perkins Brothers, performing many of Carl's compositions. His vocal style was reminiscent of **Hank Williams**, but the choppy, staccato guitar riffs owed more to the urban blues of T-Bone Walker.

In 1954 he auditioned for **Sam Phillips** at the Sun Studios, and was rewarded with a recording contract. His first three singles were 'Turn Around', 'Let The Jukebox Keep On Playing' and 'Gone, Gone, Gone', all of which were solidly country. The next record - following hot on the heels of Presley's departure for RCA - was the self-penned 'Blue Suede Shoes' (US#2, C&W#1, UK#10, 1956): the lyrics dealt explicitly with the appurtenances of rock 'n' roll and the arrangement was pure rockabilly, indicating Phillips' intention of making Perkins into as big a star as Elvis. However, later that year, en route to an appearance on the *Ed Sullivan Show*, his car crashed, gravely injuring himself and his brother, Jay, who never fully recovered from his injuries and died prematurely in 1958.

This accident put Perkins out of action for the next nine months. When he returned, Elvis had eclipsed him, and at Sun **Johnny Cash** and **Jerry Lee Lewis** were the new stars. Over the next few years, despite the consistently high standard of his material - 'Boppin' The Blues', 'Matchbox', 'Daddy Sang Bass', 'Honey Don't' and 'Everybody's Trying To Be My Baby' - alcoholism, brought about by a crisis of confidence and a susceptibility to illness, ensured that he never garnered the plaudits accorded to many lesser artists.

In the 1960s, having reverted to country, he was recruited by Johnny Cash to join his roadshow, but albums for Columbia and Mercury were uneven. Since that time he has participated in reunions - becoming a focus for every rockabilly revival, often with younger performers like Robert Gordon or Dave Edmunds - and has recorded with the elder statesmen of rock such as Eric Clapton and George Harrison. In the mid-1980s he recorded the lack-lustre *Class of '55*, with Jerry Lee Lewis, Johnny Cash and **Roy Orbison**. He remains, along with Cash, one of the few survivors of rock 'n' roll's golden age able to strut his stuff with any authority.

BORN TO ROCK, MCA, 1989
CLASSIC CARL PERKINS, Bear Family (German), 1990
EVERY ROAD, Joker (US), 1988
HONKY TONK GAL, Rounder (US), 1989
ROCKIN' THE HOUSE DOWN, Columbia, 1985
THE SUN YEARS, Sun, 1990
THE SURVIVORS (with Johnny Cash & Jerry Lee Lewis), Columbia, 1982
UP THROUGH THE YEARS, Bear Family (German), 1986

PETTY, Norman

One of the first and finest producers to have grasped the nature and production requirements of rock 'n' roll, Petty's influence provided **Buddy Holly** and **Roy Orbison** with the push that set them on the paths to stardom.

He was born on May 25, 1927, in Clovis, New Mexico, and started his career as an instrumentalist in a trio. This provided him with sufficient funds to establish a studio in his hometown; its reputation quickly spread and performers such as Buddy Knox, Roy Orbison and **Jimmy Bowen** began recording there. In 1957 he started his association with Buddy Holly, which lasted until shortly before Holly's death.

In later years he assembled the various line-ups of the Crickets for touring purposes and remastered many of the Holly outtakes for release. In 1975 he sold his publishing company, Nor-Va-Jak, to Paul McCartney. He died on August 15, 1984.

PHILLIPS, Bill

A songwriter of some distinction, William Clarence Phillips was born on January 28, 1936, in Canton, North Carolina, and learnt the guitar while still at school. On leaving school he became an upholsterer, and started broadcasting on *Old Southern Jamboree* on WMIL, Miami, in 1955. In 1957 he moved to

Nashville, and was signed to the Cedarwood publishing company, where he provided songs for artists including **Kitty Wells** and **Webb Pierce**.

This gave Columbia the necessary incentive to sign him, but hits like 'You Are The Only Reason' were modest and, in 1963, he was signed to Decca. Although he never had any massive hits, he joined the Kitty Wells roadshow and chalked up a string of medium-sellers, such as 'Put It Off Until Tomorrow' and 'The Company You Keep'. He remained a key figure in Wells's roadshow for many years.

PHILLIPS, Sam

Sam Phillips was the ultimate rock 'n' roll Svengali, discovering artists such as **Elvis Presley**, **Carl Perkins** and **Jerry Lee Lewis**. He had an instinctive knack of selecting appropriate material for his artists, and he was able to draw from a pool of session musicians that ranked among the country's finest.

Samuel Cornelius Phillips was born the son of a farmer on January 5, 1923, in Florence, Alabama. After leaving school in 1941 he started to work as a local radio announcer, while studying engineering, embalming and chiropody at evening classes. In 1942 he became a DJ on WLAY, Muscle Shoals, before moving on to WHSL, Decatur, the following year. In 1945 he moved to WLAC, Nashville, moving on again to Memphis and WREC the next year.

By 1949 he had put together sufficient cash to open studios at 706 Union Avenue, Memphis, and he began recording bluesmen like Walter Horton, Sleepy John Estes, James Cotton, Little Milton, Earl Hooker and Howlin' Wolf, leasing the tracks to labels like Modern, Meteor and Chess. In 1952 he formed the Sun label; two years later, Presley cut his famous demo, with guitarist **Scotty Moore** and bassist Bill Black (both from Doug Poindexter's group), and the world turned upside-down for Phillips.

The immediacy of Presley's success was sufficient to encourage Phillips to sign every country and rockabilly singer he could lay his hands on. These included Lewis, Perkins, **Johnny Cash**, **Charlie Feathers**, **Roy Orbison**, **Warren Smith**, **'Hardrock' Gunter** and many more. In 1955, having sold Presley's contract to RCA, he assisted both Lewis and Cash in building their careers, but his ability to capitalize on their success was found wanting - once the groundwork had been laid, each and every one of his biggest stars was tempted away to larger labels.

By 1958 Phillips had lost his momentum, and the label was kept going only by a series of instrumentals

by **Bill Justis**. The label deteriorated throughout the 1960s, until it was sold to **Shelby Singleton** in 1969, whereupon Phillips left the music industry altogether to look after substantial business interests that included a number of radio stations.

PIERCE, Webb

During the early 1950s, Webb Pierce was one of the best honky-tonk singers in country music: his tales of feckless abandonment and alcoholic amnesia were to inspire artists such as **Merle Haggard**, **Moe Bandy** and **Charlie Walker**.

He was born on August 8, 1926, near West Monroe, Louisiana. A competent guitarist, he became a regular on KMLB, Monroe, before joining the *Louisiana Hayride*, where his band included **Faron Young** and **Floyd Cramer**. In 1951 he was signed by Decca, and started to cut a string of hits with titles like 'Wondering', 'That Heart Belongs To Me' and 'Back Street Affair' (1952), 'It's Been So Long' and 'There Stands The Glass' (1953) and 'Slowly' (1954).

In 1954 he joined the *Grand Ole Opry*, having moved to Nashville and recorded songs like 'More And More' (US#22, 1954), **Jimmie Rodgers**' 'In The Jailhouse Now' (C&W#1, 1955), 'Love Love Love' (C&W#1, 1955) and 'I Don't Care' (C&W#1, 1955). » In 1956 he teamed up with **Red Sovine** for the duets, 'Why Baby Why?' (C&W#1, 1956) and 'Little Rosa' (1956), and followed it with more hits like 'Teenage Boogie' (1956), **Felice and Boudleaux Bryant**'s 'Bye Bye Love' (1957), 'Honky Tonk Song' (1957), 'Tupelo County Jail' (1958) and 'I Ain't Never' (US#24, 1959).

During the early 1960s he became more involved with overseeing his extensive business interests, which included the Cedarwood publishing company, and consequently had fewer hits: 'Walking The Streets' (1961), 'Cow Town' (1962), 'Memory No. 1' (1964) and 'Fool, Fool, Fool' (1967). In 1974 he left MCA (formerly Decca) and signed with **Shelby Singleton**'s Plantation label, where he had a brace of minor hits: 'The Good Lord Giveth' (1975) and 'I've Got Leaving On My Mind' (1976). Despite moving into retirement he cut *In The Jailhouse Now* (1982), a collection of duets with **Willie Nelson**. In his final years his house, with its guitar-shaped swimming pool, and his tasteful custom-built Cadillac - inlaid with silver dollars, gun-shaped door handles and long-horn cattlehorns mounted over the grille on the bonnet - became a major Nashville tourist attraction. He died on February 24, 1991.

CROSS COUNTRY, Stetson, 1985
THE GREAT SONGS OF WEBB PIRCE, Bulldog, 1982
I AIN'T NEVER, Charly, 1984
THE WANDERING BOY, Stetson, 1989
THE WANDERING BOY, 1951-8, Bear Family (German), 1990
WEBB, Stetson, 1986

PLAINSMEN see PARKER, Andy

POCO

Though Poco were formed out of the remnants of Buffalo Springfield, their main musical influence was the **Byrds**, of whom they became a toothless imitation. Their closest counterparts, the **Eagles**, pursued a parallel course and proved to be more successful, their songwriting capabilities far exceeding those of Poco.

Poco were formed in August, 1968, by two former members of Buffalo Springfield, Richie Furay (guitar and vocals; born on May 9, 1944, in Yellow Springs, Ohio) and Jim Messina (guitar and vocals; born on December 5, 1947, in Maywood, California), who teamed up with Rusty Young (steel guitar; born on February 23, 1946, in Long Beach, California), George Grantham (drums and vocals; born on November 20, 1947, in Cordell, Oklahoma) and **Randy Meisner** (bass and vocals). Initially calling themselves Pogo, they changed their name to Poco after incurring contractual problems with the owners of the *Pogo* comic strip.

Over the next five or so years, the group released a string of albums, including *Pickin' Up the Pieces* (1969), *Poco* (1970), *Deliverin'* and *From The Inside* (1971) and *Good Feelin' To Know* and *Crazy Eyes* (1973). Behind-the-scenes shenanigans had meanwhile resulted in a changed line-up: Meisner had left to be replaced by Timothy B. Schmidt (bass and vocals; born on October 30, 1947, in Sacramento, California); Messina had been replaced by Paul Cotten (guitar; born on February 26, 1943) from Illinois Speed Press; and Furay left to form the Souther Hillman Furay Band (see **Hillman, Chris**) in 1973.

The new four-piece line-up issued albums at fairly regular intervals, despite a change of label from Epic to ABC in 1975: *Seven* and *Cantamos* (1974), *Head Over Heels* (1975), *Poco Live* and *Rose Of Cimarron* (1976) and *Indian Summer* (1977). Another round of musical chairs resulted in Schmidt leaving to join the

Eagles in 1977, and Grantham leaving the following year to join Secrets. Their respective replacements were Charlie Harrison and Steve Chapman, and the line-up was once more increased to five with the inclusion of Kim Bullard on keyboards.

Most of Poco's country influences had by now evaporated, and they were rewarded with a couple of hit singles: 'Crazy Love' (US#17, 1979) and 'Heart Of The Night' (US#20, 1979). Further albums included *Legend* (1979), and their first for MCA, *Under The Gun* (1980), which were followed by *Blue And Gray* (1981), *Cowboys And Englishmen* and finally *Ghost Town* (1982). The group then broke up, but, in 1984, Richie Furay reunited the original line-up to record the album *Inamorata* and perform a number of gigs. Disbanding again, most of them found gainful employment as session musicians.

FROM THE INSIDE, Epic, 1974
LEGACY, RCA (US), 1989
SONGS OF RICHIE FURAY, Columbia, 1980

POOLE, Charlie

A premature death, in 1931, prevented Charlie Poole from attaining the dizzy heights of stardom that had beckoned with the offer of work on a Hollywood film soundtrack. He nonetheless succeeded in leading one of the best string bands of his era.

He was born in Alamance County, North Carolina, on March 22, 1892. After a brief schooling he worked in textile mills until 1917, when he formed the nucleus of the North Carolina Ramblers with the crippled miner and fiddler Posey Rorer (born in 1881 in Franklin County, Tennessee). Initially a duo, they added guitarist Norman Woodlieff, who was later replaced by Roy Harvey (born in 1892 in Beckley, West Virginia). In 1928 Rorer left (he died in 1936) and was replaced by Lonnie Austin.

Among their finest recordings were 'Don't Let Your Deal Go Done' (later revived by the Grateful Dead) and 'Ramblin' Blues' for Columbia. While their music was pure hillbilly, Harvey's lyrical guitar work had a bluesy edge that foreshadowed the style of **Les Paul**. Poole, who has also been touted as one of the most dedicated drinkers in the history of country music, succumbed to a massive heart attack on May 21, 1931, following an epic binge. The group disintegrated following Poole's death. Harvey died in 1958.

CHARLIE POOLE: 1926-30, Biograph (US), 1990

POSEY, Sandy

The lyrical imagery contained in Sandy Posey's 'Born A Woman' was roundly vilified at the time for hindering the progress of feminism - closer scrutiny of the lyrics reveals isolationism rather than submissiveness. In spite of the controversy, this record exemplified producer **Chips Moman**'s innate understanding of how to get the best out of a song.

Sandy Posey was born Martha Sharp on June 18, 1945, in Jasper, Alabama. In 1955 her family moved to West Memphis, and by the mid-1960s she was singing backing vocals on sessions in Muscle Shoals, and working as a receptionist at Chips Moman's American studios. With Moman she cut a number of singles, including 'Born A Woman' (US#12, UK#24, 1966), 'Single Girl' (US#12, 1966; UK#15, 1967), **John D. Loudermilk**'s 'What A Woman In Love Won't Do' (US#31, UK#48, 1967), 'I Take It Back' (US#12, 1967) and **Joe South**'s 'Something I'll Remember'.

Retiring from studio work for the next three years, she was tempted back into the studio in 1970 to record with **Billy Sherrill**. A minor country hit with 'Bring Him Home Safely To Me' (1971) was formulaic, but later country hits, with covers of the Chordettes' 'Born To Be With You' (1977) and the Dixie Cups' 'Chapel Of Love' (1978), with Moman back at the tiller, were more interesting. In 1975 'Single Girl' was re-issued by MGM and it charted again. Although she has recorded little in recent years, she still appears on the cabaret circuit and on 'Hits of the 1960s' package tours.

BEST OF SANDY POSEY AND SKEETER DAVIS, Gusto (US), 1988
VERY BEST OF SANDY POSEY, MGM (US), 1984

POSSUM HUNTERS see BATE, Doctor Humphrey

PRAIRIE RAMBLERS

The Prairie Ramblers were a phenomenally influential 1930s' string band, who, unlike many of their contemporaries, retained their essential style despite a changing line-up. The group was formed as the Kentucky Ramblers in 1932 by Chuck Hurt (mandolin and banjo), Jack Taylor (bass), Tex Atchison (fiddle) and Floyd 'Salty' Holmes (guitar, harmonica and jug). Their career started with a slot on WOC, Davenport, Iowa, which was sufficient to land them a slot on WLS's *National Barn Dance* in 1933 - a position they held until

1948 - often backing **Patsy Montana** in cowboy outfits. In 1934 they changed their name to the Prairie Ramblers and cut songs like 'Shady Grove' and 'Rollin' On'.

By 1956, when the group finally disbanded, Taylor and Hurt were the sole survivors from the original line-up: Atchison had left in 1937 to pursue a movie career on the West Coast, while playing with the bands of **Jimmy Wakely** and **Merle Travis**, among others; and Holmes had formed a duo with his wife Maddie (as Salty & Maddie), broadcasting regularly on the *Grand Ole Opry*. After the group separated Hurt, Taylor and fiddler Wally Moore played with Stan Wallowick's Polka Chips until the mid-1960s.

PRESLEY, Elvis

No single artist has captured the public imagination in quite the same way as Elvis Presley. While his post-army career was more showbusiness glitz than serious rock 'n' roll, he recorded, in the years prior to his death, material that echoed his early years as a country singer and still possessed an almost unique urgency and timing.

He was born Elvis Aaron Presley on January 8, 1935, in Tupelo, Mississippi, the son of a share-cropper. In 1948 his parents moved to Memphis and encouraged him to sing at revival meetings and the local church. After graduating from Humes High School in 1953, he started truck driving for the Precision Tool Company. That same year he made his first visit to **Sam Phillips**' Memphis Recording Services, to cut a song as a birthday present to his mother, Gladys. At the studios he met Marion Keisker, who, eager to find a white man with the feel for black music (Phillips thought such a combination a potential goldmine), took his name and address.

In early 1954 Elvis returned to the studios and met Phillips; they cut some demos together with **Scotty Moore** and Bill Black. These early demos were reputedly pretty dreadful, but, by July, 1954, they had cut **Bill Monroe**'s 'Blue Moon Of Kentucky' and Arthur Crudup's 'That's All Right, Mama'. These two songs were neither country, blues nor any other definable category, possessing the rough-hewn vigour of Elvis's other Sun records like Roy Brown's 'Good Rockin' Tonight', Kokomo Arnold's 'Milkcow Boogie' and **Arthur Gunter**'s 'Baby Let's Play House'.

Initially managed by Scotty Moore, and then Bob Neal (who secured him spots on *Louisiana Hayride* and the *Grand Ole Opry*), his career took off with the arrival of Colonel Tom Parker, the manager of **Hank**

Snow and **Eddy Arnold**, who booked him onto the Hank Snow Jamboree. In August 1955 his final Sun single 'Mystery Train' (UK#25, 1957) was released, and later that year his contract with Sun was bought out by RCA for $35,000, with Parker assuming full managerial control of his career.

Over the next three years, with producer **Chet Atkins**, he recorded a string of hits that marked him out as the authentic voice of rock 'n' roll: 'Heartbreak Hotel' (US#1, C&W#1, UK#2, 1956), 'Blue Suede Shoes' (US#20, UK#9, 1956), 'I Want You, I Need You, I Love You' (US#1, C&W#1, UK#14, 1956), 'Don't Be Cruel'/'Hound Dog' (US#1, C&W#1, UK#2, 1956), 'Love Me Tender' (US#1, UK#11, 1956), 'Love Me' (US#2, 1956), 'Too Much' (US#1, UK#6, 1957), 'All Shook Up' (US#1, UK#1, 1957), '(Let Me Be) Your Teddy Bear' (US#1, C&W#1, UK#3, 1957), 'Paralysed' (UK#8, 1957), 'Party' (UK#2, 1957), 'Jailhouse Rock' (US#1, C&W#1, 1957; UK#1, 1958), 'Don't' (US#1, UK#2, 1958), 'Wear My Ring Around Your Neck' (US#2, UK#3, 1958), 'Hard Headed Woman' (US#1, UK#2, 1958) and 'King Creole' (UK#2, 1958).

In 1958, having appeared in three films - *Loving You*, *Jailhouse Rock* and *King Creole* - he was drafted into the army. On his first weekend leave he recorded in Nashville with guitarist Hank Garland and bassist **Bob Moore**, in place of the regulars Scotty Moore and Bill Black, cutting 'One Night'/'I Got Stung' (US#4, 1958; UK#1, 1959), 'A Fool Such As I' (US#2, UK#1, 1959) and 'A Big Hunk O' Love' (US#1, UK#4, 1959). On March 5, 1960, he was demobbed, and then moved into the least satisfying phase of his career (which lasted for the best part of a decade), cutting largely indifferent material and appearing in appalling films. Among the better-known songs to appear during this period were 'Stuck On You' (US#1, UK#3, 1960), 'It's Now Or Never' (US#1, UK#1, 1960), 'Are You Lonesome Tonight' (US#1, 1960; UK#1, 1961), 'Wooden Heart' (UK#1, 1961), 'Surrender' (US#1, UK#1, 1961), '(Marie's The Name) Of His Latest Flame' (US#4, UK#1, 1961), 'Can't Help Falling In Love' (US#2, 1961; UK#1, 1962), 'Good Luck Charm' (US#1, UK#1, 1962), 'She's Not You' (US#5, UK#1, 1962), 'Return To Sender' (US#2, UK#1, 1962), '(You're The) Devil In Disguise' (US#3, UK#1, 1963) and 'Crying In The Chapel' (US#3, UK#1, 1965).

In 1968 he began to make strides towards relaunching his career as a serious rock 'n' roller with an NBC-TV special, *Elvis*, backed by Scotty Moore, Charles Hodge and D.J. Fontana. This 'special' proved beyond any doubt that Elvis still encapsulated the spirit of rock 'n' roll and that his voice was as

strong as ever. The following year he recorded *From Elvis In Memphis* at **Chips Moman**'s American studios; the sessions that produced the album provided him with some of the most commercial singles that he'd cut in years: **Mac Davis**'s 'In The Ghetto' (US#3, UK#2, 1969), 'Suspicious Minds' (US#1, UK#2, 1969) and 'Don't Cry Daddy' (US#6, 1969; UK#8, 1970).

After these sessions he began a season in Las Vegas with **James Burton** (guitar), Jerry Scheff (bass), Ronnie Tutt (drums) and **Glen D. Hardin** (keyboards), and backing vocals from the Imperials and the Sweet Inspirations. Such was the success of the show that a double album, *From Vegas To Memphis/From Memphis To Vegas*, was released, comprising live recordings from the Las Vegas shows and unissued material from the Memphis sessions. 'The Wonder Of You' (US#9, UK#1, 1970) was extracted from this double set, and was followed by the announcement of a US tour, his first since the mid-1950s.

While his later years saw him declining into a parody of his former self, his recorded output had a gravitas and poignancy that was reflected in the choice of material: 'You Don't Have To Say You Love Me' (US#11, 1970; UK#9, 1971), **Dallas Frazier**'s 'There Goes My Everything' (US#21, UK#6, 1971), 'I'm Leavin'' (US#36, UK#23, 1971), **B.J. Thomas**'s 'I Just Can't Help Believing' (UK#6, 1971), **Buffy Sainte-Marie**'s 'Until It's Time For You To Go' (US#40, UK#5, 1972), **Mickey Newbury**'s 'American Trilogy' (UK#5, 1972), **Dennis Linde**'s 'Burning Love' (US#2, UK#7, 1972) and 'Always On My Mind' (UK#9, 1972).

In 1973, a television special, *Aloha From Hawaii*, was beamed live by satellite to Japan and the Far East, with an estimated audience of 1.5 billion. The ensuing live album featured versions of James Taylor's 'Steamroller Blues' (US#17, 1973) and **Tony Joe White**'s 'Polk Salad Annie' (UK#23, 1973). This was followed by other hits, including a barnstorming version of Chuck Berry's 'Promised Land' (US#14, 1974; UK#9, 1975), 'Moody Blue'/'She Still Thinks I Care' (the latter written by **Dickey Lee**; US#21, C&W#1, UK#6, 1977), 'Way Down' (US#18, C&W#1, UK#1, 1977) and 'Guitar Man' (US#28, C&W#1, UK#43, 1981), posthumously.

In 1975 he was hospitalized with a stomach disorder, which was treated with cortisone - the most notable side effect of this drug is to make the patient appear bloated. In April 1977 he cut his final tracks in Saginaw, Michigan, and, on June 26, he made his final concert appearance at the Market Square Arena, Indianapolis, Indiana. On August 16, 1977, he was found dead in his bathroom, having died of heart failure.

Despite all the flak and adulation, the fact remains that no other performer exerted such a grasp on the popular imagination. His death has only served to tighten that grasp: the legend continues to grow from beyond the grave.

ALOHA FROM HAWAII, RCA, 1973
COLLECTION, Volumes 1-4, RCA, 1986
ELVIS LIVE AT MADISON SQUARE GARDEN, RCA, 1974
ELVIS NBC SPECIAL, RCA, 1969
FROM MEMPHIS TO VEGAS, RCA, 1984
HITS OF THE '70s, RCA, 1974
HOW GREAT THOU ART, RCA, 1967
THE KING OF ROCK 'N' ROLL: The Complete '50s Masters, RCA, 1992
MEMPHIS ALBUM, RCA, 1987

PRICE, Kenny

One of the many artists to achieve success through regular appearances on *Hee Haw*, Kenny Price was born on May 27, 1931, in Florence, Kentucky. He was raised on a farm in Boone County, where he learnt the guitar and started to perform at local dances. In the early 1950s he was drafted into the army and sent to Korea. On his discharge in 1954 he studied at the Cincinnati Conservatory of Music, before joining the *Midwestern Hayride* on WLW and eventually becoming the show's compère.

He then moved to Nashville, having already signed to the Boone label, and secured a regular slot on *Hee Haw*. This exposure generated hits like 'Walking On New Grass' and 'Happy Tracks' in 1966 and 'My Goal For Today' (1967). In 1969, 'the Round Mound of Sound' (as he was nicknamed) moved to RCA, where he had hits with 'Biloxi' and 'The Sheriff Of Boone County'. In his later years he concentrated on touring and television work, until his death on August 4, 1987, in Florence, Kentucky.

PRICE, Ray

Ray Price's reputation stems from the utter conviction of his singing, irrespective of sometimes crass or maudlin lyrics. He has also managed, through inspired choices of sidemen, to discover and employ writers and musicians at the very beginning of their careers.

Born on January 12, 1926, in Perryville, Texas, he was raised in Dallas, where he attended high school prior to joining the army. On his discharge in 1946, he trained to be a vet, but switched to play the local club circuit. His first break came with a broadcast on KRBC, Abilene, which led to a spot on the networked *Big D Jamboree*. In 1950 he was signed to the Bullet label and attracted attention with 'Jealous Lies', then joined Columbia the following year.

His first hit for the label, 'Talk To Your Heart' (C&W#3, 1952), showed the profound influence of **Hank Williams** on his style, but Price was quick to evolve his own highly personal style, with arrangements reminiscent of **Bob Wills**'s Texas Playboys set against the colourful imagery of honky-tonk. After touring with Williams' band, the **Drifting Cowboys**, he formed his own band, the Cherokee Cowboys, which included, at one time or another, such luminaries as **Roger Miller**, **Johnny Paycheck**, **Buddy Emmons**, **Willie Nelson** and **Johnny Bush**.

Throughout the 1950s he notched up hit after hit with songs like 'Don't Let The Stars Get In Your Eyes', 'Crazy Arms' (C&W#1, 1956), 'I've Got A New Heartache' (C&W#2, 1956), 'My Shoes Keep Walking Back To You' (C&W#1, 1957), **Bill Anderson**'s 'City Lights' (C&W#1, 1958), **Harlan Howard**'s 'Heartaches By The Number' (C&W#2, 1959), 'The Same Old Me' (C&W#1, 1959), 'One More Time', 'Soft Rain', **Hank Cochran**'s 'Make The World Go Away', Roger Miller's 'Invitation To The Blues', **Mel Tillis**'s 'Burning Memories' (C&W#2, 1964), 'The Other Woman' and 'Touch My Heart'.

In 1967 he edged closer to the pop market with a curious strings-laden version of 'Danny Boy', but reverted to type with **Kris Kristofferson**'s 'For The Good Times' (US#11, C&W#1, 1970), 'I Won't Mention It Again' (C&W#1, 1971), Kristofferson's 'I'd Rather Be Sorry' (C&W#2, 1972), **Mac Davis**'s 'Lonesomest Lonesome' (C&W#2, 1972), 'She's Got To Be A Saint' (C&W#1, 1972) and Jim Weatherly's 'You're The Best Thing That Ever Happened To Me' (C&W#1, 1973).

During the 1970s and 1980s he recorded gospel sides for Myrrh and recorded an album of duets, *Willie Nelson and Ray Price*, for Columbia. Also notable is his soundtrack to the Clint Eastwood movie *Honkytonk Man*. Although recording less in the last few years, he is one of the few major country stars from the 1950s still successful today, unscathed by the ravages of life on the road and the expectations of an adoring public.

GREATEST HITS, Monument, 1992
HONKY TONK YEARS: 1951-53, Rounder (US), 1988

PRIDE, Charley

One of the most successful black performers in the entertainment business, Pride cuts an unusual figure, one of only a handful of black country artists. He was born Charles Frank Pride on March 18, 1938, on a cotton farm in Sledge in the Mississippi Delta, where his parents worked the land. During his childhood, as one of eleven siblings, he worked alongside his parents on the farm, earning sufficient money to buy his first guitar. He initially intended to be a baseball player, making his debut in 1954 with the Memphis Red Sox as a pitcher. Conscripted a couple of years later, he started work on a building site on his return in 1959, and then moved on to Montana, where he obtained work in a zinc smelting factory. In the early 1960s he took another stab at professional baseball, but trials for the California Angels and the New York Mets proved abortive.

In 1963 he appeared on the same bill as **Red Foley**, who suggested that he should try to carve a career for himself as a country singer, and arranged sessions for him in Nashville with **Jack Clement**, who then persuaded **Chet Atkins** to sign him to RCA. His debut, 'Snakes Crawl At Night', was released towards the end of that year, and by April 1966 he had secured the first of many hits, including 'Just Between You And Me' (C&W#9, 1966).

Among his biggest hits were 'The Easy Part's Over' (C&W#2, 1968), **Dallas Frazier** and 'Doodle' Owens' 'All I Have To Offer You' (C&W#1, 1969) and '(I'm So) Afraid Of Losing You' (C&W#1, 1969), 'Is Anybody Going To San Antone' (C&W#1, 1970), 'Wonder, Could I Live There Anymore' (C&W#1, 1970), Dallas Frazier and 'Doodle' Owens' 'I Can't Believe That You Stopped Loving Me' (C&W#1, 1970), **Johnny Duncan**'s 'I'd Rather Love You' (C&W#1, 1971), 'I'm Just Me' (C&W#1, 1971), 'Kiss An Angel Good Morning' (US#21, C&W#1, 1971), 'It's Gonna Take A Little Bit Longer' (C&W#1, 1972), Johnny Duncan's 'She's Too Good To Be True' (C&W#1, 1972), **Merle Haggard**'s 'A Shoulder To Cry On' (C&W#1, 1973), 'Don't Fight The Feelings Of Love' (C&W#1, 1973), 'Amazing Love' (C&W#1, 1973), Dallas Frazier and 'Doodle' Owens' 'Then Who Am I' (C&W#1, 1975), 'Hope You're Feeling Me' (C&W#1, 1975), 'My Eyes Can Only See As Far As You' (C&W#1, 1976), 'She's Just An Old Love Turned Memory' (C&W#1, 1977), **Dickey Lee** and Wayland Holyfield's 'I'll Be Leaving Alone' (C&W#1, 1977), 'More To Me' (C&W#1, 1977), 'Someone Loves You Honey' (C&W#1, 1978), Jimmy Weatherly's 'Where Do I Put Her Memory' (C&W#1, 1979), 'You're My Jamaica' (C&W#1, 1979), 'Missin'

You' (C&W#2, 1979), **Hank Williams**' 'Honky Tonk Blues' (C&W#1, 1980) and 'You Win Again' (C&W#1, 1980), 'Never Been So Loved' (C&W#1, 1981), 'Mountain Of Love' (C&W#1, 1982), 'I Don't Think She's In Love Anymore' (C&W#2, 1982), 'You're So Good When You're Bad' (C&W#1, 1982), 'Why Baby Why' (C&W#1, 1983) and 'Night Games' (C&W#1, 1983).

He left RCA in 1986, and a year later he signed with producer Jerry Bradley's new label, 16th Avenue, a division of the publishing company Opryland Music. Pride provided the label with its first hit with 'Shouldn't It Be Easier Than This' and, in 1990, he celebrated twenty-five years in the record industry.

In the course of his formidably successful career, he has amassed a diverse portfolio of investments that include radio stations, interests in oil wells and the First Texas State Bank, Cecca Recording Studios, an office block and the farm in Sledge where he was raised.

AFTER ALL THIS TIME, Ritz, 1987
AMY'S EYES, Ritz, 1990
BEST OF CHARLEY PRIDE, Volumes 1-3, RCA, 1979
CHARLEY SINGS EVERYBODY'S CHOICE, RCA, 1984
DIAMOND SERIES, RCA, 1988
I'M GONNA LOVE HER ON THE RADIO, Ritz, 1988
IN PERSON, RCA International, 1976
ROLL ON MISSISSIPPI, RCA, 1981
SONGS OF PRIDE, RCA, 1978
TWENTY OF THE BEST, RCA, 1990
YOU'RE MY JAMAICA, RCA, 1979

PRINE, John

A superior songwriter with impeccable credentials, Prine suffered the setback of being compared to **Bob Dylan**. While they share folk influences, Prine generally has a much harder sound than Dylan, and, unlike Dylan, his lyrical imagery evokes the urban landscape.

He was born on October 10, 1946, in Maywood, Illinois; his father was a prominent union official who worked at the local steel foundry. After spending a couple of years in the army he started to play the local club circuit, where he was discovered by **Kris Kristofferson**. This slice of fortune eventually bore fruit in the form of a recording contract with Atlantic; his debut was produced by Arif Mardin and included songs such as 'Hello In There', 'Your Flag Won't Get You Into Heaven Anymore' and 'Six O'Clock News'. The follow-up, *Diamonds In The Rough* (1972), showed a similarity to Loudon Wainwright III, with vitriolic love-songs such as 'Yes, I Guess They Ought To Name A Drink After You'.

His next album, *Sweet Revenge*, was an altogether more sombre affair, with 'Paradise' being the key song; its evocation of a pastoral way of life overwhelmed by the march of industrialization had added poignancy when performed at miners' benefits. After *Common Sense* in 1975, he disappeared from sight only to re-emerge with the **Steve Goodman**-produced *Bruised Orange* in 1978 for Asylum. This was followed by *Pink Cadillac* (1979) and *Storm Windows* (1980).

After leaving Asylum in 1981 he formed his own Oh Boy label, and issued *Aimless Love* (1985) - a sparsely arranged and bluesy album - and *Live* (1988), the latter including a duet with Bonnie Raitt. In 1992 he returned with the aptly titled *The Missing Years*. His career has been erratic and although his songwriting is generally exemplary he has never managed to achieve wide commercial acceptance.

AIMLESS LOVE, Demon, 1985
BRUISED ORANGE, Asylum, 1978
DIAMONDS IN THE ROUGH, Atlantic, 1972
GERMAN AFTERNOONS, Demon, 1987
LIVE, Oh Boy (US), 1988
THE MISSING YEARS, This Way Up, 1992
PINK CADILLAC, Asylum, 1979
SWEET REVENGE, Atlantic, 1974

PROPHET, Chuck

Born in San Francisco in 1963, guitarist Chuck Prophet played in a variety of local bands before joining Green On Red in 1983. This band, comprising Prophet, Dan Stuart (vocals), Rene Coman (bass), David Kemper (drums) and Mike Finnigan (keyboards), quickly established themselves as one of the brighter country-rock outfits on the circuit. While successive albums with different record labels failed to yield much commercial success, their hard-edged sound won them many admirers, Stuart and Prophet's quirky songs combined with Prophet's versatile guitar work showing the influences of the **Byrds** and Tom Petty.

In 1990, while remaining a member of Green On Red, Prophet started a parallel solo career. His first two solo albums *Brother Aldo* (1990) and *Balinese Dancer* (1992) demonstrated a vocal maturity that had hitherto been overshadowed by Green On Red vocalist Dan Stuart. Furthermore, his prowess on other stringed instruments, such as the lap steel guitar,

showed that he had the potential to match country's great steel guitarists like **Buddy Emmons** and **Lloyd Green**.

BALINESE DANCER, China, 1992
BROTHER ALDO, Fire (US), 1990
GAS FOOD LODGING, (Green On Red), Demon, 1985
GREEN ON RED, Demon, 1985
HERE COME THE SNAKES, (Green On Red), China, 1990
THIS TIME AROUND, (Green On Red), China, 1989
TOO MUCH FUN, (Green On Red), China, 1992

PROPHET, Ronnie

An all-round showman, Prophet's propensity to liven up his performances with random impressions and slick guitar work has made him a highly sought-after entertainer on the Las Vegas cabaret circuit. He was born in Calumet, Quebec, Canada, on December 26, 1937, and moved to Montreal during his adolescence. After moving to Fort Lauderdale in the US, he played the club circuit until, in 1969, he moved to Nashville. Here he was signed to a management contract with Chardon (a company that looked after the careers of artists such as **Charley Pride** and **Gary Stewart**), who secured him a recording contract with RCA, and he scored with 'Sanctuary' (1977).

His debut, *Ronnie Prophet Country,* appeared in 1976, and was followed by *Ronnie Prophet* in the early months of 1977. After being dropped by RCA he recorded for independent labels such as Westwood, Audiograph and Art. Despite his popularity in the UK, Prophet is one of many country artists to earn a significant income on the cabaret circuit while making little impression on the charts.

RONNIE PROPHET, RCA (US), 1977

PRUETT, Jeanne

Born Norma Jean Bowman on January 30, 1937, in Pell City, Alabama, she married Jack Pruett and moved to Nashville in 1956. Her husband was recruited by **Marty Robbins** as a guitarist, while Jeanne concentrated on writing songs for him. In 1963 she secured a recording contract with RCA, making her debut on the *Grand Ole Opry* in 1964; in 1966 she achieved her first major success as a writer when Marty Robbins scored with 'Count Me Out'.

In 1969 she was signed to Decca and attracted attention with 'Hold Onto My Unchanging Love' two years later. In 1973 she cut 'Satin Sheets' (US#28,

C&W#1, 1973), which was followed by other hits like 'I'm Your Woman' (C&W#8, 1973), 'You Don't Need To Move A Mountain' and 'Just Like Your Daddy'. In 1979, having been dropped by MCA (formerly Decca), she returned to the charts with 'Back To Back' and 'Temporarily Yours' (1980) and 'It's Too Late' (1981) for the independent IBC label. A large following in the UK ensured that her appearances at the Country Music Festival in Wembley, London, went down well, but after cutting *Live* (1983) for the Audiograph label she gave up recording in order to run a restaurant.

JEANNE PRUETT, MCA, 1987

PUCKETT, Riley

Along with **Fiddling John Carson**, Riley Puckett was one of the first country musicians to record on a regular basis. He was born George Riley Puckett in Alpharetta, Georgia, on May 7, 1894; when he was three months old an eye infection was treated with a lead acetate solution, causing him to go blind. He was educated at the School for the Blind in Macon, where he learnt to play the banjo and the guitar.

On completion of his education he became a full-time professional musician, cutting his first sides for Columbia in 1924; these included 'Little Log Cabin In The Lane' and 'Rock All Our Babies To Sleep' - the latter was the first recorded country song to feature yodelling. Later that year he joined the **Skillet Lickers** as principal vocalist and guitarist, his resonant baritone contributing significantly to the group's popularity with audiences on WSB. After the Skillet Lickers disbanded in 1934 he resumed his solo career, cutting sides for Decca and Bluebird. He continued playing and singing, often on Southern radio stations, until his death from blood poisoning on July 13, 1946.

OLD TIME GREATS, Old Homestead (US), 1987
RED SAILS IN THE SUNSET, Bear Family (Germany), 1988

PURE PRAIRIE LEAGUE

The Pure Prairie League were one of many country-rock groups to emerge in the early 1970s. They were formed in Cincinnati in 1971 and their line-up, which has chopped and changed over the years, comprised Craig Fuller (guitar and vocals), George Powell (guitar and vocals), Jim Lanham (bass and vocals), Jim Caughlan (drums) and John David Call (steel guitar). Signed to RCA, the line-up had changed by the time the second album, *Bustin' Out*, was released in 1972, with Powell and Fuller the only original members remaining.

The group temporarily disbanded in 1973 (Fuller formed American Flyer in 1976 and then joined the re-formed line-up of Little Feat in 1986, after years of session work) but re-formed to capitalize on the success of 'Amie' (US#27, 1975), which had been reissued by RCA. This new line-up featured former members Powell and Call, Mike Reilly (bass and vocals), Michael O'Connor (keyboards), Larry Goshorn (guitar and vocals) and Billy Hinds (drums); it was shortlived as they disbanded once again.

In 1978 Powell and Call re-formed the group and, in 1980, **Vince Gill** was added to the new line-up and they were signed by Casablanca. Here they enjoyed their greatest success, with titles like 'Let Me Love You Tonight' (US#10, 1980), 'I'm Almost Ready' (US#34, 1980) and 'Still Right Here In My Heart' (US#28, 1981) launching them into the national charts. In 1983, following the sale of Casablanca to Polygram, the group was dropped and they disbanded for good, with Gill embarking on a very successful career as a country singer.

PURE PRAIRIE COLLECTION, RCA, 1981
TWO LANE HIGHWAY, RCA, 1974

PUTNAM, Norbert

In 1961, Norbert Putnam was ensconced as bassist in the Mark Vs, who became the house band at the Fame Studios in Muscle Shoals. He played bass on the recordings of artists such as Arthur Alexander, Jimmy Hughes, Tommy Roe, **Ray Stevens** and the Tams. In 1964 he was lured to Nashville by **David Briggs** and **Jerry Carrigan**, where they set up the Quadrafonic Studios. Since then he has recorded with a whole host of artists, including **Elvis Presley**, **Charley Pride**, **Waylon Jennings**, **Billy Swan** and **Kris Kristofferson**; he has also produced **John Hiatt** and Dan Fogelberg.

QUICKSILVER

Quicksilver was formed in 1979 by Doyle Lawson (mandolin), **J.D. Crowe** (banjo), Bobby Hicks (fiddle), **Tony Rice** (guitar and vocals) and Todd Phillips (guitar). Lawson, from East Tennessee, started his career with **Jimmy Martin**'s Sunny Mountain Boys, and then partnered J.D. Crowe in 1966, before moving on to the **Country Gentlemen** in 1971. The group came together in order to play the traditional bluegrass material of the 1940s and 1950s, exemplified by artists such as **Bill Monroe** and **Flatt & Scruggs**. They have cut many albums for the Sugar Hill label and become one of the best progressive bluegrass outfits around.

BEYOND THE SHADOWS, Sugar Hill (US), 1989
DOYLE LAWSON & QUICKSILVER, Sugar Hill (US), 1980
HEAVENLY TREASURES, Sugar Hill (US), 1989
HEAVEN'S JOY AWAITS, Sugar Hill (US), 1987
HYMN TIME IN THE COUNTRY, Sugar Hill (US), 1989
I HEARD THE ANGELS SINGING, Sugar Hill (US), 1989
I'LL WANDER BACK SOMEDAY, Sugar Hill (US), 1988
MY HEART IS YOURS, Sugar Hill (US), 1990
THE NEWS IS OUT, Sugar Hill (US), 1989
ONCE & FOR ALWAYS, Sugar Hill (US), 1989
QUICKSILVER RIDES AGAIN, Sugar Hill (US), 1989

RABBITT, Eddie

A country artist with middle-of-the-road tendencies, Eddie Rabbitt is one of many artists to have won massive audiences with bland and innocuous songs. He was born Edward Thomas on November 27, 1944, in Brooklyn, New York City, and raised in East Orange, New Jersey. He learnt the guitar during his childhood and made his debut on New Jersey's club circuit in 1966. After moving to Nashville in 1968 he made waves with his song 'Kentucky Rain', which was covered by **Elvis Presley** in 1970. Four years later he had another slice of luck when **Ronnie Milsap** took his composition 'Pure Love' to the top of the country charts; he was shortly after signed to the newly-formed Nashville division of the Elektra label.

Since 1976 he has strung together a succession of hits - Rabbitt co-writing many of them with songwriter Bruce 'Even' Stevens and producer David Malloy - including 'Drinkin' My Baby (Off My Mind)' (C&W#1, 1976), 'I Can't Help Myself' (C&W#2, 1977), 'Hearts On Fire' (C&W#2, 1977), 'I Don't Love You Anymore' (C&W#1, 1978), 'I Just Want To Love You' (C&W#1, 1978), 'Every Which Way But Loose' (the title song to the Clint Eastwood movie of the same name; US#30, C&W#1, 1979) 'Suspicions' (US#13, C&W#1, 1979), 'Gone Too Far' (C&W#1, 1980), 'Drivin' My Life Away' (US#5, C&W#1, 1980), 'I Love A Rainy Night' (US#1, C&W#1, 1980), 'Step By Step' (US#5, C&W#1, 1981), 'Someone Could Lose A Heart Tonight' (US#15, C&W#1, 1982), 'I Don't Know Where To Start' (US#35, C&W#2, 1982), 'You And I' (a duet with **Crystal Gayle**; US#7, C&W#1, 1982) and 'You Can't Run From Love' (C&W#1, 1983).

In 1985, having moved from Elektra to its parent company, Warner Bros., he began to produce his own work with assistance from Stevens and **Jimmy Bowen**, and scored with 'The Best Year Of My Life' (C&W#1, 1985). In 1986 he moved to RCA and started working with new producer Richard Landis. His first hit for the label was a duet with **Juice Newton**, 'Both To Each Other (Lovers And Friends)' (C&W#1, 1986); other hits followed, including 'I Wanna Dance With You' (C&W#1, 1988) and 'The Wanderer' (a cover of the Dion song; C&W#1, 1988). He has more recently been overshadowed by the young turks of New Country, but this hasn't affected his popularity.

EDDIE RABBITT, Country Store, 1988
RABBITT TRAX, RCA (US), 1986
RADIO ROMANCE, Mercury, 1983
STEP BY STEP, Mercury, 1981

RAINWATER, Marvin

Better received in Europe than in his native US, Marvin Rainwater reached his peak during the 1950s, when he cut a number of quasi-rockabilly tracks that won him a season at the prestigious London Palladium and the adulation of many. Born Marvin Percy of Indian descent on July 2, 1925, in Wichita, Kansas, he started writing songs during his childhood, but trained to be a vet on completion of his education. On the outbreak of the Second World War he was drafted into the navy as a pharmacologist. At the end of the war he started his career in the music business, adopting his mother's maiden name 'Rainwater' as a stage name.

He made his debut in 1946 on **Red Foley**'s *Ozark Jubilee Radio Show*, which was followed by a succession of tours and records, with labels like Coral and Four Star. In 1955 he appeared on Arthur Godfrey's *Talent Scouts* television show, which prompted MGM to sign him and promote him as a Cherokee Indian - complete with matching headdress!

His first hit, the self-penned 'Gonna Find Me A Bluebird' (US#18, 1957), was followed by other hits, such as 'Majesty Of Love' (a duet with Connie Francis), 'Whole Lotta Woman' (US#1, 1958), 'My Love Is Real', 'My Brand Of Blues', 'I Dig You Baby' (UK#19, 1958) and **John D. Loudermilk**'s 'Half Breed'. In 1960 he left MGM and recorded for labels such as Warner Bros. and United Artists prior to forming his own Brave label. The hits, however, dried up, and he suffered from a throat infection, which caused him to give up his career for four years. In 1971 he returned to recording and touring, but was hard-pressed to match his former glories.

ROCKIN' ROLLIN', Bear Family (Germany), 1984
WITH A HEART WITH A BEAT, Bear Family (Germany), 1984

RANDOLPH, Boots

A premier member of the Nashville session circuit, saxophonist Boots Randolph was born in Paducah, Kentucky, and first came to prominence when heard by **Homer & Jethro** at a club in Decatur, Illinois. They gave **Chet Atkins** the nod, who suggested to **Owen Bradley** that he use Randolph on a forthcoming **Brenda Lee** session. By 1957 he was a key member of the session band that comprised guitarists Atkins, **Grady Martin** and Hank Garland, pianists **Floyd Cramer** and Hargus 'Pig' Robbins, drummer Buddy Harman and bassist **Bob Moore**.

After signing to Monument as a solo artist, he cut a number of instrumentals, including 'Yakety Sax' (US#35, 1963), 'The Shadow Of Your Smile' and 'Temptation'. In 1974 he cut *Country Boots* with instrumental assistance from artists including Atkins and Maybelle Carter (see **Carter Family**). He has cut a number of other albums, all ideally suited for use in shopping malls and elevators.

RAVEN, Eddy

A successful songwriter (writing for artists such as **Don Gibson**, **Roy Acuff**, **Jeannie C. Riley**, **Roy Clark** and **Roy Orbison**), it wasn't until late in his career that Eddy Raven made an impression as a recording artist in his own right.

He was born Edward Garvin Futch in Louisiana on August 19, 1944, one of nine children whose father travelled extensively as a lorry driver and musician. A precocious musician who revealed a knack for writing lyrics during his childhood, Raven mastered the guitar by the age of seven and formed his first group when he was thirteen. In the late 1950s, while living in Georgia, he had his own show on the local radio station, WHAB, and changed his name to Eddy Raven before moving up-state to Lafayette.

He toured incessantly throughout the late 1960s, until introduced to the **Acuff-Rose** publishing house by **Jimmy 'C' Newman** in 1970. His success as a writer was immediate; as a performer it was more elusive: it wasn't until signing with RCA in 1981 (having previously recorded for Dot and Elektra) that he made an impression, with the album *Desperate Dreams*. Two years later the hits started accruing: 'I Got Mexico' (C&W#1, 1984), 'She's Gonna Win Your Heart', 'Sometimes A Lady' and 'Shine, Shine, Shine' (C&W#1, 1987).

After the death of his producer Don Gant, Raven started to work with **Barry Beckett**, who brought out the blues and R&B elements in his music. This represented a radical departure for Raven, and was vindicated by the success of singles such as **Dennis Linde**'s 'I'm Gonna Get You' (C&W#1, 1988), 'Joe Knows How To Live' (C&W#1, 1988), Linde's 'In A Letter To You' (C&W#1, 1989) and 'Bayou Boys' (C&W#1, 1989).

Though now writing less and less, Raven remains one of country's more imaginative performers through his constant experimentation with different musical styles - one of his main preoccupations being to fuse together creole, cajun and reggae.

EDDY RAVEN, La Louisiane (US), 1987
TEMPORARY SANITY, MCA, 1989

RAYE, Susan

Susan Raye was born in Eugene, Oregon, on October 8, 1944. During her schooldays she sang with a rock group, until being by auditioned by a local radio station who were looking for a vocalist and a relief DJ. This prompted her to take to the nightclub circuit, where she was spotted by **Buck Owens**' manager Jack McFadden, who arranged a meeting with Owens in Bakersfield.

In 1968 she became a full-time member of Owens' roadshow and was given a contract with the Capitol label. Over the next few years she had a number of solo hits, including 'Maybe If I Closed My Eyes', 'Put A Little Love In Your Heart', 'L.A. International Airport' (C&W#9, 1971), 'Pitty Pitty Patter' (C&W#6, 1971) and '(I've Got) A Happy Heart' (C&W#3, 1971). In addition, she regularly cut duets with Owens, which included 'We're Gonna Get Together', 'Togetherness' and 'The Great White Horse'.

Although the dizzy heights of country stardom have proved elusive, Susan Raye has made a worthy contribution through her appearances on **Buck Owens**' show and on *Hee Haw*. In recent years she has confined her activities to the cabaret circuit.

RED RIVER DAVE see McENERY, Red River Dave

REED, Jerry

One of Nashville's most versatile performers, Jerry Reed has appeared in movies, written songs and been one of the greatest guitar-pickers on the Nashville session circuit. He was born Jerry Reed Hubbard on March 20, 1937, in Atlanta, Georgia. Taught the guitar by his father, Reed performed at local dances during his teens. In 1955 Capitol signed him as a writer and one of his first compositions to find favour was 'Crazy Legs', which was covered by Gene Vincent. His own recording career was interrupted by a stint in the army and, on his return in 1962, he moved to Nashville where he was signed by Columbia.

He initially recorded instrumentals such as Leadbelly's 'Goodnight Irene' and 'Hully Gully Guitars', and this led to a steady flow of session work. In 1965 he was signed by RCA, where he cut a string of hits that continued right up to the early 1970s: 'Guitar Man' (covered by **Elvis Presley**, as was another Reed composition, 'US Male'), 'Tupelo Mississippi Flash', 'Remembering', 'Are You From Dixie', 'Georgia Sunshine', 'Amos Moses' (US#8, 1971), 'When You're Hot You're Hot' (US#9, C&W#1, 1971), 'Lord, Mr Ford' (C&W#1, 1973), 'East Bound And Down' (C&W#2, 1977) and 'She Got The Goldmine (I Got The Shaft)' (C&W#1, 1982). His albums were very patchy affairs, apart from the superb *Me And Jerry Reed* and *Me And Chet*, both of which featured duets with **Chet Atkins**.

Reed's film career took off during the 1970s with a number of memorable performances in Burt Reynolds' movies, including *WW And The Dixie Dance Kings* (1974), *Gator* (1976), *Smokey And The Bandit* (1977), *Smokey And The Bandit 2* (1980) and *Smokey And The Bandit 3* (1983). This acting career has tended to subordinate his work as a musician, which is a bit of a shame.

THE HITS OF JERRY REED, RCA (US), 1979
TWENTY OF THE BEST, RCA, 1982

REEVES, Del

Franklin Delano Reeves was born on July 14, 1933, in Sparta, North Carolina, and made his debut when he was twelve on a local radio station. After graduating from school he studied at the Appalachian State College, and then spent four years in the Air Force. After that he secured a regular slot on the Californian television show *The Chester Smith Show* and wrote for vocalists like **Roy Drusky**, **Carl Smith** and **Sheb Wooley**.

Having signed to Decca in 1961, he scored his first hit with 'Be Quiet Mind'. After unsuccessful stints with Columbia and Reprise he moved on to United Artists

in 1965, and scored with 'Girl On The Billboard' (C&W#1, 1965), 'A Dime At A Time', 'Looking At The World Through A Windshield', 'Goodtime Charlies', 'Be Glad', 'The Philadelphia Fillies' and 'On The Rebound' (a duet with **Billie Jo Spears**).

In October 1966 he joined the *Grand Ole Opry*, which was followed by his own television show, *Del Reeves Country Carnival*, and appearances in a number of undistinguished movies. His relaxed, easy style has caused many to liken him to Dean Martin.

BABY I LOVE YOU, Bear Family (Germany), 1988

REEVES, Goebel

An integral part of the blues tradition was the nomadic instinct that made many of the best-known performers, like Leadbelly and Charlie Patton, take to the open road, playing wherever they could. In country music this instinct, although not as prevalent, was still evident: **Woody Guthrie** was one of the first to describe his experiences on the road, but 'the Texas Drifter' - otherwise known as Goebel Reeves - preceded him by some years.

Reeves was born in Sherman, Texas, on October 9, 1899. During the First World War he fought in the trenches on the Western Front. After being demobbed he returned to the US and started to travel around, touring the vaudeville circuit and performing his hobo and cowboy songs. Among the best known were 'Hobo And The Cop', 'Railroad Boomer', 'Hobo's Lullaby', 'Cowboy's Prayer' and 'Bright Sherman Prayer', which were recorded for Brunswick and Okeh. After a spell with the Industrial Workers of the World, he moved into retirement in California where he died in 1959.

REEVES, Jim

'Gentleman Jim' profited more from the commercialization of the Nashville Sound than any other artist of his generation - his warm baritone perfectly matching the lush string arrangements and ethereal choirs that characterized it.

He was born James Travis Reeves on August 20, 1923, on a farm in Galloway, Texas, and made his radio debut in 1932 on a Shreveport station. Showing promise as a baseball player during high school, he was signed by the St Louis Cardinals, while attending the University of Texas in Austin. In 1947 his baseball career was brought to an abrupt halt by injury.

After finishing college he became a DJ on KGRI,

Henderson, and started to perform throughout Texas as a sideman with **Moon Mullican**, recording some sides for the Macy's label in 1949. At KGRI he became programme director, before moving on to Shreveport, where he secured work as an announcer on KWKH, the home of the *Louisiana Hayride*. His big break occurred in 1952, when he was signed to the Abbott label, for whom he had hits with 'Mexican Joe' (US#23, C&W#1, 1953) and 'Bimbo'. The former resulted in a contract with RCA and appearances on the *Grand Ole Opry* in 1955.

His records echoed the gentle crooning of **Eddy Arnold**, but his material was more traditionally-slanted than Arnold's: 'Yonder Comes A Sucker', 'According To My Heart', 'My Lips Are Sealed', 'Four Walls' (US#11, C&W#1, 1957), 'Anna Marie', 'Blue Boy', 'Billy Bayou', 'He'll Have To Go' (US#2, C&W#1, UK#12, 1960), 'I'm Getting Better' (US#37, C&W#1, 1960), 'Am I Losing You' (US#31, C&W#1, 1960), 'You're The Only Good Thing' (UK#17, 1961), 'Adios Amigo' (UK#23, 1962), 'Welcome To My World' (UK#6, 1963), 'Guilty' (UK#29, 1963), 'I Love You Because' (UK#5, 1964) and 'I Won't Forget You' (C&W#3, UK#3, 1964).

Increasing fame sucked Reeves into the movies, and he made his screen debut with *Kimberly Jim* in 1963. On July 31, 1964, he was returning to Nashville with his manager Dean Manuel when his light aircraft ran into difficulties on its approach to Nashville's Beery Field airport: the wreckage of the aeroplane was discovered two days later, in dense foliage on the outskirts of the airfield. There were no survivors.

Jim Reeves's records were assiduously marketed by RCA in the years following his death, and a string of hits resulted: 'There's A Heartache Following Me' (UK#6, 1964), 'It Hurts So Much' (UK#8, 1965), 'Not Until The Next Time' (UK#13, 1965), 'How Long Has It Been' (UK#45, 1965), 'This World Is Not My Home' (UK#22, 1965), 'Is It Really Over' (UK#17, 1965), 'Distant Drums' (UK#1, 1966), 'I Won't Come In While He's There' (UK#12, 1967), 'Trying To Forget' (UK#33, 1967), 'I Heard A Heart Break Last Night' (UK#38, 1967), 'Pretty Brown Eyes' (UK#33, 1968), 'When Two Worlds Collide' (UK#17, 1969), 'But You Love Me Daddy' (UK#15, 1969), 'Nobody's Fool' (UK#32, 1970), 'Angels Don't Lie' (UK#32, 1970) and 'Have You Ever Been Lonely (Have You Ever Been Blue)' (an electronically created duet, using overdubs, with **Patsy Cline**; C&W#5, 1981). No-one has ever managed to fill his shoes and his records are still as popular as ever.

DIAMOND SERIES, RCA, 1988
DISTANT DRUMS, RCA, 1966
GENTLEMAN JIM, Bear Family (German), 1989
GIRLS I HAVE KNOWN, RCA, 1987
GOD BE WITH YOU, RCA Camden, 1971
GOOD 'N' COUNTRY, RCA Camden, 1970
HAVE I TOLD YOU LATELY THAT I LOVE YOU, RCA Camden, 1965
I LOVE YOU MORE, Submarine, 1989
LIVE AT THE OPRY, Spectrum, 1986
SONGS OF LOVE, RCA, 1978
THERE'S ALWAYS ME, RCA, 1981
TWELVE SONGS FOR CHRISTMAS, RCA, 1990

RENO, Don

Don Reno was raised in Spartanburg, South Carolina, and was one of the most versatile performers of his generation: he mastered the guitar, steel guitar, banjo and mandolin, possessed an excellent voice and was even able to turn a step as a comedian.

Working initially with the **Morris Brothers** in the early 1940s, Reno moved on to play with **Bill Monroe** in 1948. In 1949 he formed the Tennessee Cutups, which included Arthur Lee 'Red' Smiley (born in Asheville, North Carolina); they broadcast on the local radio station in Roanoke, Virginia, before moving into a regular spot on WWVA's *Wheeling Jamboree*. Their recording career picked up momentum when they moved from Federal to its parent label, King, in 1952, cutting titles like 'I'm Going To Use My Bible For A Roadmap' and 'Let's Live For Tonight'. Developing a style characterized by Reno's three-finger banjo technique, Smiley's distinctive guitar runs and close vocal harmonies, they secured a regular spot on television's *Old Dominion Barn Dance*.

From 1954 Reno started to broaden his appeal by playing the guitar on titles such as 'Freight Train Boogie' and 'You Never Mentioned Him To Me'. In 1955 Reno and **Arthur 'Guitar Boogie' Smith** cut 'Feuding Banjos', which was later updated and included in the movie *Deliverance* as 'Duelling Banjos'.

By 1964, his full-time collaboration with Smiley had finished, as Smiley's injury (sustained during the Second World War) was aggravated by constant touring, but they continued to record and perform occasionally together right up to his death in January 1972. Reno, in partnership with vocalist Bill Harrell, played club dates, concerts and the festival circuit until his death in 1984.

COUNTRY SINGING & INSTRUMENTALS (Reno & Smiley), King (US), 1987

COUNTRY SONGS (Reno & Smiley), King (US), 1987

FAMILY & FRIENDS, Kaleidoscope (US), 1988

FASTEST FIVE STRINGS ALIVE, King (US), 1987

GOOD OLD COUNTRY BALLADS (Reno & Smiley), King, 1992

LAST TIME TOGETHER (Reno & Smiley), Starday (US), 1987

RENO & SMILEY, Volumes 1-4, Gusto (US), 1987

SIXTEEN GREATEST HITS (Reno & Smiley), Starday (US), 1988

SONGS OF YESTERDAY (Reno & Smiley), Rebel (US), 1978

TWENTY BLUEGRASS SPECIALS (Reno & Smiley), Starday (US), 1987

WORLD'S BEST FIVE STRING BANJO, King (US), 1987

RESTLESS HEART

One of many pop-country bands of the 1980s, Restless Heart were formed in 1983, under the auspices of producer Tim DuBois and co-producer Scott Hendricks, who had met guitarist Greg Jennings while studying at Oklahoma State University in 1975; and, in 1978, Hendricks met bassist Paul Gregg. When DuBois suggested the idea of a group to record some of his material, Jennings and Gregg were enlisted, while Larry Stewart (vocals), Dave Innis (keyboards), and John Dittrich (drums) were brought in to round out the group.

They were immmediately signed by RCA, making their debut with 'Let The Heartache Ride' in 1985, and starting a relentless touring schedule. The group's high profile as a live band, combined with their similarity to label-mates **Alabama**, helped to establish them as one of the premier acts on the circuit. This recognition was rewarded by a string of hits that included 'I Want Everyone To Cry' (1985), 'Heartbreak Kid' (1986), ''Til I Loved You' (1986), 'That Rock Won't Roll' (C&W#1, 1986), 'I'll Still Be Loving You' (US#33, C&W#1, 1987), 'Why Does It Have To Be (Wrong Or Right)' (C&W#1, 1987), 'Wheels' (C&W#1, 1988), 'Bluest Eyes In Texas' (C&W#1, 1988), 'A Tender Lie' (C&W#1, 1988), 'Big Dreams In A Small Town' (C&W#3, 1989), 'Say What's In Your Heart' (C&W#4, 1989) and 'You Can Depend On Me' (C&W#3, 1991).

In 1991 vocalist Larry Stewart left the group and, rather than replace him, the remaining four members split the vocal chores. *Big Iron Horses* (1991) was much better record than their previous outings, which had been too slick and over-produced. Despite the blandness of their early years, they now have the potential to be one of the better country-rock bands on the circuit.

WHEELS, RCA (US), 1986

BIG DREAMS IN A SMALL TOWN, RCA (US), 1988

FAST MOVIN' TRAIN, RCA, 1990

BIG IRON HORSES, RCA, 1991

REYNOLDS, Allen

One of the most successful producers of the 1970s and 1980s, Allen Reynolds worked for the Sun label during the early 1960s, before moving to Beaumont, Texas, where he teamed up with **Jack Clement** in 1963. Over the next few years, he worked with **Moon Mullican**, **Cliff Bruner** and **George Jones**, among others, before moving to Nashville in 1970 to found the JMI label with Clement, **Don Williams** and **Bob McDill**.

After the label folded in 1974, he worked as an independent producer, developing and guiding the careers of artists like **Daniel O'Donnell**, **Crystal Gayle**, **Kathy Mattea**, **Hal Ketchum** and **Garth Brooks**. While his production work has won him most plaudits, he has also written songs like 'Wrong Road Again', 'Somebody Loves You' and 'Ready For The Times To Get Better' for Crystal Gayle, 'Dreaming My Dreams' for **Waylon Jennings** and 'We Should Be Together' for Don Williams.

RHODES, Red

Orville J. Rhodes (born on December 30, 1930, in East Alston, Illinois) was taught the dobro as a young child. By 1945 he had become an expert steel guitarist and started to play gigs in clubs and bars with his stepfather. In 1960, he moved to Los Angeles and tapped into the lucrative studio session circuit, and by the end of the 1960s he was being employed regularly by the **Byrds**, contributing most notably to *Sweetheart Of The Rodeo*.

After **Michael Nesmith** left the Monkees, he recruited Rhodes to his First National Band, a position Rhodes held until 1973. After breaking with the First National Band, Rhodes cut a solo album, *Velvet Hammer In A Cowboy Band*, for Nesmith's Countryside label. In the 1970s and 1980s he returned to the session circuit, and established his own guitar workshop, where he builds guitars and runs a tuition masterclass.

RICE, Larry see RICE, Tony

RICE, Tony

One of the most prolific of the new wave of bluegrass artists, guitarist and vocalist Tony Rice was born in Danville, Virginia, in 1951. His career started in 1960 when he joined his brothers' (mandolinist Larry and bassist Ronnie) group, the Rice Brothers, which later added another brother, Wyatt, to the line-up. He remained with them until the early 1970s, when he joined **J.D. Crowe**'s New South, which was followed by stints with **Ricky Skaggs**, **Emmylou Harris** and **David Grisman**.

In 1979, when Doyle Lawson formed **Quicksilver**, Tony Rice was a founder member, though he has continued his solo career. His slightly nasal tenor, combined with his lightning fast picking, has contributed to the authentic sound of the group, making them one of the most significant bluegrass outfits to emerge since the **Country Gentlemen** in 1959.

ACOUSTICS, Kaleidoscope (US), 1988
BACKWATERS, Rounder (US), 1988
CHURCH STREET BLUES, Sugar Hill (US), 1983
COLD ON THE SHOULDER, Rounder (US), 1988
DELVIN', Rounder (US), 1988
GUITAR, Rebel (US), 1975
MANZANITA, Rounder (US), 1979
MAR WEST, Rounder (US), 1988
ME AND MY GUITAR, Rounder (US), 1988
NATIVE AMERICAN, Rounder (US), 1988
NEW MARKET GAP, Rounder (US), 1990
RICE BROTHERS, Rounder (US), 1989
STILL INSIDE, Rounder (US), 1988
TONY RICE, Rounder (US), 1988

RICE, Wyatt see RICE, Tony

RICE BROTHERS see RICE, Tony

RICH, Charlie

Although Charlie Rich has widespread commercial appeal as a country singer, his musical influences embrace most of the idioms of contemporary music. He was born on December 14, 1932, in Colt, Arkansas, and studied music at the state university. After graduating, he joined the Air Force and was posted to Oklahoma, where he played piano in a jazz group, the Velvetones, which featured his future wife Margaret on vocals. He then worked on his father's cotton plantation before securing work as a session pianist at **Sam Phillips**'s Sun Studios, backing artists like **Warren Smith** and Billy Lee Riley.

His first hit with Sun, 'Lonely Weekends' (US#22, 1960), was followed by collaborations with **Billy Sherrill** on 'Fool' and 'Sittin''. Sun's demise left Rich without a recording contract, but former Sun employee **Bill Justis**, who was working for the RCA subsidiary Groove, persuaded him to sign with the label. With **Chet Atkins** producing, Rich cut a number of songs, including 'Big Boss Man', the self-penned 'There Won't Be Anymore' (US#18, C&W#1, 1974), 'I Don't See Me In Your Eyes Anymore' (C&W#1, 1974) and **Harlan Howard**'s 'She Called Me Baby' (C&W#1, 1974), which were re-released and became hits after he moved to Epic.

In 1965 he was signed by **Shelby Singleton** to the Philips' subsidiary, Smash, and cut **Dallas Frazier**'s 'Mohair Sam' (US#21, 1965), but Singleton was replaced by producer **Jerry Kennedy**, who felt that Rich was primarily a rockabilly artist. After being released from his contract with Smash, he signed with the Memphis Hi label, where he cut a collection of **Hank Williams**' songs on *Charlie Rich Sings Country & Western*. In 1968 he was signed to the Epic label by Sherrill, who drew out the soulful qualities in Rich's voice and added lush string arrangements**.**

It proved a highly successful combination, and Rich notched up a series of substantial hits over the next five years: 'I Almost Lost My Mind', 'I Take It On Home', 'Behind Closed Doors' (US#15, C&W#1, 1973; UK#16, 1974), 'The Most Beautiful Girl' (US#1, C&W#1, 1973; UK#2, 1974), 'A Very Special Love Song' (US#11, C&W#1, 1974), 'I Love My Friend' (US#24, C&W#1, 1974), the self-penned 'My Elusive Dreams', 'We Love Each Other' (UK#37, 1975), 'Every Time You Touch Me (I Get High)' (US#19, 1975), 'All Over Me', 'Rollin' With The Flow' (C&W#1, 1977) and 'On My Knees' (a duet with **Janie Fricke**; C&W#1, 1978).

In 1978 he was signed to United Artists, and scored with 'Puttin' In Overtime At Home', before moving into semi-retirement in Memphis. Although his early 1970s records, with their swirling strings, today seem a mite soft, his vocal performances are just as strong as those of the late 1950s. During the 1980s he scored a minor hit with 'I'll Wake You Up When I Get Home', which was featured in the highly successful Clint Eastwood movie *Every Which Way But Loose*. In 1989 he came out of retirement and took to the cabaret circuit, signing to Warner Bros. in the early 1990s.

BEHIND CLOSED DOORS, Epic, 1974
DON'T PUT NO HEADSTONE ON MY GRAVE, ZuZazz, 1987
FOOL STRIKES AGAIN, United Artists, 1979
I LOVE COUNTRY, Epic, 1987
I'LL SHED NO TEARS, Hi, 1988
MY ELUSIVE DREAMS, Premier, 1987
NOBODY BUT YOU, United Artists, 1980
THE ORIGINAL CHARLIE RICH, Charly, 1976
ORIGINAL HITS & MIDNIGHT DEMOS, Charly, 1985
PICTURES & PAINTINGS, Warner Bros., 1992
REBOUND, Charly, 1987
ROLLIN' WITH THE FLOW, Epic, 1977

RICH, Don

An influential member of **Buck Owens**' Buckaroos during their halcyon years, Don Rich was born on August 15, 1941, in Olympia, Washington. By 1946 he had learnt the guitar and made his radio debut, and in 1951, having recently mastered the fiddle, he appeared in a talent contest and won a trip to Hollywood. Having met Buck Owens in 1958, he subsequently joined the Buckaroos, but left to qualify as a music teacher.

In 1960 he rejoined the Buckaroos as guitarist and fiddler, rounding out a complement that included **Tom Brumley**. He contributed to the embryonic Bakersfield sound with highly individual performances on tracks such as 'Faded Love', 'Turnwater Breakdown' and 'Orange Blossom Special', and also penned songs such as 'Waiting In The Welfare Line'.

In 1970 he had a modest hit with 'Cowboy Convention' (a duet with Owens' son, Buddy Alan), which was extracted from *We're Real Good Friends*. In 1974, he was named Instrumentalist of the Year by the CMA in recognition of his towering achievements as a session musician. His career was cut short on July 17, 1974, when his motorbike crashed near Morro Bay, California.

RIDERS OF THE PURPLE SAGE see WILLING, Foy

RILEY, Jeannie C.

Jeannie C. Riley exploded onto the international scene in 1968, with her trenchant exposé of small-town life in 'Harper Valley P.T.A.'. Born Jeanne Caroline Stephenson in Anson, Texas, on October 19, 1945, she began work as a secretary in Nashville. After moving around the studios, she started to cut demos,

which eventually came to the attention of **Shelby Singleton**, who signed her to his Plantation label. Her debut 'Harper Valley P.T.A.' (US#1, C&W#1, UK#12, 1968) was an immediate smash hit, and has sold over eight million copies to date. Although other hits - such as 'The Girl Most Likely', 'There Never Was A Time', 'Country Girl' and 'Good Enough To Be Your Wife' - kept her in the public eye, she became a born-again Christian in 1972 and has since worked only occasionally, recording for the Playback label.

HARPER VALLEY PTA, Topline, 1986
JEANNIE C. RILEY, Spot, 1986
TOTAL WOMAN, Sundown, 1987

RITTER, Tex

Although Tex Ritter failed to reach the heights of superstardom attained by artists like **Gene Autry**, he was an estimable student of the 'cowboy songs' genre (such was his knowledge of the Old West that he became popular on the lecture tour circuit in his later years). With an unflagging commitment to Country & Western, he helped establish the Country Music Federation and the Country Music Hall Of Fame. Seldom off the road, he did much to facilitate the career of **Marty Robbins** by promoting nostalgia for the Old West.

He was born Woodward Maurice Ritter on January 12, 1905, in Murvaul, Panola County, Texas, and studied law at the University of Texas. Always fascinated by the myths and legends of the Old West, he gave up his studies after meeting folk-song collector John Lomax, and embarked upon a career in the entertainment industry. Using songs from Lomax's collection, Ritter started to perform throughout Texas and to broadcast on KPRC, Houston.

In 1930 he went to New York and appeared on Broadway in *Green Grow The Lilacs*, later adapted as *Oklahoma!* In 1936, he moved to Hollywood and worked in a number of low-budget westerns as a Singing Cowboy, often with his touring partner **Johnny Bond**. The Capitol label was set up in 1942 and Ritter became its first country signing, providing them with a string of hits that included 'Jingle Jangle Jingle', 'Jealous Heart', 'There's A New Moon Over My Shoulder', 'I'm Wasting My Tears On You' (US#11, C&W#1, 1944), 'You Two-Timed Me One Time Too Often', 'Rye Whiskey' and 'Green Grow The Lilacs'.

In 1952 he cut the theme song for the Gary Cooper movie *High Noon* (US#12, 1952), establishing a trend among film-makers for including a theme song for most westerns. Ritter also sang the themes to *The Marshall's Daughter* (1953) and *Wichita* (1955). In later years he had other hits with songs like 'The Wayward Wind' (US#28, C&W#1, UK#8, 1956) and 'I Dreamed Of A Hillbilly Heaven' (US#20, C&W#5, 1961).

In common with other country artists like **Jimmie Davis** and **Roy Acuff**, Ritter had political aspirations which were highlighted by his attempt to win the governorship of Tennessee in 1970: the attempt was unsuccessful and he was crippled with debt for the remainder of his life. He died of a heart attack on January 2, 1974, at the Metro Gaol in Nashville, while trying to arrange bail for one of his band members who had had a disagreement with the authorities.

HIGH NOON, Bear Family (Germany), 1983
LADY KILLIN' COWBOY, Bear Family (Germany), 1986
SINGIN' IN THE SADDLE, Bear Family (Germany), 1986
SONGS FROM THE WESTERN SCREEN, Stetson, 1987

ROBBINS, Marty

With his influential *Gunfighter Ballads And Trail Songs* of 1959, Marty Robbins extended the interest in cowboy songs that had been generated by **Tex Ritter**. Robbins updated the genre in the late 1950s, making it acceptable to a new and younger audience.

He was born Martin D. Robbins on September 26, 1925, in Glendale, Arizona, and was raised in the Arizona desert to the strains of **Gene Autry** and the **Sons Of Pioneers**. After spending three years in the Navy, he sang cowboy songs in the clubs and bars of Phoenix and its environs, until given his own radio show on KPHO; this was followed by his own television show, *Western Caravan*. One of the early guests on *Western Caravan* was **Little Jimmy Dickens**, who recommended Robbins to Columbia. In 1952 he began a long and highly successful collaboration with the label.

At first Robbins veered uncomfortably from one style to another, with lachrymose ballads, rockabilly and covers of standard pop songs taking pride of place: 'Love Me Or Leave Me Alone', 'I'll Go On Alone', 'I Couldn't Keep From Crying', 'Pretty Words', Arthur 'Big Boy' Crudup's 'That's Alright Mama', Guy Mitchell's 'Singing The Blues' (US#17, C&W#1, 1956), 'Knee Deep In The Blues', 'A White Sport Coat' (US#2, C&W#1, 1957), 'The Story Of My Life' (US#15, C&W#1, 1957), 'Just Married' (US#26, 1958), 'She Was Only Seventeen' (US#27, 1958) and 'Stairway Of Love'.

In 1958 he appeared with **Webb Pierce** and **Carl Smith** in the movie *Buffalo Gun*, and the following year cut the epochal *Gunfighter Ballads And Trail Songs*, which prompted a string of hits with Western themes: 'The Hanging Tree' (US#38, 1959), 'El Paso' (US#1, C&W#1, 1959; UK#19, 1960), 'Big Iron' (US#26, UK#48, 1960), 'Is There Any Chance' (US#31, 1960), 'The Fastest Gun Around' and 'Battle Of The Alamo' (US#34, 1960).

In the early 1960s he reverted to country-pop, and had a number of hits with titles like 'Don't Worry' (US#3, C&W#1, 1961), 'Devil Woman' (US#16, C&W#1, UK#5, 1962), 'Ruby Ann' (US#18, C&W#1, 1962; UK#24, 1963), 'Begging To You', 'Ribbon Of Darkness' (C&W#1, 1965), 'Tonight Carmen', 'I Walk Alone' (C&W#1, 1968), 'My Woman, My Woman, My Wife' (C&W#1, 1970), 'El Paso City' (C&W#1, 1976) and 'Among My Souvenirs' (C&W#1, 1976).

He joined the *Grand Ole Opry* in 1954, and remained a member right up to his death in 1982, where his effortless versatility enabled him to appeal to a wide cross-section of tastes. In 1970 he underwent heart surgery and had to cut back his touring schedule, but he continued writing and recording until his death on December 8, 1982, from a heart attack.

EVERYTHING I'VE ALWAYS WANTED, Columbia, 1981
HAWAII'S CALLING ME, Bear Family (German), 1985
IN THE WILD WEST, Volumes 1-5, Bear Family (German), 1985
JUST ME & MY GUITAR, Bear Family (German), 1984
MARTY ROBBINS: 1951-62, Volumes 1-5, Bear Family (German), 1986
PIECES OF YOUR HEART, Bear Family (German), 1985
ROCKIN' ROLLIN' ROBBINS, Volumes 1-3, Bear Family (German), 1984
SONGS OF THE ISLANDS, Bear Family (German), 1983
TWENTIETH CENTURY DRIFTER, MCA (US), 1986

ROBERTS, Kenny

A magnificent yodeller, Kenny Roberts was born in Lenoir City, Tennessee, on October 14, 1927, but was better known in the Boston area and New England at the height of his career in the late 1940s and early 1950s. Despite recording for a number of labels like Dot, Starday, King, Vocalion and Coral, his better-known records are restricted to 'Chime Bells', 'She Taught Me How To Yodel' and 'I Never See Maggie Alone' (C&W#9, 1949). He slipped into obscurity after yodelling went out of fashion.

INDIAN LOVE CALL, Starday (US), 1987

ROBERTS, Rick

An alumnus of the **Byrds/Flying Burrito Brothers** axis, Rick Roberts was born in Florida on August 31, 1949, and made his debut as a session musician on the Byrds' *Untitled* in 1970. After the departure of **Gram Parsons** from the Flying Burrito Brothers, Roberts joined them and took over their musical direction in 1971.

It proved shortlived as he left the group for a solo career, signing with A&M. His debut, *Windmills* (1972), included contributions from **Chris Hillman**, Don Henley (see **Eagles**), **Linda Ronstadt** and Jackson Browne. The follow-up, *She's A Song* (1973), illustrated a new maturity in his writing. In 1974 he formed Firefall with Michael Clarke (see **Byrds**), Jock Bartley (formerly of Gram Parsons' Fallen Angels) and Mark Andes (formerly of Spirit and Jo Jo Gunne).

Their debut, *Firefall*, for Atlantic in 1976 was similar to the **Eagles** and **Poco**, and, while songs such as 'You Are The Woman' (US#9, 1976) were not as strong as those of the Eagles, they slotted perfectly into the programming schedules of AOR stations. The follow-up, *Luna Sea*, included hits such as 'Cinderella' (US#34, 1977) and 'Just Remember I Love You' (US#11, 1977). *Elan* (1978) included 'Strange Way' (US#11, 1978) and was followed in 1980 by *Undertow*, which featured 'Headed For A Fall' (US#35, 1980).

By the early 1980s, country-rock had become dated, and *Clouds Across The Sun* (featuring 'Staying With It'; US#37, 1981) and *Mirror Of The World* (1983) sounded like relics of a far-distant era. The group broke up, with Roberts moving back into session work and Mark Andes joining Heart.

ROBERTSON, Don

A fine songwriter and, more significantly, a brilliantly inventive pianist, Don Robertson was the originator of the slipped-note technique popularized by **Floyd Cramer**. He was born in Peking, China, on December 5, 1922, where his father was a doctor. After studying composition at the Chicago College of Music, he went to Los Angeles in 1947, where he obtained session work at the Capitol studios. His first successful composition, 'I Really Don't Want To Know', was co-written with Hal Blair and has been recorded by **Eddy Arnold** and **Elvis Presley**, among others.

Other successful songs have included 'I Don't Hurt Anymore' for **Hank Snow**, 'Hummingbird' for **Les Paul and Mary Ford**, 'I Love You More And More Each Day' for Al Martino and 'Please Help Me, I'm Falling' for **Hank Locklin**. He had a hit with an instrumental, 'The

Happy Whistler' (US#6, 1956), and in 1964 he cut *Heart On My Sleeve* (a collection of his most successful songs) for the RCA label. He was elected to the Songwriters' Hall of Fame in Nashville in 1972.

ROBERTSON, Eck

Eck Robertson, having cut his first sides for the Victor label back in 1922, was a founding father of recorded country music. He was born Alexander Campbell Robertson in Delaney, Arkansas, on November 20, 1887, and grew up in Amarillo, Texas. His career got under way through fiddling contests and accompanying silent westerns in film theatres.

Legend has it that he and Henry Gilliland (born in 1848 in Altus, Oklahoma) went to Virginia to perform at a Civil War veterans' reunion, and that after the show they travelled to New York, on spec, to audition for the bosses of Victor: Robertson was dressed as a cowboy and Gilliland as a Confederate soldier. That they were auditioned at all was remarkable in itself, but that they immediately cut some sides for the label indicates a level of record company tolerance that is notably absent now. One of the sides was 'Sally Gooden', which was issued in April 1923. Robertson established another first when he performed 'Sally Gooden' and 'Arkansas Traveller' on WBAP, thereby becoming the first country artist with a recording contract to promote his records on the radio. Little is known of his activities thereafter.

ROBERTSON, Jaime 'Robbie' see BAND, The

ROBISON, Carson J.

During the 1920s and 1930s, Carson Robison acquired a reputation for being one of the finest songwriters of the time. His themes were drawn with journalistic precision from the topical events of the day, and were arranged to maximize the impact of the subject matter. Like **Ralph Peer**, he had a fine business acumen, which enabled him to recognize the commercial potential of his songs. This ensured that his songs were only covered by those to whom they were suited.

He was born in Oswego, Kansas, on August 4, 1890, and started playing guitar at dances and other local events. In 1920 he moved to Kansas City and played in dance bands and on radio station KDAF, before moving to New York with the vaudevillian

Wendell Hall in 1924, where he showed his versatility by recording for Victor as a whistler. Teaming up with **Vernon Dalhart**, he cut a series of hits over the next four years which included many of Robison's compositions: 'Barnacle Bill The Sailor', 'Open Up Them Pearly Gates', 'Carry Me Back To The Lone Prairie', 'Little Green Valley', 'The John T. Scopes Trial' and 'Blue Ridge Mountain Home'.

After his partnership with Dalhart ended, he recorded with his own jazz group, the Kansas City Jack Rabbits, and with vocalist Gene Austin. In 1929, he teamed up with **Frank Luther** for a number of country-flavoured duets that included 'When It's Springtime In The Rockies', 'The Utah Trail', 'Sleepy Rio Grande' and 'Left My Gal In The Mountains', the latter featuring guitarist Roy Smeck. Robison and Luther worked together until 1932, when he left to lead the Pioneers, who later became the Buckaroos (not to be confused with **Buck Owens**' band of the same name).

He toured the world throughout the 1930s, and also broadcasted on Radio Luxembourg; in the UK, his country records were second only to **Jimmie Rodgers** in popularity. By the 1940s, as his popularity declined, he returned to radio and cut novelty items like the pithily patriotic 'We're Gonna Have To Slap That Dirty Little Jap (And Uncle Sam's The Man To Do It)' and the monologic 'Life Gets Tee-Jus Don't It'. In the 1950s, he cut the topical 'Rockin' & Rollin' With Granmaw' and some square dances with his group, the Pleasant Valley Boys. Despite slipping into obscurity in later years, he continued performing and writing until his death on March 24, 1957, in Poughkeepsie, New York.

ROCKIN' DOPSIE

One of the most significant inheritors of the cajun tradition is accordionist Rockin' Dopsie, who, since **Clifton Chenier**'s death in 1987, has, along with Queen Ida and Buckwheat Zydeco, become one of the most experienced and versatile exponents of zydeco.

He was born Alton Rubin on February 10, 1932, in Lafayette, Louisiana. Having worked at local clubs and dances from 1955, he started to record with his group, the Twisters, for the Bon Temps label in 1969; the group comprised Sherman Robertson and Paul Senegal (guitar), Alonzo Johnson (bass), David Rubin (rub-board), John Hart (saxophone) and his son, Alton Rubin Jr (drums). He finally found international recognition during the mid-1970s, when he was invited to play on the US college circuit and at festivals in Europe: this led to a contract with the Sonet label.

While none of his records have sold particularly well, *Doin' The Zydeco* (1977) and *Crown Prince Of Zydeco* (1986), for example, have kept zydeco alive. And, in 1986, Paul Simon's *Graceland* featured him to admirable effect, with the result that zydeco enjoyed considerable, but fleeting, international appeal.

BIG BAD ZYDECO, GNP (US), 1980
CROWN PRINCE OF ZYDECO, Sonet, 1987
DOIN' THE ZYDECO, Sonet, 1977
FRENCH STYLE, Sonet, 1982
GOOD ROCKIN', Sonet, 1988
HOLD ON, Sonet, 1979
ROCKIN' DOPSIE & THE TWISTERS, Rounder (US), 1988
SATURDAY NIGHT ZYDECO, Sonet, 1989
ZY-DE-BLUE, Sonet, 1978
ZY-DE-CO-IN, Sonet, 1990

RODGERS, Jimmie

Jimmie Rodgers was one of the first to be inducted into the Country Music Hall Of Fame on its foundation in 1961. The synthesis of blues and hillbilly music that he created was the catalyst in the evolution of country music.

James Charles Rodgers was born on September 8, 1897, in Meridian, Mississippi, and left school in 1911 to become a water-carrier on the Mobile and Ohio Railroad; working with black labourers, he acquired rudimentary knowledge of the guitar and the banjo. Constantly plagued by tuberculosis, he stopped working for the railroad after becoming a brakeman, and spent some time as a private detective.

In 1925 he started to perform professionally, joining a medicine show, before moving to Asheville, North Carolina, where he organized the Jimmie Rodgers Entertainers. This was a hillbilly band that comprised Rodgers (banjo), Jack Pierce (guitar), Jack Grant (mandolin) and Claude Grant (banjo). In 1927, after broadcasting on WWNC, Asheville, he heard word that **Ralph Peer** was setting up sessions in Bristol on the Tennessee-Virginia border; just as they were about to cut some sides his band left him, setting up as the Tenneva Ramblers and quickly disappearing into obscurity. Rodgers continued as a solo artist, cutting 'The Soldier's Sweetheart' and 'Sleep Baby Sleep'; they were released by Victor in October, 1927, along with sides by the **Carter Family.**

Such was the success of these tracks that Peer set up fresh sessions four months later, where Rodgers cut offerings such as 'T For Texas' (also known as 'Blue Yodel'), 'Ben Dewberry's Run' and 'Mother Was A Lady'. Rodgers' songwriting and arranging was now improving in leaps and bounds, making his style unique and immediately recognizable. Among his best-known songs from this period were 'Mississippi River Blues', 'Jimmie Rodgers' Blues', 'Peach Picking Time In Georgia', 'Waitin' For A Train', 'Jimmie The Kid', 'Brakeman's Blues', 'Tuck Away My Lonesome Blues' and 'Mother, The Queen Of My Heart'. The wide-ranging influences on his music guaranteed that he was teamed with an increasing diversity of sidemen, including Clayton McMichen of the **Skillet Lickers**, a black jazz band, the Louisville Jug Band, and even Louis Armstrong and his wife, Lil Hardin Armstrong.

While he became progressively more popular, with records selling by the truckload, he toured constantly throughout the South and southwest, appearing on the Loew's vaudeville circuit. In 1929 he appeared in a short film called *The Singing Brakeman*, and in 1930 he moved with his wife, Carrie, to San Antonio, Texas, where he began a twice-weekly radio show on KMAC. However, he was gradually wasting away with tuber-culosis, and while he chronicled the process with songs like 'TB Blues', his touring itinerary was marred by cancellations.

In 1933, he returned to Victor in New York for some more recording sessions - a bed was put in the studio so that he could rest between takes - but on May 24, 1933, he began to haemorrhage, slipping into a coma the following day and dying on May 26, 1933: his final recording was 'Fifteen Years Ago Today'. In the years since his death, his influence has permeated every facet of American music, with performers including **Woody Guthrie**, **Elvis Presley**, **Ry Cooder**, **Merle Haggard**, **Hank Williams**, **Ernest Tubb**, the Allman Brothers Band and Big Bill Broonzy paying tribute to his legacy.

MY OLD PAL, Living Era, 1989
MY ROUGH & ROWDY WAYS, Stetson, 1989
NEVER NO MO' BLUES, RCA, 1987
SINGING BRAKEMAN, Bear Family (German), 1992
TRAIN WHISTLE BLUES, Living Era, 1986
TWENTY OF THE BEST, RCA, 1984

RODRIGUEZ, Johnny
Chicano Johnny Rodriguez has eradicated all the Tex-Mex elements from his music, and come up with a tolerable alternative which shows the influence of two early benefactors, **Tom T. Hall** and **Bobby Bare**.

Juan Raoul Davis Rodriguez was born on December 10, 1951, in Sabinal, Texas, the eighth of nine children. He started to play the guitar when he was seven, and became guitarist and vocalist in a band during his high-school years. In 1969 he cut a demo in San Antonio, but the deal fell through and he started getting in trouble with the law, even-tually receiving a three-to-seven-year stretch for stealing and barbecuing a goat! He whiled away his prison-cell hours by singing, and one of the warders gave him a break by introducing him to the owner of the Alamo Village resort in Bracketville when he was paroled. Between 1970 and 1971, he did a variety of jobs at the resort, including driving a stage-coach and singing for the visitors; among them were Hall and Bare, who both encouraged him to head for Nashville.

At the end of 1971, he made the trip, and Hall employed him as a guitarist in his band, the Storytellers, and arranged an audition for him with Roy Dea at Mercury. He was immediately signed to the label, and his debut 'Pass Me By' (C&W#9, 1972) launched him into the charts. Throughout the 1970s, he featured regularly in the charts with a string of **Jerry Kennedy**-produced hits that included 'You Always Come Back (To Hurting Me)' (C&W#1, 1973), 'Ridin' My Thumb To Mexico' (C&W#1, 1973), **Lefty Frizzell**'s 'That's The Way Love Goes' (C&W#1, 1974), the Beatles' 'Something' (C&W#6, 1974), 'Dance With Me (One More Time)' (C&W#2, 1974), 'We're Over' (C&W#3, 1974), **Larry Gatlin**'s 'I Just Can't Get Her Out Of My Mind' (C&W#1, 1975), **Linda Hargrove**'s 'Just Get Up And Close The Door' (C&W#1, 1975), 'Love Put A Song In My Heart' (C&W#1, 1975), 'I Couldn't Be Without You' (C&W#3, 1977) and 'I Wonder If I Said Goodbye' (C&W#2, 1978).

In 1979 he moved to the Epic label, cutting 'Down On The Rio Grande' (C&W#6, 1979), but drug prob-lems intervened and his career hit the skids until 1983, when he returned with 'Foolin'' and 'How Could I Love Her So', both of which featured additional vocals from **Lynn Anderson**. In 1987 he signed with Capitol and scored a modest hit with 'I Didn't (Every Chance I Had)', but he has been unable to recapture the glory years of the 1970s despite the enduring popularity of his concerts.

JOHNNY RODRIGUEZ, Epic (US), 1979
THROUGH MY EYES, Epic (US), 1980

ROGERS, David

A middle-ground country singer who has never managed to translate modest hits into monsters, David Rogers was born on March 27, 1936, in Atlanta, Georgia, and the *Grand Ole Opry* was the soundtrack to his formative years. In 1956 he was drafted into the army, but his hopes for becoming an army entertainer were dashed, despite auditioning for **Roger Miller**. After being demobbed in 1958, he started to work the Atlanta club circuit, culminating in a residency at the Egyptian Ballroom in 1962, which lasted until 1968.

In 1967 he joined the cast of WWVA's *Wheeling Jamboree* and was signed by Columbia, where he had a string of modest hits that included 'I'm In Love With My Wife' (1968), 'A World Called You' (1969), 'I Wake Up In Heaven' (1970) and 'Ruby, You're Warm' (1971). In 1969, he moved to Nashville and secured regular bookings on television and the club circuit, until he was signed to the Atlantic label in 1973, charting with 'Just Thank Me' and 'Loving You Has Changed My Life'.

After Atlantic closed its Nashville division, Rogers was left without a contract, and had to content himself with minor independent labels. Still a fixture on the club circuit in and around Nashville, he lacks the vital distinctiveness which would set him apart from many other performers.

ROGERS, Kenny

During the 1970s Kenny Rogers established himself as one of the most highly paid country artists of all time. His folksy vignettes and warm baritone appealed to both pop and country audiences, and his easy professionalism guaranteed him regular spots on the lucrative Las Vegas cabaret circuit.

Kenneth David Rogers was born in Houston, Texas, on August 21, 1938, the son of a docker and younger brother of Lelan Rogers, who became a label owner and record producer. He formed his first group, the Scholars, while at school, and had a local hit with 'That Crazy Feeling' for the Carlton label. Part of the jazz combo the Bobby Doyle Trio while at the University of Houston, Rogers then joined the Lively Ones, a barbershop quartet. In 1966 he became a member of the folk group the New Christy Minstrels, formed during the folk-music boom of the early 1960s. Joining them at the tail-end of their career, he and Mike Settle (see **Stewart, John**) left to form the First Edition.

They were signed by Reprise and immediately scored with **Mickey Newbury**'s 'Just Dropped In (To See What Condition My Condition Was In)' (US#5,

1968); this was followed by other substantial hits: 'But You Know I Love You' (US#19, 1969), **Mel Tillis**'s 'Ruby Don't Take Your Love To Town' (US#6, UK#2, 1969), **Woody Guthrie**'s 'Reuben James' (US#26, 1969), **Mac Davis**'s 'Something's Burning' (US#11, UK#8, 1970), 'Tell It All Brother' (US#17, 1970) and 'Heed The Call' (US#33, 1970). By 1971 the group's popularity had declined and Rogers left to embark upon a solo career.

Although at first he failed to make an impact, by 1977, having signed with United Artists, his country-folk amalgam coalesced and he hit paydirt with 'Lucille' (US#5, C&W#1, UK#1, 1977) - the first of a series of hits that stretched into the 1990s. Among his other hits were 'Daytime Friends' (US#28, C&W#1, UK#39, 1977), 'Every Time Two Fools Collide' (a duet with **Dottie West**; C&W#1, 1978), 'Love Or Something Like It' (US#32, C&W#1, 1978), 'The Gambler' (US#16, C&W#1, 1978), 'All I Ever Need Is You' (another duet with Dottie West; C&W#1, 1979), 'She Believes In Me' (US#5, C&W#1, UK#42, 1979), 'You Decorated My Life' (US#7, C&W#1, 1979), 'Coward Of The County' (US#3, C&W#1, UK#1, 1979), 'Don't Fall In Love With A Dreamer' (a duet with Kim Carnes; US#4, C&W#3, 1980) and 'Love The World Away' (from the soundtrack of *Urban Cowboy*; US#14, C&W#4, 1980).

Ending his five-year association with producer Larry Butler in 1980, Rogers teamed up with different producers, including Lionel Richie of the R&B band the Commodores, who wrote and produced 'Lady' (US#1, C&W#1, UK#12, 1980), which was followed by 'I Don't Need You' (US#3, C&W#1, 1981), 'Share Your Love With Me' (US#14, 1981) and 'Through The Years' (US#13, 1982). He then teamed up with **Eddie Rabbitt**'s producer, David Malloy, for 'Love Will Turn You Around' (US#13, C&W#1, 1982), and the following year he joined Scottish singer Sheena Easton for a duet on the Bob Seger composition 'We've Got Tonight' (US#6, C&W#1, UK#28, 1983).

At the end of 1983 he signed a $20 million recording contract with RCA, and teamed up with the Bee Gees and their producers Karl Richardson, Albhy Galuten and Bee Gee Barry Gibb, for *Eyes That See In The Dark*, which included 'Eyes That See In The Dark', 'Islands In The Stream' (a duet with **Dolly Parton**; US#1, C&W#1, UK#7, 1983) and 'This Woman' (US#23, 1984). At the end of 1984, he cut *What About Me?*, the title track featured Carnes and soul singer James Ingram (US#15, 1984), and 'Crazy' (C&W#1, 1984) which was penned by Rogers and Richard Marx.

On January 28, 1985, Rogers joined a multitude of artists (including Richie, Michael Jackson, **Waylon**

Jennings, **Willie Nelson** and **Bob Dylan**), who together formed USA For Africa for the purpose of recording 'We Are The World' - the US music industry's contribution to Live Aid (Bob Geldof's charity for African famine relief). Later that year, Dolly Parton insisted that she duet with Rogers on 'Real Love' (C&W#1, 1985), the title track of her next album. Rogers followed this up with 'Morning Desire' (written by Dave Loggins; C&W#1, 1985) and 'Tomb Of The Unknown Love' (C&W#1, 1986) (both produced by George Martin), 'Twenty Years Ago' (C&W#2, 1986), 'I Prefer The Moonlight' (C&W#2, 1987) and Kim Carnes' 'Make No Mistake, She's Mine' (a duet with **Ronnie Milsap**; C&W#1, 1987).

In 1989 Rogers signed with Warner Bros., cutting *Something Inside So Strong*. In common with many successful country artists he has also pursued a film career, starring in movies such as *The Gambler* (1980), *The Gambler 2* (1983), *Coward Of The County* (1981) and *Six Pack* (1982).

ANTHOLOGY, Connoisseur, 1990
EYES THAT SEE IN THE DARK, RCA, 1987
FOR THE GOOD TIMES (with First Edition), Arena, 1987
GREATEST HITS, MCA (US), 1988
LADY (with Dottie West & Kim Carnes), Liberty, 1981
RUBY DON'T TAKE YOUR LOVE TO TOWN (with First Edition), Castle, 1986
SOMETHING INSIDE SO STRONG, Warner Bros., 1989
TWENTY FIVE GREATEST HITS, Liberty, 1987
VERY BEST OF KENNY ROGERS, Warner Bros., 1990

ROGERS, Roy

Best known for his roles in countless Westerns, Roy Rogers' greatest contribution was his formation of the **Sons Of Pioneers**, the band who supported him until 1948. He was born Leonard Slye on a farm in Duck Run, Ohio, on November 5, 1911, and moved with his family to California, where he worked as a peach picker. After performing locally with groups like the Rocky Mountaineers and the Hollywood Hillbillies, he formed the International Cowboys (who became the Sons Of Pioneers in 1934), and they started to support **Gene Autry** in films such as *The Old Homestead*. Having set his sights on a film career, Slye left the group and adopted the pseudonym Dick Weston, making his first appearance in this guise in *Rhythm On The Range* (1935), before assuming the Roy Rogers identity.

The Sons Of Pioneers followed him into the movies, as support to his leading role; other notable contributors to the movies included Dale Evans (born Frances Smith on October 31, 1912, in Uvalde, Texas) and his horse, Trigger. While Rogers showed himself to be a first-rate Singing Cowboy, his films were all low-budget and the best songs, such as 'Tumbling Tumbleweeds', were written by the Sons Of Pioneers. During his career he made around a hundred films and enjoyed a brief supremacy over Gene Autry in 1942, as 'King of the Cowboys'.

In 1947, he married the devout Dale Evans and began to adopt some of her religious views; the following year the Sons Of Pioneers left him and he recruited another group along similar lines called Riders Of The Purple Sage (see **Willing, Foy**). He made his final film, *Pals Of The Golden West*, for Republic in 1951, and turned to television, hosting his own show until 1954. Dale Evans turned increasingly to the Bible for inspiration and wrote many books of a religious nature.

During the 1950s, they both recorded gospel records and divorced themselves from the mainstream of the entertainment industry, until the nostalgia boom of the 1970s heralded their return and they made appearances on family television shows like *The Muppets*. In 1991 Rogers duetted with **Randy Travis** on 'Happy Trails', which was featured on Travis's *Heroes And Friends*. He has more recently taken to running the Roy Rogers And Dale Evans Museum in California.

KING OF THE COWBOYS, Bear Family (German), 1983
ROLL ON TEXAS MOON, Bear Family (German), 1986
ROY ROGERS & THE SONS OF PIONEERS, Silva Screen, 1989

ROLLING STONES

In a career lasting over thirty years, The Rolling Stones have been influenced by virtually every style of music. While the predominant influence is R&B, the guitar work of Keith Richards and the songwriting partnership of Mick Jagger and Keith Richards has strong country shadings.

These shadings first manifested themselves during the late 1960s, when 1968's 'No Expectations' from *Beggar's Banquet* established a precedent for the group as it was the first overtly country song they had recorded. By 1971, having recorded a country version of 'Honky-Tonk Women' as 'Country Honk' on *Let It Bleed*, *Sticky Fingers* illustrated the complete assimilation of country music into their overall sound with songs like 'Wild Horses' and 'Dead Flowers' being the most obvious examples; the former was reputedly co-written by **Gram Parsons** and it was mooted that Richards and Parsons were to collaborate on an album together, but Parsons' death stymied that plan.

Throughout the remainder of the 1970s and the 1980s, each album included at least one country-influenced track: 'Sweet Virginia' from *Exile On Main Street*, 'Fool To Cry' from *Black 'n' Blue*, 'Faraway Eyes' and 'Beast Of Burden' from *Some Girls* and 'Waiting On A Friend' from *Tattoo You*, for example. All that remains is for their record label to issue a definitive compilation illustrating the extent to which they have been influenced by country music.

RONSTADT, Linda

With a vocal purity that is uniquely her own, Linda Ronstadt transcends simple classification. She has performed a phenomenal diversity of material, ranging from light opera to country, from rock to jazz, and from punk to R&B.

She was born of Mexican and German extraction on July 15, 1946, in Tucson, Arizona, and spent her childhood listening to **Hank Williams**, **Jimmie Rodgers** and **Elvis Presley**. In 1964, after forming a trio with her brother and sister, she joined the Stone Poneys, who had a hit with **Mike Nesmith**'s 'Different Drum' (US#13, 1967).

After embarking on a solo career, her vocal style - which had not yet achieved the fluidity that was to distinguish her later work - was shown to good effect on *Hand Sown, Home Grown* (1969) and *Silk Purse* (1970), the latter being cut with Nashville session musicians, and including her first solo hit, 'Long Long Time' (US#25, 1970). Things began to coalesce in 1971, with the formation of a regular backing band that would later evolve into the **Eagles**. With this set-up she recorded *Linda Ronstadt* (1972), and in 1973 she teamed up with producer - and later, manager - Peter Asher for her debut on the Asylum label, *Don't Cry Now*.

Owing Capitol one last album, she cut *Heart Like A Wheel* (1974); Asher's crystal-clear production and Andrew Gold's arrangements enabled Ronstadt to extract every last drop of emotion from a diverse collection of songs, which included the Betty Everett R&B classic, 'You're No Good' (US#1, 1975), the **Everly Brothers**' 'When Will I Be Loved' (US#2, C&W#1, 1975), **Buddy Holly**'s 'It Doesn't Matter Anymore', Hank Williams' 'I Can't Help It (If I'm Still In Love With You)' (US#2, C&W#2, 1975) and Lowell George's 'Willin''. This album represented her artistic zenith - all she needed to do thereafter was apply the same formula to a different collection of songs: *Prisoner In*

Disguise (1975), *Hasten Down The Wind* (1976) and *Simple Dreams* (1977) were all strong albums - her voice was just as tremulous and her phrasing still impeccable - but the bite was temporarily gone. Each album produced a number of hits, including 'Heat Wave' (US#5, 1975), 'Tracks Of My Tears' (US#25, 1976), 'That'll Be The Day' (US#11, 1976), 'Blue Bayou' (US#3, 1977), 'It's So Easy' (US#5, 1977) and 'Poor Poor Pitiful Me' (US#31, 1978).

In 1978 she released *Living In The USA*; competently executed but lacking emotional commitment, it produced a couple of hits: Chuck Berry's 'Back In The USA' (US#16, 1978) and Smokey Robinson's 'Ooh Baby Baby' (US#7, 1978). *Mad Love* in 1980, featuring the Los Angeles band the Cretonnes, was a return to form, with Ronstadt getting to grips with material by writers like **Elvis Costello** and the Cretonnes' Mark Goldberg; it included hits like 'How Do I Make You' (US#10, 1980) and 'Hurts So Bad' (US#8, 1980).

After appearances in the Broadway production of Gilbert & Sullivan's *The Pirates Of Penzance* (1981), she cut another mediocre album, *Get Closer* (1982). A trilogy of albums - *What's New* (1983), *Lush Life* (1984) and *For Sentimental Reasons* (1986) - followed, featuring arrangements by Nelson Riddle (who had formerly worked with Frank Sinatra); they showed her vocal range on a variety of standards and lushly arranged contemporary songs, and indicated Ronstadt's growing desire to expand her musical vocabulary by paying homage to her musical antecedents.

Ronstadt reasserted her country roots in 1987, when she collaborated with **Dolly Parton** and **Emmylou Harris** on *Trio* (1987), which featured revivals of 'To Know Him Is To Love Him' (US#1, C&W#1, 1987), 'Telling Me Lies', 'Those Memories Of You' and 'Wildflowers'. She also recorded the elegiac *Canciones De Mi Padre* (Songs Of My Father) (1987), a collection of thirteen Mexican songs (all sung in Spanish) that she had been taught during her childhood. By 1989, with *Cry Like A Rainstorm* and *Howl Like The Wind*, featuring 'Don't Know Much' (a duet with Aaron Neville of the Neville Brothers; US#2, UK#2, 1989), she had become one of the best interpretative performers in the US.

CANCIONES DE MI PADRE, Asylum, 1987
DON'T CRY NOW, Asylum, 1974
GREATEST HITS, Volumes 1-2, Asylum, 1980
HEART LIKE A WHEEL, EMI (German), 1974
LIVING IN THE USA, Asylum (US), 1978
SIMPLE DREAMS, Asylum, 1987

RORER, Posey see **POOLE, Charlie**

ROSE, Fred

Fred Rose was, with **Jimmie Rodgers** and **Hank Williams**, the first to be elected to the Country Music Hall Of Fame in 1961. Significantly, he was the only executive of the three, but his influence encompassed most aspects of behind-the-scenes activity, including songwriting, producing, arranging and publishing.

He was born on August 24, 1897, in Evansville, Indiana, and started his career as a pianist in Chicago bars. Initially recording jazz, he cut piano rolls with Fats Waller for QRS, before moving on to Brunswick (where he cut early compositions such as 'Honest And Truly') and thence to join Paul Whiteman's Big Band. In 1933 he joined CBS in Chicago, before moving to Nashville, where he started to compose country songs.

Writing under the occasional pseudonyms of Floyd Jenkins and Bart Dawson, he worked with Hank Williams, **Gene Autry** and **Ray Whitley**, penning titles like 'Be Honest With Me', 'Blue Eyes Crying In The Rain', 'Tears On My Pillow', 'Kaw-Liga', 'I'll Never Get Out Of This World Alive', 'Crazy Heart', 'Take These Chains From My Heart', 'Texarkana Baby', 'We Live In Two Different Worlds', 'A Mansion On The Hill', 'No One Will Ever Know' and 'Settin' The Woods On Fire'.

In 1942 he set up the publishing company Acuff-Rose with **Roy Acuff**, and then helped to set up Broadcast Music Incorporated, which sought to assist songwriters in getting royalties for radio plays; he was also a powerful and active member of ASCAP (American Society of Composers, Authors and Publishers) right up to his death on December 1, 1954. His son **Wesley Rose** has now taken over the family business.

ROSE, Wesley

One of the founder members of the Country Music Association, Wesley Rose took over from his father, **Fred Rose**, as chief executive of Acuff-Rose in 1945, and has ensured that the publishing company has become one of the most prestigious in the world.

He was born on February 11, 1918, in Chicago, Illinois, and gained a degree in business studies and accounting from the Walton School of Commerce. He initially worked as an accountant for Standard Oil, before joining Acuff-Rose in Nashville. When his father died, he moved into record production and placed material with the major record labels, until becoming manager of the **Everly Brothers** and founding the Hickory label with **Roy Acuff** in the late 1950s. This became one of the most influential of the independent specialist country labels, signing artists like **Sue Thompson**, **Don Gibson**, **Doug Kershaw**, **Carl Smith**, Donovan, Don Everly and Acuff.

ROWAN, Peter

Peter Rowan was born in Boston, Massachusetts, in 1942, and started his career as a member of **Bill Monroe**'s Blue Grass Boys during the early 1960s; coming from a solidly middle-class, college-educated background, he represented the new breed of blue-grass musician. In 1967 he formed Earth Opera with **Dave Grisman**, and they cut a brace of albums for Elektra: *Earth Opera* (1967) and *The Great American Eagle Tragedy* (1968).

When Earth Opera split up, he started session work and reunited with fiddler Richard Greene, whom he had first met during his days with the Blue Grass Boys. They formed a jazz-oriented group called Sea Train, who recorded an eponymous debut album for A&M in 1969, before moving on to Capitol and cutting *Marbleheaded Messenger* (1971). They then moved on to form the bluegrass outfit Muleskinner with **Clarence White** in 1972, cutting *Muleskinner* for Warner Bros.; a loose aggregation of session musicians (including banjoist Bill Keith), the band members went their separate ways after the recording. Rowan then worked with Jerry Garcia (of the Grateful Dead) and Robert Hunter (lyricist with the Grateful Dead), before forming the Rowans in 1973.

The Rowans, which included brothers Chris and Lorin, cut *Rowan Brothers* for Columbia in 1973, and followed with three albums for Asylum (*The Rowans* in 1974, *Sibling Rivalry* in 1976 and *Jubilation* in 1978); while their records achieved only limited sales, they built up a significant following on the college circuit. By the early 1980s, Peter had gone back to session work and recording traditional bluegrass albums, including *Rivalry* with fiddler Tex Logan for the Waterfront label in 1986.

DUETS (Richard Greene), Rounder (US), 1988
DUST BOWL CHILDREN, Sugar Hill (US), 1990
THE FIRST WHIPPERWILL, Sugar Hill (US), 1986
MARBLEHEADED MESSENGER (Sea Train), See For Miles, 1971
MEDICINE TRAIL, Flying Fish (US), 1989
MULESKINNER, Edsel, 1972
NEW MOON RISING, Special Delivery, 1989
PETER ROWAN, Special Delivery, 1987

PETER ROWAN AND THE RED HOT PICKERS, Sugar Hill (US), 1989
PETER ROWAN AND THE WILD STALLIONS, Appaloosa, 1983
RAMBLIN' (Richard Greene), Rounder (US), 1988
RIVALRY, Waterfront, 1986
SEA TRAIN, Edsel, 1969
TEXICAN BAD MAN, Appaloosa, 1983
WALLS OF TIME, Sugar Hill (US), 1988

ROWANS see ROWAN, Peter

RUSSELL, Leon

Leon Russell achieved celebrity in the late 1960s as the *éminence grise* and bandleader of Delaney & Bonnie And Friends and Joe Cocker's Mad Dogs And Englishmen, both of which were touring outfits.

He was born Hank Wilson on April 2, 1941, in Lawton, Oklahoma, and played the piano and trumpet as a child. In 1956 he got himself a job as a musician in a Tulsa nightclub, where he played with other Tulsa musicians like **J.J. Cale**, David Gates of Bread and bassist Carl Radle. During these early years he toured with Ronnie Hawkins and **Jerry Lee Lewis**, until he moved to Los Angeles in 1958, changed his name and became a session musician, meeting and working with **James Burton**, **Dorsey Burnette**, **Glen Campbell** and Delaney Bramlett.

His first regular booking was with Bramlett and Burton as studio musicians on Jack Good's *Shindig* television show. This resulted in regular session work with producer Phil Spector at the Gold Star Studios, and then with a variety of artists like Gary Lewis & the Playboys (as arranger), the **Byrds** and Herb Alpert. In 1966 he recorded a drastically re-arranged version of the Errol Garner jazz classic, 'Misty', for A&M, and then arranged *Feelin' Groovy* for vocal group Harpers Bizarre.

In 1968 he teamed up with songwriter Marc Benno to cut *Asylum Choir* for the Smash label, but Asylum Choir II was turned down and he joined the *Delaney & Bonnie And Friends* tour, which included such luminaries as **Rita Coolidge**, Carl Radle and Eric Clapton. During this tour, Russell struck up a friendship with Joe Cocker's manager, Denny Cordell, and they set about forming the Shelter label and organizing Joe Cocker's *Mad Dogs And Englishmen* tour (which featured a cast of thousands), where Russell played the role of Master of Ceremonies; it was filmed and was, in concentrating solely on the performances, one of the best rock films of the era.

Russell's excellent eponymous debut appeared in 1970 on A&M, and featured an astonishing array of rock luminaries: Clapton, Radle, Cocker, Coolidge, George Harrison, Ringo Starr, Bill Wyman, Charlie Watts and Steve Winwood. Much of its excellence was attributable to the quality of Russell's writing, with 'Delta Lady' (dedicated to Rita Coolidge and a hit for Joe Cocker) and 'A Song For You' (later covered by **Willie Nelson** and the Carpenters) being high points. His follow-up in 1971, *Leon Russell And The Shelter People*, was issued by the A&M-distributed Shelter label; it was another star-studded affair, with Russell originals like 'Hummingbird' and 'Superstar' (covered by the Carpenters and Delaney & Bonnie) making their first appearances. The same year he appeared with George Harrison and **Bob Dylan** in the benefit concert for Bangladesh.

After suffering a breakdown brought on by overwork at the end of 1971, he acquired the tapes of *Asylum Choir II* for release by Shelter and issued *Carney*, which included 'This Masquerade' (later a hit for guitarist George Benson) and 'Tight Rope' (US#11, 1972). Having signed Tulsa chum J.J. Cale to Shelter, Russell cut *Hank Wilson's Back*, a collection of his favourite country songs; these included 'I'm So Lonesome I Could Cry' and 'Roll In My Sweet Baby's Arms' and featured session musicians such as Radle, Cale, **Pete Drake** and Billy Byrd (**Ernest Tubb**'s erstwhile guitarist).

Throughout the remainder of the 1970s, he demonstrated his eclecticism by cutting albums such as *Stop All That Jazz* (1974) and *Will O' The Wisp* (1975, including 'Lady Blue'; US#11, 1975), both of which saw him returning to the mainstream. In 1979 he joined Willie Nelson for *One For The Road*, which included an interesting version of 'Heartbreak Hotel' (C&W#1, 1979). As if to reaffirm his interest in all forms of country he cut *The Live Album* for Warner Bros. in 1981, with the progressive bluegrass band **New Grass Revival**. In 1984 he recorded *Hank Wilson Volume II*, another collection of his favourite country songs. In recent years, he has recorded less, preferring instead to concentrate on his production company Paradise Video.

THE LIVE ALBUM (with New Grass Revival), Warner Bros., 1981

RUSTY & DOUG see KERSHAW, Doug

S.K.O. see **OVERSTREET, Paul**

SAHM, Doug

Doug Sahm has been one of the guiding forces in the establishment of Tex-Mex as a major musical influence in the US. He was born Douglas Saldana on November 6, 1941, in San Antonio, Texas, and made his debut as a steel guitarist on radio KMAC in 1947. He cut his first record 'A Real American Joe' in 1955 for the Sarg label as Little Doug. In 1958, heavily influenced by fellow Texan guitarist T-Bone Walker, he formed the Knights Blues Band, playing bordertown clubs and bars and recording for a string of local labels.

After securing a residency at the prestigious Blue Note lounge, he formed the Sir Douglas Quintet, with **Augie Meyer** (organ), Jack Barber (bass), Johnny Peres (drums) and hornman Frank Morin; they were spotted here by producer **Huey Meaux**, who signed them to his Tribe label. The group's debut, 'She's About A Mover' (US#13, UK#15, 1965), was full of chunky chords and echoed the style of British groups like the **Rolling Stones** and the Pretty Things. Encouraged by the modest success of the follow-up, 'The Rains Came' (US#31, 1966), Sahm, Morin and Meyer moved to San Francisco, where they became involved in the nascent psychedelic movement and were signed by the Philips subsidiary, Smash.

Their first outing, *Sir Douglas Quintet + 2 (Honky Blues)*, showed Sahm experimenting with different rock styles; it was followed by the vociferous 'Mendocino' (US#27, 1969). *Together After Five* emerged in 1970: produced by Meaux it showed Sahm returning to a purer form of Tex-Mex on songs like 'Lawd I'm Just A Country Boy In This Great Freaky City'. *1+1+1+1=4* followed the same year, and was recorded in Nashville and produced by **Jerry Kennedy**.

After being dropped by Philips, Sahm was signed to Atlantic by Jerry Wexler, who produced *The Return Of Doug Saldana* in 1971. Sahm's eclecticism was now losing its commercial appeal and after two albums,

Doug Sahm And Band (1973) and *Texas Tornado* (1974), he was dropped by Atlantic, despite assistance from admirers like **Bob Dylan**, **David Bromberg**, **Dr John** and producers Wexler and Arif Mardin.

Over the last fifteen years, Sahm, a resident of Austin, has been one of the key figures in Tex-Mex and has been instrumental in establishing Austin as one of the great music capitals of the US. Among his later albums are *Groovers Paradise* (with Doug Clifford and Stu Cook from Creedence Clearwater Revival; see **Fogerty, John**) in 1974; the Meaux-produced *Rock For Country Rollers* on Dot in 1976; *Live Love*, on Augie Meyer's Texas Re-Cord label; *Hell Of A Spell* (1980) and *Border Wave* (1981) on John Fahey's Takoma label; and *Rio Medina* (1984) on Sonet.

In 1989 he formed the Texas Tornados with Meyer, **Flaco Jimenez** and **Freddy Fender**, cutting the live *Texas Tornados* in 1990 - an informal affair that has emphasized their commitment to playing live, which is what Sahm does best.

BACK TO THE DILLO (with Augie Meyer), Sonet, 1988
DOUG SAHM AND BAND, Edsel, 1973
DOUG SAHM LIVE, Beartracks, 1988
HANGING ON BY A THREAD (Texas Tornados), Warner Bros., 1992
JUKE BOX MUSIC, Ace, 1989
LIVE, Charly, 1987
SIR DOUGLAS: HIS FIRST RECORDINGS, Charly, 1981
SIR DOUG'S RECORDING TRIP (Sir Douglas Quintet), Edsel, 1988
TEXAS ROAD RUNNER, Moonshine, 1986
TEXAS TORNADOS, Warner Bros., 1990

SAINTE-MARIE, Buffy

An eloquent Cree Indian, Sainte-Marie has been a vociferous critic of the persecution of Indians by successive US governments. While notionally regarded as a folk singer (she started her career in that haven for folksingers, Greenwich Village), her songs have been covered by artists as diverse as **Elvis Presley**,

Bobby Bare, Glen Campbell, Cher, Bobby Darin and Joe Cocker.

She was born on February 20, 1941, in Saskatchewan, Canada, and raised by adoptive parents in Massachusetts. She played the New York club circuit during the early 1960s, before being signed to the Vanguard label and cutting a string of albums including *It's My Way* (1964) and *Little Wheel Spin And Spin* (1966), featuring compositions like 'Universal Soldier', 'Until It's Time For You To Go' and 'My Country 'Tis Of Thy People Your Dying'.

She went to Nashville in 1968, and cut *I'm Gonna Be A Country Girl Again*, the title track (UK#34, 1972) later becoming a modest hit. In 1970 she composed and sang 'Soldier Blue' (US#7, 1971), which was the theme song for the movie of the same name that dealt with the massacre of Indians by the US Army. This was followed by the album *Moonshot*, produced in Nashville by Norbert Putnam, it featured songs like 'Native North American Indian' and 'Mister Can't You See' (US#38, 1972). In 1973 she left Vanguard and signed with MCA, where she cut two up-tempo rock albums, *Buffy* and *Changing Woman*, before moving on to ABC and cutting the excellent *Sweet America* in 1976.

Out of the spotlight for the next fifteen years, she returned briefly to win an Oscar for 'Up Where We Belong', the theme song for *An Officer And A Gentleman*, which was performed on the soundtrack by Joe Cocker and Jennifer Warnes. In 1992 she returned to the limelight with *Coincidence And Other Likely Stories*, for the Ensign label, which proved to be one of the year's better albums and included the single 'Big Ones Get Away' (UK#27, 1992).

BEST OF BUFFY, Vanguard (US), 1984
BEST OF BUFFY SAINTE-MARIE, Start, 1989
COINCIDENCE AND OTHER LIKELY STORIES, Ensign, 1992
SPOTLIGHT ON BUFFY SAINTE-MARIE, Castle, 1981

SALDANA, Doug see SAHM, Doug

SATHERLEY, Art

Of English origin, Arthur Satherley was one of the founding fathers of the US record industry and was responsible for discovering a host of blues and hillbilly performers. He was born on October 19, 1889, in Bristol, Gloucestershire, England, where he was educated privately. In 1913, overcome with curiosity for

the Old West, he left the UK for America, and ended up in Wisconsin, where he worked for a lumber merchants who provided wood for the cabinets that housed Thomas Edison's phonographs. In 1918, the lumber merchants diversified and moved into the record business, starting the Paramount label, and Satherley became a producer of blues singers like Blind Lemon Jefferson.

In 1929 he went to New York to work for QRS, and then Plaza; the latter merged with other labels like Oriole and Mellotone to form the American Record Company in August 1929. Following the example of Ralph Peer, Satherley travelled down to the South on field trips to record local talent. Among the centres he visited were Dallas, Texas; Birmingham, Alabama; and Jackson, Mississippi. These visits yielded a goldmine of talent in the shape of Roy Acuff, Bob Wills, the Carlisle Brothers, Gene Autry and Big Bill Broonzy, among others.

In 1938 ARC was acquired by Columbia, and Satherley was retained in the A&R division to sign country and hillbilly artists. Those to benefit from experience were Lefty Frizzell, Marty Robbins, Little Jimmy Dickens, Spade Cooley, Al Dexter, Rose Maddox, Floyd Tillman and Ray Price. Retiring in 1952, he was elected to the Country Music Hall Of Fame in 1971, and died on June 10, 1986, in Fountain Valley, California.

SAWYER BROWN

Mark Miller (vocals) and Gregg Hubbard (keyboards) from Apopka, Florida, Bobby Randall (guitar) and Jim Scholten (keyboards) from Michigan, and Joe Smyth (percussion) from Maine, got together in 1981 in Nashville, and began a rigorous performing schedule on the club circuit. In 1983 they took first prize in the *Star Search* talent show, winning $100,000 and a recording contract.

Their debut, 'Leona', hit the Top Twenty, and they embarked on a nationwide tour opening for Kenny Rogers and Dolly Parton. Their first major hit followed with Miller's self-penned 'Step By Step' (C&W#1, 1986), with other hits like 'Used To Blue', 'Betty's Bein' Bad', 'This Missin' You Heart Of Mine', 'The Race Is On', 'The Dirt Road' (C&W#2, 1991), 'Some Girls Do' (C&W#1, 1992) and 'All These Years' (C&W#3, 1992) following in rapid succession. They tend to vindicate the old adage that putting bums on seats sells records.

CAFE ON THE CORNER, Curb (US), 1992

SCHNEIDER, John

Better known as Bo Duke in the television series *The Dukes Of Hazzard*, John Schneider came to the fore in the mid-1980s as a moderately consistent country artist. He was born on April 9, 1954, in Mount Kisco, New York, and started his acting career as a juvenile, appearing in summer stock performances of *Bye Bye Birdie* and *The Wizard Of Oz*, before landing his role in *The Dukes Of Hazzard* in 1979. His recording career started in 1981, when he was signed by the Scotti Bros. label for a re-working of the **Elvis Presley** hit 'It's Now Or Never' (US#14, C&W#4, 1981); the follow-up was the insipid honky-tonk-styled 'Them Good Ol' Boys Are Bad', which made few waves in the country charts.

By 1984, his recording career in the doldrums but his acting career flourishing, he was signed to MCA and cut 'I've Been Around Enough To Know' (a **Dickey Lee** and **Bob McDill** composition, produced by **Jimmy Bowen**; C&W#1, 1984); it revitalized his singing career and put him on the map as a bona fide country artist. It was followed by a succession of hits, including **Troy Seals** and Eddie Setser's 'Country Girls' (C&W#1, 1985), 'What's A Memory Like You (Doing In A Love Like This)' (C&W#1, 1985), 'You're The Last Thing I Needed Tonight' (C&W#1, 1986), 'At The Sound Of The Tone', 'Take The Long Way Home' and 'Love, You Ain't Seen The Last Of Me'. In 1987 his thespian instincts got the better of him, and he gave up his successful musical career to return to the silver screen.

LONG WAY, MCA (US), 1988
TOO GOOD TO STOP NOW, MCA (US), 1988
TRYIN' TO OUTRUN THE WIND, MCA (US), 1988

SCRUGGS, Earl   see FLATT & SCRUGGS

SCRUGGS, Randy

The eldest son of Earl Scruggs (See **Flatt & Scruggs**), Randy Scruggs has become one of Nashville's best guitarists and producers. His career started in 1969 when his father ended his long working relationship with **Lester Flatt** and formed the Earl Scruggs Revue. This was a loose aggregation of musicians, revolving around Earl's sons, Gary, Steve and Randy. By 1980, the three brothers had broken away to form their own band and Randy had become co-owner of the family studio in Nashville, Scruggs Sound.

While reaching high standards with his guitarwork,

it is his songwriting collaborations with **Earl Thomas Conley** that have won him most approbation: 'Your Love's On The Line', 'Don't Make It Easy For Me', 'Angel In Disguise', 'Chance of Lovin' You' and 'Love Don't Care (Whose Heart It Breaks)'. In 1988 he co-produced Conley's *The Heart Of It All*, and the following year he contributed to the **Nitty Gritty Dirt Band** album, *Will The Circle Be Unbroken? Volume 2*.

SEA TRAIN see ROWAN, Peter

SEALS, Dan

During the 1970s, Dan Seals was half of a duo with John Ford Coley, who together had hits with a number of rather innocuous, but tuneful, pop songs. Since 1983, with only a slight change of emphasis, his glossy country-pop has seldom been far from the top of the country charts.

He was born on February 8, 1950, in McCamey, Texas. After meeting John Ford Coley and Shane Keister in 1967, Dan formed the group Southwest F.O.B. After one minor hit with 'Smell Of Incense' in 1968, the group disbanded and Dan, as England Dan, continued as a duo with Coley. Over the next few years the duo toured the Midwest and southwest, until scoring with the first of their hits, 'I'd Really Love To See You Tonight' (US#2, UK#26, 1976); it was followed by 'Nights Are Forever Without You' (US#10, 1976), 'It's Sad To Belong' (US#21, 1977), 'Gone Too Far' (US#23, 1977), 'We'll Never Have To Say Goodbye Again' (US#9, 1978) and 'Love Is The Answer' (US#10, UK#45, 1979).

By the turn of the 1980s the duo had gone their separate ways, and Dan cut a series of solo albums. In 1983, having signed to Capitol, he made the transition from pop to country-pop. Working with some of the new Nashville writers, like **Paul Davis**, **Bob McDill**, Jennifer Kimball and producer Kyle Lehning, the hits started rolling in: 'My Baby's Got Good Timing' (C&W#2, 1984), 'Meet Me In Montana' (a duet with **Marie Osmond**; C&W#1, 1985), 'Bop' (C&W#1, 1985), 'Everything That Glitters (Is Not Gold)' (C&W#1, 1986), 'You Still Move Me' (C&W#1, 1986), 'I Will Be There' (C&W#1, 1987), 'Three Time Loser' (C&W#1, 1987), 'One Friend' (C&W#1, 1987), 'Addicted' (C&W#1, 1988), 'Big Wheels In The Moonlight' (C&W#1, 1988), 'They Rage On' (C&W#5, 1989), 'Love On Arrival' (C&W#1, 1990) and 'Good Times' (C&W#1, 1990). Although limited in his appeal internationally, his admirers in the US are legion, bolstered no doubt by an intensive touring schedule that ensures that he is on the road for most of the year.

BEST OF DAN SEALS, Capitol (US), 1987
ON ARRIVAL, Capitol (US), 1990
ON THE FRONT LINE, EMI America, 1987
RAGE ON, Capitol (US), 1988
SAN ANTONE, EMI America, 1987
WALKING THE WIRE, Warner Bros. (US), 1992
WON'T BE BLUE ANYMORE, Capitol (US), 1987

SEALS, Troy

Despite several attempts to get his own recording career off the ground, Troy Seals' success has come from his work as a sideman and songwriter. He was born on November 16, 1938, in Big Hill, Kentucky. After learning the guitar, he played with Lonnie Mack until marrying Jo Ann Campbell, with whom he formed a soul duo and cut 'I Found A Love, Oh What A Love', which became a minor hit in 1964. Fed up with the music industry, he worked with building contractors in Indianapolis, until moving to Nashville and writing with **Donnie Fritts** and Will Jennings.

While in Nashville he struck up a friendship with **David Briggs**, who booked him onto sessions; this resulted in regular work in the house band at the Monument Studios, with guitarists Mac Gayden and **Wayne Moss**, drummer **Kenny Buttrey** and bassist Tim Drummond.

During the early 1970s he became one of the most sought-after session musicians in Nashville, playing with artists like **Dobie Gray**, **Waylon Jennings**, **Ray Stevens** and **Brenda Lee**. After cutting some of his own demos for Monument, he joined Atlantic's short-lived Nashville operation, where he recorded Now Presenting Troy Seals. When Atlantic closed its Nashville office, he was signed to Columbia and cut Troy Seals before being dropped.

In recent years he has recorded less under his own name, preferring to work as a writer. Collaborating with Max D. Barnes, he has written hits like 'Don't Take It Away' and 'Red Neckin' Love Makin' Night' (**Conway Twitty**); 'From Seven Till Ten' and 'I Can't Love You Enough' (Conway Twitty and **Loretta Lynn**); 'Who's Gonna Fill Their Shoes' (**George Jones**); 'Drinkin' And Dreamin'' (Waylon Jennings); 'Ten Feet Away' (**Keith Whitley**); and 'There's A Honky Tonk Angel' (co-written with Denny Rice for Conway Twitty).

SEELY, Jeannie

Born in Titusville, Pennsylvania, on July 6, 1940, Jeannie Seely started her career singing on the local radio station in Meadville in 1951, and went on to broadcast on the Midwestern Hayride while at high school. She then studied finance at the American Institute of Banking, but gave up the course and moved to Los Angeles to pursue a career in the entertainment business. She signed with the Four Star music publishing company and recorded for the local Challenge label, until meeting and marrying songwriter **Hank Cochran** who suggested they move to Nashville.

In 1965 she was signed by **Buddy Killen** to his Tree publishing company and introduced to **Fred Foster** at Monument, who gave her a recording contract; here she cut Hank Cochran's 'Don't Touch Me' (1966), 'It's Only Love' (1966), 'A Wanderin' Man' (1967), 'Can I Sleep In Your Arms' (1973) and 'Lucky Ladies' (1974). In 1966, she secured a regular slot on television's **Porter Wagoner** Show, before joining **Jack Greene**'s show in 1969; with Greene she cut the duet, 'I Wish I Didn't Have To Miss You'. In recent years she has continued to make frequent appearances at the Grand Ole Opry and on the Nashville cable television network, but hit records have been elusive.

GREATEST HITS, Monument, 1992

SETTLE, Mike see STEWART, John

SHAVER, Billy Joe

While failing to make waves with his own recording career, Billy Joe Shaver's reputation as one of country's brightest songwriters was secured in 1973, when he wrote almost all the songs on **Waylon Jennings**' Honky Tonk Heroes.

Born in Corsicana, Texas, on September 15, 1941, he moved to Waco, where he was variously employed as a farmhand and a sawmill worker. Desirous of a career as a songwriter, he moved to Nashville, but initially failed to break through and returned to Texas. In 1971 he took another stab at Nashville, and this time he was rewarded by **Bobby Bare** picking up one of his songs to use as a B-side. Bare signed Shaver to his publishing company, Return Music, where Shaver became closely aligned with the Outlaws Movement; his songs also began to find favour with a host of country artists, including **Tom T. Hall**, **Dottie West**, **Jerry Reed**, and **Tex Ritter**.

In 1973, Waylon Jennings cut *Honky Tonk Heroes* and Shaver became a fully-fledged member of the Austin music community, working with luminaries like **Kris Kristofferson** and **Willie Nelson**. Signed by Monument, he cut the Kristofferson-produced *Old Five & Dimers Like Me* (1974), before recording a brace of albums for Capricorn. A regular participant at Nelson's annual picnics, he provided Nelson with 'Willie The Wandering Gypsy And Me' and **John Anderson** with 'I'm Just An Old Chunk Of Coal'.

HELL RAISERS (with Johnny Paycheck), Columbia, 1987

SHELTON BROTHERS

Bob and Joe Attlesey, better known as the Shelton Brothers, were born on a cotton farm in Rylie Springs, Hopkins County, Texas. Coming from a poor family, they began performing professionally to help raise their eight brothers, and made their debut in the Texas oil town of Longview in 1929. Later that year they performed on KGKB, Tyler, before moving on to KWKH, Shreveport, and WWL, New Orleans, where they joined forces with **Lew Childre** and **Curly Fox**.

Initially recording with Victor as the Lone Star Cowboys, they moved to Decca in 1934, where they cut 'Just Because' and 'Deep Elem Blues' and recorded with **Cliff Bruner**. They broadcast on WFAA in Dallas from 1941, and also formed a longstanding relationship with **Jimmie Davis** on KWKH - Joe Shelton becoming Davis's bandleader from 1943 until 1949. In common with many of their contemporaries, they incorporated a comic element into their act - wearing rustic garb and pulling funny faces.

Although most of their repertoire was slanted towards hillbilly material like 'Stay In The Wagon Yard' and 'Who Wouldn't Be Lonely', they also cut jazz and blues numbers, such as 'Matchbox Blues', 'Sittin' On Top Of The World' and 'Knot Hole Blues', which made good use of instrumentalists like fiddler **Johnny Gimble**. Despite the emphatic changes wrought by the arrival of Western Swing, they remained resolutely purist in their approach, forbidding their brother Merle - a rhythm guitarist - from playing bar chords on their music. They retired from the music business in the late 1940s, unable to keep pace with the changing musical climate.

SHENANDOAH

Comprising Marty Raybon (vocals), Jim Seales (guitar), Stan Thorn (keyboards), Ralph Ezell (bass) and Mike McGuire (drums), Shenandoah were known as the MGM Band when they met writer and producer Robert Byrne in 1987. After recording some demos, the group was signed to Columbia and Byrne took them to **Rick Hall**'s Fame Studios in Muscle Shoals, where they changed their name to Shenandoah.

After releasing two singles, they broke into the charts with 'She Doesn't Cry Anymore' (US#9, 1988). Adhering rigidly to the country-pop formula exemplified by bands like **Alabama** and **Restless Heart**, they have succeeded in sustaining an enviable level of consistency with titles like 'Mama Knows' (US#5, 1988), 'The Church On Cumberland Road' (US#1, 1989), 'Sunday In The South' (US#1, 1989), 'Two Dozen Roses' (written by Byrne and Mac MacAnally, who have also written for Alabama, **Ricky Van Shelton** and **T.G. Sheppard**; US#1, 1989), 'Next To You, Next To Me' (C&W#1, 1990) and 'Rock My Baby' (C&W#1, 1992). There seems little doubt that they will continue winning admirers in the US, but the likelihood of them crossing over to international audiences is remote.

LONG TIME COMING, Columbia (US), 1992
THE ROAD NOT TAKEN, Columbia (US), 1988

SHEPARD, Jean

Jean Shepard is one of a group of diehard traditionalists firmly ensconced in the honky-tonk style of country music. Although a successful exponent of that style, the strict limitations imposed upon her music create a sound which is often dated and anachronistic.

She was born in Pauls Valley, Oklahoma, on November 21, 1933. Her career started in the late 1940s as bassist in an all-girl Western Swing outfit called the Melody Ranch Girls, where she came to the attention of **Hank Thompson**. Signed by Capitol in 1953, she was teamed with **Ferlin Husky** for a brace of duets, 'Dear John Letter' and 'Forgive Me John'. In 1955 her solo career picked up momentum with 'Satisfied Mind' and 'Beautiful Lies', prompting a regular slot on *The* **Red Foley** *Show*.

By 1958 she had moved to Nashville and become a frequent guest at the *Grand Ole Opry*. In 1962 she married **Hawkshaw Hawkins**, but the marriage was cut short when Hawkins was killed in the aeroplane crash that claimed the lives of **Patsy Cline** and **Cowboy Copas**. Shepard's popularity curiously rose after Hawkins's death, and a string of hits ensued, including 'Second Fiddle (To An Old Guitar)' (1964), 'Happy Hangovers To You' (1966), 'Then He Touched

Me' (1970), 'Slippin' Away' (1973), and 'At The Time' (1974).

In 1970 she changed labels, signing with United Artists, but the hits decreased as the decade wore on. Her live performances remain as popular as always, drawing substantial audiences both in Europe and the US.

LONESOME LOVE, Stetson, 1988
SONGS OF A LOVE AFFAIR, Stetson, 1987
THIS IS JEAN SHEPARD, Stetson, 1990

SHEPPARD, T.G.

One of the most popular pop-country singers of the 1980s, T.G. Sheppard was born William Browder in Humboldt, Tennessee, on July 20, 1944, and started his first group, the Royal Tones, while still at school. In 1960 he moved to Memphis, where he worked with Travis Wammack's band as a backing singer and guitarist. He impressed the Atlantic label sufficiently to win a solo recording contract under the pseudonym Brian Stacey, but his biggest hit, 'High School Days', wasn't successful enough to stop him from being dropped by the label. With his recording prospects looking bleak, he joined the promotion department of RCA in Memphis, before forming his own promotion and production company, Umbrella.

In 1974 he picked up 'Devil In The Bottle' (C&W#1, 1974) from its writer Bobby David and, failing to place it with anyone else, cut it himself for Tamla Motown's newly established country label, Melodyland. Wishing to avoid a conflict between his promotional activities and his recording career, he adopted the name T.G. Sheppard. Although Sheppard's next single, 'Tryin' To Beat The Morning Home' (C&W#1, 1975), was a great success, Motown closed the doors of its Nashville operation in 1976, and Sheppard had to wait until Warner Bros. bought out his contract in 1977 before making his next release.

Teamed with producer **Buddy Killen** he cut a string of hits that included 'When Can We Do This Again', 'You Feel Good All Over', 'Last Cheater's Waltz' (C&W#1, 1979), 'I'll Be Coming Back For More' (C&W#1, 1980), 'Smooth Sailin'' (C&W#6, 1980), 'Do You Wanna Go To Heaven' (C&W#1, 1980), 'I Feel Like Loving You Again' (C&W#1, 1980), 'I Loved 'Em Every One' (C&W#1, 1981), 'Party Time' (C&W#1, 1981), 'Only One You' (C&W#1, 1982), 'Finally' (C&W#1, 1982), 'War Is Hell (On The Home Front Too)' (C&W#1, 1982) and 'Faking Love' (a duet with **Karen Brooks**; C&W#1, 1982). In 1983, having parted company with

Killen, he worked with Warners' Nashville head honcho, Jim Ed Norman, on 'Slow Burn' (C&W#1, 1983), 'Make My Day' (a duet with Clint Eastwood), 'Somewhere Down The Line', 'One Owner Heart' and 'You're Going Out Of My Mind', before signing with Columbia.

At the end of 1985, Sheppard started to work with producer and long-time friend **Rick Hall**. The liaison bore fruit immediately, with hits like 'Strong Heart' (C&W#1, 1986), 'Half Past Forever ('Til I'm Blue In The Heart)' (C&W#2, 1986), 'You're My First Lady' (C&W#2, 1987) and 'One For The Money' (C&W#1, 1987). Despite his popularity, Sheppard has found time to diversify, investing in a hotel, a Mexican restaurant and a Kansas City nightclub, Guitars & Cadillacs.

FINALLY, Warner Bros. (US), 1982
I LOVE 'EM ALL, Curb, 1981

SHERRILL, Billy

In the late 1950s **Chet Atkins** created the Nashville sound, which incorporated some of the features of contemporary pop into country music, making country acceptable to Top Forty radio programmers whilst preserving its essential features. By the mid-1960s, Atkins had been superseded by Billy Sherrill as the man with his finger on the pulse. Sherrill reverted to some of the more traditional characteristics of country - such as steel guitars and other stringed instruments - but balanced them against lush orchestral arrangements. As chief staff producer at Epic, he brought artists like **Tammy Wynette**, **Tanya Tucker**, **Charlie Rich** and many more into the mainstream of contemporary country. Such was the success of his production style that many singers were able to gain substantial pop hits with overtly country material: 'Stand By Your Man' and 'D-I-V-O-R-C-E' (Tammy Wynette) and 'Behind Closed Doors' (Charlie Rich) being notable examples.

Sherrill was born Philip Campbell on November 5, 1938, in Winston, Alabama. His father was an itinerant preacher and Sherrill played the piano at meetings. By 1955 he had changed his name and joined a local R&B/rockabilly outfit known as Benny Cage and the Rhythm Swingsters, which was later joined by **Rick Hall**. While playing with Cage, Sherrill and Hall formed a white soul band, the Fairlanes, and started to write songs together, which they would take up to music publishers in Nashville; **George Jones** turned one of their songs, 'Aching Breaking Heart', into a modest hit.

In 1957 they met Tom Stafford, a local writer who

managed the Princess cinema in Florence and wanted to form a music publishing company. Stafford had already established a recording studio, which became the mecca for a vast number of young local musicians that had grown up on the indigenous country, gospel and R&B: **Donnie Fritts**, **David Briggs**, **Jerry Carrigan**, **Norbert Putnam**, Roger Hawkins, Jimmy Johnson and Dan Penn.

In 1960 Sherrill moved to Nashville, having been given a job by **Shelby Singleton** at **Sam Phillips**' new Sun Studios, and left Hall to preside over the embryonic Fame Studios. Here Sherrill made his most enduring contributions, producing **Jerry Lee Lewis** and Charlie Rich. When the Sun Studios were closed in 1964, Sherrill was employed by Columbia to produce R&B and gospel artists like Ted Taylor, the Staple Singers and Otis Williams. In 1966, having started to write with **Lynn Anderson**'s husband Glenn Sutton, he was brought in to work with David Houston on 'Almost Persuaded': it became the first of a succession of Sherrill-produced hits for Houston and introduced him to Tammy Wynette.

The three-way partnership of Wynette, Sherrill and Sutton crystallized the new Nashville sound, launching Sherrill into the prestigious position as head of Columbia's Nashville operation. Other artists he worked with there included Charlie Rich (whose career was atrophying until he reforged his links with Sherrill), Tanya Tucker, George Jones, **Marty Robbins**, **Ray Charles**, **Johnny Paycheck** and **Kris Kristofferson**.

In 1977 he engineered a gospel album, *Precious Lord*, for soul singer Al Green, and then, in 1981, he produced **Elvis Costello**'s *Almost Blue*. In recent years, he has been less active, but, like Rick Hall, Jerry Wexler and **Buddy Killen**, he is one of a rare breed of producer who will take on anything that interests him, and therefore can never be written off.

SHOLES, Steve

A key executive figure in the establishment of Nashville as the centre of the country music industry, Steve Sholes was born in Washington, DC, on February 12, 1911. He started to work for RCA in 1929, only severing the relationship to attend college and join the army during the Second World War. After being demobbed in 1945, he became an A&R man with the company and signed a host of artists that included **Jim Reeves**, the **Browns**, **Elvis Presley**, **Chet Atkins** (whom he made his assistant in 1952), **Hank Snow** and **Skeeter Davis**.

Sholes was one of the guiding forces behind the establishment of the Country Music Hall Of Fame in 1961, and was instrumental in raising the funds to build a permanent home for the museum. In recognition of his achievements, he was elected to that august body in 1967, but died of a heart attack in his car on April 22, 1968, while travelling to the airport in Nashville.

SILVERSTEIN, Shel

In a long, distinguished and multifaceted career, Shel Silverstein has contributed some of country music's more eccentric lyrics. He was born in Chicago in 1932 and was initially attracted to jazz and blues. While serving in the US Army during the 1950s he became an illustrator for the army magazine *Stars And Stripes*, and after leaving the army he joined the staff of *Playboy* magazine as a cartoonist, remaining there for fifteen years. With the benefit of this experience, combined with a somewhat sardonic sense of humour, he increasingly turned his attention to songwriting.

In 1967 he released his debut, *Shel Silverstein*, on the Chess label subsidiary Cadet; and in 1969 he wrote 'A Boy Named Sue', which was covered by **Johnny Cash**. This was followed by collaborations with **Dr Hook**, whose first two albums, *Dr Hook And The Medicine Show* (1971) and *Sloppy Seconds* (1972), featured Silverstein compositions like 'Sylvia's Mother', 'The Cover Of *Rolling Stone*', 'Queen Of The Silver Dollar' and 'The Ballad Of Lucy Jordan' (later covered by **Marianne Faithfull**). Among the other artists he collaborated with were **Loretta Lynn** and **Bobby Bare**, the latter cutting an album of his songs entitled *Lullabys, Legends And Lies* in 1974.

He has also pursued a solo career, recording *A Boy Named Sue* for RCA, *Freakin' At The Freaker's Ball* for Columbia, *Inside* for Atlantic and *The Great Conch Train Robbery* for Flying Fish. Other activities have included illustrating children's books and composing the soundtrack for the film *Who Is Harry Kellerman And Why Is He Saying All Those Terrible Things About Me?* (1970).

FREAKIN' AT THE FREAKER'S BALL, Columbia, 1979
THE GREAT CONCH TRAIN ROBBERY, Flying Fish (US), 1989

SINGLETON, Shelby

Shelby Singleton was born in Waskom, Texas, on December 16, 1931. In the mid-1950s he became a promotion man for Mercury and by 1960 had become a producer, collaborating with soul singers Brook Benton and Clyde McPhatter. In 1962 he was promoted to label director of the Mercury subsidiary, Smash, and he appointed session guitarist **Jerry Kennedy** to oversee the Nashville set-up. He went on to become a vice-president of Mercury, having signed artists like **Jerry Lee Lewis**, **Tom T. Hall** and **Charlie Rich**, among others.

In 1966 he resigned to form his own labels: the country label, Plantation, which scored immediately with **Jeannie C. Riley**'s 'Harper Valley P.T.A.' and **Linda Martell**; and the soul specialist labels, Silver Fox and SSS International, which included artists like Johnny Adams, Big Al Downing and Betty LaVette. He simultaneously built up the publishing company Shelby Singleton Music, which has up to thirty writers under contract.

In 1969 he acquired the Sun catalogue and, by the mid-1970s, he had stopped recording country-soul to concentrate upon his publishing interests and to maximize the full potential of the Sun catalogue, which has an inexhaustible fund of Jerry Lee Lewis and **Johnny Cash** masters in its vaults.

SIR DOUGLAS QUINTET see SAHM, Doug

SKAGGS, Ricky

A prodigiously talented multi-instrumentalist, Ricky Skaggs achieved the seemingly impossible feat of adapting traditional features of country music to contemporary demands without any concomitant loss of authenticity. Born in Cordell, eastern Kentucky, on July 18, 1954, he had mastered the mandolin, guitar and fiddle by the age of five, and made his debut in 1961 on **Flatt & Scruggs**' television show. By 1969 he had joined Ralph Stanley's (see **Stanley Brothers**) group, the Clinch Mountain Boys, where he met and joined forces with **Keith Whitley**. In 1971, Skaggs and Whitley cut *Tribute To The Stanley Brothers*, and followed it with *Second Generation* (1972). Going their separate ways, Skaggs went on to play with the **Country Gentlemen** and **J.D. Crowe**, before forming his own bluegrass outfit, Boone Creek, who recorded for Rounder and Sugar Hill until breaking up in 1978.

The following year he made his solo debut for Sugar Hill with *Sweet Temptation*, which was followed by a collaboration with **Emmylou Harris** (as a member of the Hot Band) on *Roses In The Snow* (1980), and then with **Tony Rice** (a colleague from his days with J.D.

Crowe) on *Skaggs & Rice*. In 1981, he was signed by Epic and started a run of hits that included Flatt & Scruggs' 'Crying My Heart Out Over You' (C&W#1, 1982), **Webb Pierce**'s 'I Don't Care' (C&W#1, 1982), **Guy Clark**'s 'Heartbroke' (C&W#1, 1982), 'I Wouldn't Change You If I Could' (C&W#1, 1983), 'Highway 40 Blues' (C&W#1, 1983), 'You've Got A Lover' (C&W#2, 1983), 'Don't Cheat In Our Hometown' (C&W#1, 1983), **Mel Tillis**'s 'Honey (Open That Door)' (C&W#1, 1984), **Bill Monroe**'s 'Uncle Pen' (C&W#1, 1984), 'Something In My Heart' (C&W#2, 1984) and **Albert Lee**'s 'Country Boy' (C&W#1, 1985).

In 1985 he toured the UK, and then went on to release *Live In London*, which included 'You Make Me Feel Like A New Man', 'Cajun Moon' (C&W#1, 1986) and 'I've Got A New Heartache'. Between 1986 and 1989, Skaggs fell victim to a series of personal tragedies - including the shooting of his eight-year-old son, Andrew, by a trigger-happy trucker - but found the resources to produce **Dolly Parton**'s *White Limozeen*, and cut 'Lovin' Only Me' (C&W#1, 1989) and the *Kentucky Thunder* album with **Ricky Van Shelton**'s producer Steve Buckingham.

COMIN' HOME TO STAY, Epic (US), 1988
COUNTRY BOY, Epic, 1984
DON'T CHEAT IN OUR HOME TOWN, Epic, 1983
FAMILY & FRIENDS, Sundown, 1985
HIGHWAYS & HEARTACHES, Epic, 1982
KENTUCKY THUNDER, Epic, 1989
LIVE IN LONDON, Epic, 1986
SECOND GENERATION BLUEGRASS (with Keith Whitley), Rebel, 1975
SKAGGS & RICE (with Tony Rice), Sundown, 1987
SWEET TEMPTATION, Ritz, 1985
THAT'S IT, Sundown, 1986

SKILLET LICKERS

An influential string band with a distinguished cast, the Skillet Lickers were formed by Gid Tanner in 1926 in Atlanta, Georgia. A competent fiddler who often made use of comic routines, Tanner was born James Gideon Tanner on June 6, 1884, in Thomas Bridge, Georgia. After starting his recording career in 1924, Tanner met **Riley Puckett** and they began working together on sessions. In 1926, having been signed by **Frank Walker** at Columbia, the Skillet Lickers came into being when Tanner and Puckett were joined by fiddlers Clayton McMichen (born on January 26, 1900, in Allatoona, Georgia) and Bert Layne and banjoist Fate Norris.

Broadcasting on WSB, their combination of minstrel songs, breakdowns and good-natured banter brought them popular acclaim; their fame spread and the group expanded its membership to include Gid's brother Arthur Tanner (banjo and vocals), **Hugh Cross** (guitar) and fiddler Lowe Stokes. Something of a floating aggregation, key members of the band founded their own spin-off groups, with Clayton McMichen forming the Melody Men and Stokes forming the North Georgians. These two groups contrasted strongly with Tanner's Skillet Lickers by taking a more progressive approach and incorporating jazz tunes into their repertoires.

By 1934 the Skillet Lickers had broken up, with McMichen forming the Georgia Wildcats with guitarist Slim Bryant. In later years **Merle Travis** was a member of the Georgia Wildcats, and McMichen was so widely revered that he was the National Fiddling Champion from 1934 until 1949. His recording career included sessions with **Jimmie Rodgers**, and records under his own name for Columbia, Crown and Decca. He continued playing on radio and television until 1954, when he retired; he died on January 3, 1970, in Battletown, Kentucky.

After the break up of the group, Gid Tanner went on to record with his son Gordon, also a fiddler, Puckett and mandolinist Ted Hawkins, cutting the million-selling 'Down Yonder' for Bluebird. Gid Tanner died on May 13, 1960, and Gordon went on to establish himself as a fiddle-maker. Shortly before his death in 1982, Gordon assembled a new line-up of the Skillet Lickers for some recording sessions for the Folkways label.

HEAR THESE NEW SOUTHERN GUITAR AND FIDDLE RECORDS (Gid Tanner), Rounder (US), 1977
KICKAPOO MEDICINE SHOW (Gid Tanner), Rounder (US), 1988

SMITH, Arthur 'Guitar Boogie'

Arthur Smith was born on April 1, 1921, in Clinton, South Carolina. He came to prominence as a regular contributor to broadcasts on WBT, Charlotte, achieving success with 'Guitar Boogie' (US#25, 1948), which was initially issued on Superdisc and then re-issued in 1947 on MGM. It was a substantial hit and earned him his nickname. In spite of his undoubted expertise, later records for Starday, Dot and Monument failed to match the superiority of 'Guitar Boogie'. He opened his own studios in the 1950s and composed gospel songs.

Smith has more recently come to prominence through the piece 'Duelling Banjos' which appeared in the 1972 film *Deliverance*; performed by Eric Weissberg (see **Greenbriar Boys**) and Steve Mandel, it was based on the **Dan Reno** and Arthur Smith composition 'Feuding Banjos'.

ARTHUR 'GUITAR BOOGIE' SMITH & VOICES, Stetson, 1986
JUMPIN' GUITAR, Relaxed Rabbit, 1988
MISTER GUITAR, Starday (US), 1987

SMITH, Fiddlin' Arthur

An occasional collaborator with **Sam & Kirk McGee**, Fiddlin' Arthur Smith was born in Humphreys County, Tennessee, and started his working life on the railroad. He made his debut on WSM's *Barn Dance* in 1927, and from 1932 regularly broadcast with the McGees. He went on to tour with the **Delmore Brothers** between 1935 and 1936, became a regular contributor to the *Grand Ole Opry*, and worked with the **Shelton Brothers** on KWKH's *Louisiana Hayride* during the early 1940s.

After moving to the West Coast he toured and was filmed with the **Jimmy Wakely** Band until 1947. The 1950s were a fallow period for Smith, and he had to wait until the folk-boom of the early 1960s for his rediscovery, when Mike Seeger (see **New Lost City Ramblers**) organized some sessions, reuniting him with the McGees for the Folkways' album, *The McGee Brothers And Arthur Smith* (1963). He was then drawn into the festival circuit, where sparkling renditions of self-composed tunes, like 'There's More Pretty Girls Than One', 'Red Apple Rag' and 'Beautiful Brown Eyes', were object lessons in fiddling.

SMITH, Cal

Cal Smith was born Calvin Grant Shofner on April 7, 1932, in Gans, Oklahoma. After moving to the West Coast in 1943, he landed a regular spot on television's *California Hayride*, which led to club dates and spells as a DJ. His big break came in 1962, when he was recruited by his mentor **Ernest Tubb** to fill the vocalist and MC vacancy in his band the Texas Troubadours.

He remained with Tubb until 1967, when he was signed to the Kapp label and cut sides such as 'The Only Thing I Want' and 'Heaven Is Just A Touch Away'. In 1971 he moved to the Decca label (of which Kapp was a subsidiary), cutting 'I've Found Someone Of My Own' (C&W#4, 1972), **Bill Anderson**'s 'The Lord Knows I'm Drinking' (C&W#1, 1973), 'Country

Bumpkin' (C&W#1, 1974), 'It's Time To Pay The Fiddler' (C&W#4, 1975), 'She Talked A Lot About Texas' (1975) and 'I Just Came Home To Count The Memories' (1977). Out of the spotlight in recent years, Smith continues to tour throughout the south; his most recent outing was *Stories Of Life* in 1986 for the Step One Label.

SMITH, Carl

A successful exponent of western-style songs and honky-tonk ballads, **Carl Smith** was born on March 15, 1927, in Maynardsville, Tennessee, and worked as a gardener to pay for his first guitar. Having played at local functions and dances, he made his debut on WROL, Knoxville in 1949. He was invited to appear on WSM's morning show in 1950, which provided him with the necessary opening to the *Grand Ole Opry*.

That same year he signed with Columbia, cutting a string of hits that included 'Let's Live A Little' (1950), 'If Teardrops Were Pennies' (1951), 'Mr Moon' (1951), 'Let Old Mother Nature Have Her Way' (C&W#1, 1952), 'Don't Just Stand There' (C&W#1, 1952), 'Are You Teasing Me' (1952), 'Hey Joe' (1953), 'Loose Talk' (1954), 'Kisses Don't Lie' (1955), 'There She Goes' (1955) and 'Ten Thousand Drums' (1959). As his recording career boomed, he made more television appearances on programmes like ABC's *Four Star Jubilee* and his own *Country Music Hall* - the latter was Canadian in origin and widely syndicated throughout the US. He also appeared in low-budget westerns, including *The Badge Of Marshall Brennan* (1957).

In 1974, he signed with **Wesley Rose**'s Hickory label. After his marriage to **June Carter** broke up, he married **Goldie Hill**. His final album *A Way With Words* appeared in 1977, after which he left the music industry in 1977 to concentrate on running his six-hundred-dred acre ranch.

GREATEST HITS, Gusto (US), 1980
OLD LONESOME TIMES, Rounder (US), 1988

SMITH, Connie

Connie Smith was born on August 14, 1941, in Elkhart, Indiana, one of sixteen children. She learnt the guitar during a spell in hospital, and performed at local church events and parent-teacher functions throughout her adolescence. After her marriage, she continued to perform until being discovered in 1963

by **Bill Anderson**, who secured her a contract with RCA. Her debut, 'Once A Day' (C&W#1, 1964), written by Anderson, catapulted her to stardom. She made her television debut on *The **Little Jimmy Dickens** Show* and joined the *Grand Ole Opry* the following year.

Over the next ten years, she notched up one hit after another: 'Then And Only Then', 'Tiny Blue Transistor Radio' and 'I Can't Remember' (1965); 'Ain't Had No Lovin'' and 'The Hurtin's All Over' (1966); 'Burning A Hole In My Mind' (1967); 'I Never Once Stopped Loving You' (1970); 'Just One Time' (1971); 'If It Ain't Love' and 'Just For What I Am' (1972); 'Love Is What You're Looking For' (1973); and 'I Don't Wanna Talk About It' (1976).

Having recorded extensively for RCA, she moved to Columbia where she cut mainly gospel records. Despite having recorded little in recent years, Connie Smith maintains a steady touring schedule - travelling the world and promoting the gospel - and retains solid popularity with those who share her intense religious convictions.

GREATEST HITS, Monument, 1992
TWENTY OF THE BEST, RCA International, 1985
WHERE IS MY CASTLE?, Stetson, 1989

SMITH, Margo

Born Betty Lou Smith on April 9, 1942, in Dayton, Ohio, Margo Smith was adopted by an uncle and aunt in 1944. After leaving school she went to college to study for a degree in teaching. On graduation she began teaching in a kindergarten, where her interest in music proved to be a bonus for her classes and encouraged her to pursue a career in the music industry.

Adopting the name Margo Smith, she was signed to the 20th Century label, where she scored with her first single, 'There I Said It' (1975), the beginning of a brief spell of stardom. The following year she signed with Warner Bros. and notched up a number of hits with titles like 'Don't Break The Heart That Loves You' (C&W#1, 1978), 'Little Things Mean A Lot' (C&W#3, 1978), 'It Only Hurts For A While' (C&W#1, 1978), 'Still A Woman' (1979) and 'If I Give My Heart To You' (1979).

In 1982 she moved to Nashville, toured regularly and recorded for independent labels, before signing with MCA in 1986 and cutting *The Best Of The Tennessee Yodeller* (1987). The following year, she started a leisure-wear company and reduced her touring schedule. She remains one the few country singers to draw upon the older traditions of the genre, incorporating dying arts such as yodelling in her performances.

THE BEST OF THE TENNESSEE YODELLER, MCA (US), 1987
MARGO SMITH, MCA (US), 1986

SMITH, Sammi

Sammi Smith achieved some kudos as a crossover artist in the early 1970s with her rendition of **Kris Kristofferson**'s 'Help Me Make It Through The Night'. Though she was unable to sustain this early success, she has subsequently worked with artists like **Waylon Jennings** and **Willie Nelson.**

She was born in Orange County, California, on August 5, 1943, and grew up in Oklahoma, where she started playing the club circuit at the age of twelve. Encouraged by Gene Sullivan, who owned a recording studio in Oklahoma, she moved to Nashville and was signed by Columbia, where she cut titles like 'So Long Charlie Brown' and 'Brownsville Lumberyard'.

In 1970 she moved to the independent Mega label, recording songs like 'He's Everywhere', 'Help Me Make It Through The Night' (US#8, C&W#1, 1971), 'Then You Walk In' (1971) and **Merle Haggard**'s 'Today I Started Loving You Again' (1975). Latterly, she has been less active in the studio, but has continued to forge a career on the Texas club circuit.

SMITH, Warren

A distinguished rockabilly artist, Warren Smith failed to achieve the international renown of many of his contemporaries. His most important sides for Sun, cut during the 1950s, remain some of the toughest examples of rockabilly, and illustrate the extent of its derivation from country.

Born in Louise, West Memphis, on February 7, 1932, he moved to Memphis in 1953 after leaving the Air Force, and started to sing with Clyde Leoppard's Snearly Ranch Boys at West Memphis's Cotton Club. Spotted at the Cotton Club by **Sam Phillips**, he made some recordings for the Sun label. After cutting the local hit 'Rock 'n' Roll Ruby' (1956), he went on to record other tracks which remained unreleased for several years, followed by 'Black Jack David', 'Ubangi Stomp' and his biggest hit, 'So Long, I'm Gone'.

In 1959, he left Sun and started label-hopping, moving from Liberty to Mercury to Skill to Jubal, before leaving the music industry to work for a heating company in Longview, Texas. In 1976, he cut *The Legendary Warren Smith* for the independent Lake County label, before going on a brief tour of the UK with other rockabilly artists like **Charlie Feathers** and Sleepy LaBeef. He died of a heart attack on January 30, 1980.

CALL OF THE WILD, Bear Family (Germany), 1990
THE LAST DETAIL, Charly, 1981
REAL MEMPHIS ROCK 'N' ROLL, Charly, 1988
SO LONG I'M GONE, Charly, 1987
WARREN SMITH, Sun, 1990

SNOW, Hank

Hank Snow is one of the longest–established country artists in the music business. While his recent disenchantment with the commercialism of country music sounds rather hollow (given his popularization of gaudy western outfits in the 1930s), he is an original, who has managed to straddle the fine line between out-and-out commercialism and authentic traditional styles.

Born Clarence Eugene Snow on May 9, 1914, in Liverpool, Nova Scotia, Canada, he left home in 1926 to enter the merchant navy. After four years of service, he returned to Nova Scotia to play the club circuit, which resulted in his own radio programme on CHNS, Halifax. Signed to Bluebird in 1936 - where he was known as Hank the Yodelling Ranger - he moved to the US in 1944, where he was signed by RCA and known as the Singing Ranger. In spite of the approval of artists like **Ernest Tubb**, and of broadcasts on WWVA's *Wheeling Jamboree* and the *Grand Ole Opry*, Snow initially failed to penetrate the cliquey country-music scene.

Following the release of 'Marriage Vow' in 1949, Snow found a home on Dallas's *Big D Jamboree*, was taken to the bosom of the *Opry*, and recorded strings of hits that lasted well into the 1970s. These included 'I'm Moving On' (C&W#1, 1950), 'Golden Rocket' (C&W#1, 1950), 'Rhumba Boogie' (C&W#1, 1951), 'I Don't Hurt Anymore' (C&W#1, 1954), 'Let Me Go, Lover' (C&W#1, 1955), 'I've Been Everywhere' (C&W#1, 1962) and 'Hello Love' (C&W#1, 1974).

He has cut over a hundred albums - many with **Chet Atkins** - and has been instrumental in keeping alive the memory of his hero **Jimmie Rodgers** by recording innumerable tributes to him. He was elected to the Country Music Hall Of Fame in 1979, and stopped recording for RCA in 1986. He stills makes intermittent appearances at the *Grand Ole Opry*.

COUNTRY MUSIC HALL OF FAME, RCA, 1981
DIAMOND SERIES, RCA, 1988
THE SWINGING RANGER, Bear Family (Germany), 1990
THE SWINGING RANGER: I'M MOVING ON, Bear Family (Germany), 1988

SONS OF PIONEERS

The Sons Of Pioneers remain one of the finest vocal-harmony groups in the history of country, their treatment of western songs and ballads inspiring other performers, like **Johnny Bond**, **Marty Robbins** and **Jimmy Wakely**, to draw from their extensive repertoire.

The group was formed in 1933 in Los Angeles by Leonard Slye, Bob Nolan (guitar and vocals; born Robert Clarence Nobles on April 1, 1908, in New Brunswick, Canada) and Tim Spencer (banjo; born Vernon Spencer on July 13, 1908, in Webb City, Missouri). All three had worked together in the Rocky Mountaineers and were contemporaries of the Beverly Hillbillies (see **Manners, Zeke**), making their first broadcasts on KFWB, Hollywood, as the Pioneer Trio. In 1934 fiddler Hugh Farr (born Thomas Hubert Farr on December 6, 1903, in Llano, Texas) joined the group and they became the Sons Of Pioneers.

Starting a recording career with Decca, they cut tuneful ditties like 'Tumbling Tumbleweeds', which featured the precise harmonizing that would later win them so many appearances in movies. In 1935 they added Hugh's brother Karl (guitar; born Karl Marx Farr on April 25, 1909, in Rochelle, Texas; died on September 20, 1961, in West Springfield, Massachusetts) and made their first movie appearance in *The Old Homestead*. The following year they worked in a couple of **Gene Autry** movies and with Bing Crosby in *Rhythm Of The Range*. In 1937, having added vocalist Lloyd Perryman (born on January 29, 1917, in Ruth, Arkansas; died on May 31, 1977, in California), Slye became **Roy Rogers**, and was replaced by bassist Pat Brady (born Robert Ellsworth O'Brady on December 31, 1914, in Toledo, Ohio; died on February 27, 1972, in Colorado Springs).

By 1940 the group had started to tour and to broadcast from Chicago, stimulating a demand for songs like 'Cool Water'. When the US joined the war effort, both Brady and Perryman joined the army, to be replaced by Ken Carson (born Hubert Kenneth Carson in Colgate, Oklahoma) and bassist/comedian Shug Fisher (born George Clinton Fisher on September 26, 1907, in Chickasha, Oklahoma). They re-formed after the war and signed with RCA, re-recording their most popular hits, 'Tumbling Tumbleweeds' and 'Cool Water'.

In 1949, the group had its final significant hit with 'Room Full Of Roses', and both Nolan and Spencer left the group. Nolan, after managing the group until 1955, continued to work as a songwriter until his death on June 15, 1980, and Spencer died on April 26, 1974 in Apple Valley, California. Their respective replacements were Ken Curtis (born Curtis Wayne Gates on July 2, 1916, in Lamar, Colorado) and Spike Doss (born Lloyd Thomas Doss on September 26, 1920, in Weiser, Idaho).

The new group was used by film director John Ford in a clutch of John Wayne movies, including *Wagon Master* (1950), *Rio Grande* (1950) and *The Searchers* (1956). In 1953, Curtis left to join the cast of the television series *Gunsmoke* as 'Festus', and his replacement was Dale Warren (born on June 1, 1925, in Summerville, Kentucky). In 1954 they were signed by the Coral label, before returning to RCA, where they remained until 1975. During those years they cut innumerable albums, embracing all styles from country to gospel.

The line-up became increasingly volatile, the most notable additions being guitarist Roy Lanham and fiddler Wade Ray. Older former members rejoined during the 1960s, to tour and to appear on television. They have become the most durable western group of their generation.

COOL WATER: 1945-6, Bear Family (Germany), 1987
COWBOY COUNTRY, Bear Family (Germany), 1984
HUNDRED & SIXTY ACRES: 1945-46, Bear Family (Germany), 1987
LAND BEYOND THE SUN: 1949-50, Bear Family (Germany), 1987
RADIO TRANSCRIPTIONS, Volume 1-4, Outlaw, 1987
RIDERS IN THE SKY: 1947-49, Bear Family (Germany), 1987
SONS OF PIONEERS & FRIENDS: 1950-51, Bear Family (Germany), 1987
TEARDROPS IN MY HEART: 1946-47, Bear Family (Germany), 1987
THERE'S A GOLDMINE: 1951-52, Bear Family (Germany), 1987

SOUTH, Joe

Joe South was born on February 28, 1940, in Atlanta, Georgia. A proficient guitarist by the age of eleven, he joined up with **Pete Drake** in 1958 for the minor novelty hit 'The Purple-People Eater Meets The Witch Doctor', a take-off of **Sheb Wooley**'s 'The Purple-

People Eater'. After becoming a DJ, he continued to record intermittently as a session musician until meeting up with Bill Lowery, who was beginning to assemble a roster of R&B artists, such as the Tams and Tommy Roe. With Lowery, he began to develop his writing skills, penning 'What Kind Of Fool (Do You Think I Am)' and 'Untie Me' for the Tams.

In 1965 he began work with fellow Atlantan Billy Joe Royal, who recorded some of South's songs and had hits with 'Down In The Boondocks', 'I Knew You When', 'I've Got To Be Somebody' and 'Hush'. As his reputation grew, South was enlisted for session work by **Bob Dylan**, **Marty Robbins**, **Eddy Arnold**, Simon & Garfunkel and Aretha Franklin, among others, and, in 1968, he signed a contract with Capitol as a solo artist. His 1969 album *Introspect* remains a fine example of country-soul, and included 'Games People Play' (US#12, UK#6, 1969), 'Rose Garden' (later covered by **Lynn Anderson** and **Elvis Presley**) and 'These Are Not My People' (a modest hit for **Freddy Weller**).

The follow-up, *Don't It Make You Want To Go Home?*, included 'Walk A Mile In My Shoes' (US#12, 1970), and the title track was covered by R&B vocalist Brook Benton. After cutting *So The Seeds Are Growing* (1971), his brother Tommy died; South retired and moved to Hawaii, where he stayed until 1975. On his return, he recorded *Midnight Rainbows* (1975) and *To Have, To Hold And To Let Go* (1976) for the Island label, backed by various members of the Atlanta Rhythm Section. Discouraged by the failure of both of these albums, he has languished in obscurity since.

INTROSPECT, See For Miles, 1986

SOVINE, Red

Red Sovine and **Dave Dudley** have both become widely regarded as the arch-exponents of truckers' songs. Adhering to the spoken narrative, Sovine imbued his songs with a degree of pathos lacking in Dudley's melodic format.

He was born Woodrow Wilson Sovine in Charleston, West Virginia, on July 17, 1918, and started to play the guitar in his childhood. He made his radio debut on WCHS, Charleston in 1935 as a member of Jim Pike's Carolina Tar Heels, before joining WWVA's *Wheeling Jamboree*, where he played with Johnny Bailes of the **Bailes Brothers**. After leaving the Carolina Tar Heels, he formed the Echo Valley Boys, who were given their own show on WCHS. In 1949, they moved over to join the regular cast of the *Louisiana Hayride*, filling the position vacated by **Hank Williams**.

He stayed with the *Hayride* for five years, recording for Starday and forming a friendship with **Webb Pierce**; together they cut duets including 'Why Baby Why' (C&W#1, 1956) and 'Little Rosa'. In 1964, after several years of comparative obscurity, he hit the top with 'Giddy Up Go' (C&W#1, 1965), which was followed by 'Phantom 309' (C&W#9, 1967) and the appalling 'Teddy Bear' (US#40, C&W#1, 1976; UK#4, 1981).

While **C.W. McCall** paved the way for the national popularity of CB radios with 'Convoy', Sovine helped to consolidate that appeal. He died on April 4, 1980, of injuries sustained in a car crash.

BEST OF RED SOVINE, Starday (US), 1987
CLASSIC NARRATIONS, Starday (US), 1987
GREATEST HITS, Starday (US), 1987
THE ONE AND ONLY, Official, 1989
SUPER COLLECTION, Starday (US), 1988
TEDDY BEAR, Starday (US), 1980

SPEARS, Billy Jo

A somewhat middle-of-the-road performer, Billy Jo Spears has always sustained a much larger audience in the UK than in her native US. She was born in Beaumont, Texas, on January 14, 1938. After graduating from high school she worked in a variety of jobs, until prompted to visit Nashville by songwriter Jack Rhodes in 1964. Here she auditioned for producer Larry Butler, who signed her to United Artists. Moving quickly on to Capitol, she had her first hit with 'He's Got More Love In His Little Finger', followed by 'Mr Walker It's All Over' (C&W#4, 1969) and 'Marty Gray'.

A hiatus ensued, until she re-signed with United Artists in 1974 and recorded a string of hits that included 'Blanket On The Ground' (C&W#1, UK#6, 1975), 'What I've Got In Mind' (C&W#5, UK#4, 1976), 'Sing Me An Old Fashioned Song' (UK#34, 1976), 'Silver Wings And Golden Rings', 'Misty Blue', 'On The Rebound' (a duet with **Del Reeves**) and 'I Will Survive' (UK#4, 1979).

In 1981 she left United Artists, and recorded for different labels like Premier and Ritz, both of which focused on her European popularity. Recording little of late, her personal appearances remain as popular as ever.

BILLIE JOE SPEARS, Ritz, 1983
COUNTRY COLLECTION, Knight, 1990
IT COULD HAVE BEEN ME, Castle, 1986

STAMPLEY, Joe

Joe Stampley was one of the beneficiaries of a group of labels set up by the Shreveport entrepreneur Stan Lewis, who, noting the success of KWKH's *Louisiana Hayride*, set up the Ronn, Paula and Jewel labels. While Jewel concentrated on bluesmen like Lowell Fulson and Lightnin' Hopkins, and Ronn signed R&B/soul acts like Ted Taylor and Toussaint McCall, Paula signed pop acts like John Fred and his Playboys and Joe Stampley and the Uniques.

Stampley was born in Springhill, Louisiana, on June 6, 1943. Inspired by **Jerry Lee Lewis** and the **Everly Brothers**, Stampley recorded for the Chess label before forming the Uniques, who had minor hits with 'Not Too Long Ago' and 'All These Things'. While working with the Uniques, he started a solo career, recording for the Dot label; in 1971 he had his first country hit with 'Takes Time To Know Her'; this was followed by 'If You Touch Me (You've Got To Love Me)', 'Soul Song' (US#37, C&W#1, 1972) and 'All These Things' (C&W#1, 1976), among others.

In 1975 he moved to the Epic label, retaining the services of producer Norro Wilson, and scored with 'Roll On Big Mama' (C&W#1, 1975); 'Red Wine And Blue Memories', 'If You've Got Ten Minutes (Let's Fall In Love)' and 'Do You Ever Fool Around' (1978); 'Just Good Ol' Boys' (a duet with **Moe Bandy**; C&W#1, 1979); 'Put Your Clothes Back On' (1979); 'I'm Gonna Love You Back To Loving Me Again' (1981); and 'Double Shot' (1984). Despite the paucity of recent hits, he remains firmly ensconced on the club and cabaret circuit.

GREATEST HITS, Astan (US), 1984
JOE STAMPLEY, Audio Fidelity (US), 1984

STANLEY BROTHERS

The **Stanley Brothers** occupy a special niche in the development of bluegrass that ranks them alongside other great originals like **Bill Monroe** and **Flatt & Scruggs**. Like Monroe and Flatt & Scruggs, they too provided a vital training-ground for many young performers who later achieved international recognition. Their repertoire has been a vital source of material and inspiration for artists like **Emmylou Harris**, **Chris Hillman**, **J.D. Crowe** and **Quicksilver**.

Carter Glen was born on August 27, 1925, in McClure, Virginia, and Ralph was born on February 25, 1927, in Stratton, Virginia. After being taught the rudiments of the guitar and banjo, they were raised against the austere backdrop of the Baptist church, where they received formal voice training - their magnificent use of harmony was to set them apart throughout their career. After finishing their stints in the army in 1946, they became professional musicians with Roy Sykes & the Blue Ridge Mountain Boys, but left shortly after, taking mandolinist Pee Wee Lambert with them to form the Clinch Mountain Boys.

They secured a regular slot on WNVA, Norton, Virginia, before moving to WCYB, Bristol, on *The Farm And Fun Time Show*. They cut their first sides for a local label, and recorded titles such as 'Man Of Constant Sorrow', 'Little Glass Of Wine' and 'Molly And Tenbrooks'. In 1949 they moved to WPTF, Raleigh, and were signed by **Art Satherley** to Columbia; they stayed with Columbia for three years, during which time they recorded songs including 'A Vision Of Mother', 'Lonesome River', 'The Fields Have Turned To Brown' and 'The White Dove'. They were never as inventive as Flatt & Scruggs, but Carter Glen's vocal talents emphasized his maturity as a songwriter: his mournful tones evoked the splendour of the rolling hills of Virginia and images of childhood desolation.

After leaving Columbia, they were signed by Mercury, where Ralph's high tenor and the propulsive prowess of bassist George Shuffler came into their own. These Mercury sides established their impeccable bluegrass credentials, but the emergence of rock 'n' roll militated against their acceptance on a national scale. In 1958 they left Mercury to record for Starday, and moved to Florida, from where they toured and broadcast on various radio stations.

During the 1960s they recorded for the King label, cutting tracks including 'How Mountain Girls Can Love' and 'Clinch Mountain Backstep', and then started to work the international folk festival circuit. In 1966 they appeared at London's Royal Albert Hall, but on December 1, 1966, the rigours of constant touring finally took their toll and Carter Glen died.

The following year Ralph started to reorganize the line-up with a string of young musicians, including the Ohio-born guitarist Larry Sparks, Kentuckian Roy Lee Centers (who was murdered on May 2, 1974), **Ricky Skaggs** and **Keith Whitley**. They all contributed to the group's high standing the during the 1970s, and did much to endow bluegrass with its contemporary appeal. Throughout the 1980s and 1990s, Ralph continued to lead different incarnations of the Clinch Mountain Boys while touring and recording for the independent Rebel label.

BANJO IN THE HILLS, King (US), 1987
BEST OF THE STANLEY BROTHERS, Starday (US), 1987

BLUEGRASS ORIGINALS, Starday (US), 1987
LIVE IN JAPAN (Ralph Stanley), Rebel, 1987
SONGS THEY LIKE THE BEST, King (US), 1987
STANLEY BROTHERS, Volumes 1-2, Rounder (US), 1988
STANLEY BROTHERS & THE CLINCH MOUNTAIN BOYS, King (US), 1987
STANLEY BROTHERS SING BLUEGRASS FOR YOU, Old Homestead (US), 1987
STANLEY SOUND TODAY (Ralph Stanley), Rebel, 1987

STANTON, Harry Dean

Thought by many to be the most interesting country music prospect never to make an album, actor Harry Dean Stanton has contributed to some of the most thought-provoking movies of the last twenty years. Born on July 14, 1926, in Kentucky, he attended the State University.

After many years in the actors' wilderness, he came to prominence co-starring with **Kris Kristofferson** in *Cisco Pike* (1971) and *Pat Garrett And Billy The Kid* (also starring **Bob Dylan**; 1973). His enigmatic persona went on to grace dozens of films, including *Dillinger* (1973), *Missouri Breaks* (1976), *Alien* (1979), *Wise Blood* (1980), *One From The Heart* (1982), *Paris, Texas* (1984), *Repo Man* (1984), *The Last Temptation Of Christ* (1988) and *Wild At Heart* (1990).

His musical dalliances have been sporadic, performing on the Los Angeles radio station KCRW and opening for **k.d. lang** in an early San Francisco gig. He contributed a verse in Spanish to 'Borderline' on **Ry Cooder**'s *Get Rhythm* album, and has appeared with Cooder in concert, most notably at London's Wembley Arena. He is known for his haunting renditions of Mexican folk songs, one of which can be heard on the Cooder-composed soundtrack album to *Paris, Texas*.

STATLER BROTHERS

The Statler Brothers reigned supreme throughout the mid-1970s as the most popular male vocal group in country music. They were formed as the gospel trio the Kingsmen by Lew DeWitt (born in Roanoke, Virginia, on March 8, 1938), Philip Balsley (born in Augusta County, Virginia, on August 8, 1939) and Harold Reid (born in Augusta County, Virginia, on August 21, 1939) in Lyndhurst Methodist Church in Staunton in 1955. By 1960, Harold's brother Don (born in Staunton, Virginia, on June 5, 1945) had joined the group as lead vocalist. Three years later, they joined the **Johnny Cash** roadshow as the Statler Brothers, which led to a contract with Columbia recording under their own name and as backing vocalists for Cash.

Continuing to tour with Cash, they had their first hit with 'Flowers On The Wall' (US#4, C&W#2, 1965), which was followed by other lesser hits like 'Ruthless' and 'You Can't Have Your Kate and Edith Too' (1967). In 1970 they were signed to Mercury by producer **Jerry Kennedy**, and they started to string together a number of hits, such as 'Do You Remember These' (C&W#2, 1972), 'I'll Go To My Grave Loving You' (C&W#3, 1975), 'Do You Know You Are My Sunshine' (C&W#1, 1978) and 'How To Be A Country Star'.

By 1982, co-founder member Lew DeWitt, who was suffering from Crohn's disease, was compelled to leave the group: he died on August 15, 1990, in Waynesboro, Virginia. His replacement was Jimmy Fortune, who was to become one of the group's principal songwriters. The group continued notching up hits with songs like 'Whatever', 'Elizabeth' (C&W#1, 1984), 'My Only Love' (C&W#1, 1985) and 'Too Much On My Heart' (C&W#1, 1985).

In recent years, they have been partially eclipsed by the **Oak Ridge Boys**, but they have retained the purism and authenticity of their gospel roots.

BEST OF THE STATLER BROTHERS, Volume 2, Mercury (US), 1988
FOUR FOR THE SHOW, Mercury, 1986
MAPLE STREET MEMORIES, Mercury, 1987
PARDNERS IN RHYME, Mercury, 1985
STATLER BROTHERS, Country Store, 1988
TODAY, Mercury, 1983

STEAGALL, Red

A staunch devotee of Western Swing and the music of **Bob Wills**, Russell 'Red' Steagall was born in Gainsville, Texas. During his youth his left arm was crippled by polio, but after intensive physiotherapy he regained almost total control of it and learnt to play the guitar. On leaving school he attended West Texas State University, where he studied animal husbandry and played the local bars and clubs.

His first job after graduation was at an oil company as a soil analyst, but in 1967 **Ray Charles** covered Steagall's 'Here We Go Again', and Steagall took to the open road with his group, the Coleman County Cowboys, playing at rodeos, bars and dance halls. In 1969 he obtained a recording contract with the Dot label, but went on to join Capitol, where he cut a number of modest hits: 'Party Dolls And Wine',

'Somewhere My Love', 'Someone Cares For You' and 'If You've Got The Time, I've Got The Song'.

In 1976 he rejoined Dot and had immediate hits with 'Lonestar Beer And Bob Wills Music' and 'Texas Red'. Despite having slipped out of the public eye, he remains one of Wills's greatest champions and continues to tour throughout the southwest, particularly on the rodeo circuit.

COWBOY FAVOURITES, Delta, 1985

STEWART, Gary

A forerunner of New Country artists such as **Steve Earle**, Gary Stewart has the capacity to be one of the most important songwriters in Nashville. He was born the son of a coal miner in Letcher County, Kentucky, on May 28, 1944, one of nine children. In 1956 the family moved to Fort Pierce, Florida, and by 1960 he had started his career in the music industry. He made his recording debut in 1964 with 'I Love You Truly' for the local Cory label, and was later spotted by **Mel Tillis** at the Wagon Wheel in Okeechobee. Tillis advised him to move to Nashville and pursue a songwriting career.

After working the club and bar circuit in Nashville, he was signed by Jerry Bradley to the Forrest Hills Publishing Company in 1970. This move resulted in his compositions being covered by **Nat Stuckey**, **Kenny Price**, **Jack Greene**, **Warner Mack**, **Hank Snow** and **Billy Walker**; he also landed a job as pianist in **Charley Pride**'s band. The following year, he cut some demos of country versions of Motown classics before returning to Florida. Roy Dea at RCA heard the demos and encouraged Stewart to return to Nashville. Over the next five years he had a string of hits, including a reworking of the Allman Brothers' 'Ramblin' Man' (1973), 'Drinking Thing' (C&W#10, 1974), 'Out Of Hand' (C&W#4, 1975), 'She's Acting Single (I'm Drinking Doubles)' (C&W#1, 1975), 'In Some Room Above The Street' (1976) and 'Your Place Or Mine' (1978).

By the end of the 1970s his career had hit a stormy patch, which was exacerbated by a brief flirtation with drugs and a refusal to knuckle under and embrace Nashville's star-making machinery. In the early 1980s, he collaborated with songwriter Dean Dillon and scored minor hits with 'Brotherly Love' and 'Smokin' In The Rockies'. While Dillon went on to achieve wider distinction in Nashville, Stewart resolutely stuck to the bar circuit, where his observant honky-tonk-style vignettes, detailing the seamier side of life, were in

their element. In 1988, he was signed by the Hightone label and cut *Brand New*. More recently, he returned to the obscurity of the club circuit.

TWENTY OF THE BEST, RCA, 1984

STEWART, John

The songs of John Stewart evoke pastoral images of an America that has now gone forever, and perhaps was only ever there in the imaginations of writers and movie-makers: there is the unmistakeable whiff of the woodsmoke and wide-open spaces in his early work.

He was born on September 5, 1939, in San Diego, California. After completing school, he flirted briefly with rock 'n' roll in a group called the Furies, before turning his attention in 1958 towards songwriting and folk music (which was undergoing something of a renaissance). Compositions like 'Molly Dee' and 'Green Grasses' were immediately picked up and covered by the Kingston Trio, while Stewart formed the Cumberland Three with John Montgomery and Mike Settle (born on March 20, 1941). The Cumberland Three recorded three albums for the Roulette label, before Stewart went on to replace Dave Guard in the Kingston Trio; Settle joined the New Christy Minstrels, before leaving to form the First Edition with **Kenny Rogers** in 1968.

Stewart remained with the Kingston Trio until 1967; he then planned to work with John Phillips of The Mamas And The Papas, but ended up cutting demos of his songs with **John Denver**. His first big hit came in 1967 when the Monkees covered 'Daydream Believer'; this prompted him to launch a solo career, teaming first with Buffy Ford for the Capitol album *Signals Through The Glass* and then with producer Nik Venet and Mike Settle for *California Bloodlines* (1969) and *Willard* (1970): fine records, but commercial turkeys.

His next outing was the splendid *The Lonesome Picker Rides Again* for Warner Bros., which included a sparse and languorous version of 'Daydream Believer'. Dropped by Warner Bros., he signed with RCA in 1973, cutting *Cannons In The Rain* (1973), *Wingless Angels* (1974) and *The Phoenix Concerts* (1974). Another gap ensued, until his return in 1979 with the almost commercial *Bombs Away Dream Babies* for the RSO label; this featured contributions from Stevie Nicks and Lindsay Buckingham of Fleetwood Mac, and included three hit singles: 'Gold' (US#5, UK#43, 1979) and 'Midnight Wind' (US#28,

1979), both of which were duets with Nicks, and 'Lost Her In The Sun' (US#34, 1980).

Throughout the 1980s, he recorded for a variety of independent labels without achieving any great degree of success, but 1987's *Punch The Big Guy*, featuring a duet with **Nanci Griffith**, showed that he could still cut the mustard. In 1992 he re-emerged with *Bullet In The Hour Glass* for the Shanachie label.

AMERICAN ORIGINALS, Capitol (US), 1993
BLONDES, Line (Germany), 1990
BULLET IN THE HOUR GLASS, Shanachie, 1992
CALIFORNIA BLOODLINES/WILLARD, Bear Family (Germany), 1989
CANNONS IN THE RAIN/WINGLESS ANGELS, Bear Family (Germany), 1989
THE LONESOME PICKER RIDES AGAIN, Linea, 1990
THE PHOENIX CONCERTS, RCA (Germany), 1989
SUNSTORM, Linea, 1990
TRANCAS, Sunstorm, 1984

STEWART, Redd

Born Henry Redd Stewart on May 27, 1921, in Ashland, Tennessee, Redd Stewart started to write in 1935, when he penned a jingle for a local car showroom. After playing in various local bands, he was recruited by **Pee Wee King** as a pianist in 1937. In 1938, Stewart became King's vocalist (after **Eddy Arnold** had left to pursue a solo career), and also started to write with King. Apart from the 'Tennessee Waltz', they composed such monsters as 'Slow Poke' and 'You Belong To Me', while Stewart himself composed 'A Soldier's Last Letter' (covered by **Ernest Tubb**), and re-arranged the old standard, 'Bonaparte's Retreat'.

'Tennessee Waltz' has been adopted as the State Anthem, has been covered by countless people, including Patti Page, whose version reputedly sold in excess of six million, and **Lacy J. Dalton**, and was partially responsible for establishing its publishers, **Acuff-Rose**, as one of the largest and most lucrative operations in the business.

STEWART, Wynn

Wynn Stewart was one of the first country singers and songwriters to settle in Bakersfield, thereby instigating the California-based country circuit. He gave **Merle Haggard** his first big break by employing him as a bassist in his band.

He was born in Morrisville, Missouri, on June 7,

1934, and made his debut as a five-year-old in his local church. In 1947, he made his first broadcasts on KWTO, Springfield, Missouri; two years later he moved to the West Coast with his family. Initially signed by Capitol, he moved to Jackpot, a subsidiary of Challenge, where he scored hits with 'Wishful Thinking' (1959), 'Big Big Day' (1961) and 'Another Day Another Dollar' (1962). It was during this period that **Buck Owens** covered Stewart's composition 'Above And Beyond', while Stewart established the Nashville Nevada Club in Las Vegas and was given his own television show.

During the mid-1960s, he returned to California and re-signed with Capitol, scoring with a number of honky-tonk ballads like 'It's Such A Pretty World Today' (C&W#1, 1967), "Cause I Have You' (1967), 'Love's Gonna Happen To Me' (1967), 'Something Pretty' (1968), 'In Love' (1968), 'World Wide Travellin' Man' (1969), 'It's A Beautiful Day' (1970) and 'After The Storm' (1976). Less active in his later years, he was preparing for a comeback tour when he died of a heart attack on July 17, 1985, in Hendersonville, Tennessee.

THE CHALLENGE YEARS: 1958-63, Bear Family (Germany), 1988
THE SONGS OF WS, Stetson, 1989

STONE, Cliffie

Best known for guiding the career of **Tennessee Ernie Ford**, Cliffie Stone was born Clifford Gilpin Snyder on March 1, 1917, and brought up by a professional banjo-playing father. After leaving school, Stone joined Freddy Slack's Orchestra as bassist before joining the *Hollywood Barn Dance* as an announcer, and then moving over to KXLA, Pasadena, where he had a daily variety show, *Dinner Bell Roundup*.

After the formation of the Capitol label in 1946, Stone joined as an A&R man, meeting up with Ford and taking over as his manager. Stone stayed with Capitol for over twenty years, becoming a recording artist in his own right and cutting a number of albums, featuring compositions written with **Merle Travis**, including 'No Vacancy'.

Despite his executive role, he continued broadcasting on *Hometown Jamboree* from Legion Stadium, El Monte, California; but by the 1960s he was spending most of his time running his publishing company, Central Songs, which he sold to Capitol in 1969. His activities have been reduced somewhat since the death of Ford in 1991, but he continues to run the Granite label which he set up in 1976.

STONE CANYON BAND see NELSON, Rick

STONEMAN, Ernest V.

'Pop' Stoneman occupies a special place in the annals of country music, as the head of a clan that was as influential in its own way as the **Carter Family**. He was born on May 25, 1893, in Carroll County, Virginia. During his adolescence he mastered a range of instruments, including the jew's harp, harmonica, banjo, autoharp and guitar. After finishing his education he became a carpenter, until, in 1924, he secured an audition with **Ralph Peer** at Okeh, who allowed him to cut some demos. The following year, 'The Sinking Of The Titanic' became an immediate hit, and over the next five years he and various members of his family, under the name of the Dixie Mountaineers, cut over two hundred sides for Okeh, Gennett, Victor and Paramount. On these sides, he often used other local musicians like **Riley Puckett**, **Uncle Dave Macon** and Clayton McMichen (see **Skillet Lickers**).

Stoneman's career was seriously hit by the Depression, and his wife, Hattie, had to raise their thirteen children on a shoestring. They moved to Washington, DC, where Pop returned to carpentry work at a naval factory. By the end of the war, Stoneman had become a leading and revered collector of rural tunes, and was widely regarded as one of the pioneers of bluegrass.

By 1956, he was appearing on Connie Gay's *Gaytime Show* and on the *Grand Ole Opry*. His band, the Stoneman Family, included various members of his family, with Pop at the epicentre of the group's activities (it was through his endeavours that successive contracts were made with labels like MGM, Starday and Folkways). During the 1960s, the family moved en masse to Nashville and started to appear on television shows like The **Little Jimmy Dickens** *Show*; in 1966 they were given their own show, *Those Stonemans*.

The following year they won the Country Music Association award for Best Vocal Group; at this time the group comprised Pop, Scott (fiddle), Jim (bass), Van (guitar), Donna (mandolin) and Roni (banjo). By 1968 Pop had become ill with a stomach affliction: he died on June 14, 1968. His legacy has continued through the activities of his children and grandchildren, most notably Scott, who has worked with progressive bluegrass outfits like the Kentucky Colonels (see **White, Clarence**).

ERNEST V. STONEMAN AND THE BLUE RIDGE CORN SHUCKERS, Rounder (US), 1982

STRAIT, George

Although **Garth Brooks** has become the most celebrated performer of the New Country artists (generating enough column inches in the popular international press to make one suppose that he is the natural heir to **George Jones**'s throne), George Strait has the versatility and the vision to encompass most styles of country music with total conviction and credibility.

He was born in Pearsall, Texas, on May 18, 1952, the son of a teacher and a rancher. While in the army, he started to sing, modelling his style on the great honky-tonk singers such as **Lefty Frizzell**, **Merle Haggard**, **Hank Thompson** and George Jones. Demobbed in 1975, he studied agriculture and recorded some sides with the Ace In The Hole Band for the local D label, while touring throughout the southwest. On the Texas club circuit he met Erv Woolsey, who started doing promotional work for MCA. Strait was signed to MCA in 1980, with Woolsey taking over as his manager.

Since 1981, he has been one of the most consistent hitmakers in country music: 'Unwound' (C&W#6, 1981), 'If You're Thinking You Want A Stranger (There's One Coming Home)' (C&W#3, 1982), 'Fool Hearted Memory' (C&W#1, 1982), 'A Fire I Can't Put Out' (C&W#1, 1983), 'You Look So Good In Love' (C&W#1, 1983), 'Right Or Wrong' (C&W#1, 1984) and **Dickey Lee**'s 'Let's Fall To Pieces Together' (C&W#1, 1984).

In May 1984 he changed producer (having previously worked with Blake Mevis and Ray Baker), turning to **Jimmy Bowen** to co-produce 'Don't Fort Worth Ever Cross Your Mind' (C&W#1, 1984), 'The Cowboy Rides Again', 'The Fireman', **Hank Cochran** and Dean Dillon's 'The Chair' (C&W#1, 1985), 'Nobody In His Right Mind Would've Left Her' (C&W#1, 1986), 'It Ain't Cool To Be Crazy About You' (C&W#1, 1986), Hank Cochran and Dean Dillon's 'Ocean Front Property' (C&W#1, 1987), 'All My Ex's Live In Texas' (C&W#1, 1987), 'Am I Blue' (C&W#1, 1987), 'Famous Last Words Of A Fool' (C&W#1, 1988), 'Baby Blue' (C&W#1, 1988), **Tommy Collins**'s 'If You Ain't Loving (You Ain't Livin')' (C&W#1, 1988), 'Baby's Gotten Good At Goodbye' (C&W#1, 1989), 'What's Going On

In Your World' (C&W#1, 1989), 'Ace In The Hole' (C&W#1, 1989), 'Love Without End, Amen' (C&W#1, 1990), 'I've Come To Expect It From You' (C&W#1, 1990), 'If I Know Me' (C&W#1, 1991), 'So Much Like My Dad' (C&W#3, 1992) and 'I Cross My Heart' (C&W#1, 1992).

By 1992, he had made the inevitable transition to the silver screen, starring in the movie *Pure Country*. At the end of the 1980s, he was voted Entertainer of the Decade by the CMA, having picked up the Male Vocalist Award in successive years.

BEYOND THE BLUE MOON, MCA (US), 1989
DOES FORT WORTH EVER CROSS YOUR MIND, MCA (US), 1985
THE ESSENTIAL GEORGE STRAIT, MCA, 1990
IF YOU LOVIN' YOU AIN'T LIVIN', MCA (US), 1988
LIVIN' IT UP, MCA, 1990
NUMBER 7, MCA (US), 1986
OCEAN FRONT PROPERTY, MCA, 1987
PURE COUNTRY (film soundtrack), MCA, 1992
RIGHT OR WRONG, MCA (US), 1983
SOMETHING SPECIAL, MCA, 1985
STRAIT COUNTRY, MCA (US), 1981
STRAIT FROM THE HEART, MCA (US), 1982

STRINGBEAN

Stringbean was a fine banjo player in the mould of **Uncle Dave Macon**. He was born David Akeman on June 17, 1915, in Annville, Kentucky. His father, although not a professional, taught him the rudiments of banjo-playing, and Stringbean built his own instrument before he was twelve. After the Depression, he started to work the clubs, bars and dances of Lexington, until joining the Lonesome Pine Fiddlers. With this group he regularly broadcast on local radio, acquiring the moniker Stringbean from a radio announcer because of his gangling stature.

During the late 1930s, he hooked up with **Charlie Monroe**, before joining **Bill Monroe**'s Blue Grass Boys on the *Grand Ole Opry* in 1942. After leaving Monroe in 1945, he continued his appearances at the *Opry* for some years, often with **Lew Childre**. Having developed a comic gormlessness for his act, he was a natural choice as regular cast member of the television show *Hee Haw*. He and his wife, Estelle, were murdered by intruders on November 10, 1973, after returning home from an appearance at the *Opry*.

SALUTE TO UNCLE DAVE MACON, Starday (US), 1987

STUCKEY, Nat

Little known beyond the US, Nat Stuckey has been a frequent visitor to the lower reaches of the country charts. He was born in Cass County, Texas, on December 17, 1937. After studying at Arlington State College in Dallas, he became a radio announcer, before joining a jazz group in 1957. The following year, he changed over to country and formed the Corn Huskers. When the Corn Huskers split up, he played with the Louisiana Hayriders, until leaving for a solo career with the Sims label.

In 1966, **Buck Owens** covered Stuckey's 'Waiting In The Welfare Line', which became a monster hit and encouraged Stuckey to sign up with Stan Lewis's Paula label: he immediately scored with 'Sweet Thang'. In 1968 he moved on to RCA, where more modest hits followed: 'Plastic Saddle', 'Cut Across Shorty', **Gary Stewart**'s 'Sweet Thang And Cisco', 'Young Love' (a duet with **Connie Smith**) and 'Take Time To Love Her'. By 1975 he had signed with MCA, charting with 'What I've Got In Mind', but consistency remains elusive.

SUMMEY, James Clell   See COUSIN JODY

SWAN, Billy

Billy Swan has for over twenty years been one of the most dependable and inspiring session musicians on the Music City circuit. Unlike many other session musicians, Swan's stab at personal celebrity paid dividends, in the shape of 'I Can Help', a fine slice of country-tinged rock 'n' roll that coursed its way to the top of the charts in 1974.

He was born in Cape Girardeau, Missouri, on May 12,1942. His first success came in 1958, when, as a member of Mirt Mirley and the Rhythm Steppers, he wrote 'Lover Please', which became a big hit for R&B singer Clyde McPhatter in 1962. After moving to Nashville, he took a job at the Columbia studios as janitor - a position that **Kris Kristofferson** would later hold - and got work as a session musician at the Monument studios. After playing guitar on sessions he was nominated to produce **Tony Joe White**, for whom he produced three albums, none of which sold in any quantity and spawned only one hit single, 'Polk Salad Annie'. Around the same time, he hooked up with Kristofferson, becoming a member of his touring band, before touring and recording with **Kinky Friedman**'s band.

In 1974 **Fred Foster** signed him to Monument; his first hit 'I Can Help' (US#1, C&W#1, UK#6, 1974) was a welcome relief in a musical climate dominated by absurd costumes and platform shoes. Other lesser hits, like 'Don't Be Cruel' (UK#42, 1975) and 'Everything's The Same', soon followed. Later albums such as *Rock 'n' Roll Moon* and *Billy Swan* were critical successes, but commercial disasters. By 1978, he had moved to A&M and cut *You're OK, I'm OK*, before returning to the Nashville session circuit. During the mid-1980s, he resumed work with Kristofferson's band, appearing on *Repossessed* (1986) and *Third World Warrior* (1990). Despite the lack of commercial acceptance afforded his own records, he remains a stalwart of the session circuit and very much the musicians' musician.

SYLVIA
Born Sylvia Kirby Allen in Kokomo, Indiana, on December 9, 1956, she moved to Nashville in 1976 and found work as a receptionist for producer Tom Collins at his music publishing company, Pi-Gem. After doing the rounds of record companies, which included auditioning for the role of Sugar in the duo **Dave & Sugar**, and singing back-up vocals for **Janie Fricke**, she was signed to RCA by Jerry Bradley.

In 1980 she had her first hit with 'Tumbleweed', which was followed by 'Drifter' (C&W#1, 1981), 'The Matador', 'Heart On The Mend', 'Nobody' (US#15, C&W#1, 1982), 'Like Nothing Ever Happened' (C&W#2, 1982) and 'Read All About It'. Since 1985, she has been developing her own songwriting abilities and has duetted with **Michael Johnson** on 'I Love You By Heart', but hasn't yet recaptured her earlier level of success.

ONE STEP CLOSER, RCA (US), 1985
SWEET YESTERDAY, RCA, 1983

TALLEY, James

Despite comparisons with **Woody Guthrie**, **Ramblin' Jack Elliott** and Pete Seeger, James Talley's synthesis of blues, R&B and country has been greeted apathetically by the record-buying public.

He was born in Tulsa, Oklahoma, on November 9, 1943, and was raised in a trailer, before settling in Albuquerque, New Mexico, in 1951. He studied at UCLA and the University of New Mexico, majoring in American Studies, before working as a social worker with Chicanos. By the late 1960s he had moved to Nashville, where he continued his social work in the black communities.

In the early 1970s, he took the plunge and started to play on the college circuit, and in 1974 he financed the cutting of his debut, *Got No Bread, No Milk, No Honey, But We Sure Got Love*, which aroused the interest of Capitol and got him a contract. Other albums, like *Trying Like The Devil* (1976) and *Blackjack Choir* (1977), followed: while featuring session men like **Johnny Gimble** and dobroist Buck Graves, they were greeted with total indifference. After being dropped by Capitol, he recorded *American Originals* (1985) for the Bear Family label. Still performing regularly on the club circuit, his biggest following is in Europe.

AMERICAN ORIGINALS, Bear Family (Germany), 1985
BLACKJACK CHOIR, Bear Family (Germany), 1977
TRYING LIKE THE DEVIL, Bear Family (Germany), 1976
LOVE SONGS AND THE BLUES, Bear Family (Germany), 1989

TANNER, Gid see SKILLET LICKERS

TARLTON, Jimmie

During the 1920s, Jimmie Tarlton and Tom Darby exemplified the influence of the blues on country artists. Predating the arrival of the steel guitar by some years, Tarlton adopted the bottleneck technique favoured by bluesmen like Charley Patton.

Tarlton was born in Chesterfield County, South Carolina, in 1892, the son of a sharecropper. During his youth he mastered the banjo, harmonica and guitar, was taught traditional folk songs by his mother, and was influenced by the work-songs of the black cotton-pickers. After leaving home he travelled around the US and ended up in Texas, where he got work in the oilfields, before returning to Carolina and the cotton mills.

In 1926, having taken to the road once again, he met Tom Darby, a native of Columbus, Georgia, and they started performing together as a duo. The following year, they recorded 'Birmingham Jail' and 'Columbus Stockade Blues' for Columbia; over the next three years, they cut songs like 'Where The River Shannon Flows', 'Lowe Bonnie' and 'Slow Wicked Blues'. After another spell at the cotton mill in 1931, they resumed the partnership in 1932, recording for Victor and ARC. By 1933, Darby had returned to farming, while Tarlton continued to play in bars and at dances.

After years of obscurity, he was rediscovered in the late 1950s by Mike Seeger of the **New Lost City Ramblers**, and encouraged to come out of retirement to play the college and festival circuit. He died in 1973.

TAYLOR, Chip

Chip Taylor was born James Wesley Voight in 1940 in Westchester County, New York, the younger brother of actor Jon Voight. During the late 1950s, he recorded as a rockabilly singer for **Syd Nathan**'s King label, before turning his attention to songwriting.

Over the next twelve years, he penned a string of hits for a vast number of different artists, including 'Wild Thing' (the Troggs, Jimi Hendrix & Fancy), 'I Can't Let Go' (the Hollies), 'Any Way That You Want Me' (the Troggs and American Breed), 'I Can Make It With You' (Jackie De Shannon), 'Angel Of The Morning' (P.P. Arnold, Merilee Rush and **Juice Newton**), 'Sweet Dream Woman' (**Waylon Jennings**), 'Just A Little Bit Lower On Down The Line' (**Bobby Bare**), 'If You Were Mine Mary' (**Eddy Arnold** and **Jim Ed Brown**) and 'The Long Walk Home' (**Floyd Cramer**).

In 1967, in partnership with Al Gorgoni, he produced James Taylor and the Flying Machine's debut, before they both linked up with Trade Martin to cut two albums for Buddah: *Gorgoni, Martin And Taylor* (1971) and *Gotta Get Back To Cisco* (1972). Still signed to Buddah, he lauched his solo career with *Gasoline*, which included his langourous version of 'Angel Of The Morning'.

Signing with Warner Bros., Taylor continued to write and record regularly, although his efforts were only appreciated by a handful of people. *Chip Taylor's Last Chance* (1973), featuring 'I Read It In *Rolling Stone*', among others, was as fine an example of country-rock as anything else to emerge during that period. Other albums like *Some Of Us* (1974) followed, as did a change in record labels. By 1979, having moved from Warner Bros. to Columbia and then to Capitol, he seemed to give up, as nothing has emerged in recent years.

TAYLOR, Tut

A virtuoso dobroist, Robert 'Tut' Taylor was born in Milledgeville, Georgia, on November 20, 1923, and showed his precocity by learning the mandolin, autoharp, dulcimer, fiddle and banjo before he was twelve.

Starting off as a guitar and stringed-instrument maker, he went on to establish his own guitar shop in Nashville. In the early 1960s, he began to play the club circuit and record with various groups like the Folkswingers and the Dixie Gentlemen. Together with **Vassar Clements**, Taylor established himself on the session circuit and contributed to the growth of interest in bluegrass.

In 1972, he linked up with **John Hartford** and **Norman Blake**, forming the nucleus of the Dobrolic Plectral Society, which was a loose aggregation of musicians that played the festival circuit. By the late 1970s he was cutting solo albums like *Friar Tut* for Rounder and *The Old Post Office* for Flying Fish. In recent years, his public performances and recording commitments have given way to running his shop, which is now a mecca for guitar collectors and enthusiasts.

FRIAR TUT, Rounder (US), 1977

TENNEVA RAMBLERS see **RODGERS, Jimmie**

TEXAS PLAYBOYS see **BRUNER, Cliff**

TEXAS RUBY see **FOX, Curly**

THOMAS, B.J.

Best known for recording the Oscar-winning 'Raindrops Keep Falling On My Head' in the movie *Butch Cassidy And The Sundance Kid*, B.J. Thomas has recorded in a variety of styles, incorporating country and gospel, as well as mainstream pop.

He was born Billy Joe Thomas on August 27, 1942, in Hugo, Oklahoma, and was raised in Houston, Texas. Forming the Triumphs in 1957, he played bars and dances until 1965, when they cut a version of **Hank Williams**'s 'I'm So Lonesome I Could Cry' (US#8, 1966) for the local Pacemaker label. It was picked up for national distribution by Scepter, who turned it into a million-seller.

Having left the group in 1966 for a solo career, he cut a string of hits for Scepter that included 'Mama' (US#22, 1966), 'Billy And Sue' (US#34, 1966), 'The Eyes Of A New York Woman' (US#28, 1968), 'Hooked On A Feeling' (US#5, 1968), 'Raindrops Keep Falling On My Head' (US#1, 1969; UK#38, 1970), 'Everybody's Out Of Town' (US#26, 1970), 'I Just Can't Help Believing' (US#9, 1970), 'Most Of All' (US#38, 1971), 'No Love At All' (US#16, 1971), 'Mighty Clouds Of Joy' (US#34, 1971) and 'Rock 'n' Roll Lullaby' (which featured guitarist Duane Eddy; US#15, 1972).

After a brief spell with Paramount, he joined ABC (later to become MCA) and cut a number of country hits with producer **Chips Moman**, including '(Hey Won't You Play) Another Somebody Done Somebody Wrong Song' (US#1, C&W#1, 1975). After becoming a born-again Christian in 1976, he cut the gospel album, *Home Where I Belong*, for the Myrrh label, while continuing to cut country material: 'Don't Worry Baby' (US#17, 1977), 'Some Love Songs Never Die', 'Whatever Happened To Old-Fashioned Love' (C&W#1, 1983), 'New Looks From An Old Lover' (C&W#1, 1983), 'Two Car Garage' (C&W#3, 1984), 'The Whole World's In Love When You're Lonely' (C&W#10, 1984) and 'Rock 'n' Roll Shoes' (a duet with **Ray Charles**). More recently, he has returned to the mainstream, cutting items like the theme to the television series *Growing Pains*.

BEST OF B.J. THOMAS, Creole, 1984
GREATEST HITS, Gusto (US), 1988
NEW LOOKS, Epic, 1983

THOMPSON, Hank

During the 1950s and 1960s Hank Thompson led a band called the Brazos Valley Boys. Using Western Swing as a loose framework for their material they became, in spite of occasional lapses into the formulaic, an inspiration for artists like **Asleep At The Wheel**, **Commander Cody** and **George Strait**.

He was born Henry William Thompson on September 3, 1925, in Waco, Texas, and made his radio debut on the local station while still at school. After doing his stint in the navy during war, he returned to Waco to form the Brazos Valley Boys, and was immediately co-opted to broadcast on KWTX. Fuelled by the success of this venture, he started gigging throughout Texas and landed himself and his group a recording deal with the Globe label in 1946. The following year he recorded briefly for another local label, Bluebonnet, before being signed by Capitol in 1948.

He remained with Capitol until 1966, during which time he chalked up over a dozen hits: 'Humpty Dumpty Heart' (C&W#2, 1948), 'Today', 'Whoa Sailor' (originally recorded for Globe in 1946), 'Green Light', 'Waiting In The Lobby Of Your Heart', 'Wild Side Of Life' (C&W#1, 1952), 'Rub-A-Dub-Dub' (C&W#1, 1953), 'Wake Up Irene' (C&W#1, 1953), 'You Can't Have My Heart', 'Squaws Along The Yukon' (C&W#2, 1958), 'She's A Whole Lot Like You', 'Oklahoma Hills', 'Hangover Tavern', 'On Tap', 'In The Can Or In The Bottle', 'Next Time I Fall In Love (I Won't)' and 'I've Come Awful Close'.

His records riding high, his lighthearted concert performances and festival and rodeo-circuit appearances were also successful. After the termination of his contract with Capitol, he signed with Warner Bros., before moving to the Dot label in 1968, where he cut the excellent *Back In The Swing Of Things* (1976). Although he has recorded little over the last dozen years or so, his regular performances with a slimmed-down version of the band are still greeted with unbridled enthusiasm.

BEST OF THE BEST OF HANK THOMPSON, Gusto (US), 1988
HANK THOMPSON, Capitol, 1989
HANK THOMPSON, MCA, 1987
HANK THOMPSON: 1952, Country Routes, 1990
IN THE STUDIO, ON THE ROAD, See For Miles, 1989

THOMPSON, Sue

Sue Thompson was born Eva Sue McKee on July 19, 1926, in Nevada, Missouri, and was raised on a farm. In 1933 she was given a guitar and began to play at church socials. After winning a talent contest in San Jose, she appeared in vaudeville, and was later engaged to appear on Dude Martin's KGO-TV show *Hometown Hayride* in San Francisco. After marrying and divorcing Martin, she married **Hank Penny** and became the lead singer of his band during his sojourn in Las Vegas.

Her marriage to Penny broke up in the late 1950s, and she moved to Los Angeles, appearing in cabaret and guesting on the *Grand Ole Opry* with **Red Foley**. In the early 1960s she was signed to **Wesley Rose**'s Hickory label, where she had a string of national hits, including 'Sad Movies (Make Me Cry)' (US#5, UK#46, 1961), 'Norman' (US#3, 1962), 'Have A Good Time' (US#31, 1962), 'James (Hold The Ladder Steady)' (US#17, 1962) and 'Paper Tiger' (US#23, UK#30, 1965). Although she continues to tour with an increasingly country-ish output, her true *métier* remains the cabaret circuit.

SWEET MEMORIES, Sundown, 1985

THOMPSON, Uncle Jimmy

Born in 1848 in Smith County, Tennessee, Uncle Jimmy Thompson won many fiddle contests prior to his first broadcast on WSM's *Barn Dance* at the invitation of **George Hay**. After his first broadcast, many listeners wrote to the radio station requesting auditions, prompting Hay to rename the show the *Grand Ole Opry*.

He remained a regular of the *Grand Ole Opry* until 1928, during which time he never played the same tune twice. Although he toured and recorded for Vocalion and Columbia, the mainstay of his income was farming. He died on February 17, 1931.

TILLIS, Mel

Mel Tillis has for over thirty years been one of country's most versatile songwriters and performers, achieving the unusual feat of writing successful material both for himself and for other artists, and establishing himself on the lucrative Las Vegas cabaret circuit.

He was born in Tampa, Florida, on August 8, 1932, and grew up Pahokee, Florida. During his high-school years, he was a drummer in the school band, before changing over to study the violin. He set his musical aspirations aside to pursue a career as a footballer, but this had to be put on hold when he went into the US Air Force.

Discharged from the Air Force, he went to Nashville to develop a career as a songwriter, and had immediate success as artists flocked to record his compositions: 'Detroit City' (**Bobby Bare**); 'Ruby Don't Take Your Love To Town' (**Kenny Rogers** & the First Edition); 'Honey (Open That Door)' (**Ricky Skaggs**); 'All The Time' (**Jack Greene**); 'Heart Over Mind', 'One More Time' and 'Burning Memories' (**Ray Price**); and 'Honky Tonk Memories' and 'Tupelo County Jail' (**Webb Pierce**).

As a performer, he landed a contract with Columbia in 1958 and cut 'The Violet And The Rose' and 'Finally'. After moving to the Ric label, he had a minor hit with 'Wine' in 1965, and then signed with Kapp, where he scored minor hits with 'Who's Julie', 'These Lonely Hands Of Mine', 'She'll Be Hanging Around Somewhere' and 'Heart Over Mind'. In 1968, he was fired from The **Porter Wagoner** Show over a minor infraction, but was recruited to The **Glen Campbell** Goodtime Hour.

By 1970 he had changed label again, signing with MGM and scoring with 'Commercial Affection', 'Heaven Everyday', 'The Arms Of A Fool', 'Brand New Mister Me', 'I Ain't Never' (C&W#1, 1972), 'Sawmill' (C&W#2, 1973), 'Midnight, Me And The Blues' (C&W#2, 1974), 'Stomp Them Grapes' and 'The Woman In The Back Of My Mind'. Another change of label came in 1976, when he signed with MCA and entered the most successful phase of his career, with **Jimmy Bowen** producing 'Good Woman Blues' (C&W#1, 1976), 'Heart Healer' (C&W#1, 1977), 'I Believe In You' (C&W#1, 1978), 'Ain't No California', 'Send Me Down To Tucson' (C&W#2, 1979) and 'Coca Cola Cowboy' (C&W#1, 1979).

In 1979, having started a parallel career as an actor, appearing in movies like Smokey And The Bandit, he moved to the Elektra label with producer Bowen in 1979, where he charted with 'Blind In Love', 'Lying Time Again', 'Your Body Is An Outlaw', 'Southern Rain' (C&W#1, 1981), 'A Million Old Goodbyes', 'One Night Fever', 'In The Middle Of The Night' and 'New Patches'. In 1984, Tillis moved back to MCA with Bowen. Charting less often over the past decade, Tillis has continued to make regular cabaret appearances in Las Vegas, as he has done since the early 1970s.

THE GREAT MEL, Gusto (US), 1988
NEW PATCHES, MCA, 1984
THE VERY BEST OF MEL TILLIS, MCA (US), 1986

TILLIS, Pam

Daughter of **Mel Tillis**, Pam Tillis represents the new breed of female country singer, whose influences are drawn from rock and folk music, as well as traditional country styles. She was born in Plant City, Florida, on July 24, 1957, and made her debut on the Grand Ole Opry when she was eight with her father. After attending the University of Tennessee, where she fell under the spell of groups like Little Feat, the **Charlie Daniels** Band and the **Eagles**, and singers like **Linda Ronstadt**, she formed a duo with a jazz pianist and moved to the West Coast; intriguingly, in hindsight, she says this duo sounded 'like **Dolly Parton** meets Flora Purim'.

During the 1980s, she signed with Warner Bros., cutting an album which included a country song called 'It Ain't Easy Being Easy'. It sunk without a trace, and she returned to Nashville and began to work as a session singer. In 1990, she signed a songwriting deal with **Buddy Killen**'s Tree publishing house, which led to a recording contract with the newly-opened Nashville branch of Arista. Her debut album Put Yourself In My Place yielded hits like 'Don't Tell Me What To Do' and 'Maybe It Was Memphis' (C&W#3, 1991); the follow-up Homeward Looking Angel performed creditably with hits like 'Shake The Sugar Tree' (C&W#3, 1992), 'Let That Pony Run' (C&W#5, 1992) and 'Cleopatra: Queen Of Denial'. Apart from her successful recording career, she has had her songs covered by Chaka Khan, **Conway Twitty** and the **Forester Sisters**, among others.

HOMEWARD LOOKING ANGEL, Arista (US), 1992
PUT YOURSELF IN MY PLACE, Arista (US), 1991

TILLMAN, Floyd

One of the finest songwriters of the 1930s, Floyd Tillman's 'It Makes No Difference Now' became a standard within months of its composition, establishing the cheating song as one of country music's most popular forms.

He was born in Ryan, Oklahoma, on December 8, 1914, and became a messenger for Western Union in 1927. During the early 1930s he joined Adolph Hofner's band, before joining Leon Seph's Blue Ridge Playboys, where he met **Cliff Bruner**. In 1938 he penned 'It Makes No Difference Now'. With a lyrical strength able to withstand any amount of interpretation, it was covered by **Jimmie Davis** and Hofner, among many others, and quickly attained classic status.

After joining Bruner's Texas Playboys, where he became the lead vocalist, Tillman embarked on a solo career with Decca. He quickly established himself, becoming one of the most successful vocalists of the war years with 'They Took The Stars Out Of Heaven' and 'Each Night At Nine'. After the war he signed with Columbia, cutting 'Drivin' Nails In My Coffin', 'I Love You So Much It Hurts' and the million-seller 'Slippin' Around'.

In 1954 he left Columbia and recorded for a bunch of minor labels, before joining Liberty in 1960, where he had another substantial hit with 'It Just Tore Me Up'. In 1966, having earlier sold a percentage of the copyright of 'It Makes No Difference Now' to Jimmie Davis, he regained the full copyright when it came up for renewal. In later years he cut *Floyd Tillman And Friends* for **Mickey Gilley**'s label, Gilley's, which included duets with **Merle Haggard**, among others.

In retirement over the last few years; he became a member of the Country Music Hall Of Fame in 1984. Many of his songs are still performed by other artists.

TOMPALL and the Glaser Brothers

The country music establishment took quite a blow when Tompall and the Glaser Brothers - who had always pursued their career along very traditional lines - aligned themselves with **Willie Nelson** and **Waylon Jennings** in the Outlaw Movement. Raised on a farm in Spalding, Nebraska, the brothers comprised Tompall (born on September 3, 1933), Chuck (born on February 27, 1936) and Jim (born on December 16, 1937). They became professional musicians during their adolescence, and moved to Nashville, where they were signed to **Marty Robbins**' label in 1957, having won first place on Arthur Godfrey's *Talent Scouts* show.

The following year they were signed to the Decca label as Tompall and the Glaser Brothers. Their debut album, *This Land*, combined elements of folk as well as country, which satisfied the record company but aroused the group's displeasure. However, they continued to tour and record with Robbins, and joined the prestigious **Johnny Cash** roadshow.

In 1963 they were signed by Kapp, before moving over to MGM in 1966, where they had hits with **John Hartford**'s 'Gentle On My Mind' and 'Rings', among others; they also started to establish their own independent publishing and management operation.

Tompall wrote titles such as 'Stand Beside Me' and 'Streets Of Baltimore' with **Harlan Howard**, and Chuck set up the Nova booking agency and started to produce artists like Hartford and **Kinky Friedman**.

In the early 1970s, Tompall and **Jim Glaser** started to pursue solo careers; Tompall was the more successful with hits like 'Take The Singer With The Song' and 'Lay Down Beside Me'. In 1976, having hitched his flag to the Outlaw Movement with Nelson, Jennings and **Jessi Colter**, he collaborated with them on *Wanted: The Outlaws*. The following year, dissatisfied with MGM, Tompall moved to the Dot label, cutting *Tompall And His Outlaw Band*.

By 1981 Tompall and the Glaser Brothers had reformed and signed with Elektra, scoring with **Kris Kristofferson**'s 'Loving Her Was Easier Than Anything I'll Ever Do Again' (C&W#2, 1981). It was a shortlived affair, as Chuck, who had suffered a stroke in 1975, was preoccupied with production and running the booking agency, while Jim remained committed to a solo career. Although less successful as solo performers than in the group, both Chuck and Tompall have become good administrators, representing the interests of country mavericks like Waylon Jennings and **Billy Joe Shaver**.

LOVIN' HER WAS EASIER THAN ANYTHING I'LL DO AGAIN, Elektra, 1981
NIGHTS ON THE BORDERLINE, MCA (US), 1987
TOMPALL AND THE GLASER BROTHERS, Country Store, 1988

TRASK, Diana

In 1968, Diana Trask (born in Melbourne, Australia, on June 23, 1940) cut *Miss Country Soul* for the Dot label. Produced by **Buddy Killen** and consisting of songs written by soul singer Joe Tex, it illustrated the very fine line between country and soul. That it was an Australian who made the connection between the two was quite extraordinary.

The album sold few copies, but it did generate a few modest hits: 'I Fall To Pieces', 'Beneath Still Waters' and 'The Choking Kind'. It failed to catapult her into the upper echelons of country, and by the mid-1970s she had sunk into the obscurity of the nightclub circuit, both in the US and Australia.

TRAVELLING WILBURYS see ORBISON, Roy

TRAVIS, Merle

A prodigiously talented musician, Merle Travis's innovative finger-picking technique revolutionized country guitar-playing. He was born in Rosewood, Muehlenburg County, Kentucky, on November 29, 1917, and learnt the rudiments of the guitar from two local musicians, Mose Rager and Arnold Schultz. After finishing school he played in bars all over the country, developed his unique style - using the thumb and index finger - and ended up with Clayton McMichen's (see **Skillet Lickers**) band, the Georgia Wildcats, in 1937. He then moved to WLW, Cincinnati, where he broadcast on the *Boone County Jamboree* and then the *Midwestern Hayride*, and began recording with **Grandpa Jones**, the **Delmore Brothers** and the gospel group, the Brown's Ferry Four.

Joining the Marines during the war, he moved out to the West Coast after his discharge in 1944; here he worked with **Cliffie Stone**, **Ray Whitley** and **Jimmy Wakely**. Initially signing with King, where he cut some sessions with **Hank Penny**, he was then signed to Capitol, where his compositional skills flourished in titles like 'Divorce Me C.O.D.', 'So Round, So Firm, So Fully Packed', 'Dark As A Dungeon', 'Sixteen Tons', 'No Vacancy' (with Cliffie Stone) and 'Smoke! Smoke! Smoke (That Cigarette)!' (with **Tex Williams**). While his songwriting gained fresh admirers, with artists like **Tennessee Ernie Ford** and **Rose Maddox** covering his material, his guitar work was emulated by the likes of **Les Paul**, **Doc Watson** and, most notably, **Chet Atkins**.

During the 1950s and 1960s, he was an inspiration to many of the emerging young players, including **Jerry Reed** and **Scotty Moore**. His fame increasing, he played a sailor in Fred Zinnemann's *From Here To Eternity* (1954), and then had a spell as a cast member of the *Grand Ole Opry*. Among his later records were *The Atkins-Travis Travelling Show* (with Chet Atkins, and produced by Reed), *Country Guitar Giants* (with **Joe Maphis**) and *Walkin' The Strings*. After contributing to the **Nitty Gritty Dirt Band**'s influential *Will The Circle Be Unbroken?* (1971) he went full-circle with *The Merle Travis Story*, which teamed him with veteran session men like **Johnny Gimble** and steel guitarist Herb Remington.

During the late 1940s, he designed a solid-body electric guitar, which was later mass-produced by Leo Fender. In 1977, he was belatedly elected to the Country Music Hall Of Fame, but died on October 20, 1983.

BACK HOME, Stetson, 1987

COUNTRY GUITAR GIANTS (with Joe Maphis), CMH (US), 1979
FOLK SONGS OF THE HILLS, Bear Family (Germany), 1993
GREAT SONGS OF THE DELMORE BROTHERS (with Johnny Bond), Stetson, 1989
MERLE TRAVIS, Capitol, 1993
MERLE TRAVIS: 1944-46, Country Routes, 1990
ROUGH, ROWDY & BLUE, CMH (US), 1985
TRAVIS, Stetson, 1988
TRAVIS PICKIN', CMH (US), 1982

TRAVIS, Randy

Randy Travis, along with **Garth Brooks**, **Clint Black** and **George Strait**, represents a new breed of country artist. Widely respected, he has, in a relatively short period, garnered an awesome array of musical awards and plaudits from peers such as **Merle Haggard** and **George Jones**.

He was born Randy Bruce Traywick in Marshville, North Carolina, on May 4, 1961. Having learnt to play the guitar when he was eight, he spent his early adolescence on the brink of delinquency, but was kept afloat by his interest in music. He met Libby Hatcher in the early 1980s, and she started to mastermind his career, overseeing his performances on the club circuit. For several years he honed his act, and in 1986, when working as a general factotum at the Nashville Palace (a Hatcher-owned entertainment complex in the environs of Music City), he got the opportunity to perform some songs for producers Kyle Lehning and Keith Stegall. After cutting some demos, he was signed to Warner Bros. by A&R director Martha Sharp.

His debut, **Paul Overstreet** and Don Schlitz's 'On The Other Hand', was a minor hit, and was followed-up by '1982' (C&W#6, 1985) and the re-release of 'On The Other Hand' (C&W#1, 1986). He was now on course for a string of hits that stretched into the 1990s: Overstreet and Al Gore's (not the Vice-President!) 'Diggin' Up Bones' (C&W#1, 1986), Overstreet and Schlitz's 'Forever And Ever, Amen' (C&W#1, 1987), **Troy Seals** and Max Barnes's 'I Won't Need You Anymore (Always And Forever)' (C&W#1, 1987), 'Too Gone, Too Long' (C&W#1, 1988), 'I Told You So' (C&W#1, 1988), 'Honky Tonk Moon' (C&W#1, 1988), Overstreet and Schlitz's 'Deeper Than The Holler' (C&W#1, 1988), 'Is It Still Over' (C&W#1, 1989), 'It's Just A Matter Of Time' (C&W#1, 1989), 'Point Of Light' (C&W#1, 1991) and 'If I Didn't Have You' (C&W#1, 1992).

While appealing to younger audiences, he has also

engendered the respect of his peers, as evidenced by his album *Heroes And Friends*, which consists of a series of duets with some of country's most charismatic characters, including George Jones, **Roy Rogers**, **Willie Nelson**, **Tammy Wynette**, **Chet Atkins**, Merle Haggard and B.B. King.

ALWAYS AND FOREVER, Warner Bros., 1987
GREATEST HITS, Volume 1-2, Warner Bros., 1992
HEROES AND FRIENDS, Warner Bros., 1990
HIGH LONESOME, Warner Bros., 1991
NO HOLDING BACK, Warner Bros., 1989
OLD 8 x 10, Warner Bros., 1988
STORMS OF LIFE, Warner Bros., 1986

TRITT, Travis

One of the best New Country writers and performers, Travis Tritt has adopted a similarly unorthodox approach to his career as **Willie Nelson**. He was born and bred in Marietta, Georgia, graduating from high school in 1981 and working for a trucking company thereafter. Although he rose through the ranks of the trucking company to a management position, at heart he wanted to be a musician.

Having sung in a neighbourhood choir during his childhood, learnt the guitar at eight, and written his first song at fourteen, he started to to play the local club circuit where he came to the attention of Warner Brothers' A&R man, Danny Davenport. After two years of demoing material, Davenport took Tritt's tapes to the label, who signed him up immediately and issued his debut *Country Club* in 1990. The debut yielded four hits: 'Country Club', 'Help Me Hold On' (C&W#1, 1990), 'I'm Gonna Be Somebody' (C&W#2, 1990) and 'Drift Off To Dream' (C&W#3, 1991).

After the release of the debut, Tritt took to the open road and toured from coast to coast, building a solid reputation. The follow-up *It's All About to Change* included 'Here's A Quarter (Call Someone Who Cares)' and 'The Whiskey Ain't Workin'' (a duet with Marty Stuart; C&W#2, 1991) and contributions from Little Feat, among others. More touring followed and he made his debut on the *Grand Ole Opry* in February 1992. His most recent offering *T-R-O-U-B-L-E* was released in August 1992, and included 'Can I Trust You With My Heart'.

A strong writer who draws influences from the Allman Brothers, **Charlie Daniels** and **Merle Haggard**, his lyrics reflect his assertion that 'country music is the soundtrack to the lives of working people'.

COUNTRY CLUB, Warner Bros. (US), 1990
IT'S ALL ABOUT TO CHANGE, Warner Bros. (US), 1991
T-R-O-U-B-L-E, Warner Bros. (US), 1992

TUBB, Ernest

A hugely influential figure, Ernest Tubb promulgated the cause of Texan music and established the honky-tonk tradition through the simple but gruelling process of constant touring. Born on February 9, 1914, in Crisp, Texas, Tubb's hero was **Jimmie Rodgers**. Inspired by Rodgers to pursue a career in country, he began playing on radio KONO, San Antonio, in 1934. The following year he befriended Rodgers' widow, Carrie, who gave him her husband's guitar and introduced him to the head honchos at RCA, who signed him on the strength of two demos: 'The Passing Of Jimmie Rodgers' and 'Jimmie Rodgers' Last Thoughts'. After his stint in San Antonio, he moved onto other stations in Fort Worth and San Angelo. While his professional career was on the up, his personal life suffered its share of drawbacks: his second son Roger died within weeks of his birth in 1938.

The following year, he won sponsorship from the Universal (Gold Chain Flour) Mills for a series of programmes on Fort Worth's KGKO as the Gold Chain Troubadour, and the Decca label offered him a new contract. His career now took off, and with the formation of his band, the Texas Troubadours, he became one of Texas's finest performers. Among his hits were 'Walking The Floor Over You', 'Blue Christmas', 'Letters Have No Arms', 'Slippin' Around' and 'I Ain't Goin' Honky Tonkin' Anymore'.

Now increasingly famous, he notched up a string of acting credits in films like *Fightin' Buckaroos* (1941), *Ridin' West* (1942), *Jamboree* (1943) and *Hollywood Barn Dance* (1947). During that period he opened his record store in Nashville, where his tireless promotion of younger artists reflected a policy that he had always exercised in his own group. Those to benefit from his patronage included **Hank Snow**, **Hank Williams**, **Patsy Cline**, **Willie Nelson**, **Loretta Lynn**, **Jack Greene** and **Cal Smith**.

During the 1950s and 1960s, his remorseless touring schedule ensured that he was seldom out of the charts: 'Goodnight Irene' (a duet with **Red Foley**), 'I Love You Because', 'Missing In Action', 'Two Glasses Joe', 'Half A Mind', 'Thanks A Lot', 'Mr And Mrs Used-To-Be' (a duet with Loretta Lynn), 'Waltz Across Texas' and 'Another Story, Another Time, Another Place'. In 1965 he was elected to the Country Music Hall Of Fame, and in 1979

The Legend And Legacy was released, celebrating his sixty-fifth birthday, and featuring contributions from **George Jones**, **Merle Haggard**, the **Wilburn Brothers** and Loretta Lynn. He continued broadcasting his show, *Ernest Tubb Midnight Jamboree*, from his record store on Demonbreun Street in Nashville right up to his death on September 6, 1984, from emphysema.

COUNTRY MUSIC HALL OF FAME, MCA, 1979
ERNEST TUBB STORY, MCA (US), 1986
FAVOURITES, Stetson, 1986
HONKY TONK CLASSICS, Rounder (US), 1988
THE IMPORTANCE OF BEING ERNEST, Stetson, 1985
MIDNIGHT JAMBOREE, Stetson, 1987

TUBB, Justin

The eldest son of **Ernest Tubb**, Justin Tubb (born in San Antonio, Texas, on August 20, 1935) has always been a vehement upholder of the traditional values of country music. He started his career while still at school and formed a group with two of his cousins in 1952, playing bars in and around Austin. After spending a year at the University of Texas, he moved to Nashville and started work at WHIN as a DJ, where he both played records and sang songs!

In 1953 he was signed by Decca, where he had modest hits with 'Looking Back To See' and 'Sure Fire Kisses', both of which were duets with **Goldie Hill**. In 1959 he signed with Challenge, went on to Starday, and then joined RCA in 1962, where he scored with 'Take A Letter, Miss Gray', 'Hurry, Mr Peters', 'We've Gone Too Far Again' and 'But Wait There's More'.

While his records have never sold in vast quantities, he has toured extensively and written songs, including 'Lonesome 7-7203' (a big hit for **Hawkshaw Hawkins** in 1963). One of his father's staunchest supporters, he stage-managed the *Ernest Tubb Midnight Jamboree*, which was broadcast live from his father's Nashville record store on Demonbreun Street.

JUSTIN TUBB, MCA (US), 1987
STAR OF THE GRAND OLE OPRY, Official, 1988

TUCKER, Tanya

Tanya Tucker briefly flirted with rock music in the late 1970s, with a brace of albums produced by Mike Chapman (who had previously worked with groups like Blondie and Sweet). The gamble didn't pay off, and she reverted to country music, having been heartily vilified by the country music establishment.

She was born Tanya Denise Tucker on October 10, 1958, in Seminole, Texas, but grew up in Phoenix, Arizona. When she was nine she started to perform at local events, and in 1971 got a small part in the movie *Jeremiah Johnson*. The following year she was signed by **Billy Sherrill** to the Columbia label, cutting hits like **Alex Harvey**'s 'Delta Dawn', 'Love's The Answer' (C&W#5, 1972), **Dallas Frazier** and Earl Montgomery's 'What's Your Mama's Name' (C&W#1, 1973), 'Blood Red And Goin' Down' (C&W#1, 1973) and **David Allan Coe**'s 'Would You Lay Me Down (In A Field Of Stone)' (C&W#1, 1974).

In 1975 she moved to the MCA label where, produced by Tommy 'Snuff' Garrett, she had a brace of hits with 'Lizzie And The Rainman' (US#37, C&W#1, 1975) and 'San Antonio Stroll' (C&W#1, 1975). After recording in Los Angeles, she returned to Nashville to work with Jerry Crutchfield, who produced 'Don't Believe My Heart Can Stand Another You' (C&W#4, 1976), 'You've Got Me To Hold On To' (C&W#3, 1976), 'Here's Some Love' (C&W#1, 1976), 'Texas (When I Die)' (C&W#5, 1978) and 'Can I See You Tonight' (C&W#4, 1981).

After her unsuccessful foray into rock music, she left MCA and recorded little for three years, returning in 1985 to sign with Capitol. Still produced by Crutchfield, she notched up more hits with **Paul Overstreet** and **Paul Davis**'s 'One Love At A Time' (C&W#3, 1986), Paul Davis's 'Just Another Love' (featuring backing vocals by Davis and **Vince Gill**; C&W#1, 1986), Paul Overstreet and Don Schlitz's 'I Won't Take Less Than Your Love' (featuring Overstreet and Davis; C&W#1, 1988), 'If It Don't Come Easy' (C&W#1, 1988), and 'Strong Enough To Bend' (C&W#1, 1988). By 1992, she had side-stepped from Capitol to Liberty, where she cut *Can't Run From Yourself*, which included a duet with **Delbert McClinton** on 'Tell Me About It'.

CAN'T RUN FROM YOURSELF, Liberty, 1992
GREATEST HITS, Capitol, 1990
LIZZIE AND THE RAINMAN, Cottage, 1975
TANYA TUCKER, Country Store, 1987
TANYA TUCKER'S GREATEST HITS, MCA (US), 1988
TENNESSEE WOMAN, Capitol, 1990
WHAT DO I DO WITH ME, Liberty, 1991
TNT, MCA (US), 1979

TUTTLE, Wesley see MANNERS, Zeke

TWITTY, Conway

Initially a rockabilly singer in the **Elvis Presley** mould, Conway Twitty's roots were firmly grounded in country music, to which he successfully returned in the late 1960s. He was born Harold Lloyd Jenkins (named after the silent movie star) on September 1, 1933, in Friars Point, Mississippi, the son of a Mississippi riverboat pilot. During his teens he formed a country band, the Phillips County Ramblers, before being enlisted to serve in Korea. When he left the army in 1955, he changed his name to Conway Twitty ('Conway' after a town in Arkansas, and 'Twitty' after a town in Texas) and auditioned abortively for **Sam Phillips**.

Signed to Mercury in 1957, he cut 'I Need Your Lovin'', before moving on to MGM, where he had considerable success in the national charts: 'It's Only Make Believe' (US#1, UK#1, 1958), 'The Story Of My Love' (US#28, UK#30, 1959), 'Mona Lisa' (US#29, UK#5, 1959), 'Danny Boy' (US#10, 1959), 'Lonely Blue Boy' (US#6, 1960), 'What Am I Living For' (US#26, 1960), 'Is A Blue Bird Blue?' (US#35, UK#43, 1960) and 'C'est Si Bon' (US#22, UK#40, 1961). After a lull in his career, he went back to country music, via the cabaret circuit, and signed with Decca, with guidance from **Harlan Howard** and production from **Owen Bradley**. In 1966, having settled in Oklahoma City, he started the syndicated television programme *The Conway Twitty Show*.

Over the next twenty years, he notched up one hit after another, many of them self-penned: 'The Image Of Me', 'Next In Line' (C&W#1, 1968), 'I Love You More Today' (C&W#1, 1969), 'To See My Angel Cry' (C&W#1, 1969), 'Hello Darlin'' (C&W#1, 1970), 'Fifteen Years Ago' (C&W#1, 1970), 'How Much More Can She Stand' (C&W#1, 1971), '(Lost Her Love) On Our Last Date' (C&W#1, 1972), **Don Gibson**'s 'I Can't Stop Loving You' (C&W#1, 1972), 'She Needs Someone To Hold Her (When She Cries)' (C&W#1, 1973), 'Baby's Gone' (C&W#2, 1973), 'You've Never Been This Far Before' (US#22, C&W#1, 1973), Denny Rice and **Troy Seals**' 'There's A Honky Tonk Angel (Who'll Take Me Back In)' (C&W#1, 1974), 'I See The Want-To In Your Eyes' (C&W#1, 1974), 'Linda On My Mind' (C&W#1, 1975), 'Touch The Hand' (C&W#1, 1975), 'This Time I've Hurt Her More Than She Loves Me' (C&W#1, 1975), 'After All The Good Is Gone' (C&W#1, 1976), 'The Games That Daddies Play' (C&W#1, 1976), 'I Can't Believe She Gives It All To Me' (C&W#1, 1976), 'Play Guitar Play' (C&W#1, 1977) and 'I've Already Loved You In My Mind' (C&W#1, 1977).

In 1979, after fifteen years of working with producer Owen Bradley, he started to produce his own records with assistance from arranger David Barnes; he also started to use session musicians like guitarists **Chips Moman** and Reggie Young, keyboards player Bobby Wood and bassist Mike Leech. His next hits, influenced by these session musicians, introduced elements of black music into Twitty's country style: Troy Seals and Max D. Barnes's 'Don't Take It Away' (C&W#1, 1979), **Bill Anderson** and **Buddy Killen**'s 'I May Never Get To Heaven' (C&W#1, 1979), 'Happy Birthday Darlin'' (C&W#1, 1979), 'I'd Love To Lay You Down' (C&W#1, 1980), Bee Gee Barry Gibb's 'Rest Your Love On Me' (C&W#1, 1981), 'Tight Fittin' Jeans' (C&W#1, 1981) and Troy Seals and Max D. Barnes's 'Red Neckin' Love Makin' Night' (C&W#1, 1981).

Outside of his immensely successful solo career, Twitty also regularly duetted with **Loretta Lynn**, a liaison which had first started at the Wembley Country Music Festival in London during the late 1960s. They established their own booking agency, United Talent, and recorded a series of classic titles: 'After The Fire Is Gone' (C&W#1, 1971), 'Lead Me On' (C&W#1, 1971), 'Louisiana Woman, Mississippi Man' (C&W#1, 1973), 'As Soon As I Hang Up The Phone' (C&W#1, 1974), 'Feelins' (C&W#1, 1975), 'The Letter' (C&W#3, 1976), 'I Can't Love You Enough' (C&W#2, 1976), 'It's True Love' (C&W#5, 1979) and 'I Still Believe In Waltzes' (C&W#2, 1981).

At the beginning of 1982 he moved from MCA to Elektra, where he teamed up with producer **Jimmy Bowen**, and continued his run of hits with 'The Clown' (C&W#1, 1982), 'Slow Hand' (C&W#1, 1982), 'The Rose' (C&W#1, 1983), 'Lost In The Feeling' (C&W#2, 1983), 'Somebody's Needin' Somebody' (C&W#1, 1984) and Harlan Howard's 'I Don't Know A Thing About Love' (C&W#1, 1984). In 1985, having moved to Warner Bros. from Elektra, he took over the production chores with his former production assistant, Dee Henry, as Bowen had moved to MCA, and the strike-rate continued apace: 'Ain't She Something Else' (C&W#1, 1985), 'Don't Call Him A Cowboy' (C&W#1, 1985), 'Desperado Love' (C&W#1, 1986), 'Fallin' For You For Years' (C&W#2, 1986), 'Julia' (C&W#2, 1987), 'I Want To Know You Before We Make Love' (C&W#2, 1987) and 'I Wish I Was Still In Your Dreams' (C&W#4, 1989).

Twitty's success placed him among the top five best-selling country artists of all time. He diversified his business interests, taking a stake in a fast-food chain, and opened a theme park, Twitty City, in 1983. On June 5, 1993, he collapsed and died on his tour bus during a rest stop in Springfield, Missouri.

BEAT GOES ON, Charly, 1985
BORDERLINE, MCA, 1987
CLASSICS, Volumes 1-2, MCA (US), 1988
CONWAY & LORETTA (with Loretta Lynn), MCA (US), 1988
CROSSWINDS, MCA (US), 1979
GREAT COUNTRY HITS, MCA, 1985
HOUSE ON OLD LONESOME ROAD, MCA (US), 1989
MGM YEARS, Bear Family (Germany), 1985

TYLER, T. Texas

Initially a hillbilly entertainer, T. Texas Tyler achieved a certain distinction in the late 1940s with updated monologues that often drew their inspiration from traditional folk ballads and stories.

He was born David Luke Myrick on June 20, 1916, near Mena, Arkansas, and was educated in Philadelphia. From 1930 onwards he travelled widely, performing a mixture of traditional songs and ballads at hoedowns, dances, church functions and, from 1942, on KWKH'S *Louisiana Hayride*. After serving in the army during the war, he settled in Hollywood, formed the T. Texas Western Dance Band and started to perform at the Venice Pier Ballroom, alongside artists such as **Spade Cooley**.

In 1948, he cut an old English folk song, retitled 'Deck Of Cards' (later covered by **Tex Ritter**, Wink Martindale and Max Bygraves). After the success of 'Deck Of Cards' he recorded other monologues, like 'Dad Gave The Dog Away' and his theme song, 'Remember Me'. Thereafter his career declined, despite frequent television appearances on programmes like *Range Round-Up*. He died in Springfield, Missouri, on January 28, 1972.

T. TEXAS TYLER, Sing, 1988

U V

UNCLE HENRY'S ORIGINAL KENTUCKY MOUNTAINEERS

'Uncle Henry' Warren was an enthusiast who, with entrepreneurial zeal, ran an old-time band long after other such bands had faded into obscurity. Born in 1903, in Taylor County, Kentucky, he started his group in 1928, playing the dual roles of MC and comedian. From then until the late 1940s, he and his band held down successive spots on different radio stations, including KVLV, Rockford, Illinois; *Morning Jamboree* on WHAS, Louisville; WNOX, Knoxville; WLAP, Lexington; and, WHIS, Bluefield, West Virginia. In 1940 they moved to the *Suppertime Frolic* on WJJD, Chicago, where they remained until the late 1940s.

They cut sides for Capitol, but none of these have survived. Their most celebrated alumnus is Uncle Henry's son, Jimmy Dale Warren, who was lead vocalist with the **Sons Of Pioneers**.

VAN DYKE, Leroy

Born in Spring Fork, Missouri, on October 4, 1929, Leroy Van Dyke studied agriculture and gained a BSc at the University Of Missouri. Serving with US Intelligence during the Korean War, he became a livestock auctioneer and journalist after being demobbed. In 1955 he won a talent contest, where he performed the self-penned 'The Auctioneer', and was rewarded with a recording contract with the Dot label. 'The Auctioneer' (US#19, 1956) sold 2.5 million copies, and he became a regular on **Red Foley**'s *Ozark Jubilee*.

In 1961, he was signed to Mercury and scored with 'Walk On By' (US#5, 1961; UK#5, 1962), which was followed by 'Big Man In A Big House' (UK#34, 1962), 'If A Woman Answers' (US#35, 1962) and 'Black Cloud'. After leaving Mercury in 1965, he recorded for Warner Bros., Kapp and Decca, with little success, and appeared in the movie *What Am I Bid?* (1967). In recent years he has become one of many performers on the cabaret circuit.

THE ORIGINAL AUCTIONEER, Bear Family (Germany), 1988

VAN SHELTON, Ricky

One of the few New Country artists to have overtly paid homage to predecessors like **Ernest Tubb**, Ricky Van Shelton was born in Grit, Virginia, in 1952. After working as a builder, he moved to Nashville in 1984, looking after his children by day and auditioning at various clubs by night. After spending two years on this thankless merry-go-round, his live act at **Buddy Killen**'s club, the Stock Yard, was spotted by two Columbia executives, who lined him up to record some demos.

The three songs he demoed were 'Wild-Eyed Dream', 'Crime Of Passion' and 'Somebody Lied' (C&W#1, 1987). The latter established his reputation, and he followed it up with titles like **Harlan Howard**'s 'Life Turned Her That Way' (C&W#1, 1988), **Roger Miller**'s 'Don't We All Have The Right' (C&W#1, 1988), **Wayne Kemp**'s 'I'll Leave This World Loving You' (C&W#1, 1988), **Ned Miller**'s 'From A Jack To A King' (C&W#1, 1989), **Felice and Boudleaux Bryant**'s 'Hole In My Pocket' (C&W#3, 1989), 'Living Proof' (C&W#1, 1989), 'I've Cried My Last Tear For You' (C&W#1, 1990), 'I Meant Every Word He Said' (C&W#2, 1990), 'Rockin' Years' (a duet with **Dolly Parton**; C&W#1, 1991) and 'Backroads' (C&W#2, 1992). He won the CMA's Male Vocalist of the Year award in 1989. Much of his success is due to the fact that he appeals to the middle-of-the-road country fan and that his live shows are packaged like rock concerts.

DON'T OVERLOOK SALVATION, Columbia, 1990
GREATEST HITS PLUS, Columbia (US), 1992
LIVING PROOF, Columbia, 1988
WILD-EYED DREAM, Columbia, 1987

VAN ZANDT, Townes

A superior Texan songwriter from Fort Worth, Townes Van Zandt, along with **Guy Clark** and **Willie Nelson**, was one of the inspirational forces behind the development of the New Country movement. After joining the Peace Corps in the 1960s, he started to work with

★

Guy Clark and **Jerry Jeff Walker**, cutting a string of distinguished albums for the independent Poppy label, his debut, *For The Sake Of A Song*, appearing in 1968 and displaying his superb lyrical skills. Among his other albums for Poppy were *Delta Mama Blues* (1971) and *The Late, Great Townes Van Zandt* (1973); the latter included his composition 'Pancho And Lefty', which was covered as a duet by **Merle Haggard** and Willie Nelson in 1983.

During the 1970s he started to record for the Tomato label, cutting *Live At The Old Quarter* (1977), which captured the spirited essence of his concerts. Although Tomato went down the tubes shortly after, he continued recording, cutting *Live And Obscure* for the independent Heartland label in 1985. In 1987 he cut *At My Window* for the Sugar Hill label, with veteran producer **Jack Clement** at the mixing desk.

Despite his lack of popularity with the general public, his songs have been covered by **Emmylou Harris** and **Don Williams**, among others, and his concerts possess an intimacy rare for contemporary gigs.

AT MY WINDOW, Edsel, 1987
DELTA MOMMA BLUES, Decal, 1979
FLYING SHOES, Decal, 1979
FOR THE SAKE OF THE SONG, Poppy (US), 1990
HIGH LOW AND IN BETWEEN, Decal, 1979
THE LATE, GREAT TOWNES VAN ZANDT, Decal, 1979
LIVE AT THE OLD QUARTER, Decal, 1989
LIVE & OBSCURE, Heartland (US), 1985
OUR MOTHER THE MOUNTAIN, Decal, 1989
PANCHO & LEFTY, Edsel, 1992
RAIN ON A CONGA DRUM, Exile, 1992
TOWNES VAN ZANDT, Decal, 1979

VIRGINIA BOYS See **JIM & JESSE**

WAGONER, Porter

Porter Wagoner was born on August 12, 1930, in West Plains, Missouri, and broke into the music business while working behind the counter in a grocer's shop. During quiet periods at work, he used to play his guitar and sing, encouraging the owner of the store to engage his services for a radio advertising campaign. This eventually led to a weekly series on Springfield's KWTO in 1951, and then to a spot on KWTO-TV's *Ozark Jubilee* with **Red Foley**.

By 1955, he had been signed by RCA, and scored immediately with 'A Satisfied Mind' (C&W#1, 1955); it was followed by other hits, such as 'Eat Drink And Be Merry', 'What Would You Do (If Jesus Came To Your House)', 'Your Old Love Letters', 'Misery Loves Company' (C&W#1, 1962), 'Cold Dark Waters', 'I've Enjoyed As Much Of This As I Can Stand', 'Sorrow On The Rocks', 'Green Green Grass Of Home', 'Skid Row Joe', 'The Cold Hard Facts Of Life', 'Carroll County Incident' and 'Big Wind'.

After joining the *Grand Ole Opry* in 1957, he moved to Nashville where he started the long-running TV series, *The Porter Wagoner Show* in 1960, with his group the Wagonmasters and resident singer **Norma Jean**. The show was initially syndicated throughout the South and the Midwest, but by the late 1960s was being syndicated throughout the US and Canada, making Wagoner one of the most highly paid and heavily promoted artists on the country circuit. After the departure of Norma Jean in 1967, he recruited **Dolly Parton** as her replacement. This was to prove to be Parton's career breakthrough, and it pushed Wagoner up into the big league with a series of hit duets: 'The Last Thing On My Mind', 'We'll Get Ahead Someday', 'Just Someone I Used To Know', 'Please Don't Stop Loving Me' (C&W#1, 1974) and 'Is Forever Longer Than Always'.

An acrimonious split came in 1974: Wagoner felt that his influence upon her career obligated her to stay with his show. He sued, and Parton was obliged - as part of the repararations - to participate in another album of duets, *Porter & Dolly* (1980), which included 'Making Plans' (C&W#2, 1980). After some years the

rift was papered over: Wagoner appeared on Parton's television show in 1988, and in 1989 they duetted on stage at the opening of her 'Dollywood' theme park. Since her departure Wagoner has continued touring with his roadshow, but his chart appearances have been rare.

BLUEGRASS STORY, Stetson, 1989
HITS OF DOLLY PARTON & PORTER WAGONER, RCA, 1977
HITS OF PORTER WAGONER, RCA, 1978
PORTER WAGONER, MCA (US), 1986

WAKELY, Jimmy

The Jimmy Wakely Band established itself during the 1940s and 1950s as one of the premier country bands on the West Coast. Playing on radio and at the flourishing ballrooms, like Venice Pier, his style of crooning gave him fleeting supremacy over Bing Crosby and Frank Sinatra.

He was born on February 16, 1914, in Mineola, Arkansas, and educated in Oklahoma. After finishing his schooling he took a variety of menial jobs, before becoming a journalist and then a professional musician. In 1937 he formed the Jimmy Wakely Trio, with **Johnny Bond** and Scotty Harrell, kicking off his long radio career with daily broadcasts on WKY, Oklahoma City. In 1940, **Gene Autry** guested on Wakely's show and liked the band so much that he took them to Hollywood to appear on his *Melody Ranch* programme.

A hugely popular show, *Melody Ranch* enabled Wakely to pick up a substantial following, and led to appearances in over seventy movies. By 1948 he had firmly established his own band, which was to include such luminaries as **Merle Travis**, **Spade Cooley** and **Cliffie Stone**. Having signed with Capitol, he notched up a string of hits that included **Floyd Tillman**'s 'Slippin' Around' (a duet with Margaret Whiting), 'One Has My Name, The Other Has My Heart', 'I Love You So Much It Hurts', 'I Wish I Had A Nickel', 'My Heart Cries For You' and 'Beautiful Brown Eyes'.

Between 1952 and 1957 he hosted his own radio show on CBS, but by 1958 his style had become outdated. Although co-hosting a television series with **Tex Ritter** in 1961, his drawing power had diminished and he was left to ply his trade, albeit very lucratively, on the Las Vegas and Los Angeles cabaret circuit. He died on September 23, 1982.

SANTA FE TRAIL, Stetson, 1989

WALKER, Billy

Billy Walker's career took off amid a blaze of publicity surrounding his designation as the first masked singer. He was born William Marvin Walker in Ralls, Texas, on January 14, 1929, and attended Whiteface High School, New Mexico. In 1944, he won a local talent contest, whose first prize was a fifteen-minute slot on Clovis's KICA station. By 1949, he had joined Dallas's *Big D Jamboree* as the Masked Singer, which gained him a recording contract with Columbia.

Throughout the 1950s, he broadcast and appeared on a variety of radio and television shows, including KWKH's *Louisiana Hayride*, television's *Ozark Jubilee* and the *Grand Ole Opry*, but Walker had to wait until 1962 to score a major hit, with 'Charlie's Shoes' (C&W#1, 1962). Thereafter, he had a string of Top Twenty hits that included 'Willie The Weeper', 'Circumstances', 'Cross The Brazos At Waco' and 'Matamoros'. In 1966 he changed label to Monument, and continued his string of hits with 'A Million And One', 'Bear With Me A Little Longer', 'Anything Your Heart Desires', 'Ramona' and 'Thinking About You Baby'.

In 1970 Wakely moved to MGM, where he scored with 'When A Man Loves A Woman' (C&W#3, 1970), 'I'm Gonna Keep On Loving You' (C&W#3, 1971) and 'Sing A Love Song To Baby'. In 1975, he switched to RCA and had a couple of modest hits with 'Don't Stop The World' and 'Love You All To Pieces'. His Masked Singer disguise having gone by the board some years previously (prompted no doubt by a brace of film appearances), he moved increasingly towards gospel during the 1980s. Having changed label yet again, signing with MCA, he cut *Billy Walker* in 1986, which teamed him with **Barbara Fairchild** for 'Answer Game' and a reworking of the **Everly Brothers**' classic 'Bye Bye Love'.

BEST OF BILLY WALKER, Monument, 1992
BEST OF THE BEST OF BILLY WALKER, Gusto (US), 1988
BILLY WALKER, MCA, 1987
FOR MY FRIENDS, Bulldog, 1987

WALKER, Charlie

Had it not been for his abilities as a country singer, Charlie Walker would have made the grade as a professional golfer. This expertise has been underlined in his later years by his shrewd, analytical comments as a golfing broadcaster.

He was born in Collins County, Texas, on November 2, 1926, and proved his talent early on as a vocalist, joining **Bill Boyd**'s Cowboy Ramblers in 1943. After leaving Boyd, he served in Japan, before being demobbed and picking up a number of jobs as DJ or announcer with a succession of radio stations.

He was signed to the Columbia label in 1956, and between 1958 and 1970 he had about half a dozen hits: **Harlan Howard**'s 'Pick Me Up On Your Way Down', 'Who'll Buy The Wine', 'Wild As A Wildcat', 'Close All The Honky Tonks', 'Don't Squeeze My Sharmon', 'Honky Tonk Season' and the **Rolling Stones**' 'Honky Tonk Woman'. Recording with RCA from 1970, he joined the Las Vegas cabaret circuit, appearing regularly at the Golden Nugget. In 1986 he released *Charlie Walker* for MCA, but his musical career had already given way to his golfing activities.

CHARLIE WALKER, MCA (US), 1986

WALKER, Frank

A producer and talent scout of great perspicacity, Frank Walker, along with **Art Satherley** and **Ralph Peer**, was responsible for signing some of the most influential hillbilly performers of the 1920s, and during the 1940s signed **Hank Williams**.

He was born in Fly Summit, New York, in 1889, and started his career as a banker, before joining the army to serve in the First World War. After the war he became a promoter, and then an A&R man at Columbia. While he remained essentially a businessman, he was sufficiently creative to spot the potential of younger artists and to provide them with the chance to record.

In 1925 he founded a special division of the label, devoted to popularizing country music; among the earliest beneficiaries were the **Skillet Lickers**, **Charlie Poole**, **Bob Miller**, **Riley Puckett** and **Vernon Dalhart**. During the late 1930s Walker joined RCA as vice-president, before joining MGM in 1945 and signing Hank Williams. Eventually becoming president of MGM, he continued to do consultancy work for Loew's (the owners of MGM) after his retirement. He died in New York in 1965.

WALKER, Jerry Jeff

Best known for his composition 'Mr Bojangles' (a tribute to the legendary tap and street dancer Bill 'Bojangles' Robinson), Jerry Jeff Walker relocated to Austin in the early 1970s and became one of the key figures in its flourishing music community, alongside **Willie Nelson**, **Guy Clark**, **Townes Van Zandt**, **Michael Martin Murphey** and **Doug Sahm**.

He was born Paul Crosby on March 16, 1942, in Oneonta, New York. He finished high school in 1959 and became a folk singer, performing in clubs and bars all over the US prior to forming the folk-rock group Circus Maximus with Bob Bruno in 1966. They cut two albums, *Circus Maximus* and *Neverland Revisited*, for Vanguard before splitting up in 1968.

Still signed to Vanguard, he made his solo debut with *Driftin' Way Of Life* in 1969. Later that year he joined the Atlantic subsidiary, Atco, cutting 'Mr Bojangles' after meeting him in a New Orleans jail. The song was immediately covered by the **Nitty Gritty Dirt Band**. Shortly after, Walker settled in Austin and was signed by MCA; despite the consistent quality of albums like *Jerry Jeff Walker* and *It's A Good Night For Singing*, he failed to achieve commercial acceptance. Backed by the Lost Gonzo Band, he toured incessantly, appearing at festivals and on the college circuit, until in 1978, having parted company with MCA, he reverted to solo performances.

Signed to Elektra he cut two albums, in which he attempted to establish himself within the prevailing singer-songwriter genre: both albums suffered from over-production. In 1981 he moved back to MCA and cut *Reunion*, a sympathetically produced album with sparse arrangements, emphasizing the reflective nature of the lyrics. Still a regular performer on the club circuit, he now tours frequently with other Austin residents like Townes Van Zandt and Guy Clark, while also being associated with New Country performers like **Steve Earle** and **Lyle Lovett**.

DRIFTIN' WAY OF LIFE, Vanguard, 1969
GYPSY SONGMAN, TM, 1989
HILL COUNTRY RAIN, Rykodisc, 1992
LIVE AT GRUENE HALL, Rykodisc (US), 1989

WALLACE, Jerry

Born on December 15, 1933, in Kansas City, Missouri, Jerry Wallace was raised partly in Kansas and then in Glendale, Arizona, before completing his education in California. After recording for the Allied label in 1951, he served in the Navy, before making his mark with 'How The Time Flies' (US#11, 1958) for the Challenge label. Other hits followed, including 'Primrose Lane' (US#8, 1959), 'Little Coco Palm' (US#36, 1960), 'There She Goes' (US#26, 1961), 'Shutters And Boards' (US#24, 1962) and 'In The Misty Moonlight' (US#19, 1964). Possessing a velvet sound resembling that of Nat 'King' Cole, Wallace was dubbed 'Mr Smooth'.

Failing to consolidate the success of the early records, Wallace moved over to country. With little initial success, he finally broke through in 1972, when 'If You Leave Me Tonight I'll Cry' (US#38, C&W#1, 1972) was featured in an episode of the television series *Night Gallery*. This briefly rekindled his career, and other hits followed, including 'Do You Know What It's Like To Be Lonesome' (C&W#2, 1973), 'Don't Give Up On Me' and 'My Wife's House'. In 1975, embroiled in a legal battle with his management, Wallace's recording career went on hold, but he continued to work as an actor and to provide jingles for commercials. His recording career never regained its momentum, but he still performs on television and the club and cabaret circuit.

WARINER, Steve

Steve Wariner is one of country's more rock-oriented performers, who has kept pace with **Clint Black** and **Alan Jackson**, among others, by developing his songwriting abilities and by drawing on the wealth of material emanating from lesser-known writers.

He was born on December 25, 1954, in Indianapolis, Indiana, and made his 1971 debut at the Nashville Country Club, Indianapolis, while still in high school. Later opening for **Dottie West**, he was recruited as bassist in her touring outfit and remained with her for three years, before moving on to **Bob Luman**'s band for a further two and a half years. While playing with Luman, he was signed by **Chet Atkins** to RCA as a solo performer.

Initially produced by Atkins, he went on to secure a run of hits under the tutelage of **Ronnie Milsap**'s producer Tom Collins: 'Your Memory', 'By Now' and 'All Roads Lead To You' (C&W#1, 1981). After parting company with Collins, he started to work with Tony Brown, who, by toughening up his sound and encouraging him to use different writers, revitalized his chart career with 'Midnight Fire' (C&W#5, 1983) and Bob Luman's 'Lonely Women Make Good Lovers' (C&W#4, 1984). At the beginning of 1985 he moved to MCA, where he was teamed with Brown (who had recently left RCA) and **Jimmy Bowen**.

At MCA he started to record his own material, and

achieved a level of consistency with 'Some Fools Never Learn' (C&W#1, 1985), 'You Can Dream Of Me' (C&W#1, 1986), 'Life's Highway' (C&W#1, 1986), 'Small Town Girl' (C&W#1, 1987), 'The Weekend' (C&W#1, 1987), 'Lynda' (C&W#1, 1987), 'Baby I'm Yours' (C&W#2, 1988), 'I Should Be With You' (C&W#2, 1988), 'Where Did I Go Wrong' (C&W#1, 1989) and 'I Got Dreams' (C&W#1, 1989). In 1992, he joined Arista and scored with 'The Tips Of My Fingers' (C&W#1, 1992) and 'Like A River To The Sea' (1993).

I AM READY, Arista (US), 1992
I GOT DREAMS, MCA, 1989
LAREDO, MCA, 1990
LIFE'S HIGHWAY, MCA, 1988
ONE GOOD NIGHT DESERVES ANOTHER, MCA, 1988
STEVE WARINER, MCA, 1988

WATSON, Doc

A fine flat-picker in the mould of **Grady Martin**, **Merle Travis** and **Dan Reno**, Doc Watson spent many years in obscurity assiduously assimilating different styles of picking, and finally achieved recognition during the folk boom of the early 1960s.

Arthel Watson was born blind on March 2, 1923, in Deep Gap, North Carolina. During his childhood he learnt to play the harmonica and the banjo, before graduating to the guitar. He first distinguished himself at a fiddlers' convention in Boone, North Carolina, but this coincided inopportunely with the emergence of rock 'n' roll and the decline of traditional rural music. Throughout the 1950s he played with a string of pop groups, doing covers of hit-parade material, until in 1960 he came to the attention of Ralph Rinzler (see **Greenbriar Boys**), who was organizing the Folkways' sessions that would result in *Old Time Music At Clarence Ashley's*.

These sessions were enthusiastically received, and Watson became an immediate fixture on the Greenwich Village club circuit, and then went on to appear at the Newport Folk Festival in 1963. The following year he was signed by Sam Charters to the Vanguard label, where he remained for the better part of the decade. In 1965, he joined forces with his son, Merle Watson (born on February 8, 1949, in Deep Gap, North Carolina), cutting albums of duets, such as *Doc Watson And Son* (1965), *Southbound* (1966) and *Home Again* (1967).

Object lessons in instrumental virtuosity, they drew their material from a variety of sources: the blues, Appalachian ballads and traditional English and American folk songs. He also continued his association with the Folkways label, recording with folk singers like Jean Ritchie. In 1971, Watson was the catalyst for the **Nitty Gritty Dirt Band**'s *Will The Circle Be Unbroken?* project, which was followed by two more collaborations with Merle for the independent Poppy label: *Then And Now* (1973) and *Two Days In November* (1974), both of which won Grammy awards.

They continued to broaden their scope throughout the 1970s, drawing from the repertoires of **Bob Dylan**, **Elvis Presley**, **Hank Williams** and **Gram Parsons**, and recording for independent labels such as Flying Fish, Magnum, Sundown and Topic, and in 1980 Doc cut *Reflections* with **Chet Atkins**. On October 23, 1985, in Lenoir, North Carolina, Merle was killed in a farming accident, hastening Doc's decision to retire.

BALLADS FROM DEEP (with Merle Watson), Vanguard, 1990
DOWN SOUTH, Sugar Hill (US), 1985
THE ESSENTIAL DOC WATSON, Volume 1-2, Vanguard, 1979
FOLK & COUNTRY LEGEND, L&R, 1982
GUITAR ALBUM (with Merle Watson), Flying Fish (US), 1988
IN THE PINES, Sundown, 1984
OLD TIMEY CONCERT, Vanguard, 1990
ON PRAYING GROUND, Sugar Hill (US), 1990
PICKIN' THE BLUES (with Merle Watson), Flying Fish (US), 1986
PORTRAIT, Sugar Hill (US), 1988
RED ROCKIN' CHAIR (with Merle Watson), Flying Fish (US), 1988
RIDIN' THE MIDNIGHT, Sugar Hill (US), 1988
SONGS FOR LITTLE PICKERS, Sugar Hill (US), 1990

WATSON, Gene

Since his emergence in 1975, Gene Watson has had a series of traditional hard country hits, characterized by prominent steel guitar. Born on October 11, 1943 in Palestine, Texas, and raised in Paris, Texas, he moved to Houston in 1963, where he obtained work in a number of clubs and held down a variety of day jobs. After securing a residency at Houston's Dynasty Club, he started to record for a succession of labels, including Uni, Wild World and Resco. At Resco he cut 'Love In The Afternoon' (C&W#4, 1975), which became a massive regional hit.

Capitol picked it up for national distribution and signed him up, setting in train a string of medium-sized hits that stretched well into the 1980s: 'Where Love Begins', 'You Could Know As Much About

A Stranger', 'Because You Believed In Me', 'Paper Roses', 'Farewell Party' (C&W#3, 1979), 'Should I Come Home (Or Should I Go Crazy)', 'You're Out Doing What I'm Here Doing Without', 'Fourteen Carat Mind' (C&W#1, 1981), 'Memories To Burn' and 'Don't Waste It On The Blues'. After joining MCA in 1980, he switched to Epic in 1985 and continued touring with his Farewell Party Band, joining up with **Tammy Wynette** for a duet on her *Higher Ground* album.

Despite his pre-eminence as an exponent of honky-tonk, his unwillingness to cross over into the more populist areas of country-pop has adversely affected his international career, with Ireland being the only country outside the US to fully appreciate him.

GREATEST HITS, MCA (US), 1986
HEARTACHES LOVE & STUFF, MCA (US), 1984
I AM READY, Broadland (US), 1992
IN OTHER WORDS, Mercury (US), 1992
LITTLE BY LITTLE, MCA, 1984
SOMETIMES I GET LUCKY, MCA (US), 1986

WATSON, Merle see WATSON, Doc

WEISSBERG, Eric see GREENBRIAR BOYS

WELLER, Freddy
Formerly a member of Paul Revere & the Raiders, Freddy Weller went on to write a brace of bubblegum hits - 'Dizzy' and 'Jam Up, Jelly Tight' - for Tommy Roe in the late 1960s, before starting a reasonably successful career as a country singer.

He was born on September 9, 1947, in Atlanta, Georgia, and was a member of Paul Revere & the Raiders (signed to Columbia) from 1967 to 1971, during which time he penned Roe's two hits. In 1969 he started his solo career as a country singer, cutting **Joe South**'s 'Games People Play' (C&W#2, 1969), 'These Are Not My People', Chuck Berry's 'Promised Land', 'Indian Lake' and 'Another Night Of Love', as well as producing 'Stolen Moments' for **Razzy Bailey**.

After leaving Paul Revere & the Raiders, he joined Joe South's touring unit as bassist, before joining Billy Joe Royal's band. In 1974 he was signed to the Dot label, before returning to Columbia. Dropped by Columbia in 1980, Weller has since kept a low profile;

it is rumoured that he has rejoined Paul Revere & the Raiders on 'oldies' tour' packages.

BACK ON THE STREET, Bulldog, 1987

WELLS, Kitty
For many years the undisputed Queen of Country, Kitty Wells came to prominence at the beginning of the 1950s, and reigned supreme until **Tammy Wynette**'s emergence in the mid-1960s.

She was born Muriel Deason on August 30, 1918, in Nashville, Tennessee, and started to sing gospel in church as early as 1925. By 1932, she had learnt to play the guitar and was playing at church functions and various civic events. In 1936 she made her radio debut on WXIX, broadcasting on the *Dixie Early Birds* programme; two years later she met **Johnny Wright** (at that time performing with Jack Anglin, as Johnny & Jack), who suggested that she change her name to Kitty Wells - in reference to the **Carter Family**'s song, 'I'm A Goin' To Marry Kitty Wells'.

In 1938 he did marry Kitty Wells, and with Johnny & Jack and their touring band, the Tennessee Mountain Boys, Wells toured the radio stations and concert halls of the South. Her unaffected delivery (on material that ranged from hillbilly to contemporary), retaining the inflexions and intonations of her native Tennessee, was regularly broadcast on WBIG, Greensboro, North Carolina, and WNOX, Knoxville's *Mid-Day Merry-Go-Round*. The embodiment of the local girl made good, she joined the *Grand Ole Opry* in 1947, before moving to the recently established *Louisiana Hayride* on KWKH.

Within five years she had moved back, settling into a regular spot on the *Grand Ole Opry* and securing a recording contract with Decca. Her years with Decca established her beyond any doubt as country's premier female performer, with a string of hits that included 'It Wasn't God Who Made Honky Tonk Angels' (C&W#1, 1952), 'Paying For That Back Street Affair', 'Making Believe' (C&W#2, 1955), 'Searching' (C&W#4, 1956), 'Jealousy', 'Mommy For A Day', **John D. Loudermilk** and Wells's 'Amigo's Guitar', 'Left To Right', 'Heartbreak USA' (C&W#1, 1961), 'Unloved, Unwanted', 'Password' and 'You Don't Hear Her'.

Her solo career continuing apace, she also recorded a number of duets, including 'One By One' and 'As Long As I Live' with **Red Foley**; 'We'll Stick Together' with Johnny Wright; and others with **Webb Pierce**, **Roy Drusky** and **Roy Acuff**. She also became one of country's first high-profile television

241

performers, with her programme, *The Johnny Wright And Kitty Wells Show*, and regular appearances on Red Foley's *Ozark Jubilee*, **Carl Smith**'s *Country Music Hall*, *The **Little Jimmy Dickens** Show* and Johnny Carson's *Tonight*.

In 1974, she terminated her contract with MCA (formerly Decca) and signed with Capricorn, cutting *Forever Young*; and in 1976 she was elected to the Country Music Hall Of Fame. Performing less in recent years, she still makes the occasional appearance with her son **Bobby Wright**.

GOLDEN YEARS, Rounder (US), 1988
GOLDEN YEARS: 1949-57, Bear Family (Germany), 1987
KITTY WELLS STORY, MCA (US), 1986
KITTY'S CHOICE, Stetson, 1986
MAKIN' BELIEVE, Colorado, 1985
ORIGINAL QUEEN OF COUNTRY MUSIC, Bulldog, 1982

WEST, Dottie

During the 1970s and early 1980s, Dottie West became one of the most effective exponents of country-pop, her slick stage show enabling her to play the Las Vegas cabaret circuit as well as traditional Nashville venues like the Grand Ole Opry.

She was born Dorothy Marie Marsh on a cotton and sugar-cane farm in McMinnville, Tennessee, on October 11, 1932. While studying music at Tennessee Technical College, she met her future husband, Bill West, and they moved to Ohio on graduation, where they performed as a duo on local television, with Bill playing the steel guitar. After their marriage they returned to Nashville, where Dottie was initially signed by Starday, and then moved on to Atlantic.

In 1963 she was signed to RCA and started to work with artists including **Patsy Cline** and **Roger Miller**, as well as writing 'Is This Me' for **Jim Reeves**. Her first hit, 'Let Me Off At The Corner', came in 1963, and a year later she wrote 'Here Comes My Baby', which was a big hit for Perry Como and won her a Grammy. Her degree in music stood her in good stead as an arranger with the Memphis and Kansas City Symphony Orchestra, and in 1970 she wrote 'Country Sunshine', which was subsequently used on a Coke commercial.

Among her most significant hits were 'Would You Hold It Against Me', 'Paper Mansions', 'Country Girl', 'Forever Yours', 'Country Sunshine' (C&W#2, 1973) and 'Last Time I Saw Him' (C&W#8, 1974). In 1976 she was signed by United Artists, and cut 'When It's Just You And Me' and 'A Lesson In Leavin'' (C&W#1,

1980). Moving on to Liberty, she continued - albeit erratically - to notch up hits, which included 'Are You Happy Baby' (C&W#1, 1981) and 'What Are We Doin' In Love' (US#14, C&W#1, 1981).

She also recorded a number of duets: **Justin Tubb**'s 'Love Is No Excuse' with Jim Reeves; 'Rings Of Gold' (C&W#2, 1969) and 'There's A Story Goin' Round' (C&W#7, 1969) with **Don Gibson**; 'Every Time Two Fools Collide' (C&W#1, 1978), 'Anyone Who Isn't Me Tonight' (C&W#2, 1978), 'All I Ever Need Is You' (C&W#1, 1979) and ''Til I Can Make It On My Own'' (C&W#3, 1979) with **Kenny Rogers**.

In 1966 her first marriage broke up and she married drummer Byron Metcalf. During the 1970s, she appeared in several movies and became a regular on the Las Vegas cabaret circuit, but by the mid-1980s her career was hampered by cancer, from which she died on September 4, 1991.

CLASSICS (with Kenny Rogers), Capitol (US), 1979
I FALL TO PIECES, Gusto (US), 1988

WEST, Shelley

The daughter of **Dottie West**, Shelley West was born in Cleveland, Ohio, on May 23, 1958. She made her debut singing back-up vocals in her mother's road-show in 1975, and remained with the outfit until 1977. In 1978, Shelley married Allen Frizzell - a member of her mother's roadshow, and the brother of **Lefty** and **David Frizzell** - and they moved to the West Coast, working the club circuit with David Frizzell.

This led to a recording contract for Shelley and David with Snuff Garrett's Viva label; their first single 'You're The Reason God Made Oklahoma' (C&W#1, 1980) was included on the soundtrack of the Clint Eastwood movie *Any Which Way You Can*. Three more hit singles followed: 'A Texas State Of Mind', 'Another Honky-Tonk Night On Broadway' and 'I Just Came Here To Dance'.

In 1983, having divorced Allen, she cut 'Jose Cuervo' (C&W#1, 1983), 'Flight 309 To Tennessee' and 'Another Motel Memory', but left the music business to look after her family and care for her terminally ill mother.

WEST, Speedy

During the 1940s and 1950s, pedal steel guitarist Speedy West was one of country's most sought-after session musicians. Born Wesley Webb West on January 25, 1924, in Springfield, Missouri, he started playing the steel guitar at thirteen and, after serving in the army during the war, joined the migration of musicians out to the West Coast. In 1948 he worked with **Hank Penny** and **Spade Cooley**, and established his credentials as one of the more inspired and subtle players on the circuit. Over the next five years he went on to work with nearly every major country artist of the time, including **Tennessee Ernie Ford**, **Johnny Horton**, **Merle Travis**, **Hank Thompson**, **Tex Williams**, **Tex Ritter**, **Rex Allen** and **Slim Whitman**. In recent years he has confined his activities to reunions, but still cuts the occasional album, including *Two Guitars: Country Style*, a collaboration with guitarist Jimmy Bryant.

GUITAR SPECTACULAR, Stetson, 1989

WESTERNERS see MASSEY, Louise

WHITE, Clarence
Along with **Gram Parsons**, Clarence White was one of the prime movers in the **Byrds**' shift from country-rock to a more authentic country sound. He was also a founder-member of the Kentucky Colonels, one of the first progressive bluegrass outfits to emerge in the early 1960s.

Born in Lewiston, Maine, on June 7, 1944, White was raised in California with his two brothers Roland and Eric, with whom he formed the Country Boys. By 1961, the group had evolved into the Kentucky Colonels, the line-up comprising Clarence (guitar), Roland (mandolin), Roger Bush (bass; see **Country Gazette**), Billy Ray Latham (banjo) and Leroy Mack (dobro). In 1966, after recording *Kentucky Colonels* for World Pacific, White left to form Nashville West with **Gene Parsons**.

He joined the Byrds in late 1968 and remained with them until 1973, when he left to re-form the Kentucky Colonels. He was killed by a drunken driver on July 14, 1973, while loading his van after a gig.

KENTUCKY COLONELS (with Clarence White), 1966, Shiloh (US), 1979
KENTUCKY COLONELS FEATURING CLARENCE WHITE, Rounder (US), 1988
ON STAGE (Kentucky Colonels), Sundown, 1984

WHITE, Tony Joe
For a brief spell in the late 1960s, Tony Joe White held centre-stage as the sole practitioner of swamp-rock, which, despite his abilities as a writer and guitarist, failed to catch on. He was born on July 23, 1943, in Oak Grove, Louisiana and formed his first group, Tony and the Mojos, in the late 1950s, before moving briefly to Texas, where he led Tony and the Twilights. In 1968, he moved to Nashville and was signed by **Fred Foster** to the Monument label, with **Billy Swan** producing. His debut *Black And White* (1969) included 'Polk Salad Annie' (US#8, 1969), which was covered by **Elvis Presley**; the follow-ups, despite their artistic merits, failed to raise the public's pulse, with 'Groupie Girl' (UK#22, 1970) being the only hit.

Dropped by Monument, he was signed by Warner Bros. for the Peter Asher-produced *Tony Joe White*. Later albums saw him collaborating with such fine producers as Tom Dowd and Jerry Wexler, but success continued to be elusive. In 1991, he launched a comeback, under the expert guidance of Tina Turner's manager, Roger Davies, cutting *Closer To The Truth* for the Remark label.

CLOSER TO THE TRUTH, Remark, 1991

WHITLEY, Keith
Keith Whitley is a rare example of a bluegrass musician who made it to the top without compromising his devotion to the traditional aspects of country music. Born in Sandy Hook, Kentucky, on July 1, 1954, he was a competent guitarist by the age of six and was broadcasting on local radio in West Virginia when he was nine. In 1971, he joined **Ricky Skaggs** in Ralph Stanley's (see **Stanley Brothers**) Clinch Mountain Boys, where both made their debut with *Cry From The Cross: A Tribute To The Stanley Brothers* for the Jalna label. Remaining with Stanley until 1977, he went on to join **J.D. Crowe**'s band, New South, as lead vocalist, before moving to Nashville in 1983, where he won a recording contract with RCA.

His label debut, *A Hard Act To Follow*, was released the following year, and in 1986 he cut *LA To Miami*, which included four hits: 'Miami, My Amy', 'Ten Feet Away', 'Homecoming '63' and 'Hard Livin''. After shelving an album's worth of material, he scored his first major hit with **Bob McDill**'s 'Don't Close Your Eyes' (C&W#1, 1988), **Paul Overstreet** and Don Schlitz's 'When You Say Nothing At All' (C&W#1, 1988), **Sonny Curtis**'s 'I'm No Stranger To The Rain' (C&W#1, 1989), 'I Wonder Do You Think Of Me' (C&W#1, 1989) and 'I'm Over You' (C&W#2, 1990). Married to **Lorrie Morgan**, his blossoming career ended suddenly on May 9, 1989, when he died of alcoholic poisoning.

DON'T CLOSE YOUR EYES, RCA, 1989
GREATEST HITS, RCA, 1991

WHITLEY, Ray

Ray Whitley had a chequered career until his mid-1930s' debut as a Singing Cowboy on *Barn Dance* on New York's WHN. He was born in 1901 in Atlanta, Georgia, and joined the Navy before moving to Philadelphia, and then New York, working as an electrician and in the steel works. He became joint host of *Barn Dance* with **Tex Ritter** in 1935, while recording for ARC and Decca and having hits with 'Blue Yodel Blues' and 'The Last Flight Of Wiley Post'.

The following year he joined the migration to Hollywood, where his vocal skills found favour with RKO and Universal. Appearing in scores of westerns, he still found time to front his own Western Swing-type band - who performed regularly at the Culver City, Baldwin Park, Compton and Venice Pier Ballrooms - and to record for labels like Conqueror, Okeh and Decca. He also took up songwriting - sometimes with **Fred Rose** - and penned hits for **Gene Autry** like 'Back In The Saddle Again', 'Lonely River' and 'I Hang My Head And Cry'.

In later years, he managed **Jimmy Wakely** and the **Sons Of Pioneers**, while acting as a consultant for the Gibson guitar company (who were building the J-200, a perennial favourite with country musicians) and making guest appearances at California film festivals.

WHITMAN, Slim

Always more popular in Europe than in his homeland, Slim Whitman's effortless crooning has encompassed a wide range of styles, giving him an enduring appeal to middle-aged audiences. He was born Otis Dewey Whitman on January 20, 1924, in Tampa, Florida, and planned to be a baseball player. After leaving school, he worked at a meat-packing plant, before getting work in a shipyard in Tampa. In 1943, he joined the Navy and served on the *USS Chilton*, until being demobbed in 1945. The following year, he joined the Plant City Berries baseball team and sang to supplement his income, winning a regular spot Tampa's WDAE.

This led to a recording contract with RCA, where he scored a minor hit with 'Casting My Lasso To The Sky', which created the opening for him to join the *Louisiana Hayride* on KWKH in 1950. By 1952 he had joined Imperial, where he scored with the classic yodelling tune, 'Indian Love Call' (US#9, C&W#2, 1952; UK#7,

1955) from the operetta *Rose Marie*; the operetta proved to be a rich vein, as Whitman later scored with 'Rose Marie' (at thirteen weeks, the longest-running UK No.1 before Bryan Adams's 'Everything I Do I Do It For You' deposed it in 1991; UK#1, 1955).

Among his other hits were 'Keep It A Secret', 'North Wind', 'Secret Love', 'Cattle Call', 'China Doll' (UK#15, 1955), 'Tumbling Tumbleweeds' (UK#19, 1956), 'I'm A Fool' (UK#16, 1956), 'Serenade' (UK#8, 1956), 'I'll Take You Home Again Kathleen' (UK#7, 1957), 'More Than Yesterday', 'Guess Who', 'Something Beautiful' and 'Happy Anniversary' (UK#14, 1974).

While his current singles seldom chart, he still issues occasional albums (at present for Epic), and continues to tour Europe. In the UK, his greatest-hits collections are regularly re-issued and promoted on television, usually pushing them to the top of the album charts.

50 ORIGINAL TRACKS, EMI, 1993
IRISH SONGS, EMI, 1988

WHITTER, Henry

Along with **Eck Robertson** and **Fiddling John Carson**, Henry Whitter was one of country music's first recording artists, cutting sides for **Ralph Peer** as early as 1923. He was born on April 6, 1892, in Fries, Virginia, where he worked in a cotton mill after leaving school. Having learnt the harmonica, fiddle, guitar and piano, he played at local functions in his spare time. In 1923 he went to New York and cut two unreleased sides for the General Phonograph Company. When Okeh scored considerable interest with Fiddling John Carson's sides, Whitter was invited to cut 'The Wreck Of The Ole '97', which received universal acclaim and became one of the biggest-selling songs of the 1920s when covered by **Vernon Dalhart**.

Despite performing with the Virginia Breakdowners in 1924 and the blind fiddler George Banman Grayson between 1927 and 1929, Whitter quickly returned to obscurity. His partnership with Grayson was brought to an abrupt end when the latter died in a car crash during the mid-1930s. Whitter continued to perform, but his health deteriorated and he died from diabetes on November 10, 1941, in Morganton, North Carolina.

WILBURN BROTHERS

Doyle (born July 7, 1930) and Teddy Wilburn (born November 30, 1931) were born in Thayer, Missouri. An enduring vocal duo, they made their debut on the

Grand Ole Opry in the early 1940s with their elder brothers, Leslie and Lester.

In 1951 Teddy, Leslie and Lester joined **Webb Pierce**'s Southern Valley Boys, but Doyle, Teddy and Leslie were drafted for military service in the Korean War the following year, while Lester joined the Johnny & Jack roadshow (see **Wright, Johnny**). After their war service, Doyle and Teddy formed the Wilburn Brothers and toured with **Faron Young** from 1953 until 1955, cutting their first sides as a duo for Decca in 1954. They scored their first hit in 1956 with 'Go Away With Me' and went on to chart into the 1970s with titles like 'Which One Is To Blame', 'Somebody Back In Town', 'A Woman's Intuition', 'Trouble's Back In Town', 'Tell Her So', 'It's Another World', 'Someone Before Me' and 'Hurt Her One For Me'.

Furthering **Loretta Lynn**'s career by featuring her on their syndicated television show, they also founded the Sure-Fire music publishing company and the Wil-Helm Talent Agency. Regular contributors to the *Grand Ole Opry*, they still record periodically for the independent First Generation label, but have been unable to match their early success.

CITY LIMITS, Stetson, 1988
COUNTRY GOLD, Stetson, 1985
TEDDY & DOYLE, Stetson, 1987
THE WILBURN BROTHERS SHOW, Stetson, 1986

WILLIAMS, Doc

A longstanding contributor to WWVA's *Wheeling Jamboree*, Doc Williams was born Andrew Smid in Central Europe on June 26, 1914, and was raised in Pennsylvania, where he became a coal miner. Assuming the name Doc Williams, he started to perform in and around Cleveland from 1934 until 1936. In 1937 he made his debut on the *Wheeling Jamboree* and remained with show for over forty years.

While never achieving national celebrity, he became one of the the most popular performers in Canada and the northeast - brief spells at WREC, Memphis, did little to enhance his reputation in the South. In 1948 he married Jessie Wanda Crupe, who became a central figure in his band, the Border Riders. That same year he also set up the Wheeling label, cutting titles like 'Beyond The Sunset' and 'Willie Roy The Crippled Boy', which were modest local hits. A staunch traditionalist, Williams has stood aloof from the new trends in country music.

WILLIAMS, Don

In the mid-1970s, Don Williams came to prominence in Europe as a result of Eric Clapton's alleged enthusiasm for his music. His warm baritone filled the void created by **Jim Reeves**'s death some years earlier, appealing to a vast audience that weren't really country fans.

He was born on May 27, 1939, in Floydada, Texas, but was raised in Corpus Christi. After military service he formed the folkish Pozo Seco Singers, with Susan Taylor and Lofton Kline, scoring with 'I Can Make It With You' (US#32, 1966) and 'Look What You've Done' (US#32, 1967) on Columbia. In 1971, the group split up and Don Williams moved to Nashville to work as a songwriter. After signing with **Jack Clement**'s JMI publishing company, his reputation as a writer began to develop with his songs being covered by artists such as **Tompall and the Glaser Brothers**, **Lefty Frizzell**, **Jeanne Pruett**, **Dickey Lee** and **Kenny Rogers**.

In 1973, he teamed up with producer **Allen Reynolds** for *Don Williams: Volume 1*, which was released to considerable acclaim on Clement's JMI label. The following year JMI shut down; Williams moved to ABC-Dot and the hits started to roll in: 'I Wouldn't Want To Live If You Didn't Love Me' (C&W#1, 1974), 'You're My Best Friend' (C&W#1, 1975; UK#35, 1976), **Bob McDill**'s '(Turn Out The Light And) Love Me Tonight' (C&W#1, 1975), ''Til The Rivers All Run Dry' (C&W#1, 1976), 'I Recall A Gypsy Woman' (UK#13, 1976), McDill's 'Say It Again' (C&W#1, 1976), 'Some Broken Hearts Never Mend' (C&W#1, 1977), 'I'm Just A Country Boy' (C&W#1, 1977) and 'Tulsa Time' (C&W#1, 1978).

In 1979, ABC was absorbed into the parent company MCA, and Williams's records were duly issued on that label: McDill's 'It Must Be Love' (C&W#1, 1979), 'Love Me Over Again' (C&W#1, 1979), 'I Believe In You' (US#24, C&W#1, 1980), 'Lord, I Hope This Day Is Good' (C&W#1, 1982), 'If Hollywood Don't Need You' (C&W#1, 1982), Roger Cook and **John Prine**'s 'Love Is On A Roll' (C&W#1, 1983), 'Nobody But You' (C&W#2, 1983), Benny Gallagher and Graham Lyle's 'Stay Young' (C&W#1, 1984) and 'That's The Thing About Love' (C&W#1, 1984).

By 1985 he had moved to the Capitol label, but Williams, suffering from a back injury, put his career on hold for eighteen months or so. On his return, his succession of hits continued with 'Heartbeat In The Darkness' (C&W#1, 1986), 'We've Got A Good Fire Goin'', 'Then It's Love' and 'I Wouldn't Be A Man'. In 1989 he moved to RCA, scoring with 'One Good Well',

'I've Been Loved By The Best' and 'Back In My Younger Days' (C&W#2, 1990). Apart from his musical activities, he has appeared in two films: *W.W. And The Dixie Dance Kings* (1975) and *Smokey And The Bandit II* (1980).

AS LONG AS I HAVE YOU, RCA, 1989
CAFE CAROLINA, MCA, 1984
CURRENTS, RCA, 1992
GREATEST HITS, Volumes 1-4, MCA (US), 1988
I BELIEVE IN YOU, MCA, 1980
LOVERS AND BEST FRIENDS, MCA, 1987
NEW MOVES, Capitol, 1986
TRACES, Capitol, 1987
TRUE LOVE, RCA, 1990
YOU'RE MY BEST FRIEND, MCA, 1984

WILLIAMS, Hank

The influence of Hank Williams upon successive generations of performers is of such magnitude that there are few who haven't been touched in some way by his music. He was born Hiram King Williams on September 17, 1923, in Georgiana, Alabama, and joined the local church choir in 1929. By 1936 he had won a talent contest in Montgomery - singing 'WPA Blues' - which prompted him to form the **Drifting Cowboys**. For the next ten years he fronted the Drifting Cowboys on WSFA, Mongomery, and was then signed by the Sterling label in December, 1946, where he was backed by the **Willis Brothers**. The following year, he was signed by **Frank Walker** to the MGM label, and became a regular on the *Louisiana Hayride*.

From 1949, in tandem with his producer and occasional co-writer **Fred Rose**, he started a run of hits with 'Lovesick Blues', which was followed by 'Wedding Bells', 'Mind Your Own Business', 'You're Gonna Change', 'My Buckets Got A Hole In It', 'I Just Don't Like This Kind Of Living', 'Long Gone Lonesome Blues', 'Why Don't You Love Me', 'Why Should We Try Anymore', 'Moaning The Blues', 'Cold Cold Heart', 'Howlin' At The Moon', 'Hey Good Lookin'', 'Crazy Love', 'Baby We're Really In Love', 'Honky Tonk Blues', 'Half As Much', 'Jambalaya', 'Settin' The Woods On Fire' and 'I'll Never Get Out Of This World Alive'. He also adopted the pseudonym of Luke The Drifter for a number of monologues.

Despite his formidable popularity, he was beset by personal problems: he was fired from the *Grand Ole Opry* in August 1952 because of excessive drinking, and the same problem caused his wife, Audrey

Shepherd, to divorce him the same year. On January 1, 1953, he was booked into a gig in Canton, Ohio, and, with a chauffeur driving him, fell asleep in the back of the car. He died of a heart attack en route.

After his death, MGM issued 'Your Cheatin' Heart', 'Take These Chains From My Heart', 'I Won't Be Home No More' and 'Weary Blues From Waiting', all of which became big hits. His band, the Drifting Cowboys, went on to back **Ray Price**, who proved himself to be a good interpreter of Williams's songs.

In the years since his death Williams's reputation has increased several-fold, with performers of all musical persuasions covering his material, and some - like **Gram Parsons** and **Keith Whitley** - emulating his life-style and following him to an early death. His songs remain as poignant and touching today as they did forty years ago, and have been covered by **Ray Charles**, **Dwight Yoakam**, **Randy Travis**, Mitch Miller, Tony Bennett and Jo Stafford, among others. He was elected to the Country Music Hall Of Fame in 1961, and the biopic *Your Cheatin' Heart* was made in 1964, with George Hamilton playing the part of Williams, and his son, **Hank Williams, Jr,** singing on the soundtrack. Several biographies have appeared: Chet Flippo's *Your Cheatin' Heart* (1981) is probably the best.

BEYOND THE SUNSET, Polydor, 1988
GREATEST HITS, Polydor, 1978
HANK WILLIAMS AND THE DRIFTING COWBOYS, Flyright, 1987
HEY GOOD LOOKIN', Polydor, 1992
I AIN'T GOT NOTHING BUT TIME, Polydor, 1988
I WON'T BE HOME NO MORE, Polydor, 1987
I'M SO LONESOME I COULD CRY, Polydor, 1987
LET'S TURN BACK THE YEARS, Polydor, 1987
LIVE AT THE GRAND OLE OPRY, MGM, 1987
LONG GONE LONESOME BLUES, Polydor, 1987
LOST HIGHWAY, Polydor, 1986
LOVESICK BLUES, Polydor, 1986
ON THE AIR, Polydor, 1988
RARE TAKES AND RADIO CUTS, Polydor, 1988

WILLIAMS, Jr, Hank

It is very much to his credit that Hank Williams, Jr, has not buckled under the burden of his distinguished father **Hank Williams**'s reputation. There are very few performers who have had such enormous expectations thrust upon them - expectations that were not purely artistic: for years he was expected to carry on his father's hedonistic life-style.

He was born Randall Hank Williams, Jr, on May 26, 1949, in Shreveport, Louisiana, but grew up in Nashville. His natural athleticism enabled him to become proficient at a number of different sports, including boxing, football and swimming. He formed his first band, Randall and the Rockets, while still at school, before joining his mother, Audrey Williams, in the *Caravan Of Stars* roadshow, performing many of his father's best-known songs. In 1964 he was recruited to perform his father's songs on the soundtrack to the film *Your Cheatin' Heart*; this enabled him to secure a contract with MGM, where he scored with a string of hits, including 'Long Gone Lonesome Blues', 'Endless Sleep', 'Standing In The Shadows', 'It's All Over But The Crying', 'Cajun Baby', 'I'd Rather Be Gone', 'All For The Love Of Sunshine' (C&W#1, 1970) and 'Eleven Roses' (C&W#1, 1972).

In 1974 he moved away from Nashville in an attempt to develop his own sound, cutting *Hank Williams Jr And Friends*, which included contributions from **Charlie Daniels**, Chuck Leavell (of the Allman Brothers Band) and Toy Caldwell (of the Marshall Tucker Band). Just before its release, he sustained dreadful head injuries in a hunting accident that put him out of action for almost two years. On his return he joined Warner Bros., distancing himself still further from the shadow of his father, and consolidating his own musical identity with the **Waylon Jennings**–produced *New South*, which aligned him with country's Outlaw Movement. While this was part of an overall plan, the music he produced sounded contrived, as evidenced by the wry references to his father's influence: Waylon Jennings's 'Are You Sure Hank Done It This Way', **Kris Kristofferson**'s 'If You Don't Like Hank Williams' and Williams's 'Kaw Liga'.

Throughout the 1980s he notched up one hit after another, having moved to Elektra and producer **Jimmy Bowen**. Among his biggest hits, many of them self-penned, were 'Texas Women' (C&W#1, 1981), 'Dixie On My Mind' (C&W#1, 1981), 'All My Rowdy Friends (Have Settled Down)' (C&W#1, 1981), 'A Country Boy Can Survive' (C&W#2, 1982), Hank Williams's 'Honky Tonkin'' (C&W#1, 1982), 'I'm For Love' (C&W#1, 1985), 'This Ain't Dallas' (C&W#4, 1985) and Fats Waller's 'Ain't Misbehavin'' (C&W#1, 1986).

In 1986 he ended his five-year partnership with Bowen, which had spawned a series of commercially successful albums of extremely high quality - in 1982 he had nine albums listed in the country charts, a feat only equalled by **Elvis Presley**. Bowen's replacements were **Barry Beckett** and Jim Ed Norman (the

Nashville head of Warner Bros.). This arrangement worked equally well, with Williams matching his former consistency: 'Country State Of Mind' (C&W#2, 1986), Hank Williams's 'Mind Your Own Business' (featuring evangelist Reverend Ike, **Reba McEntire** and Tom Petty; C&W#1, 1986), 'Born To Boogie' (C&W#1, 1987) and 'There's A Tear In My Beer' (a duet with his late father). In 1990 he cut the impressive *Lone Wolf*, featuring a duet with the cajun singer **Jimmy 'C' Newman**, which was followed by a string of complete turkeys, such as the execrable *Out Of Left Field*.

ARE YOU SURE HANK DONE IT THIS WAY?, Warner Bros. (US), 1985
BEST OF HANK & HANK (with Hank Williams), Curb (US), 1992
BEST OF HANK WILLIAMS Jr: Roots and Branches, Polydor, 1992
BEST OF HANK WILLIAMS Jr, Warner Bros., 1989
GREATEST HITS, Elektra (US), 1984
OUT OF LEFT FIELD, Capricorn (US), 1993

WILLIAMS, Leona

Leona Williams and her husband **Merle Haggard** co-wrote 'Someday When Things Are Good', which proved to be one of his biggest hits of the 1980s. Born Leona Helton in Vienna, Missouri, on January 7, 1943, she was inducted into the family band comprising mother, father, four brothers and seven sisters, before securing her own radio show *Leona Sings* on KWOS, Jefferson City, Missouri. In 1958, she married bassist Ron Williams and they joined the **Loretta Lynn** roadshow. After her marriage broke up, she secured a contract with the Hickory label and was contracted to the **Acuff**-**Rose** publishing company.

In 1974, having joined MCA, she cut *San Quentin's First Lady* in front of an audience of prisoners, before joining Merle Haggard's group, the Strangers, as a backing vocalist. In 1978 she married Haggard, and cut an album of duets, *Heart To Heart*, for Mercury in 1983, but they split up the same year. After the divorce, she married Dave Kirby, a former member of the Strangers, and retired to look after her family in her former hometown, Vienna, Missouri.

LEONA WILLIAMS AND HER DIXIE BAND, Retrieval, 1979

WILLIAMS, Lucinda

One of the better singer-songwriters, Lucinda Williams seems to be able to draw from, and adapt to, any style she chooses. She was born in Lake Charles, Louisiana, and grew up in different towns throughout the South, as her father was a poet and visiting professor of literature at innumerable colleges and universities below the the Mason-Dixon line.

By the late 1970s, having honed her skills on the folk-club circuit, she recorded a brace of albums for the Folkways label - *Ramblin' On My Mind* (1979) and *Happy Woman Blues* (1980) - that gave the erroneous impression that she was just a folk singer. More years on the club circuit followed until the mid-1980s, when she moved to Los Angeles and cut the excellent *Lucinda Williams*. This proved to be a watershed, as the enthusiastic critical response encouraged Warner Bros. to sign her. *Sweet Old World* (1992) showed that she, like **Mary-Chapin Carpenter**, is one of the most mature songwriters of the 1990s.

LUCINDA WILLIAMS, Rough Trade, 1989
SWEET OLD WORLD, Warner Bros., 1992

WILLIAMS, Tex

Co-writer of 'Smoke! Smoke! Smoke (That Cigarette)!' with **Merle Travis**, Tex Williams was born Sol Williams on August 23, 1917, in Ramsey, Illinois, and started his career as a Singing Cowboy on local radio in 1930, accompanying himself on banjo and harmonica. After moving to California in 1935, he began to make appearances in westerns alongside **Tex Ritter** and Charles Starrett, a career which was to continue right up to 1955.

During the late 1930s he joined **Spade Cooley**'s band as lead vocalist, and sang on Cooley's biggest hit 'Shame On You'. He remained with him until 1946, when he formed his own outfit, Western Caravan, and became one of the first signings to the Capitol label. His third release was 'Smoke! Smoke! Smoke (That Cigarette)!', which became a monster hit (and was later a hit for **Commander Cody**), launching him into a constant round of radio and television engagements. Although his brand of Western Swing tended to be over-arranged, he cut several other hits, including the pithy 'Don't Telephone, Don't Telegraph, Tell A Woman' and 'Bluebird On Your Windowsill', and accompanied vocalists Jo Stafford and Dinah Shore on many of their ballroom dates.

During the 1960s, having been signed to the Boone label, he scored again with 'Bottom Of A Mountain' (1966); moving to Monument his success continued with 'It Ain't No Big Thing' (1970) and 'The Night Miss Nancy Ann's Hotel For Single Girls Burned Down'

(1971). He continued making appearances until his death on October 11, 1985.

ROMPIN', STOMPIN', SINGIN', SWINGIN' (with Spade Cooley), Bear Family (Germany), 1983
TEX WILLIAMS IN LAS VEGAS, Stetson, 1989

WILLING, Foy

During the 1930s, the trail-blazing success of Singing Cowboys like **Gene Autry** and **Roy Rogers** encouraged many others to follow their example. Foy Willing, while never achieving the success of Autry and Rogers, put together, in Riders Of The Purple Sage, a cowboy group second only to the **Sons Of Pioneers**.

Born Foy Willingham in 1915 in Bosque County, Texas, he broadcast on local radio throughout his high-school years, moving to New York in 1933 where his radio show was sponsored by the Crazy Water Crystals Company. In 1935 he returned to Texas, before moving to California in 1940, where he formed the Riders Of The Purple Sage, which included **Jimmy Wakely** alumnus Scotty Harrell.

From 1942 the group regularly appeared with Monte Hale and Roy Rogers in a succession of Westerns (made by the Republic film company) and broadcast on *Hollywood Barn Dance*, *The Andrews Sisters Show* and *The Roy Rogers Show*. They also recorded extensively, cutting 'No One To Cry To' and 'Cool Water' for Majestic, and 'Texas Blues' and 'Ghost Riders In The Sky' for Capitol. In 1952, Willing disbanded the group and retired from the music industry. In later years, he re-emerged to cut the odd album and to make special appearances at rodeos and film festivals.

FOY WILLING AND THE RIDERS OF THE PURPLE SAGE, Outlaw, 1987

WILLIS BROTHERS

Comprising Guy (born in Alex, Arkansas, on July 15, 1915), Skeeter (born in Coalton, Oklahoma, on December 20, 1917) and Vic (born in Schulter, Oklahoma, on May 31, 1922), the Willis Brothers had a long and distinguished career in their own right, but achieved greater distinction as session musicians.

Initially known as the Oklahoma Wranglers, they made their radio debut on KGEF, Shawnee, Oklahoma, before joining *Brush Creek Follies* on Kansas City's KMBC in 1940. Joining the army during the war years, they re-grouped in 1946 and became regulars on the *Grand Ole Opry*, forging a relationship with **Eddy Arnold**. They worked with Arnold over the next eight years, backing him on his syndicated television show and also performing their own act; they also backed **Hank Williams** on his few sessions for the Sterling label at the end of 1946.

Recording with a string of different labels, such as MGM, Coral, RCA and Mercury, they hit their commercial peak with Starday in the mid-1960s with a bunch of minor hits that included 'Give Me Forty Acres', 'Bob' and 'Somebody Loves My Dog'. These hits prolonged their stay at the *Grand Ole Opry* well into the 1970s. Although Skeeter died of cancer in 1976, Vic and Guy continued working into the 1980s.

BEST OF THE WILLIS BROTHERS, Starday (US), 1987

WILLS, BOB

Bob Wills was one of the most significant contributors to the evolution of that quintessentially American musical form, Western Swing, which was a synthesis of many disparate influences, including ragtime, traditional fiddling, jazz and the black work-songs of the Deep South.

Bob Wills was born in Limestone County, Texas, on March 6, 1905. His father was a fiddler, and it was his early influence that imbued Wills with his appreciation of music. He began his career playing with the **Light Crust Doughboys**, which was sponsored by a local flour company and featured vocalist **Milton Brown**. In 1932 Wills and Brown cut 'Nancy Jane' - previously recorded by Big Bill Broonzy's group, the Famous Hokum Boys - for RCA, under the name of the Fort Worth Doughboys, and started to broadcast on the radio station KFJZ.

By 1933 Wills had formed the nucleus of what was to become the Texas Playboys: with frequent changes of line-up, **Leon McAuliffe** (steel guitar), Al Stricklin (piano), Eldon Shamblin (guitar) and **Tommy Duncan** (vocals) remained key members in the early incarnations of the group. They secured a residency at Cain's Dancing Academy in Tulsa, and frequently featured on the local radio station, KVOO. With this regular exposure, they started to tour the Deep South and southwest. In 1935 they were signed by the Vocalion label and cut a string of sides, including 'Steel Guitar Rag', 'That's What I Like About The South' and 'New San Antonio Rose'; the latter was to become a massive hit for Bing Crosby in 1941.

After the outbreak of the Second World War, Wills boosted his national popularity by moving to the West

Coast and touring the dancehalls of Los Angeles. Now recording for Columbia, he also recorded sessions for national broadcast. The Playboys now featured fiddlers such as Louis Tierney, as well as steel guitarists Herb Remington and Noel Boggs. Wartime success gave way to declining popularity, as Wills began hitting the bottle with a vengeance. He left Columbia in 1947, and recorded for MGM, Decca, Liberty, Longhorn and Kapp.

In 1968 he was elected to the Country Music Hall Of Fame, and was honoured by the State of Texas the following year. By 1970, he was beginning to reap the benefits of his near-legendary status, but his health was deteriorating rapidly. Other artists now began to acknowledge the influence of Wills by recording tributes: **Waylon Jennings** wrote 'Bob Wills Is Still The King', and **Merle Haggard** recorded *A Tribute To The Best Damn Fiddle Player In The World* (1970), which included contributions from former Texas Playboys such as **Johnnie Lee Wills**, **Johnny Gimble**, Leon McAuliffe and Al Stricklin; **Commander Cody** and **Asleep At The Wheel** showed their debt to Wills in their output.

In 1973, Merle Haggard organized a reunion of the group, but Wills had a stroke and fell into a coma in the middle of the session; he never regained consciousness and died eighteen months later on May 13, 1975, in Fort Worth, Texas. In the aftermath of his death, reunions led by former members of the band became commonplace, with the line-ups often supplemented by fans from younger bands such as Asleep At The Wheel.

BEST OF BOB WILLS, Volume 1-2, MCA (US), 1986
BEST OF THE TIFFANYS, Edsel, 1990
BOB WILLS AND HIS TEXAS PLAYBOYS, Charly, 1988
GOLDEN ERA, Columbia, 1988
PAPA'S JUMPIN', Bear Family (Germany), 1987
TIFFANY TRANSCRIPTIONS, Volumes 1-8, Edsel, 1990
TIME CHANGES EVERYTHING, Stetson, 1986
VERY BEST OF BOB WILLS AND THE TEXAS PLAYBOYS, Liberty, 1984

WILLS, Johnnie Lee

Despite failing to achieve the pre-eminence of his older brother **Bob Wills**, Johnnie Lee was, for a number of years, a distinguished bandleader with several different groups. He was born in 1912, in Limestone County, Texas, and joined the **Light Crust Doughboys** as the tenor banjo player. When Bob left the Doughboys to form the Texas Playboys, Johnnie

Lee also left, forming his own outfit, Johnnie Lee Wills and his Boys.

By 1940, Johnnie Lee's band was riding on the crest of a wave whipped up by the success of the Texas Playboys; this enabled them to secure a contract with Decca, for whom they cut an excellent version of 'Milk Cow Blues'. During the war years, they managed to keep up appearances in Tulsa and started to record for RCA and Bullet. Johnnie Lee had two more sizeable hits, with 'Rag Mop' and 'Peter Cottontail', before being hit by the slump in popularity of Western Swing during the 1950s.

After his retirement from full-time performing, he opened a clothing shop specializing in cowboy outfits. In 1970 he came out of retirement to participate on the sessions for **Merle Haggard**'s *A Tribute To The Best Damn Fiddle Player In The World* with other former Texas Playboys like **Johnny Gimble**, **Leon McAuliffe** and Al Stricklin. During the 1970s and early 1980s there were two different line-ups of the Texas Playboys on the circuit, each playing reunion concerts: one was led by Johnnie Lee, the other led by McAuliffe. Johnnie Lee resumed recording once again, cutting *Reunion* for Flying Fish in 1978, and *Dance All Night* for Delta in 1980. He died on October 25, 1984, in Tulsa, Oklahoma.

OPERATOR'S SPECIAL, Topic, 1979
REUNION, Flying Fish (US), 1979
ROMPIN', STOMPIN', SINGIN', SWINGIN', Bear Family (Germany), 1984
TULSA SWING, Rounder (US), 1988

WISEMAN, Mac
One of the finest bluegrass singers and guitarists, Mac Wiseman has dedicated his musical career to the preservation of the old-time songs from the Shenandoah Valley, near Waynesboro, Virginia. Born in the valley on May 23, 1925, he attended the Shenandoah Conservatory of Music in Dayton, and went on to become an announcer at WSVA, Harrisburg, Virginia. In 1946 he started to work with **Molly O'Day**, before joining *Farm And Fun Time* on WCYB, Bristol, Virginia, as MC. While working on WCYB he met **Flatt & Scruggs**, who had just left **Bill Monroe** and who enlisted him as lead vocalist in their new band, the Foggy Mountain Boys. In 1949 he left the group to work on *Barn Dance* on WSB, Atlanta; the following year, he joined Monroe's Blue Grass Boys for a spell before launching his solo career in 1951.

Signed to the recently formed Dot label, and regularly appearing on the *Louisiana Hayride*, he started notching up hits: 'Shackles And Chains', ''Tis Sweet To Be Remembered', 'Jimmy Brown The Newsboy', 'Ballad Of Davy Crockett' and 'Love Letters In The Sand'. By 1953 he had joined the cast of the *Old Dominion Barn Dance* on WRVA, Richmond, before taking over the A&R directorship of the Dot label in 1957 - a post he held until 1961. Over the next eight years, Wiseman signed with several different labels, until joining RCA in 1969 and teaming up with Lester Flatt for *On The South Bound* and *Lester 'n' Mac*.

During the 1960s and 1970s, he championed old-time and bluegrass on college campuses and at festivals, contributing to the renewal of interest in traditional country music. He went on to secure highly prestigious gigs at venues like Carnegie Hall, the Hollywood Bowl and London's Royal Albert Hall. After leaving RCA he signed with the specialist bluegrass label Country Music Heritage, reworking the old Dot recordings on *The Mac Wiseman Story*. In 1986 he returned to Dot, cutting *Once More With Feeling* for the label's new owners, MCA. He runs an annual bluegrass festival in Renfro Valley, Kentucky.

BLUEGRASS FAVOURITES, Stetson, 1987
CONCERT FAVOURITES, Stetson, 1989
EARLY DOT RECORDINGS, Volumes 1-2, County (US), 1985
GOLDEN CLASSICS, Gusto (US), 1979
GRASSROOTS TO BLUEGRASS, CMH (US), 1990
MAC WISEMAN STORY, CMH (US), 1976

WISEMAN, Scotty see LULU BELLE & SCOTTY

WOLF, Kate
A fine songwriter and singer, little known beyond the US, Kate Wolf was born Kathryn Louise Allen on January 27, 1942. During the 1970s and 1980s she toured extensively on the West Coast, developing a reputation and recording for Kaleidoscope. Despite the excellence of albums, such as *Safe At Anchor*, *Give Yourself To Love* and *Gold In California*, she remained a secret to all but a handful of admirers. In 1985, she contributed, along with Pete Seeger, Sweet Honey In Rock and Jesse Colin Young (formerly of the Youngbloods), to the compilation *Out Of The Darkness: Songs For Survival*. On December 10, 1986, she died of leukaemia.

BACKROADS, Kaleidoscope (US), 1988
CLOSE TO YOU, Kaleidoscope (US), 1988
EVENING IN AUSTIN, Kaleidoscope (US), 1990
GIVE YOURSELF TO LOVE, Kaleidoscope (US), 1988
GOLD IN CALIFORNIA, Kaleidoscope (US), 1988
LINES ON THE PAPER, Kaleidoscope (US), 1988
POET'S HEART, Kaleidoscope (US), 1988
SAFE AT ANCHOR, Kaleidoscope (US), 1988
WIND BLOWS WILD, Kaleidoscope (US), 1988

WOOD, Tommy see Noack, Eddie

WOOLEY, Sheb

A spirited and versatile entertainer, Sheb Wooley is most noted for his acting abilities. He was born on April 10, 1921, on a farm in Erick, Oklahoma, and formed his first group while at high school. After leaving school, he studied at the Jack Koslyn School of Acting and worked in the oilfields, before moving to Nashville and cutting some sides for the Bullet label. In 1946 he moved to Fort Worth, Texas, where he wrote and performed jingles for one of the local radio stations.

By 1948 he had moved to Hollywood and won a recording contract with MGM. He made his film debut in *Rocky Mountain* (starring Errol Flynn; 1950), which was followed by appearances in over forty other movies, including *High Noon* (1952) and *Giant* (1956), and a five-year stint as co-star in the television series *Rawhide*, with Clint Eastwood.

His film and television career booming, he also recorded a number of novelty hits: 'The Purple People Eater' (US#1, UK#12, 1958) and 'That's My Pa' (C&W#1, 1962) under his own name, and 'Don't Go Near The Eskimos', 'Almost Persuaded No. 2', 'Harper Valley P.T.A. (Later That Same Day)' and '15 Beers Ago' under the name Ben Colder. With his acting career showing little sign of decline, he still makes regular contributions to Nashville shows such as the *Grand Ole Opry* and *Hee Haw*.

BLUE GUITAR, Bear Family (Germany), 1985
COUNTRY BOOGIE, WILD 'N' WOOLEY, Bear Family (Germany), 1985

WORTH, Billy see ASHWORTH, Ernie

WRIGHT, Bobby

A member of one of country music's best-known families, Bobby Wright was born on March 30, 1942, in Charleston, West Virginia, the son of **Kitty Wells** and **Johnny Wright**. He made his first appearance on the *Louisiana Hayride* at the age of eight, and signed to Decca in 1953. After completing his education at Middle Tennessee State University, he held a part in the television series, *McHale's Navy*, for four years, and also started to appear on the *The Kitty Wells And Johnny Wright Family Show*. After a couple of minor hits, 'Lay Some Happiness On Me' (1967) and 'Here I Go Again' (1971), he cut an album of Johnny & Jack material (see **Wright, Johnny**) for Starday in 1977. He continues to tour and to make appearances on television.

WRIGHT, Johnny

Johnny Wright (born in Mount Juliet, Tennessee, on May 13, 1914) was surrounded by country music from birth: his grandfather was a fiddler and his father a banjo player. In 1933 he moved to Nashville, where he met and married **Kitty Wells**, and formed the Johnny & Jack duo with guitarist Jack Anglin (born in Columbia, Tennessee, on May 13, 1916) in 1938. The duo had their first break on WSIX, Nashville, and then formed the Tennessee Mountain Boys, with Wells as featured singer.

During the 1940s they toured constantly, broadcasting regularly on WBIG, Greensboro, North Carolina, and WNOX, Knoxville, Tennessee; they made their debut on the *Grand Ole Opry* in 1947, and secured a residency on the *Louisiana Hayride*. In 1952, with Kitty Wells's career on the up, they returned for another spell at the *Grand Ole Opry*, which consolidated their position as one of the most prestigious country acts on the circuit.

Initially signed to the R&B label Apollo, they cut 'Jolé Blon' and 'Paper Boy', and in 1949 they moved to RCA, where they scored with hits like 'Poison Love' (C&W#5, 1951), 'Crying Heart Blues' (1951), 'Oh Baby Mine (I Get So Lonely)' (C&W#1, 1954), 'Beware Of It' (1954), 'Goodnight, Sweetheart, Goodnight' (1954), 'Stop The World' (1958), 'Lonely Island Pearl' (1958), 'Sailor Man' (1959) and 'Slow Poison' (1962). On March 8, 1963, the partnership was broken when Jack was killed in a car accident on his way to **Patsy Cline**'s funeral.

Johnny then formed a new touring group, which included his son **Bobby Wright**, and started to record as a solo artist - his biggest hit being 'Hello Vietnam' (C&W#1, 1965). In 1969 he started to appear in the syndicated television series *The Kitty Wells And Johnny Wright Family Show*, and in 1977 he cut an album of Johnny & Jack material with his son Bobby, for Starday. He is semi-retired now.

TENNESSEE MOUNTAIN BOYS, Stetson, 1988

WYNETTE, Tammy

Tammy Wynette is one of those country singers whose lives mirror the melodrama of their songs: a tendency which seems to have enhanced her popularity. Often vilified by feminists for the apparent subservience of her lyrics, she has established herself as one of country's most successful female singers.

Born Virginia Wynette Pugh on May 5, 1942, near Tupelo, Mississippi, she was brought up by farming grandparents after the death of her father. She sang in the local church as a child, and was married after leaving school, aged only seventeen. She had three children, the youngest of whom developed spinal meningitis, and Tammy became a beautician in Birmingham in order to help pay the hospital bills.

In 1966 she moved to Nashville, becoming the featured vocalist on WBRC-TV's *Country Boy Eddy Show* and making occasional appearances on **Porter Wagoner**'s syndicated television programme. She started to audition for record companies like United Artists, Kapp and Hickory, and was finally signed to the Epic label by producer **Billy Sherrill**. Sherrill was quick to spot the similarity of her voice to that of **Patsy Cline**, and he set about providing her with emotionally charged material that would get the best out of her crying style.

Over the next ten years, she notched up one hit after another, many of which were penned by Sherrill and Glenn Sutton (**Lynn Anderson**'s husband): **Johnny Paycheck**'s 'Apartment No. 9', 'Your Good Girl's Gonna Go Bad' (C&W#3, 1967), 'My Elusive Dreams' (a duet with **David Houston**; C&W#1, 1967), 'I Don't Wanna Play House' (C&W#1, 1967), 'Take Me To Your World' (C&W#1, 1968), 'D-I-V-O-R-C-E' (C&W#1, 1968; UK#12, 1975), 'Stand By Your Man' (C&W#1, 1968; UK#1, 1975), 'Singing My Song' (C&W#1, 1969), 'The Ways To Love A Man' (C&W#1, 1970), 'He Loves Me All The Way' (C&W#1, 1970), 'Run Woman Run' (C&W#1, 1970), 'We Sure Can Love Each Other' (C&W#2, 1971), 'Good Lovin' (Makes It Right)' (C&W#1, 1971), 'Bedtime Story' (C&W#1, 1972), 'My Man (Understands)' (C&W#1, 1972), ''Til I Get It Right' (C&W#1, 1973), 'Kids Say The Darnedest Things' (C&W#1, 1973), 'Another Lonely Song' (C&W#1, 1974), 'Woman To Woman' (C&W#4, 1974), '(You Make Me Want To Be) A Mother' (C&W#4, 1974), ''Til I Can Make It On My Own' (C&W#1, 1976) and 'You And Me' (C&W#1, 1976).

Aside from her solo work, her seven-year marriage to **George Jones** (from 1968 to 1975) resulted in a number of impressive duets: 'We're Gonna Hold On' (C&W#1, 1973), 'Golden Ring' (C&W#1, 1976), 'Near You' (C&W#1, 1976), 'Southern California' (C&W#1, 1977) and 'Two-Storey House' (C&W#2, 1980). Many of the sides they recorded together documented the trials and tribulations of their own relationship, lending poignancy to material that could otherwise have seemed mawkish and sentimental.

After her divorce from Jones, she edged further into the mainstream, appearing in the US television soap, *Capitol*, and recording material like 'I Just Heard A Heartbreak' and 'Sometimes When We Touch'; despite these divergences, she was locked firmly into the traditions of Country & Western, unlike artists such as **Dolly Parton**. The 1987 album *Higher Ground* included a duet with one of the young turks of the New Country brigade, **Ricky Skaggs**, and in 1991 she collaborated with the UK techno outfit, KLF, on 'Justified And Ancient' (UK#2, 1992), a project which contained more than a hint of self-mockery, particularly in the kitsch promotional video. In 1982, her autobiography *Stand By Your Man*, was filmed.

CLASSIC COLLECTION, Epic, 1982
COUNTRY STARS LIVE (with George Jones), Platinum, 1990
HEART OVER MIND, Epic, 1990
HIGHER GROUND, Epic, 1987
IT SURE IS GOOD (with George Jones), Premier, 1987
NEXT TO YOU, Epic, 1989
TEARS OF FIRE: The 25th Anniversary Collection, Epic, 1992

WYNONNA see JUDDS

YEARWOOD, Trisha

One of the brightest of the new crop of country artists, Trisha Yearwood was born in Monticello, near Atlanta, Georgia, in 1966. After moving to Nashville in 1985, she attended Belmont College, while working in publicity at the MTM label. At MTM, she started to sing on sessions and to cut demos, and met producer Garth Fundis, who encouraged her to audition for MCA.

Her debut, *Trisha Yearwood*, featured compositions by **Garth Brooks** and included vocal support from **Vince Gill**. Her first single, 'She's In Love With The Boy' (C&W#6, 1991), was followed by 'That's What I Like About You' and 'Lonesome Dove'. Throughout 1991, she opened for Brooks on his US tour, before issuing *Hearts In Armour* the following year, which included contributions from Brooks, Gill and the ubiquitous **Emmylou Harris**.

HEARTS IN ARMOUR, MCA, 1992
TRISHA YEARWOOD, MCA, 1991

YOAKAM, Dwight

A genuine honky-tonk singer in the New Country mould, Dwight Yoakam was born in Pikesville, Kentucky, on October 23, 1954, and was raised on gospel, singing in the church choir. After attempting to break into the country music circuit in Nashville in 1976, he moved to Los Angeles and spent six years as a truck-driver. He then started working with bands like Los Lobos and the Blasters, and made his debut in 1985 with the superb EP *Guitars, Cadillacs, Etc., Etc.*, which featured contributions from steel guitarist J.D. Maness and **Glen D. Hardin**.

Snapped up by Warner Bros., the EP was re-released with four additional tracks tacked on, and included covers of **Johnny Horton**'s 'Honky Tonk Man', **Harlan Howard**'s 'Heartaches By The Number' and 'Guitars, Cadillacs'. Featuring compositions like 'Bury Me' (a duet with Maria McKee) and 'South Of Cincinnati', the record also showcased Yoakam's fine songwriting skills.

After *Hillbilly Deluxe* (1987), Yoakam recorded *Buenas Noches From A Lonely Room*, which included 'Streets Of Bakersfield' (a duet with **Buck Owens**; C&W#1, 1988) and 'I Sang Dixie' (C&W#1, 1989). In 1990 he released *If There Was A Way*, which featured 'It Only Hurts When I Cry' (co-written with **Roger Miller**) and 'Send A Message To My Heart' (a duet with **Patti Loveless**). In 1992 he put out *La Croix D'Amour*, which gathered together previously unissued material and a few new tracks, including versions of 'Suspicious Minds' and Lennon & McCartney's 'Things We Said Today'. Touring Europe at the end of 1992, he established himself in the minds of international audiences as one of the least formulaic of all the New Country singers.

BUENAS NOCHES FROM A LONELY ROOM, Reprise, 1988
GUITARS, CADILLACS, ETC., ETC., Reprise (US), 1987
HILLBILLY DELUXE, Reprise (US), 1987
IF THERE WAS A WAY, Reprise, 1990
JUST LOOKING FOR A HIT, Reprise, 1989
LA CROIX D'AMOUR, Reprise, 1992
THIS TIME, Reprise, 1992

YOUNG, Donny see PAYCHECK, Johnny

YOUNG, Faron

Among the top ten best-selling country artists of all time, Faron Young has been a successful bandleader, performer, songwriter and entrepreneur. He was born in Shreveport, Louisiana, on February 25, 1932, and was raised on his family's farm. While at high school, he learnt the guitar and started to play at local functions. On completion of his education, his reputation had developed to such an extent that he was invited to broadcast on the *Louisiana Hayride*, where he was spotted by **Webb Pierce** and recruited as his lead vocalist in 1950. The following year he joined the Gotham label as a solo artist, cutting 'Tattle Tale Tears' and 'Have I Waited Too Long'. Between 1952 and 1954, he served in the army in Korea, joining the

Grand Ole Opry on his return and signing with the Capitol label.

With Capitol, he started to consolidate his position with a string of hits that included **Ted Daffan**'s 'I've Got Five Dollars And It's Saturday Night', 'Going Steady' (C&W#2, 1953), 'Live Fast, Love Hard, Die Young' (C&W#1, 1955), 'Sweet Dreams', 'Alone With You' (C&W#1, 1958), 'Country Girl' (C&W#1, 1959) and **Willie Nelson**'s 'Hello Walls' (US#12, C&W#1, 1961). He also appeared in a succession of low-budget Westerns, including *Hidden Guns*, *Daniel Boone* and *Raiders Of Old California*.

In 1961 he moved over to the Mercury label and to producer **Jerry Kennedy**, and the hits continued to roll: 'Backtrack', 'Three Days', 'The Comeback', 'Down By The River', 'The Yellow Bandanna', 'You'll Drive Me Back (Into Her Arms Again)', 'Walk Tall', 'Unmitigated Gall', 'Your Time's Comin'', 'Keepin' Up With The Joneses' (a duet with Margie Singleton), 'It's Four In The Morning' (C&W#1, UK#3, 1972), 'This Little Girl Of Mine' and 'Just What I Had In Mind'.

During the 1960s, he toured Europe regularly and expanded his business interests to include film production, music publishing and property (he owns the Young Executive Building, a skyscraper near Music Row in Nashville). Young also publishes country music's trade paper, *Music City News*. In the late 1970s he moved to the MCA label, but with less success.

FOUR IN THE MORNING, Charly, 1986
THE SHERIFF, Allegiance, 1984
TALK ABOUT HITS, Stetson, 1987
THIS IS FARON YOUNG, Stetson, 1989

ACKNOWLEDGEMENTS

Books of this nature don't happen without extensive guidance and assistance from all sorts of different people and agencies. I have been very fortunate in having had the enthusiasm and knowledge of Allegra Huston of Weidenfeld & Nicolson at my disposal. She has always been positive and constructive in her suggestions and her considerable understanding of country music has been a great bonus. Shunil Roychaudhuri has knocked my unwieldy text into shape sympathetically (although he wouldn't let me give Roy Rogers' horse Trigger a proper mention).

Furthermore, I would like to thank the following who have offered words of wisdom and enthusiasm (some have had to put up with the occasional bout of intransigence, I am ashamed to say): Catrina Barnes (FBM), Elizabeth Blumer (Weidenfeld & Nicolson), Stuart Booth, Chris Briggs (Compulsion), Bob Cotton (Fit Vision), Sara Jane Coxon, Christopher Fagg, Graham Fletcher (Fit Vision), Keren Greenwell (MCA), Brenda & Oliver Gregory, Howard Jones (Sheridans), Irving Mildener (Clayman & Co.), Jonathan Morrish (Sony, UK), Kay Mumford (Fit Vision), Lorne Murdoch (MCPS), National Sound Archive, Tim Noakes, Thierry Pannetier (EMI), Chrissy Pierce, Caffy St. Luce (Hall Or Nothing), Martin Satterthwaite (Country Music Association), George Scott (Fit Vision), Lucy Stacey (EMI), Phil Straight (Warner Bros.), Judith Wheaterston (Arista) and Richard Wootton (Manor House).

255

INDEX